Governing by Consent

AN INTRODUCTION TO AMERICAN POLITICS

Governing by Consent

AN INTRODUCTION TO AMERICAN POLITICS

John F. Bibby
University of Wisconsin, Milwaukee

CQ PRESS Congressional Quarterly Inc.
Washington, D.C.

Printed in the United States of America

Second Printing

Permissions for copyrighted materials not credited on the page where they appear
are listed in the acknowledgments section beginning on page 639. This section is
to be considered an extension of the copyright page.

Jacket and text design by Kachergis Book Design, Pittsboro, North Carolina

Cover photo supplied by Folio, Inc., Washington, D.C.

LIBRARY OF CONGRESS CATALOGING-IN-PUBLICATION DATA
Bibby, John F.
    Governing by consent : an introduction to American politics / John F. Bibby.
        p.   cm.
    Includes bibliographical references and index.
        ISBN 0-87187-527-6
        1. United States — Politics and government.   I. Title.
    JK274.B54   1992
    320.973 — dc20   91-30076
                                                                                CIP

Contents

Part III ❧ Governmental Institutions

Politics along the Potomac   339

Part IV ❧ Politics and Public Policy

❧ Reference Materials

❧ Tables, Figures, and Boxes

Tables

Figures

❧ Boxes

❧ Preface

Although Americans periodically complain that their government leaders are too heavily involved in playing "politics" and that the country is getting off on the wrong track, Americans generally are upbeat when compared with citizens of other nations about the prospects for improving their lives and those of their families. Many are cynical about government processes and institutions—bewildered, perhaps, by the seeming snail's pace of Congress or the inefficiency of the bureaucracy—but most Americans take pride in their country and its myriad economic, social, and foreign policy achievements.

Ironically, Americans often take for granted the singular accomplishment that stands above all others: the creation and development of a political order based on the principles set out in the Declaration of Independence that governments are instituted to protect human rights and that they derive "their just powers from the consent of the governed." Indeed, as failed experiments with representative government and the repression of human rights around the globe sadly testify, the United States has achieved an impressive feat in establishing a representative government that is adaptable, generally protective of individual liberties, responsive to societal concerns, and capable of enduring for more than two hundred years.

Governing by Consent: An Introduction to American Politics was designed to help students of political science understand and appreciate the unique American system. The book examines the processes of American politics, the behavior of political actors, and the functioning of governmental institutions, as well as the problems within the polity. But it goes beyond mere descriptive accounts of how candidates win elections, Congress passes a bill, the president shapes public opinion, or cases reach the Supreme Court. It probes deeply into the fundamental issues of why the political process operates as it does and what the consequences of that process are for the American people.

Concept and Organization
of this Book

Governing by Consent is a comprehensive, basic text that embodies a somewhat different approach to the study of American government: its straightforward, balanced presentation and relatively compact size offer flexibility to instructors who want to supplement with thematic or topical material of their own choosing, while knowing that students have been exposed to a thorough analysis of the American system.

The text is organized traditionally: legal framework—political processes—governmental institutions—public policy. The chapters were written to stand alone, however, so they can be assigned in a different sequence without jeopardizing comprehension.

Part I focuses primarily on the Constitution—the legal basis and framework for American government and politics. Not surprisingly, the constitutional arrangements forged by the nation's Founders in 1787 continue to profoundly influence politics in the 1990s. The constitutional separation of powers—the division of government into the legislative, executive, and judicial branches—imposes on policy makers a difficult task. Former secretary of state George Shultz aptly captured the enduring impact and challenge of this when he commented: "Separation of powers . . . means we have to learn how to share power. Sharing power is harder, and we need to work at it harder than we do. But that's the only way."[1] Part I completes its look at the constitutional foundations by examining federal-state relations as well as civil liberties and civil rights.

In Part II attention is turned to the *process* of governing by consent. Public opinion and the ways in which citizens' concerns become government concerns—through political participation, political parties, elections, interest groups, and the mass media—are analyzed. Over time and in many cultures the right to rule has often been seized by people on the basis of family, birth, religion, class, or wealth. Such claims have been challenged in modern times by the demand for greater participation in the governing process. Broadened participation requires that institutions, such as political parties, be capable of mobilizing citizens and contesting elections. As pointed out by V. O. Key, Jr.: "The political party becomes the instrument for organization of support in societies founded on the

---

1. Quoted by Hedrick Smith, *The Power Game: How Washington Works* (New York: Random House, 1988), 726.

doctrine of consent of the governed. Inherent in that is the idea of popular displacement of governments and the substitution of other rulers preferred by the people."[2] Key also reminded us of the essential role of interest groups, another subject analyzed in Part II. Indeed, he called group interests "the animating forces in the political process" and observed that the governing process "consists in large degree in the advancement of legitimate group objectives, in the reconciliation and mediation of conflicting group ambitions, and in the restraint of group tendencies judged to be socially destructive."[3]

The book moves on in Part III to a discussion of the governing institutions: the Congress, presidency, bureaucracy, and judiciary. The relationships between each institution and the public—for example, popular support as a basis for presidential power and the impact of the political environment on the Supreme Court—are explored. The internal operations of each branch of government are analyzed as well, along with the politics of interbranch relations—how the various institutions have adapted to what Edwin Corwin has called the Constitution's "invitation to struggle."[4]

Part IV provides an overview of U.S. public policy, a framework for analyzing the stages in the policy process, and classifications of the types of policies emanating from government. Several critical questions are also addressed: Are the policies produced by the system adequate? Is the process truly democratic? Is reform of the system needed?

Finally, to help readers gain a feel for national politics and sense its drama and significance, a special essay on the Washington political community has been written to open Part III. This relatively informal account of the milieu within which government decision makers operate provides insights into political life "along the Potomac" and illustrates the influence of the Washington environment on government policy making.

An instructor's manual, test bank, and diskette of test questions and lecture notes accompany the text. Two reports on the 1992 elections—one compiled by the editors of *Congressional Quarterly Weekly Report* and the other by this author—will be available after the elections.

2. V. O. Key, Jr., *Politics, Parties, and Pressure Groups*, 5th ed. (New York: Crowell, 1964), 199–200.
3. Ibid., 17.
4. Edwin S. Corwin, *The President: Office and Powers*, 4th ed. (New York: New York University Press, 1957), 171.

Acknowledgments

In preparing this text, many individuals contributed generously of their time, skills, and expertise. I wish to thank, while absolving from all blame, the following professional colleagues who reviewed the manuscript and provided wise counsel: Judith Baer, Lawrence Baum, Donald Baumer, Gary Bryner, Bradley Canon, Robert Carp, Allan Cigler, Timothy Conlan, M. Margaret Conway, Lawrence Dodd, Maureen Drummy, Louis Fisher, John Gates, Doris Graber, Cole Blease Graham, Jr., James Guth, William Keefe, Donald Kettl, Stephanie Greco Larson, James Lester, Michael Maggiotto, Kenneth Meier, Richard Niemi, Bruce Oppenheimer, Lawrence O'Toole, Jr., Mark Peterson, Leroy Rieselbach, Randall Ripley, Michael Robinson, David Rohde, Barbara Salmore, Robert Spitzer, Harold Stanley, Norman Thomas, Thomas Walker, Richard Watson, and Nancy Zingale.

Sabra Bissette Ledent was particularly skillful (and good humored) while editing the manuscript. I also want to thank developmental editor Phyllis Fisher and Joanne Daniels, former director of CQ Press, for their work during the early stages of the book. Throughout this project, the staff of CQ Press—especially Brenda Carter, Nancy Lammers, David Tarr, and Jerry Orvedahl—have been supportive and generous with their assistance. Though she professes no expertise in political science other than that which a husband has shared with her, my wife, Lucile, has provided skillful reading, common sense, and, most important, support and encouragement for which I am most grateful.

Governing by Consent

AN INTRODUCTION TO AMERICAN POLITICS

PART I

The Context
of American Politics

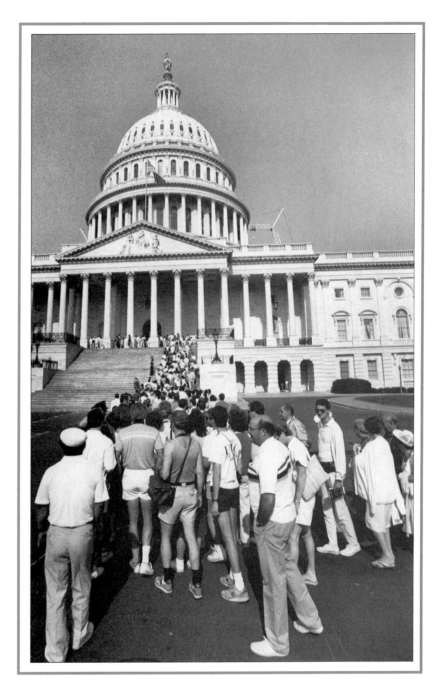

1. Politics and Democracy in America

L IVING UNDER one of the world's oldest and stablest demo-cratic governments, Americans are, in general, satisfied with their system of government and the quality of their lives. This rosy picture, however, masks periodic dissat-isfaction with the country's leaders and doubts about the capacity of government to cope with societal problems. Indeed, in a recent public opinion survey 56 percent of respondents (51 percent of men and 57 percent of women) said that the country was seriously on the wrong track.[1] Forty percent of respondents said government was the problem; 31 percent found government the answer; and 15 percent said government was both the problem and the answer.[2]

Such survey results are not unusual. They reflect both a desire for change in government policy and skepticism about the capacity of government to remedy societal problems. Is the country seriously off track? Is government the problem or the answer? Are institutional reforms in order? How can policy change be achieved, if indeed it is needed? How can the most desirable features of the political order be preserved? Responses to these questions depend substantially on the information available about politics and government. Before peo-ple can assess the need for change or stability, identify appropriate policy alternatives, and engage in political activity that has a rea-sonable chance of achieving its stated goals, they need to know how politics works, how it is changing, and just what the forces of change and stability are.

Most people acquire information about how the political process operates in, at best, a rather sporadic and casual manner. They watch television newscasts when they can and catch brief news re-ports on the car radio. They scan the newspapers and perhaps sub-scribe to *Time* or *Newsweek*. But the difficulties encountered in absorbing the knowledge needed for informed political discussion and action in no way diminishes the need for such knowledge. This book describes and analyzes what political scientists—those who an-alyze and teach about politics and government on a full-time basis—have discovered about how American government works, why it works the way it does, and what the consequences of its operations are.

1. *American Enterprise,* January/February 1991, 92.
2. *Public Opinion,* November/December 1987, 32.

The Nature of Politics and Government

Politics

Politics and government influence the very basics of life—an individual's standard of living, freedoms, and future opportunities. The political process and the consequent government policies are important because of what government can do for—and to—anyone. Government can provide financial assistance to attend college, withhold money from paychecks, provide medical care, send a person to prison, and even plunge the country into war. Anything that can affect people so dramatically requires a closer, serious examination.

What is **politics**? As used in everyday language, "politics" conjures up all kinds of rather unsavory images. Indeed, frequently it refers to the unseemly machinations of the ambitious and self-serving to gain personal advantage over others. Being called a "politician" is seldom intended as a compliment. Candidates for office may claim, in fact, that one of their main qualifications is that they are not politicians. Indeed, President Harry Truman once noted that "a President needs political understanding to run the government, but he may be elected without it." And in what may be one of today's most revealing statements on the profession of politics, a company has even produced a board game called "Lie, Cheat, Steal: A Game of Political Power." Promotional materials describe it as "a game of political power that lets you play scrupulously fair or devilishly devious!" Generally then, anyone accused of "playing politics" or acting out of political motivations is suspected of having afoot something less than wholesome activities.

But *politics,* it must be quickly pointed out, has its more favorable associations as well. As far back as Aristotle, it has been recognized that political activity "exists for the sake of noble actions" and that genuine good can be achieved by political leaders. George Washington, Thomas Jefferson, James Madison, and Alexander Hamilton played leading roles in founding the nation. Abraham Lincoln took actions to save the Union and free the slaves. And Franklin Roosevelt's leadership pulled the country through a depression and world war. One look at American history reveals that our greatest national heroes have been politicians. Ordinary citizens as well have banded together to influence national policy for the better—the suffragists early in this century and the civil rights marchers in the 1960s are two prominent examples.

Political leaders who fight for especially noble causes—Washington, Jefferson, Lincoln—are often elevated to the rank of statesman in the public's mind. The label *statesman* may even be applied to much-admired contemporary leaders, while others are relegated to the category of just being "politicians." But when value-laden connotations are removed, the essence of politics is *power*—the ability of one person to get another person to behave in a desired manner. And leaders—whether viewed as statesmen or politicians—are engaged in gaining and exercising power. Politics and the use of power inevitably involve *conflict* because people have different values and goals and because life's prized objectives—wealth, security, deference, safety, knowledge, and power itself—do not exist in sufficient quantity to satisfy everyone. In its most fundamental sense, politics is concerned with "who gets what, when, how."[3]

How well a political system works depends largely on whether society's inevitable political conflicts among competing interests, parties, and individuals can be resolved and managed via negotiation, bargaining, and compromise. If these processes permit competing interests to get enough of what they want, these interests can continue competing and yet not disrupt the whole legal structure of government. Politics can therefore be viewed as a process of *conflict management*.

But there is more to politics than just keeping the lid on the simmering kettle of political conflict. Politics is also the process through which individuals and groups organize and act together to achieve social objectives—individual freedom, national security, public health and safety, economic opportunity, improved education, clean air and water. Through collective action, environmental and health groups, for example, successfully pressured Congress to enact clean air legislation.

When politics is thus stripped of both its negative and positive connotations and viewed in its essentials, it becomes a basic, inevitable social process involving the acquisition, retention, and exercise of power; the management of conflicts; and collective action.

Government

The **government** is an institution that through its actions has ultimate authority to allocate values in society—to decide "who gets what, when, how." For example, neither the United States Chamber of Commerce nor the AFL-CIO (American Federation of Labor and Congress of Industrial Organizations) has final authority to decide

3. Harold D. Lasswell, *Politics: Who Gets What, When, How* (New York: Meridian Books, 1958).

on the minimum wage for workers or whether workers will be entitled to parental leave from their jobs. The authority to set such policies rests with government officials—with Congress to enact the legislation, the president to see that the law is carried out, and the courts to interpret it. Both the Chamber of Commerce and the AFL-CIO can try to influence congressional, presidential, and judicial decisions, but ultimately it is the government that makes the policy decisions. Government decisions are distinguished from those of other organizations by the fact that they are binding for all of society. By contrast, the decisions and policies of private organizations are enforceable within their own memberships but not beyond. Governments, moreover, have a monopoly on the legitimate use of force. The federal government, for example, can if necessary use physical force—the Federal Bureau of Investigation, federal marshals, Treasury agents, the Coast Guard, and even the military—to compel compliance. State and local governments have the state patrol, sheriff departments, and local police to enforce their laws. No other organizations in this society can legitimately use physical force.

Because government decisions are authoritative for all of society, this book is primarily concerned with the politics of government rather than that of nongovernmental organizations. We will, however, occasionally consider the internal politics of nongovernmental organizations—interest groups, political parties, the media—because these organizations have an impact on government decisions.

The Political Process: Never-Ending

When the World Series is over each October, we know which team is the world champion. The decision is final; the baseball season is at an end, and nothing can be done to reverse the outcome. But unlike major league baseball, the political season has no end, and no decision is really final.

Our political system offers individuals, groups, interests, and parties ample opportunities to change existing government policies. Those who lose a policy struggle in one political arena always have a chance to win in another. Moreover, there is the possibility that the ongoing turnover—both voluntary and involuntary—in government officials will bring about the sought-after policy changes. The examples of ways in which government policies can be changed are many:

• Laws enacted by Congress can be repealed and modified by a succeeding Congress.

- Presidents can veto acts of Congress and influence how statutes are administered.
- Bureaucrats can implement laws of Congress in a manner that may or may not conform to the intent of Congress or the president.
- The courts can invalidate an act of Congress; they also can interpret it in a narrow or expansive manner.
- The courts can nullify decisions of the president and the bureaucracy.
- Supreme Court decisions can be reversed or modified by constitutional amendments and legislation, or by the lower courts when they implement Supreme Court decisions.
- Elections can result in changes in government personnel, which in turn can cause the government to change its policies.

Those who win a legislative victory in Congress must normally be prepared to defend their victory before the administration, courts, and future Congresses. Those who initially lose the policy struggle in Congress still have a chance to regain part or all of their loss via the administration, the courts, or a future Congress. No decision is really final—that is, *all government decisions should be seen as interim or temporary*. No matter how important it seems at the time, each government decision is just one stage in an ongoing struggle over public policy.

The Politics of Democracy

Politics is found in all government systems whether they be democratic, authoritarian, or totalitarian. In this book, however, we will look primarily at a particular brand of politics: the American style of democratic politics.

The Many Meanings and Forms of Democracy

The term **democracy** has a variety of meanings. The Soviet bloc countries of the cold war era and some Third World nations have been said to have had democratic systems of government because government decisions were allegedly made in the real interests of the people, whether or not they had an opportunity to participate in choosing their leaders. In the Greek city-states of antiquity and New England town meetings of today, democracy means direct citizen participation in government decision making. This is **direct democracy**. In the United States and most Western nations, democracy is a system of government in which officeholders acquire the power to make decisions by means of a competitive struggle for the people's vote. This is **representative democracy**.

Representative democracies come in a variety of forms. The United States has a *presidential system* in which a chief executive is elected independently of the national legislature. In the *parliamentary systems* of most Western European nations, the chief executive (called a prime minister, premier, or chancellor) is selected by the majority party or coalition of parties in the national legislature. Democracies also differ in how they divide power between the national government and regional governments. The United States, Canada, Australia, and Germany are organized on a *federal* basis—that is, they divide governmental power between the national government and the states. But in Britain and France all governmental authority resides with the national government. Democracies differ as well in the extent to which they provide their citizens with social welfare benefits. In Sweden, for example, the government assumes a much larger share of the responsibility for peoples' economic security and social welfare than is true in the United States.

Even with these significant differences among the Western democracies, all measure up to a basic test of a democracy: *their citizens have a relatively high degree of control over the actions of their leaders*.[4] Citizen efforts to influence political leaders are expected, accepted, and frequently successful. This sets Western democracies in stark contrast to such regimes as the People's Republic of China where open opposition to government policies is not permitted.

Leadership Succession through Elections

Traditionally, one of the most vexing problems of government has been that of leadership succession to government offices.[5] In hereditary monarchies, leadership succession was handled through a sort of biological lottery—when the monarch died, the heir succeeded to the throne. Sometimes this worked well (Elizabeth I of England); at other times disaster ensued (Elizabeth's Stuart successors, James I and Charles I). In both traditional monarchies and modern-day dictatorships, succession often has been achieved through revolution, assassination, or a *coup d'état*.

Transferring governmental authority without seriously disrupting

4. Fred I. Greenstein and Frank B. Feigert, *The American Party System and the American People*, 3d ed. (Englewood Cliffs, N.J.: Prentice-Hall, 1985), 2.
5. The discussion of the characteristics of democratic governments and their institutions draws heavily on the writing of V. O. Key, Jr., *Politics, Parties, and Pressure Groups*, 5th ed. (New York: Crowell, 1964), 4–11.

Democracy requires the peaceful and orderly transfer of power through elections. Incoming Republican president Ronald Reagan (left) accepts the congratulations of the man he defeated in 1980, outgoing Democratic president Jimmy Carter (right), at Reagan's inauguration at the Capitol. Reagan's wife, Nancy, is between them, back to the camera.

the life of the state has been a long-standing problem of governance. The democratic solution to this problem is elections. Experience has shown that elections operate most effectively when (1) there is a tradition of elections and the citizens are fully familiar with the process, and (2) there is widespread agreement within society about the substance of public policy and political procedures. Fortunately, these conditions are present in the United States.

In a democracy, elections are more than a matter of filling government posts when they become vacant. Elections ensure that posts will become vacant at periodic intervals without the "messiness of beheading or the inconvenience of revolution."[6] As that distinguished scholar of American politics V. O. Key, Jr., has observed,

The democratic technique for the determination of succession is . . . combined with a method for the termination of the life of a government. An election poses the questions whether the ruling clique shall be continued in power and, if not, by whom shall it be succeeded. Democratic orders merge into a single ritual a substitute for older techniques of determining the heir

6. Ibid., 6.

Consent of the Governed

to authority and a functional equivalent for the varieties of ways by which peoples rid themselves of unwanted rulers.[7]

In democracies, governments derive their power from the people. This basis for governmental authority differs sharply from the older theory of the *divine right of kings* in which the ruler derived power from God and acted as God's temporal agent on earth. In a representative democracy, the rulers, or the government, are expected to defer to the views and interests of the ruled—that is, act with the consent of the governed. And elections are an essential way in which the government can consult with the people or their representatives and the people can express their consent to government action.

A corollary of the doctrine of government by consent of the governed is the freedom to express dissent against the actions of the government. In a democracy, not only is there the freedom to dissent, but also there is the expectation that protests will be heard and considered, though not necessarily heeded, and that no reprisals will be taken against the protesters. The freedom to dissent is accompanied by the right to join with others to seek redress of grievances by ousting officeholders through the electoral process.[8]

The Politics of Limited Objectives
and Hope for Tomorrow

Democratic procedures operate best when there is the expectation that policy changes in the short run will be modest and relatively narrow, and there will be no wholesale changes in the economic order or the governmental system. Losers of an election need not fear being liquidated or deprived of their liberty without process. They know that all concerned will be able to continue the struggle in the next election. There is, in other words, a societal consensus on the limits of the political struggle. Americans, for example, operate on the assumption that politics will continue to function within the existing constitutional order. They further assume that the economic system will be primarily a free-enterprise one. But within these areas of fundamental agreement, Americans dispute narrower issues such as the level of the minimum wage, the need to take military action in the Persian Gulf, appropriate sentences for convicted drug dealers, and the amounts to be spent on defense, health care, and education.

Ironically, if democracy works best when the political battles are over such limited objectives, a durable democracy holds out hope at

7. Ibid.
8. Ibid.

the same time for far-reaching changes in the long run. Again, in Key's words,

The mystique of democracy nourishes a belief that the wrongs of today, persistent though they may seem, will be corrected in some remote tomorrow. Any regime that struggles for stability must implant such expectations in the minds of its people. ... [D]emocratic doctrine seems especially adapted to encouragement of such a faith, for it contemplates an evolving system in which the dispossessed of today may hope to become the top dogs of tomorrow.[9]

The Institutions of Democracy

No single set of institutions is required for a democratic order. All Western-style democracies, however, supplement the executives, courts, and councils found in any government—nondemocratic as well as democratic—with institutions and processes that link the ruled with the rulers, permit consultation with the governed, manage succession of authority, and reconcile competing interests within society. Although the exact nature of the institutions and processes that carry out these functions varies from one representative democracy to another (the American representative democracy, of course, has its own distinctive features), most democratic orders have the following elements in common:[10]

- *Political parties* to contest elections, mobilize public support for or opposition to the government's policies, and handle the succession of power
- *An elected legislature* to serve as the agent and advocate of the representatives' constituents, to symbolize consultation with the governed, and to act as a conduit for communication of approval of and dissent from official policy
- *Electoral procedures* to express mass approval or disapproval of government policy, to set limits on the course of government policy, and to renew leaders' terms of office or dismiss them
- *Nonparty associations and groups* (interest groups) to supplement the formal system of representation in the legislature, to communicate their members' views to government officials, and to act as a means of consultation between the governed and the governors
- *Additional linkages between the government and its citizens* to provide supplementary means of communications through guarantees of freedom of the press, the right to petition the government for

9. Ibid., 8.
10. Ibid., 9–11.

redress of grievances, and protection against official reprisals for dissent against government actions.

The Setting for American Politics

American politics functions always within the shadow of the Constitution, which sets the legal framework for the government (see Chapter 2). But by itself, the Constitution does not explain America's unique brand of democracy or its stability. Other nations, especially in Latin America, have copied our constitutional system, but they have not developed stable democratic political orders. Rather, these countries are subject to occasional periods of free elections and civilian rule, followed by military coups, authoritarian rule, and instability.

Few would question that at the time of the founding, circumstances in the United States were favorable to the development of democracy. This vast subcontinent with its abundant natural resources and fertile land had had no history of feudalism, no titled aristocracy, and no monopoly of landownership by a privileged few. Governments imposed few limitations on those seeking to improve their lots in life in the early years of settlement and nationhood. For those for whom opportunities seemed limited, the vast western frontier was available for starting a new life. Indeed, noted historian Frederick Jackson Turner observed that the frontier environment, with its cheap or free land, promoted democracy, individualism, and nationalism. But the frontier and the prospect of free land and a new life in the West did not last forever. By 1900, the western frontier was largely closed, and America was becoming an industrialized nation whose people were increasingly crowded into teeming cities. Yet despite these and more recent challenges, American democracy has shown a remarkable capacity for adaptability and durability.

The forces molding the uniquely American brand of politics involve more than geophysical conditions, accidents of history, and a remarkable Constitution, although each of these has affected and continues to affect politics. American politics is also shaped by the cultural and socioeconomic environment of the nation: the values and attitudes that people have, the size and composition of the population, the distribution of wealth and income, the class structure, where people live, living patterns, and the issues that divide as well as unite the people.

The Declaration of Independence and the Constitution, enshrined at the National Archives in Washington, D.C., embody fundamental principles of government that are the cornerstones of the nation's political system.

The term **political culture** refers to people's fundamental beliefs and assumptions about how government and politics should operate. Scholars have debated the content of the American political culture and have recognized that some beliefs are more strongly held by certain elements of society than by others. Most agree, however, that five beliefs are deeply rooted in the American psyche: popular sovereignty, an obligation to political participation, individual rights, individualism, and equality. These beliefs influence our behavior, expectations, and evaluations of politicians and policies. They also impose limits on which policy alternatives can be seriously considered. A policy that violates a basic value—such as the right to own private property—does not have a realistic chance of being adopted.

The Preamble to the Constitution begins with the words "We the People of the United States." Embedded in these words is the belief that the people, not some hereditary monarch, are the source of governmental power. As every schoolchild learns, Lincoln's Gettysburg address asserts that ours is a "government of the people, by the people, and for the people." This phrase captures one of our most fundamental beliefs: *popular sovereignty.* The primacy of this belief is reflected in the importance attached to periodic free elections and the role of public opinion in policy making. Government officials who can claim that they have a public mandate to act gain legitimacy for their policies.

The doctrine of popular sovereignty not only bestows the right to participate in the nation's political life but also carries with it a civic duty to participate. *Political participation* is important to Americans. Indeed, a criticism of the era of "Big Government" with its numbing bureaucracies is that these phenomena inhibit meaningful citizen participation. One of the appealing aspects of local and state governments is that they are thought to be "close to the people."

Despite their commitment to popular sovereignty and participation, Americans do have some reservations about democracy. Many fear that voters may be misled by demagogues—leaders who play on voters' prejudices, fears, and baser emotions. In addition, the value attached to strong presidential leadership is proof that people believe they may not always be capable of choosing the best policies by themselves.[11]

As for the widespread belief in *individual rights,* the Declaration of Independence proclaims that it is "self-evident, that all men are

11. Raymond E. Wolfinger, Martin Shapiro, and Fred I. Greenstein, *Dynamics of American Politics,* 2d ed. (Englewood Cliffs, N.J.: Prentice-Hall, 1980), 102.

. . . endowed by their Creator with certain unalienable Rights, that among these are Life, Liberty and the pursuit of Happiness." "Liberty" is the right to make one's own decisions and live one's life freely without undue government restraints. The people's basic right to liberty constitutes a limitation on the power of the majority over individuals and groups. Also well-ingrained into American thinking is the belief in the fundamental right to hold private property. The commitment to private property and individual economic initiative has been so strong in the United States that socialism has made little headway, unlike in some other Western democracies. The largest share of votes ever gained by a socialist candidate for president was the 6 percent (900,369 votes) won by Eugene V. Debs in 1912. No socialist presidential candidate has ever carried a single state.

Individualism is deeply imbedded in the American culture as well. According to the Declaration of Independence, governments exist to fulfill an individual's right to "Life, Liberty and the pursuit of Happiness." When a government fails to provide these rights, it loses its reason to exist. Also part of our culture is the belief that people should make it on their own. They should be rewarded on the basis of their own merit, efforts, and achievements and not on the basis of their family or class positions. It is just such beliefs that force politicians from wealthy, high-society backgrounds to stress their identification with the concerns of average Americans. This commitment to individualism also colors how the middle class views government assistance programs such as welfare and public housing. Such programs are less than universally popular with members of this class.

Even before asserting that people have "unalienable Rights," the Declaration of Independence states that "all men are created equal." In American thinking, *equality* and individual rights are closely linked—if all people are equal, they must have the same rights. Equality has several dimensions. In the Declaration of Independence, Jefferson was referring to political equality. To provide for this kind of equality, the Constitution and statutes contain provisions ensuring that all citizens of legal age have the right to vote, and the Fourteenth Amendment requires the states grant all people the "equal protection of the laws."

Many Americans also are concerned about equality of opportunity. They want people to have the necessities of life and children to have a chance to better themselves. This concern is manifested in the government's expanded role in providing the poor with money, food, housing, education, health care, and legal services. But despite a commitment to equality of opportunity, most Americans do not believe that everyone should be equally well off; rather, everyone should have a relatively equal chance to become better off than his or her neighbors. Americans are quite prepared in fact to accept large disparities in the economic status of their fellow citizens.

A commitment to equality also implies racial equality. In America, the goal of racial equality has not been met, and this failing is a source of continuing frustration, particularly for minority groups. There have been some accomplishments—political discrimination in voting has been largely eliminated since the 1960s, and overt discrimination based on government statutes and rules (for example, requiring segregated schools, restaurants, and theaters) is no longer tolerated—but minorities have not yet achieved full social and economic equality in America. Moreover, there is no consensus on how to deal with the plight of racial minorities. One government-sponsored remedy, affirmative action programs, has stirred deep emotions in both its proponents and opponents. These programs seek to ensure that minorities (and women) are fairly considered for employment and college admission, and, in their most controversial form, they use procedures that give minorities a greater chance of being hired or admitted to educational institutions than their credentials alone would give them. Proponents see these programs as a way to compensate for past acts of discrimination and to give minorities a chance to live the American dream. But opponents see affirmative action programs as violations of society's commitment to awarding people on the basis of merit and as reverse discrimination.

But America's inability to assure its racial minorities of equality should not obscure the importance of the public's commitment to equality. The history of race relations and government civil rights policies in the United States would be much different had the American creed not included such a commitment. That commitment has been and continues to be a source of change as people are forced to confront the inconsistencies between their creed and the treatment accorded racial minorities.

The distinctive blend of beliefs and ways of thinking about politics described here gives America a unique political culture that is interwoven into its political life. American politics, however, also must be viewed in its socioeconomic context for a more well-rounded picture.

The Socioeconomic Context of Politics

To preside over a stable democracy, a government must respond to the needs and wishes of its people. America's people are a diverse lot from all parts of the globe. They differ in their ethnic and racial backgrounds, social statuses, wealth, ages, occupations, religious preferences, lifestyles, and places of residence. Americans live in places as dissimilar as the Bronx in New York City; Midland, Texas; Minot, North Dakota; Beverly Hills, California; and Canton, Mississippi. This diversity produces a myriad of interests as well as conflicts within society—the raw materials of politics. In this section, we will explore the important social and economic features of American society that affect politics.

A look at the *distribution of wealth and income* in American society reveals one of that society's most important characteristics: the vast majority of Americans are not poor. In 1988, the median family household income—the point that separates the upper 50 percent of families from the lower 50 percent—was $31,135 (see Figure 1.1). In the same year, 13.1 percent of families had incomes that fell below the official government poverty level (see Figure 1.2). These data help explain one of the basics of American politics: the poor are a distinct minority in the United States. They cannot rely, therefore, on the traditional weapon of the underprivileged—superior numbers—to achieve their political goals. Instead, they must make alliances with and gain the support of the nonpoor. Indeed, government programs to assist the needy must be supported by large segments of the middle class and by interests that are not poor.

The median incomes of white, black, and Hispanic households (including family and nonfamily) differ substantially. In 1988, the median white household income stood above the national average of $25,986 at $27,427; for black households this figure was $15,475 and for Hispanic households $19,305 (see Figure 1.1). Such income disparities between white, black, and Hispanic households create pressures within the black and Hispanic communities for government assistance programs and income redistribution. These income disparities also help explain why blacks and Hispanics exhibit patterns of voting behavior different from that of whites (see Chapter 6, Political Parties).

As for their *national origins*, over 93 percent of the American population was born in the United States, yet except for Native Americans, the nation descended from immigrants. Until the late 1800s, immigrants came primarily from northern and western Europe, with

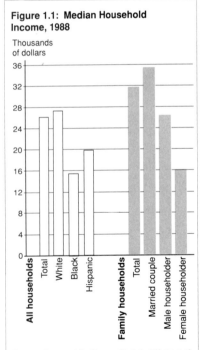

Figure 1.1: Median Household Income, 1988

Thousands of dollars

Source: Bureau of the Census, *Statistical Abstract of the United States: 1990* (Washington, D.C.: Government Printing Office, 1990), 420.
  Note: Hispanic persons may be of any race. For the categories "Male householder" and "Female householder," there is no spouse present.

Figure 1.2: Americans Living Below the Poverty Level, 1959-1988

Percent

Black — All races
Hispanic — White

Source: Bureau of the Census, *Statistical Abstract of the United States: 1990* (Washington, D.C.: Government Printing Office, 1990), 420.
Note: Hispanic persons may be of any race. "All races" includes those races not shown separately.

the largest percentage from Great Britain and Ireland. The wave of "new immigration" in the late 1800s and early twentieth century was quite different, however. It was dominated by former inhabitants of eastern and southern Europe—Italians, Poles, Czechs, Slavs, Greeks, and Russian Jews (see Figure 1.3). Their ethnicity tended to set them apart from native-born Americans and constituted a source of psychological identification. During the late 1920s and 1930s, these new immigrants, who were largely urban, working class, and Catholic, became politically aware and active—so much so, in fact, that their impact on politics was profound. But as the descendants of immigrants from eastern and southern Europe have become assimilated into American life and better off economically, their voting patterns have become less distinct and their traditional support of Democratic candidates is no longer assured. Like other people of European heritage, they have become less conscious of their ethnicity, with the result that their ethnicity is less relevant to them politically (see Chapter 5, Public Opinion and Participation).

It is estimated that between 1981 and 1990 the flow of legal immigrants equaled or surpassed the 8.7 million immigrants that entered the country between 1901 and 1910, the previous high point for immigration into the United States.[12] This latest wave of immigration is dramatically changing the ethnic and racial composition of the nation. Primarily from Latin America and Asia (see Figure 1.3), these new immigrants are concentrated in California, Texas, Florida, and New York. Indeed, it is expected that within the next twenty to twenty-five years, non-Hispanic whites will become a minority in California.[13] The influx of Asian and Latin American immigrants is transforming American politics as well. In the 1988 elections, both the Republican and Democratic parties made special efforts to woo these non-European immigrants, and they have become a critical voting bloc in states with large electoral votes such as California and Texas.

Hispanic immigrants, who can be of any race, hail from countries where Spanish is the dominant language. Because of their high immigration and birth rates, the number of Hispanic-Americans is increasing rapidly—today they make up 8.9 percent of the population. Twenty-seven percent, however, live below the poverty level. A closer

12. Center for Immigration Studies data, reported by Zita Arocha, "1980s Expected to Set Mark as Top Immigration Decade," *Washington Post,* July 23, 1988, A1.

13. Felicity Barringer, "Census Shows Profound Change in Racial Makeup of the Nation," *New York Times,* March 11, 1991, 1, national edition.

Figure 1.3: Immigration to the United States, 1820-1985

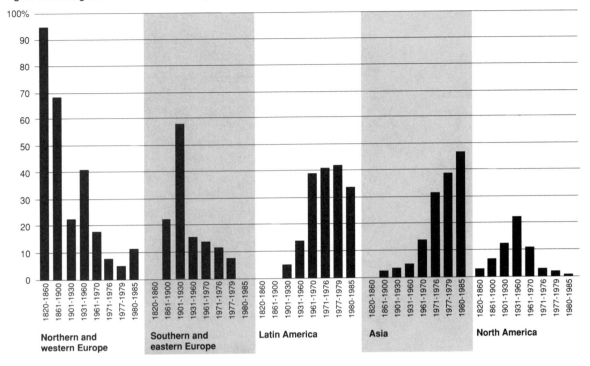

Source: Based on Population Reference Bureau and Bureau of the Census data reported in *New York Times*, June 30, 1986. Copyright © 1986/91 by the New York Times Company. Reprinted by permission.
Note: Percentage of immigrants by region of birth in each period. After 1979, figures for all of Europe are combined into the northern and western Europe category.

look at the political orientations of Hispanics reveals distinct differences. Those of Mexican and Puerto Rican heritage tend to be heavily Democratic in their voting patterns. Cuban-Americans, however, who are better off economically and ardent anticommunists, tend to be Republicans.

Race is another feature of American society (Figure 1.4). Blacks, most of whom are descendants of African slaves, constitute 12 percent of the U.S. population. Unlike Europeans, for whom ethnicity has declining political relevance, blacks are highly conscious of their ethnicity. They have done less well economically than European immigrants, and over 31 percent live below the poverty level. Blacks tend to be concentrated in inner-city neighborhoods and poor rural areas and to feel the continuing effects of racial discrimination. Government policies that combat poverty and deal with civil rights issues are high on the list of political concerns for blacks, who are a critical element of the Democratic party's electoral coalition.

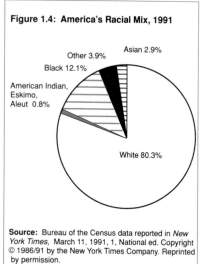

Figure 1.4: America's Racial Mix, 1991

Other 3.9%   Asian 2.9%

Black 12.1%

American Indian,
Eskimo,
Aleut 0.8%

White 80.3%

Source: Bureau of the Census data reported in *New York Times*, March 11, 1991, 1, National ed. Copyright © 1986/91 by the New York Times Company. Reprinted by permission.
Note: Hispanic people can be of any race. They make up 9 percent of the population.

According to population projections, the share of the voting age population held by blacks and other minorities will continue to grow (Figure 1.5). We can, therefore, anticipate that the concerns of these minorities will become increasingly important to Democratic and Republican leaders ever mindful of the importance of winning elections.

Age must not be forgotten in any examination of the socioeconomic context of politics. The proportions of the population that are young, middle-aged, and elderly significantly affect the issues government must confront. As Americans have smaller families and people live longer, the population, on the whole, is aging. Thus, this growing elderly segment of the population is putting heavy pressure on the government to provide it with services, particularly in the areas of pensions and health care. As an increasingly well-organized electoral force, the elderly have effectively blocked any proposal to reduce Social Security retirement benefits for the purpose of trimming the federal budget deficit. And because of the growing numbers of this age group, their concerns will be high on the government's agenda in coming years. It is even possible that generational conflicts in politics will surface as younger Americans balk at paying a large share of the bill for elderly services.

In other policy areas, generational differences are already apparent. Teenagers and those "twentysomething" are more liberal on social issues than their elders. They are more likely to favor busing for school integration, legalization of marijuana, sex education in schools, and careers for women, and be tolerant of premarital sex. Thus, advocates of a conservative social agenda for the nation may encounter opposition as younger voters assume a larger leadership role in society.

Violent clashes between Catholics and Protestants in Northern Ireland and between Christians and Moslems in Lebanon are proof that worldwide *religion* can cause bitter internal political strife as well. Fortunately, in the United States religious differences have never raised the same kind of passions, even though substantial religious diversity exists. Religion can, however, affect voting patterns. As we will see in Chapter 5, Protestants are predominantly Republican; Catholics have traditionally been strongly Democratic, although in the 1980s a majority voted Republican for president; and Jews have been overwhelmingly Democratic. In recent elections, Protestant fundamentalists have become increasingly active in politics and have tended to support Republican candidates for president.

Although social scientists can neatly place people in a particular

The public agenda of the 1990s arises from changing lifestyles, shifts in the composition of the population, concern for the environment, and economics. Growing numbers of women working outside the home give salience to the issues of sex discrimination and day care for children; the preference of many middle-class Americans for life in the suburbs contributes to the decay of central cities; an aging population means that increased resources will be required to care for the elderly; and America's expanding need for energy poses continuing economic and environmental challenges.

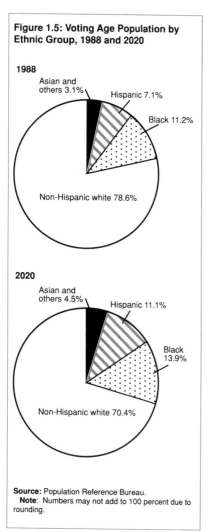

Figure 1.5: Voting Age Population by Ethnic Group, 1988 and 2020

1988

Asian and others 3.1%
Hispanic 7.1%
Black 11.2%
Non-Hispanic white 78.6%

2020

Asian and others 4.5%
Hispanic 11.1%
Black 13.9%
Non-Hispanic white 70.4%

Source: Population Reference Bureau.
Note: Numbers may not add to 100 percent due to rounding.

social class based on such criteria as income or occupation, most Americans are not class-conscious. After reviewing polling data on the demands that different income groups place on government, the editors of *Public Opinion* magazine concluded that there are "class differences, but no class divide."[14] Furthermore, they discovered only small differences of opinion on such issues as housing discrimination, the value of social welfare programs and public schools, the government's role in combating poverty, and the level of taxation.

American political parties draw support from voters in all social classes and at all income levels. Even so, there are differences in the extent to which the various income groups support the Republican and Democratic parties (see Chapter 5). Generally speaking, as one moves up the socioeconomic ladder, one is more likely to support the Republicans.

One of the potentially significant changes in the class composition of the United States is the emergence of a growing "new class" of college-trained professionals—engineers, computer experts, economists, research analysts, lawyers, and scientists. While political scientists are not certain about the political implications of this increasingly prominent group, its members' opinions, candidate preferences, and level of political participation will significantly affect the future of American politics.[15]

Changing lifestyles and changes in the way people earn their livings have significant political implications as well. One of the most important changes in American society has been the growing proportion of women entering the labor force. Indeed, the Bureau of Labor Statistics reported that between 1970 and 1988 this proportion jumped from 49 percent to over 67 percent for women ages twenty-five to sixty-four. Particularly striking is the proportion of working mothers.[16] In 1988, over 72 percent of mothers with children ages 6–17 were in the work force, and a majority of women with children under six were working.[17] Just as the growing number of older Americans has forced politicians to pay attention to the concerns of the elderly, the dramatic upswing in the number of women in the work force also has put pressure on the government to, for example, provide day-care facilities and ensure the right to parental leave in cases of pregnancy and family illness.

14. *Public Opinion,* May/June 1987, 24–25.
15. Everett Carll Ladd, "Pursuing the New Class: Social Theory and Survey Data," in *The New Class?* ed. B. Bruce Briggs (New Brunswick, N.J.: Transaction Books, 1979), 101–122.
16. Bureau of the Census, *Statistical Abstract of the United States: 1990* (Washington, D.C.: Government Printing Office, 1990), 379.
17. Ibid., 385.

Place of residence is yet another factor in America's political equation. For most of its history, the United States has been a predominantly rural nation with most of its citizens living on farms and in small towns. But today, over three-fourths of Americans live in a metropolitan area (a central city of at least fifty thousand and its surrounding suburbs) and slightly over half of the nation's population resides in metropolitan areas with a population exceeding one million. Within metropolitan areas, population growth has been concentrated in the suburbs.

The regional distribution of the population has changed as well. The population is growing most rapidly in the South, Southwest, and Pacific coast (especially California), while the proportion of the population living in the New England, Middle-Atlantic, midwestern, and Plains states is declining.

Such population changes have political consequences. As increasing numbers of white, middle-class Americans have migrated to the suburbs and exurbia, the central cities have becoming increasingly occupied by the poor, blacks, and other minorities. Also with the exodus of the middle class, cities' tax bases have diminished, yet the proportion of city residents needing government social services has expanded. It is not surprising then that city officials have been at the forefront of those pressing for increased federal government assistance to urban areas and the poor.

The changing composition of the population of these central cities has its partisan implications as well. Because the middle class has largely left the central cities, few Republicans now represent central city congressional districts, which have become solidly one-party, Democratic areas. As a result, members of Congress—both white and black—from these districts are amassing congressional seniority and moving into leadership positions within the Democratic party in the House of Representatives.

The political power equations in Congress also are being altered in the shifts in population among the states. For example, in 1950 California had thirty members in the House of Representatives, but after 1990 its population will entitle it to fifty-two representatives— the largest state delegation in the House. Indeed, California will have more representatives than the fourteen states in the Rocky Mountain and Plains states combined. New York, by contrast, saw its House representation shrink from forty-three to thirty-one between 1950 and 1990.

The electoral fortunes of the Republican and Democratic parties have felt the effect, too, of population shifts among the states. The

Figure 1.6: Regional Differences in Voters' Political Orientations

ABC News: "Regardless of the party you may favor, do you lean toward the liberal side or the conservative side politically?"

New England: 24% / 37% / 39%

Middle Atlantic: 27% / 37% / 37%

East North Central: 21% / 37% / 42%

West North Central: 18% / 36% / 46%

South Atlantic: 18% / 33% / 49%

East South Central: 15% / 38% / 47%

West South Central: 18% / 34% / 48%

Mountain: 16% / 37% / 46%

Pacific: 25% / 37% / 38%

National: 21% / 36% / 43%

Lean toward the liberal side politically

Somewhere in between

Conservative side

Source: 1984 ABC News survey reprinted in *Public Opinion*, January/February 1988, 26. Reprinted with the permission of the American Enterprise Institute for Public Policy Research, Washington, D.C.

Note: Sample = 11,023 voters. Numbers may not add to 100 percent due to rounding.

migration of northerners carrying their Republicanism with them has contributed to a breakdown of the once solidly Democratic South. Indeed, after the 1990 elections Republicans held one-third of the region's congressional seats, and southern Republicans constituted the largest regional bloc within the House Republican party. This increase in southern Republican representation and decrease in the number of House Democrats from the South have had a significant impact on the policy orientation of both congressional parties: House Republicans have become more conservative, and House Democrats more liberal.

Although America's regions are becoming more homogeneous in their political viewpoints, regional differences in political orientations continue to exist. People living in the New England, Middle-Atlantic, and Pacific Coast states are, on the whole, more liberal politically than those in other regions (Figure 1.6).

The Public Policy Context

A government's policy making is strongly affected by its past decisions. These decisions create the conditions and public expectations with which today's leaders must deal. As government's role in society has expanded to provide services to virtually every interest in American life, beneficiaries and their supporters have begun to expect that their programs will continue and perhaps expand. Farmers expect continued price supports and crop insurance; students expect loans and grants; car owners expect interstate highways; professors expect research grants; backpackers expect wilderness areas to be preserved; the poor and their defenders expect welfare programs, food stamps, Medicaid, and housing assistance; and the list goes on. Given the constituencies of support that nearly every government program and policy develop, it is small wonder that the politicians in Washington find it difficult to make sweeping changes in government policy.

Probably the most significant of the past national policy decisions in terms of consequences for current and future government policy making have been those made about the federal budget—taxes and spending. During the 1980s and early 1990s, the federal budget deficit was allowed to rise to unprecedented levels—$318 billion in fiscal year 1991. As a result of this flood of red ink, national policy making has become "fiscalized"—that is, policy proposals in both domestic and defense areas are being judged more on how they will affect the federal budget deficit than on their merits. In the face of

(1) swelling budget deficits, (2) public reluctance to support either reductions in long-familiar services or higher taxes, and (3) elected officials' fears of incurring the public's wrath for either cutting programs or raising taxes, it has become extremely difficult to advocate expanding existing programs or to propose new ones. For the government to embark on major new spending programs in this budgetary environment, the money to fund such activities must be taken from already hard-pressed existing programs. The prospects for major policy changes or innovations in the 1990s are thus extremely dim.

Economists are in near agreement that the government's huge federal budget deficits are having adverse consequences on the domestic economy and on America's position in the international economy. The budget deficits also are believed to be threatening the nation's long-term economic health. Coping with these deficits, however, requires confronting a series of equally unattractive policy choices: raising taxes or cutting spending. Tax increases to raise additional revenues send shivers down the spines of many elected officials (Figure 1.7 shows where the federal government obtains and spends its funds). Cutting or reducing the rate of growth in existing domestic programs is an extremely difficult option as well because the largest share of the budget (41 percent) is tied up in **entitlements** (direct payments to individuals who meet certain criteria) for such popular programs as Social Security and Medicare, as well as such safety net programs for the poor as food stamps, Medicaid, Aid to Families with Dependent Children (welfare), and housing assistance (see Figure 1.7).

With the decline in the threat from the Soviet Union, the Pentagon budget has become a prime target for budget cutters. But uncertain world conditions (of which the 1991 war in the Persian Gulf was a reminder) make many Washington policy makers reluctant to tamper too severely with Department of Defense budgets. In addition, members of Congress strenuously resist military expenditure cutbacks if they think it will mean a loss of jobs in their own districts or states. Proposals, then, to close military bases or to stop production on even unneeded aircraft and weapons confront tough opposition within Congress.

Further complicating the problem of cutting expenditures is the growing share (14 percent) of the budget that must go toward paying the interest on the federal debt. As the prolonged and at times acrimonious conflict of 1990 between the Bush White House and Congress over taxes and spending in the 1991 budget demonstrated,

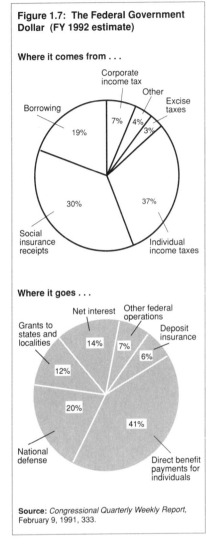

Figure 1.7: The Federal Government Dollar (FY 1992 estimate)

Where it comes from . . .

Corporate income tax

Other

Excise taxes

Borrowing

7%

4%

3%

19%

37%

30%

Social insurance receipts

Individual income taxes

Where it goes . . .

Net interest

Other federal operations

Grants to states and localities

Deposit insurance

14%

7%

6%

12%

20%

41%

National defense

Direct benefit payments for individuals

Source: *Congressional Quarterly Weekly Report*, February 9, 1991, 333.

policy making in the 1990s has been profoundly affected by what political scientist Paul Peterson has called "new politics of deficits."[18]

It is not just in the domestic area that past policy decisions impose constraints on and influence current policy making; past foreign policy decisions also affect today's decisions. For example, for over forty years America has provided support for and leadership of the North Atlantic Treaty Organization (NATO), and it has committed U.S. ground troops to the defense of Western Europe. A strong NATO alliance has been the cornerstone of American policy for Western Europe. Adapting that policy and NATO to an increasingly unified and economically vibrant Western Europe that no longer senses an immediate Soviet military threat, however, is proving to be extremely difficult for U.S. policy makers.

The Durable and Unique American Political System

Stripped down to its basics, politics is the pursuit and exercise of power as well as the process through which society expresses and manages its conflicts. But American politics does not take place in a vacuum. It is affected on a daily basis by the legal structure imposed by the Constitution, society's cultural values and socioeconomic characteristics, as well as the government's past policy decisions.

Americans take pride in their creative accomplishments—their technological inventiveness which resulted in Henry Ford's Model T, bringing the automobile within reach of ordinary people, and in the electronics technology that has enabled students to have hand-held calculators; retailing inventions like the supermarket and the shopping mall; and an economic system that has produced a high standard of living for many in this country. Yet Americans rarely brag about the U.S. political system. Instead, on the Fourth of July, America's great national day, the country celebrates its creation as a new and independent nation with parades, speeches, family picnics, ball games, fireworks, and, for most people, a day off from work. But there is a certain irony that it is independence that commands so much celebration and commemoration. As British political scientist Anthony King has reminded us, achieving national independence is no great trick, especially when the colonial power is three thousand miles away, half-hearted about holding onto its colony, and internally

18. Paul E. Peterson, "The New Politics of Deficits," in *The New Directions in American Politics*, ed. John E. Chubb and Paul E. Peterson (Washington, D.C.: Brookings, 1985), chap. 13.

divided.[19] After all, almost ninety nations have achieved independence since 1945.

Much more impressive is the feat of establishing a set of governmental institutions that are highly adaptable, liberal rather than repressive, and capable of enduring for more than two hundred years. Testimony to the political system's remarkable record of stability is the fact that the United States has held its elections on schedule even in the midst of a civil war, two world wars, and major economic depressions. Indeed, the American political system's record of adaptability and durability is such that if the readers of this book are still alive in one hundred years, they would be confidently looking forward to the election of the president, the entire House of Representatives, and one-third of the Senate—in 2092.

At least a partial explanation for this expectation of continuity rests with the Constitution, which provides a legal framework for America's unique and durable political system. The Constitution, therefore, is the subject of the next chapter.

For Review

1. Politics is a natural and inevitable social process through which society expresses and manages its conflicts. The political process is never-ending. Every government decision is therefore an interim one.

2. Under a democratic government, citizens have a relatively high degree of control over their leaders. All democracies, however, do not structure their governments in the same manner. The United States, for example, has a presidential system, but most Western-style democracies utilize a parliamentary form of government.

3. Democratic governments have these elements in common: guarantees of freedom of the press and speech and protection against official reprisals for dissent; political parties to contest elections and mobilize support for and opposition to the government's policies; an elected legislature; and nonparty associations and groups to supplement the formal system of representation in the legislature.

4. A nation's politics is profoundly affected by its political culture—people's fundamental beliefs and assumptions about how government and politics should operate. Among the fundamental values of the American political culture are popular sovereignty, the obli-

19. Anthony King, "The American Polity in the 1990s," in *The New American Political System,* 2d ed., ed. Anthony King (Washington, D.C.: American Enterprise Institute, 1990), 287.

gation of civic participation, individual rights, individualism, and equality.

5. The socioeconomic characteristics of the people also have significant consequences for American politics. Changes in the population's ethnic and racial composition, age distribution, places of residence and work, and lifestyle are creating new problems and demands for shifts in government policy.

6. The current policy-making process is affected by the government's past decisions as well. Today, the massive government budget deficits impose severe constraints on policy makers and make it difficult to expand existing government programs or institute new ones.

For Further Reading

Almond, Gabriel A., and Sidney Verba. *Civic Culture: Political Attitudes and Democracy in Five Nations*. Princeton, N.J.: Princeton University Press, 1963. A classic study comparing the political culture of five nations, including the United States.

Bureau of the Census. *Statistical Abstract of the United States*. Washington, D.C.: Government Printing Office, published annually. A compendium of useful information about political, economic, and social trends in the United States.

de Tocqueville, Alexis. *Democracy in America*. Translated by Phillips Bradley. New York: Knopf, Vintage Books, 1945. Originally published in 1835, an important portrait of American political culture.

Huntington, Samuel P. *American Politics: The Promise of Disharmony*. Cambridge, Mass.: Harvard University Press, 1981. A fascinating analysis of America's democratic creed of liberty, equality, and hostility to authority and how it has affected the functioning of government institutions.

Lipset, Seymour Martin. *The First New Nation: The United States in Historical and Comparative Perspective*. Rev. ed. New York: Norton, 1979. An exploration of how the values of equality and achievement developed in American culture and their impact on American politics.

2. The Constitution

CONSTITUTIONS grant powers to public officials, distribute powers among the branches and levels of government, and impose limits on government itself. Indeed, the basic principle of **constitutional government** calls for imposing recognized and enforced limits on the government's powers.[1] Constitutions are therefore a special type of law— a law above ordinary statutes passed by the national legislature, the executive orders of a president or prime minister, or the administrative regulations of the bureaucracy. And all parts of the government are expected to abide by this higher law. A country's constitution embodies the fundamental political philosophy of its citizens, outlines the basic structure and functions of its government, and describes the relationships between individuals and their government.

The American brand of democracy has its roots in the Constitution of the United States. The organization and actions of the Congress, presidency, and judiciary reflect how officials in each branch of government have interpreted their powers under the Constitution. Because it provides the legal framework within which our political system functions, the Constitution has exerted a profound influence on American government for over two centuries. In this chapter, we explore the origins and basic principles of this remarkable and enduring document, as well as the processes of constitutional interpretation and change.

Origins of the American Constitution

The Constitution was written by fifty-five men gathered at a constitutional convention in Philadelphia during the summer of 1787. The document they produced reflected, of course, their personal philosophies of governance. It also reflected their reactions to the problems America had experienced as a colony of England and was experiencing as a newly independent nation. But to produce such a document, the Framers had to resolve through compromise the internal conflicts and divisions that existed within their own ranks.

The English Political Heritage

The Constitution of the United States, with its provisions for **limited government**, a representative legislature, and government by consent of the governed, owes much to America's English heritage.

1. Charles H. McIlwain, *Constitutionalism: Ancient and Modern* (Ithaca, N.Y.: Cornell University Press, 1940), 23.

For centuries before the writing of the Constitution in 1787, the English had been evolving and experimenting with constitutional government. As early as 1215, with the signing of the Magna Carta (the Great Charter), King John had been forced to accept limits on the monarch's powers, including the principle that extraordinary taxes could not be levied without the consent of a council of noblemen from all over his realm. This council was the forerunner of the modern British Parliament. By 1688, almost one hundred years before the convening of the Constitutional Convention in Philadelphia, the British Parliament had twice deposed kings who had sought to rule without Parliament and had violated the basic rights and liberties of English citizens. In compelling King William to agree to the Bill of Rights in 1689 as a condition to his becoming the monarch, Parliament affirmed the rights of English citizens to petition their government, to be tried by a jury of their peers, and to be free from excessive bail, fines, and cruel or unusual punishments.[2] Moreover, the English Bill of Rights banned the king from suspending laws of Parliament or interfering with free speech in the proceedings of Parliament and guaranteed frequent meetings of the Parliament. Over the centuries, England also had been developing a judicial system that sought to treat individuals fairly and to hold public officials to previously established rules of conduct. The English colonists carried these traditions to America and incorporated them into the governments of the thirteen original colonies. Although there were differences among the colonies in governmental structures, each had a governor, a council composed of key executive officials, an elected legislature, and a judiciary.

Until the 1770s, the colonists did not consider themselves to be "Americans." Rather, they were English citizens living in the New World. Their sense of national identity only began to develop after the French and Indian War, which ended in 1763. With its victory over the French and their Indian allies, the British government sought to have the colonies share in paying for the cost of the war, which the British believed had been fought largely for the benefit of the colonists. The British also wanted the colonies to pay the costs of their own administration. The resulting taxes enacted by a parliament across the Atlantic in London created the bases for conflict between the colonies and the mother country.

2. For a concise account of the crown-parliamentary struggle that culminated in the revolution that produced the English Bill of Rights, see Stuart E. Prall, *The Bloodless Revolution: England, 1688* (Madison: University of Wisconsin Press, 1985).

The Founding of a New Nation

1763 British defeat the French in North America in the French and Indian War.

1765 Britain imposes the Stamp Act on the colonies.

1773 Britain enacts the Tea Act, and colonists in Massachusetts stage the Boston Tea Party.

1774 First Continental Congress meets in Philadelphia and asserts that the British Parliament has no authority over the colonies' internal affairs.

1775 Battles of Lexington and Concord.

1776 Second Continental Congress adopts the Declaration of Independence.
New state constitutions adopted between 1776 and 1784.

1777 Second Continental Congress adopts the Articles of Confederation.

1781 British surrender at Yorktown.
States complete ratification of the Articles of Confederation.

1786 Shays's Rebellion.
Annapolis Convention petitions the Continental Congress to call a constitutional convention.

1787 Constitutional Convention meets in Philadelphia and drafts the Constitution of the United States of America.

1787–1788 Eleven states ratify the Constitution, including the large states of New York and Virginia.

1789 First elections held under the Constitution.
The First Congress convenes, and George Washington is inaugurated the nation's first president.
North Carolina ratifies the Constitution.

1790 Rhode Island becomes the last of the thirteen original states to ratify the Constitution.

1791 Bill of Rights is ratified by the states.

The Declaration of Independence

Among the taxes imposed by the British government were the Sugar Act, which levied a duty on foreign molasses and threatened the rum trade; the Stamp Act, which imposed a tax on all legal documents, newspapers, almanacs, dice, and playing cards; and the Quartering Act, which required colonists to help support English troops by providing them with living quarters, food, and beer. From the colonists' viewpoints, however, these taxes deliberately denied them their rights as English citizens. Being such, they believed that it was their right not to be taxed except by their own elected representatives. They were, however, being taxed by the English Parliament in London where they had no representatives. Particularly distressing was the denial in the Sugar and Stamp acts of their rights as English citizens to a trial by a jury of their peers. Special courts, which operated without juries and considered the defendant guilty until proved innocent, were used to try violators of the Sugar and Stamp acts. These and other actions by the British government encouraged the colonists to see their interests as distinct from those of England, and a sense of common interest among the colonists developed.

To protest the 1773 Tea Act, which gave a commercial advantage to England's East India Company over American traders, a band of colonists, disguised as Indians, staged the Boston Tea Party and dumped 342 chests of tea into the harbor. The English responded by closing the Port of Boston. American resistance to British rule then intensified, and armed hostilities broke out in nearby Lexington and Concord in 1775. But earlier, in 1774, the first Continental Congress had been convened to air the colonies' grievances, and on July 4, 1776, it approved the **Declaration of Independence**. By this act, the American colonies ended their allegiance to Great Britain.

The colonies' justification for the Revolution was set forth in the Declaration of Independence. This declaration went beyond a statement of the particular facts surrounding the eighteenth-century struggle between the British government and its colonies and alleged that the colonists' basic rights had been violated repeatedly. The enduring quality of the document results from its citing basic principles under which the new nation would be governed. Much of the spirit of the declaration is captured in the opening lines penned by its drafter and member of the Continental Congress, Thomas Jefferson:

We hold these truths to be self-evident, that all men are created equal, that they are endowed by their Creator with certain unalienable Rights, that among these are Life, Liberty and the pursuit of Happiness. That to secure these rights, Governments are instituted among Men, deriving their just powers from the consent of the governed.

In drafting the declaration, Jefferson drew heavily on the writing of John Locke, an English political philosopher. Locke believed that there was a natural law that bestowed on all people **natural rights** to life, liberty, and property. To protect these basic rights, people agree to form a government through a **social compact**. If a government persistently violates its citizens' natural rights, however, it then loses its legitimacy, and people have the right, in Jefferson's phrasing, "to alter or to abolish it, and to institute a new Government, laying its foundations on such principles and organizing its powers in such form, as to them shall seem most likely to effect their Safety and Happiness." In utilizing Locke's philosophy, Jefferson articulated

Hostility to British rule of the American colonies was inflamed by the "Boston Massacre" of March 5, 1770, when troops fired on an unruly mob of tax protesters. This incident in which seven protesters were killed was given a sensationalized portrayal in this engraving by Paul Revere.

basic concepts of government that are cornerstones of the American political system: that the major purpose of government is to protect people's rights to life, liberty, and the pursuit of happiness, and that governments derive their power from the people.

Traditionally, kings have ruled by divine right, claiming that they derive their power from the Almighty and that they are acting as God's temporal agents on earth. The Declaration of Independence swept away the divine-right-of-kings rationale for governmental authority and replaced it with a new and radical doctrine—that governments derive their powers from the *consent of the governed*. The people are the source of a government's power. Over two hundred years later, the principles of the Declaration of Independence have continuing appeal and special relevance both to those groups in the United States struggling for their rights and to those around the world asserting individual rights against authoritarian governments.

Governing the New Nation:
State Constitutions

The revolutionary break with Great Britain required the thirteen former colonies to write new state constitutions to replace the colonial charters that had been granted by the Crown and that had constituted the basis for the colonial governments' authority. Power in the new post-Revolution state governments was concentrated in their legislatures. Gubernatorial and judicial authorities were reduced from their former levels in the colonial charters because these authorities had been sources of royal influence and Americans had become wary of a strong executive and judges. Under the post-Revolution state constitutions, governors were elected by the state legislatures, which also could override judicial decisions. The new state constitutions not only strengthened the legislative branch but also contained bills of rights and liberalized most property-owning and taxpaying qualifications for voting.

In framing the Constitution a decade later, the drafters drew on their experiences under post-Revolution state constitutions. These experiences led them to conclude that the executive and judicial powers within the states were too weak to offset the tendency of each legislature to draw all power "to its impetuous vortex" and become despotic.[3] As a result, they sought in the Constitution to create a government in which the legislative, executive, and judicial branches would check each other.

3. E. M. Earle, ed., *The Federalist* (New York: Modern Library, 1937), No. 48, 322–324.

At the national level, a union of the thirteen states was formed under a new constitution, **the Articles of Confederation,** which was ratified unanimously by the states in 1781.[4] The articles vested all powers of the national government in a one-chamber Continental Congress in which each state was entitled to one vote, regardless of size of population. There were no national judiciary and no national executive to coordinate the implementation of congressional policy. Important legislation required the support of nine of the thirteen states, and any amendments to the original thirteen articles needed the unanimous approval of the states.

Among its significant accomplishments during its eleven years (1777–1788) under the articles, the United States won its independence; made commercial treaties with European countries; created the executive departments of the Post Office, Treasury, Foreign Affairs, and War (defense); and approved the Northwest Ordinance, which established the principles that guided territorial expansion until the end of the nineteenth century. The ordinance established procedures for admitting new states to the Union and embodied governmental principles essential for democracy, including a ban on slavery, freedom of religion, and encouragement of public education. There were, however, at least three serious weaknesses inherent in the articles that made effective governance of the Union virtually impossible.

First, *the national government was dependent on the states.* The national government created under the articles was a **confederation**—a "League of Friendship and Cooperation" among the several states of the Union. This meant that the national government had to exercise its authority *through the states* and could not deal directly with individual citizens. The national government, therefore, was dependent on the states to carry out many of its policies, yet it lacked the power to compel the states to comply with its statutory enactments. To raise an army and a navy, the Continental Congress had to request troops from the states, which often did not provide the required manpower. As a result, the national government could do little to combat hostile acts by foreign governments. In 1784, for example, Spain closed the lower Mississippi to foreign navigation, and Britain's King George III secretly ordered British military gar-

---

4. A distinguished study of the articles is that by Merrill Jensen in *The Articles of Confederation* (Madison: University of Wisconsin Press, 1940).

risons and trading posts to remain in the American territory west of the Appalachians. A government that could not provide for the common defense of its citizens did not inspire confidence or loyalty.

Having to rely on state compliance to carry out national policies also created problems in raising revenue. Because Congress could not tax individual citizens, it assessed the states. The states, however, frequently did not pay their assessments. Efforts to increase national revenues through a tax on imports revealed a further problem with the Articles of Confederation: an amendment to the articles could be implemented only by unanimous consent of all the states. Twice a single state blocked congressional efforts to amend the articles to permit taxing imports. The government under the Articles of Confederation thus lacked two essential resources required for governing: a military force and revenues.

Second, *the national government had no power to regulate foreign and interstate commerce.* In addition to its unworkable dependence on the states for military manpower and revenues, the Continental Congress lacked the power to regulate commerce among the states and with foreign nations. The states, therefore, acted independently to impose tariffs and other barriers to trade with foreign countries as well as with their sister states. The result was economic chaos. The government lacked revenues it might have derived from nationally imposed tariff duties; there was no uniform commercial policy; and the states imposed restrictions on trade to protect special interests within their boundaries. Such state-imposed restrictions on interstate trade limited both the economic development of the nation and the development of a sense of a national identity.

Third, *the national government had a weak executive and judiciary.* Congress did establish executive departments presided over by secretaries, but there was no strong, unifying executive to coordinate national policy. And as there was no independent or separate national judiciary, the judicial functions of the government were carried out by the state courts. There was, however, no regularized method for dealing with disputes among the states.

But the problems of the post-Revolution period were not just problems with the national government; there were also serious problems of economic and political instability within the states. Some of the states failed to adopt sound measures to deal with the depressed economy and responded to demands of debtors by printing excessive amounts of paper money. Such actions created inflation, which devalued the worth of the currency and caused people of means to believe that the sanctity of private property was threatened. In Rhode Island, creditors hid from their debtors seeking to pay off debts with nearly worthless paper currency.

In those states that refused to adopt inflationary measures, debt-ridden citizens threatened with foreclosure on their farms became violent in some instances. Indeed, the militia in New Hampshire had to disperse a mob that descended on the state legislature, and in Massachusetts, crowds of angry citizens led by Daniel Shays tried to prevent courts from foreclosing on the mortgages of farmers and even sought to seize a government arsenal. This incident, known as Shays's Rebellion (1786), was put down by the militia, but it provided an additional impetus for reform of the Articles of Confederation because it seemed to demonstrate the inherent instability of a system that vested most governmental power in the legislature and had a weak executive and judiciary.

Reforming the Articles of Confederation

The leaders of the movement to reform the articles recognized the government's inability to exercise national powers. They believed that the new nation needed a stronger national government to promote economic development and to deal with the political instability within the states. Their experience with state governments dominated by popularly elected legislatures had convinced them that stable and effective representative government required some restraint on popular rule and legislative power.

The immediate impetus for reform came out of interstate trade controversies. A conference on trade was held in Annapolis, Maryland, in 1786 under the auspices of then-retired general George Washington and James Madison, member of the Virginia House of Delegates. At the urging of Alexander Hamilton, a New York lawyer who had been agitating for constitutional reform for years, the five states represented at the Annapolis Convention petitioned the Continental Congress to call a constitutional convention. After initially ignoring this request, the Congress, in response to pressures from such states as Virginia and fears created by Shays's Rebellion, issued a call for a convention to meet in Philadelphia in 1787 for the purpose of revising the Articles of Confederation.

The Constitutional Convention: Creating a New Governmental Order

In 1787, precisely because it was fearful of a *constitutional* convention, the Continental Congress worded its call to the states carefully: the convention was for the "sole and express purpose of revising the Articles of Confederation." Thus, in deciding to draft a wholly new constitution for the United States, the delegates to the convention disregarded the mandate given them by the Continental Congress and set about the business of creating a government strong enough to govern, while preserving individual rights and a major role for the states.

The Framers of the Constitution began their task on May 25, 1787, at the State House in Philadelphia. George Washington was chosen unanimously president of the Constitutional Convention. After four months of deliberations over a sweltering summer, delegates drafted the document known today as the Constitution of the United States. But fashioning this blueprint for American government involved lengthy debate and conflict—conflict so intense at times it was feared the convention would break up without completing its task. Reflected, then, in the Constitution are the numerous compromises required to resolve the philosophical, economic, and regional differences among the delegates; the basic principles of governance in which the writers believed; as well as their practical solutions to problems facing the new nation.[5]

The Delegates

From the beginning, the convention was controversial. The revolutionary leader from Virginia Patrick Henry "smelled a rat" and, fearing that the convention would endorse the centralization of government power, stayed away from Philadelphia. Rhode Island, a center of paper money interests, even refused to send delegates. Indeed, only fifty-five of the seventy-four delegates to the Constitutional Convention actually attended. But those delegates who did convene in Philadelphia were a distinguished group of men experienced in government. There were seven former governors, thirty-nine former members of the Continental Congress, and eight individuals who had helped write state constitutions. Despite their experience, they were relatively young, with an average age of forty-two.

As a group, they were also men of considerable status and wealth who had advanced beyond the positions of their fathers. Only William Few of Georgia could be considered a representative of the small farmers who constituted a majority of the free, nonslave population. The leaders of the convention included James Madison of

5. For a discussion of the background and intellectual underpinnings for the writing of the Constitution, see Vernon L. Parrington, *Main Currents of American Thought,* vol. 1 (New York: Harcourt, Brace, 1927). Also see Clinton Rossiter, *1787: The Grand Convention* (New York: Macmillan, 1966).

George Washington, whose presence lent an aura of legitimacy to the proceedings, presided at the Constitutional Convention of 1787 in Philadelphia. Alexander Hamilton (seated in foreground) and James Madison (seated in front of Washington) played critical roles in arranging for the convention and in securing ratification. Madison also drafted much of the document. Eighty-one-year-old Benjamin Franklin (seated in foreground) played the role of conciliator among the convention's factions.

Virginia, who at age thirty-six had served in the Continental Congress, drafted the Virginia constitution, and made a thorough study of history and political theory preparatory to the convention; Alexander Hamilton of New York, who at age thirty-one had fiercely aristocratic tendencies and strongly supported a national government with expanded authority; George Washington, the Virginia planter and general whose prestige and status lent credibility to the deliberations; Benjamin Franklin of Pennsylvania, a man of wit, experience, and charm, who helped moderate the disputes and found bases for compromise among the conflicting factions of the convention and who at age eighty-one was the oldest delegate present; James Wilson of Pennsylvania, an attorney who played a major role in drafting sections of the Constitution relating to the presidency and executive power; and Gouverneur Morris, another Pennsylvanian, who as the head of the committee on style drafted much of the final language of the document.

The men who wrote the Constitution were the heirs to seventeenth-century English republicanism, with its opposition to monarchy, military dictatorship, and arbitrary rule, as well as its faith in representative government and belief in **popular sovereignty**—that the people are the source of governmental authority.[6] Like John Locke, they believed that the laws of nature entitled each person to life, liberty, and property, and that governments had as their first responsibility the protection of these rights. Because of their experiences with a powerful colonial government in London, they were fearful of concentrations of governmental power.

But for all these beliefs and fears, the writers of the Constitution had counterbalancing concerns. Like the seventeenth-century English philosopher Thomas Hobbes and the Protestant reformer and theologian John Calvin, they distrusted human nature. They saw humans as atoms of self-interest. This was more than a matter of philosophy; as practical men of affairs, the Founders had observed human nature in the marketplaces, legislative halls, and courts, and on the battlefields. Their experiences had convinced them of human frailty and caused them to be wary of what they perceived were excesses of popular rule.

The Founders believed that a sound constitution was needed to control people's natural tendencies toward evil, selfishness, and contentiousness. Writing such a constitution, however, posed a difficult dilemma. They believed that governments rested on the consent of the governed, who were the source of governmental authority, yet they were convinced that human beings were unchangeable creatures of self-interest. Thus, the Constitution writers feared democracy. Hamilton was quoted as saying, "Your people, sir, are a great beast." The Founders sought a government that was capable of governing— a government of expanded powers and one that could control the inherent flaws in human nature. But they did not want that government to be too strong lest it endanger the basic liberties and rights for which they had fought a revolution.

Consensus, Conflict, and Compromise

On some key constitutional provisions, the delegates quickly reached a consensus. During the first week of their deliberations, they agreed that the new government would consist of three

6. For a concise discussion of the Founders' beliefs, see Richard Hofstadter, *The American Political Tradition* (New York: Vintage Books, 1954), chap. 1.

branches—a supreme national legislature, an executive, and a judiciary—and that the national government would have powers wider than those exercised under the Articles of Confederation. The principle of representative government based on an elected legislature was accepted, while Hamilton's plan for a hereditary body like the English House of Lords was rejected. It was further agreed that the national legislature would be *bicameral*—consisting of two chambers. One chamber would represent the aristocracy and the other would represent the ordinary citizen. The executive branch was to consist of one person, elected, it was thought initially, by the legislature. The need for an independent national judiciary, comprised of a supreme court and lower federal courts with judges appointed for life, also was accepted.

Although the delegates quickly established a consensus on many key elements of the new government, there also were major conflicts among them as they sought to protect their states' interests. These conflicts were, however, successfully resolved through a series of major compromises.

A major dispute arose over the basis on which representation in the new Congress would be apportioned among the states. The larger states favored the **Virginia Plan**, which called for a bicameral legislature with the lower house elected by the voters and the upper house chosen by the lower house from nominees submitted by the state legislatures. Representation in both houses would be based on each state's population. This plan would have assured the large and more populous states—Virginia, New York, Pennsylvania, and Massachusetts—of a majority in the legislature. The small states countered with the **New Jersey Plan**. It called for retaining the *unicameral*—single chamber—legislature in place under the Articles of Confederation in which each state had equal representation. This large-versus-small-state dispute was resolved by the Connecticut Compromise, also known as the **Great Compromise**. It called for a bicameral legislature with the House of Representatives elected by the voters and its membership based on each state's population and the Senate elected by the state legislatures with each state having two senators. The House of Representatives would have the power to initiate all tax legislation.

An additional controversy about congressional representation arose over slavery. The South wanted slaves to count in a state's population when determining the number of representatives a state was entitled to have in the House of Representatives. But southern delegates did not want slaves counted in apportioning direct taxes

(taxes paid directly to the national government by individuals) among the states. Northern delegates, however, wanted slaves counted in apportioning direct taxes but did not want them counted for purposes of determining representation. This thorny issue was settled through the **Three-fifths Compromise**, under which it was agreed that slaves would count as three-fifths of a person for purposes of apportioning both representation and taxes among the states.

Further conflict between the North and South arose over the power of the national government to regulate interstate and foreign commerce, including the slave trade. The North, which was developing a commercial and manufacturing economy, was anxious to have a government capable of regulating and promoting interstate and foreign commerce. Northern delegates also favored a ban on the importation of slaves. The more agrarian South, dependent on trading its commodities for imported goods, feared that a new government with extensive trade powers would harm its interests. Southern delegates also wanted the slave trade continued. This dispute was resolved through the **Commerce and Slave Trade Compromise** in which the North gained a strong central government with the power to regulate foreign and interstate commerce. But to protect the South's export trade, the national government was prohibited from levying any taxes on U.S. exports. Furthermore, the South was guaranteed protection against harmful trade treaties by a provision that required a two-thirds vote of the Senate to ratify treaties. In addition, Congress was banned from prohibiting the importation of slaves before 1808.

The presidency also posed a serious problem for the Founders. Initially, they accepted the notion of having the chief executive chosen by the Congress. There was concern, however, that this method of selection would make the president subservient to Congress. In addition, the smaller states believed that a congressionally elected president would permit the larger states to control the office. Because of the distrust they had developed for the post-Revolution state legislatures, the delegates rejected selection of the president by these bodies. Their distrust of the general public also led them to reject direct popular election by the voters. The compromise solution to the presidential selection issue was the **electoral college** in which the president (and vice president) would be chosen by a majority of the electors. According to this plan, each state would choose, in a manner to be determined by the state legislatures, a number of electors equal to its number of representatives and senators in Congress. If no candidate received a majority of the electors' votes, the House of Representatives would then select the president from among the three candidates receiving the largest number of electoral votes. This compromise assured the states and the Congress of a role in presidential selection yet maintained a buffer between the general public and the nation's highest executive.

Basic Principles of the Constitutional System

The drafters of the Constitution faced a series of complex governance problems (Table 2.1). They were seeking to create a government that derived its powers from the people, avoided potential excesses of democracy, protected individual liberties and property, had sufficient power to govern effectively, and preserved state autonomy within a strengthened union. But devising such a government required finding constitutional devices that would permit reconciling these sometimes conflicting objectives. The combination of features in the Constitution can be viewed, therefore, as the Founders' solution to the still vexing problems of representative government.

Popular Sovereignty and Representative Government Tempered by Indirect Election

The Founders' belief that the people should be the source of government power—*popular sovereignty*—is embodied in the Preamble to the Constitution, which states: "We the People of the United States, . . . do ordain and establish this Constitution for the United States of America." The commitment to popular sovereignty is reinforced in more concrete terms by the provision in Article I for direct election of the House of Representatives by the voters every two years.

In providing for an elected House of Representatives and a Senate chosen by the state legislatures, the Founders affirmed their commitment to representative government. They rejected monarchy (a hereditary kingship), aristocracy (rule by a hereditary elite), and direct democracy (rule by the masses).

Fears of mob rule and excessive democracy led the delegates to insulate the new government from the public through a series of indirect selection procedures (see Figure 2.1 for the Founders' system of leadership selection through a combination of direct election, indirect election, and appointment methods). The Founders believed that an indirectly elected Senate would provide a check on imprudent

Table 2.1 The Constitutional Balance

Problems Confronting the Drafters of the Constitution	Constitutional Features Designed to Resolve the Problems
Creating a government based on the consent of the governed while avoiding the evils of factions and excesses of democracy	A government of divided powers • Separation of powers and checks and balances • Federalism (the constitutional division of governmental powers between the national government and the states) • Bicameral legislature An appointed judiciary System of direct popular elections and indirect elections
Creating a government capable of governing while preventing that government from becoming too strong and a threat to individual liberties	Granting extensive powers to the national government while imposing constitutional limits on governmental authority Dividing government powers to make it difficult for any group, faction, or temporary majority to gain control of government
Creating a union out of relatively independent states while preventing the creation of too powerful a national government and permitting state autonomy	Federal supremacy doctrine Federalism
Creating representative government while preventing the legislative excesses that characterized the post-Revolution period	Direct popular election of the House of Representatives, with indirect election of the Senate by the state legislatures Separation of powers to check the legislature Explicit limits on legislative power
Creating an executive strong enough to coordinate the operations of the government and check the legislature while preventing the executive from becoming an arbitrary ruler	Creating the office of president with specified powers Separation of powers to check executive power Election of the president for a fixed term; no hereditary executive

actions inspired by any momentary passions that might sweep through the popularly elected House of Representatives. (It was not until 1913 and ratification of the Seventeenth Amendment that all the states chose their senators through direct popular election—see Chapter 10, Congress.) The presidency was to be insulated from public opinion by its fixed four-year term of office and selection by the electoral college. Each state was free to determine how its electors would be chosen, and, until the 1830s, most states delegated this responsibility to their state legislatures rather than to the voters. To ensure the independence of the judiciary, judges were to serve life terms after being appointed by the president and confirmed by the Senate rather than be elected by the voters.

Limited Government

Like John Locke, the Framers believed that governments were instituted to protect basic individual rights. Thus, they sought to impose limits on governmental power by making explicit grants of authority to the national government. Article I, section 8, of the Constitution contains a list of powers delegated to Congress. When Congress passes legislation, it must be able to trace its authority back to this list or to powers that can be implied from these listed powers. Congress may not act just because it thinks a proposed bill is needed. The Constitution's grants of authority to Congress, however, are stated in broad, general terms—for example, Congress is empowered to pass legislation to provide for the "general Welfare" and to make laws "necessary and proper" to carry out its delegated powers. As a result, the Congress has substantial leeway in fashioning legislation.

Limitations on government also were achieved through specific prohibitions. The national government, for example, is denied the power to tax exports, and both the national government and states are banned from passing either **bills of attainder** (criminal punishment without benefit of a trial) or **ex post facto laws** (retroactive criminal statutes making something a crime that was not a crime at the time it was committed). The **Bill of Rights** was added later to the Constitution to provide additional and explicit limits to the national government's power (see Chapter 4, Civil Liberties and Civil Rights). The First Amendment, for example, says that "Congress shall make no law respecting an establishment of religion, or prohibiting the free exercise thereof; or abridging the freedom of speech, or of the press; or the right of the people peaceably to assemble, and to petition the Government for a redress of grievances."

Separation of Powers with Checks and Balances

A key element in the thinking of the Founders was the belief that a concentration of power leads to tyranny. They feared that some faction, group, or temporary majority might gain enough power to dominate the government and thereby threaten the basic rights of others. Thus, they divided the government's power among three separate branches of government: Congress, vested with legislative authority by Article I; the president, authorized by Article II to exercise executive powers; and the federal courts, vested with judicial power by Article III (specifically, such power is vested in "one supreme Court, and in such inferior courts as the Congress may from time to time ordain and establish").

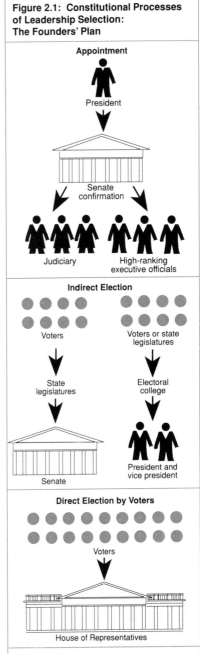

Figure 2.1: Constitutional Processes of Leadership Selection: The Founders' Plan

Appointment

President

Senate confirmation

Judiciary   High-ranking executive officials

Indirect Election

Voters   Voters or state legislatures

State legislatures   Electoral college

Senate   President and vice president

Direct Election by Voters

Voters

House of Representatives

Note: Two important changes have been made over the years in this plan. First, since 1836 the election of presidential electors by a statewide, winner-take-all popular vote has been the almost universal state practice. Second, the Seventeenth Amendment (1913) permits direct election of senators by the voters.

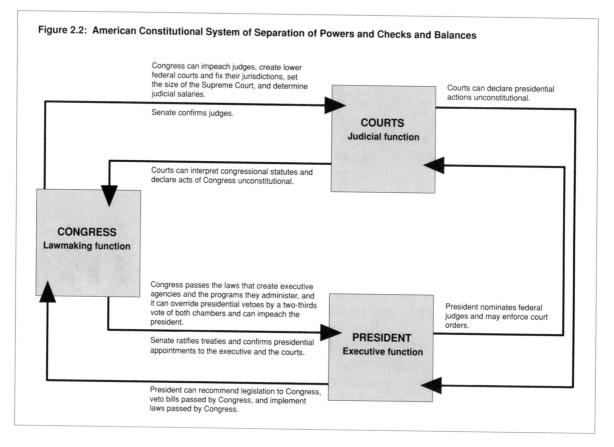

Figure 2.2: American Constitutional System of Separation of Powers and Checks and Balances

To ensure that no one branch could dominate the government and that the government would use restraint in exercising its powers, each branch was required to share some of its powers with the other branches. Under this system of **checks and balances** (described in Figure 2.2), the president has the power to recommend legislation to Congress and to veto bills to indicate presidential disapproval. To check the president, Congress has authority to override presidential vetoes by a two-thirds vote, create executive agencies, impeach the president, confirm appointees to the executive and judicial branches, and ratify treaties negotiated by the president. The judiciary can check both the Congress and the president by declaring their acts unconstitutional, even though this power was not expressly granted by the Constitution. Both the Congress and president have power over the judiciary. The president nominates judges, subject to Senate confirmation, and the Congress may determine the organization and jurisdiction of the federal courts. Through **separation of powers** with checks and balances, the Founders believed that they had found a constitutional device that would prevent any faction or interest that might temporarily dominate a branch of government from infringing on basic rights.

Federalism

The writers of the Constitution succeeded in extending the powers of the national government beyond those under the Articles of Confederation. Congress was now empowered to levy taxes, regulate interstate and foreign commerce, coin money, maintain an army and navy, and provide for the common defense and general welfare. Important matters no longer required virtually the unanimous consent of all the states. Although the national government was strengthened, the states were retained as key governmental units. Actually, the Founders had little choice in this matter. The state legislatures had to ratify the draft constitution prepared by the convention in Philadelphia, and the states could hardly be expected to agree to their own demise. The Founders, therefore, created a government based on the principle of **federalism**. In a federal system the powers of government are constitutionally divided between the national government and the states, with each exercising significant powers. The powers of the national government were to be those enumerated— and those implied by that enumeration—in the Constitution, whereas the states were to exercise reserved powers, which were those not prohibited to the states (for example, the Constitution bans the states from entering into treaties or alliances with foreign countries or coining money) nor granted to the national government. In practical terms, this division of powers has meant that today the states have the major responsibility for such governmental activities as public education, local government, intrastate highway transportation, protection of public health and safety, and family relations.

But in a system in which powers are divided between the national government and the states, it is inevitable that conflicts will arise between national and state laws. To deal with this problem, Article VI contains a **federal supremacy clause**, which makes the Constitution and the laws and treaties passed under it the "supreme Law of the Land." This provision means that all state laws, executive orders, and judicial decisions must conform to the Constitution, treaties, and laws of the United States, or they are invalid.

Where the Constitution draws the line between national and state governmental authority has always been both fuzzy and controversial. In the case of the Civil War, the nation's ongoing controversy over the extent of federal versus state power turned to violence as the South sought to secede from the Union. The manner in which

American federalism has evolved and the controversies over the extent of national versus state power are considered in Chapter 3.

Judicial Review

The federal courts exercise the power of **judicial review**—the power to declare acts of Congress and the president unconstitutional. This principle is firmly embedded in the American constitutional system, even though there is no explicit grant of this authority to the federal courts in the Constitution. Led by Chief Justice John Marshall, the Supreme Court established the precedent for judicial review in 1803 in the case of *Marbury v. Madison* (described in more detail in Chapter 13, The Judiciary).[7] But the Court has used this power sparingly. In the fifty years following the *Marbury* decision, for example, it did not hold any federal laws unconstitutional. Judicial review is exercised only when a specific case is brought before the courts. The judiciary does not give advisory opinions to the Congress or the president.

The Struggle for Ratification

To avoid entrenched opposition within the state legislatures, the drafters provided for ratification of the new Constitution by special constitutional conventions in the states. Ratification by nine of the thirteen states was required before the Constitution could be put into effect.

The backers of the Constitution, who supported a strong national government, were called **Federalists**. James Madison, Alexander Hamilton, and John Jay, a New Yorker who later became chief justice of the Supreme Court, were leaders in this cause. Under the pen name "Publius," they anonymously wrote, published, and circulated eighty-five letters to the public that appeared in New York newspapers beginning in October 1787. Later collected to form the *Federalist Papers,* these writings, which are counted among the classics of political theory, today provide insights into how the drafters of the Constitution envisioned the new government would function. The more immediate purpose of the *Federalist Papers,* however, was to counter the arguments of the **Antifederalists**, who opposed the Constitution.

The Antifederalists feared that the Constitution would create a national government that would endanger personal liberties and sub-

7. *Marbury v. Madison,* 1 Cr. 137 (1803).

Table 2.2 The First Ten Amendments to the Constitution:
Bill of Rights

Amendment	Purpose
I	Guarantees freedom of religion, speech, assembly, and press, and the right of people to petition the government for redress of grievances
II	Protects the right of states to maintain a militia
III	Restricts quartering of troops in private homes
IV	Protects against "unreasonable searches and seizures"
V	Assures the right not to be deprived of "life, liberty or property, without due process of law," including protections against double jeopardy, self-incrimination, and government seizure of property without just compensation
VI	Guarantees the right to a speedy and public trial by an impartial jury
VII	Assures the right to a jury trial in cases involving the common law
VIII	Protects against excessive bail or cruel and unusual punishment
IX	Provides that people's rights are not restricted to those specified in Amendments I–VIII
X	Reiterates the Constitution's principle of federalism by providing that powers not granted to the national government nor prohibited to the states are reserved to states and to the people

merge the state legislatures under the supremacy of Congress.[8] They focused their fire on the absence of a bill of rights in the Constitution and the threat they believed this omission posed for basic liberties. The Federalists argued that a bill of rights was not required because the national government would be restricted to exercising the powers granted to it by the Constitution. They decided, however, to concede this issue in order to secure ratification of the Constitution and agreed to incorporate a bill of rights into the Constitution as the first ten amendments (see Table 2.2).

By June 1788, the required nine states had ratified the Constitution but not included among them were Virginia and New York,

8. See Cecelia M. Kenyon, ed., *The Antifederalists* (Indianapolis: Bobbs-Merrill, 1966).

whose support was essential if the Union was to succeed. Led by Madison in Virginia and Hamilton in New York, the Federalists late in 1788 won narrow and hard-fought victories in both states (with only a three-vote margin in New York).[9] North Carolina (1789) and Rhode Island (1790) later made ratification by the thirteen original states unanimous. The Bill of Rights was ratified on December 15, 1791.

Changing and Interpreting the Constitution: An Enduring Document

In 1987, the Constitution celebrated its two hundredth anniversary, an unusual record of durability for such a document. One reason for its longevity is its relative lack of detailed provisions or statutory-type language that could become quickly outmoded, necessitating frequent changes in its language through amendments. Rather, each branch of government has been able to interpret the Constitution and adapt it to changing circumstances. The records of most state constitutions have been quite different. Most are lengthy documents heavily laden with detailed language that becomes outdated. Frequent amendment or even total revision therefore has been required. Louisiana, for example, has had eleven constitutions; Georgia, nine; and South Carolina, seven. The California constitution has been amended over 430 times, and the current constitutions of eighteen states have been amended over a hundred times. By contrast, the Constitution of the United States has been amended only twenty-six times (Table 2.3).

The Formal Amending Process

The formal amending process has two stages: *proposal* and *ratification* (Figure 2.3). According to the Constitution, amendments may be proposed either by a two-thirds vote of both houses of Congress or by a constitutional convention called by Congress on petition of two-thirds of the states. Ratification is achieved by securing the approval of either three-fourths of the state legislatures or constitutional conventions held in three-fourths of the states.

Stage 1: Proposal. To date, the only method of proposal used successfully has been House and Senate approval by a two-thirds vote of resolutions proposing amendments. Congressional resolutions proposing constitutional amendments are not subject to presidential vetoes. Presidents may, however, exert substantial informal influence

9. For an account of Alexander Hamilton's role in securing ratification by New York, see Clinton Rossiter, *Alexander Hamilton and the Constitution* (New York: Harcourt, Brace, 1964).

Table 2.3 Constitutional Amendments Added after Ratification of the Bill of Rights

Amendment	(Date)	Purpose
Amendments Changing the Powers of the National and State Governments		
XI	(1795)	Removed cases in which a state was sued without its own consent from the jurisdiction of the federal courts
XIII	(1865)	Abolished slavery and authorized Congress to pass legislation implementing its abolition
XIV	(1868)	Granted citizenship to all persons born or naturalized in the United States; banned states from denying any person life, liberty, or property without due process of law; and banned states from denying any person the equal protection of the laws
XVI	(1913)	Empowered Congress to levy an income tax
XVIII	(1919)	Authorized Congress to prohibit the manufacture, sale, and transportation of liquor
XXI	(1933)	Repealed the Eighteenth Amendment and empowered Congress to regulate the liquor industry
Amendments Changing Government Structure		
XII	(1804)	Required presidential electors to vote separately for president and vice president
XX	(1933)	Shortened the time between a presidential election and inauguration by designating January 20 as Inauguration Day; set January 3 as the date for the opening of a new Congress
XXII	(1951)	Limited presidents to two full terms in office
XXV	(1967)	Provided for succession to the office of president in the event of death or incapacity and for filling vacancies in the office of the vice president
Amendments Extending the Suffrage and Power of the Voters		
XV	(1870)	Extended voting rights to blacks by outlawing denial of the right to vote on the basis of race, color, or previous condition of servitude
XVII	(1913)	Provided for the election of U.S. senators by direct popular vote instead of by the state legislatures
XIX	(1920)	Extended the right to vote to women
XXIII	(1961)	Granted voters in the District of Columbia the right to vote for president and vice president
XXIV	(1964)	Forbade requiring the payment of a poll tax to vote in a federal election
XXVI	(1971)	Extended the right to vote to eighteen-year-olds

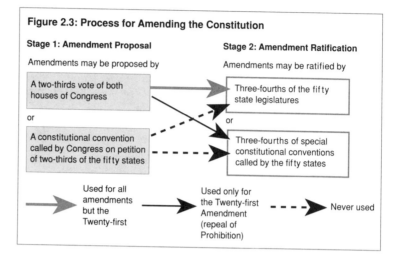

Figure 2.3: Process for Amending the Constitution

Stage 1: Amendment Proposal

Amendments may be proposed by

A two-thirds vote of both houses of Congress

or

A constitutional convention called by Congress on petition of two-thirds of the fifty states

Stage 2: Amendment Ratification

Amendments may be ratified by

Three-fourths of the fifty state legislatures

or

Three-fourths of special constitutional conventions called by the fifty states

Used for all amendments but the Twenty-first

Used only for the Twenty-first Amendment (repeal of Prohibition)

Never used

during congressional consideration of amendments. During the 1950s, President Dwight Eisenhower, for example, lobbied Congress forcefully and successfully to reject the so-called Bricker amendment, which would have severely limited the president's treaty-making authority.

Although the alternative method of proposal—a constitutional convention called by Congress on petition of two-thirds of the states—has never been used successfully, in several instances this procedure has appeared to be on the verge of implementation. For example, by 1986 thirty of the needed thirty-four states had petitioned Congress for a constitutional convention to propose an amendment requiring a balanced federal budget. Use of this method of proposal raises a series of important constitutional questions that have not been resolved. For example, how long can a petition from a state remain pending before Congress? Can Congress be compelled by the courts to call a constitutional convention if it fails to do so after two-thirds of the states have filed petitions? Can a constitutional convention propose amendments on topics other than those contained in the states' petitions or in the congressional call for the convention? This latter question stems from fears of a "runaway" convention that might engage in wholesale constitutional revision and mischief. Congress has therefore considered, but not yet acted on, measures that would limit constitutional conventions to the subject matter specified in the state petitions to Congress. The fact that Congress has managed thus far to adhere to the two-thirds-vote-of-Congress method of proposal reflects the national legislature's determination to maintain control of the amending process and not surrender it to a temporary convention.

Stage 2: Ratification. Congress normally specifies in its resolution proposing an amendment the length of time the states have for completing the ratification process. The customary time limit has been seven years. On occasion, however, Congress has extended the deadline, which it did in the case of the Equal Rights Amendment (ERA). In 1979, its deadline was extended three years when it became apparent that the three additional states needed for ratification would not approve the amendment within the seven-year time limit. Even with this extension, however, the ERA was not ratified.

The ratification process reflects the constitutional principle of federalism by requiring three-fourths of the states to ratify proposed amendments. All amendments to the Constitution have been ratified by the state legislatures except the Twenty-first, which repealed Prohibition. State constitutional conventions were used to ratify this amendment because the advocates of repeal feared that a large number of state legislatures were dominated by "Drys," the advocates of Prohibition. Most states permit their legislatures to ratify amendments by a simple majority vote, although in seven states either a three-fifths or two-thirds majority is required.

Congressional Interpretation

Whenever Congress acts, it is making an interpretation of its powers under the Constitution. Article I, section 8, lists the powers of Congress in exceedingly general terms—for example, "to regulate Commerce with foreign Nations, and among the several States." In implementing its power to regulate commerce, Congress has taken an expansive view of its authority. The commerce clause has been used to ban discrimination in places of public accommodation, to regulate working conditions, to authorize the Federal Bureau of Investigation to participate in kidnapping cases, to regulate the amount of crops farmers can plant and the prices they will receive for them, to allocate television channels and radio frequencies, to restrict monopolies and trusts, to guarantee home mortgages, to protect investor savings in banks and savings and loans—and the list goes on. Backed by court decisions endorsing broad interpretations of its constitutional powers, Congress has gradually extended its authority so that there are few aspects of American life that are safe from the long arm of Congress.

Presidential Interpretation

Like Congress, presidents also interpret the meaning of the Constitution, and in the process they have expanded significantly the scope of presidential power. The constitutional provisions in Article II state presidential powers in extremely broad terms. For example, the president is designated the "Commander in Chief of the Army and Navy" and charged with responsibility for taking "Care that the Laws be faithfully executed."

Such grants of authority, as well as those in Article I giving the president power to propose legislation and veto acts of Congress, have been utilized by the occupants of the White House to increase vastly the influence of their office. As commanders in chief of the armed forces, presidents have committed American forces to battle on foreign soil and the high seas to protect American citizens, fulfill treaty obligations, and protect American interests—all without a declaration of war by Congress. Thus through their war powers, presidents may commit the United States to a course of action that Congress will find extremely difficult to reverse should it wish to do so.

And many presidents have used their war powers. For example, during the Civil War Abraham Lincoln suspended the writ of habeas corpus (a court order requiring government officials to bring a prisoner before a court and show cause for his or her detention), ordered a blockade of southern ports, and called up the state militia at the beginning of the war. James K. Polk's 1846 dispatch of American troops into disputed territory in what is now Texas helped precipitate the Mexican War. In more recent times, Harry Truman supported United Nations forces after communist North Korea invaded South Korea in 1950. John Kennedy's 1962 imposition of a military blockade on Cuba to prevent the Soviets from setting up an offensive missile base was followed by the commitment of American forces to Vietnam under three presidents in the 1960s and 1970s. Finally, in the Middle East, Ronald Reagan bombed Libya in 1986 in retaliation for Libyan support of international terrorism, and in 1990 George Bush deployed ground and naval forces in the Persian Gulf region after Iraq's August invasion of Kuwait.

It is not just in the realm of foreign policy that presidents have extended their powers through constitutional interpretation. The veto power over legislation was initially used sparingly, only when presidents thought a law was either unconstitutional or technically defective. But modern presidents frequently veto legislation they find objectionable either in whole or in part. They also regularly use the threat of a presidential veto to induce Congress to pass laws more to their liking. Just as Congress has been able to extend its authority without formal amendment, presidents also have found the Constitution sufficiently pliable to permit significant expansion of their powers.

Judicial Interpretation

The meaning of the Constitution depends heavily on its interpretation by the judiciary, especially the Supreme Court. We saw earlier in the case of *Marbury v. Madison* (1803) that it was the Supreme Court that read into the Constitution the power of the courts to declare acts of Congress unconstitutional. Even though the original Constitution did not provide for judicial review, it is now a firmly established principle. It was also the Supreme Court that established the tradition of interpreting the Constitution's grant of powers to Congress in a broad manner. In the case of *McCulloch v. Maryland* (1819), the Court established the principle of *implied powers*—that Congress could do those things necessary and proper to execute its enumerated powers.[10]

Like the president and Congress, the courts are asked constantly to interpret the Constitution. For example, in 1986 the Supreme Court ruled that a provision of the so-called Gramm-Rudman-Hollings budget deficit reduction law was unconstitutional. The act mandated the comptroller general, an agent of Congress, to implement budget cuts if Congress failed to meet statutory deficit reduction targets. But because the law gave to an agency of Congress functions that were within the constitutional province of the executive branch, the Court ruled that this provision of the law violated the Constitution's separation of powers principle.

The Supreme Court is also heavily involved in ongoing controversies over the meaning of the Fourteenth Amendment's guarantee that the "equal protection of the laws" will be denied to no one. In interpreting this so-called equal protection clause, the courts have banned state-supported racial discrimination in public schools and state universities, required state legislatures to create congressional and state legislative districts that are as nearly equal in population as practicable, and determined the permissible limits of affirmative action in hiring practices, government contracting procedures, and admission to institutions of higher education. Because the courts share their constitutional interpretation responsibilities with other branches of government, Charles Evans Hughes, who later became chief justice, probably was exaggerating when he observed in 1907, "We are under a Constitution, but the Constitution is what the

10. *McCulloch v. Maryland,* 4 Wheat. 316 (1819).

Traditions and Practices

judges say it is." Few would dispute, however, that the judiciary plays a prominent role in deciding the meaning of the Constitution.[11]

American constitutional government also has been shaped by traditions and practices that have grown up outside the formal government. The Founders made no provision in the Constitution for political parties and were opposed to their development. Yet today, political parties profoundly affect the operation of the governmental system in ways not envisioned by the Constitution writers. National party conventions nominate presidential candidates. Presidential electors are chosen on partisan slates and almost invariably vote for their party's candidate. Moreover, candidates for the House and Senate are nominated in party primary elections, and Congress is organized on a partisan basis. Finally, presidential appointees to the federal courts are overwhelmingly of the same party as the president.

In spite of the Framers' fear of factions, interest groups have become a highly regularized part of the political process; they represent organized interests before the Congress, administration, and courts. They also have become an increasingly important and controversial source of campaign money for House and Senate candidates—especially incumbents—through their political action committees (PACs).

A Government of Divided Powers and Diverse Goals

The writers of the Constitution were not bent on creating an activist government. Rather, they wanted primarily to protect individual rights and achieve political stability. To protect individual and property rights, they created a system of limited government through a written constitution that made grants of authority to the national government and imposed prohibitions on both the national and state governments. To protect further the rights of the individual from temporary and potentially impetuous majorities, government power was divided between the national government and the states (federalism); among the legislative, executive, and judicial branches (separation of powers); and between the House and Senate (bicameralism). Different methods of selection were specified for the president (electoral college), Senate (election by state legislatures), House (popular election), and judiciary (presidential appointment with confirmation by the Senate). The Framers of the Constitution did

11. For an informed analysis of the process of constitutional interpretation, see Louis Fisher, *Constitutional Dialogues: Interpretation as Political Process* (Princeton, N.J.: Princeton University Press, 1988).

not try to design a strictly majoritarian system in which government policies would be based on the opinions of a majority of the citizenry. Rather, they sought a system that would restrain majorities and require the formation of broad coalitions and consensus for the government to act.

Indeed, the Founders' principal goals were neither equality nor democracy. As surprising as it may appear today, assuring equality was simply not one of their priorities. The Constitution even left the institution of slavery intact. Since 1787 and the drafting of the Constitution, however, one of the most compelling movements in American society has been the cause of political and social equality (also see Chapter 4, Civil Liberties and Civil Rights). The movement for greater equality has resulted in a series of constitutional amendments which, while not altering the fundamental structure of American government created by the Founders, has advanced the cause of equality. For example, voting rights were extended to black males (the Fifteenth Amendment outlawed denial of the right to vote on the basis of race, color, or previous condition of servitude), women (Nineteenth), residents of the District of Columbia (to vote in the presidential elections, Twenty-third), and eighteen-year-olds (Twenty-sixth). And in a related area, the Seventeenth Amendment granted voters, instead of state legislators, the power to elect U.S. senators, and the Twenty-fourth Amendment abolished the poll tax as a requirement for voting in federal elections. Slavery was prohibited in 1865 by the Thirteenth Amendment, followed several years later by the Fourteenth Amendment, which prohibited the states from denying citizens due process of the law and the equal protection of the laws.

As the Constitution enters its third century, there is little support for fundamental change in the constitutional order devised in 1787. Yet the American Constitution, like any set of governmental procedures, carries with it both costs and benefits.[12] Critics and reformers have argued that government under the Constitution is often one with divided leadership—a president from one political party and a majority in Congress from another. The result can be policy deadlocks and excessive partisan maneuvering. Even under the best of circumstances, it is argued that the American system of divided power makes it difficult for government to cope in a timely manner

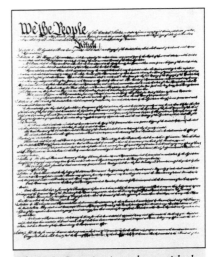

The U.S. Constitution, along with the Bill of Rights, serves as the framework for relations between the federal government and the states; the three branches of government; and, ultimately, the government and the people. Written in 1787 and ratified the following year, the Constitution is noted for its adaptability; there have been only twenty-six amendments to the original document.

12. For evaluations of the Constitution on the occasion of its two hundredth anniversary, see "The Constitutional Order: 1787–1987," a collection of essays published in *Public Interest* 86 (Winter 1987); Robert A. Goldwin and Art Kaufman, eds., *Separation of Powers—Does It Still Work?* (Washington, D.C.: American Enterprise Institute, 1986); and James L. Sundquist, *Constitutional Reform and Effective Government* (Washington, D.C.: Brookings, 1986).

with societal and world problems. For example, since 1987, Republican control of the White House and Democratic control of the Congress have complicated the already formidable and intensely political task of reducing the federal budget deficit. It is further claimed that decisive government policies are almost impossible to achieve because so many interests must be accommodated within the separation of powers system. Thus, government institutions have been frustrated in their attempts to develop a comprehensive and coherent energy policy, for example, because of conflicts between energy-producing and -consuming regions, environmentalists and energy producers, pro- and antinuclear power forces, and hordes of other organized interests. Critics of the constitutional system also claim that with governmental authority so scattered, the voters find it extremely hard to hold any group or party responsible for government policy. Popular control of government through elections is thereby frustrated.

Defenders of the constitutional order tend to stress its contributions to political stability and public consensus, as well as its protections against any group, faction, party, or individual becoming too powerful. They acknowledge that rapid, decisive action is difficult in a system of divided powers. But they also argue that divided power and the extensive bargaining, negotiation, and compromise required for government action tend to result in policies conducive to wide public acceptance (though not necessarily support). For example, after lengthy and extensive negotiations among members of Congress, the Reagan administration, and a wide range of interest groups, a major overhaul of the federal tax code was approved in 1986. While no tax bill can be expected to win universal praise, the 1986 tax reform law has at least been accepted by a diverse array of taxpayers. All this bargaining, negotiation, compromise, and consensus-seeking, it is maintained, contributes to political stability.

A government of divided powers also provides citizens and groups with many possible points of access to the political process where their voices may be heard. Groups who find the Congress unresponsive can appeal to the executive and the courts. And when any of the three branches has seemed to assert power unduly, the separation of powers system has worked to restrain the overzealous.

Whatever the merits of the debate over the Constitution's strengths and weaknesses, it is a document that is widely accepted and glorified by Americans. Barring some cataclysmic event, it will not, therefore, be changed significantly in the near future. The Constitution is the legal cornerstone of American politics.

For Review

1. The Constitution reflects America's heritage as a British colony, as well as the lengthy evolution of representative government in Great Britain. Its contents also mirror the problems the young nation faced after the Revolution, the conflicts waged and the compromises offered at the Constitutional Convention of 1787, and the struggle over ratification.

2. The Constitution embodies five basic principles: popular sovereignty and representative government, tempered by indirect election; limited government; separation of powers and checks and balances; federalism; and judicial review.

3. The unusually long life and durability of the Constitution owes much to its concise yet flexible text, which has allowed Congress, the president, and the courts to interpret the Constitution in ways appropriate for changing conditions. Because the Constitution has proven so adaptable, it has not been necessary to change it frequently through formal amendment.

4. The drafters of the Constitution sought to create a government capable of governing, promoting economic development, and protecting individual rights. Since they wrote the original document, however, a movement toward greater political and social equality has resulted in a series of amendments that has advanced the cause of equality while leaving the fundamental structure of the government unaltered.

5. The Constitution, like all governmental rules and procedures, is not neutral in its impact. By dividing government power among three branches of government and between the national government and the states, it has made quick, decisive, and comprehensive policy making difficult. But at the same time, divided governmental power has provided citizens with multiple points of access to decision makers; encouraged policy making through negotiation, bargaining, and compromise; and proven resistant to authoritarian rule.

For Further Reading

"The Constitutional Order: 1787–1987," *Public Interest* 86 (Winter 1987). A collection of essays written by leading scholars on the occasion of the Constitution's bicentennial.

Farrand, Max, ed. *The Records of the Federal Convention of 1787*. New Haven, Conn.: Yale University Press, 1913 (last reprinted in 1986). A documentary of the Constitutional Convention.

Goldwin, Robert A., and Art Kaufman, eds. *Separation of Powers—Does It Still Work?* Washington, D.C.: American Enterprise Institute, 1986.

A collection of essays assessing the consequences of the Constitution's separation of powers principle.

Hamilton, Alexander, James Madison, and John Jay. *The Federalist Papers*. Available in a variety of editions. An exposition of the ideas underlying the Constitution by leading participants in the Constitutional Convention, written in support of ratification.

Lipset, Seymour Martin. *The First New Nation: The United States in Historical and Comparative Perspective*. Rev. ed. New York: Norton, 1979. A political sociologist's analysis of the impact of the values of achievement and equality on the development of the American character.

Peltason, J. W. *Understanding the Constitution*. 11th ed. New York: Holt, Rinehart, and Winston, 1988. An excellent reference guide to the meaning of the Constitution.

Rossiter, Clinton. *1787: The Grand Convention*. New York: Macmillan, 1966. A readable account of the writing of the Constitution and the struggle for ratification.

Wood, Gordon S. *The Creation of the American Republic, 1776–1787*. New York: Norton, 1972. An informative history of America's early years.

3. Federalism

THE RELATIONSHIP of the national government to the states and their local units of government affects virtually every American political institution from the political parties to the judiciary. It also affects many aspects of people's daily lives—the quality of the education they receive, the quality and quantity of their health care, the steps taken to protect their environment, as well as their welfare, housing, and transportation. Moreover, intergovernmental relationships influence the extent to which federal, state, and local governments pay for these services.

The national-state government relationship was of paramount concern to the writers of the Constitution. The failings of the governmental order under the Articles of Confederation stemmed in large part from the national government's weaknesses. It was subservient to the states and dependent on them for the revenues needed to perform even the most basic governmental functions such as providing for the common defense and maintaining domestic order. The national government also lacked authority to deal effectively with the chaotic economic conditions created by each state regulating its own foreign and interstate commerce and printing its own currency. Thus, the economic development of the new nation was being strangled in a web of conflicting and confusing state laws, while the national government, bound by the Articles of Confederation, lacked the authority to respond.

The Founders' solution to these problems was to abandon the flawed system of the Articles of Confederation and create a new *federal system* that substantially strengthened the authority of the national government while also reserving important powers to the states. But the American federal system is not all neat and tidy. The line between national and state powers and responsibilities is not always clear, and there are ongoing conflicts over which level of government should engage in particular kinds of activities. But at the same time, there is also a great deal of cooperation and sharing of responsibility among the various levels of government. This chapter explores the nature of the American federal system. Specifically, we will examine its constitutional basis; the changes that have taken place since 1787, especially post-1960 developments; and, most important, how federalism has affected and continues to affect American government and politics.

What is Federalism?

Federalism is a constitutional division of the powers of government between the national government and regional governments (states in the United States), with each exercising significant powers. Both the national government and the states exercise governing authority over the same people and territory. As a result, each American lives under two governmental jurisdictions—the government of the United States and the government of the state in which he or she resides. Both the national and state governments have their own officers and structures. Thus, the legislatures, governors, courts, and bureaucracies of the states are separate from those of the national government. The national and state governments do, however, share and cooperate in carrying out their functions.

A governmental order more common than federalism is one in which all governmental power is vested in a national government from which regional and local governments derive their powers. In these **unitary government** systems, the national government can alter or even abolish regional governments without their consent. In Britain, for example, the Conservative-dominated House of Commons abolished the Labour party-controlled Greater London Council in 1984 when the latter pursued policies sharply at odds with those of Prime Minister Margaret Thatcher. By contrast, under the American federal system, states derive their powers from the Constitution, and they cannot be abolished or have their boundaries altered by an act of Congress without their consent. Most state governments, however, are organized on a unitary principle. All local units of government—counties, cities, villages, townships, school districts—are legal creatures of the states and derive their powers from the states.

The weakest form of national government is found in a *confederation,* such as the United States under the Articles of Confederation and the southern Confederacy during the Civil War. In such a system, the states are sovereign (independent of external control) and free to join or withdraw from the nation as they choose. The national government may exercise only those powers delegated to it by the states. As a creature of the states, the national government in a confederate system must work through the states to effect domestic policies since it is not empowered to exert its authority directly upon individuals.

American federalism has been described as the "price of union." By introducing federalism into the Constitution, the drafters balanced the need for a stronger national government than had existed under the Articles of Confederation with the need to maintain the states as vital instruments of self-government. Had the Founders not authorized the states to retain substantial policy-making authority, the Constitution probably would not have been ratified by the thirteen original states and there would have been no Union.

The Founders also viewed federalism as a way of preventing tyranny. Because federalism diffuses power among the national and various state governments, the Constitution writers believed that this diffusion would make it difficult for any faction, group, or party to gain control of the entire government and exercise unrestrained power. In *Federalist* No. 10, James Madison captured this argument when he observed that if "factious leaders . . . kindle a flame within their particular states," the spread of the "conflagration into other states" may be checked by national leaders.[1]

In such countries as the United States, Canada, India, Mexico, and Germany, which have substantial cultural, social, religious, and economic diversity, federalism permits a sense of national identity to develop while also permitting a high degree of regional autonomy. The spirit of federalism is captured in the Latin phrase on American coins, *e pluribus unum* (out of many, one). Indeed, federalism is a means of achieving unity without uniformity. It permits the states, while abiding by the Constitution and national laws, to develop distinctive ways of organizing their governments and dealing with their citizens' concerns. For example, Nebraska operates with a unicameral (one-house) legislature; all other states have a bicameral body. Arkansas, New Hampshire, Vermont, and Rhode Island elect their governors for two years rather than the four years favored elsewhere. In California, supreme court judges are initially appointed by the governor, whereas in most of the states they are elected. As for nonpolitical matters, Massachusetts, unlike other states, requires employers to provide most of their workers with health insurance. And in fourteen states, including Michigan, Iowa, Minnesota, and Wisconsin, there is no death penalty for serious crimes, but this is not

1. E. M. Earle, ed., *The Federalist* (New York: Modern Library, 1937), No. 10. For an informed summary of the Founders' reasons for creating a federal system in the Constitution, see Arthur N. Holcombe, *Our More Perfect Union* (Cambridge, Mass.: Harvard University Press, 1950), chaps. 1 and 2.

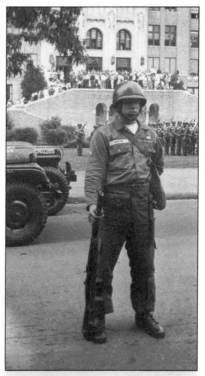

Federalism inevitably leads to clashes between the national government and the states. The national government may, however, use force to see that the Constitution and federal laws are enforced. In 1957, facing massive resistance in the South, President Dwight Eisenhower ordered federal troops to enforce desegregation of Central High School in Little Rock, Arkansas.

the case in a majority of states. Finally, most states levy an income tax on wages, but, as of 1992, nine states, including Alaska, Nevada, New Hampshire, and Florida, do not.

The Constitutional Basis
of Federalism

American federalism has its basis in the Constitution, whose provisions relate to the powers of the national government, the powers of the state governments, federal guarantees to the states, and relationships among the states (the division of powers between the national government and the states, including the restrictions on each, is shown in Table 3.1).

*Scope of the National
Government's Power*

Article I, section 8, of the Constitution enumerates at length the powers of the national government. Congress is empowered, for example, to lay and collect taxes, regulate foreign and interstate commerce, raise armies, maintain a navy, coin money, establish rules for naturalization of citizens, regulate bankruptcies, and create lower federal courts. In addition to these **delegated powers**, Article I further provides that "the Congress shall have the Power . . . to make all Laws which shall be necessary and proper for carrying into Execution the foregoing Powers, and all other Powers vested by this Constitution in the Government of the United States." This is the so-called **necessary and proper clause**, also known as the elastic clause.

Conflicts arose almost immediately after the Constitution was put into effect over the extent of federal power granted to Congress by Article I. These conflicts aligned the Federalists, who advocated a strong national government capable of encouraging commercial development and exercising discipline over the states, against the Antifederalist advocates of states' rights. In one of its most important early decisions, *McCulloch v. Maryland* (1819), the Supreme Court came down strongly on the side of those who favored interpreting constitutional grants to the national government in a broad manner.[2]

The *McCulloch* case arose over the refusal of the cashier of the United States Bank branch in Baltimore to pay a tax levied by the state of Maryland on the bank. Maryland argued that the Congress had no right to create the bank since the Constitution makes no mention of such a power in Article I. In writing the Supreme Court's

2. *McCulloch v. Maryland*, 4 Wheat. 316 (1819).

Table 3.1 Constitutional Allocation of Powers to the National and State Governments

	Examples of Powers Permitted		
National Government (Delegated, Implied, and Inherent Powers)	**National and State Governments (Concurrent Powers)**	**State Governments (Reserved Powers)**
Regulate foreign and interstate commerce	Levy taxes	Regulate intrastate commerce
Coin money	Borrow money	Establish local government systems
Establish post offices	Spend for general welfare	Administer elections
Provide an army and navy	Establish courts	Protect the public's health, welfare, and morals
Declare war	Enact and enforce laws	
Establish federal courts below the Supreme Court		
Conduct foreign relations		

	Examples of Powers Denied		
National Government	**National and State Governments**	**State Governments**
To violate the Bill of Rights	Enact ex post facto laws or bills of attainder	Tax imports or exports
Alter state boundaries	Grant titles of nobility	Coin money
Tax exports	Permit slavery	Enter into treaties or alliances
	Deny the right to vote on basis of race, color, previous condition of servitude, or sex	Deny people the equal protection of the laws or due process of law

opinion, Chief Justice John Marshall, an ardent Federalist, rejected Maryland's call for a strict and literal interpretation of the grant of powers to Congress in the Constitution. He noted that it was entirely reasonable for Congress to decide that it was "necessary and proper" to create a national bank in order to carry out its delegated powers to impose taxes, borrow money, and care for the property of the United States. Marshall thereby established in *McCulloch v. Mary-*

Chief Justice John Marshall States the Doctrine of Implied Powers

At an early and critical stage in the development of the Constitution, the Supreme Court interpreted Article I, section 8, in a manner that vastly expanded the powers of Congress. In the case of *McCulloch v. Maryland* (1819), Chief Justice John Marshall interpreted the necessary and proper clause to give the national government *implied powers*. He wrote that

we think the sound construction of the constitution must allow to the national legislature that discretion, with respect to the means by which the powers it confers are to be carried into execution, which will enable that body to perform the high duties assigned to it, in the manner most beneficial to the people. Let the end be legitimate, let it be within the scope of the constitution, and all means which are appropriate, which are plainly adapted to that end, which are not prohibited, but consistent with the letter and spirit of the constitution, are constitutional.

land the doctrine of **implied powers**, which states that the national government may exercise powers that can be reasonably implied from its delegated powers.

In later years, the Supreme Court used the precedent for the doctrine of implied powers supplied by Marshall in *McCulloch* to provide the legal justification for sweeping extensions of the national government's powers. By virtue of the implied powers doctrine, the national government has been empowered to provide support for public schools, welfare programs, farm prices, public housing, community development, crime control, and unemployment compensation; regulate working conditions and collective bargaining; fix a minimum wage; ban discrimination in housing, places of public accommodation, and employment; and even affect highway speed limits and the legal drinking age.[3]

In the realm of foreign affairs, the national government is permitted to exercise **inherent powers**—powers that do not depend on constitutional grants of authority. Rather, they derive from the very existence of the national government. These inherent powers include the authority to discover and occupy territory, make treaties, and conduct foreign relations with other nations. The Supreme Court has ruled that the national government would have these powers even if the Constitution were silent on these matters because they are the powers that all national governments exercise under international law.[4]

Role and Powers of the States

As we noted in Chapter 2, the Constitution accords a special role to the states in the governmental system by guaranteeing each state equal representation in the Senate, permitting electors chosen by each state to elect the president, and requiring that three-fourths of the states ratify all constitutional amendments. The permanent bond of the states to the Union was settled once and for all by the Civil War. As the Supreme Court declared in a post-Civil War case, the United States is "an indestructible Union composed of indestructible states."[5]

3. For a concise account of how the Court used the doctrine of implied powers to greatly expand the national government's powers under the commerce clause, see C. Herman Pritchett, *The American Constitution*, 3d ed. (New York: McGraw-Hill, 1977), 194–201.

4. *United States v. Curtiss-Wright Export Corp.*, 299 U.S. 304 (1936). For a definition of inherent powers, see J. W. Peltason, *Understanding the Constitution*, 11th ed. (New York: Holt, Rinehart, and Winston, 1988), 19.

5. *Texas v. White*, 7 Wall. 700 (1869).

When powers are not granted exclusively to the national government by the Constitution, the states may exercise those powers concurrently, provided there is no conflict with federal law. Among the **concurrent powers** of the states are the power to levy taxes, borrow money, and establish courts.

The states are authorized by the Tenth Amendment to exercise **reserved powers**—powers not granted to the national government and not prohibited to the states by the Constitution. But there is no specific listing of states' reserved powers in the Constitution. Thus, they constitute an undefined residuum of powers, including responsibility for education, intrastate commerce, local government, conduct of elections, family relations, and regulations to protect the public's health, safety, and morals.

Over the years, the Supreme Court has issued different interpretations of the extent to which the Tenth Amendment protects the powers of the states from encroachment by the national government. Until the late 1930s, the amendment was treated as an assertion of states' rights that severely restricted the national government's power. For example, in 1918 the Supreme Court declared a federal anti-child labor statute unconstitutional because it acted as a regulation of intrastate commerce, an area reserved to the states.[6] But the Court subsequently reversed such rulings as its 1918 child labor decision and held in 1941 that the Tenth Amendment and the reserved powers of the states imposed no limit on the national government in exercising powers granted to the Congress.[7]

Since the mid-1970s, however, the Court has shown some uncertainty about how to interpret the Tenth Amendment when federal laws are applied directly to the states. For example, in a 1976 case in which the minimum wage and maximum hours restrictions of the Fair Labor Standards Act were imposed on state and local government employees, the Court ruled that such an application of the law was unconstitutional. The grounds for this ruling were that the law impaired "the state's integrity" and "ability to function effectively in the federal system."[8] Nine years later, however, when Justice Harry Blackmun changed his position, the Court overruled its earlier decision and held by a narrow 5–4 margin that federal minimum wage and maximum hours legislation could be applied to state and local government employees.[9] The Court's changing interpretations

6. *Hammer v. Dagenhart*, 247 U.S. 251 (1918).
7. *United States v. Darby Lumber Co.*, 312 U.S. 100 (1941).
8. *National League of Cities v. Usery*, 426 U.S. 833 (1976).
9. *Garcia v. San Antonio Metropolitan Transit Authority*, 469 U.S. 528 (1985).

of the Tenth Amendment demonstrate that the meaning of the amendment and the nature of American federalism are far from settled issues. The national-state relationship of American federalism is constantly evolving.

While the Constitution assures the states of a significant role in the governmental order, it also imposes limitations on the states. Thus, they are prohibited from making treaties with foreign governments; authorizing private persons to raid and seize the shipping and commerce of enemy nations; and coining money, issuing bills of credit, or making anything but gold or silver legal tender. In addition, the states may not do any of the following without the consent of Congress: tax imports or exports; tax foreign ships; maintain troops or ships in peacetime, except for a state militia or national guard; enter into compacts or agreements with other states or foreign governments; and engage in war unless actually invaded or in imminent danger.

National Government
Obligations to the States

In Article IV, the Constitution specifies a series of obligations on the part of the national government to the states.

In obliging the national government to *guarantee a republican form of government,* the drafters of the Constitution used the term *republican government* to distinguish the American system from either monarchy or direct democracy. Congress, rather than the courts, enforces this guarantee when it permits representatives and senators of a state to take their seats in the Congress.

The national government also must *protect states against foreign invasion and domestic violence.* At the request of a state for assistance, the president may send in federal troops to quell domestic violence. The president need not wait for such a request, however, to enforce federal law or court orders. For example, in 1957 President Dwight Eisenhower sent federal troops to enforce a federal court's order that Little Rock (Arkansas) Central High School be desegregated.

Finally, the Constitution specifies that to *protect states from dismemberment,* no new state may be formed from the territory of an existing state, nor may a state be formed by combining two or more states, without the consent of the Congress and of the legislatures of the states concerned.

Because the operation of the federal system inevitably brings the states into contact with each other, the Constitution specifies in Article IV the obligations of the states to each other.

The **full faith and credit clause** (section 1) requires each state to honor the civil acts, judgments, and public documents of every other state. Thus, wills, contracts, and civil judgments of a state court must be enforced in the other states. The full faith and credit clause does not apply to matters of criminal law.

The **privileges and immunities clause** (section 2) prevents the states from discriminating against out-of-state residents in such matters as protection of the laws, access to the courts, and taxation. States may, however, enforce reasonable regulations to protect their citizens' health and safety through licensing requirements for doctors, dentists, lawyers, nurses, and teachers. It is also permissible for a state to increase fees for out-of-state residents wishing to enroll in state-supported universities or to buy hunting and fishing licenses.

In providing for **extradition**, Article IV, section 2, specifies that states are responsible for apprehending fugitives who have fled across a state line and returning them to the state having jurisdiction over the crime.

Article I, section 10, of the Constitution does permit the states to engage in cooperative arrangements by drawing up *interstate compacts* or agreements. Through such compacts, which must be approved by Congress, states may form interstate agencies and work together to solve mutual problems. Interstate compacts have been used to resolve interstate tax disputes, share higher education facilities, and administer transportation facilities. The states of New York and New Jersey, for example, jointly administer transportation facilities in the New York City metropolitan area through the Port of New York Authority, while out West, the Upper Colorado Basin Compact has enabled states to work out problems about the division of water in that region, and in the Midwest, Minnesota and Wisconsin permit each other's residents to attend state universities without paying out-of-state tuition fees.

The Ever-Changing Nature of Federal-State Relations

In the over two hundred years of America's history under the Constitution, the pattern of federal-state government relations has undergone continual change. This evolving pattern of intergovernmental relations has reflected governments' responses to the new

New Hampshire's
Residency Law for
Lawyers Runs Afoul
of the Constitution's
Privileges and
Immunities Clause

In exercising their powers to protect the health, welfare, and safety of their citizens, states regulate professions through licensing. As the following case illustrates, these regulations can raise constitutional issues under the privileges and immunities clause (Article IV, section 2).

In this case, Kathryn A. Piper, an attorney living four hundred yards across the Connecticut River from New Hampshire in the community of Lower Waterford, Vermont, passed the New Hampshire bar examination. New Hampshire, however, required that attorneys, in addition to passing the state bar examination, be state residents to practice law in the state courts. Thus, because Piper was not a state resident, she was not allowed to practice in New Hampshire. Attorney Piper brought suit, charging that New Hampshire's residency requirement for lawyers violated the constitutional provision that the "Citizens of each State shall be entitled to all Privileges and Immunities of Citizens in the several States." But New Hampshire argued that its residency requirement for attorneys helped maintain high standards of ethics and competency and ensured the availability of lawyers for court hearings, disciplinary matters, and public service programs.

In its ruling in the case, the U.S. Supreme Court rejected New Hampshire's claims and agreed with Piper that her rights under the privileges and immunities clause had been violated. Justice Lewis Powell wrote that the purpose of this constitutional provision was to "create a national economic union" and to prevent "economic protectionism" on the part of the states. Under this ruling, states may still require nonresidents to pass bar examinations, but they may not impose residency requirements as a prerequisite for admission to practice in state courts.

Supreme Court of New Hampshire v. Piper, 470 U.S. 274 (1985).

problems faced by citizens and the shifting alignments of political power among the contending forces in society. The basic trend in federal-state relations has been away from separate and distinct areas of responsibility for national and state governments and toward shared powers and responsibilities.

Early Federalism: Separate Spheres of Federal and State Responsibility

For most of the period leading up to the Civil War, Americans had little contact with the national government; its functions were limited. It carried out foreign policy, defended the shores, delivered the mail, levied tariffs on imports, administered public lands, and supported some public works projects such as roads, canals, and harbors. Criminal justice, health, welfare, transportation, education, and regulation of business were handled largely by state and local governments.

The Civil War was a critical turning point in federal-state relations as it settled with finality the question of whether states could secede from the Union or nullify national government policies with which they disagreed. Indeed, the doctrine of federal supremacy was firmly established by the North's victory in the war. In the aftermath of the Civil War, a series of constitutional amendments—the Thirteenth, Fourteenth, and Fifteenth—were approved with the intent of protecting the rights of the newly freed black Americans. The longer-term impact of these amendments—especially the Fourteenth Amendment's ban on state actions that deny people due process of law or the equal protection of the laws—has been to give the national government authority to invalidate state laws.[10]

Although the Civil War amendments had given the national government additional authority, the national and state governments continued until early in this century to operate in largely separate spheres of authority, without interference from the other level of government. There were, however, a few instances of intergovernmental activity through federal land grants to the states. For example, the Morrill Act of 1862 provided land grants to the states for the purpose of creating agricultural and technical colleges. America's great land-grant colleges such as Ohio State, Iowa State, Texas A&M, and Kansas State, and the agriculture schools at Cornell University and the University of Wisconsin have their origins in this legislation. Federal land grants also were made for roads, canals, and railroads, but, for the most part, the domains of the national and state governments were separate and distinct.

Expansion of Federal Economic Regulatory Activity

During the twentieth century, the pressures for an expanded role for the federal government intensified. These pressures developed because of the changed nature of American society. By the turn of the century, America had been transformed by technological and economic developments from an agrarian, rural society into an urban, industrial society. The country's population tripled between 1870 and 1920, and huge cities with populations running into the millions

10. Henry J. Friendly, "Federalism Forward," *Yale Law Review* 86 (May 1977): 1020.

grew up. Such corporate giants as U.S. Steel and Standard Oil emerged. The societal problems created by the new industrial order were not within the power of the states to resolve, and there was a demand for increased governmental regulation of the economy to protect consumers and workers. For example, it was not possible for the states to cope with the monopolistic practices of huge corporate trusts which operated on a nationwide basis. Nor could the states effectively ensure the purity of food being consumed in cities far from where it was produced. Congress, at the urging of President Theodore Roosevelt, responded to the latter problem by passing in 1906 the Pure Food and Drug Act and the Meat Inspection Act. In response to demands for greater governmental control over business practices, federal regulatory activity continued to expand during the administration of Woodrow Wilson with the enactment of the Federal Reserve Act (1913), Federal Trade Commission Act (1914), and Clayton Anti-Trust Act (1914).

The federal government's early twentieth-century ventures into economic regulatory activity were but precursors of a much more extensive federal role that was to develop under President Franklin Roosevelt's leadership during the Great Depression of the 1930s.

The New Deal: A Tidal Wave
of Federal Programs

The demand for government action to relieve the hardships created by the depression of the 1930s was intense. The Roosevelt administration responded with what has been called a "tidal wave" of federal programs (the so-called **New Deal**) that permanently changed the balance of power within the American federal system.[11] President Roosevelt's New Deal policies expanded the government's economic regulatory role through the creation in 1933 of the Securities and Exchange Commission to protect investors and ensure orderly stock exchange procedures and the passage of the National Labor Relations Act in 1935 to guarantee workers the right to organize unions and engage in collective bargaining.

At Roosevelt's urging, Congress also enacted a series of measures designed to provide relief and spur economic recovery. Most of these measures involved joint action between the federal government and the states that vastly increased the role and power of the federal government. To receive the benefits of such programs as unemployment compensation, public housing, Aid to Families with Dependent Children, and public works projects, states were frequently required to

11. Ibid., 1023.

The human misery created by the depression of the 1930s, portrayed by this massive breadline, prompted a demand for government action that resulted in President Franklin Roosevelt's New Deal, an unprecedented array of federal programs.

provide administrative personnel, abide by federal regulations, and put up some money of their own. Through the "carrot and stick" technique of providing federal funds and programs in return for state cooperation and adherence to federal regulations, the federal government was able to extend its influence over the states.[12]

Further Expansion of the Federal Role in the 1960s and 1970s

During the 1960s, the pattern of an expanding role in providing social welfare benefits was given a dramatic push forward by the administration of President Lyndon Johnson.[13] His administration pushed through a willing Congress a wide array of legislation providing federal funds to the states and localities for such purposes as cleaning up the environment, making grants and loans to college students, providing health care to the poor, expanding urban transit,

12. James T. Patterson, *The New Deal and the States: Federalism in Transition* (Princeton, N.J.: Princeton University Press, 1969).

13. For an account of the grant explosion of the 1960s and 1970s, see John E. Chubb, "Federalism and the Bias for Centralization," in *The New Direction of American Politics,* ed. Chubb and Paul E. Peterson (Washington, D.C.: Brookings, 1985), 277–286.

combating crime, and improving housing. The 1960s and 1970s were also a period in which the federal government again increased its economic regulatory activities through such measures as the Occupational Safety and Health Act, Consumer Product Safety Act, Federal Coal Mine Health and Safety Act, Consumer Protection Act, and a series of environmental protection measures, including the Clean Air Amendments of 1970, Water Quality Improvement Act, Safe Drinking Water Act, and Resource Conservation and Recovery Act.

Federal Protection of Civil Rights

Federalism, which gives state governments wide leeway on many aspects of public policy, enabled the southern states in particular for much of the nation's history to engage in acts of racial discrimination—denying blacks the right to vote, maintaining separate white and black school systems, and segregating facilities of public accommodation. In the 1950s and 1960s, however, national public opinion shifted toward a position supportive of enforced civil rights, and government policy reflected this change (also see Chapter 4, Civil Liberties and Civil Rights). The federal courts took the lead in moving against racial discrimination mandated by state governments. A major judicial breakthrough in this area was the 1954 Supreme Court decision in *Brown v. Board of Education of Topeka,* which declared unconstitutional separate state-supported school systems for whites and blacks.[14] When court decisions were resisted by southern states, as they were at Central High School in Little Rock, Arkansas, and at the University of Alabama, Presidents Eisenhower and Kennedy mobilized troops and sent federal marshals to bring about state compliance with federal court orders to desegregate.

The federal role in the protection of civil rights for minorities was further expanded when Congress passed the Civil Rights Act of 1964, banning discrimination in places of public accommodation—restaurants, motels, theaters—and the Voting Rights Act of 1965, empowering the federal government to send registrars into southern states to register voters when there was a past record of racial discrimination. On these issues, the advocates of a national standard for civil rights enforced by the federal government carried the day, and the proponents of a states' rights position had to give way.

14. *Brown v. Board of Education of Topeka,* 347 U.S. 483 (1954).

Modern Cooperative Federalism: The Grant-in-Aid System

Thus, the New Deal era marked the end of a 150-year period during which American federalism had been characterized by the national and state governments operating in largely separate and distinct spheres of authority. With the advent of the New Deal and subsequent extensions of the national government's role, federal-state relations began to be characterized by **cooperative federalism**—a sharing of responsibilities among the federal, state, and local governments.

When the federal government becomes involved in a domestic policy area, it does not normally set up a federal agency—such as the U.S. Postal Service, National Park Service, or Coast Guard—to directly administer its programs. More frequently, federal policies are carried out in cooperation with state and local governments. This pattern of administering federal programs through state and local governments has meant that, even though the federal government has increased its role in society, federal employment has remained relatively stable. At the same time, however, state and local government employment has increased dramatically and constitutes over 82 percent of the civilian government work force. This growth (shown in Figure 3.1) reflects both the impact of the transfer of federal funds to the states and the resulting expansion in state and local government services.

Cooperative federalism frequently takes the form of the federal government providing money (so-called **grants-in-aid**) to states and localities to carry out a government activity in a manner that follows federal policy guidelines but also permits some state and local flexibility in administration. As a result of this system, today there are few policy areas that are exclusively either federal, state, or local responsibilities. Rather, responsibilities are shared, and nearly all government activity, except such things as printing currency, minting coins, and maintaining the national defense, are intergovernmental in character (Figure 3.2).[15] But even with the shared responsibilities inherent in cooperative federalism, the net effect of the growth in federal regulatory activity and the operation of domestic programs

15. Donald F. Kettl, "The Maturing of American Federalism," in *The Costs of Federalism*, ed. Robert T. Golembiewski and Aaron Wildavsky (New Brunswick, N.J.: Transaction Books, 1984), 73.

Figure 3.1: Rising Federal Expenditures and State and Local Government Employment Versus Stable Federal Employment, 1960-1990

— · State and local government employment

· · · · Federal expenditures

—— Federal civilian employment

Sources: Bureau of the Census, *Statistical Abstract of the United States:1978* (Washington, D.C.: Government Printing Office, 1978); and *Statistical Abstract of the United States: 1990.*

Figure 3.2: Sharing the Cost of Government-Provided Services: Federal and State/Local Expenditures, 1987

Federal (% of expenditures) ▪
State and local (% of expenditures) ▫

Source: Advisory Commission on Intergovernmental Relations, *Significant Features of Fiscal Federalism, 1989 Edition* (Washington, D.C.: Advisory Commission on Intergovernmental Relations, 1989), 2:19; Bureau of the Census, *Statistical Abstract of the United States: 1990* (Washington, D.C.: Government Printing Office, 1990), 274.

through grants to state and local governments has been a centralization of governmental decision making at the national level.[16]

The grant-in-aid system of shared federal and state and local funding, primarily state and local government administration, and federal supervision has developed and grown in this century for a variety of reasons.[17]

• Federal grants-in-aid provide a means of meeting and coping with a societal need or problem. For example, Medicaid grants are a method of providing health care to the poor, and mass transit grants are a way in which to maintain public transportation systems in urban areas.

• Because the fiscal resources and willingness of the states and localities to provide their citizens with services vary tremendously, federal grants are a means of making essential services available to all citizens regardless of the state in which they reside.

• Americans prefer local over federal administration of government programs, although they readily accept federal aid to state and local governments.

• The federal income tax is the most productive government revenue raiser available. It provides the federal government with the economic underpinning required to fund an extensive grant-in-aid program.

• Members of Congress can deliver benefits to their constituents by enacting grant-in-aid programs that channel funds to state and local governments in their districts.

• Both Democratic and Republican presidents have found that grants-in-aid are a means of achieving their policy and political aims. Even as conservative a president as Ronald Reagan, who opposed centralization of power in the federal government, supported requiring states to set the legal drinking age at twenty-one to qualify for federal highway funds. He also supported grants for drug enforcement, abuse prevention, and rehabilitation.

The growth in federal grant-in-aid programs since the 1930s has meant that federal funds constitute a large share of the expenditures of state and local governments—indeed, ranging from 18 to over 25 percent of state and local expenditures during the 1980s (see Figure 3.3). This means, of course, that state and local governments are heavily dependent on federal grants to meet their programmatic re-

16. See Chubb, "Federalism."
17. Deil S. Wright, *Understanding Intergovernmental Relations,* 3d ed. (Pacific Grove, Calif.: Brooks/Cole, 1988), 208–210.

sponsibilities. Any change in federal grant policy—particularly budgetary reductions or even a slowdown in the growth of federal grant monies—can have far-reaching and painful consequences for state and local governments.

There are three principal types of grants-in-aid: (1) categorical grants, (2) project grants, and (3) block grants.[18] Each type of grant differs in the extent to which control over government policy resides with the federal government or state and local governments.

Categorical grants are the oldest form of federal grant-in-aid to the states and localities. These grants provide funds to state and local agencies (such as libraries, hospitals, schools, and state highway departments) for a particular category of government activity. In 1991, 478 federal categorical grant programs were distributing over $100 billion for specific activities. These programs enable the federal government to prescribe a general policy for dealing with a problem, to provide funds for that purpose, and to then turn over to state and local governments the responsibility for carrying out the policy at the grass roots. States and local governments wishing to participate in categorical grant programs are normally required to put up some of their own money (to provide some proportion of *matching funds*) and to follow federal policy guidelines in administering the program. State and local governments have some flexibility in implementing categorical grants, however. For example, Aid to Families with Dependent Children (AFDC) is a categorical grant program under which states must comply with federal guidelines to qualify for funds. It has still been possible, however, for the states to develop widely varying welfare programs under AFDC in such areas as the level of welfare benefits provided and the work (Workfare) and educational (Learnfare) requirements for receipt of benefits.

Project grants are a special form of categorical grant developed to target funds more precisely in order to better fulfill program objectives. Instead of distributing funds to the states or localities under the fixed formulas used in categorical grants, project grants provide variable levels of funding. Project grants have been used to support aid to the handicapped, to combat drug abuse, and to provide bilingual education. Applicants—which may be nongovernmental agencies, such as a local United Way agency, as well as state and local governments—submit proposals to the federal agency administering a project grant program and then compete for funding. Skill in prep-

18. For a description of different types of grants and the administrative, policy, and political implications of each, see ibid., chap. 6.

Figure 3.3: Federal Grants-in-Aid, 1950-1990

As a percent of federal domestic expenditures
As a percent of state and local expenditures
As a percent of gross national product (GNP)

Source: Executive Office of the President, Office of Management and Budget, Special Analyses, *Budget of the United States Government, Fiscal Year 1990* (Washington D.C.: Government Printing Office, 1989), H-22.

aration of a grant proposal and political influence in Washington—so-called grantsmanship—are often critical factors in determining how project grant funds are awarded. To enhance their abilities to influence the awarding of project grants, states, cities, and universities maintain liaison offices in Washington and try to enlist the assistance of their states' congressional delegations.

Block grants are given to the states for a general functional area of government activity (for example, job training or community development). States receiving block grants are responsible for developing a program within this general field of policy, but following federal guidelines. Block grants give the states greater policy-making discretion in developing programs to fit their specific needs than do categorical grants, which have a narrower focus and many federal conditions attached. The Partnership in Health Act of 1966, the first block grant program enacted by Congress, combined several categorical grant programs designed to combat specific illnesses. Other examples are block grants for job training of disadvantaged youth, urban mass transit, maternal and child health care, criminal justice, and community development.

The Politics of
Grant-in-Aid Programs

While any description of the different types of grants may seem rather technical and uninteresting, they have in fact been the subjects of many fiercely fought political battles. Each type of grant has different consequences in terms of which level of government and which interests exert a dominant influence over government policy. Indeed, powerful alliances of interest groups, government administrators, and interested members of Congress form to generate, defend, and expand grant-in-aid programs in which they have a stake.

The differences between the Republican and Democratic parties in their approach to government are also reflected in their approaches to grant-in-aid policy. Republicans in both the White House and Congress have consistently favored decentralization of governmental decision making by reducing the number of the federal strings attached to grants-in-aid and allowing state and local governments greater discretion. By contrast, Democrats have advocated centralized decision making and a strong federal role.[19]

Categorical grants vest substantial authority in federal officials, who determine the specific purposes for which the funds will be used and set guidelines for their expenditure. Thus, these grants are the

19. John E. Chubb, "The Political Economy of Federalism," *American Political Science Review* 79 (December 1985): 1005.

predominant type of federal grant-in-aid because they provide members of Congress with a way to deliver benefits and services to their constituents by assisting state and local governments.[20] Not surprisingly, representatives and senators view providing benefits to constituents an essential element in gaining reelection. Moreover, the state and local agencies that receive and spend such categorical grants, the beneficiaries of the services provided through grants, and federal administrators constitute powerful interest group alliances in support of categorical grant programs.

Because block grants require that the federal grant money be spent within a general field of governmental responsibility, they give wide discretion to state authorities and shift influence away from Washington. Governors have tended to favor consolidation of categorical grants into block grants because such a policy shifts substantial decision-making power to the state governments. Of course, the current beneficiaries of categorical grant programs and members of Congress have tended to resist proposals for block grants, especially if acceptance of those proposals would mean a reduction in the amount of federal funds available for grants.

When President Bush proposed in his 1991 state-of-the-union address that $15 billion in existing categorical grant programs be converted into a large block grant to be administered by the states, the contending forces in the politics of grants-in-aid were clearly revealed. The fiscally hard-pressed governors responded favorably to the prospect of having additional federal funds channeled through state governments under Bush's expanded block grant proposal. Mayors, however, were apoplectic and called the president's plan an "assault on America's cities" because it meant that municipalities would no longer receive aid for targeted programs directly from the federal government through categorical grants. Rather, the cities would have to seek funds for such programs as community development (housing, street repairs, parks, child care, and shelters for battered women) from state governments, which would be administering the federal block grant. Since local governments have a long history of battling state governments for what they consider a fair share of state revenues, it is not surprising that their leaders reacted negatively to the Bush proposal. Nor were the committees of Congress receptive to giving up their existing control over the content of categorical grant programs by turning them over to the states.

Governments in the United States— By the Thousands

Federal government	1
State governments	50
Local governments	83,186
Counties	3,042
Municipalities	19,200
Townships and towns	16,691
School districts	14,721
Special districts	29,532
Total governments	83,237

SOURCE: Bureau of the Census, *Statistical Abstract of the United States: 1990* (Washington, D.C.: Government Printing Office, 1990), 272.

20. Chubb, "Federalism," 286. For a perceptive account of the use of grants by members of Congress to claim credit with constituents and distribute benefits, see David R. Mayhew, *Congress: The Electoral Connection* (New Haven, Conn.: Yale University Press, 1974), 129–130.

The political forces favoring centralization and an expanded federal role tended to be ascendent from Roosevelt's New Deal of the 1930s until at least the late 1960s. The pattern since the Nixon administration took office in 1969, and particularly during the Reagan and Bush administrations of the 1980s and 1990s, has been toward decentralization—fewer federal dollars for grants, consolidation of categorical grants into block grants, and reduced federal restrictions.

The Politics of Federalism from the Nixon Years to the Bush Presidency

Since the 1960s, the functioning of American federalism has been central to domestic politics. The legacy of expanded federal programs and regulatory activity from the New Deal and Johnson administration was challenged as Republican administrations sought to shift policy-making responsibility away from Washington to the state capitols.

The Nixon Administration's Approach

When the Nixon administration took office in 1969 after a period of dramatic growth in federal grant-in-aid programs, 98 percent of all federal aid to state and local governments was in the form of categorical grants. Criticism of these grants had begun to mount, however, on the grounds that they imposed excessive administrative costs and that they distorted state and local budgetary priorities because they encouraged state and local governments to give priority to securing grants over meeting their own priorities.

President Richard Nixon was sensitive and sympathetic to these criticisms. He believed that if decision making was decentralized so that state and local governments played a larger role, government would be more efficient and creative. He was not antigovernment, but he did distrust the federal bureaucracy and sought to weaken it by proposing general **revenue sharing** and the consolidation of categorical grants into block grants.

At Nixon's urging, Congress enacted in 1972 a program of general revenue sharing, which provided states and local governments with federal grants totaling more than $6 billion a year. Unlike other grant-in-aid programs, revenue-sharing funds could be used for whatever purpose state and local governments thought appropriate, as long as the funds were not used in a way that discriminated on the basis of race, sex, age, religion, or physical handicap. Because it

President Richard Nixon, an advocate of revenue sharing and block grants, meets with Republican governors in February 1973 to rally support for his New Federalism proposals.

gave state and local officials unprecedented flexibility in spending federal grant money, revenue sharing was enormously popular with state and local officials. But it was never popular with Congress. It tended to reduce congressional influence on grant-in-aid programs and members' capacities to claim credit for directing government benefits to particular groups of constituents and interest groups. Moreover, fiscal conservatives were skeptical of the program; they believed that the federal government, with its large budget deficits, really had no revenue to share. As these budget deficits swelled ominously in the 1980s, Nixon's experiment in governmental decentralization via revenue sharing was eliminated as an economy measure in fiscal year 1987.

Along with congressional approval of revenue sharing, Nixon also succeeded in securing a block grant program for comprehensive employment and training and community development. But approval of these block grant programs by a Democratic-controlled Congress had its cost; Nixon was forced to accept increased levels of federal funding for domestic programs. Moreover, his achievements in the

block grant field were limited by Congress. It killed his grant consolidation initiatives in education, law enforcement, rural development, and transportation.[21]

Despite his reputation for budgetary penury, the Nixon presidency was a period of dramatic growth in federal domestic spending,
especially in the areas of food stamps, housing supplements, and
medical care for the poor.[22] The Nixon administration also presided
over and contributed to an unparalleled expansion of federal regulation of state and local governments. The most dramatic of these
regulatory actions was in the field of environmental protection. Under the National Environmental Policy Act of 1969, federal agencies
and federal grant recipients were required to file detailed environmental impact statements before undertaking construction or other
projects with environmental consequences. Even more important
were the Clean Air Act amendments of 1970, which established national air quality standards to be implemented by state governments.

The Nixon administration thus sought to increase state and local
power within the intergovernmental system, but, ironically, the net
effect of federal actions during his presidency was quite the opposite:
federal spending rose dramatically, and the federal regulatory presence became more pervasive. Despite his modest successes with
block grants and revenue sharing, the federal system was more centralized when he left office than when he entered.[23]

Reagan's New Federalism

Although in response to budgetary pressures a slowdown in federal funding for grant-in-aid programs began in the last years of the
Carter administration (1977–1981), even more restrictive actions
accompanied the Reagan administration (1981–1989). Like Nixon,
President Ronald Reagan wanted to decentralize government decision making. In addition, and unlike Nixon, Reagan wanted to
reduce government domestic spending and regulatory activity significantly. This reflected his fundamental discomfort with the modern welfare state.[24]

The most dramatic Reagan proposal was the New Federalism
package that he put forward in 1982. It called for revamping the
federal system by realigning federal and state government functions.
In return for the federal government taking over the full cost of the

21. Chubb, "Federalism," 287.
22. For an account of the Nixon administration's approach to federalism, see
Timothy J. Conlan, *New Federalism: Intergovernmental Reform and Political Change
from Nixon to Reagan* (Washington, D.C.: Brookings, 1988), part I.
23. Ibid., chap. 5.
24. Ibid., 220.

increasingly expensive Medicaid program (health care for the poor), the Reagan administration proposed that the states assume full responsibility for welfare, food stamps, and other selected grant programs. To help the states fund these new responsibilities, the federal government would turn over to the states such revenue sources as excise taxes, tobacco and alcohol taxes, and the windfall profits tax on oil production.

But Reagan's New Federalism ran into firm opposition from state and local officials who asserted that they could not fund the programs they would be assigned with the revenue sources to be available to them. Supporters of the existing categorical grant programs also lined up in opposition to the plan, and the New Federalism proposal died for lack of support. One reason the plan was never enacted was that it combined two quite different objectives: (1) sorting out the confusing mix of federal and state responsibilities, and (2) reducing federal domestic spending. Some advocates of creating a more rational federal system by sorting out federal and state government functions wanted higher levels of federal spending for social programs. They, then, opposed the New Federalism. Others feared that shifting greater responsibility to the states would endanger the very programs they had pushed Congress to enact and fund. They therefore also opposed the Reagan proposal.

Although Reagan's New Federalism proposals were never enacted, his presidency was a period of dramatic change in the operation of the American federal system. Approximately eighty categorical grants were consolidated into block grants, and several grant programs, including general revenue sharing, were eliminated. As a result, administration and policy-making responsibilities for programs once closely controlled by Washington passed to the states.

The most noteworthy impact of the Reagan years, however, was on federal spending on grant-in-aid programs. Because of federal fiscal policies enacted with presidential support in 1981, the federal government has annually run up massive budget deficits. These deficits have created an environment for policy making that virtually precludes enactment of any major new domestic spending programs or significant expansions of existing programs. The large federal budget deficits also have put spending for existing grants-in-aid under heavy pressure as the executive branch and Congress have sought to limit the hemorrhaging red ink in the federal budget.

Deficit reduction measures resulted in cuts in grants-in-aid in the 1980s, both as a percentage of federal expenditures and as a percentage of state and local government expenditures (see Figure 3.3).

Between 1980 and 1988, for example, federal grants-in-aid fell from 23.3 percent of federal outlays for domestic programs to 18.9 percent and from 25.8 percent of state and local expenditures to 18.2 percent. The consequences for state and local governments have been profound as they have sought to compensate for the shrinking pool of federal dollars either through cutbacks in services or increased taxes.[25]

In spite of the dramatic changes in grant-in-aid policies during the Reagan years, the net effects of the 1980s for American federalism were mixed. On the one hand, President Reagan's efforts to reduce the size and activities of the welfare state were more successful than most analysts thought possible when he took office. Yet the basic character of cooperative federalism remained intact. While President Reagan sought major spending reductions and block grant consolidations, Congress never abandoned categorical grants as the dominant form of federal grants-in-aid to state and local governments. Rather, it tempered proposed budget cuts in grants and resisted Reagan administration attempts at large-scale grant consolidation.

Just as Richard Nixon's attempts to revise the federal system had paradoxical consequences, so too did Ronald Reagan's. The public underpinnings of support for the welfare state were in some respects stronger when Reagan left office than when he entered the White House. The Reagan agenda trimmed questionable programs and seemingly answered public concerns about uncontrolled government growth. As a result, opinion surveys revealed a rebound in public confidence in the federal government and broad support for government spending.[26]

Federal Budget Politics and Federalism during the Bush Presidency

Because of the Reagan administration's legacy of diminished grant-in-aid support for state and local governments, the Bush administration entered office in 1989 faced with pent-up demands for additional financial assistance from governors, state legislators, mayors, and other local officials.[27] The large federal budget deficit, however, effectively restrained both George Bush and the Congress from

25. For a detailed exploration of the impact of New Federalism on state and local governments, see Peter K. Eisinger and William Gormley, eds., *The Midwest Response to the New Federalism* (Madison: University of Wisconsin Press, 1988).

26. Conlan, *New Federalism,* chap. 11.

27. David Shribman, "Among the Generalizations, Bush Gives a Few Signals to the States and Localities," *National Journal,* January 1989, 19.

attempting to expand grant-in-aid spending. Indeed, the lengthy and often bitter budget battle of 1990 between the Republican president and Democratic-controlled Congress resulted in an agreement that put the states under intensified fiscal pressure. While not increasing grant-in-aid funds to the states, the budget for 1991 imposed additional and costly responsibilities on the states. The law mandated that Medicaid coverage be expanded to cover more poor children, pregnant women, and elderly, but the states were required by Congress to pick up the tab for these expanded services without receiving additional federal funds. The federal budget agreement further compounded the states' fiscal problems by increasing federal taxes on tobacco, liquor, and luxuries. As a result, the ability of states to tax these traditional sources of state revenue was severely restricted.

In 1991, the Bush administration demonstrated that, like the Nixon and Reagan administrations, it too was committed to decentralizing government decision making by giving the states greater flexibility in utilizing federal grants. Its most far-reaching proposal was the previously noted $15 billion block grant, which would replace a series of existing categorical grants. But in another move, Secretary of Transportation Samuel Skinner proposed a federal highway program that would give the states greater leeway in the use of federal transportation funds. The Bush administration made it clear, however, that it expected the states to shoulder a greater share of the costs. Its highway and mass transit proposals reduced the federal share of matching grants to as low as 60 percent for many highways outside the interstate system and for mass transit programs. In addition, the administration proposed eliminating all mass transit operating subsidies in areas of over one million people.

These transportation initiatives were immediately attacked by state officials because they shifted costs onto state taxpayers. State highway officials, for example, complained that to generate the revenues needed to receive federal matching grants, they would have to raise state gasoline taxes. And not to be outdone, mass transit interests complained that the proposals would downgrade mass transit and thereby worsen traffic congestion, energy waste, and air pollution problems. Clearly, the respective roles of the federal and state governments are anything but settled issues in the 1990s.[28]

A Resurgence of the States

While the Reagan administration was seeking to reduce government's role in American life, the states responded to cuts in federal

28. Mike Mills, "Bush Releases Highway Plan," *Congressional Quarterly Weekly Report*, February 16, 1991, 412–413.

grant programs by expanding their activities and levels of spending. Indeed, political commentators have stressed that it was at the state level during the late 1980s that major policy innovations were occurring. As the percentage of the federal budget devoted to grants-in-aid declined, the states devised ways—including use of their own tax revenues—to maintain higher levels of social services than would have been the case under federal budget reductions.[29] And while the Reagan administration followed a policy of deregulating the economy, many of the state governments became activists in such areas as education reform, environmental protection, plant closing restrictions, securities regulation, medical insurance, auto insurance, consumer protection, employee drug testing, family and parental leave policy, and the minimum wage.

This is not the first time that the states have played an activist role during a conservative era at the federal level. During the "Normalcy" era of the 1920s and the administrations of Presidents Warren Harding and Calvin Coolidge, the states also energized the federal system by enacting child labor and unemployment insurance laws while expanding state social services.

Federalism, the Constitution, and Public Policy

Federalism was incorporated into the Constitution to achieve the practical governing objectives of the Founders. By dividing governmental power between the national government and the states, the drafters of the Constitution believed it would be possible to prevent any one group, faction, or party from becoming too powerful. Moreover, retaining the states as powerful governing units within the constitutional order was viewed as essential to having those same states ratify the new Constitution. The Founders believed as well that the strengthened national government created under a federal system would promote economic development, provide an improved national defense, and ensure domestic order.

The nature of the relationship between the national government and the states has changed dramatically over the past two centuries. Whereas the national government initially had little contact with its citizens, today its activities directly touch the lives of every citizen. But the development of cooperative federalism has meant that the functional lines of responsibility for government activities have be-

29. Richard P. Nathan and Fred C. Doolittle, *Reagan and the States* (Princeton, N.J.: Princeton University Press, 1987).

come increasingly fuzzy. Moreover, with the maturing of federalism, virtually every unit of government in the United States has a major stake in seeing that it gets its slice of the federal financial pie.[30]

Decisions about which level of government will perform a particular function and how the costs of that function will be shared by federal, state and local governments are issues over which intense battles have been and continue to be fought. These issues of federalism are important because over time different parties and interests achieve ascendancy within the federal government and within the states. And whether Democrats or Republicans, liberals or conservatives control a level of government will affect policy. For example, the election of President Ronald Reagan, a conservative Republican, resulted in policies at the federal level designed to limit the federal government's role in providing social services through grants-in-aid. As a result, the states assumed increased responsibility for maintaining existing programs and for devising new domestic policy initiatives. These developments at both the federal and state levels caused liberal and conservative policy planners alike to rethink their traditional views about the desirability of centralizing decision-making authority in the federal government or decentralizing decision-making authority among state and local units. Since the depression of the 1930s, liberals on social issues have tended to favor action by the federal government on the grounds that it is more supportive of their policies and values than the states. By contrast, conservatives have favored strategies that devolved governmental responsibility from the federal government to the states and localities. With the presidency in recent years in conservative hands, liberals have found that they can no longer achieve their goals by relying on the federal government and that some of their objectives can be achieved only through the states. At the same time, conservatives have learned that they should be cautious about strengthening the states, lest they fall under liberal control and engage in governmental activism. How federalism operates, therefore, is much more than just a matter of constitutional law. Decisions about the shape of federalism—which level of government will dominate policy making in a particular area of government activity and who will pay how much for that activity— go a long way toward determining who wins and loses in the American political system.

30. Kettl, "The Maturing of American Federalism," 73–74.

For Review

1. Federalism is a constitutional division of the powers of government between the national government and the regional governments (states), with each exercising significant powers.

2. Federalism was the "price of union"—a necessary means for creating one nation out of thirteen highly independent states.

3. Until the 1930s, American federalism was characterized by the national and state governments operating in largely separate and distinct spheres of authority. But with the advent of the New Deal in the 1930s and subsequent extensions of the federal government's role, federal-state relations have been characterized by cooperative federalism, in which responsibilities are shared among the federal, state, and local governments.

4. An essential element of cooperative federalism is the grant-in-aid system, which transfers funds from the federal government to the states and localities for the purpose of carrying out federal policies. Federal grants have enabled state and local governments to expand their services but also have made them heavily dependent on the federal government for funds.

5. As federal budget deficits have mounted since 1981, the federal government has been unable to embark on new domestic grant-in-aid programs. In the 1980s, then, the states became major policy innovators within the federal system. Nevertheless, the declining share of the federal budget going to grants-in-aid has put the states under increased fiscal pressure.

6. Because of the expanded role of the federal government since the 1930s, the federal system of the 1990s is clearly more centralized than anything envisioned by the writers of the Constitution. Although the role of the federal government has expanded, the states have expanded their levels of activity as well and continue to play a major policy-making role in the system. Which level of government should perform which functions and how those functions should be paid for are continuing sources of conflict, however, within the American federal system.

For Further Reading

Advisory Commission on Intergovernmental Relations. *Intergovernmental Perspective.* A periodical containing timely data as well as articles of thought and opinion on the state of American federalism.

Conlan, Timothy J. *New Federalism: Intergovernmental Reform and Political Change from Nixon to Reagan.* Washington, D.C.: Brookings,

1988. A detailed analysis of the often paradoxical consequences of federalism reform under two conservative presidents.

Eisinger, Peter K., and William Gormley, eds. *The Midwest Response to the New Federalism*. Madison: University of Wisconsin Press, 1988. A collection of studies analyzing state and local government responses to the federal government policies during the Reagan era.

Elazar, Daniel J. *American Federalism: A View from the States*. 3d ed. New York: Harper and Row, 1984. A thoughtful consideration of the role of the states by one of the leading students of federalism.

Nathan, Richard P., and Fred C. Doolittle. *Reagan and the States*. Princeton, N.J.: Princeton University Press, 1987. An analysis of the impact of Reagan administration domestic policies and the resurgence of the states as a consequence of those policies.

Wright, Deil S. *Understanding Intergovernmental Relations*. 3d ed. Pacific Grove, Calif.: Brooks/Cole, 1988. A comprehensive analysis of intergovernmental relations.

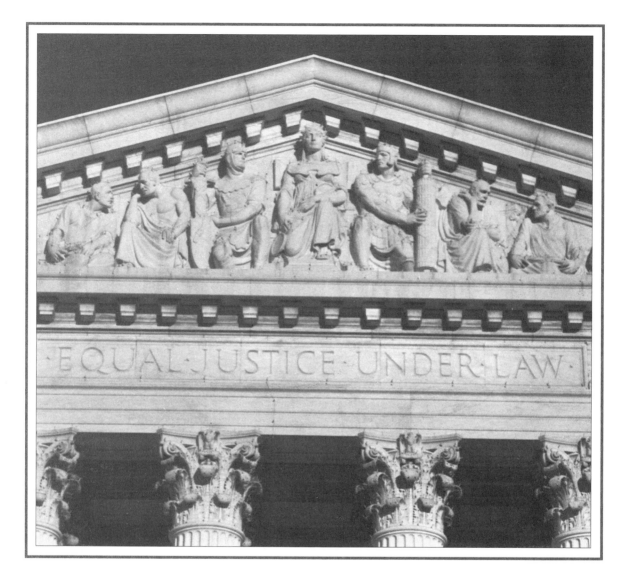

4. Civil Liberties and Civil Rights

THE DRAFTERS of the Constitution stated in its Preamble that their purpose was to "establish Justice" and "secure the Blessings of Liberty to ourselves and our Posterity." But despite these intentions, controversy immediately arose within the states over whether or not the new Constitution did in fact protect people's basic liberties. This controversy, as well as the desire to secure ratification of the new Constitution, resulted in the addition of a bill of rights to that document. Then, as now, people perceived a direct connection between the basic liberties guaranteed by the Bill of Rights and the existence of a free society. Although most Americans take their basic liberties and rights under the Constitution pretty much for granted, they are nevertheless repelled by television news pictures that depict the governments of China and South Africa, for example, repressing their citizens.

Despite the public's almost unanimous endorsement of basic civil liberties, these liberties have been a continual source of controversy in American political life. The issue is not whether it is desirable to have freedom of speech, press, or assembly. Rather, controversy is created by the actual application of such straightforward language in the First Amendment as "Congress shall make no law . . . abridging the freedom of speech, or of the press; or the right of the people peaceably to assemble."

As this chapter will demonstrate, there are no absolutes in a government's civil liberties policies. To the contrary, the actual application of the civil liberties guaranteed in the Constitution is ever-changing, ambiguous, and delicate—and even creates controversies when highly cherished values collide with each other. For example, what are the values of a free press versus those of protecting national security? Should the press be allowed to print documents whose release will be, in the government's opinion, a threat to national security? Or what are the values of a fair trial versus those of the need for public safety and order? Should an individual clearly guilty of a serious crime go free because the police seized evidence without a proper search warrant? And how does one weigh the right of privacy against the need to protect an unborn human life? Does a woman have the right to an abortion, or can the government limit abortions to protect the unborn? These are the kinds of issues that the Supreme Court is forced to confront when applying the Bill of Rights to specific cases.

Because they involve conflicts over deeply held values, civil liberties issues are not only complicated but also highly contentious.

For example, when the Supreme Court declared in 1989 that burning the American flag was a constitutionally protected form of free expression and subsequently declared a law banning desecration of the flag to be unconstitutional, a major political controversy was created. It pitted President George Bush, who advocated a constitutional amendment protecting the flag, against Democratic congressional leaders and such groups as the American Civil Liberties Union.

This chapter considers civil liberties and civil rights policy making in three areas: *First Amendment rights*—basic human freedoms considered essential to a free society such as freedom of speech, the press, and religion; *procedural rights*—guarantees of due process or fairness (for example, the right to a lawyer in a criminal trial or protection from unreasonable searches and seizures) when the government seeks to deny a person life, liberty, or property; and *guarantees of equal protection of the laws*—protection against discrimination based on unreasonable considerations such as race or sex.

Nationalizing the Bill of Rights

Initially, the Bill of Rights was interpreted by the Supreme Court (*Barron v. Baltimore*, 1833[1]) to apply only to the national government and not to the states. As a result, basic rights protected against violation by the national government were not protected from violations by state governments. Beginning in the 1920s, however, the Supreme Court began to interpret the Fourteenth Amendment in a manner that protected people from state infringement on most of the rights guaranteed by the Bill of Rights. According to the Fourteenth Amendment, no *state* shall "deprive any person of life, liberty, or property, without due process of law."[2] The Supreme Court interpreted this to include most of the rights protected by the Bill of Rights. The Court thereby engaged in **selective incorporation** of the Bill of Rights into the Constitution (see Table 4.1).

It began by declaring in *Gitlow v. New York* (1925) that freedom of speech and freedom of the press were protected from state infringement[3] and gradually extended Fourteenth Amendment protection to most of the guarantees in the Bill of Rights of a fair trial.

1. *Barron v. Baltimore,* 7 Peters 243 (1833).
2. The nationalization of the Bill of Rights through interpretation of the Fourteenth Amendment's due process clause is described by Richard C. Cortner, *The Supreme Court and the Second Bill of Rights: The Fourteenth Amendment and the Nationalization of Civil Liberties* (Madison: University of Wisconsin Press, 1981).
3. *Gitlow v. New York,* 268 U.S. 652 (1925).

Table 4.1 Selective Incorporation of the Bill of Rights into the Fourteenth Amendment

Amendment and Right Incorporated	Supreme Court Decision
First	
Free speech	*Gitlow v. New York* (1925)
Free press	*Near v. Minnesota* (1931)
Peaceable assembly	*DeJonge v. Oregon* (1937)
Free exercise of religion	*Cantwell v. Connecticut* (1940)
No establishment of religion	*Everson v. Board of Education* (1947)
Fourth	
No unreasonable searches and seizures	*Wolf v. Colorado* (1949)
Exclusionary rule	*Mapp v. Ohio* (1961)
Fifth	
Protection from self-incrimination	*Malloy v. Hogan* (1964)
Protection from double jeopardy	*Benton v. Maryland* (1969)
Right to counsel in capital cases	*Powell v. Alabama* (1932)
Sixth	
Right to know nature of accusations	*Cole v. Arkansas* (1948)
Right to public trial	*In re Oliver* (1948)
Right to counsel in noncapital felony cases	*Gideon v. Wainwright* (1963)
Right to confront accusers	*Pointer v. Texas* (1965)
Right to speedy trial	*Klopfer v. North Carolina* (1967)
Right to jury trial in felony cases	*Duncan v. Louisiana* (1968)
Eighth	
Protection from cruel and unusual punishment	*Robinson v. California* (1962)

Today, all of the provisions of the Bill of Rights apply to the states except the right to bear arms and have a militia (Second Amendment), the protection against quartering troops in private homes (Third Amendment), the right to a grand jury indictment (Fifth Amendment), the right to trial by jury in civil cases (Seventh Amendment), and the protection against excessive bail and fines (Eighth Amendment). The present Supreme Court appears unlikely to adopt a "total incorporation" theory of the Fourteenth Amendment. Rather, it has adopted a case-by-case approach to determining whether a fair trial has been afforded defendants.

First Amendment Rights

The rights to freedom of speech, press, assembly, and religion contained in the First Amendment are, in the words of Justice Benjamin Cardozo (*Palko v. Connecticut*, 1937), "the very essence of ordered liberty . . . [they are the] fundamental principles of liberty and justice which lie at the base of all our civil and political institutions."[4] But the essential character of basic civil liberties principles has not made their application to specific circumstances any less difficult or controversial. Freedom of speech, as the following discussion demonstrates, can clash with other closely held values.

Freedom of Expression

In protecting freedom of expression, the First Amendment specifies that Congress may not impose restrictions on the rights of the people and the press to speak out or on the right of the people to gather peacefully and to petition the government when they feel they have been wronged. Without these freedoms, governments cannot be responsive to the needs of the citizenry and free elections become impossible. Freedom of expression is, therefore, more than a personal right to say what one wishes. One also has the right to hear conflicting views, to conclude what is truth and what is not as ideas clash in the free marketplace, and to organize with fellow citizens to influence government policy. Freedom of expression is an essential cornerstone of and prerequisite for a democratic order.

In spite of the need to maintain a free marketplace of ideas, the Supreme Court has not interpreted the First Amendment to mean there are no limits on freedom of expression. Libelous and slanderous statements may be penalized. Obscenity and child pornography do not enjoy constitutional protection, nor do "fighting" words— words uttered in circumstances that by their utterance injure or provoke acts of violence. Justice Oliver Wendell Holmes observed, for example, that no one has a right to cry "Fire!" in a crowded theater.[5] The onerous task of developing doctrines that distinguish between constitutional and unconstitutional limitations on freedom of expression has fallen largely to the Supreme Court. The doctrines used by the Court have changed over time in response to changing national and world conditions.

One of the best-known doctrines has been the **"clear and present danger" test** developed in 1919 when the Court was confronted with a case in which a man had been arrested for distributing leaflets urg-

4. *Palko v. Connecticut*, 302 U.S. 319 (1937).
5. *Schenck v. United States*, 249 U.S. 47 (1919).

ing young men to resist the draft during World War I. According to the Court, in deciding such cases it was necessary to take into account the circumstances in which the seemingly dangerous speech occurred. Speech could be restricted only if the words used created "a clear and present danger" that they would bring about substantive evils that Congress had a right to prevent.[6] The clear and present danger test thus stressed the likelihood and proximity of the threat posed by the speech in question. The burden of proof rested with the government; it had to show that freedom of expression constituted a serious and immediate threat to society.

In 1925, the Court modified the clear and present danger test and adopted a **"bad tendency" test**, which permitted restrictions on speech deemed to have a tendency to lead to illegal acts. The bad tendency test made it significantly less difficult for the government to justify limitations on speech. By the 1940s, however, the Court had adopted a much tougher standard for judging the constitutionality of restrictions on free expression: the **preferred position doctrine**. This doctrine holds that the rights of free expression are so crucial to a democratic order as to be in a preferred position. It is therefore assumed that restrictions on political speech are unconstitutional unless the government can demonstrate that the speech constitutes an imminent and serious threat to create a substantive evil.

When the values of national security and freedom of expression have seemed to collide, the Court has been confronted with particularly troublesome decisions. In 1940, with World War II looming on the horizon, Congress passed the Smith Act, which made it a crime to knowingly advocate, advise, teach about, or print or distribute written material advocating the overthrow of the U.S. government. It also made it illegal to knowingly become a member of a group advocating the overthrow of the government. In the context of the Cold War that followed World War II, when the threats of Soviet espionage and aggression seemed real to most Americans, eleven of the top American Communist party leaders were arrested and convicted of violating the Smith Act. And in *Dennis v. United States* (1951), the Supreme Court upheld their convictions. On the basis of their activities and membership in the Communist party, the Court held that the government was justified in restricting the communist leaders' rights to freedom of speech. Using a rather relaxed version of the clear and present danger test, the Court upheld the

6. Ibid., at 52.

Even Flag Burning Is Protected Communication under the First Amendment

In 1989, the Supreme Court threw out the conviction under Texas law of Gregory Johnson, who had burned the American flag at the 1984 Republican National Convention to protest the policies of President Ronald Reagan *(Texas v. Johnson)*. In making this decision, the Court held that Johnson was engaged in symbolic speech protected by the First Amendment. As a consequence of this unpopular decision, there were demands, endorsed by President George Bush, for a constitutional amendment banning desecration of the flag. In an effort to head off such an amendment, Congress responded by passing the Flag Protection Act of 1989. This law made it a punishable offense to mutilate, deface, physically defile, burn, or trample the flag of the United States.

When people protesting passage of the law burned the U.S. flag in Washington, D.C., in 1989, they were arrested for violating the Flag Protection Act. While noting that the defendants' desecration of the flag was "deeply offensive to many," the Supreme Court reasserted its view in *U.S. v. Haggerty,* 110 S.Ct. 2404 (1990), that "[i]f there is a bedrock principle underlying the First Amendment, it is that the Government may not prohibit the expression of an idea simply because society finds the idea itself offensive or disagreeable." It concluded by saying, "Punishing desecration of the flag dilutes the very freedom that makes this emblem so revered, and worth revering."

Communists' convictions under the Smith Act by emphasizing the gravity of the evil to be prevented (in this case the overthrow of the government) and discounting the likelihood of the evil actually occurring.[7] Since the *Dennis* decision, the Court has significantly restricted the scope of the Smith Act. Mere membership and statements of belief have ceased to be a basis for prosecution, as opposed to advocacy of imminent action that is likely to produce unlawful acts.

Today, the Court essentially adheres to the preferred position doctrine and maintains a high level of skepticism about any restrictions on expression, particularly on political speech—whether spoken,

7. *Dennis v. United States,* 341 U.S. 494 (1951) at 510–511.

written, or portrayed through pictures and demonstrations. It is therefore possible to hold meetings, rallies, or demonstrations in support of virtually any cause without political speech being restricted. This even extends to demonstrations that burn or desecrate the American flag. The Court has held that however distasteful these actions may be to most Americans, such demonstrations are constitutionally protected. The changing doctrines adopted by the Supreme Court during the twentieth century, however, are testimony to the fact that the First Amendment rights of freedom of expression are not absolute and that the principle of free expression must be applied constantly to specific and diverse circumstances.

Freedom of the Press

Like freedom of speech, an unfettered press is considered a prerequisite for democracy. The media play an essential role in keeping people informed about government actions and issues. But it is also true that the media are in a position to exercise great influence on public opinion and government policy. As a result, periodic attempts are made to restrict the press—attempts that inevitably provoke controversy and pose thorny issues, particularly in times of war. During the Persian Gulf War of 1991, for example, the U.S. military severely restricted media access to the battle zone by utilizing a "pool" system. Under this arrangement, small groups of tightly controlled correspondents accompanying U.S. troops in Kuwait and Iraq reported back to their more than seven hundred colleagues confined to bases in Saudi Arabia. In addition, press reports were censored. The Pentagon defended these restrictions as essential for effective prosecution of the war and for protection of the lives of American military personnel. Reporters and media representatives objected strenuously, claiming that the public was not being permitted to see and hear the full story of what their military forces were doing in an action that would have profound consequences for years to come. The media's objections, however, did not change Pentagon policy, and the public demonstrated scant concern over the media's complaints. Because the freedom of the press issues the Persian Gulf War raised are not new, they demonstrate how the meaning of the First Amendment is constantly being reinterpreted.

Prior Restraint. Although the government did restrict reporters' abilities to report battle-front news during the Persian Gulf War, the courts generally have taken a tough line against such government attempts at **prior restraint** as censorship and preventing the publication of information that the government finds objectionable.[8] The Supreme Court's hostility to prior censorship by the government was made clear in the 1971 *Pentagon Papers* case in which the U.S. attorney general sought a court injunction against publication by the *New York Times, Washington Post,* and other newspapers of classified Pentagon documents relating to American involvement in the Vietnam War.[9] The Court, however, held that the government had failed to demonstrate that publication of the documents would cause immediate and specific damage to national security.

Freedom of the press means not only that the government may not engage in prior censorship but also that it may not dictate the content or form of what the press prints. The Supreme Court has held that a command by the government to print specific material collides with the First Amendment. Thus when Florida passed a law that forced publishers to give free space to people who had been criticized in the pages of a newspaper, the Supreme Court voided the law, thereby extending constitutional protection to the editorial judgments of newspaper writers.[10]

Libel. Even though virtually all prior censorship is banned, people are not without legal recourse against the press. Citizens can sue the media for **libel** when they can demonstrate that what was published was false and that the publisher knew it was false or published it without regard to whether or not it was true. Public figures, such as politicians, have a more difficult time obtaining libel judgments against the media than do private citizens. Since 1964 and *New York Times v. Sullivan,* the Supreme Court has held that public figures lose some of their rights to privacy by virtue of their positions and, therefore, must prove not only that what was published about them was false and defamatory, but also that it was published with "reckless disregard" for the truth.[11] This test has made it extremely hard for public figures to win libel cases against the media. In 1988, for example, the Supreme Court ruled that the leader of Moral Majority, the Reverend Jerry Falwell, could not collect libel damages from *Hustler* magazine, which he claimed had intentionally caused him great emotional distress by publishing a merciless parody of the evangelical Christian minister. In ruling against Falwell, the Court stated that the magazine's cartoon depiction of Falwell could hardly be consid-

8. Freedom of the press, including freedom from prior censorship, was incorporated into the Fourteenth Amendment in *Near v. Minnesota,* 283 U.S. 697 (1931).

9. *New York Times Co. v. United States,* 403 U.S. 713 (1971).

10. *Miami Herald Publishing Co. v. Tornillo,* 418 U.S. 241 (1974).

11. *The New York Times v. Sullivan,* 376 U.S. 254 (1964).

ered a portrayal of actual events or facts.[12] The Court's restrictive attitude toward permitting public figures to win libel judgments stems from its concern that burdensome libel laws could stifle valued public debate.

Obscenity. Obscene materials do not enjoy constitutional protection. But, because people's views on what constitutes obscenity vary widely, it has been extremely difficult to develop workable definitions of obscenity for use by law enforcement officials. The definition of obscenity developed by a majority of the Supreme Court in 1973 involves a three-part test:[13]

1. Would an average person applying the contemporary standards of a particular community find that the work taken as a whole appeals to prurient interests?

2. When taken as a whole, does the work lack serious literary, artistic, political, or scientific value?

3. Does the work depict or describe sexual conduct in a patently offensive way?

In devising these tests for obscenity, the Court indicated that although the same standards did not have to be applied in every community, it did not intend for local enforcement officials and juries to have carte blanche in determining what constituted obscene material. Indeed, anti-obscenity laws must define specifically what constitutes obscenity in a manner that avoids vague language; vaguely drawn obscenity statutes provide no guidance to booksellers and theater managers of what could constitute a violation of the law. In addition, sellers of allegedly obscene materials must be shown to have knowingly offered such materials for sale. It is not enough merely to have obscene material in one's possession. Although the Court has explicitly denied constitutional protection to obscene material, developing statutes and then prosecuting offenders within the confines of the First Amendment have proven to be no easy task.

The conflicts between the advocates of freedom of artistic and political expression and the various groups anxious to protect the public, especially the more vulnerable members of society, are continuing and serious. For example, women's groups have sought to restrict hard-core sex publications on the grounds that they degrade women and encourage violence against women.[14] A particularly

12. *Hustler Magazine v. Falwell,* 485 U.S. 46 (1988).
13. *Miller v. California,* 413 U.S. 15 (1973).
14. The issue of the women's movement and pornography is considered by Donald A. Downs, *The New Politics of Pornography: The First Amendment's Encounter with a Dilemma* (Chicago: University of Chicago Press, 1989).

troublesome issue is the access of children to sexually oriented material in print, movies, television, and records. Tipper Gore, a concerned mother and the wife of Democratic senator Albert Gore, Jr. (Tenn.), has gained substantial publicity (both highly critical and laudatory) by advocating warning labels on records containing sexually explicit lyrics to protect children. Some civil liberties advocates and the record industry charge that such actions amount to censorship and would have the effect of limiting the rights of adults. These conflicts over obscenity and freedom of the press are not likely to go away because they involve prized, but often clashing, values.

Shield Laws for the Press. Another controversial area surrounding freedom of the press is whether or not reporters should be required to testify during criminal trials and divulge the sources of their information. Those who favor requiring reporters to testify argue that reporters are not exempt from the obligations of citizenship imposed on all Americans. But press groups have urged legislatures to adopt shield laws that would prevent reporters from being compelled to divulge their sources. Reporters claim that their sources will dry up and that they will not be able to gain access to vital news if their sources can be revealed in a court of law. Thus far, the courts have not granted reporters the right to withhold information in criminal prosecutions, and, as a result, some reporters have gone to jail rather than reveal their information sources.

Freedom of Religion

The First Amendment guarantees religious freedom in two ways: through the **establishment of religion clause**, which bans the establishment of an official state-sanctioned religion and erects a "wall of separation" between church and state, and through the **free exercise of religion clause**, which protects people's right to practice their religion. As with the rights of free speech and a free press, neither clause has been interpreted in absolute terms. For example, in spite of the so-called establishment clause, the government is not totally separated from religion. The House and Senate have official chaplains, who open each session with prayer, and the military has chaplains on the payroll as well. Similarly, the so-called free exercise clause does not exempt a person from obeying otherwise nondiscriminatory laws such as those banning the practice of polygamy or requiring parents to provide medical care for their children.

The relationship between the government and religion is complex and often controversial because it involves balancing the constitutional mandate for religious freedom and separation of church and state against America's deep religious heritage and the commitment many have to their faiths. It is therefore inevitable that issues involving the relationship of the government to church organizations and religious practices would enter the political arena. For example, should parents, who on religious grounds do not believe in medicine, be required to immunize their children? Is it a violation of the establishment clause to permit prayer in public schools or to pay for textbooks used in nonreligious classes in parochial schools with tax funds? These and other vexing, and sometimes emotional, issues confront anyone seeking to determine the appropriate relationship of the government to religion.

Establishment of Religion. The drafters of the Constitution clearly wanted to prevent the creation of a state-sponsored and -supported religion such as the Church of England. Today, however, issues of church-state relations are raised by the more indirect involvement of the government in religion.[15] For example, in 1947 the Supreme Court was confronted with an establishment of religion case when the constitutionality of a New Jersey law providing free bus transportation to children attending parochial schools was challenged (*Everson v. Board of Education*).[16] While stating that the government should not be involved in the affairs of religious organizations, the Court upheld New Jersey's law on the grounds that it provided aid to students rather than to religious organizations. Similar reasoning has been applied to permit government support of school lunches and nonsecular textbooks for children attending parochial schools.

Since 1971 and the case of *Lemon v. Kurtzman,* the Supreme Court has used a three-part test to determine whether or not government involvement in religion violates the establishment clause. A law is said not to violate the establishment clause if (1) it has a secular rather than a religious purpose; (2) its actual effect is neutral— neither promoting nor inhibiting religion; and (3) it does not cause excessive government involvement in religion.[17] Using the *Lemon* test, the Court has declared unconstitutional state sponsorship and encouragement of religion through such means as a nondenominational prayer at the opening of the school day and a devotional Bible reading. State bans on teaching the theory of evolution, which of-

15. For a detailed discussion of the establishment of religion clause, see Leonard W. Levy, *The Establishment Clause: Religion and the First Amendment* (New York: Macmillan, 1986); and Robert A. Goldman and Art Kaufman, eds., *How Does the Constitution Protect Religious Freedom?* (New York: University Press of America, 1988).
16. *Everson v. Board of Education,* 330 U.S. 1 (1947).
17. *Lemon v. Kurtzman,* 403 U.S. 602 (1971).

fends the religious sensitivities of some fundamentalist Protestants, also have been declared unconstitutional. Government-sponsored religious displays—such as nativity scenes at Christmas—are permitted when done in a secular holiday context, but displays of the crèche in a manner that suggests state support for a particular religion have been declared to be in violation of the First Amendment.

A particularly complex area is state financial aid to parochial schools. In applying the *Lemon* test on a case-by-case basis, the Court has held that states may not subsidize the salaries of parochial schoolteachers, even when they teach only nonreligious subjects. Nor may states pay for counseling, audiovisual equipment, field trips, or maintenance of facilities in parochial schools. The Court has permitted, however, state financial assistance to pay for textbooks, lunches, transportation to and from school, diagnostic tests, and remedial assistance. Tax deductions and credits by parents for the cost of tuition at nonpublic schools also have been permitted.

As these examples demonstrate, the "wall of separation" between church and state so strongly advocated by Thomas Jefferson can be penetrated. A government that is actively involved in the lives of its citizens inevitably interacts with religious organizations. Supreme Court policy has tended to be one of accommodating constitutional guarantees to religious traditions and practices. But as long as government remains a powerful force in society and the nation becomes more diverse in its religious faiths and practices, controversy about interpretation of the establishment of religion clause will continue.

Free Exercise of Religion. The free exercise clause of the First Amendment, which prohibits the federal government from interfering in people's right to practice their religion, has been incorporated by the Supreme Court into the Fourteenth Amendment for protection against state infringement. People have an absolute right to believe whatever they wish. The government therefore cannot compel a particular religious belief or penalize people because of their beliefs or lack of religious faith.

The right of people to practice their religion freely has been interpreted by the courts in a less absolute manner than a person's right to believe as he or she sees fit. Yet the Supreme Court has been highly protective of the rights of various religious groups. Thus, a state law requiring a flag salute in public schools was declared unconstitutional because Jehovah's Witnesses claimed it conflicted with their faith's prohibition on the worship of graven images. Nor can Jehovah's Witnesses be required to display on their New Hampshire license plates the state motto, "Live Free or Die." And Amish parents cannot be required to send their children to school after the eighth grade. The Court has upheld other legislation, however, including Sunday closing laws for businesses, compulsory vaccination of children, bans on polygamy, bans by the military on such religious headgear as the Jewish yarmulke, and requirements that the Amish collect and pay Social Security taxes on their employees, even though some religious groups asserted that these laws interfered with their free practice of religion.

*Freedom of Assembly
and Association*

The right of people to assemble peaceably, including demonstrations, parades, and other types of symbolic speech, is constitutionally protected. But this protection does not extend to incitements to violence, nor are governmental entities helpless in dealing with the problems associated with crowd control—such as blocked highways and sidewalks or the disruption of such public facilities as schools or courthouses. Reasonable regulations governing the time, place, and manner of demonstrations, for example, have been permitted by the courts, as well as the arrest of protesters who deliberately made noise that disrupted the peace and good order of a school.[18] Such restrictions, however, cannot be applied in a discriminatory manner.

The courts have been particularly protective of people's rights of assembly on or in such public property as parks, sidewalks, squares, and buildings. There is, however, no constitutional right of assembly on private property. The owners of shopping centers, for example, may restrict the distribution of political campaign materials and financial solicitations. But the Supreme Court has allowed state and local governments to require shopping centers to permit political activities that do not interfere with business.

The Supreme Court also has ruled that the right to freedom of assembly along with the right to freedom of speech implies a right to freedom of association. This means that people are free to associate with whom they please and to form organizations espousing diverse causes as long as they do not constitute an immediate threat to society. Thus, people have a constitutional right to form political parties as well as religious, charitable, social, ethnic, and racial organizations.

18. *Grayned v. Rockford,* 408 U.S. 104 (1972).

The Right to Privacy

Although the Constitution does not state explicitly that people have a right to privacy, the Supreme Court has determined that the First Amendment, taken together with the Third, Fourth, Fifth, Ninth, and Fourteenth amendments, provides the basis for this right. The Third Amendment bans quartering troops in private homes; the Fourth Amendment protects against unreasonable searches and seizures; the Fifth and Fourteenth amendments provide protection against being deprived of liberty without due process of law, and the Ninth Amendment provides that the enumeration of rights in the Constitution does not imply that other natural rights have been abandoned.

The most significant court decisions relating to the right to privacy have dealt with sexual relations and reproduction. In 1965 (*Griswold v. Connecticut*), the Supreme Court declared unconstitutional a Connecticut law that made it a crime for married or unmarried couples to use birth control devices or medication. The same law also made it illegal to provide a person with birth control information. The court considered marital relations so personal and intimate a matter as to be "within the penumbra of special guarantees of the Bill of Rights."[19]

By far the most controversial application of the right of privacy has been to abortion. In *Roe v. Wade* (1973), the Supreme Court held that a woman has the right to an abortion during the first three months (or first trimester) of pregnancy and that for a state to interfere with that right violates her right to privacy.[20] But the Court did permit reasonable regulation of abortions during the second trimester, and during the third trimester, when life outside the womb is possible, state prohibitions on abortion were permitted. The *Roe* decision, involving as it did the highly emotional issue of a woman's right to control her own body and the right of the unborn fetus to life, set off an intense controversy over government policy.

As the membership of the Court became more conservative during the 1980s, it became more tolerant of state restrictions on a woman's right to an abortion during the first trimester. In *Webster v. Reproductive Health Services* (1989), it held that a state can prohibit the use of state resources in performing abortions and that reasonable state regulations could be imposed to ensure that abortions

19. *Griswold v. Connecticut*, 381 U.S. 479 (1965).
20. *Roe v. Wade*, 410 U.S. 113 (1973).

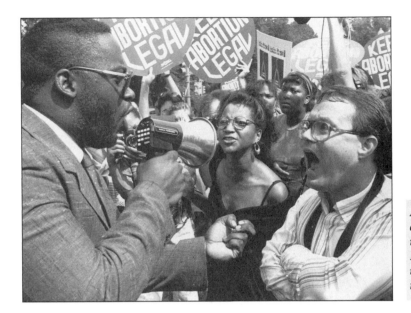

Abortion foes and advocates confront each other over the Supreme Court's rulings on the issue, beginning with Roe v. Wade in 1973, which prevented states from denying women the right to an abortion.

are not carried out once the fetus is viable.[21] This highly controversial decision was followed by another in 1990 permitting states to require parental notification before performance of abortions on girls under the age of eighteen.[22] While not overruling the *Roe* decision with its assertion of a woman's right to an abortion, the Court has in recent decisions significantly restricted its initial scope by giving the states greater latitude in regulating abortions. Thus, the political struggle over the issue has intensified and shifted increasingly to electoral and legislative arenas. Activists on both sides are seeking to elect supporters of their cause and are lobbying state legislatures to influence the content of state abortion legislation.

The Bill of Rights and Criminal Proceedings

The authors of the Bill of Rights were all too familiar with government actions that arbitrarily deprived people of life, liberty, and property. Therefore, they included in the Bill of Rights detailed guarantees of **procedural due process** or fairness to people accused of criminal wrongdoing. These guarantees include the Fourth Amendment's prohibition against "unreasonable searches and seizures," the Fifth Amendment's prohibition against double jeopardy (trying

21. *Webster v. Reproductive Health Services*, 109 S.Ct. 3040 (1989).
22. *Ohio v. Akron Center for Reproductive Health*, 110 S.Ct. 2972 (1990).

a person twice for the same offense) and protection of defendants from self-incrimination, the Sixth Amendment's guarantee of trial by jury and the right to an attorney, and the Eighth Amendment's interdiction against "cruel and unusual punishments." Although these protections initially were intended to apply only to the federal government, they are now applicable to the states through the doctrine of selective incorporation.

In applying these amendments to specific cases, the judicial system is often confronted with the delicate issue of balancing the rights of the accused with society's need for order and protection. A continuing question that arises in procedural due process cases is whether or not to let a guilty person go free because law enforcement officials failed to observe the procedural guarantees of the Bill of Rights. Under the leadership of Chief Justice Earl Warren, the Supreme Court moved in the 1960s to define more clearly and extend the rights of the accused. These actions brought praise from civil liberties advocates and sharp criticism from those who believed the Court was unduly hampering law enforcement. The Burger Court of the 1970s and 1980s did narrow some of the Warren Court doctrines, but for the most part it maintained the guarantees enunciated during the Warren era.

Protection from Unreasonable
Searches and Seizures

The Fourth Amendment protects an individual's privacy in guaranteeing security from unreasonable searches and seizures. Under most circumstances, it requires that a judge issue a search warrant authorizing law officers to search for and seize evidence of criminal activity. Warrants can be issued only when there is *probable cause* to believe the search will produce criminal evidence. In 1914, the Supreme Court adopted the **exclusionary rule**, which barred evidence seized illegally from being used in a criminal trial,[23] and in 1961 (*Mapp v. Ohio*) the Warren Court made this rule applicable to state as well as to federal criminal proceedings through the Fourteenth Amendment's **due process clause**.[24] This decision stirred criticism of the Court on the grounds that criminals could be let free on procedural technicalities. The rationale of the Court, however, was that law enforcement officials should have no incentive to obtain evidence illegally in order to obtain convictions.

Since 1961, the Burger and Rehnquist Courts have narrowed significantly the application of the exclusionary rule. Under the doctrine

23. *Weeks v. United States,* 232 U.S. 383 (1914).
24. *Mapp v. Ohio,* 367 U.S. 643 (1961).

of "objective good faith" adopted by the Court in 1984, when the police seize evidence with a search warrant that was obtained in objective good faith that it was valid, the evidence is admissible in a trial even if it is later demonstrated that the warrant contained a technical flaw that made the search illegal. The Court has further weakened the exclusionary rule through the doctrines of "inevitable discovery" and "independent evidence." Otherwise illegally seized evidence may be introduced into a trial if it would have been discovered "inevitably," or if a search warrant is obtained after the fact on the basis of "independent evidence." Clearly, in balancing the rights of the accused with society's interest in convicting lawbreakers, the exclusionary rule has been weakened substantially.

An individual is protected under the Fourth Amendment from warrantless police searches in places where one has a legitimate right to expect privacy, including one's home, office, hotel room, desk, or file cabinets. But a person does not have Fourth Amendment protection in all places where he or she has a legitimate right to be. Thus, the Court has permitted stopping and searching automobiles when there is probable cause to believe that the car is carrying something illegal. There are, however, limits on police authority to search cars. For example, if the police stop a car they believe is carrying illegal aliens, they are not then authorized to search containers or suitcases for drugs. But the police are permitted to stop cars for traffic offenses and conduct a full search of the driver. In other areas, owners of fenced or open fields on which marijuana is growing do not enjoy Fourth Amendment protection, but the Court has held that police may not tap phones without a court order.

Protection from Self-incrimination

The Fifth Amendment states that no person shall "be compelled in any criminal case to be a witness against himself." Initially, the courts interpreted this amendment to be protection against defendants being required to testify in their own criminal trials, and judges banned prosecuting attorneys from commenting on the fact that a defendant had chosen not to testify. Not all self-incrimination occurs in the courtroom under cross-examination, however. After taking prisoners into custody, police may fail to inform them of their constitutional rights and subject them to third-degree tactics to coerce confessions.

In an effort to put an end to such practices, the Warren Court in the landmark case of *Miranda v. Arizona* (1966) took the position that police custody is inherently threatening and that confessions obtained during custody can be admitted as evidence only if subjects have been (1) advised of their constitutional right to remain silent, (2) warned that what they say may be used against them in a trial, (3) informed of the right to have an attorney paid for by the state if they cannot afford one and to have that attorney present during interrogation, and (4) told of the right to terminate the interrogation at any time.[25] Failure by law enforcement authorities to abide by these *Miranda* rules can result in the courts excluding as evidence the statements made by a suspect.

Many law enforcement officials and politicians, including Richard Nixon in his 1968 presidential campaign, severely criticized the *Miranda* decision for handcuffing the police and undermining law and order. With their more conservative membership in the 1970s and 1980s, the Burger and Rehnquist Courts narrowed the scope of the *Miranda* decision. The Burger Court ruled that statements made without the *Miranda* warnings being given could still be admitted as evidence in order to contest the credibility of a defendant's testimony. For example, if statements made by a defendant in court contradict statements made without a prior *Miranda* warning, prosecutors may use the earlier statements to challenge the credibility of the defendant's court testimony. Further limits on the *Miranda* decision occurred in 1984, when the Court held that the *Miranda* warning need not be given if public safety is threatened. In 1991, the Court even went so far as to rule that the use of a coerced confession in a trial does not automatically invalidate a conviction if it can be shown that other evidence, obtained independently of the coerced confession, was also introduced at the trial and was adequate to sustain a guilty verdict.[26] In 1990, however, the Court reiterated the importance of protection against self-incrimination when it held in *Minnick v. Mississippi* that suspects held in custody who ask to consult a lawyer when police try to interrogate them may not be approached later for questioning when their lawyers are not present.[27]

As with the exclusionary rule, Court policy regarding self-incrimination is not fixed, and the seemingly explicit meaning of constitutional language is not absolute. The broad extensions of rights designed to preserve a defendant's presumption of innocence, introduced in the 1960s under the Warren Court, have met with powerful

25. *Miranda v. Arizona*, 384 U.S. 436 (1966). For an account of the decision and the controversy it created, see Liva Baker, *Miranda: Crime, Law and Politics* (New York: Atheneum, 1983).
26. *Arizona v. Fulminante*, 111 S.Ct. 1246 (1991).
27. *Minnick v. Mississippi*, 111 S.Ct. 486 (1990).

opposition from those concerned about the government's obligation to protect public safety. In balancing these highly prized values, the Burger and Rehnquist Courts have tended to tilt the balance in the direction of public safety needs.

Right to an Attorney

Lawyers have a saying that "he who defends himself has a fool for a client." This adage is testimony to the accused's need for an attorney if there is to be any hope for a fair trial. This need is explicitly recognized by the Sixth Amendment, which states that defendants in criminal trials shall have the right "to have the Assistance of Counsel." The right to counsel was first incorporated into the Fourteenth Amendment in the case of the so-called Scottsboro boys in 1932. In this case, nine young black defendants were charged with raping two white women in Alabama. Noting that this case involved a capital crime (one punishable by death), the Supreme Court ruled that the defendants—who were poor, illiterate teenagers—were entitled to an attorney paid for by the state.[28]

In 1963 in *Gideon v. Wainwright,* the Warren Court extended the right to an attorney to any poor state defendant charged with a felony (a serious criminal offense punishable by death or imprisonment for a year). In this case, Clarence Gideon sent a handwritten petition to the Supreme Court from his Florida prison cell claiming that his five-year prison sentence was unconstitutional because he had been too poor to hire an attorney and had been required to defend himself at his trial. The Court agreed that his constitutional right to counsel had been denied.[29] In a new trial, at which he was provided with counsel, Gideon was acquitted. The Court's *Gideon* decision has been responsible for the development and growth of public defender programs within the states.

In the 1970s, the Burger Court extended the right of indigent defendants to counsel to include misdemeanor offenses that would result in a jail sentence. But the Court has not required states to provide counsel to poor defendants in civil cases involving custody of children or loss of property.

Protection from Excessive Bail and Cruel and Unusual Punishment

According to the Eighth Amendment, "Excessive bail shall not be required, nor excessive fines imposed, nor cruel and unusual pun-

28. *Powell v. Alabama,* 287 U.S. 45 (1932).
29. *Gideon v. Wainwright,* 372 U.S. 335 (1963). For an engrossing and complete account of the *Gideon* case, see Anthony Lewis, *Gideon's Trumpet* (New York: Random House, 1964).

Clarence Earl Gideon

You Need a Lawyer: Justice Hugo Black Speaks

During the 1960s, the Supreme Court was actively involved in extending the protection of the Bill of Rights to defendants in state courts. A dramatic example of this protection was evident in the 1963 case of *Gideon v. Wainwright,* in which an indigent, Clarence Earl Gideon, who after being denied a court-appointed attorney, tried to defend himself against a charge of breaking into a Florida pool hall. The Supreme Court ruled that by denying Gideon an attorney, Florida had violated the due process clause of the Fourteenth Amendment, which requires that all persons charged with serious crimes be provided with the aid of an attorney. Justice Hugo Black explained the reasoning of the Court:

[R]eason and reflection require us to recognize that in our adversary system of criminal justice, any person haled into court, who is too poor to hire a lawyer, cannot be assured a fair trial unless counsel is provided for him. This seems to us to be an obvious truth. . . . Lawyers to prosecute are everywhere deemed essential to protect the public's interest in an orderly society. . . . That government hires lawyers to prosecute and defendants who have the money hire lawyers to defend are the strongest indications of the widespread belief that lawyers in criminal courts are necessities, not luxuries. (*Gideon v. Wainwright,* 372 U.S. 335 at 343-344, 1963)

ishments inflicted." Because the bail provision of the Eighth Amendment has not been incorporated into the Fourteenth Amendment, state judges can set bail at high levels to keep prisoners in jail until a trial has been concluded. Such a measure is a type of preventive detention. But this practice has been criticized because defendants, who are presumed to be innocent until proven guilty under our system of justice, are subject to all the indignities of prison life before being convicted, and, indeed, they may ultimately be acquitted. Preventive detention is defended as a reasonable way to protect the public from dangerous criminals and to prevent the accused from jumping bail. In 1984, Congress enacted the Bail Reform Act, which authorized the use of preventive detention through the denial of bail in federal court cases in which the judge determines that the defendant is a threat to public safety.

The Eighth Amendment ban on cruel and unusual punishment raises the question of the meaning of "cruel and unusual." As society's standards for judging cruelty have changed, the meaning of the phrase has evolved. But the amendment clearly bans the torture practices that were condemned by English common law when the Bill of Rights was drafted. In addition, the federal courts have ruled that such conditions in state prisons as excessive crowding, improper diets, poor sanitation, or denials of needed medical care are violations of the Eighth Amendment. On rare occasions, the Supreme Court also has ruled that the severity of a punishment was out of proportion to the seriousness of the offense. But the Court has been reluctant to second-guess legislative decisions in this area and has upheld a forty-year sentence and a $20,000 fine for the crime of intending to distribute nine ounces of marijuana. Yet in a related area, the Supreme Court ruled in the 1962 case of *Robinson v. California* that a state law making it a crime to be a drug addict violated the constitutional protection against cruel and unusual punishment because the law made it a crime for a person to have an illness.[30]

Most contemporary controversies have revolved around the death penalty. Now-retired justices William Brennan, Jr., and Thurgood Marshall considered the death penalty to be a cruel and unusual punishment. The majority of the Court, however, has not accepted this view. While permitting the death penalty when a person kills, intends to kill, or tries to kill another person, the Court has imposed limits on the use of this severest of all punishments. When imposed in an arbitrary and discriminatory manner (as was true in a 1972 case in

30. *Robinson v. California,* 370 U.S. 660 (1962).

Georgia, where juries had such wide discretion that racial bias entered the process), the death penalty has been considered cruel and unusual punishment. But statistics showing that blacks convicted of murdering whites have a greater chance of receiving a death sentence than whites convicted of killing blacks have not been considered sufficient evidence of a violation of the Eighth Amendment.[31] As long as it has been shown that the accused had a fair trial and was convicted under a valid death penalty law, the Court has declined to throw out a conviction.

The Quest for Equality

The Declaration of Independence includes Thomas Jefferson's affirmation that the new nation was to be based on the principle of equality: "We hold these truths to be self-evident, that all men are created equal." The Constitution of 1787, however, did not guarantee that the government will treat all citizens equally. It was not until 1868 that equality gained a formal place in the Constitution with the ratification of the Fourteenth Amendment, which provides that "no state shall deny any person the *equal protection of the laws*" (emphasis added). This amendment was intended to protect the newly freed slaves from state acts of discrimination (unequal treatment of individuals based on such arbitrary classifications as race), and the federal government was given enforcement authority. With its broad language, however, the **equal protection clause** has over time come to be interpreted as banning government acts of discrimination based on gender, religion, or national origin, as well as those based on race. Although the Fourteenth Amendment does not prohibit discrimination by private citizens, it does ban private acts of discrimination when supported by government actions (for example, state court enforcement of real estate deed restrictions that prohibit the sale of property to nonwhites).

Although equality is a broadly accepted part of the American creed, it has several dimensions, some of which are a source of continuing debate.[32] The least controversial is the notion of *equality under the law,* which asserts that the government should treat everyone the same and not make arbitrary distinctions among people based on such criteria as race, sex, national origin, or religion. For some Americans, however, equality has a more expansive meaning. It can encompass *equality of opportunity*—that all people should have the

31. *McCleskey v. Kemp*, 481 U.S. 279 (1987).
32. See Sidney Verba and Gary Orren, *Equality in America: The View from the Top* (Cambridge, Mass.: Harvard University Press, 1985).

same chance in life regardless of the color of their skin, sex, national origin, or religion. Most Americans accept the notion of providing some minimum standard of living and education so that people can compete and achieve a better life for themselves and their children. The most controversial conception of equality is *equality of outcomes*—that equality exists when all people share the benefits of society regardless of race, sex, national origin, or religion. Advocates of equality of outcomes have endorsed preferential treatment in education and hiring for disadvantaged groups to compensate for past acts of discrimination or deprivation. But such **affirmative action** policies have created sharp divisions within society as America continues to debate the meaning of its commitment to equality.

Racial Equality

To combat the discriminatory laws (so-called black codes) passed by southern states after the Civil War, a series of constitutional amendments protecting the rights of black Americans also were proposed and ratified in the years after the war. The Thirteenth Amendment (1865) banned slavery and involuntary servitude; the Fourteenth Amendment (1868) contained guarantees of "equal protection" and "due process of law" and declared blacks to be citizens of the United States and the states in which they resided; and the Fifteenth Amendment (1870) guaranteed that the right to vote could not be abridged on the basis of race or previous condition of servitude. In addition, Congress passed a series of civil rights laws, including the Civil Rights Act of 1875, which banned discrimination in places of public accommodation such as hotels and restaurants as well as in jury service.[33]

Rise of Jim Crow Laws and the "Separate but Equal" Doctrine. During the 1870s through the 1940s, the rights that these federal actions were intended to protect were gradually eroded. The Supreme Court narrowed the applicability of federal civil rights legislation and racist state legislatures passed so-called Jim Crow laws requiring segregation of blacks and whites in schools, parks, restrooms, transportation facilities, and other places of public accommodation. To make certain that blacks did not challenge segregation via the ballot box, they were effectively disenfranchised. One means of disenfranchisement used by southern states was the "poll tax," a head tax a citizen was required to pay in order to vote. These taxes hit poor blacks particularly hard, especially since normally there was a provision for payment of back taxes before voting for the first time.

33. This act was later declared unconstitutional by the Supreme Court. See *Civil Rights Cases*, 100 U.S. 3 (1883).

Literacy tests also were adopted as a qualification for voting. These tests were often administered in a discriminatory manner that effectively prevented blacks from registering to vote. To further insulate the electoral process from black influence, southern states instituted what they called a white primary, which excluded blacks from the primary elections of the dominant party in the region, the Democratic party.

The Supreme Court gave constitutional status to the Jim Crow system in 1896 when it stated in the case of *Plessy v. Ferguson* that segregation did not violate the equal protection clause.[34] The case arose when Homer Plessy, who was seven-eighths white, appealed his conviction for having violated Louisiana's segregation laws by sitting in a "whites only" railroad car. In upholding Plessy's conviction, the Court adopted the so-called **separate but equal doctrine**, which held that government-enforced segregation of the races was constitutional as long as the facilities for blacks and whites were equal. With this constitutional endorsement of segregation, Jim Crow laws proliferated, notably in education at both the elementary and secondary levels and in universities.

Blacks were clearly relegated to second-class citizenship and, even worse, were subjected to intimidation and violence if they sought to assert their rights to equality under the law. Ku Klux Klan cross burnings, beatings, and vigilante lynchings were used to enforce the system of segregation by private means.

Brown v. Board of Education of Topeka and the Desegregation of Public Education. In the 1930s, the Supreme Court, under prodding from cases brought before it through the efforts of the National Association for the Advancement of Colored People (NAACP), began to cast a more critical eye on segregation. The Court began to enforce the requirement that facilities for blacks and whites actually be equal, and in a series of cases it required that blacks be admitted to state university law schools since no comparable legal education was available elsewhere for blacks.[35] It also declared the white primary to be a violation of the Fifteenth Amendment because a party primary is an integral part of the electoral process.[36]

The real revolution in Court policy toward government-enforced segregation occurred in 1954 in the case of *Brown v. Board of*

34. *Plessy v. Ferguson,* 163 U.S. 537 (1896).
35. See *Missouri ex rel. Gaines v. Canada,* 305 U.S. 337 (1938); *McLaurin v. Oklahoma State Regents for Higher Education,* 339 U.S. 637 (1950); and *Sweatt v. Painter,* 339 U.S. 629 (1950).
36. *Smith v. Allwright,* 321 U.S. 649 (1944).

The Birth and Death of "Separate but Equal"

Although the Preamble to the Declaration of Independence proclaims the equality of all people, the drafters of the Constitution, in deference to the slave-holding South, omitted a definition of equality and permitted slavery to continue. The Civil War and the constitutional amendments that followed the war—especially the Fourteenth, which banned the states from denying any person the "equal protection of the laws"—sought to correct that omission. But in 1896, the Supreme Court delivered a mighty blow to racial equality in the case of *Plessy v. Ferguson* (163 U.S. 537, 1896). In this case, the Court held that a Louisiana law requiring "equal but separate accommodations" on public transportation was constitutional. In reconciling state-enforced segregation with the Fourteenth Amendment's equal protection clause, the Court adopted the infamous "separate but equal" formula—that is, state-enforced segregation was to be permitted so long as the facilities for blacks and whites were equal. Justice Henry Brown sought to justify the Court's position by saying that

in the nature of things [the Fourteenth Amendment] could not have been intended to abolish distinctions based upon color, or to enforce social, as distinguished from political equality, or a commingling of the two races upon terms unsatisfactory to either.

In protest to this line of constitutional interpretation, Justice John Marshall Harlan dissented, saying that "our Constitution is colorblind and neither knows nor tolerates classes among citizens." It was not until fifty-eight years later that Harlan's principles of equality were em-braced by the Supreme Court and the law was brought into closer conformity with the ideals of the Declaration of Independence. In *Brown v. Board of Education of Topeka* (347 U.S. 483, 1954) the Court ruled that state-enforced segregation was unconstitutional. The case concerned young Linda Brown, who because of Kansas state law and local segregation rules was required to travel a mile outside her neighborhood to attend a segregated black school. In 1950, when her father sought to enter her in the white school closer to their home, he was refused. The National Association for the Advancement of Colored People (NAACP) took up Linda's cause and carried her case to the Supreme Court. A unanimous Supreme Court led by Chief Justice Earl Warren explicitly reversed the *Plessy* decision. The chief justice stated, "We conclude that in the field of public education the doctrine of 'separate but equal' has no place. Separate educational facilities are inherently unequal."

In the years since Linda Brown's father, with the assistance of the NAACP, successfully challenged the "separate but equal" doctrine, the federal government has been embroiled in one controversy after another over how to combat discrimination by state and local governments, school boards, and some private sector employers.

Linda Brown

Education of Topeka. In this case, Oliver Brown, on behalf of his eight-year-old daughter, Linda, challenged Topeka's school segregation policy, which was permitted under Kansas law. Since the black and white schools of the city were presumed to be equal, the Court was not able to decide the case by determining whether the two school systems were in fact equal. Rather, it had to confront the issue of segregation per se and decide its constitutionality. In a unanimous decision, the Court threw out the old doctrine of "separate but equal," pointing out that in public education "the doctrine of 'separate but equal' has no place. Separate educational facilities are inherently unequal."[37] This case was followed by an enforcement decision that recognized the difficulty of achieving integrated schools and called for desegregation to occur "with all deliberate speed."[38]

Integration of southern school systems did not occur voluntarily. It required the filing of numerous lawsuits seeking federal court orders to desegregate. At times, southern opposition to court orders to desegregate public schools was both massive and violent. In 1957 in Little Rock, Arkansas, Gov. Orval Faubus used National Guard troops to block black students from entering Central High School. A federal court, however, ordered desegregation to continue and the guard to be withdrawn. President Dwight Eisenhower then sent in U.S. Army troops to protect the black students from harassment by white mobs. The various tactics used by southern states to postpone the inevitable desegregation of their school systems were so effective that a decade after the *Brown* decision, schools in the eleven states of the old Confederacy remained overwhelmingly segregated. Finally, the Supreme Court lost its patience with delays. In 1969 it stated that "[t]he time for mere 'deliberate speed' has run out. . . . Delays in desegregating school systems are no longer tolerable." The Court then demanded that every school district terminate dual school systems.[39]

The Civil Rights Movement and the Civil Rights Act of 1964. As the desegregation of public schools proceeded slowly ("with all deliberate speed") in the face of white southern opposition during the 1950s and early 1960s, the civil rights movement gathered momentum as blacks demonstrated against centuries of injustice. Lunch-counter sit-ins protesting segregated eating facilities, bus boycotts protesting requirements that blacks sit at the back of buses, a massive march on Washington to dramatize support for federal civil rights legislation, and marches for voting rights captured public attention, and whites became increasingly aware of the gap between the American creed of equality and the reality of the black experience. As the civil rights movement, led by the Reverend Martin Luther King, made headway, pressure mounted in Congress for passage of civil rights legislation.[40] A major legislative breakthrough occurred with the

37. *Brown v. Board of Education of Topeka,* 347 U.S. 483 (1954). For an account of the events leading up to the *Brown* case, see Richard Kluger, *Simple Justice: The History of Brown v. Board of Education and Black America's Struggle for Equality* (New York: Knopf, 1976).
38. *Brown v. Board of Education of Topeka,* 349 U.S. 294 (1955).
39. *Alexander v. Holmes Board of Education,* 396 U.S. 19 (1969).
40. For an account of the civil rights movement, see Taylor Branch, *Parting the Waters: America in the King Years 1954–63* (New York: Simon and Schuster, 1988).

passage of the Civil Rights Act of 1964, which banned racial discrimination in places of public accommodation. It also authorized the Department of Justice to enter into the integration battle by filing desegregation suits. Moreover, the law required that federal funds be cut off when any person shall "on the basis of race, color, or national origin be subjected to discrimination under any program or activity receiving federal financial assistance." Since public schools received federal financial assistance, the act provided the government with a powerful weapon to require desegregation. Through the combined enforcement activities of the Office of Civil Rights in the Department of Health, Education and Welfare and the Justice Department, school desegregation proceeded rapidly so that by 1972 the number of blacks in the South attending all-black schools had dropped to 9 percent.

School Integration in the North. The problems of school desegregation in the North proved even more difficult than those in the South. The Fourteenth Amendment bans *governmental* acts of discrimination—that is, **de jure segregation**. Since segregated schools in the South stemmed from state laws that mandated dual school systems for blacks and whites, the courts could order the schools to be integrated. But in the North, state laws did not require segregated schools; such schools occurred largely as a result of residential housing patterns—that is, **de facto segregation** based on practices, not state laws. Thus for the federal courts to order the integration of northern schools, they had to demonstrate that segregation occurred as a result of government actions that violated the equal protection clause. When prior government actions did indeed result in racial imbalances in the schools, the Supreme Court held in 1971 that federal judges could order remedial actions be taken to redress the imbalances. This frequently meant busing children to distant schools—a highly controversial and politically explosive issue in many communities.

Today in most metropolitan areas, the existence of separate central city and suburban school districts, as well as demographic patterns, work against racial integration of the schools. Expanding black and Hispanic populations in city centers coupled with white migration to the suburbs have created central city schools dominated by minority students and largely white suburban schools. In these situations, busing of children within only the central city school district is unlikely to create racially balanced schools. Thus, the Supreme Court has held that cross-district busing is an appropriate remedy if it can be demonstrated that school district lines have been

Major Civil Rights Legislation

Date	Act	Major Provisions
1875	Civil Rights Act	Bans discrimination in places of public accommodation (declared unconstitutional in 1883)
1963	Equal Pay Act	Bans wage discrimination based on race, sex, color, religion, or national origin
1964	Civil Rights Act	Bans discrimination in places of public accommodation Authorizes Justice Department to bring school integration suits Bans discrimination in federally funded programs Bans racial- and gender-based discrimination in private employment
1965	Voting Rights Act	In states and counties with literacy tests or where less than 50 percent of the population was registered to vote on November 1, 1964 —Federal registrars could register voters and ensure that those registered could exercise their right to vote. —Any changes in voting laws must be approved by the attorney general for the U.S. District Court for the District of Columbia.
1967	Age Discrimination Act	Bans discriminatory employment practices based on age
1968	Civil Rights Act, Title VIII	Bans racial discrimination in sale or rental of housing
1972	Higher Education Act, Title IX	Forbids discrimination based on sex by universities and colleges receiving federal aid
1974	Equal Credit Opportunity Act	Bans discrimination in granting credit based on sex, marital status, race, age, or receiving public assistance
1974	Housing and Community Development Act	Bans housing discrimination based on sex
1990	Americans with Disabilities Act	Bans discrimination in employment, transportation, public accommodations, and telecommunications against persons with physical or mental disabilities

defined in a discriminatory manner.[41] But when government involvement in creating and operating segregated school systems cannot be demonstrated, the Court stated in a case involving the Detroit area that federal judges may not order cross-district busing to achieve

41. *Swann v. Charlotte-Mecklenburg County Board of Education,* 402 U.S. 1 (1971).

racial balance in the schools.[42] In interpreting the Fourteenth Amendment's equal protection clause to mean that proof of government actions that achieve or perpetuate segregation is needed to enforce desegregation, the Supreme Court has significantly limited the extent to which school integration can be achieved through judicial action.

Federal Legislation to Combat Discrimination in Public Accommodations, Employment, and Housing. The Civil Rights Act of 1964 stands as one of the most significant and lasting achievements of the civil rights movement. It contains provisions designed to eliminate private acts of discrimination that are not covered by the Fourteenth Amendment. The act's ban on discrimination based on race, religion, or national origin in places of public accommodation is derived from the commerce clause in Article I of the Constitution, which gives Congress the power to regulate foreign and interstate commerce. Through vigorous enforcement of the act, persons of color are no longer denied access to such public facilities as hotels, restaurants, theaters, service stations, and sports arenas.

The Civil Rights Act of 1964 also sought to combat discrimination in employment by banning businesses and unions involved in interstate commerce and employing fifteen or more workers from discriminating in their employment practices on the basis of race, color, religion, national origin, or sex. Since 1964, the same protection has been extended to the handicapped, armed services veterans, and people over forty years of age.

In 1968, Congress passed the Fair Housing Act, which, as amended in 1988, banned discrimination in housing offered for sale or rent. Small rooming and apartment houses in which the owner maintains a residence, private clubs and religious organizations providing housing for their members, and homeowners selling their property without a real estate agent are exempt from the law's coverage, however. Although the enforcement provisions of the law were strengthened in 1988, racial discrimination by individuals and businesses has meant that the goal of equal access to housing has remained unfulfilled.

Sexual Equality

Women have long been subjected to discriminatory actions by governments and private organizations. But it was not until 1920 and ratification of the Nineteenth Amendment that women were guaranteed the right to vote throughout the United States. Never-

42. *Milliken v. Bradley*, 418 U.S. 717 (1974).

theless, educational and employment opportunities, access to credit, and wages and salaries for women continued to be severely restricted. Even into the 1960s, for example, some school districts maintained separate salary schedules for women and men and paid women less than men.

As women entered the work force in larger numbers in the 1960s and the women's movement gained strength, public and government policy became more sensitive to discrimination based on sex. The Supreme Court began the process of striking down gender-oriented statutes in 1971 when it declared unconstitutional an Idaho law requiring that men be given preference when hiring individuals to administer estates.[43] This law and others that distinguished between women and men on an unreasonable basis have been declared in violation of the Fourteenth Amendment's equal protection clause. The courts have not, however, banned all legislation that makes distinctions between the sexes. Male-only registration for the draft, for example, has gained Supreme Court approval, and the military, while often assigning women to hazardous duty in the Persian Gulf War, has consistently restricted the role of women in combat.

In an effort to correct the inequity in paying women at a lower rate than men for the same work, Congress passed in 1963 the Equal Pay Act. It requires that those who do the same work be paid the same without regard to race, color, religion, national origin, or sex.

This legislation did nothing, however, to remove the barriers to employment that had tended to confine women to traditionally female occupations—teaching, nursing, and clerical work. The way was opened for increased employment opportunities for women by the inclusion in the Civil Rights Act of 1964 of Title VII, which prohibited employment discrimination based on sex. Interestingly, this provision was proposed by the leader of the southern anti-integration forces in Congress, Rep. Howard Smith (D-Va.). Smith believed that by adding what he considered to be an outrageous amendment to the Civil Rights Act, the entire bill would be defeated. But his ploy failed, and the entire bill, including his anti-sex discrimination amendment, passed. After several years during which its enforcement proved difficult, Title VII became an effective weapon in gaining employment opportunities for women and in forcing companies to cease discriminatory pay policies.

Congress followed its actions in the employment field with those designed to advance women's educational opportunities. One of the

43. *Reed v. Reed,* 404 U.S. 71 (1971).

most important pieces of legislation was Title IX of the Higher Education Act of 1972, which forbids discrimination on the basis of sex by colleges and universities receiving federal aid.

Also in the early 1970s, the women's movement, led by the National Organization for Women (NOW), pressed for adoption of a constitutional amendment that read: "Equality of rights under the law shall not be denied or abridged by the United States or by any State on account of sex." Congress responded in 1972 by approving the so-called Equal Rights Amendment (ERA) by the necessary two-thirds vote and sending it on to the states for ratification. But the ERA fell three states short of the thirty-eight needed for ratification and died on June 30, 1982, the extended deadline for ratification set by Congress. In the ratification struggle, feminist groups confronted antifeminist organizations led by conservative activist Phyllis Schafly, who asserted, among other things, that the ERA would guarantee a woman's right to an abortion and thereby sought to enlist the support of right-to-life groups in opposing the amendment.[44] Although the ERA was defeated, sixteen states have equal rights amendments in their state constitutions, and most of the protections sought by advocates of the amendment have been achieved by judicial and legislative actions.

Other Claims to Equality:
Gays, Disabled, Elderly, Voters

Although gays and lesbians have become increasingly militant in fighting discrimination and asserting claims to equality, to date the Supreme Court has not determined the rights of homosexuals under the equal protection clause. In 1986, however, the Court ruled that there is no constitutional right to engage in homosexual sodomy, and therefore it upheld a Georgia law that made sodomy a crime. Laws have been passed by various states and localities granting antidiscrimination rights to gays.

In seeking protection for the disabled, Congress in 1990 passed overwhelmingly the Americans with Disabilities Act, the most sweeping piece of antidiscrimination legislation since the Civil Rights Act of 1964. It requires that (1) businesses with twenty-five workers or more adapt their physical plants to accommodate disabled employees; (2) new buses, trains, and subway cars be accessible to people in wheelchairs; (3) renovated or new hotels, retail stores,

44. For an account of the ERA battle, see Jane Mansbridge, *Why We Lost ERA* (Chicago: University of Chicago Press, 1986). Also see Gilbert Y. Steiner, *Constitutional Inequality: The Political Fortunes of the Equal Rights Amendment* (Washington, D.C.: Brookings, 1986).

and restaurants be accessible to people in wheelchairs and that existing barriers be removed where it is "readily achievable"; and (4) telephone companies provide within three years relay services that would allow the hearing-impaired or voice-impaired possessing special telephones to place and receive calls from ordinary telephones.

With their relatively high levels of voter turnout and political activity, Americans aged sixty-five and over are an influential segment of the total population, of which they constitute approximately 12 percent. Congress responded to older Americans' concerns about age discrimination in the workplace by enacting the Age Discrimination Act of 1967. Unless age is essential to job performance, the act prohibits employers from giving preference to younger workers in hiring, firing, or benefits. Congress has also banned mandatory retirements at age seventy in most occupations.

Voters, too, have claimed equality. The equal protection clause has been used to advance equality of representation—that is, to have each person's vote count the same as that of every other person. It is not possible to adhere to a strict one person, one vote standard under the Constitution because of the provision for equal representation for each state in the Senate. But the federal courts have used the equal protection clause to prevent the states from engaging in **gerrymandering**—drawing congressional, state legislative, judicial, and municipal election district boundaries in a manner that violates the one person, one vote principle or discriminates against particular groups in society (see Chapter 10, Congress, for a discussion of the role of the courts in preventing gerrymandering).

Advocates of the Americans with Disabilities Act of 1990 rally to show their support for this major civil rights bill.

Affirmative Action

The principle stated by Supreme Court Justice John Marshall Harlan in his famous dissent in *Plessy v. Ferguson* that the "Constitution is colorblind" and that the government should prevent acts of discrimination has gained wide acceptance since the 1960s. Advocates for more rapid progress toward equality for disadvantaged groups have argued, however, that it is not enough for the government to be neutral and prohibit acts of discrimination. It also should take positive steps (*affirmative action*) to achieve equality of outcomes for the victims of past acts of discrimination. For example, employers have been required to advertise job openings widely and to advise applicants that they are "equal opportunity employers." These requirements are intended to break up "old boy" hiring networks and prevent discriminatory hiring practices by making the application process open to all. Much more controversial are government programs based on explicit racial and gender distinctions, which give preference in government contracting, university admissions, or employment to minorities and women, even if the individuals themselves have not been personally discriminated against. Proponents of such programs believe that they are essential to overcoming sexism and racism in society and achieving real progress toward equality for women and minorities. Opponents consider these affirmative action programs to be *reverse discrimination,* which is banned by the equal protection clause and the Civil Rights Act of 1964.

The constitutionality of affirmative action programs based on racial and sexual classifications was first confronted by the Supreme Court in the case of Allan Bakke, a white male applicant to the University of California at Davis Medical School. Although qualified for admission, Bakke was rejected and minority applicants with lower grades and interview ratings were admitted under a special program designed to overcome underrepresentation of minorities in the student body. Bakke then claimed reverse discrimination and denial of equal protection under the Constitution. In 1978, the Supreme Court agreed with Bakke and declared the University of California at Davis admission system unconstitutional.[45] It found the university's quota system for admissions to be unreasonable. The Court, however, did not ban all affirmative action programs and held that race could be considered along with other factors in university admissions procedures.

After *Bakke,* the Court further restricted affirmative action programs that imposed strict quotas in the absence of proof of past records of discrimination. Thus in a Richmond, Virginia, case in 1989, the Court held as unconstitutional a city affirmative action plan that required 30 percent of all city contracts to be awarded to minority contractors.[46] In ruling against Richmond's program, the Court indicated that racially based measures would be subjected to strict judicial scrutiny and that to be upheld they would have to be designed carefully to deal with demonstrated past acts of discrimination.

Despite its recent rather skeptical attitude toward some state and local government affirmative action programs, the Court has been more tolerant of race-conscious programs mandated by Congress. In 1980, it upheld a federal public works project that reserved 10 percent of its funds for minority contractors.[47] And in a 1990 de-

45. *University of California Regents v. Bakke,* 438 U.S. 265 (1978).
46. *City of Richmond v. J. A. Croson Co.,* 109 S.Ct. 706 (1989).
47. *Fullilove v. Klutznick,* 448 U.S. 448 (1980).

cision that surprised many Court watchers, a narrow 5-4 majority of justices upheld a Federal Communications Commission (FCC) program that made minority ownership a special consideration in granting new station licenses and in buying stations that were in danger of losing their licenses. The FCC program was not designed to rectify past acts of discrimination but rather was aimed at promoting minority ownership in the future. The decision of the Court in the FCC case has been interpreted by constitutional lawyers as signaling a green light for federally initiated affirmative action programs.[48]

The narrow division and sharp disagreements among Supreme Court justices on affirmative action cases mirror the divisiveness of this issue within the public. Only the most reactionary would suggest that no programs are needed to assist minorities in achieving greater economic equality. But whether race- or gender-conscious remedies are appropriate, constitutional, or effective is a source of continuing debate.[49]

Civil Liberties and Civil Rights, the Constitution, and Politics

The principles of basic civil liberties, procedural rights, and equality are enshrined in the Constitution. The language of the Constitution, however, requires application and interpretation. Much of this responsibility has fallen to the Supreme Court, which, since the 1930s, has taken on the role of protecting and expanding the liberties and rights of Americans. But in spite of the simple and straightforward language of the Constitution, Bill of Rights, and such amendments as the Fourteenth, our civil liberties and civil rights under the Constitution appear to be anything but absolute. Indeed, most government decision making in this field reflects a balancing of the competing claims of deeply held traditional values. As a result, civil liberties and civil rights issues often create emotionally charged controversies such as those over abortion, prayer in school, flag burning as free speech, and affirmative action. It is not surprising, therefore, that the nature and scope of constitutionally protected

48. See the analysis of the FCC decision by Linda Greenhouse, "Justices Bolster Race Preferences at Federal Level," *New York Times*, June 28, 1990, A1, A12, National edition; and Neil A. Lewis, "Ruling on Minority Broadcasting Seen as Aiding Affirmative Action," *New York Times*, July 4, 1990, 8Y, National edition.

49. For a discussion of the controversy surrounding affirmative action programs, see W. John Moore, "After the Marching," *National Journal*, June 23, 1990, 1525–1530.

liberties and rights have changed over time and will continue to change in response to changing political conditions—shifts in public thinking, membership changes in the courts, and congressional and presidential decision making. Even fundamental liberties and rights that are the cornerstone of American democracy are defined through the political process. It is therefore appropriate that the next chapter of this book begins an analysis of the forces that affect the political process of decision making.

For Review

1. The Bill of Rights was added to the Constitution to protect individual rights from encroachment by the federal government. Since the 1920s, the Fourteenth Amendment's due process clause has been interpreted to include most of the protections guaranteed in the Bill of Rights and to prevent the states from infringing on those rights. This process is known as "selective incorporation." While most of the basic rights—such as freedom of speech, religion, press, and assembly—have been incorporated into the Fourteenth Amendment, a few of the rights included in the Bill of Rights do not apply to the states (for example, indictment by a grand jury).

2. The rights conferred by the Constitution are not absolute, and the extent of protection afforded by the Constitution has varied over time depending on political conditions, including the composition of the Supreme Court. The Court, however, has played a major role, particularly in the twentieth century, in guaranteeing individual rights and liberties.

3. Controversies over civil rights issues normally occur when cherished values appear to come into conflict—for example, the right of freedom of the press versus the need for national security or the right of a person to a fair trial.

4. With the Supreme Court's abandonment of the separate but equal doctrine in 1954 and the rise of the civil rights and women's movements, the federal government has leaned toward policies aimed at tearing down the barriers represented by racial and other forms of discrimination. These policies, however, continue to stir major controversies within society as illustrated by the ongoing debate over affirmative action programs.

5. Ultimately, the nature of the rights and liberties enjoyed by Americans is determined through the political process.

For Further Reading

Bullock, Charles S., III, and Charles M. Lamb, eds. *Implementation of Civil Rights Policy.* Monterey, Calif.: Brooks/Cole, 1984. Analyses of the implementation of federal civil rights legislation in the areas of voting, housing, education, and employment.

Cortner, Richard C. *The Supreme Court and the Second Bill of Rights: The Fourteenth Amendment and the Nationalization of Civil Liberties.* Madison: University of Wisconsin Press, 1981. A comprehensive account of the process of incorporating the Bill of Rights into the Fourteenth Amendment.

Kluger, Richard. *Simple Justice: The History of Brown v. Board of Education and Black America's Struggle For Equality.* New York: Knopf, 1976. An account of the struggle for racial equality with emphasis on the 1954 landmark school desegregation case.

Lewis, Anthony. *Gideon's Trumpet.* New York: Random House, 1964. A detailed account of the Supreme Court's decision to extend the right to counsel to noncapital cases.

Peltason, J. W. *Understanding the Constitution.* 11th ed. New York: Holt, Rinehart, and Winston, 1988. An excellent reference that describes how the courts have interpreted the Constitution and Bill of Rights.

PART II

Political Participation and Mobilizing Political Influence

5. Public Opinion and Participation

BECAUSE AMERICAN DEMOCRACY is built on the assumption that the people are the source of all government authority, public opinion has a special importance to our citizens. The Framers of the Constitution acknowledged a role for public opinion by calling for popular election of the House of Representatives. Their confidence in the public's ability to decide government policy, however, was not sufficient for them to create a strictly majoritarian democracy. As we noted in Chapter 2, the Framers sought instead to create a government somewhat insulated from the popular passions of the day through a series of constitutional devices that included separation of powers, checks and balances, indirect election of senators, election of the president by an electoral college, and a judiciary appointed for life.

As the Framers envisioned, the government does not necessarily run the country on the basis of the public's preferences. Indeed, American government institutions—the Congress, president, and courts—frequently differ in how and to what extent they respond to public sentiments. Public opinion is nonetheless an important ingredient in American politics. People's opinions influence their political behavior—whether and how they vote, which political party they support, which interest groups they join, whether they contribute money to a cause or candidate, whether they run for public office. The behavior of public officials, who periodically must face the voters in elections, is also affected by public opinion. For example, when members of Congress find their constituents strongly supportive of the president, they, too, tend to back the chief executive's policies.

Public officials not only take public opinion into account when framing public policy but also try to shape it. For example, President Franklin Roosevelt, through his "fireside chat" radio addresses in the depths of the depression and World War II, and President Ronald Reagan, through television and radio in the 1980s, strengthened their presidencies because of their communications skills.

Because public opinion has such far-reaching consequences for the governing process, this chapter explores the nature of public opinion, how it is measured and shaped, as well as its impact on policy making. The depth and breadth of public influence, however, involve more than citizens just having opinions on issues of public policy; they also must act on the basis of their opinions. Government decisions are affected by who actually participates in the political process and by the nature and extent of that participation. Thus, public participation, another essential ingredient of a democratic order, is the focal point of this chapter as well.

What Is Public Opinion?

The term **public opinion** is invoked constantly in political discourse: "Public Opinion Demands All-out War on Drugs!" "Public Opinion Opposes New Sales Tax!" "Public Opinion Supports Increased Federal Funding for the Homeless!" But invocations of the public's views offer little information about the nature of public opinion. What is the meaning of this concept? *Public opinion* is people's attitudes on an issue or question. As students of political science, we are particularly concerned about political public opinion—what people think about the issues surrounding politics and government. Such issues are always changing, however, depending on events and circumstances. For example, abortion was rarely a matter of major public concern in the 1950s. But by the 1980s, heightened concerns about the rights of women and the unborn had made abortion a highly divisive issue within society.

The General Public and Issue Publics

Public opinion is often viewed as a semiorganic entity that goes through a process of deliberation before reaching a collective decision on an issue. Indeed, the formation of public opinion is likened to the traditional New England town meeting. But large nation-states such as the United States do not operate through national town meetings that discuss, debate, and decide public issues. It is the rare issue that attracts the attention of a majority, let alone all, of the adults in this country. It is seldom, then, that the *general public*—the adult population—takes an interest in an issue.

For most issues, the public consists just of those people who are affected by or aware of the issue. Thus, there are in fact many publics, each created by an issue that generates interest. These **issue publics** exist for the whole range of public issues—taxes and spending, law and order, health care, welfare, civil rights, education, relations with the Soviet Union, the environment. An individual can be part of many different issue publics simultaneously.

Public Opinion Polling

Americans are confronted, and often surprised, daily by polling statistics that tell them what they, the public, think about an assortment of public issues. Indeed, public opinion polls themselves are big business in modern-day American politics and corporate life.

Polls are conducted by commercial organizations that sell the results of their work to clients—newspapers, corporations, interest groups—anxious to know the public's thinking. The Gallup, Roper, Harris, and Yankelovich organizations are the best known of the nation's pollsters. Campaign consultants engage in opinion polling as well for their political clients. In fact, few serious candidates for a major elected office undertake campaigns without the advice of pollsters. Major newspapers, news magazines, and television networks also do extensive polling, and the results are a regular feature of their coverage. Even academic institutions, such as the Center for Political Studies (CPS) at the University of Michigan, survey opinion regularly in an effort to develop a database for theoretical explanations of human behavior. Political scientists utilize all of these sources in their work and rely heavily on the CPS studies of voting behavior.

Surveying the Public: A New Science. Knowledge of public opinion has been advanced tremendously by the development in the twentieth century of scientific public opinion surveys or polls. Before scientific polling, it was almost impossible to measure public sentiment reliably.

Most polling organizations rely on telephone polls rather than in-person interviews because they are more economical. Since most American households now have telephones, this survey method does not significantly distort polling results. The recent increased reluctance of people to be interviewed over the phone, however, is worrisome to public opinion analysts. One form of in-person interviewing that has figured more and more in election day surveys is *exit polling*—surveying voters as they leave the polling place about how they voted.

Pollsters normally interview between one thousand and two thou-

BLOOM COUNTY
by Berke Breathed

sand people in a national survey. But how can such a small group of respondents accurately reflect the views of an entire nation? The answer: it cannot unless the people being interviewed constitute a representative sample of the population whose opinion is being sought. To create such a sample, pollsters utilize a **probability sampling** procedure in which every individual in the population being surveyed has the same chance of being chosen for an interview as everyone else.

A classic example of a nonrepresentative sample that resulted in a distorted picture of public opinion was the 1936 *Literary Digest* poll that predicted that Kansas governor Alfred Landon would win over President Franklin Roosevelt in the presidential election. The *Digest*'s sample had been selected from phone books and automobile registrations, overlooking the fact that in the depths of the depression people with phones and cars were only a fraction of the electorate and certainly not a cross section of American voters.

Drawing a probability sample is a technical matter for which reasonably reliable methodologies have now been developed. All responsible polling organizations take great care to determine that they have a representative sample of the population they are studying. Preelection polls pose special problems for pollsters because not all of the eligible voters will actually vote on election day. Thus, a poll that reports the preferences of all eligible voters presents a potentially inaccurate prediction of the election outcome. To deal with this problem, polling organizations try to interview those people who are most likely to vote.

Most polling organizations rely on *random-digit-dialing* to overcome the problems associated with unlisted telephone numbers—30 percent or more in some areas. Random-digit-dialing typically involves using a computer random-number generator or table of random numbers to select the last four digits of the phone numbers to be called after the area codes and exchanges (the first three digits of a seven-digit phone number) in the area to be surveyed have been identified.

Survey interviews can last from a few minutes to as long as an hour, depending on the amount of information being sought. Most questions are *closed-ended*—that is, the respondent chooses from a predetermined set of possible answers, thereby enhancing the comparability of the responses. A small number of questions may be *open-ended*. Here respondents are allowed to answer questions in their own words. Open-ended questions may elicit subtle distinctions in people's opinions, but they substantially complicate interpretation and analysis of interview data.

Table 5.1 Accuracy of Gallup Poll in Presidential Elections, 1960–1988 *(percent)*

Year	Final Gallup Survey		Election Result		Deviation
1960	51.0	Kennedy	50.1	Kennedy	+0.9
1964	64.0	Johnson	61.3	Johnson	+2.7
1968	43.0	Nixon	43.5	Nixon	−0.5
1972	62.0	Nixon	61.8	Nixon	+0.2
1976	48.0	Carter	50.0	Carter	−2.0
1980	47.0	Reagan	50.8	Reagan	−3.8
1984	59.0	Reagan	59.2	Reagan	−0.2
1988	53.0	Bush	54.0	Bush	−1.0

SOURCES: *Gallup Report,* No. 271, April 1988, 31; and *Congressional Quarterly Weekly Report,* November 12, 1988, 3244.

Particular care must be taken that the wording of questions does not bias or influence respondents' answers, which would affect the results of the poll. For example, when voters participating in a 1982 poll conducted by the Advisory Commission on Intergovernmental Relations were asked in a series of closed-ended questions how to reduce state and local budgets, only 8 percent said "aid to the needy" should be slashed. But when "public welfare programs" was substituted for "needy," 39 percent opted to cut welfare.[1]

Accuracy of Polls. As polling techniques have improved, their accuracy has improved. The Gallup poll, for example, has had an average deviation from the actual winning vote in the eight presidential elections since 1960 of only 1.4 percentage points (see Table 5.1).[2] Inaccurate polls might stem from a **sampling error**—the degree to which the sample can be expected to vary from the total population being studied. National surveys typically have a sampling error of about 4 percent. This means that if 55 percent of the respondents prefer the Republican candidate, the actual value is likely to be in the range of 51 to 59 percent (55 percent plus or minus 4 percent).[3] Inaccurate poll results also might stem from a faulty questionnaire, sloppy interview procedures, and mistakes in interpreting and analyzing survey responses.

Polls cannot reliably predict what the public's opinions or behavior might be at some future time; a poll is only a snapshot of opinions

1. Herbert Asher, *Polling and the Public: What Every Citizen Should Know* (Washington, D.C.: CQ Press, 1988), 42.
2. *Gallup Report,* No. 271, April 1988, 31.
3. Asher, *Polling and the Public,* 58–64.

at the time it was taken. Thus, polls undertaken before the 1980 presidential election did not predict Ronald Reagan's 10-percentage-point victory over Jimmy Carter because they could not pick up the last-minute shifts in Reagan's favor.

Dimensions of Public Opinion

In 1989, members of the House of Representatives voted to reject a 50 percent raise in their own pay. Underpaid compared with individuals in the private sector, they nevertheless bowed to public opposition to the salary boost. Why did they turn down what a government panel and many political commentators saw as a justified raise? The answer: an overwhelming proportion of the public was strongly opposed, and elected officials take the direction, intensity, and other dimensions of public opinion into account in their decision making.

The *direction* of public opinion is simply whether people view an issue or action favorably or unfavorably. Surveys of public opinion can provide information on the yes-no dimension: how people align themselves on such issues as the death penalty, affirmative action, military action against Iraq for invading Kuwait, or imposing a trade embargo on South Africa because of its policy of racial apartheid.

A related and critical aspect of public opinion is the *distribution,* or extent, of agreement or consensus on an issue, with opinions clustering on one side or the other of the yes-no dimension. Like the congressional pay raise controversy, some issues evoke high levels of agreement. Other issues are highly divisive (see the examples in Figure 5.1). When a high level of consensus exists on an issue, government policy makers usually find it necessary to follow public opinion. For example, with a January 1988 Gallup poll showing that 77 percent of the public supported the U.S.-Soviet treaty to eliminate intermediate-range nuclear weapons (INF treaty), Senate ratification of the treaty was achieved by an overwhelming vote. When opinions divide and the public's feelings are intense, outcomes are less certain. This was illustrated by the Reagan administration's policy of providing military aid to the contra rebels fighting the Sandinista government of Nicaragua—a policy that deeply divided the American people. Reflecting this lack of consensus, Congress followed an inconsistent policy of first providing military aid and then opposing it while providing humanitarian aid.

The *saliency,* or importance, of an issue is another dimension of public opinion. Individuals differ in the extent to which they consider an issue salient. For National Rifle Association (NRA) members, for example, gun control is extremely salient. In the same way, retired people care more about cost-of-living adjustments to Social Security benefits than do working parents, who find tax deductions for child care expenses more important than do retirees. For the public as a whole, the saliency of issues changes over time. Thus at the beginning of the Reagan administration in 1981, the Gallup poll reported that 72 percent of Americans believed inflation to be the most important problem facing the nation, but by 1988, when the inflation rate was down to 4.1 percent from 13.5 percent, only 2 percent of the people gave it such importance.[4]

The *intensity* of public opinion can vary as well—people may feel strongly about some issues and less strongly about others. Such issues as abortion, which involve moral questions, are most likely to generate intense opinions.[5] People who feel strongly about an issue are more likely to act on their sentiments and participate in the political process than those whose views are weakly held. The impact of public opinion is, therefore, influenced by the strength of commitment people give to a cause. Small but intense minorities frequently can have an influence well out of proportion to their numbers. Understanding the intensity with which people hold and act on their opinions helps explain why policy positions opposed by a majority of the people can become public policy. For example, polls show that a majority of the public supports tougher gun control legislation.[6] But deeply committed opponents, led by the National Rifle Association, have blocked most new bills that would strengthen gun control laws and have even succeeded in weakening previously passed laws. The NRA efforts have included advertising campaigns, campaign contributions, and aggressive lobbying, with their members deluging members of Congress with mail against gun control. By contrast, people favoring tougher gun laws have generally not felt strongly enough about the issue to act on their convictions.

A final dimension of public opinion is its *stability*—the public's opinion on an issue can change over time, occasionally with amazing rapidity. President George Bush discovered this in the fall of 1990 when his approval rating fell 23 percentage points, from 76 to 53 percent, after he dropped his "Read my lips, no new taxes" campaign pledge and engaged in a protracted struggle over the budget with Congress.[7] But in the aftermath of the coalition victory in the

4. Gallup poll data, reported in *Public Opinion,* July/August 1988, 34–35.
5. Robert E. Lane and David O. Sears, *Public Opinion* (Englewood Cliffs, N.J.: Prentice-Hall, 1964), 9.
6. National Opinion Research Center surveys, reported in *Public Opinion,* November/December 1988, 27.
7. Gallup surveys reported in *American Enterprise,* November/December 1990, 92, and March/April 1991, 91.

Figure 5.1: Consensus Versus Divisiveness

Consensus on Arms Control Treaty
Question: "Do you favor or oppose ratification of the treaty between the U.S. and Soviet Union to eliminate their intermediate-range nuclear weapons?"

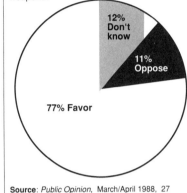

12% Don't know
11% Oppose
77% Favor

Source: *Public Opinion,* March/April 1988, 27 (Gallup Organization survey for Times Mirror Company in January 1988).

Divisiveness of Abortion
Question: "As you know, the state of Idaho recently considered a new law which would make it illegal for any woman to have an abortion except in four cases: 1—rape reported to police within seven days of the rape, 2—incest where the woman is under 18, 3—where the fetus is deformed, and 4—where there is a physical threat to the health of the mother. Would you favor or oppose the state where you live passing the law?"

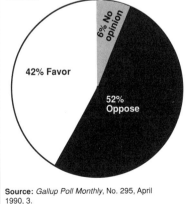

6% No opinion
42% Favor
52% Oppose

Source: *Gallup Poll Monthly,* No. 295, April 1990, 3.

Persian Gulf War, his approval rating jumped to 89 percent. Similarly, America stopped embracing an isolationist foreign policy in one day on December 7, 1941, when the Japanese bombed Pearl Harbor. Although these examples suggest a high level of volatility in public opinion, studies show that American opinion on many issues exhibits a substantial level of stability and that change in public attitudes tends to occur gradually.[8] Thus since 1977, the public has overwhelmingly supported allowing a woman to have an abortion when her own health is endangered by the pregnancy or when the pregnancy occurred because of rape. At the same time, a majority of Americans have consistently opposed permitting abortions sought for other reasons such as because a woman is not married or does not want to marry.[9]

Another aspect of the stability dimension is that a public once divided on an issue can over time achieve a high level of agreement. For example, in 1942 only 30 percent of whites said that they thought white and black students should go to the same schools. Yet by 1984, 90 percent of whites said that they accepted integrated schools. Analysis of these data, however, showed that whites were not monolithic in their racial attitudes. Differences in attitudes were derived from people's diverse social backgrounds and life experiences.[10] This exploration of public opinion, therefore, must consider **political socialization**—the process through which people acquire political attitudes.

Acquiring Political Attitudes: Political Socialization

As people go through life, they acquire an awareness of, facts about, and values related to politics. This is the process of **political socialization**. Much of this political learning process is incidental as, for example, children observe, listen to, and imitate their parents. Although early childhood is important in shaping such basic attitudes as one's attachment to one's country and feelings toward government and authority, political socialization is a lifelong process. Among the agents of political socialization are family, schools, peers, mass media, and leaders.

8. Benjamin I. Page and Robert Y. Shapiro, "Changes in American Policy Preferences, 1935–1979," *Public Opinion Quarterly* 46 (Spring 1982), 24–42.

9. National Opinion Research Center data, reported in *Public Opinion,* November/December 1987, 40.

10. Tom W. Smith and Paul B. Sheatsley, "American Attitudes toward Race Relations," *Public Opinion,* November/December 1984, 15, 51–53.

Childhood Socialization

The impact of the family on political attitudes is profound. It is the family that first interprets the world for a child and, presumably, acquaints that child with certain moral, religious, social, economic, and political values. Moreover, when parents are interested in politics, this interest tends to be passed on to their children.[11]

Parents also often pass on to their children a political attitude that is important in understanding political behavior: **party identification**—a feeling of attachment to and sympathy for a political party. As early as the third grade, children frequently think of themselves as Democrats or Republicans. Family influence on party identification is greatest when both parents agree on their partisan preference. When the father and mother do not agree, mothers are likely to have a greater influence than fathers (reflecting the traditional tendency of mothers to spend more time with children than fathers). Although the maternal influence is present for both boys and girls, it is especially strong on the daughters of college-educated, politically active mothers.[12]

The parental influence on a child's party identification is strong, but research indicates that this influence decreases as children get older and are subjected to influences outside the family. Indeed, political scientists Kent Jennings and Richard Niemi found in one study that shared partisanship between parents and children declined from 56 percent to 47 percent over a nine-year period.[13] Parents' influence on their child's party identification is strengthened when it is reinforced, or at least not contradicted, by the messages received from other participants in the child's environment such as friends or neighbors.[14]

Political learning occurs in the schools as well. Schools normally

11. W. Russell Neuman, *The Paradox of Mass Politics: Knowledge and Opinion in the American Electorate* (Cambridge, Mass.: Harvard University Press, 1986), 113–114.

12. M. Kent Jennings and Kenneth P. Langton, "Mothers versus Fathers: The Foundations of Political Orientations among Young Americans," *Journal of Politics* 31 (May 1969): 329–358. Important studies of children's political socialization include Fred I. Greenstein, *Children and Politics* (New Haven, Conn.: Yale University Press, 1965); and Robert D. Hess and Judith V. Torney, *The Development of Political Attitudes in Children* (Chicago: Aldine, 1967).

13. M. Kent Jennings and Richard G. Niemi, *Generations and Politics: A Panel Study of Young Adults and Their Parents* (Princeton, N.J.: Princeton University Press, 1981), 90.

14. Russell J. Dalton, "Reassessing Parental Socialization: Indicator Unreliability versus Generational Transfer," *American Political Science Review* 74 (June 1980): 421–431. Also see Robert C. Luskin, John P. McIver, and Edward G. Carmines, "Issues and the Transmission of Partisanship," *American Journal of Political Science* 33 (May 1989): 440–458.

Political socialization occurs throughout life. Here high school students get a taste of politics by holding a mock national convention.

do not make a conscious effort to promote a preference for a political party or a specific viewpoint on issues. Rather, they tend to present children with the facts about their country and its political system and, in the process, foster patriotism and support for the institutions of government. The picture presented of American government in the early grades is beneficent and positive, with the president often viewed as a benevolent leader. Although the high schools continue the process of political education through American history and civics courses, they have been found to have only a modest influence on students' political interest, tolerance for differing opinions, trust in government, or inclination to participate in politics.[15]

Adolescents' almost slavish conformity in their clothing and hairstyles, as well as their musical tastes, is strong evidence of the impact that peer pressure, too, has on young people's attitudes and behavior. This influence is more limited, however, in the realm of political attitudes. For example, parents tend to have more influence than peers on which political party teenagers identify with. One of the factors contributing to the only modest influence that peers have on adolescent political attitudes is the relatively low salience of politics to adolescents' lives. It has little to do with their day-to-day concerns or their status in the peer group. But on issues of immediate relevance to teenagers, such as the right of eighteen-year-olds to vote, peer pressure tends to be more powerful than parental influence.[16]

Politics is apt to take on greater relevance at the college level, and there peer pressures can have a substantial impact on students' political attitudes. In his classic study of peer group influence, Theodore Newcombe examined the political attitudes of women attending Bennington College, an exclusive liberal arts college in Vermont, in the 1930s. These students' political attitudes were affected significantly by Bennington's politically liberal culture. Indeed, during their years there many of the women students became significantly more liberal than their generally well-to-do and conservative parents. Twenty-five years later in a follow-up study, Newcombe found that Bennington alumnae retained the liberalism of their college days because it was reinforced by their spouses and adult peers.[17]

Finally, television viewing begins at an early age and its influence

15. Kenneth P. Langton and M. Kent Jennings, "Political Socialization and the High School Civics Curriculum in the United States," *American Political Science Review* 62 (September 1968): 852–877.

16. M. Kent Jennings and Richard G. Niemi, *The Political Character of Adolescence* (Princeton, N.J.: Princeton University Press, 1974), 243.

17. Theodore M. Newcombe, *Persistence and Social Change: Bennington College and Its Students after Twenty-five Years* (New York: Wiley, 1967).

interacts with that of parents, schools, and peers in shaping political attitudes. Although "Sesame Street" and "Mr. Rogers" provide children with positive images of such authority figures as police officers, young people pick up negative connotations about political figures from other television programming such as newscasts. Nevertheless, research demonstrates that young people who are heavy users of the media show a greater interest in current political events and a greater understanding of and support for basic American values such as freedom of speech and the right to equal and fair treatment (see Chapter 9 for a more detailed look at the role of the media in American politics).[18]

Adult Socialization

The shaping of basic political beliefs, values, and attitudes does not stop with graduation from high school or college. But the influences that were important in youth—parents, school, childhood peers—recede and are replaced by daily events and experiences, political leaders, and new peer groups such as coworkers, neighbors, friends, and fellow church and club members.

As people grow older, they have experiences that are politically relevant. They encounter the Internal Revenue Service, military recruiting, banking regulations, air travel regulations, government-influenced mortgage rates, and Social Security and Medicare. People also observe politically relevant events on television and read about them in newspapers and magazines. The impressions gained from these experiences and interactions with peers continue to shape people's political attitudes.

Daily events during the depression of the 1930s, for example, caused people to change their views about the role of government in regulating the economy and providing basic social services. People demanded and came to expect the government to manage the economy and provide social services. Likewise, fifty years later people's assessment of their own and the nation's well-being played a major role in the presidential election victories of Ronald Reagan in 1980 and 1984. Double-digit inflation, high interest rates, rising unemployment, and foreign policy setbacks, such as the seizure of American hostages at the U.S. Embassy in Iran, contributed to public dissatisfaction and Reagan's 1980 defeat of President Jimmy Carter. Four years later, more favorable economic and world conditions helped President Reagan to a landslide reelection.

18. The impact of the media on childhood socialization is ably summarized by Doris A. Graber, *Mass Media and American Politics,* 3d ed. (Washington, D.C.: CQ Press, 1989), 150–152.

Events also may trigger latent attitudes in the public. For example, during the early 1960s Americans' basic values of equality and fairness were offended by the use of fire hoses, fierce dogs, beatings, and other forms of intimidation to break up peaceful demonstrations for black voting rights and desegregation of public facilities in the South. The result was a swelling of public support for federal voting rights and civil rights legislation.

People's attitudes are affected as well by the actions and statements of political leaders, particularly the president. One of the most dramatic changes in public opinion began in the early 1970s when President Richard Nixon, a man whose entire public career had been built on staunch anticommunism, began the process of normalizing diplomatic relations with the communist government of the People's Republic of China. Virtually overnight, American opinion changed from one of overwhelming opposition to one of heightened tolerance toward and interest in the communist government on mainland China. The actions of successive presidents to strengthen diplomatic, economic, and cultural ties with China continued to garner widespread public support until June 1989 when the communist government brutally repressed pro-democracy demonstrations.

Presidential leadership of public opinion is most effective when the president is riding a crest of popularity. During times of declining popular support, however, the president finds it difficult to sway the public. This was true for both Presidents Carter and Reagan. With his standing in the polls falling, Carter was unable in 1979 to rally support for the SALT II treaty with the Soviets, which would have limited strategic nuclear weapons. Even as effective a communicator as Reagan could not—as his popularity fell during the 1982 recession—muster support for a constitutional amendment permitting prayer in the public schools.[19]

Social Groups and Political Opinions

No two Americans have identical political socialization experiences. People with similar social backgrounds, however, are apt to share some political opinions, which are likely to differ from the views of people with different backgrounds. Differences in education, income or class, ethnicity, race, religion, region, and gender can produce distinctive political orientations.

19. Benjamin I. Page, Robert Y. Shapiro, and Glenn R. Dempsey, "What Moves Public Opinion?" *American Political Science Review* 81 (March 1987): 37.

Table 5.2 Level of Education and Public Opinion *(percent)*

Issue	College Graduate	College Incomplete	High School Graduate	Did Not Complete High School
Approve of increased government spending for food programs for low-income families	36	44	45	53
Approve of increased government spending to improve medical and health care for Americans generally	62	64	70	74
Approve raising personal income taxes to reduce the federal deficit	34	29	21	21
Approve of increased spending for the space program	33	30	24	15
Approve of development of a space-based "Star Wars" system to protect the U.S. from nuclear attack	41	41	40	28
Approve of relaxing pollution controls to reduce costs to industry	14	18	31	32
Favor prayer in the public schools	57	64	77	77
Favor a ban on abortions except in cases of rape, incest, or when the life of the mother is endangered	34	45	47	52

SOURCE: *Gallup Report,* No. 274, July 1988, 5–17.

Education

Education increases people's interest in and understanding of politics and affects the political attitudes that they develop. College graduates, on the one hand, profess greater support for civil liberties and have more tolerant racial attitudes than people who attended but did not graduate from college.[20] Better-educated individuals also are more likely to support environmental protection measures, space research, and affirmative action hiring programs for women and minorities. But, on the other hand, the more highly educated appear to be less supportive of extending the government's role in providing social services. They also are less likely to support such conservative social policy agenda items as permitting prayer in the public schools or banning abortions (see Table 5.2).

20. On the effect of education on support for civil liberties, see Herbert McClosky and Alida Brill, *Dimensions of Tolerance: What Americans Believe about Civil Liberties* (New York: Russell Sage Foundation, 1983), 250–251, 370–371, 420–422.

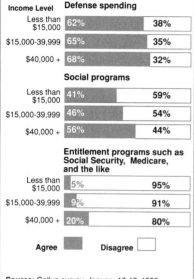

Figure 5.2: Class-based Differences on Issues—But No Great Divide

Issue: The federal budget should be reduced by cutting

Income Level	Defense spending	Agree	Disagree
Less than $15,000		62%	38%
$15,000-39,999		65%	35%
$40,000 +		68%	32%

Social programs

Income Level	Agree	Disagree
Less than $15,000	41%	59%
$15,000-39,999	46%	54%
$40,000 +	56%	44%

Entitlement programs such as Social Security, Medicare, and the like

Income Level	Agree	Disagree
Less than $15,000	5%	95%
$15,000-39,999	9%	91%
$40,000 +	20%	80%

Agree ▨   Disagree ☐

Source: Gallup survey, January 10-13, 1986, summarized in *Public Opinion*, May/June 1987, 24. Reprinted with permission of the American Enterprise Institute for Public Policy Research, Washington, D.C.

Income/Class

Differences of opinion emerge among social classes on such questions as the role of government in providing services and reducing disparities in income between the rich and the poor. As would be expected, well-to-do people react less favorably to such schemes than those with low incomes. But class-based differences on such issues as government spending do not greatly divide American society (Figure 5.2). Surveys of public opinion also show relatively low levels of class-based resentment against people who have gained positions of influence and prominence in the United States.[21]

Ethnicity and Race

America is frequently called a nation of immigrants, and with each new wave of immigration, the mix of nationalities becomes more varied. Most of the earliest settlers came from England, Scotland, and Wales, followed by those from Ireland, Germany, and Scandinavia. During the late nineteenth and early twentieth centuries, immigrants from eastern and southern Europe—Poles, Italians, Russians—predominated. The cultural and religious differences between immigrants with eastern and southern European backgrounds and those of English heritage have been a basis for political division within the United States. For example, immigrants from eastern and southern Europe provided essential support for the New Deal Democratic coalition forged by President Franklin Roosevelt in the 1930s, and those of British heritage traditionally have constituted an important base of Republican voting strength.

Although differences in voting patterns among voters of European heritage are still detectable, these differences are diminishing as these older immigrant groups become assimilated into American society. Public opinion surveys do show modest differences in thinking, however, among European ethnic groups on issues of government responsibility for health care, improved living standards for the poor, and a more equitable distribution of income (see Table 5.3).[22]

The current tide of immigrants from Spanish-speaking (Hispanic) countries in this hemisphere—particularly Mexico and Central America—and from Asia is showing distinctive political attitudes and partisan preferences as well. Reflecting the relatively less well-off economic positions of these "new ethnics," Mexican-Americans,

21. For a summary of surveys dealing with class-based differences on issues, see *Public Opinion*, May/June 1987, 21–31.
22. For a survey of attitudes by ethnic groups, see *Public Opinion*, October/November 1984, 26–27.

Table 5.3 Ethnic and Racial Group Differences on the Role of Government *(percent agreeing)*

Issue	Black	English/ Scottish/ Welsh	Italian	East European/ Soviet	Scandinavian	German/ Austrian	Irish	Hispanic
Government should do more to solve our country's problems.	50	15	32	34	18	19	24	42
Government should do everything possible to improve living standards of all poor Americans.	56	20	36	34	27	23	34	52
Government should do something to reduce income differences between rich and poor.	66	34	47	49	42	45	48	56
It is the responsibility of government to help pay for doctors' and hospital bills.	60	38	55	51	34	39	49	54

SOURCE: "Summaries of National Opinion Research Center Surveys," *Public Opinion*, October/November 1984, 24–25. Reprinted with the permission of the American Enterprise Institute for Public Policy Research, Washington, D.C.

for example, are more highly supportive of extending government services and of the Democratic party than are the "old ethnics" from eastern and southern Europe. The political attitudes of Mexican-Americans also differ from those of another Hispanic group, the Cuban-Americans, who, with their fierce anticommunist stance and generally higher standard of living, are predominantly Republican.

Blacks constitute the country's largest racial minority (over 12 percent) with other nonwhites (Asians and American Indians) making up approximately 3 percent. Both blacks and Asians are expanding segments of the population. According to numerous surveys conducted by the National Opinion Research Center, blacks and other racial minorities tend to have some political attitudes in common. In contrast to older European ethnics and Hispanics, blacks are more likely to believe that government should assume a large responsibility for solving the country's problems, helping the poor, reducing income differences between rich and poor, and providing health care (see Table 5.3).

Religion

America is a predominantly Protestant nation with 59 percent professing a Protestant religious preference, followed by Catholics, 27 percent; Jewish, 2 percent; other religions, 4 percent; and no religious preference, 8 percent. Some of the differences in attitudes and partisan preferences found among people of various religious faiths can be traced to historic causes. Most Catholic immigrants, for example, arrived in the United States at a time when Protestants and Republicans dominated the nation's political and economic life. This fact, as well as the limited discrimination to which Catholics were once subjected, has left traces of liberal and pro-Democratic sentiment among Catholics. The 1928 election also helped forge an electoral bond between Catholics and the Democratic party. In that year, the Democratic governor of New York, Al Smith, became the first Catholic to become a major party presidential nominee. The unique history of Jews as a persecuted minority also has had an impact on their political views; centuries of antisemitism have tended to drive them in a liberal direction, especially on civil liberties issues.

Doctrinal differences among religions have political relevance as well. The Catholic church has taken a strong stand against abortion and birth control, and the emphasis Protestants place on individual responsibility for one's economic and spiritual well-being may predispose them toward conservative positions on economic issues. Fundamentalist Protestants show a particularly conservative orientation. They overwhelmingly favor prayer in public schools and oppose both abortion and the Equal Rights Amendment.

Region

Regional differences of opinion have been periodic sources of conflict since the earliest days of the American political system.[23] The Civil War, of course, was the most dramatic instance in American history of issues aligning one region against another, and that war and its aftermath left their marks on American politics for over a century. After the war, small-town, white Protestant, middle-class conservatives, who might otherwise have been Republicans, created a one-party Democratic stronghold in the South. But, as the memories of the Civil War faded, northerners migrated to the South, and the region's per capita income disadvantages began to diminish after World War II, the partisanship of whites changed and some of the distinctiveness of southern attitudes receded. Southerners, however, continue to hold more conservative views on most issues than people from other regions. They are more likely to consider themselves conservatives, to trust the Republicans to deal with the country's most important problems, to oppose abortion, to favor prayer in the public

23. For a detailed analysis of sectional conflicts in American politics, see Richard F. Bensel, *Sectionalism and American Political Development, 1880–1980* (Madison: University of Wisconsin Press, 1984).

schools, to oppose homosexual relations, and to oppose the nuclear freeze movement.[24]

As for other regions of the United States, political analyst William Schneider has identified a pronounced anti-Washington, D.C., feeling that surfaces periodically in the Plains and Mountain states. He notes that these regions, with their predominantly native-born and rural milieus, never experienced the levels of class conflict that occurred in the Northeast and South and around the Great Lakes during the late nineteenth and early twentieth centuries. They never, therefore, developed Left-leaning, class-based protest movements. Their protest movements have tended instead to be directed against outside forces like the federal government, as during the 1970s and 1980s when the so-called Sagebrush Rebellion protested federal regulation of undeveloped western lands.[25]

Gender

Because men and women go through differing processes of political socialization even though they may share common racial, social class, ethnic, and religious backgrounds, they do not have the same attitudes about some issues. The most frequently noted difference in attitude has been toward the Democratic party: in the 1980s, a higher proportion of women than men supported Democratic candidates. As a result, the term *gender gap* entered the political vocabulary. Women are less apt than men to be supportive of military expenditures and the use of force in international affairs and more apt to be supportive of gun control and social welfare spending.[26] Not all issues, however, are gender-sensitive. On the question of increased spending for education, no significant gender differences emerge (see Table 5.4).

Political Ideology in America

Thus far we have examined the forces that shape our values and the differences of opinion that exist among various demographic groups in American society. Now we will consider the beliefs that structure people's political thinking. Such an organized and coherent set of attitudes about government and public policy is known

24. Regional attitudes on a range of social and foreign policy issues are summarized in *Public Opinion,* January/February 1988, 28–29.

25. William Schneider, "Democrats and Republicans, Liberals and Conservatives," in *Party Coalitions in the 1980s,* ed. Seymour Martin Lipset (San Francisco: Institute for Contemporary Studies, 1981), 203–204.

26. For a concise consideration of gender and political opinions, see Robert S. Erikson, Norman R. Luttbeg, and Kent L. Tedin, *American Public Opinion,* 4th ed. (New York: Macmillan, 1991), 198–201.

Table 5.4 Differences in the Political Opinions of Male and Female Registered Voters *(percent)*

Issue	Males	Females
Favor U.S. support of guerilla forces (contras) opposing Marxist government of Nicaragua	36	18
Favor development of a space-based "Star Wars" system to protect the U.S. from nuclear attack	45	31
Favor increased spending for the U.S. space program	34	17
Support increased government spending to improve medical and health care for Americans generally	64	70
Support increased government spending for food programs for low-income families	40	47
Support increased government spending to improve the quality of public education	65	67
Voted for George Bush for president	57	50
Approve of U.S. having gone to war against Iraq	84	68

SOURCES: *Gallup Report*, No. 274, July 1988, 5–17; No. 261, June 1987, 10; No. 275, August 1988, 4; *New York Times*, Nov. 10, 1988, 18Y, National edition; *American Enterprise*, March/April 1991, 86; *New York Times*/CBS exit poll, November 10, 1988; and ABC News/*Washington Post* poll, January 16, 1991, reported in *American Enterprise*, March/April 1991, 86.

as a **political ideology**. In America, people with a liberal ideology traditionally have supported a strong national government that actively promotes social welfare and equality and intervenes to regulate the economy. Conservatives, by contrast, have believed that government should have a limited role in regulating the economy and providing social services. They have stressed that individuals are primarily responsible for their own welfare.

Ideological Self-identification

Americans' descriptions of their own ideological positions changed relatively little through the 1970s and 1980s (see Figure 5.3). Although there was some growth of conservative sentiment in the 1980s, the proportions of the public considering themselves liberal, moderate, and conservative tended to remain stable, with moderates consistently constituting the largest category. The significance of such ideological self-identification data is limited, however, because many people do not understand the meaning of the categories. For example, some self-identified conservatives are supportive of such "liberal" policies as increased federal spending for health, the elderly, and education.[27]

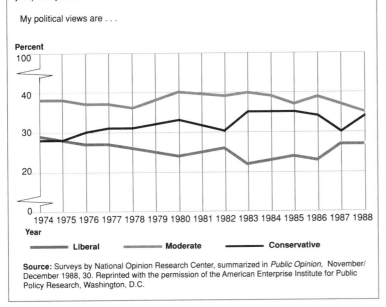

Figure 5.3: Americans' Ideological Self-Identification: Liberal, Moderate, or Conservative?

Question: "We hear a lot of talk these days about liberals and conservatives. I'm going to show you a seven point scale on which the political views that people might hold are arranged from extremely liberal—point 1—to extremely conservative—point 7. Where would you place yourself on this scale?"

My political views are . . .

Source: Surveys by National Opinion Research Center, summarized in *Public Opinion,* November/December 1988, 30. Reprinted with the permission of the American Enterprise Institute for Public Policy Research, Washington, D.C.

Dimensions of Liberalism and Conservatism

A further difficulty in determining the meaning of people's ideological self-identification stems from the way in which political discourse has changed since the 1950s. During the 1950s and until the mid-1960s, **liberalism** and **conservatism** pertained primarily to a single dimension of public policy—the scope of government involvement in the economy and society. Since the 1960s, however, this traditional distinction between liberalism and conservatism has been overlaid with additional policy dimensions. In foreign policy, for example, conservatism is now equated with support for military expenditures, a greater willingness to use military force in international

27. For an early confirmation of Americans' tendencies to view themselves as conservatives in the abstract but to be liberal regarding specific policies, see Lloyd Free and Hadley Cantril, *The Political Beliefs of Americans* (New York: Simon and Schuster, 1968), chap. 3.

affairs, and according primacy to the president for formulating policy in international affairs. By contrast, liberalism is equated with giving less priority to military expenditures, exhibiting greater reluctance to use military power, and according a substantial role to Congress in the shaping of foreign policy. There is also a social policy dimension to use of the terms *liberalism* and *conservatism*. On so-called lifestyle issues—abortion, law and order, prayer in the public schools, women's rights, gay rights, pornography—conservatives show a greater willingness to permit government intervention to regulate human conduct than do liberals.[28]

The multidimensional nature of liberalism and conservatism in current political discourse makes it increasingly difficult for people to place themselves accurately on a liberal-conservative continuum. It also means that a person might take a traditionally liberal position on issues relating to the government's social welfare responsibilities, yet at the same time support such conservative lifestyle positions as advocating prayer in the public schools, taking a hard line on law and order, and opposing abortion. Indeed, it was just such lifestyle issues that gave more recent Republican presidential candidates Richard Nixon, Ronald Reagan, and George Bush an opening wedge with which to split off traditional Democratic voters from their party.

Extent of Ideological Thinking in America

Students of public opinion have engaged in a lively debate about the extent of the ideological thinking of the American public. The evidence, however, indicates that the level of ideological thinking among Americans is not high. In 1988, only 18 percent of the voters used such terms as *liberal* or *conservative* in evaluating candidates and issues; the number was even lower—12 percent—in 1956.[29] But surveys done in the 1960s and 1970s found a higher level of ideological awareness among Americans. For example, in their study Norman Nie and his associates showed a steady increase in ideology-based evaluations of presidential candidates and parties between 1956 and 1972. Indeed, they reported that in 1972, 36 percent of

28. A discussion of how the meanings of liberalism and conservatism have changed since the 1950s is included in Herbert A. Asher, *Presidential Elections and American Politics: Voters, Candidates, and Campaigns Since 1952* (Chicago: Dorsey, 1987), 24–29.

29. Angus Campbell, et al., *The American Voter* (New York: Wiley, 1960), chap. 10.

voters evaluated the two parties on an ideological basis compared with 17 percent in 1956.[30]

The reasons for this rise in ideological thinking are not altogether clear, but it is likely that the high-intensity political environment of the 1960s and 1970s had an impact. The 1964, 1968, and 1972 elections took place in the highly charged and often polarizing atmosphere of civil rights demonstrations, urban riots, and the Vietnam War. Moreover, these elections were characterized by sharp policy differences between the presidential candidates. For example, the 1964 Republican nominee, conservative senator Barry Goldwater (Ariz.), offered Americans "a choice not an echo" as he campaigned against a committed liberal Democrat, President Lyndon Johnson. Not all public opinion analysts, however, are prepared to acknowledge that Americans became more ideological in the 1960s and 1970s. Some skeptics believe that reworded survey questions were responsible for the findings of an increased incidence of ideological thinking.[31]

This controversy among students of public opinion is just one more indication of the complexity and changing nature of public opinion. Although some analysts claim that ideological thinking has been on the rise, the thrust of political science research is that most Americans do not view politics from an ideological perspective. To the extent that they do, however, education is a contributing factor.[32] An education helps people better understand political issues and government's role in society and thus the links between issues.

Although most Americans do not view politics ideologically and are more likely to consider an issue from the perspective of individual or group self-interest, it is important to distinguish between the mass public and *political elites*—individuals active and influential in political decision making. Candidates, for example, are more likely than the average citizen to have coherent views on current political affairs. They also are more likely to rely on ideological criteria in evaluating issues and political events.

Analysts also have discovered that in their political ideologies po-

30. Norman H. Nie, Sidney Verba, and John R. Petrocik, *The Changing American Voter* (Cambridge, Mass.: Harvard University Press, 1976), 112–113.

31. W. Lance Bennett, *Public Opinion in American Politics* (New York: Harcourt, 1980), 48–56; Christopher H. Achen, "Mass Attitudes and the Survey Response," *American Political Science Review* 69 (December 1975): 1218–1231; and John L. Sullivan, James E. Pierson, and George E. Marcus, "Ideological Constraint in the Mass Public," *American Journal of Political Science* 22 (May 1978): 233–249.

32. Nie, et al., *Changing American Voter,* 121.

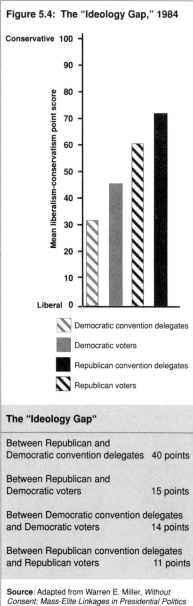

Figure 5.4: The "Ideology Gap," 1984

Democratic convention delegates

Democratic voters

Republican convention delegates

Republican voters

The "Ideology Gap"

Between Republican and Democratic convention delegates	40 points
Between Republican and Democratic voters	15 points
Between Democratic convention delegates and Democratic voters	14 points
Between Republican convention delegates and Republican voters	11 points

Source: Adapted from Warren E. Miller, *Without Consent: Mass-Elite Linkages in Presidential Politics* (Lexington: University of Kentucky Press, 1988), 35. © 1988. Reprinted with permission.

litical activists are less moderate than the rank-and-file voters. This ideological difference is revealed by a comparison of the liberal-conservative scores of delegates to national conventions and those of rank-and-file voters. According to Figure 5.4, not only is there a major "ideology gap" between Republican and Democratic national convention delegates, but also Republican delegates are considerably more conservative than rank-and-file Republicans, and Democratic delegates are more liberal than their party's voters.[33] This, of course, has implications for presidential nominating politics. Republican presidential aspirants must demonstrate their conservative credentials (as George Bush sought to do in 1988) to have a chance of being nominated, and candidates for Democratic presidential nominations must show their liberal bona fides. Thus, centrist candidates in past elections who might have been quite attractive to the general electorate, such as Republican senator Howard Baker of Tennessee (1980) and Democratic senator John Glenn of Ohio (1984), were unable to get their campaigns off the ground and dropped out of the race early.

Ideology and the American Political Process

The functioning of American politics is profoundly influenced by the scant attention most people pay to ideological concerns and their failure to divide themselves neatly into distinct liberal or conservative groups. Instead of a situation in which liberals and conservatives stand united against each other, people tend to fall into either the liberal or conservative camp depending on the domestic or foreign policy issue at stake. Economically liberal auto workers, for example, may fight business interests on such issues as raising the minimum wage or requiring health insurance for workers. Later, however, they may find themselves arm in arm with the "Big Three" auto makers in jointly opposing tougher government clean air standards for auto emissions because they believe these standards pose an economic threat to American auto manufacturers. Thus, people who are at odds on one issue today may find themselves allies on another issue tomorrow, making it difficult for cumulative antagonisms to build up through a series of confrontations. The overlapping and inconsistent belief systems that characterize the American public, there-

33. For an analysis of mass-elite differences and linkages, see Warren E. Miller and M. Kent Jennings, *Parties in Transition: A Longitudinal Study of Party Elites and Supporters* (New York: Russell Sage Foundation, 1986); and Warren E. Miller, *Without Consent: Mass-Elite Linkages in Presidential Politics* (Lexington: University of Kentucky Press, 1988).

fore, reduce the intensity of political conflict. At the same time, however, these overlapping belief systems also make it hard to form political alliances based on common attitudes. This in turn contributes to the government's frequent difficulty in reaching policy decisions.[34]

The public's lack of ideological perspectives on many issues also has meant that it often settles for the easier route of simple party allegiance (discussed more fully in Chapter 7, Elections, Campaigns, and Voters). Party allegiance is an important component of the political thought process for many Americans and a basis for their election day decisions.

Public Opinion and Government Policy

Public opinion has its most obvious impact on government decision making through elections. In the United States, however, elections are usually held to vote for candidates for public office and not for specific policies, except in those states (such as California) that permit voters to enact laws through initiative and referendum. Clear electoral mandates from the voters are rare in American politics because candidates take stands on scores of issues and thus collect voters for different and even conflicting reasons; elections are seldom dominated or decided by just one or two issues. In addition, the candidates' positions on salient issues are not always clear nor are they necessarily in opposition to each other.

But even if it is hard to discern a clear policy mandate from the voters on election day, a verdict on the past performances of incumbent officeholders is frequently rendered. Indeed, the public can affect the general direction of government policy by changing the people and parties in control of government institutions. In the 1980 election, for example, the public gave a negative verdict on President Jimmy Carter's handling of an economy reeling under double-digit inflation, higher interest rates, and rising unemployment. But in rejecting Carter and replacing him with Reagan, the public did not necessarily signal its approval of Reagan's specific policy proposals. It did, however, indicate that it was prepared to give him a chance to solve the nation's problems, and Reagan's Republican administration certainly followed a policy course little like that of its Democratic predecessor.[35]

34. See the discussion of the inconsistent nature of Americans' political opinions and the implications of this phenomenon for American politics in V. O. Key, Jr., *Public Opinion and American Democracy* (New York: Knopf, 1961), chap. 7.

35. See the analysis of Reagan's electoral mandate by William Schneider, "The

Public opinion can determine not only who governs but also the context within which political leaders must act. Thus, a president whose public approval rating is declining will find it difficult to lead the nation and convince other political leaders such as members of the Congress to support presidential policies. A prominent example of a president debilitated by low public approval ratings was Richard Nixon, who was forced to resign in 1974 as the Watergate scandal and the threat of impeachment engulfed his administration.

Public opinion has its greatest impact on policy when people have clear preferences and feel strongly about an issue. A study by Alan Monroe found that on issues particularly important to the public, government policy and public opinion were in agreement over two-thirds of the time.[36] One of the most striking examples of the impact of public opinion on national policy was the congressional pay raise controversy of 1989. Overwhelming and vehement public opposition caused a reluctant Congress to reject the 50 percent salary increase proposed by a bipartisan, blue-ribbon commission and endorsed by Presidents Reagan and Bush.

There are, of course, instances when public opinion and government policy are not consistent. Such inconsistencies may stem from the influence of well-organized and intense interest groups (also see Chapter 8, Interest Groups). For example, a popular majority favored tougher clean air laws in the 1980s, yet Congress was unable to enact such legislation. This inaction reflected the ability of auto makers, utilities, several unions, and key legislators to mobilize opposition to clean air bills. Inconsistencies between public opinion and government policy also occur because the public cares little about an issue. Polls have repeatedly shown, for example, that Americans favor abolishing the electoral college system for electing the president, but this is not something about which the public feels strongly. As a result, the likelihood of Congress proposing a constitutional amendment to abolish the electoral college seems remote.

Public opinion does then influence public policy in the United States, but only through a complicated and often indirect process. It takes more than a majority of the public registering its approval

November 4 Vote for President: What Did It Mean?" in *The American Elections of 1980,* ed. Austin Ranney (Washington, D.C.: American Enterprise Institute, 1981), 240–248; and Everett Carll Ladd, "The Brittle Mandate: Electoral Realignment and the 1980 Presidential Election," *Political Science Quarterly* 96 (Spring 1981): 1–26.

36. Alan D. Monroe, "Consistency between Public Preferences and National Policy Decisions," *American Politics Quarterly* 7 (January 1979): 3–21. For further evidence of the consistency between public opinion and government policy, see Benjamin I. Page and Robert Y. Shapiro, "Effect of Public Opinion on Policy," *American Political Science Review* 77 (March 1983): 175–190.

or disapproval in a poll to affect policy. People's policy preferences are translated into government policy only when individuals act on opinions—that is, when they actually participate in politics.

Citizen Participation in Politics

For most Americans, political participation simply means exercising their right to vote. But many other avenues of participation are available, requiring a higher level of political involvement. For example, millions open their checkbooks each year and contribute to the Republican and Democratic parties, preferred candidates, or interest groups such as Planned Parenthood, the Sierra Club, or the National Conservative Political Action Committee. Thousands work on campaigns, distributing campaign literature, staffing phone banks, and putting up lawn signs. Parents work through their local parent-teacher associations to improve schools; environmentalists support the Wilderness Society or the Nature Conservancy to protect wilderness areas from development; and doctors join the American Medical Association to have their say about health policy. Concerned citizens contact their representatives, senators, and local officials to express their views on such issues as gun control, abortion, or Social Security. Unusually committed persons take part in demonstrations—for gay rights, the homeless, and women's rights, as well as against rising property taxes, higher university tuitions, and CIA recruiting on university campuses. Some citizens seek to make their protests especially dramatic by participating in such illegal acts as damaging research facilities to protest scientific research using animals or blocking entrances and even physically attacking workers at abortion clinics.

Although there are abundant opportunities for political participation, most Americans are not consumed by an overwhelming interest in politics.[37] Job and family responsibilities, friends, and recreational activities have a much higher priority than politics for the average citizen.

Extent of Political Participation

Ironically, the United States, with its open and participatory political culture, ranks below most Western democracies in its rate of voter turnout in elections (the causes and consequences of voter turn-

37. For a landmark study of participation, see Sidney Verba and Norman H. Nie, *Participation in America: Social Equality and Political Democracy* (New York: Harper and Row, 1972). For a more recent survey, see M. Margaret Conway, *Political Participation in the United States,* 2d ed. (Washington, D.C.: CQ Press, 1991).

out are considered in Chapter 7). A 1987 comparative study of voter turnout by Robert Jackman revealed that America's average voter turnout rate of 54 percent was at least 20 percentage points below those for elections to the national legislatures in France, Germany, Italy, Sweden, Israel, and the United Kingdom.[38] But Americans are more likely to join and work in community organizations than the citizens of other countries.[39]

Beyond voting, which involves only registering and getting to the polls on election day, almost three-quarters of the U.S. adult population engage in at least one political activity (for example, contributing money to candidates; attending campaign rallies; joining an organization concerned with a local, state, or national issue; or contacting government officials), and a majority engage in at least two political activities. Among their political activities, Americans are drawn more to community organizations than to party or campaign work (see Table 5.5).

What Influences a Person's Level of Participation?

People's levels of political participation are affected by their social and economic status, age, their political beliefs and attitudes, and the influence of any groups to which they belong.

People with higher *social and economic status*—whether measured by level of educational attainment, income, or occupation—participate more actively in politics than those with lower social and economic status.[40] Education is, however, the most important socioeconomic characteristic influencing political participation. People with higher levels of education are more likely to understand how the political process works, to be aware of how government actions might affect their lives, to move in social environments in which politics is discussed, and to be subjected to social pressures to participate. In addition, education helps people acquire the skills necessary to participate.

Age affects participation as well. Young people are less likely to

38. Robert W. Jackman, "Political Institutions and Voter Turnout in Industrial Democracies," *American Political Science Review* 80 (June 1987): 405–423. Also see the analysis of America's relatively low voter turnout rates in G. Bingham Powell, "American Voting Turnout in Comparative Perspective," *American Political Science Review* 80 (March 1987): 17–43.

39. Norman H. Nie and Sidney Verba, "Political Participation," in *Handbook of Political Science,* ed. Fred I. Greenstein and Nelson W. Polsby (Reading, Mass.: Addison-Wesley, 1975), 4: 24–25.

40. Verba and Nie, *Participation in America,* 125. For a survey of the impact of social and economic characteristics on participation, see Conway, *Political Participation,* 15–40.

vote and engage in election-related activity than middle-aged and older citizens, but they are more likely than their elders to take part in unconventional forms of political participation such as protest demonstrations.

In the past, significant differences in political participation were related to *gender and race,* with women and blacks lagging behind men and whites. Today, however, the differences between men and women have largely disappeared.[41] The gap between white and black participation rates has been narrowed as the right of black Americans to vote has been protected, educational and economic mobility have been enhanced, and black political awareness has increased. Black participation rates are now similar to those of whites, when differences between the races in educational attainment and socio-economic status are taken into consideration.

Political participation is affected as well by people's *political beliefs and attitudes.* Among the attitudes related to participation are a sense of civic duty (a feeling of obligation to participate), an interest in politics, a sense of **political efficacy** (a feeling of personal political effectiveness), and a sense of party identification.[42] These attitudes are indicators of whether or not a person is predisposed to participate in politics, but, aside from party identification, they do not indicate which issues or candidates will receive that person's attention. In addition to such long-term attitudes as ideology and party identification, short-term influences—the salient issues of the day and the qualities of particular candidates—have an impact on the nature of participation as well. Thus in the period leading up to Senate ratification of the 1988 treaty reducing the number of U.S. and Soviet intermediate-range nuclear missiles (INF treaty), a liberal activist might have campaigned actively for a nuclear freeze. But as the nuclear issue declined in salience after ratification of the treaty, the same activist might have turned to a domestic concern such as the well-publicized plight of the homeless.

People's *group affiliations* and their sense of identification with a group also affect the extent to which they participate in politics. The rate of increase in black participation, for example, was slowed in the 1980s by the decline of community organizations and networks

Table 5.5 Participation Rates in Political Activities, 1987

Activity	% Participating
Voted regularly in presidential elections	58
Voted always in local elections	35
Persuaded others how to vote	47
Worked actively for party or candidate	26
Attended a political meeting or rally	19
Contributed only to party or candidate	23
Joined a political club	4
Worked with others on a local problem	34
Participated in a community problem-solving organization	34
Formed a group to solve a local problem	14
Contacted a local official about an issue	24
Contacted a state or national official about an issue	22

SOURCE: Adapted from Norman H. Nie, et al., "Participation in America: Continuity and Change" (Paper presented at the annual meeting of the Midwest Political Science Association, Chicago, April 14–16, 1988), table 1.

41. Interestingly, women are less likely than men to seek to persuade people how they should vote. See Ronald B. Rapoport, "The Sex Gap in Political Persuading: Where the 'Structuring Principle' Works," *American Journal of Political Science* 25 (February 1981): 32–48.
42. For a summary of the psychological components of participation, see Conway, *Political Participation,* 41–68. Also see Verba and Nie, *Participation in America.*

in America's inner cities.[43] As the bulwarks of these groups—the black middle class and stable working class—moved out of the inner cities, they left behind a large number of isolated, disadvantaged citizens.[44] By contrast, in the 1960s, before the outmigration of the middle and working classes, the inner cities had a rich organizational life that formed a basis for political mobilization. Today, however, that rich organizational life has been depleted, thereby hampering black political participation.

Conventional and Unconventional Forms of Political Participation

The distinction between conventional and unconventional forms of participation is admittedly difficult to make. Conventional participation comprises such traditionally accepted activities as voting, assisting with campaigns, contributing campaign funds, running for office, working in community organizations and interest groups, and making one's views known to public officials. Unconventional participation is more unusual, often dramatic, outside the normal government channels, and sometimes even illegal. Among the less conventional kinds of activities are demonstrations, protests, civil disobedience, and, occasionally, violence.

Conventional Activities. Other than voting, the most common form of political activity is persuading others how to vote (see Table 5.5). Almost half of the public engages in this activity. Other forms of campaign activity, however, such as contributing money, working for a candidate, attending political meetings, or belonging to political clubs, are popular only with a much smaller group of political activists. A person's level of campaign activity is strongly related to such basic political orientations as his or her interest in and attentiveness to politics, sense of party identification, and belief that participation contributes to community welfare.[45]

As important as elections are in a democracy, politics is more than elections; it also includes influencing government officials between elections. Important vehicles for such influence are interest groups (considered in detail in Chapter 8). Most Americans are members of some organized group that seeks regularly to shape government policy. A labor union or manufacturers' trade association, for example,

43. Norman H. Nie, et al., "Participation in America: Continuity and Change" (Paper presented at the annual meeting of the Midwest Political Science Association, Chicago, April 14–16, 1988).

44. See William J. Wilson, *The Truly Disadvantaged: The Inner City, the Under Class, and Public Policy* (Chicago: University of Chicago Press, 1987).

45. Nie and Verba, "Political Participation," 17–20.

Public participation in policy issues takes many forms and changes with the times. In the 1960s and early 1970s, protests against U.S. military involvement in Vietnam were a regular occurrence around the Capitol (above), but in 1991 flag-waving citizens showed their support for the troops of Operation Desert Storm.

may seek protection against Japanese imports through trade legislation; churches may advocate enactment of civil rights laws; Planned Parenthood may work actively to block the appointment of a Supreme Court nominee whose views on abortion law it opposes; or a neighborhood association may try to obtain a higher level of police protection and city services. Unlike campaign activity, community involvement is not closely associated with a strong sense of partisan identification. Rather, it stems from people's interest in politics and their concern for the overall welfare of the community.[46]

Another conventional form of political participation is contacting government officials. In contrast to the fixed schedules of voting and campaign activities and the largely controlled lists of issues raised in campaigns, the timing, content, and targets of citizen-initiated contacts with government officials are determined by individuals themselves or by the leaders of the organized groups to which they belong. Interestingly, while voter turnout has been declining since 1960, the number of citizens contacting public officials has been increasing.[47] Communications advances such as computerized direct mail enable

46. Ibid., 20–21.
47. Richard A. Brody, "The Puzzle of Political Participation in America," in *The New American Political System,* ed. Anthony King (Washington, D.C.: American Enterprise Institute, 1978), 317.

interest groups to contact their members almost instantaneously and urge them to write, phone, or fax their representative or senator. The result can be a literal avalanche of communications pouring into a legislator's office. As with other forms of political participation, people with more prestigious occupations, higher incomes, and better educations are most apt to contact public officials and to be active in other ways.

Unconventional Activities. Protest marches, demonstrations, and acts of civil disobedience—refusing to obey the law on the grounds that it is immoral—have been used throughout our history as means of political expression, publicity, and citizen mobilization. The civil rights marchers and the anti-Vietnam War protesters of the 1960s and the Persian Gulf War protesters of the 1990s, for example, were following in the tradition of the patriots who dumped tea in Boston Harbor, the abolitionists before the Civil War, the suffragists at the turn of the century, as well as the veterans' groups and labor unions during the depression of the 1930s.

Unconventional political activity often attracts substantial media attention. Indeed, one reason participants find protest activities worth the cost and effort is the media's tendency to cover these events—farmers using their tractors to block traffic in Washington to protest low prices for their products; a sit-in at a college president's office to protest the investment of college funds in firms doing business in South Africa; erection of a tent city in Lafayette Park across the street from the White House to dramatize the plight of the homeless. However dramatic such activities may be, it is useful to remember that only a tiny fraction of the citizenry participates in such protests and that the issue at stake by and large determines the social backgrounds and ideological orientations of the protesters. For example, activists who chain themselves to trees to prevent logging or lie down in front of bulldozers to prevent development are dedicated environmentalists; antiapartheid demonstrators are mainly blacks and white liberals; and antibusing protesters are primarily white, lower-middle-class urban residents. There is not, therefore, a cadre of active protesters who moves from issue to issue.

Protests require a high level of commitment. Only those who are deeply affected by an issue (and, in reality, only a fraction of these people) are likely to engage in protests.[48] The most likely participants are people who feel a sense of distrust of the political system, but who also have a sense of political efficacy—the belief that they can

48. Ibid., 316–317.

have an impact on politics.[49] The mobilization of such individuals to participate in protests usually falls to organized groups—for example, right-to-life groups might organize the picketing of abortion clinics; civil rights groups might stage antiapartheid demonstrations; or Mothers Against Drunk Driving (MADD) might hold vigils to dramatize the death toll caused by intoxicated drivers.

Although Americans are normally unmoved by unconventional political action, under some circumstances it can be most effective. The civil rights demonstrations of the 1960s—bus boycotts, lunch-counter sit-ins, and marches for voting rights—helped mold public opinion and build broad support for civil rights and voting rights legislation. These demonstrations dramatized, where more conventional political activity had failed, the extent to which American society was not yet living up to its creed of equality. But protest activity that does not strike a responsive chord with the public and that does not have the organized support of a group to back it up is not likely to succeed.

Public Opinion, Participation, and Governing

This chapter has examined the nature of public opinion as well as the forces that shape people's political thinking. Public opinion is important because it is the basis for citizen political action or participation. But understanding how the American government works and the role of citizens in that government requires moving beyond the realm of public opinion and participation to explore in more detail how citizens connect with their government. Thus, the intermediary groups and processes—political parties, interest groups, and elections—through which citizens channel their views to their government are the focus of the upcoming chapters.

For Review

1. Public opinion is the population's attitudes on an issue or question. It can be measured with a relatively high degree of accuracy by using scientific polling techniques that include interviewing carefully selected samples of the population.

2. To understand the nature of public opinion on an issue, one

49. Stephen C. Craig and Michael A. Magiotto, "Political Discontent and Political Action," *Journal of Politics* 43 (May 1981): 514–522.

must understand the various dimensions of public opinion: direction, distribution, saliency, intensity, and stability.

3. Political socialization is the process through which people acquire an awareness of, the facts about, and values concerning politics. It is a lifelong process. Among the agents of political socialization are the family, schools, peers, and the mass media.

4. Political attitudes vary in America depending on such socioeconomic characteristics as education, income/class, ethnicity and race, religion, region, and gender.

5. A political ideology is an organized, coherent set of attitudes on government and public policy. Liberal and conservative ideologies have taken on a multidimensional character, reflecting not only the traditional concern for government's role in society but also social and foreign policy concerns. Most Americans do not approach politics from an ideological perspective.

6. Public opinion has its greatest impact on governmental decision making when people feel strongly about clear-cut preferences. Although government policy tends to coincide with public opinion, this may not always be the case, particularly when a well-organized interest group intervenes or public apathy is evident.

7. Most Americans are not highly interested or intensely involved in politics. Level of involvement is strongly influenced by one's social and economic status, level of education, political attitudes such as party identification and political efficacy, and group affiliations.

For Further Reading

American Enterprise. A bimonthly magazine published by the American Enterprise Institute in Washington, D.C., featuring summaries of public opinion surveys in each issue.

Asher, Herbert. *Polling and the Public: What Every Citizen Should Know.* 2d ed. Washington, D.C.: CQ Press, 1992. A citizen's guide to understanding public opinion polling.

Conway, M. Margaret. *Political Participation in the United States.* 2d ed. Washington, D.C.: CQ Press, 1991. A concise survey of political science research on participation.

Dalton, Russell J. *Citizen Politics in Western Democracies.* Chatham, N.J.: Chatham House, 1988. A comparative study of public opinion and its role in the United States and three European democracies.

Huntington, Samuel P. *American Politics: The Promise of Disharmony.* Cambridge, Mass.: Harvard University Press, 1981. A provocative analysis of the impact of underlying American values on political reform and foreign policy.

Jennings, M. Kent, and Richard G. Niemi. *Generations and Politics: A Panel Study of Young Adults and Their Parents.* Princeton, N.J.: Princeton

University Press, 1981. A longitudinal study of the political socialization of young people and their parents.

Moore, Stanley W., James Lare, and Kenneth A. Wagner. *A Child's Political World*. New York: Praeger, 1988. A longitudinal study of children's political learning starting with kindergarten.

Neuman, W. Russell. *The Paradox of Mass Politics*. Cambridge, Mass.: Harvard University Press, 1986. An analysis of voters' interests in politics, their knowledge, and their level of conceptualization.

Verba, Sidney, and Norman H. Nie. *Participation in America: Political Democracy and Social Equality*. New York: Harper and Row, 1972. A benchmark study of political participation in the United States.

6. Political Parties

POLITICAL PARTIES were not part of the Founders' plan for America. Indeed, James Madison warned in the *Federalist* against the "mischiefs of faction," and the first president, George Washington, used his "Farewell Address" to caution that a spirit of party is divisive, "foments occasionally riot and insurrection," and "opens the doors to foreign influence and corruption." Yet wherever free elections have been conducted on a regular basis at the national and regional levels, political parties have been part of that process. Political parties have developed as suffrage has been extended and the need has arisen for organizations that can mobilize voters. Because the United States was one of the first nations to extend voting rights to all free men, it also was one of the first to develop political parties.

Even though parties are an integral part of American-style democracy and two-thirds of voters consider themselves either Democrats or Republicans, people tend to be suspicious of such organizations. A 1984 survey revealed broad support for the proposition that "it would be better if in all elections we put no party labels on the ballot," and only 29 percent disagreed with the statement that "parties do more to confuse the issues than to provide a clear choice on issues."[1] Reflecting the public's distrust, the federal and especially state governments impose severe regulatory restrictions on parties. The state statutes, for example, specify party nominating procedures and frequently stipulate how parties must organize themselves and elect their officers.

What Is a Political Party and What Does It Do?

Although political parties are a fixture of the political process, political commentators have found them difficult to define. In 1770, Edmund Burke, the English parliamentarian and philosopher, defined a **political party** by stressing the common ideology of its members: "Party is a body of men united, for promoting by their endeavors the national interest, upon some particular principle in which they are all agreed."[2] But Burke's conception of parties has little relevance to today's Republican and Democratic parties. Both

1. Jack Dennis, "Public Support for the Party System, 1964–1984" (Paper presented at the annual meeting of the American Political Science Association, Washington, D.C., August 28–31, 1986).
2. Edmund Burke, "Thoughts on the Cause of the Present Discontents," in *The Works of Edmund Burke* (Boston: Little, Brown, 1871), 151.

include in their ranks conservatives, moderates, and liberals. As former Speaker of the House of Representatives Thomas ("Tip") O'Neill (D-Mass.) remarked about his party, "We Democrats are all under one tent. In any other country we'd be five splinter parties."

More recently, political scientist Leon Epstein has managed to provide a definition of *political party* that is well adapted to the American experience: "Any group, however loosely organized, seeking to elect governmental officeholders under a given label."[3] The essential elements of this definition are that, first, political parties are preoccupied with contesting elections and, second, only parties run candidates *under their own labels*. Epstein's conception of parties takes into account the absence of ideological and policy unity that characterizes our parties. It also accommodates the widely varying types of party organizations found in the United States—such as the patronage-based and centrally controlled machine of the late mayor Richard Daley in Chicago, the well-financed suburban operations such as the Nassau County (Long Island, New York) Republicans, the ideological Democratic reformers in Los Angeles and New York, the professionally staffed headquarters of the Republican and Democratic national committees, and the poorly funded and understaffed local party committees in hundreds of communities.

One reason analysts have found political parties so difficult to define is their complex, overlapping social structures, which have these components: (1) *the party in the electorate*: voters who identify with, vote for, or register a preference for a particular party; (2) *the party organization*: party officers, committee members, paid staff, and volunteer workers; and (3) *the party in government*: government officeholders of a party and a party's nominees for office.[4] Each of these elements is an essential component of a political party, but none by itself constitutes the whole of a party. Within a party are found the most weakly committed voter, the dedicated party worker, the paid professional staffer, and even, perhaps, the president of the United States.

Act as an Intermediary between Citizens and Their Government

Parties serve as linkages or intermediaries between citizens and their government. They bring the scattered elements of the public

3. Leon D. Epstein, *Political Parties in Western Democracies* (New York: Praeger, 1967), 9.

4. This tripartite conception of American political parties was developed by V. O. Key, Jr., *Politics, Parties, and Pressure Groups*, 5th ed. (New York: Crowell, 1964), 163–164. Also see Frank J. Sorauf and Paul Allen Beck, *Party Politics in America*, 6th ed. (Glenview, Ill.: Scott, Foresman/Little, Brown, 1988), 8–12.

together to define objectives, support candidates, and achieve common goals through government policy. The parties' role as linkages between the citizens and their government was held so important by political scientist E. E. Schattschneider that he observed in his 1944 classic study that "political parties created democracy and modern democracy is unthinkable save in terms of parties."[5] More recently, political scientist Samuel Huntington concluded after a multi-nation study that parties organize participation, bring together different groups in society, and "serve as a link between social forces and the governments."[6] Parties, of course, are not the only intermediary institutions in the political system. They must compete for influence with interest groups, political action committees (committees established by business groups, ideological groups, and unions to distribute money to candidates), and the mass media. But even if the statements of Schattschneider and Huntington may have overstated the role of parties, it is evident that parties are involved in every aspect of government. After all, it is men and women elected as Democrats and Republicans who make the laws and decide whether and at what level government benefits should be available to the poor, elderly, veterans, students, farmers, businesses, and local governments. It is also Democrats and Republicans who determine who will pay how much for these benefits through taxes.

Nominate Candidates

The **nomination** of candidates—determining which candidates' names will appear on the general election ballot—is a critical phase in the electoral process. For candidates, the nomination is a hurdle that must be crossed for election to public office. For all practical purposes, the nominating process also restricts the voters' choices on election day to the candidates of the Republican and Democratic parties.

Party nominating procedures narrow the field of candidates. Without a party nomination, it is virtually impossible to win major elective office. Indeed, since the emergence of modern parties in 1800, every president has been a major party nominee. Between 1978 and 1990, every member of the Congress was either a Republican or Democrat except for Socialist Bernard Sanders (Vt.), who was elected to the House in 1990. And since 1942 only three persons (two in 1990—Lowell Weicker in Connecticut and Walter Hickel in

5. E. E. Schattschneider, *Party Government* (New York: Holt, Rinehart, and Winston, 1944), 10.

6. Samuel Huntington, *Political Order in Changing Societies* (New Haven, Conn.: Yale University Press, 1980), 91.

Alaska) have been elected governor as an independent. At the same time, however, nomination procedures in the United States permit broad voter participation, making it difficult for party leaders to control the nomination process.

Contest Elections and
Mobilize Voters

Parties and their candidates contest elections by mobilizing the electorate. In spite of cultural diversity, rapid social change, competing interests, and simultaneous elections in fifty states and thousands of communities, the two major parties have been remarkably successful in channeling the vote and dominating electoral competition. But voters have been less guided by partisan commitments since the 1970s than they were in prior decades.[7] This is reflected in the tendency of many voters to engage in **ticket-splitting**—electing Republican presidents while voting Democratic in congressional elections.

Organize the Government

To carry out their responsibilities, government institutions must have leaders, procedural rules, and divisions of labor. Most government institutions are organized along party lines. Congress, for example, is organized on a partisan basis. Because Democrats held a majority of the seats in the House and Senate after the 1990 elections, they controlled the institution's most powerful leadership positions. Members of Congress also tend to be guided by party positions when casting their votes on the floors of the House and Senate. The executive branch is organized in a partisan manner as well. Presidential appointees—department secretaries and assistant secretaries, White House staff, and agency heads—are almost exclusively members of the president's party.

When different parties control the executive and legislative branches, as has very often been the case since 1968, the institutional rivalries created by the separation of powers system are intensified. For example, executive-congressional conflicts during the 1980s and 1990s have been intensified by Republican control of the White House and Democratic control of Congress. But when the same party controls both branches, the prospects for presidential–congressional cooperation are enhanced. Partisanship can thus help bridge the separation of powers.

7. See Martin P. Wattenberg, *The Decline of American Political Parties, 1952–1984* (Cambridge, Mass.: Harvard University Press, 1986).

Act as Agents of
Public Accountability

Parties contribute to democracy by providing voters with a means of holding public officials accountable for their actions. The political world within which the average citizen must function is incredibly complex—multiple and interrelated issues, political power divided by separation of powers and federalism, and a lengthy election day ballot that includes candidates from the president to the county registrar of deeds. Making informed choices in this kind of tangled environment is almost mind-boggling. Fortunately, a lengthy, in-depth study of politics is not necessary to make rational electoral choices; political parties provide the voter with a few simple criteria that help make election day decision making manageable.

Because parties simplify voters' choices on election day by structuring the election into a contest between Democrats and Republicans, voters can vote for the candidates from the party they feel is closest to their viewpoints. Voters also may use their ballots to hold elected officials accountable for the conduct of the government. With all elected officials wearing a party label—a political brand name— the voters are in a position to assign blame or credit for the state of the Union to the party that controls the government. Elected officials' fears of being held responsible for adversity and their desires to be credited for good times tend to make them responsive to society's needs. But without political party labels, it would be much more difficult to achieve public accountability through elections.

This process of citizen control over their government leaders is, of course, indirect and imperfect. Elections do not tell elected officials what specific policies the voters favor. Rather, they provide an opportunity to register a general reaction to a party's stewardship in office or the general direction of future policy. Thus, when the Republicans in 1976 and the Democrats in 1980 were forced to vacate the White House, the voters were not telling the respective new presidents what specific policies they should follow. They were instead expressing their dissatisfaction with the incumbent parties' performances and giving the new administrations a chance to deal with the country's most pressing problems.

Manage Conflicts in Society

In a society composed of people and groups with different goals, interests, and values, conflict is inevitable. But when conflict gets out of hand, it can make living conditions intolerable. A stable democratic order, therefore, requires some means of managing and resolving the conflicts that naturally arise.

Political parties help manage societal conflict in America. They are in the business of winning elections, and electoral majorities require fashioning broad-based voter coalitions. But such coalitions inevitably contain contentious elements—for example, the **New Deal Democratic coalition** forged by President Franklin Roosevelt in the 1930s comprised southern white Protestants, northern urban Catholics, blue-collar workers, Jews, and blacks. Yet in spite of this variety, the party's leadership was able to work out intracoalition compromises that allowed it to dominate American elections from the 1930s into the 1970s. Similarly, the Republican coalitions that elected Ronald Reagan and George Bush in the 1980s included such unlikely partners as well-educated, northern suburbanites and southern fundamentalist Protestants. Thus, by settling some of society's conflicts *within the parties,* American parties have helped manage conflict and thus have contributed to political stability.

The Party Struggle in America

Despite the Founders' forecast that the establishment of political parties would have dire consequences for the new Republic, parties quickly became an institutionalized part of the political process. By the 1830s, presidential candidates were nominated by party conventions, presidents were selected by partisan slates of presidential electors, and Congress was organized on a partisan basis. Indeed, the history of political conflict in the United States reveals the durability of political parties in spite of public misgivings about their influence, frequently inhospitable federal and state regulations, and changing social and economic conditions (see Table 6.1).[8]

The First Party System, 1789–1824

Although the government under the Constitution did not begin with organized political parties, they came into being in its early days when conflicts arose between the congressional followers of Secretary of the Treasury Alexander Hamilton and of Secretary of State Thomas Jefferson in the Washington administration. It was the followers of Jefferson who first sought to expand their activities beyond the halls of Congress. Organizing at the state and local levels, they ran candidates for Congress and the electoral college under the banner of the Democratic-Republican party. Reluctantly, the Federalist

8. An excellent short summary of party history is found in Key, *Politics, Parties, and Pressure Groups,* 166–198. A more detailed account is contained in Everett Carll Ladd, *American Political Parties: Social Change and Political Response* (New York: Norton, 1970).

Table 6.1 American Party Systems

Party System	Years	Major Parties	Characteristics and Major Events
First	1789–1824	Federalist Democratic-Republican	Political parties emerge in 1790s. War of 1812 Democratic-Republicans dominate, 1800–1824.
Second	1828–1854	Democratic Whig	Factional conflicts develop within Democratic party, 1828–1836. Whigs emerge as opposition to Democrats in 1830s. Two-party competition results, with the Democrats stronger electorally. Sectional conflicts between North and South intensify and create schisms within Democratic and Whig parties.
Third	1856–1896	Democratic Republican	Republican party emerges as major opposition to Democrats in 1850s. Lincoln elected in 1860; Civil War and Reconstruction follow. Republicans dominate, 1864–1874; two-party competition characterizes 1874–1896. Agrarian unrest surfaces; Populist party contests 1892 election.
Fourth	1896–1932	Democratic Republican	Republicans dominate, 1896–1910. Progressive movement develops; Progressives split away from GOP and run Theodore Roosevelt for president, but Democrat Woodrow Wilson is elected. South becomes solidly Democratic. World War I and Normalcy of 1920s Republicans dominate nationally, 1920–1928.
Fifth	1932–	Democratic Republican	Great Depression of 1930s, World War II New Deal Democratic coalition forms; Democrats dominate electorally in 1930s and 1940s. Korean and Vietnam wars After 1950s, Democratic electoral coalition is weakened; Republicans dominate presidency and Democrats dominate Congress in 1970s and 1980s.

supporters of Hamilton and President John Adams (1797–1801) followed the Jeffersonian example of local political organizing to influence elections.

Federalists supported a strong national government capable of protecting and stimulating business development. Thus, they were strongest in the Northeast and along the seaboard and among well-to-do business and tradespeople. They also tended to favor England and oppose the revolutionary government in France. Jefferson's

To broaden the party's electoral appeal and compensate for deep divisions within its own ranks, the Whigs nominated military heroes William Henry Harrison (top) in 1840 and Zachary Taylor (bottom) in 1848 and won the White House both times. Nominating a candidate whose appeal extends beyond party loyalists continues to be a goal of party strategists today.

Democratic-Republicans drew their support from less well-to-do elements and were defenders of agrarian interests. They feared a strong national government that supported business development. In foreign policy, they tended to favor France over England.

In the election of 1800, the Democratic-Republicans won an overwhelming victory, and the Federalists then went into a steady decline. As the party of the elite elements of society, the Federalists had failed to adapt to the more democratic style of politics that was emerging in the early decades of the nineteenth century as the right to vote was extended to all white males.[9]

The Second Party System, 1828–1854

In 1828, Andrew Jackson, running as a Democrat, defeated President John Quincy Adams and then was reelected in 1832. The forces opposed to Jackson had coalesced by 1834 to form the Whig party. Thereafter for two decades, the Democrats and the Whigs engaged in bitter electoral struggles in all regions of the country. Both organized state and local party organizations and ran full slates of candidates for public office. In this atmosphere of party competition, voters began to think of themselves as Democrats or Whigs, yet throughout this period the Democrats were the dominant party, with the minority Whigs winning presidential elections only when they nominated such military heroes as William Henry Harrison in 1840 and Zachary Taylor in 1848.

Both parties were broad electoral coalitions that sought to balance the interests of farmers, manufacturers, and merchants; the native-born and immigrants; and Protestants and Catholics. The Whigs attracted proportionally more support from manufacturing and trading interests, planters, and old Protestant stock, and the Democrats did best among western farmers, newly enfranchised voters, immigrants, and Catholics.

During the second party system, national conventions became the standard method for nominating presidential candidates and writing party platforms. Before the 1830s, presidential candidates had been nominated by their parties' members of Congress, the congressional caucuses.

Racial and slavery issues became increasingly divisive during the

9. For accounts of the early development of political parties in the United States, see William Nisbet Chambers, *Political Parties in a New Nation* (New York: Oxford University Press, 1963); and Richard Hofstadter, *The Idea of a Party System: The Rise of Legitimate Opposition in the United States* (Berkeley: University of California Press, 1969).

1850s and split both the Democrats and Whigs along a North-South axis. Neither party was capable of resolving this sectional conflict, and America entered its third party system era with the emergence of the Republican party.

The Third Party System, 1856–1896

Between 1854 and 1860, the electorate went through a major **realignment**—a significant change in the partisanship of the electorate and in the underlying bases of the parties' electoral support. The Whigs dissolved; the Democrats split into northern and southern factions; and the Republican party—made up of abolitionists, Free-Soilers (an 1848 third-party movement opposed to the extension of slavery to the newly acquired territories in the West), and dissident northern Whigs and Democrats—emerged. In 1860, Abraham Lincoln, a former Whig, captured the presidency for the new Republican party, and the period 1864–1874 was one of Republican electoral dominance.

The electoral base of the Republican party (also known as the "Grand Old Party" or GOP) was in the North, where for decades after the Civil War it effectively campaigned using the emotional symbols of the war: the Union, emancipation, and the martyred president. The GOP's dominant electoral coalition comprised diverse interests—Union veterans, farmers, northern business interests, and working people in the cities.

The Civil War and the Reconstruction policies of the Republicans alienated that party from the South, which became strongly Democratic. In addition to its southern base, the Democratic party gained the support of scattered elements of the business community through its commitment to free trade and of the new and largely Catholic immigrant groups in the cities.

After 1874 and the end of Reconstruction in the South, the Democrats and Republicans began to compete on a more even basis and alternated control of the presidency and Congress up until 1896. Overall, however, the post-Civil War era was a period of Republican dominance of the national government and of sectional conflict between the southern-based Democrats and the northern-based Republicans.

The Fourth Party System, 1896–1932

America was transformed socially and economically in the second half of the nineteenth century. Urbanization created cities with populations of over one million; transcontinental railroads spanned the

After failing to win the Republican presidential nomination in 1912, former president Theodore Roosevelt ran on his own "Bull Moose" Progressive ticket. This split the Republican vote between Roosevelt and President William Howard Taft and contributed to Democrat Woodrow Wilson's election to the presidency.

nation; mammoth corporations such as Standard Oil and U.S. Steel emerged; and waves of immigrants from non-English-speaking nations reached American shores. The social dislocations and discontent caused by these social changes reverberated through the political system and spawned third-party protest movements. The most significant was the People's (Populist) party of 1892, whose platform of agrarian radicalism called for an income tax, nationalization of railroads and telephone/telegraph companies, and inflation through unlimited coinage of silver. The popular unrest demonstrated by the 1892 election set the stage for the capture of the Democratic party in 1896 by the Populist movement.

The election of 1896, which found the Democrats nominating a prairie Populist, William Jennings Bryan, and the Republicans selecting as their candidate a traditional conservative, William McKinley, was a watershed in American political history. Running on a platform of "Prosperity—Sound Money—Good Markets and Employment for Labor—A Full Dinner Pail," McKinley was elected with the support of business classes who were scared by Bryan's populism. Working people in the cities also supported McKinley because they believed that the Republican policy of a high protective tariff would shield their jobs.

The political landscape was transformed by the 1896 election. The Republican electoral coalition, which had been weakened after 1874, gained an infusion of voters, especially among urban residents in the Northeast. The Democrats were severely weakened in much of the North and were forced to rely on their southern base. Thus, the fourth party system of 1896–1932 was dominated by the Republicans, except when a split within the GOP permitted Democrat Woodrow Wilson to win the presidency in 1912 and gain reelection in 1916.

The Fifth Party System, 1932–?

In the first year of Herbert Hoover's administration, the stock market crashed, signaling the beginning of the depression of the 1930s. The once-dominant Republicans were crushed in the elections of 1932 and 1936 as the electorate realigned itself and the nation entered a long period of Democratic ascendancy. Indeed, the new president, Franklin Roosevelt, had the support of his remarkably diverse New Deal Democratic coalition and his leadership of the nation during World War II strengthened support for the Democratic party as well.

But by the 1950s, the New Deal Democratic coalition had begun to show signs of strain as Republican Dwight Eisenhower won the presidency in 1952 and 1956. Although the electoral alignments of the 1930s were still visible, the erosion of the Democrats' electoral base intensified from the late 1960s into the 1980s, especially among white southerners. At the same time, however, black voters came to constitute a larger and loyal component of the Democratic coalition.

During the 1980s, America developed a two-tiered electoral system. Republicans won five of six presidential contests, between 1968 and 1988, but Democrats continued to dominate the congressional elections and to control the bulk of the governorships and state legislative chambers. In addition, a plurality of voters continued to consider themselves Democrats rather than Republicans. As a result, the post-1968 period of divided party control of government has been characterized as a time of "incomplete realignment"—significant changes in the parties' electoral bases of support but not of sufficient magnitude to constitute a thorough realignment.[10]

10. See Paul Allen Beck, "Incomplete Realignment: The Reagan Legacy for Parties and Elections," in *The Reagan Legacy and Performance*, ed. Charles O. Jones (Chatham, N.J.: Chatham House, 1988), 145–171. For further analysis of the electoral and party system that emerged in the 1980s, see Thomas E. Cavanagh and James L. Sundquist, "The New Two-Party System," in *The New Directions in Amer-*

Interparty Competition

The nature of the competition among political parties has varied significantly over time. Between 1800 and 1990, three distinct patterns characterized interparty competition. The first, *balanced two-party competition,* was evident in the Democratic-Whig confrontations of 1836–1854 and in Republican-Democratic struggles since World War II. The second, *sustained one-party dominance* of national politics, characterized the Republican era of 1896–1910 and the Democratic New Deal period of 1932–1946. And, third, *intraparty factionalism and pluralism* describe the factional battles between progressive and conservative Republicans from 1910 to 1912 and the multiparty politics of the 1850s and early Civil War years.[11] Interestingly, all three types of electoral competition have existed in this century, but the period since World War II has been the longest period of sustained balanced interparty competition in American history.

Over 130 Years of Democratic-Republican Electoral Dominance

One of the most remarkable features of the history of American political parties has been the way two parties—the Democrats and Republicans—have dominated electoral politics since 1856. Indeed, this record of two-party durability and electoral dominance is unmatched in the world's democracies. The two parties have survived demoralizing defeats and adapted to the dislocations in society caused by a civil war, two world wars, depressions, waves of immigrants, industrialization, urbanization, suburbanization, and a communications revolution.

Among the reasons for the Democratic and Republican parties' amazing record of durability is their *capacity to absorb protest.*[12] Although third-party protest movements have flowered periodically, they usually have withered as their causes and supporters have been incorporated into the major parties. Thus, the 1892 Populists were absorbed into the Democratic party in 1896, and Theodore Roosevelt's "Bull Moose" Progressives of 1912 moved back into the GOP in 1916. The **direct primary** method of nominating candidates is one of the reasons parties are able to absorb protest. The direct

ican Politics,* ed. John E. Chubb and Paul E. Peterson (Washington, D.C.: Brookings, 1985), 33–68; and Everett Carll Ladd, "The 1988 Elections: Continuation of the Post-New Deal System," *Political Science Quarterly* 104 (Spring 1989): 1–18.

11. Samuel J. Eldersveld, *Political Parties in American Society* (New York: Basic Books, 1982), 35–36.

12. Ibid., 40–41.

primary takes the power over nominations out of the hands of party leaders and permits voters to select their party's nominees. As a result, dissidents can work *within* the established parties to achieve their goals instead of having to form **third parties**.[13]

The electoral dominance of the Republican and Democratic parties has been further enhanced by election procedures that work to the disadvantage of third parties. Members of the Congress and most state legislators are elected from **single-member districts** under a **winner-take-all system**—whoever receives a plurality of the vote is the winner. This is in contrast to **proportional representation** systems in which parties win a share of the seats in the legislature directly proportionate to their share of the popular vote. Thus, if party A receives 40 percent of the popular vote, party B gets 30 percent, party C 20 percent, and party D 10 percent, party A would be entitled to 40 percent of the seats in the legislature; party B would be entitled to 30 percent; and so on. Under proportional representation, parties have little incentive to form broad coalitions since they are virtually assured of some representation in the legislature. Under America's winner-take-all system of single-member districts, however, only two parties normally have a reasonable chance of victory; third or minor parties are condemned to perpetual defeat. As a result, there is an incentive in countries using single-member constituencies to form broadly based parties capable of winning pluralities in legislative districts.

The electoral college system for choosing presidents also discourages the development of strong third parties. To be elected president, a candidate must receive an absolute majority of the electoral votes—an almost impossible feat for a minor party. In addition, states' electoral votes are allocated on a winner-take-all basis—that is, the candidate receiving a plurality of a state's popular votes receives all of its electoral votes. Like the single-member district system, this winner-take-all system works to the disadvantage of minor parties.

Democratic-Republican electoral dominance also has been sustained by the parties' *ideological pragmatism*. Thus, rather than adhere to a strict ideology, both parties have shifted their policy orientations in response to changing conditions. The Democrats have gone from populism in 1896, to conservatism in 1904, to Woodrow Wilson's New Freedom progressivism in 1912, to New

13. Leon D. Epstein, *Political Parties in the American Mold* (Madison: University of Wisconsin Press, 1986), 131–133, 243–245.

Deal liberalism in the 1930s and 1940s, to Jimmy Carter moderation in the 1970s, and to Walter Mondale and Michael Dukakis liberalism in the 1980s. The Republicans have shown similar flexibility: McKinley-style conservatism in the 1890s, Theodore Roosevelt progressivism at the turn of the century, "normalcy" (business domination of government and a retreat into isolationism) in the 1920s, moderate Republicanism in the 1940s and 1950s, and Reagan-Bush conservatism in the 1980s.

Finally, the parties have demonstrated *coalitional flexibility*—an ability to attract voters from all segments of society, even those normally thought to support the opposition. In 1988, for example, Republicans showed a capacity to win a majority of Catholics and 49 percent of blue-collar workers even though these groups generally are thought to be in the Democratic camp.[14] Likewise, earlier, the Democrats, with Jimmy Carter of Georgia as their 1976 presidential nominee, won a larger than normal share of the southern white Republican vote. Party coalitions thus are not static. As political scientist Samuel Eldersveld has observed, "The history of American parties is one of breakup, modification, and reconstruction of socioeconomic coalitions."[15]

Two-Party Competition: More than Meets the Eye

With the Republicans and Democrats dominating the political landscape, the phrase "American two-party system" accurately describes the overall pattern of electoral competition. But it also masks a great deal of variation in the nature and extent of interparty competition. Most statewide elections—contests for a state's electoral votes as well as its senatorial and gubernatorial elections—tend to be confrontations between the Republicans and Democrats. A large proportion of congressional (House) districts, however, are safe havens for one party. In 1990, for example, 87 percent of the contested seats were won by votes of 60 percent or more. Elections for some state officials also may lack authentic **two-party competition**. For example, an analysis (Figure 6.1) of the level of interparty competition in the fifty states between 1981 and 1988—taking into account each party's percentage of the gubernatorial vote and the proportion of state legislative seats controlled by each party—reveals that over half the states failed the test of two-party competitiveness.

Comparative state studies have shown that socioeconomic diversity within a state's population contributes to two-party competi-

14. *New York Times*/CBS poll, reported in the *New York Times,* Nov. 10, 1988, 18Y, National edition.
15. Eldersveld, *Political Parties in American Society,* 42.

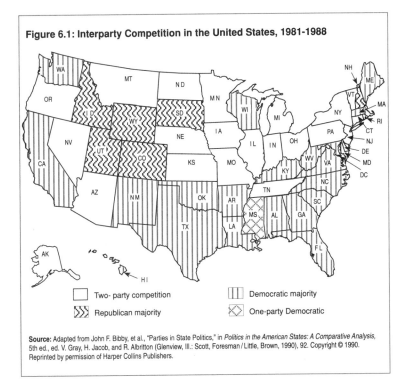

Figure 6.1: Interparty Competition in the United States, 1981-1988

Legend:
- ☐ Two-party competition
- ▨ Republican majority
- ⦀ Democratic majority
- ⊠ One-party Democratic

Source: Adapted from John F. Bibby, et al., "Parties in State Politics," in *Politics in the American States: A Comparative Analysis*, 5th ed., ed. V. Gray, H. Jacob, and R. Albritton (Glenview, Ill.: Scott, Foresman/Little, Brown, 1990), 92. Copyright © 1990. Reprinted by permission of Harper Collins Publishers.

tion.[16] A socially diverse population provides a basis for differences over government policy and allows both parties to build up support among selected groups. The changeover of the South from a one-party Democratic region to one characterized by increased interparty competition, especially in statewide elections, illustrates what happens when a society becomes more diverse. Until the 1950s, the southern electorate was relatively homogeneous, sharing common ethnic, religious, and economic characteristics. Indeed, it was overwhelmingly white (blacks had been disenfranchised), Anglo-Saxon, and Protestant. The economy of the South was primarily agrarian, and its people tended to live in rural areas and small towns. Such homogeneity, therefore, offered little basis for the development of two parties. Real two-party competition did not come to the region until industrialization, unionization, urbanization, the enfranchisement of blacks, and the inmigration of northerners created divisions within society that enabled the Republicans to gain a basis of support.

16. See Sarah McCally Morehouse, *State Politics and Policy* (New York: Holt, Rinehart, and Winston, 1981), chap. 2.

Table 6.2 The Fate of Third Parties

Year	Third Party	% of Popular Vote for President	No. of Electoral Votes	Status in Next Election
1832	Anti-Masonic	7.8	7	Endorsed Whig candidate
1848	Free-Soil	10.1	0	Received 4.9% of vote
1856	American (Know-Nothing)	21.5	8	Party dissolved
	Republican	33.1	114	Won presidency
1860	Southern Democrat	18.1	72	Party dissolved
	Constitutional Union	12.6	39	Party dissolved
1892	Populist	8.5	22	Endorsed Democratic candidate
1912	Progressive (T. Roosevelt)	27.4	88	Returned to Republican party
	Socialist	6.0	0	Received 3.2% of vote
1924	Progressive (R. LaFollette)	16.6	13	Returned to Republican party
1948	States' Rights Democratic	2.4	39	Party dissolved
	Progressive (H. Wallace)	2.4	0	Received 0.23% of vote
1968	American Independent (G. Wallace)	13.5	46	Received 1.4% of vote
1980	John B. Anderson	7.1	0	Did not run

SOURCE: Congressional Quarterly, *Guide to U.S. Elections,* 2d ed. (Washington, D.C.: Congressional Quarterly Inc., 1985).

Third and Minor Parties:
At Times a Critical Impact

Although American politics is dominated by two major parties, third parties have at times had a critical impact on our history (see Table 6.2).[17] For example, the new Republican party of the 1850s helped focus national debate on the slavery issue. Indeed, its election victory in 1860 precipitated the Civil War. The Republican party also was a factor in the dissolution of the Whig party.

Unlike the Republicans, most third parties do not become major parties. They can, however, affect election outcomes and electoral alignments. Most third parties in this century have been **splinter parties**—offshoots of the major parties—which formed to protest the policies of their parent party's dominant faction. Theodore Roosevelt's 1912 Progressive ("Bull Moose") party, for example, was born

17. For an analysis of how third parties emerge and why people vote for their candidates, see Steven J. Rosenstone, Roy L. Behr, and Edward H. Lazarus, *Third Parties in America: Citizen Response to Major Party Failure* (Princeton, N.J.: Princeton University Press, 1984).

because of a split in the GOP. As a result, the Republican vote was divided in the 1912 election, and Democrat Woodrow Wilson was elected president with less than a majority of the popular vote. In 1968, Alabama's Democratic governor George Wallace ran on the American Independent ticket. His populist, antiestablishment, and hawkish military policies won 13 percent of the vote, siphoned off votes from both the Republican and Democratic candidates, and contributed to one of the closest presidential elections in the twentieth century. The most recent third-party movement was led by Rep. John B. Anderson (R-Ill.) in 1980. Although a Republican, Anderson assumed a generally liberal issue stance, thereby taking votes mainly from President Jimmy Carter and aiding the Republican challenger, Ronald Reagan.

Strong third-party movements are normally a signal of substantial discontent within the country. This was certainly true of the Populists in 1892, the LaFollette Progressives in 1923 (Wisconsin senator Robert LaFollette, its founder, ran for the presidency in 1924, losing to Republican Calvin Coolidge), and Wallace's American Independent party in 1968. Faced with such evidence of social unrest, at least one of the highly adaptive major parties normally has sought to accommodate the protest group within its ranks (for example, the Democrats adopted the Populist program in 1896).[18]

Some minor parties such as the Socialists and Libertarians are characterized by strong policy or ideological orientations. Their goals are not to win elections; rather, they use the electoral process to publicize their cause in the hope that eventually some of their policies will be adopted by the major parties.

Characteristics of American Parties

The American party system shares many traits with those in other Western democracies. These include long-established parties; a limited number of major parties; electoral alignments organized around national issues; and class-, religious-, and regionally based patterns of electoral support. The American party system, however, encompasses a particular combination of characteristics that makes it distinctive.

18. For a discussion of the role of third parties in electoral realignments in American history, see Walter Dean Burnham, *Critical Elections and the Mainsprings of American Politics* (New York: Norton, 1970), 27–33.

Decentralized Power Structure

Power within American parties is fragmented and scattered among thousands of elected and party officials at the national, state, and local levels. American parties thus are not hierarchical or centralized organizations. Elected officials, including the president, as well as party officers, such as the national chairmen, do not have the power to order fellow party officials about. A number of factors contribute to the decentralized power structure of American parties. Two factors—separation of powers and federalism—are constitutionally mandated. Yet two other factors—party nominating procedures and campaign practices—originate within the parties themselves.

Bases of the Party Power Structure. In countries with a **parliamentary system** such as Great Britain, the chief executive or prime minister is chosen by the majority party or a coalition of parties in the national legislature. If the legislators of the prime minister's party fail to support their leader's policies, new parliamentary elections may be called or a new prime minister and cabinet may be appointed. Thus in a parliamentary system, party members in the legislature and in the executive have an incentive to remain united.

Under America's separation of powers principle, however, members of the president's party in Congress may oppose presidential policies without risking either having to stand immediately for reelection or forcing the resignation of the president and the cabinet. Operating on a different election schedule than the president and running in separate constituencies, members of Congress have an incentive to look after their own reelection needs first; support for their party's president is secondary. The separation of powers principle is embedded as well in state constitutions and its party-fragmenting consequences are therefore present at the state level.

In creating a bewildering array of government units and elected officials, federalism, too, has contributed to the decentralization of power in political parties. Parties must organize not only to win the presidency but also to win offices in the thousands of constituencies found in the fifty states. Each of these election districts has its own party organization, elected officials, and candidate organizations. Frequently, the interests and priorities of these state and local politicians are quite different from those of their party's national leadership. For example, when the Democratic leader in New York City's Bronx was asked whether he was concerned about the outcome of the presidential election, he responded: "It [presidential politics] doesn't affect our life one bit. National politics—President and such—are too far removed from the bread and butter things that matter to local leaders and mayors and governors. The local leader cares about a senior citizen center, a local concern."[19] Thus, by creating thousands of distinct party organizations and separately elected state and local officials, the American brand of federalism has made centralized control of the parties virtually impossible.

The decentralizing consequences of separation of powers and federalism are reinforced by the manner in which nominations are made and elections are conducted. As we saw earlier, party nominations for state, local, and congressional offices are made through a system of popular elections (*direct primaries*). Because the voters, not the party leaders, thus control the nominating process, candidates build personal—not party—organizations to compete in the primaries. Knowing that it is their *personal* campaign efforts and organizations that win primary elections, elected officials rarely feel a strong sense of obligation to their party organization.

Indeed, electoral survival requires building a personal organization and not depending on popular presidents or a party organization to carry one to victory. Individual candidates are responsible for raising their own campaign war chests. Armed with adequate financing, a candidate can then secure the other resources essential to a campaign—media experts, pollsters, computer specialists, direct-mail specialists, accountants, lawyers, campaign managers, and consultants. With candidates largely on their own in securing the needed campaign resources, it is not surprising that they emerge from elections believing that the party's role in their victory was minor and that they can operate quite independently of party leaders.

A Countertrend. Although American parties remain decentralized institutions, important countertrends should be noted. Since the 1970s the national organizations of both the Republican and Democratic parties have been strengthened significantly. The Democratic National Committee (DNC), backed by Supreme Court rulings, has aggressively asserted authority over its state affiliates in matters pertaining to the selection of delegates to the **national nominating conventions**. The DNC requires, for example, that all delegation selection procedures used in the states conform with national party

19. Maurice Carroll, "For Once, a Primary Unites a Party," *New York Times*, March 25, 1984, 6E, National edition.

rules. Failure to conform can result in a state's delegation not being seated at the convention.

Both the national Democratic and Republican organizations, especially the Republicans, have developed highly efficient fund-raising operations. With millions of dollars in their treasuries, the national parties have been able to provide financial and technical assistance to state-level candidates and party organizations. In dispensing these favors, the national party has gained increased influence over party organizations at the state level.[20]

Broad-based Electoral Support

In some parts of the world, partisan attachments closely parallel social and economic divisions within society—Catholics versus Protestants, Christians versus Moslems, rich versus poor, workers versus management, city versus countryside, immigrants versus the native-born. When political and socioeconomic splits coincide, political conflicts tend to be intense, sustained, and even violent. The tragic histories of Northern Ireland and Lebanon illustrate this pattern.

In sharp contrast, American political parties are coalition-type parties that can count on significant levels of support from virtually every major socioeconomic group. While both parties can anticipate some support from most social groups, there are important differences in the levels of support provided by various voter groups (see Table 6.3).[21] This table also reveals the changes in the composition of the Republican and Democratic electoral coalitions since the 1950s. The Republican party has become more southern and white, while the Democratic party has become distinctly less southern, with blacks and Hispanics constituting a growing share of its adherents.[22]

As we noted in Chapter 5, differences in income and class, religion, race and ethnicity, and gender produce distinctive political orientations and thus patterns of support for political parties. More specifically, low-wage earners, union members, and blue-collar workers traditionally have supported the Democratic party, and peo-

---

20. See John F. Bibby, "Party Renewal in the Republican Party," in *Party Renewal in America: Theory and Practice,* ed. Gerald M. Pomper (New York: Praeger, 1980), 102–115; A. James Reichley, "The Rise of National Parties," in Chubb and Peterson, *New Directions,* 175–202; and Paul Herrnson, *Party Campaigning in the 1980s* (Cambridge, Mass.: Harvard University Press, 1988).

21. A comprehensive analysis of party electoral coalitions is found in John R. Petrocik, *Party Coalitions: Realignments and the Decline of the New Deal Party System* (Chicago: University of Chicago Press, 1981).

22. For an analysis of the changing voting patterns of socioeconomic groups, see Ladd, "The 1988 Elections."

Table 6.3 Profile of Democratic and Republican Electoral
Coalitions Since the 1950s *(percent)*

	Democratic Party Identifiers					
	1950s	*1960s*	*1970s*	*1980*	*1984*	*1988*
White Protestants	18	20	17	16	17	15
Catholics	14	16	17	14	14	14
Northern union households	22	16	19	17	16	14
White southerners	31	26	23	23	22	23
Jews	4	4	3	5	3	4
Blacks	9	13	16	18	17	22
Hispanics	1	2	2	3	7	5
All others	2	2	3	4	5	3
Total	100	100	100	100	100	100

	Republican Party Identifiers					
	1950s	*1960s*	*1970s*	*1980*	*1984*	*1988*
White Protestants	51	50	43	37	38	37
Catholics	10	12	12	14	14	16
Northern union households	16	11	14	16	12	12
White southerners	15	21	23	22	25	25
Jews	1	1	1	1	1	2
Blacks	5	2	2	3	2	4
Hispanics	0	—	1	2	4	2
All others	2	3	3	5	5	3
Total	100	100	100	100	100	100

SOURCE: John R. Petrocik, "Issues and Agendas: Electoral Coalitions in the 1988
Election" (Paper presented at the annual meeting of the American Political Science
Association, Atlanta, August 31–September 3, 1989).

ple in professional, business, and managerial occupations have tilted
toward the Republicans. In general, as income, level of education,
and occupational status rise, the tendency to support Republicans
increases (see Table 6.4). But these general tendencies should not obscure the fact that both parties receive significant support from the
other party's core support groups—for example, in the 1988 presidential election Democrats received 40 percent of the vote of professional and managerial personnel, and Republicans received 42
percent of the union household vote.

Religion traditionally has provided a basis for partisan alignments
in the United States. Since the New Deal era of the 1930s, Catholics

Table 6.4 Voting Patterns of Socioeconomic Groups, 1988 Presidential Election

	% of Vote by Party		Rep./Dem. Advantage (%)
	Dem.	Rep.	
Age			
18–29	47	52	+ 5 R
30–44	45	54	+ 9 R
45–59	42	57	+15 R
60+	49	50	+ 1 R
Sex			
Men	41	57	+16 R
Women	49	50	+ 1 R
Occupation			
Professional/ management	40	59	+19 R
White collar	42	57	+15 R
Blue collar	50	49	+ 1 D
Union household	57	42	+15 D
Ethnicity/race			
White	40	59	+19 R
Black	86	12	+74 D
Hispanic	69	30	+39 D
German/Austrian[a]	40	60	+20 R
English/Scotch/Irish[a]	37	63	+26 R
Italian[a]	49	51	+ 2 R
Scandinavian[a]	47	53	+ 6 R
Asian[b]	39	52	+13 R
Religion			
Protestant[c]	40	60	+20 R
Catholic	47	52	+ 5 R
Jewish	64	35	+29 D
White evangelical or fundamentalist Christian	18	81	+63 R
Income			
Under $12,500	62	37	+25 D
$12,500–24,999	50	49	+ 1 D
$25,000–34,999	44	56	+12 R
$35,000–49,999	42	56	+14 R
$50,000–100,000	38	61	+23 R
$100,000+	33	65	+32 R
Education			
Less than high school	56	43	+13 D
High school graduate	50	49	+ 1 D
Some college	42	57	+15 R
College graduate	37	62	+25 R
Postgraduate	48	50	+ 2 R

SOURCE: *New York Times*/CBS poll, *New York Times*, Nov. 10, 1988, 18Y, National edition. Copyright © 1988 by The New York Times Company. Reprinted by permission.
[a]ABC News/*Washington Post* exit poll, reported in *Public Opinion*, January/February 1989, 32.
[b]*Los Angeles Times* exit poll, reported in *Public Opinion*, January/February 1989, 32.
[c]*New York Times*/CBS exit poll, reported in *Public Opinion*, January/February 1989, 30.

and Jews (overwhelmingly) have tended to be Democrats and white Protestants have tended to be Republicans. (Among Catholics, the tendency to vote Democratic declined in the 1980s, with the Republicans gaining a plurality among these voters. And, unlike other social groups, Jews tend to vote Democratic regardless of their socioeconomic status.) Moreover, an increasingly significant component of the GOP since 1980 has been white fundamentalists or evangelical Christians, who voted 81 percent Republican in 1988.

The influences of race and ethnicity on partisan choices are fairly clear-cut as well. Although from the post-Civil War era until the 1930s blacks supported Republicans as the party of emancipation, they have been overwhelmingly Democratic in recent decades (averaging 87 percent in the 1980s). The shift to the Democrats began during the depression of the 1930s and was accelerated by the 1964 election campaign, during which the Republican presidential nominee, Sen. Barry Goldwater (Ariz.), opposed major civil rights legislation proposed by President Lyndon Johnson. Hispanic voters have a definite but less pronounced tendency to support the Democratic party. Cuban-Americans, however, many of whom have achieved economic prosperity and are adamantly anticommunist, show strong pro-Republican tendencies. Asian-Americans are a smaller, but rapidly expanding, element of the population. The politically active among the new Asian immigrants have tended to be disproportionally drawn from professional and educated classes; they voted 52 percent Republican in 1988.[23] Interestingly, as blacks, Hispanics, and Asians are emerging as critically important voter groups of the 1990s, the political influence of European ethnic groups is declining. As such groups have been assimilated into American society, their voting patterns have become less distinct.

Until the 1980s, gender was not a basis for political divisions in the United States. In the 1980, 1984, and 1988 presidential elections, however, more men voted Republican than women. Indeed, according to a *New York Times*/CBS poll, in 1988 a 15-percentage-point "gender gap" surfaced, with men favoring George Bush over Michael Dukakis by 16 percentage points and women favoring Bush by only 1 percentage point (Table 6.4). Much of the publicity surrounding the so-called gender gap has focused on the tendency of the Democrats to embrace the policies advocated by organized fem-

23. *Los Angeles Times* exit poll, reported in *Public Opinion*, January/February 1989, 32.

inists. Survey research, however, indicates that economic and defense issues are causing the electoral divisions between men and women.[24]

Nonprogrammatic Policy Orientation

Although American political parties have an interest in influencing government policy, they are not highly programmatic in their orientation. Unlike European labor and socialist parties, their approach to policy is not guided by a social theory to which the party is expected to adhere. American party positions on issues tend to be adopted to meet immediate problems or electoral circumstances and are not based on achieving long-range goals. Neither major party has a clear image of the type of society it wishes to foster, and neither is committed to either unfettered capitalism or socialism.

Their broad-based electoral coalitions, moreover, make it difficult for political parties to adopt highly ideological and consistent policy positions. They must appeal to both labor and management, farmers and consumers, central city and suburban dwellers, Catholics and Protestants, homeowners and renters, whites, Hispanics, blacks, and Asians. Even if their diverse followings permitted a strongly ideological approach to politics, political parties would find it difficult to achieve the internal unity needed to enact their programs because of their decentralized character.

Although their nonprogrammatic approach to public policy makes them moderate or centrist rather than doctrinaire extremists of the Left or Right, the Republican and Democratic parties differ significantly in their policy orientations. Republicans, for example, tend to be less supportive of economic planning, redistribution of wealth, and social welfare benefits than Democrats (see Table 6.5 for a comparison of the 1988 party platforms).

Party Organization

The primary task of party organizations is winning elections. Parties are, therefore, organized around geographic election districts, beginning with the local unit of election administration (called a precinct in most states) and ascending through city/village/town committees, county committees, legislative district committees, congressional district committees, state central committees, and the national committee. The relationship of one level of committee to another is not hierarchical; higher-level committees do not have con-

24. Arthur H. Miller, "The Emerging Gender Gap in American Elections," *Election Politics* 1 (Winter 1983–1984): 7–12.

Table 6.5 Comparison of Selected Policies in the Republican and Democratic Party Platforms, 1988

Policy	Republican Party	Democratic Party
Health care	Reduce the government's role and preserve voluntary institutions.	Institute national health insurance program with coordination and leadership.
Abortion	Support human life amendment and oppose public funding of abortions.	Guarantee right of reproductive choice regardless of ability to pay.
Minimum wage	Oppose raising minimum wage as inflationary and job-destroying.	Favor indexing minimum wage to lift families out of poverty.
Taxes and budget	Oppose any attempts to increase taxes and support balanced budget amendment.	Have America reinvest in its people and significantly increase funding for education.
Strategic Defense Initiative	Commit to rapid and certain deployment.	Ban space weapons in their entirety.

trol over those at a lower level. Rather, the party organizational structure is a series of layers (see Figure 6.2).[25] Each layer concentrates on the election campaign in its jurisdiction but also may cooperate in campaigns at a higher level, such as those for governor or president. Each stratum of the party is more or less autonomous in its operations. A midwestern Republican state party chairman captured the essence of party organization when he described his relationship with the county party chairmen: "At best we are a loose confederation. I have no jurisdiction over county chairmen. I'd have resented a state chairman telling me what to do when I was county chairman."[26]

National Party Organizations

The national party organizations reflect the decentralized character of American parties. The Republican and Democratic national organizations both consist of a series of largely autonomous orga-

25. See Eldersveld, *Political Parties in American Society,* 133–136.
26. Interview conducted by the author as part of a National Science Foundation-funded study of state parties.

nizations: the national committee, the congressional campaign committee, and the senatorial campaign committee. Each committee has a separate membership and specific set of elections on which it concentrates its activities.

National Committees. The highest governing authorities of the two major parties are their national conventions, which meet every four years to nominate presidential candidates. During the long intervals between conventions, the national affairs of the parties are managed by their national committees: the Republican National Committee (RNC) and the Democratic National Committee (DNC).

Each national committee is composed of representatives of state party organizations, as well as representatives of various voter groups and such elected officials as members of Congress, state legislators, and governors. Because the national committees are large bodies (the RNC has 162 members, and the DNC has a variable roster of slightly over 400 members) which meet only a few times per year, the real work of the committees is carried out by their national chairmen and headquarters staff.

The national chairman is formally elected by the national committee. For the party of the president (the "in-party"), however, the president actually makes the selection. Thus in 1989, President Bush designated his campaign manager, Lee Atwater, to be RNC chairman. When a later-fatal illness forced Atwater to relinquish the post, the president picked his secretary of agriculture, Clayton Yeutter, as Atwater's successor, and in January 1991 the RNC formally ratified Bush's choice. In-party chairmen normally operate in strict accordance with White House directives and have little freedom of action. "Out-party" leaders are normally chosen in contested elections as various party factions seek to gain control of the national committee. Because they are not beholden to the White House, out-party chairmen have more leeway and can have much more impact than in-party leaders on their party's image and level of organizational activity.

National committees arrange for and manage national conventions, raise funds, carry out research, provide financial and technical assistance to state parties and candidates, and conduct polling and public relations. Through their highly successful direct-mail programs for soliciting small contributions and their efforts to gain large contributions, the national committees have been able to raise huge campaign war chests. In the 1987–1988 election cycle, for example, the RNC reported receipts of $91 million and the DNC receipts of $53.3 million.

The superior fund-raising capacity of the RNC has meant that it

Figure 6.2: How Political Parties Are Organized

National committee

State committees

Congressional district and state legislative district committees

County committees (townships in Northeast; parishes in Louisiana; districts in Alaska)

Rural areas Town, village rural township committees

Urban areas City committee

Ward committee

Precinct leaders

Source: John F. Bibby, *Politics, Parties, and Elections in America* (Chicago: Nelson-Hall, 1987), 83.

is a much more important campaign resource for assisting GOP candidates and state parties than is the DNC for its candidates and state affiliates. Under the leadership of chairs Paul Kirk (1985–1989) and Ronald Brown (1989–), the DNC significantly expanded its services to candidates and state parties, but it still lags well behind the RNC.[27]

Senatorial and Congressional Campaign Committees. The Republican and Democratic senatorial and congressional campaign committees are composed of incumbent senators and representatives whose function is to elect fellow partisans to Congress. Each committee has a professional staff that recruits candidates, raises campaign funds, and provides technical assistance to candidates. Like the national committees, the Republican congressional and senatorial committees have greater fund-raising capacities than their Democratic counterparts. In the 1987–1988 election cycle, these Republican committees raised $100 million and the Democratic committees raised $29 million.[28]

In addition to their role in supporting congressional and senatorial candidates, these committees make large-scale transfers of funds to state and local parties. These funds are used for party building and get-out-the-vote activities that indirectly assist candidates vying for seats on Capitol Hill.

State Committees

Each state has a Republican and Democratic state central committee. Membership is determined by state law and party rules. Committee members frequently represent congressional districts, legislative districts, or counties, as well as such auxiliary groups as the Young Democrats or the Federation of Republican Women. The size of central committees varies from approximately twenty in Iowa to over a thousand in California. Because of the size and periodic meeting schedules of these committees, their leadership normally falls to the state's party chairs and the headquarters staffs.

In the decades before the 1960s, state parties commonly had neither a permanent headquarters nor a paid, full-time staff. Over the past two decades, however, state parties have operated out of permanent headquarters, and their professional staffs have dealt with

27. Reichley, "The Rise of National Parties"; Larry J. Sabato, *The Party's Just Begun: Shaping Political Parties for America's Future* (Glenview, Ill.: Scott, Foresman, 1988), chap. 3; and James Barnes, "Reinventing the RNC," *National Journal,* January 14, 1989, 67–71.
28. Federal Election Commission data.

fund-raising, research, public relations, and the provision of technical assistance to candidates and local party organizations. Just as Republican national party organizations are stronger than their Democratic counterparts, Republican state organizations tend to be stronger than Democratic state parties.[29] For example, the Florida state Republican organization operates a high-tech headquarters crammed with computer hardware, telephone banks, and printing facilities and in 1988 had a budget of $6 million.[30]

Counterparts of the senatorial and congressional campaign committees exist at the state level. State legislative campaign committees, composed of incumbent legislators who provide support to their parties' candidates, have become increasingly important in state politics. Indeed, in some states they are a more significant source of support for legislative candidates than the regular state central committees.

County and Local Committees

When people think of local party organizations, they often envision a traditional urban machine such as that of the late mayor Richard Daley of Chicago. By dispensing 35,000 patronage jobs and other government favors to its supporters, Daley's Democratic machine maintained a hierarchically organized network of ward and precinct captains capable of mobilizing voters on election day. But such organizations are fast fading from the political landscape and are far from typical.[31]

Most county and local party organizations operate without a headquarters, using volunteer leaders and workers. Their activities are highly cyclical and concentrated during campaign periods. While normally short-handed, underfunded, and hardly models of professionalism or efficiency, local parties do manage to carry off many kinds of campaign activities—distributing campaign literature, raising funds, and getting out the vote.[32]

29. For a detailed consideration of state party organizations, see Cornelius P. Cotter, et al., *Party Organizations in American Politics* (New York: Praeger, 1984). Also see John F. Bibby, "Party Organization at the State Level," in *The Parties Respond: Changes in the American Party System,* ed. L. Sandy Maisel (Boulder, Colo.: Westview Press, 1990), 21–39.

30. Barnes, "Reinventing the RNC," 70; and Sabato, *Party's Just Begun,* 90.

31. For a discussion of the decline of the Chicago Democratic organization and other urban machines, see Sorauf and Beck, *Party Politics in America,* 83–91.

32. The organizational status of local parties is analyzed utilizing a national survey in James L. Gibson, et al., "Whither the Local Parties," *American Journal of Political Science* 29 (February 1985): 139–160; and James L. Gibson, John P. Frendries, and Laura L. Vertz, "Party Dynamics in the 1980s: Change in County Party Organizational Strength, 1980–1984," *American Journal of Political Science* 33 (February 1989): 67–90.

Nominations for
Congressional and
State Offices

On election day, a voter essentially chooses between Republican and Democratic candidates because, as we saw earlier, only the nominees of the two major parties have a realistic chance of being elected. The functioning of American democracy is, then, dramatically affected by the Republicans' and Democrats' nominating decisions.

The Rise of the Direct Primary

In most Western democracies, nominations are the responsibility of the party organizations; the ordinary voters play no role in the process. The American practice is quite different. Candidates for congressional and state offices are nominated via a *direct primary* in which the voters pick the nominees who will represent each party.[33]

In the nineteenth century, nominations were made by each party organization meeting in a **caucus** or convention. These procedures fell into disrepute early in this century, however, because of allegations of corrupt boss rule, and the direct primary spread across the country as a reform designed to give ordinary voters a voice in choosing party nominees. An additional reason for introducing the direct primary was the absence of real interparty competition after the 1890s in the solidly Democratic South and in GOP-dominated areas of the North. Primary elections provided a way for the voters to participate in the electoral choice that in one-party areas was most important—the selection of the dominant party's candidate.

Types of Direct Primaries

Because each state regulates by statute how primaries will be conducted for congressional and state candidates, primaries operate quite differently in each state. Most states utilize a form of **closed primary**, which restricts participation in primaries to people who either register as party affiliates or declare publicly the party primary in which they wish to participate. Advocates of a mandatory public declaration of party preference before voting in a primary believe that party nominations should be made by party adherents and that the process should not be contaminated by people who are either members of the opposition party or independents.

33. On the development of the direct primary and its consequences, see Key, *Politics, Parties, and Pressure Groups*, chap. 14; and Epstein, *Political Parties in the American Mold*, chap. 6.

A minority of the states choose their candidates without requiring public declarations of party preference. In the nine states using an **open primary** procedure, voters decide in the secrecy of the polling booth in which party's primary they wish to vote. They may vote in only one party's primary, but the party primary in which they voted is secret. The open primary permits wider participation in the nominating process. Its critics argue that it also encourages **cross-over voting**—voting in the primary of the party to which the voter does not belong. In open primary states, voters tend to participate in the party primary that has the hottest contests.

Alaska and Washington operate a wide-open primary—a **blanket primary**—which permits citizens to vote in more than one party's primary by switching back and forth between parties from office to office, provided they vote for only one candidate per office.

Under Louisiana's unique *"nonpartisan" primary,* all candidates for each office, regardless of party affiliation, are listed on the primary ballot. If a candidate receives a majority of the vote, that candidate is automatically elected. If no candidate receives a majority, the top two finishers run against each other in the general election.

In most states, the candidate who receives the most votes (a plurality) wins the primary and is given a place on the general election ballot. In nine of the southern and border states, however, a candidate is required to win a majority of the primary vote to qualify as the party nominee on the general election ballot. If no candidate receives a majority of the votes in the primary, a **runoff primary** is held between the top two finishers. This practice developed in the South earlier in this century when there was no meaningful Republican competition in the general election. Winning the Democratic primary, therefore, was the equivalent of being elected.

*Consequences of
the Direct Primary*

Weakened party organizational control over nominations was the intended consequence of the direct primary, and it succeeded. Party organizations rarely have sufficient influence to control the outcome of primary elections. They often recruit candidates for primaries, discourage others from running, and provide support for preferred candidates, but ultimately it is the primary voters who pick party nominees. Without control over nominations, parties lack the power to discipline maverick officeholders by denying them a nomination and a place on the general election ballot.

The reformers who urged adoption of the direct primary also envisaged high levels of voter turnout in primary elections, but low voter turnout has been the reality. In northern states, only about 30 percent of the eligible electorate participates in primaries. Participation has been higher in the South because its one-party Democratic traditions made the Democratic primary the real election in the region. But as Republican electoral strength has grown and made many general elections real interparty contests, primary turnout as a proportion of the general election vote has fallen.[34]

The sponsors of the direct primary expected as well substantial competition in such contests, but the advantages that incumbents carry into campaigns tend to discourage serious opposition in the primaries. As a result, for most incumbents the primary is like the common cold—a nuisance but unlikely to be fatal. Over 90 percent of all incumbent governors, senators, and representatives gain renomination. When no incumbent is seeking renomination—an open seat—there is frequently a hotly contested primary, especially in the party with the best prospects for winning the general election.

Presidential Nominations

Presidential nominees of the Republican and Democratic parties are formally nominated by national conventions held in the summers of presidential election years. These conventions, which are the culmination of a long season of campaigning, are composed of delegates representing the fifty states, the District of Columbia, Puerto Rico, and the territories.

Methods of Delegate Selection

National convention delegates are chosen within each state under procedures spelled out in state laws or state party rules. Because each state legislature or party organization devises its own delegate selection procedures, the exact procedures of the states vary widely. But in cases in which statutes or party rules violate national party rules, the national party reigns supreme and the national convention may refuse to seat the offending state's delegation.

The national Democratic party has been particularly active in developing, revising, and vigorously enforcing its complicated delegate rules. As a result, it has come into periodic conflict with state party organizations whose delegate selection procedures were found to be in violation of national party rules. The most prominent case in-

34. Larry J. Sabato, *Goodbye to Goodtime Charlie: The American Governorship Transformed,* 2d ed. (Washington, D.C.: CQ Press, 1983), 124.

volved Wisconsin's use of an open presidential primary to select its delegates—a procedure contrary to a national Democratic rule banning this type of presidential primary. Strict enforcement of this rule meant that Democrats in Wisconsin—which had the oldest presidential primary law in the nation (enacted in 1903)—were forced in 1984 to abandon their traditional open presidential primary and use a system of party caucuses to select convention delegates. For the 1988 national convention, the national party sought to reduce the intraparty conflict created by this situation and granted Wisconsin an exemption from the ban on open primaries. The national Republican party's delegate selection rules are much more lenient than those of the Democrats and give the state parties wide latitude in devising delegate selection procedures.[35]

Three principal methods of selecting national convention delegates are used (Figure 6.3). They are (1) the presidential primary, (2) state party caucuses and conventions, and (3) for the Democrats only, automatic selection based on an individual's holding a party or elected office.

Presidential Primaries. A **presidential primary** is an election in which the voters of a state have the opportunity to cast a ballot in favor of a preferred candidate for their party's presidential nomination or for delegates pledged to support that candidate. In 1988, three-fourths of the Republican delegates and two-thirds of the Democratic delegates were chosen through presidential primaries (Table 6.6). It is therefore essential that presidential contenders contest virtually all of the primaries.

Presidential primaries have an importance that extends beyond the number of delegates at stake. Primary outcomes reveal to party leaders, the media, and the public a candidate's popularity, electability, and campaign momentum. Thus, it is particularly important that candidates do well in the early primaries—most notably in New Hampshire's first-in-the-nation primary and on "Super Tuesday" three weeks later when most southern states and several northern and western states hold their primaries and caucuses.

But to do well in the presidential primaries, held from February to June in presidential election years, and to compete ably for a majority of the national convention delegates at stake, candidates must

35. For a thoroughgoing analysis of delegate selection procedures and their impact on national conventions, see Byron E. Shafer, *Bifurcated Politics: Evolution and Reform in the National Party Convention* (Cambridge, Mass.: Harvard University Press, 1988).

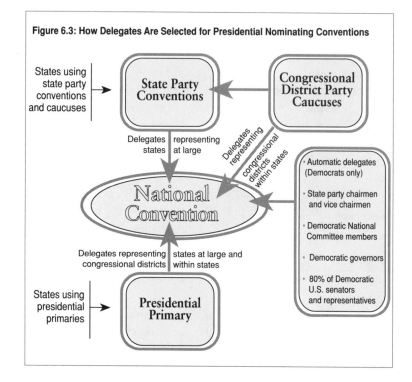

Figure 6.3: How Delegates Are Selected for Presidential Nominating Conventions

be extremely well organized on a nationwide basis and well financed. It is not surprising, then, that Republican George Bush and Democrat Michael Dukakis, the candidates who had both the strongest organizations and superior financing, succeeded in winning their parties' nominations in 1988.[36]

State Party Caucuses and Conventions. In states using the caucus and convention system of delegate selection, the process normally starts with party meetings at the local level (for example, at the precinct or county level). These local meetings select people to represent the local party at congressional district caucuses and state conventions. Individuals attending the congressional district caucuses select delegates to represent their congressional districts at the national convention; the state convention selects national convention delegates to represent the state at large.

This progression of party meetings involves a relatively small proportion of the electorate. Those attending party caucuses tend to be

36. See the discussion of Bush's organizational and financial advantages over his principal rival, Sen. Robert Dole, in E. J. Dionne, "Bush vs. Dole: Behind the Turnaround," *New York Times,* March 17, 1988, 13Y, National edition.

Table 6.6 Presidential Primary Results, 1988

	No. of Primaries on Ballot	No. of Primaries Won	Total Vote	%	Best Showing (%)
Democrats					
Michael Dukakis (Mass.)	36	22	9,848,579	42.4	W.Va. (78.9)
Jesse Jackson (Ill.)	36	7	6,769,019	29.1	D.C. (80)
Albert Gore, Jr. (Tenn.)	35	5	3,182,669	13.7	Tenn. (72.3)
Richard Gephardt (Mo.)	30	2	1,392,510	6.0	Mo. (57.8)
Paul Simon (Ill.)	35	1	1,082,059	4.7	Ill. (42.3)
Gary Hart (Colo.)	27	0	405,902	1.8	Puerto Rico (7.5)
"Uncommitted"	20	0	235,435	1.0	Ark. (7.1)
Bruce Babbitt (Ariz.)	23	0	89,472	0.4	N.H. (4.6)
Others	—	0	224,880	0.7	—
Total vote			23,230,525		
Republicans					
George Bush (Texas)	37	37	8,219,059	67.9	Puerto Rico (97.1)
Robert Dole (Kan.)	33	1	2,312,058	19.1	S.D. (55.2)
Pat Robertson (Va.)	34	0	1,095,233	9.1	Okla. (21.1)
Jack Kemp (N.Y.)	25	0	327,513	2.7	N.H. (12.8)
"Uncommitted"	15	0	56,788	0.5	Idaho (10.2)
Pierre du Pont, IV (Del.)	22	0	49,766	0.4	N.H. (10.1)
Alexander Haig, Jr. (Va.)	23	0	26,964	0.2	N.M. (2.4)
Others	—	0	14,786	0.1	—
Total vote			12,102,167		

SOURCE: *Congressional Quarterly Weekly Report,* July 9, 1989, 1892.

party activists and enthusiastic supporters of the presidential candidates. Thus, the candidates who do best in the caucus states are those who have strong organizations capable of mobilizing supporters to attend the meetings (Bush for the Republicans and Dukakis for the Democrats in 1988), and who instill passionate support among their loyalists (Jesse Jackson for the Democrats and Pat Robertson for the Republicans in 1988).[37]

Automatic Delegates. In an effort to achieve higher levels of involvement by their elected and party officials, the Democrats began in 1984 to give these leaders **automatic delegate** status. In 1988, the 645 so-called super-delegates included 80 percent of the Democratic

37. Rhodes Cook and Dave Kaplan, "In 1988, Caucuses Have Been the Place for Political Passion," *Congressional Quarterly Weekly Report,* June 4, 1988, 1523–1527.

The Reverend Jesse Jackson joins hands with members of his family after finishing second to Gov. Michael Dukakis in the 1988 New York Democratic presidential primary. A strong showing in this delegate-rich primary enabled him to stay in the race for the nomination.

members of the Senate and House, Democratic governors, members of the Democratic National Committee, and the state party chairmen and vice chairmen. By giving overwhelming support to Michael Dukakis, the automatic delegates were an important source of his victory margin over Jesse Jackson. The Republicans do not have any automatic delegates. Republican party and elected officials must be selected through the normal primary or caucus processes.

Stages in the Nominating Process

Gaining a major party nomination is often an almost full-time, four-year undertaking. Because it is such an all-consuming activity, it is difficult for politicians having major government responsibilities to enter the contest. Aside from incumbents, the major contestants for presidential nominations have either been out of office—former governor Jimmy Carter in 1976, former governor Ronald Reagan in 1980, former vice president Walter Mondale in 1984, and Jesse Jackson in 1984 and 1988—or elected officials with sufficiently limited leadership responsibilities to permit full-time campaigning—Sen. Gary Hart (D-Colo.) in 1984 and Sen. Albert Gore (D-Tenn.), Sen. Paul Simon (D-Ill.), Rep. Richard Gephardt (D-Mo.), Rep. Jack Kemp (R-N.Y.), and Vice President George Bush in 1988. Kansas senator Robert Dole, the Republican minority leader, and Governor Dukakis of Massachusetts were exceptions in 1988. The marathon struggle that such contestants must confront for the nomination can be divided into a series of stages.[38]

38. A summary of 1988 presidential nominating politics is found in Michael Nel-

Stage One: Building a Base of Support and Entering Preliminary Contests. The planning and preparation for a nomination campaign normally begin shortly after a presidential election with the recruitment of an experienced campaign staff. Candidates also customarily create political action committees (PACs) and tax-exempt foundations to help fund their preliminary campaign activities.[39] These activities include crisscrossing the nation to speak to state party meetings, congressional candidate fund-raisers, trade associations, unions, and college groups. Because Iowa and New Hampshire (as well as Michigan for the Republicans) hold the earliest delegate selection events, the itineraries of the candidates normally include a concentration of stopovers in these states. Well-publicized trips abroad to confer with foreign leaders are yet another standard part of the process of becoming a nationally known leader.

In the year of the midterm congressional and state elections (for example, 1986, 1990), the pace of campaigning normally picks up. The candidates blanket the country to appear at events in support of their party's congressional and state candidates and in the process to gain the backing of key party leaders and elected officials.

Following the midterm elections, the candidates begin to enlarge and perfect their campaign staffs and to concentrate their campaign efforts on the states holding early primaries and caucuses. These also are days of candidate testing as the national media begin to pay closer attention to the activities, issue positions, backgrounds, and personalities of the candidates. Revelations of past indiscretions or recent errors in judgment can damage a campaign beyond repair as the news media have become increasingly aggressive in investigating the private lives of candidates. Gary Hart, the early Democratic front-runner in the 1988 race, saw his nomination drive collapse within a month of its formal opening when revelations of his extramarital adventures with an attractive model on a yacht named *Monkey Business* created a storm of publicity.

In the year before the national conventions, the candidates are brought into face-to-face contests during candidate debates and straw polls conducted at state party gatherings. In 1988, there was a proliferation of candidate debates in which Republican opponents

son, ed., *The Elections of 1988* (Washington, D.C.: CQ Press, 1989), chap. 2. For a more complete description of the stages in the presidential nomination process, see John F. Bibby, *Politics, Parties, and Elections in America* (Chicago: Nelson-Hall, 1987), chap. 6.

39. For an example of the use of presidential candidate political action committees, see Dan Morgan, "PACs Stretching Election Law Limits," *Washington Post*, Feb. 5, 1988, A1, A10.

of George Bush sought to undermine his front-runner status, and seven Democratic candidates tried to establish themselves as serious contenders for the nomination. As for the straw polls, a good showing is extremely important in the early stages of a campaign because strong poll results encourage financial contributions and help in recruiting campaign workers.

Stage Two: Competing in Early Primaries and Caucuses. The early events in the delegate selection process have a significance that goes well beyond the number of convention delegates at stake. The Iowa caucuses, New Hampshire primary, and Super Tuesday primaries and caucuses follow one another in quick succession in February and March of presidential election years. By weeding out the weaker candidates, these events narrow the field of candidates. The early contests also provide the more successful candidates with campaign momentum—standing in the polls, campaign contributions, and volunteer workers—which help them sustain their campaigns during the long grind of primaries and caucuses that stretch from February to June. In 1988, for example, Vice President Bush's successive victories in New Hampshire and in the Super Tuesday primaries and caucuses mortally wounded the candidacy of his chief rival, Sen. Robert Dole, and allowed him to coast to victory in most of the remaining primaries and caucuses.

Although in 1988 the early primaries and caucuses narrowed the field of Democrats, the initial delegate selection events were less decisive than was the case for the Republicans. Because none of the Democratic candidates except Jesse Jackson were well known nationally, the early primaries were indecisive. Three candidates registered impressive primary showings and emerged as serious contenders after Super Tuesday: Governor Dukakis by virtue of his wins in New Hampshire, Florida, and Texas; Sen. Albert Gore for his strong showing in southern states on Super Tuesday; and Jackson by virtue of his victories on Super Tuesday in the South and his base of support among minority voters.

Throughout the primary season, but especially during the early primaries, the news media play an important role in interpreting the meaning of primary outcomes. The media determine winners and losers—which candidates made strong or stronger-than-expected showings and which candidates did less well than expected. After Bush's weak third-place showing behind Senator Dole and evangelist Pat Robertson in the Iowa caucuses of 1988, campaign momentum was on Dole's side and the news media were preparing Bush's political obituary. Bush's come-from-behind victory in the New Hampshire primary, however, reestablished his credibility as a candidate. At the same time, Dole's defeat and Robertson's weak showing were seen as severe blows to their chances of gaining the GOP nomination.

Stage Three: Competing in Later Primaries and Caucuses. After the mid-March primaries and caucuses, the serious contenders left in the race try to sustain their early momentum and win the maximum number of delegates. In the later primaries and caucuses, the front-runner does not have to win all or even most of the contests, but he or she must continue to gain a significant share of the delegates being contested. Jimmy Carter in 1976 and Walter Mondale in 1984, for example, failed to win a majority in the later primaries, but their strong showings in the early primaries and their abilities to win a significant portion of the delegates in the later primaries, even in states they did not carry, enabled them to gather a majority of the convention delegates.

In the 1988 Republican contest, George Bush administered the final blow to the Dole candidacy by defeating the Kansas senator in the Illinois primary on March 15. Governor Dukakis did not come out on top in the Democratic race until later in the primary season when he won April primaries in Wisconsin, New York, and Pennsylvania.

Because candidates' organizations run slates of candidates for delegate positions in both the primary and caucus states and amass pledges of support from delegates as they are chosen, it is usually apparent before the end of the primary and caucus season in June which candidate will have sufficient delegate strength to be the nominee of the national convention. It was, therefore, certain in the weeks before the 1988 Republican and Democratic conventions that George Bush and Michael Dukakis would be the nominees of their respective parties (a summary of 1988 presidential primary results is provided in Table 6.6).

Stage Four: Confirming the Nomination at the National Convention. National conventions are not deliberative bodies whose delegates carefully weigh the merits of various candidates before casting their votes on the presidential nomination roll call.[40] To the contrary, the vast majority of the delegates have already announced and pledged their support to a candidate. It is their function to ratify and legitimize the decisions that have been made in the presidential primaries and caucuses across the nation. As for its other duties, the convention adopts the party platform and makes rules governing party operations for the next four years.

40. On the role of the modern-day convention, see Shafer, *Bifurcated Politics.*

The principal significance of the national convention is that it kicks off the presidential election campaign. It is an opportunity for the party to showcase its presidential nominee while it has the attention of the television networks and to establish campaign themes for the fall campaign. As David Broder, respected *Washington Post* political reporter, has commented:

Convention week is important, not because it marks the end of the nominating period, but because it is the start of the general election. It is the time when most voters take their first serious look at the candidates and their parties and begin to focus on the choice they will make in November.[41]

Conventions also are places for working out the compromises that will unify the party for the upcoming campaign. The winning faction can make concessions to the losers on key provisions in the platform, on party rules, and on the personnel who will run the campaign. In 1988, the Dukakis organization made concessions to Jesse Jackson in each of these areas in an effort to enlist his enthusiastic support of Dukakis in the general election.

Particularly important for party unity is the selection of a vice-presidential nominee. Presidential nominees usually select their vice-presidential running mates from a faction of the party different than their own. Such choices are aimed at unifying the party for the campaign and adding vote-getting appeal to the ticket. In 1988, for example, Governor Dukakis picked Sen. Lloyd Bentsen (D-Texas), prominent member of the moderate wing of the Democratic party, to be his vice-presidential candidate. George Bush's surprising selection of youthful senator Dan Quayle (R-Ind.) was done with an eye toward reassuring conservative activists and appealing to younger voters.

Although the outcome of convention nomination contests are normally known well in advance of the event, conventions are seldom dull affairs. The front-running candidates usually continue to court the delegates to ensure their eventual nomination. The underdog candidates frequently seek test votes on issues that, on the surface, appear to be matters of fairness or ideology rather than contests between the candidates for the nomination. Such issues include convention rules, platform planks, and the seating of delegates whose status is being challenged on legal grounds. The underdog candidates hope to use such issues to cast doubt on the strength of the front-runner and to demonstrate their own support among the delegates.

41. David Broder, "A Chance to Be 'Presidential,'" *Washington Post*, July 15, 1984, A8.

An example of this strategy occurred at the 1980 Democratic convention when Sen. Edward Kennedy (D-Mass.) was seeking to derail President Jimmy Carter's bid for renomination. The Kennedy forces sought a rules change that would have freed delegates from their pledges of candidate support made at the time they were selected, enabling them to vote for whomever they chose on the nomination roll call. When Carter handily defeated this Kennedy tactic, it was clear to all that Carter would be renominated, and Kennedy withdrew from the contest. These fights over rules, the platform, and delegate seating (credentials) are the most crucial events of a convention. Their outcomes foreshadow who will win the convention's nomination.

Financing Presidential Nomination Campaigns

The disclosures of campaign finance irregularities made during the Watergate investigations of the Nixon presidency culminated in passage of major reform legislation, the Federal Election Campaign Act (FECA) amendments of 1974. This law has dramatically changed the financing of presidential nomination campaigns so that it is no longer possible to fund such campaigns by relying on a few large contributors or "fat cats." Strict contribution limits have been imposed: $1,000 for individuals and $5,000 for political action committees. Candidates must raise funds through broad-based efforts that rely upon small and medium-sized contributions.

One of FECA's most significant innovations is a provision making it possible for major party candidates to receive **federal matching funds**. Under this system, the Federal Election Commission (FEC) will match private contributions in amounts up to $250 with federal funds. To be eligible for federal matching funds, candidates must raise at least $5,000 through individual contributions (not to exceed $250 each) in each of at least twenty states; abide by a nationwide spending limit which is adjusted before each presidential campaign for inflation (in 1988, the limit was $23 million); abide by individual state spending limits based on a formula of 16 cents plus an inflation factor per eligible voter; and disclose all contributions and expenditures of $200 or more.

The FECA reforms have not made money less important in presidential nominations than it was before 1974, but the rules of the game for raising it are now different. Without adequate private contributions to generate matching funds, campaigns can quickly run out of gas and stall as Jack Kemp, Richard Gephardt, Paul Simon, and Gov. Bruce Babbitt of Arizona discovered in 1988.

An additional consequence of FECA has been a requirement that candidates impose tightfisted budgetary control over their campaigns in every state. Indeed, every campaign organization must comply with a national spending limit as well as with individual state spending limits. The task of staying within the law is complicated by three factors: (1) the total of all state spending limits is less than the national spending ceiling; (2) the state spending limits do not take into account whether a state chooses its delegates by primary or by caucus (primary campaigns are much more expensive); and (3) state spending limits are based on the number of eligible voters in the state and not on the state's strategic importance (the spending limit for New Hampshire's first-in-the-nation primary is the same as that for Guam's caucus!). Presidential nomination campaigns are, therefore, characterized by centralized control exercised by the candidates' national headquarters.

American Political Parties: Unrivaled Record of Durability

American political parties, while sharing many characteristics with the parties found in other Western democracies, are still quite distinct. They tend to be weaker organizationally and to have less influence over party nominations because of the direct primary. Not based on a mass dues-paying membership, American parties also show a distinct lack of internal unity, and they have a nonprogrammatic or nonpolicy-oriented approach to politics.

Despite the handicaps under which they have been forced to operate, American parties have demonstrated an unrivaled record of durability. Indeed, the same two parties have dominated electoral politics since 1856. Among the handicaps the Republican and Democratic parties have surmounted are the Constitution's provisions for separation of power and federalism which fragment the parties, such reforms as the direct primary, and hostile public attitudes toward parties and party leaders. Yet through a civil war, depressions, world wars, waves of immigration, scandals, and technological and social change, the parties have survived. They have melded diverse elements of society into their ranks and sought to compromise and reconcile their differences, achieving a remarkable record of durability and adaptability. Indeed, it was only a decade ago that some scholars and commentaries were lamenting the passing of parties as viable participants in the political process. As this chapter has demonstrated, however, the uniquely American style of political party is still very much alive and is showing at the national level unprecedented strength as a fund-raising and campaign support agency.

Parties also help citizens exercise indirect control over their government. In the American system, candidates for major national and state offices—incumbents and challengers—must wear party labels. This simplifies the voter's choice. These labels also make it possible for voters to force some accountability on elected officials. The party in control of the government—especially the executive branch—is usually held accountable for the state of the Union during its tenure in office. And because public officials like to keep their jobs and parties want to control the White House and Congress, both have an incentive to deal with and even anticipate societal problems. They do this out of fear that the voters will throw them out if domestic and foreign conditions deteriorate, as well as in the hope they will be rewarded by the voters for their successes in office.

Parties, of course, are not a perfect mechanism for ensuring public accountability by elected officials. They are, however, the most broadly based institution found in democracies for mobilizing voters and for replacing the "ins" with the "outs" in a peaceful manner.

For Review

1. Parties are complex social structures composed of the party in the electorate, the party organization, and the party in the government. They developed in the United States as suffrage was extended and the need for institutions to mobilize voters developed.

2. Parties serve as linkages between citizens and their government and perform such functions as nominating candidates, contesting elections, serving as agents for holding public officials accountable for their actions, and managing societal conflicts.

3. The two-party competitive model accurately describes the electoral competition for president and many state elections. Below the state level, however, the ideal of meaningful two-party competition often goes unrealized.

4. American political parties are characterized by decentralized power structures, broad-based electoral support, and relatively nonprogrammatic policy orientations.

5. Nominations for state and congressional offices are made via the direct primary, which severely weakens party organization control over the nomination process and encourages candidates to rely on personal campaign organizations.

6. Presidential nominations are made formally by national conventions. Party organizations do not control presidential nominations, and candidates form personal campaign organizations. The crucial events in the nomination process are presidential primaries.

For Further Reading

Bibby, John F. *Politics, Parties, and Elections in America.* 2d ed. Chicago: Nelson-Hall, 1992. A brief description of the functioning of parties in the electoral and governmental processes.

Epstein, Leon D. *Political Parties in the American Mold.* Madison: University of Wisconsin Press, 1986. An analysis of American parties that considers their distinctive characteristics, development, durability, and adaptability.

Herrnson, Paul S. *Party Campaigning in the 1980s.* Cambridge, Mass.: Harvard University Press, 1988. An analysis of the expanding electoral role of national party committees.

Jewell, Malcolm E. *Parties and Primaries: Nominating State Governors.* New York: Praeger, 1984. The most complete account of the operation of direct primaries available.

Jewell, Malcolm E., and David M. Olson. *Political Parties and Elections in American States.* 3d ed. Pacific Grove, Calif.: Brooks/Cole, 1987. A comparative description and analysis of the electoral process and parties at the state level.

Key, V. O., Jr. *Politics, Parties, and Pressure Groups.* 5th ed. New York: Crowell, 1964. A classic text written by the leading twentieth-century student of American political parties.

Maisel, L. Sandy, ed. *The Parties Respond: Changes in the American Party System.* Boulder, Colo.: Westview Press, 1990. A collection of essays by leading scholars describing changes in party organizations, the party in government, and the party in the electorate.

Polsby, Nelson W. *The Consequences of Reform.* New York: Oxford University Press, 1983. A critique of party reform efforts since the late 1960s.

Reichley, A. James, ed. *Elections American Style.* Washington, D.C.: Brookings, 1987. The role of parties in elections is analyzed, and provocative suggestions for reform are considered.

Sabato, Larry J. *The Party's Just Begun: Shaping Political Parties for America's Future.* Glenview, Ill.: Scott, Foresman, 1988. A concise description of the functioning of American parties with a discussion of proposals to strengthen parties.

Shafer, Byron E. *Bifurcated Politics: Evolution and Reform in the National Party Convention.* Cambridge, Mass.: Harvard University Press, 1988. A comprehensive analysis of changes in presidential nominating politics.

Sorauf, Frank J., and Paul Allen Beck. *Party Politics in America.* 6th ed. Glenview, Ill.: Scott, Foresman/Little, Brown, 1988. A comprehensive text on political parties.

Wayne, Stephen J. *The Road to the White House.* New York: St. Martin's, 1987. A comprehensive treatment of presidential nomination and election politics.

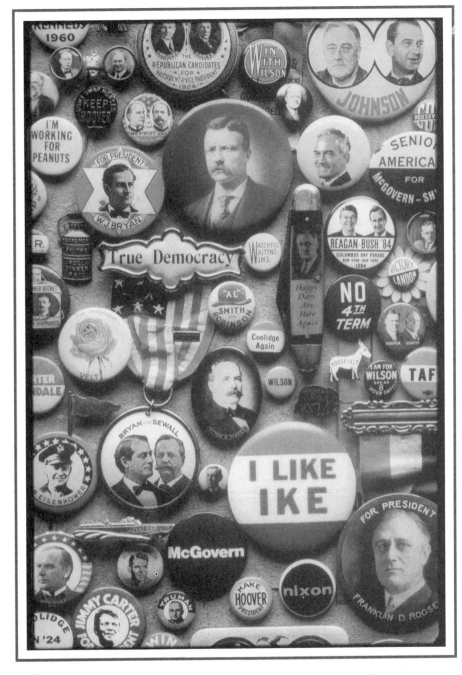

7. Elections, Campaigns, and Voters

B Y CASTING their votes in elections, Americans make their most important collective decisions. They determine who will lead their government—who will decide when and where to use military force, what taxes to impose, what services to provide, and how to regulate the economy and social relations. With their election day choices, voters can demonstrate their displeasure as well as their satisfaction with the state of the Union, with the performance of public officials, and with how their own lives are going. By either terminating or renewing leaders' leases to government offices, voters can hold public officials accountable for their actions and indirectly affect government policy.

Periodic free elections are democracy's solution to the problems that have plagued government regimes for ages: how to arrange a peaceful succession to government posts and an end to the life of a government without having to rely on a *coup d'état,* execution, or revolution. Americans have the opportunity to participate in elections more frequently and for more offices than the citizens of most democracies. They vote for their president, senator, representative, governor, state legislator, and a host of other state and local officials. They vote in presidential years and midterm years, in general elections and primaries, and on referendums.

This chapter explores the American electoral process—the formal rules governing how elections are conducted, the nature of campaigns (especially presidential campaigns), the behavior of the voters, and the meaning and significance of elections (elections for congressional seats are considered in Chapter 10, Congress).

How America Conducts Its Elections

U nder America's federal system, the responsibility for regulating elections is shared by the national and state governments. The states make many of the important decisions about how elections will be conducted, including who is eligible to vote, what regulations are applied to political parties, how elections are administered, and how votes are counted. The federal government's role is largely one of setting the times for federal elections, preventing discrimination in the exercise of the right to vote (also known as **suffrage** or **franchise**), and regulating campaign finance in federal elections.

The Right to Vote

Suffrage qualifications are set by the states, subject to constraints imposed by the Constitution and Congress. Congress, for example, has used its constitutional power to regulate the "Times, Places and Manner of holding Elections" for federal officials (1) to set a uniform date across the country for the election of representatives, senators, and presidential electors, and (2) to set age requirements for voting in federal elections. Since the 1980 elections, Congress has periodically debated legislation to fix a common poll closing time across the nation. This legislation is designed to prevent television networks from projecting election outcomes while polls are still open on the West Coast. Critics of the networks charge that these projections discourage voter **turnout**.

Extending the Right to Vote. When the Constitution was ratified, the states imposed severe restrictions on the right to vote by demanding that voters meet certain property-owning or tax-paying requirements. As a result, the eligible electorate was confined to adult white males with property, leaving an estimated three-quarters of adult males not eligible to vote. But by the 1830s, the states had largely abolished economic qualifications for voting so the United States could claim that it had universal white manhood suffrage. This easing of restrictions, of course, still left large portions of the adult population—including women and blacks—unable to cast their votes.

In the continuing struggle to make the right to vote a reality for all adult citizens, the states have ratified constitutional amendments and Congress has passed legislation aimed at eliminating state-imposed barriers to voting. The Fourteenth and Fifteenth amendments forbid the states from imposing unreasonable and racially based qualifications; the Nineteenth Amendment capped the long battle for women's suffrage; the Twenty-fourth Amendment bans denial of the right to vote because of failure to pay a state-imposed poll tax, and the Twenty-sixth Amendment forbids denying the right to vote to eighteen-year-olds.

But as we saw in Chapter 4, states found ways to prevent blacks from participating in the electoral process even after ratification of the Fourteenth and Fifteenth amendments. Eventually, however, the heightened public concern for civil rights issues in the early 1960s, as well as the use of violence and intimidation in the South to prevent black voter registration drives, led to passage of the Voting Rights Act of 1965. This law suspended literacy tests in all states and counties in which less than 50 percent of the voting age population was registered to vote in 1964 and authorized federal registrars to register voters and supervise elections in these areas. To prevent manipu-

Supporters of the Nineteenth Amendment picket the White House in 1916, while their adversaries mobilize from their headquarters.

lation of election laws in an effort to disenfranchise blacks, officials in these states were required to gain Department of Justice approval for all election law changes.

The enfranchisement of black voters has had a dramatic effect on American politics. In 1965, there were only a few hundred black elected officials; by 1990 there were almost eight thousand. With their greatly expanded numbers and their overwhelming support for Democratic candidates, the black electorate has become a critical voting bloc within the Democratic electoral coalition (see Chapter 6, Political Parties). This same electorate also played an important role in enabling Jesse Jackson to become the first member of his race to compete seriously for the presidential nomination.

Voter Registration. Although constrained by constitutional and congressionally enacted restrictions, the states play a major role in regulating and administering elections. Their most important regulations apply to voter registration. Even though justified as a means of preventing fraud (for example, when people vote more than once or a voter uses the name of someone deceased) and protecting the integrity of elections (some states impose restrictions on voting by convicted felons, aliens, and the mentally incompetent), registration requirements also can work to depress voter turnout.[1] These re-

1. See Raymond E. Wolfinger and Steven J. Rosenstone, "The Effect of Registration Laws on Voter Turnout," *American Political Science Review* 72 (March 1978):

quirements vary widely among the states, with the most lenient states permitting voters to register at the polls on election day and the stricter states requiring would-be voters to register in person at such government buildings as a courthouse or city hall. Among the world's democracies, the United States is unique in that here individual citizens are responsible for getting themselves registered. By contrast, in most democracies the government assumes responsibility for voter registration.

Election administration—printing ballots, providing polling places and poll workers, setting hours the polls will be open, counting ballots, certifying outcomes, providing for recounts, and regulating campaign practices on election days—is largely the responsibility of state and local governments.

Types of Ballots. States also determine the type of ballot to be used. Either of two basic ballot forms is usually found in U.S. polling booths. Twenty-one states use the *party column ballot,* which arranges the names of the candidates so that all those from one party are in one column or row. In this way, the voter can cast a vote for one party's candidates by simply marking an "X" at the top of the party's column or by pulling a lever on the voting machine. The party column ballot encourages straight-ticket voting. The *office bloc ballot,* used in twenty-nine states, arranges the names of candidates according to the office they are seeking. The office bloc ballot tends to discourage straight party line voting and encourages candidates to campaign as individuals rather than as part of a party slate.

The Electoral College

When Americans were choosing between George Bush and Michael Dukakis on November 8, 1988, they were actually voting for slates of presidential electors who would cast their states' electoral votes for a president and vice president. American presidents are elected through an indirect system that relies on electoral votes, not popular votes (also see Chapter 2, The Constitution).

To be elected president, a candidate must receive an absolute majority (270) of the 538 votes in the *electoral college,* where each state's electoral votes equal its total number of senators and representatives. Thus, California with two senators and fifty-two representatives has fifty-four electoral votes, and Delaware with two

22–48. Also see G. Bingham Powell, "American Turnout in Comparative Perspective," *American Political Science Review* 80 (March 1986): 17–43.

senators and one representative has three. The District of Columbia, which was granted the right to vote for president by the Twenty-third Amendment, has three electoral votes.

The allocation of a state's electoral votes among presidential candidates is determined on a winner-take-all basis—whichever candidate receives the most popular votes (a plurality) receives that state's entire complement of electoral votes.[2] Thus, all of Pennsylvania's twenty-five electoral votes in 1988 went to George Bush, who received 107,000 more votes (51 percent) than Michael Dukakis out of the almost four and a half million votes cast.

In the event no candidate receives the 270 electoral votes required for election, the election is thrown into the newly elected House of Representatives, which chooses from among the three candidates who received the largest number of electoral votes. In making its selection, the House votes by state delegation, with each state having one vote and with a majority of states required to elect a president.[3] When no vice-presidential candidate has a majority in the electoral college, the Senate chooses one of the two candidates having the largest number of electoral votes.

Because of the winner-take-all system for deciding which candidate will receive a state's electoral votes, the big states, in terms of population, take on critical significance in electing presidents. This is true even though sparsely populated states such as North and South Dakota have more electoral votes than a population-based system of electoral vote apportionment would entitle them. A vote cast in California holds the potential of determining which candidate will win that state's fifty-four electoral votes. By contrast, a vote cast in South Dakota can influence only which candidate will win three electoral votes. The ten most populous states control 257 out of the 270 electoral votes needed to elect a president, and the thirteen least populous states have only forty-six electoral votes—fewer than the largest state, California (the map in Figure 7.1 shows the relative importance of each state's electoral votes). In these circumstances, it is not surprising that presidential candidates normally concentrate their campaign efforts on winning as many of the most thickly populated states as possible.

2. The only exceptions to the winner-take-all rule are Maine and Nebraska, which allocate their electoral votes on the basis of two electoral votes to the candidate who receives a statewide plurality and one electoral vote to the winning candidate in each of the state's congressional districts.
3. The House has selected a president only twice (after the elections of 1800 and 1824), before the United States developed a stable two-party system.

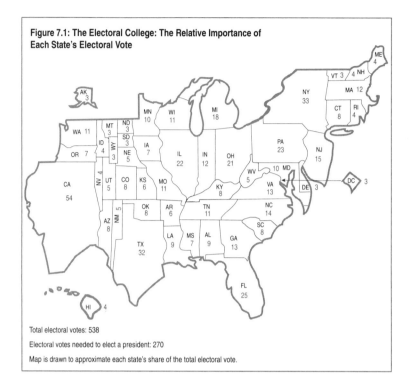

Figure 7.1: The Electoral College: The Relative Importance of Each State's Electoral Vote

Total electoral votes: 538

Electoral votes needed to elect a president: 270

Map is drawn to approximate each state's share of the total electoral vote.

A persistent criticism leveled at the electoral college is that a candidate can win a plurality of the popular vote and still not be elected president because of failure to gain an electoral college majority. This happened in 1824, 1876, and 1888. Thus, would-be presidents Andrew Jackson (1824), Samuel J. Tilden (1876), and Grover Cleveland (1888)—each of whom received a plurality of the popular vote— found their aspirations dashed when they failed to receive a majority of the electoral college vote (happily for Jackson and Cleveland, they succeeded in occupying the White House after their second runs for the office). Normally, however, the electoral college system exaggerates the popular vote winner's margin of victory. In the cliffhanger election of 1960, for example, John Kennedy received 49.7 percent of the popular vote, but his electoral vote percentage was a more comfortable 56.4 percent. Similarly, in 1988 George Bush gained 54 percent of the popular vote but won 79 percent of the electoral votes. The reason for this pattern: the winning candidate normally carries a number of states by narrow margins and, because of the winner-take-all system, collects all of those states' electoral votes. Since newly elected presidents usually have substantial majorities in the electoral college, they can then claim electoral mandates from the voters even though their popular vote pluralities may have been relatively modest.

Although it has not happened for over a hundred years, the possibility of a person being elected who did not receive a popular vote plurality bothers many Americans because it seems to violate democratic principles. As a result, calls are heard periodically for a constitutional amendment that provides for direct popular election of the president. Defenders of the electoral college believe that the current system has worked reasonably well and see potential risks in moving to direct election. One of those risks is that splinter parties would be encouraged to run candidates in the popular election, thereby altering the character of the party system. Opponents of change also are concerned that campaigns would be conducted differently; candidates would have an even greater incentive to run national media-oriented campaigns that pay little attention to voters on a state-by-state basis.[4] All this being said, because in recent history there has been no instance in which a popular vote winner failed to win a majority of the electoral college, attempts to revise the procedure for electing the president have received little sustained effort. Indeed, proponents of change have failed to muster the necessary two-thirds majorities in Congress needed to propose a constitutional amendment.

The Campaign: Electing a President

Campaigns are a crucial part of the struggle for political power in the United States. But to be successful, campaigns must have smoothly run organizations and well-thought-out strategies. In spite of their importance, campaign organizations are highly transitory structures. Presidential campaign organizations, which spend millions of dollars and enlist thousands of people, are erected quickly to contest the election and then disbanded even more rapidly whether the candidate has won or lost.

Traditionally, presidential campaigns have kicked off formally around Labor Day after the July and August national conventions. For example, Democratic presidential nominees have frequently

4. For a discussion of the issues involved in electoral college reform, see Nelson W. Polsby and Aaron Wildavsky, *Presidential Elections: Contemporary Strategies of American Electoral Politics,* 7th ed. (New York: Free Press, 1988), 275–284. Also see Neal R. Pierce and Lawrence D. Longley, *The People's President,* rev. ed. (New Haven, Conn.: Yale University Press, 1981); and Wallace S. Sayre and Judith H. Parris, *Voting for President: The Electoral College and the American Political System* (Washington, D.C.: Brookings, 1970).

started their campaigns with massive rallies in Cadillac Square in Detroit. As was noted in Chapter 6, however, the real opening of the general election campaigns occurs at the national conventions where each party tries to present its candidate to the television audience in the most positive manner possible. In 1988, neither party waited for the traditional Labor Day opening of the campaign. Democratic presidential nominee Michael Dukakis and his running mate Lloyd Bentsen hit the road the first day after the convention, campaigning in Bentsen's (and George Bush's) home state of Texas. Using sophisticated market research to identify issues likely to inflict the most damage on its opponent, the Bush organization launched its campaign in late summer with almost daily attacks on Dukakis.

Campaign strategies can significantly affect election outcomes. During the 1988 presidential campaign, Democrat Michael Dukakis saw his lead in the polls over Republican George Bush go from a 17-percentage-point advantage in July to a 5-percentage-point deficit in November. Analysts attributed Dukakis's slide in part to the aggressive Republican media strategy that portrayed Dukakis as a liberal who was sympathetic to criminals, unconcerned about the victims of crime, and unappreciative of the need for a strong defense. Dukakis's campaign was further damaged by his organization's lack of experience in national campaigns and inability to find an effective campaign theme.[5]

When the Voter Decides

Most voters make up their minds well before election day. In the presidential elections held since 1960, on average over 60 percent of the voters made up their minds before or during the nominating conventions. In 1988, 62 percent of the voters made up their minds before the last month of the campaign (see Figure 7.2). Such percentages, however, can be a bit misleading. A sizable share of voters do make their choices late in the campaign, and in close elections these voters' choices can decide the election. In presidential elections, key states are often won by margins of less than 5 percent of the vote, and the 1988 election was no exception. George Bush carried twelve states by a margin of 54 percent or less of the vote. In such circumstances, a late surge of support for his opponent could have reversed the outcome of the election. Thus, campaigns and how they are organized can make a difference.[6]

5. See David Schribman and James M. Perry, "Dukakis's Campaign Was Marred by a Series of Lost Opportunities," *Wall Street Journal*, Nov. 8, 1988, A1, A8; and Paul R. Abramson, John H. Aldrich, and David W. Rohde, *Change and Continuity in the 1988 Elections* (Washington, D.C.: CQ Press, 1990), chap. 2.
6. For a comprehensive consideration of campaign strategy, see Stephen A. Sal-

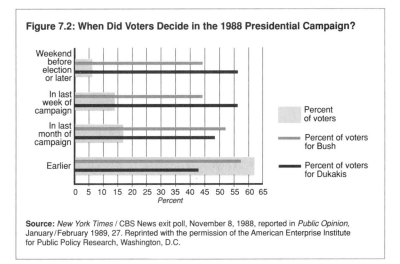

Figure 7.2: When Did Voters Decide in the 1988 Presidential Campaign?

Percent of voters

Percent of voters for Bush

Percent of voters for Dukakis

Source: *New York Times* / CBS News exit poll, November 8, 1988, reported in *Public Opinion,* January/February 1989, 27. Reprinted with the permission of the American Enterprise Institute for Public Policy Research, Washington, D.C.

Organizing and Running the Campaign

According to journalist Theodore White, a presidential campaign "starts with a candidate, a handful of men, a theme and a plan. By November of election year it has enlisted hundreds of thousands of volunteers, politicians, state staffs, national staffs, media specialists and has become an enterprise."[7] Creating a presidential campaign organization is indeed a mammoth undertaking, requiring establishment of a headquarters and recruitment of a staff of experienced, savvy professionals capable of developing and implementing a campaign plan and mobilizing thousands of campaign volunteers.[8]

Staffing the Campaign Organization. In the 1988 race, the Bush organization had an edge over the Dukakis team in terms of experience in national politics and organizational discipline. The Bush team was headed by former White House chief of staff and secretary of the Treasury James Baker, who had played a major role in three previous presidential races. He was backed up by campaign manager Lee Atwater, a professional campaign consultant and deputy campaign manager of Ronald Reagan's 1984 successful reelection drive; Robert Teeter, a respected Republican pollster; and Roger Ailes, a media consultant whose experience in presidential media campaigns

---

more and Barbara G. Salmore, *Candidates, Parties, and Campaigns,* 2d ed. (Washington, D.C.: CQ Press, 1989).

7. Michael P. Riccards, *A Republic, If You Can Keep It: The Foundation of the American Presidency, 1700–1800* (New York: Greenwood Press, 1987), 101.

8. For a discussion of campaign organizations and the development of strategy, see John H. Kessel, *Presidential Campaign Politics,* 4th ed. (Pacific Grove, Calif.: Brooks/Cole, 1992), chaps. 3 and 4.

dated back to the 1960s. Baker's tight control over the organization enabled the campaign to utilize such techniques as emphasizing one carefully calculated message per day, to execute its tactics efficiently, to avoid outside distractions, and to court the news media. In contrast to the Bush operation, the Dukakis staff was largely Massachusetts-based with less experience in national campaigns. It also was plagued by internal problems, which hampered its ability to make timely and crucial campaign decisions and to master the many strategic considerations so vital to running a successful campaign.

Developing Campaign Themes and Issues. Effective campaign themes embody the declared political and policy commitments of the candidates in ways that appeal to public support. The themes and issues developed by campaigns reflect the records and experience of the candidates, their objectives and those of their supporters, and the campaign organization's assessments of current political conditions. In 1980, for example, as inflation and interest rates reached double-digit levels, unemployment rose, and people felt frustrated by the Carter administration's seeming inability to free American hostages captured when Iran seized the U.S. Embassy in Teheran, Ronald Reagan asked voters to "Vote Republican for a change!" and pledged to lower taxes, cut domestic spending, and increase military expenditures. Twenty years earlier, when the American economy was in a slump and Americans were worrying at the height of the Cold War about the adequacy of the country's defenses, Democrat John Kennedy had promised to "get the country going again" and to erase the alleged "missile gap" by bolstering defense capabilities.

The 1988 Republican campaign quite naturally associated Vice President Bush with the popular incumbent president, Ronald Reagan, and claimed for the Reagan-Bush administration a record of economic growth, military strength, and peace. The campaign also sought to differentiate Bush from Dukakis on social issues: the mandatory "Pledge of Allegiance" in public schools, capital punishment, and school prayer, all of which Bush supported; and gun control, abortion rights, and the Massachusetts prison furlough program, all of which Bush opposed. Using the phrase "Read my lips!" for emphasis, Bush promised "no new taxes" and hammered Dukakis for failing to make a similar pledge. A series of hard-hitting negative television ads also sought to portray Dukakis as an out-of-the-mainstream liberal who was soft on crime and national defense and who favored higher taxes. In contrast to these candidate-maiming tactics was the softer side of the Bush campaign. The candidate called for a "kinder and gentler America," high standards of ethics in government, and racial tolerance as he backed away from the hardline, anti-welfare state conservatism of President Reagan.

Dukakis hoped to increase his party's appeal to moderate and conservative voters by selecting Sen. Lloyd Bentsen from Texas, a moderate conservative, as his running mate and by shying away from positions that would label him a liberal. He sought to associate his candidacy with the American dream of opportunity for all—a point he personalized by recounting his origins as the son of Greek immigrants. Dukakis accused the Reagan administration of limiting the opportunities of middle- and lower-income citizens while extending the advantages of the wealthy. A central theme of his campaign was "good jobs at good wages for every citizen." In playing out his theme, Dukakis sought to downplay ideology and stress his competence and claims of success in job creation and balancing budgets as governor of Massachusetts. He asserted, "This election isn't about ideology. It's about competence."

In a period of peace abroad—and relative economic prosperity and aggressive attacks from the Bush campaign at home—the Dukakis organization found it difficult to establish campaign themes that appealed to the average voter. During the last three weeks of the campaign, Dukakis admitted that he was a liberal and adopted populist themes using the new slogan "I'm on your side." While this new emphasis improved his poll ratings, the change of themes occurred too late to affect the outcome of the election. The Dukakis campaign also was hampered by organizational problems (for example, an inability to decide on a television advertising strategy and power struggles among key aides) that made it difficult to respond to Bush's attacks.[9]

Getting the Message Across. In a television age, careful coordination of the various elements of a campaign—particularly public opinion polling, media advertising, and candidate appearances—is essential to getting out the intended message to the voters. The 1988 Bush campaign was unusually well disciplined at this task and more experienced than the Dukakis organization. Polling was done every night of the campaign, with the results available for James Baker's daily 7:30 A.M. senior staff meetings. At these meetings, polling data were reviewed, and campaign activities were carefully planned for each day and week, using the campaign message of the day or

9. For an overview of 1988 campaign strategies and issues, see Paul J. Quirk, "The Election," in *The Elections of 1988,* ed. Michael Nelson (Washington, D.C.: CQ Press, 1989), chap. 3. For an informed discussion of the problems of the Dukakis campaign, see Schribman and Perry, "Dukakis Campaign Was Marred."

While "Keep Cool with Coolidge" posters, banners, and buttons may have gotten the message across in 1924, today candidates rely on television advertising, such as George Bush's use of this image of his opponent in 1988.

week—for example, the environment, crime, or national defense. The candidate's public appearances were then scheduled to highlight the chosen message visually and create positive images for the evening news. Media advisers even went so far as to insert snappy lines in the speeches—tested in advance, of course—to ensure they were included as "sound bites" on news programs. To complete the media package, television commercials were designed to back up the chosen message. But before being aired, each commercial was tested on a group of citizens ("focus group") whose reactions to the commercial were carefully analyzed by a panel of advertising executives. The Bush campaign also tried to limit news conferences with reporters, lest the free-wheeling and often adversarial nature of these sessions result in messages being communicated to the voters that were different from those contained in the campaign plan. Thus, the campaign was designed to exert maximum control over what the voters would see and hear of George Bush on television, people's most important source of news. The Dukakis campaign also had its media consultants, but they were less experienced than Bush's and they were working with a less cooperative candidate.[10] As a result, the

10. For a summary of the media campaigns of Bush and Dukakis, see Marjorie Randon Hershey, "The Campaign and the Media," in *The Election of 1988: Reports and Interpretations,* ed. Gerald Pomper et al. (Chatham, N.J.: Chatham House, 1989), chap. 3. Also see James M. Perry and Monica Langley, "Bush Thrives on One-a-Day TV-Message Capsules Prescribed by His Skilled Poli-Tech Image Makers," *Wall Street Journal,* Oct. 27, 1988, A16; and David Hoffman, "The Bush Campaign's Controlling Factor," *Washington Post,* Oct. 4, 1989, A1, A16.

Bush campaign was successful in framing the issues of the campaign to its advantage.

Using the Incumbency Advantage. It is impossible for anyone in American political life to match the publicity and symbolic advantages of an incumbent president. The office carries with it symbols of the nation and of power—the presidential seal, the Oval Office with its massive desk and flags of the military services bedecked with battle ribbons, *Air Force One,* and the strains of "Hail to the Chief," which is played for ceremonial occasions. There is a presidential aura that surrounds each incumbent which no challenger can match. Just by carrying out their official duties, presidents are able to transcend the appearance of mere politicians campaigning for office; rather, they appear to be servants of the people—all the people. For example, President Reagan's 1984 visit to the Normandy beaches of France to celebrate the fortieth anniversary of D-Day (the Allied invasion of Europe during World War II) provided him with a dramatic and emotional setting for television coverage on the eve of his 1984 reelection campaign. Less dramatic, but nonetheless effective, are bill-signing ceremonies and gatherings in the White House Rose Garden to honor foreign dignitaries, Super Bowl champions, and astronauts. A further advantage of **incumbency** is the ability of an administration to make policy decisions that will help win support for the incumbent president's party—for example, approving contracts for military procurement or public works projects in states considered essential for an electoral college majority.

Incumbent presidents and their vice presidents, like George Bush, are in a position to claim credit for all the good things that happened during their terms. Presidents Dwight Eisenhower and Ronald Reagan, as well as Vice President Bush, all ran on themes of peace and prosperity. But when the economy turns sour and international affairs go against American interests, it is the president who stands alone, exposed and accountable. It does not matter that presidents cannot control all aspects of our domestic and foreign affairs. President Jimmy Carter's defeat in 1980 can be attributed primarily to his being held accountable for the troubled state of the economy and the nation's embarrassment at having its embassy in Teheran seized and Americans held hostage by Iranian revolutionaries for over a year.

Arranging Televised Debates. Televised debates now go hand in hand with presidential elections. For nonincumbent and underdog candidates, such debates are potentially advantageous because they place these candidates on equal footing with a president, vice pres-

With Vice President George Bush leading in the polls, Gov. Michael Dukakis needed an impressive showing in the 1988 presidential debates. Dukakis, however, was unable to score a decisive victory. In this photograph, Bush responds to a question posed by the panel of journalists in the foreground.

ident, or front-running candidate. On an unadorned stage, both candidates stand alone as equals before the television audience, poised to answer the questions to come. Not only are presidents and vice presidents robbed of the aura of the White House, but their claims of superior experience can be quickly eroded during the debate by challengers who are credible and clever—which most are.

Because the news media give prime-time coverage to debates, candidates tend to see them as the make-or-break events of the campaign.[11] In fact, extended negotiations between campaign managers over the format of the debates are usually the rule—all aimed, of course, at preventing the opposition from gaining any procedural advantage. While negotiating arrangements for the 1988 debates, the Bush campaign successfully insisted on limiting the number of presidential debates to two, squeezing the debates into a short period in early fall, and confining the candidates' statements to responses to questions initiated by a panel of reporters. These conditions, it was believed, would limit the risks for the incumbent vice president.

Even with the limitations imposed by the debate format, the Dukakis organization hoped that the debates would give its candidate a major boost. After the first debate, a consensus of political analysts pronounced Dukakis the winner because he had kept Bush on the defensive; the polls rated the event a draw or slight edge for Dukakis.

11. Social scientists disagree about the impact of presidential debates. See John G. Geer, "The Effects of Presidential Debates on the Electorate's Preference for Candidates," *American Politics Quarterly* 16 (October 1988): 486–501.

That debate did nothing, however, to overcome his passionless and somewhat gloomy image and was more an opportunity lost than a campaign boost. In the second debate, Dukakis again failed to make any emotional headway with the voters, while a more confident and relaxed Bush succeeded in getting across his message that Dukakis was a liberal. In response, the media declared the race virtually over and speculated about the size of Bush's victory.[12]

Overall, presidential debates seem to reinforce support for candidates among their supporters. For independents and weak partisans, debates can stimulate interest in their campaigns and color perceptions of the candidates. Thus in 1960, the debates helped John Kennedy stir up support for his campaign and ease doubts about his youth and inexperience.

Dealing with the Political Geography of the Electoral College. Because electoral, not popular, votes determine the winner, presidential elections are in reality fifty-one separate contests for the electoral votes of each state and the District of Columbia. The candidates' campaign organizations must, therefore, devise strategies and allocate their campaign resources among the states in a way that will produce a majority in the electoral college. In 1988, this posed a particularly difficult problem for the Dukakis campaign. With the Republicans holding what appeared to be a lock on the South and most of the western states, the Democratic nominee was forced to concentrate his efforts on winning a combination of eighteen states with 272 electoral votes. This was an almost impossible task since in some of the eighteen target states the two parties were highly competitive. The Republican electoral college strategy was quite different. With comfortable leads in the South and West and the cushion of electoral votes they provided, the Republican strategists calculated that they needed to win only three of the so-called Big Eight battleground states—California, New York, Illinois, Michigan, Pennsylvania, Ohio, New Jersey, and Texas—to achieve an electoral college victory. Based on past voting history and political demographics, they determined that their best chances were in New Jersey, Texas, and Ohio. These states thus were singled out for intensive campaign efforts. In Ohio alone, Vice President Bush made eighteen campaign appearances between August 20 and election day,[13] and his strategy

12. Hershey, "The Campaign and the Media," 89–91; and Abramson et al., *Change and Continuity,* 47–50.

13. Paul Taylor, "GOP Strategist 'Carpet-Bombs' Buckeye State," *Washington Post,* Nov. 4, 1988, A21.

Figure 7.3: Electoral Votes by State, 1988

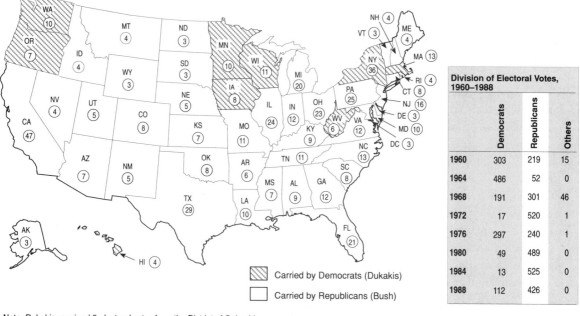

Division of Electoral Votes, 1960–1988			
	Democrats	Republicans	Others
1960	303	219	15
1964	486	52	0
1968	191	301	46
1972	17	520	1
1976	297	240	1
1980	49	489	0
1984	13	525	0
1988	112	426	0

Carried by Democrats (Dukakis)

Carried by Republicans (Bush)

Note: Dukakis received 3 electoral votes from the District of Columbia.

proved effective as he carried all three target states (see Figure 7.3 for the state-by-state outcomes of the 1988 election).

Financing Presidential Elections

A credible presidential campaign costs a lot of money. Money purchases a headquarters, staff, consultants, pollsters, advertising, research, and jet travel. Paying for campaigns has always been a troublesome aspect of the electoral process, and today that is particularly true. The expense of television time and new technologies—computer-based analyses of voting behavior and nightly telephone polls tracking candidate support levels—have caused the costs of campaigns to escalate dramatically. Moreover, the candidates and their parties differ in their abilities to raise campaign funds from private sources. But of even greater concern is the possibility that in the eagerness of the candidates to fill their campaign coffers, the government process may be corrupted by large contributors seeking access to and influence with government officials.

Faced with unprecedented levels of spending by President Nixon's 1972 Committee to Re-elect the President and charges of improprieties in the raising of those funds, Congress enacted in 1974 a major campaign finance reform act. The 1974 amendments to the Federal Election Campaign Act (FECA) seek to relieve presidential candidates of the need to spend time raising money, provide the public with information about the sources of campaign funds, limit the role of a few large contributors and interest groups in funding campaigns, and reduce the role of money in elections.

The most important provision of the act affecting presidential elections pertains to public funding of campaigns.[14] Major party presidential candidates may elect to accept federal funding of their campaigns. Candidates accepting public funding ($46.1 million in 1988), however, must agree not to accept or spend any additional campaign funds other than up to $50,000 of their own personal money. The national committees of the parties also are limited in the amount ($8.3 million in 1988) they can spend to support their presidential nominees, but state and local party organizations can spend without limit on party building and get-out-the-vote activities (posters, yard signs, bumper stickers, voter registration drives, phone banks).

Since 1976 when the 1974 FECA amendments went into effect, every Republican and Democratic presidential nominee has accepted public funding for their campaigns. In practice, however, the FECA has not been effective in limiting the cost of campaigns or the role of nonpublic funds in presidential elections. Indeed, despite FECA's cap on candidate expenditures, an estimated $300 million was spent on the 1988 presidential campaign.[15] This level of spending stemmed from the fierce struggle between the Democratic and Republican national party organizations for private contributions to supplement the public funds. The two parties raised an estimated $45–$60 million (some in contributions of as much as $100,000), which was channeled to state and local party organizations for party-building activities in support of the presidential campaign.

In addition to these party expenditures, private groups and individuals are permitted to make *independent expenditures* in support of the candidates of their choice—but without the collusion of the candidate's campaign organization. The Supreme Court has ruled that the First Amendment protects such expenditures and that

14. For an analysis of the operation of public funding in presidential elections, see Frank J. Sorauf, *Money in American Elections* (Glenview, Ill.: Scott, Foresman, 1988), chap. 7.

15. Herbert E. Alexander, "The Price We Pay for Our President," *Public Opinion*, March/April 1989, 46.

Current Laws Regulating Presidential Campaign Finance

The following provisions regulating presidential campaigns are listed in order of the progress of the nomination and general election campaigns.

- **Federal regulation.** The Federal Election Commission (FEC) is the federal agency responsible for enforcement of campaign laws.
- **Disclosure.** Presidential candidates must file regular reports with the FEC listing campaign contributions and expenditures. Donors of $200 or more must be listed in the reports. Any organization spending more than $5,000 on campaigns must establish formal political action committees. Candidates must establish a single organization for their campaigns. Certain expenses of local party organizations such as get-out-the-vote drives and voter education activities do not have to be reported.
- **Political action committees (PACs).** Corporations and labor unions may establish separate units to promote political ends and not be in violation of federal prohibitions on direct contributions.
- **Taxpayer checkoff.** Citizens may indicate on their tax forms that they would like $1 ($2 for joint filings) of their tax money to be put into the Presidential Election Campaign Fund. This fund has been used to help finance nomination and general election campaigns.
- **Matching funds during primaries.** Candidates may receive federal matching funds if they raise at least $100,000 in twenty or more states. Each of those states must contribute a total of at least $5,000 to the candidate in individual donations of $250 or less.
- **Limits on contributions.** Citizens may contribute only $1,000 to each primary or general election campaign, a total of $25,000 to federal candidates overall, and $20,000 to committees of national parties. Candidates may spend only $50,000 of their own or their family's money on their campaigns if they accept federal funding. Multicandidate committees—most commonly PACs—may contribute only $5,000 per candidate and $15,000 to committees of the national parties.
- **Federal funding of national conventions.** The parties receive funding for their summer conventions.
- **Spending limits.** Candidates receiving federal matching funds may spend limited amounts during the nomination season and other limited amounts in each of the states (state limits are determined by population).
- **Federal funding of general election campaigns.** The federal government offers the nominees of the major parties equal sums of money for the general election campaign. Candidates who accept the money may not raise or use additional campaign funds. The figure was $46.1 million in 1988; the amount has been adjusted each election year according to the inflation rate.

the provisions in the FECA that sought to limit these expenditures were unconstitutional.[16] In 1988, the Federal Election Commission, the regulatory agency responsible for enforcing campaign finance laws, reported that over $13 million in independent expenditures was used to support the Bush and Dukakis campaigns.

Voter Turnout in Elections

Although elections are the underpinning of a democratic order, a relatively small percentage of Americans actually take advantage of their right to vote.[17] In the 1988 presidential election, 50.1 percent of the voting age population cast ballots—the lowest percentage in sixty-four years (Figure 7.4). Voter **turnout** is even lower in midterm elections for the House of Representatives and Senate. In the 1990 midterm elections, for example, just one-third of the eligible voters went to the polls (see Figure 7.4).

With their saturation media coverage and complex strategies, presidential campaigns bombard voters with stimuli to vote. Midterm elections, however, tend to have much less media coverage and, in many congressional districts, lackluster contests when the incumbent representative is largely unchallenged. Voter disinterest and lower turnout than in presidential contests are the result. Since 1952, the falloff in turnout from each presidential election to the next midterm election has averaged −18 percent.

The states vary widely in their rates of voter turnout—in 1988 Minnesota had a 66.3 percent turnout and Georgia only 38.8 percent (see Figure 7.5). These widely different rates can be attributed to three factors, the first of which is a combination of *levels of interparty competition, intensity of campaigning, and voter mobilization efforts.* When there is genuine electoral competition between the Republicans and Democrats and an intense campaign effort on the part of candidates, parties, and interest groups to reach the voters within a state, voter participation is increased.[18] A second factor is *state voter registration requirements.* The states differ greatly in their registration requirements. North Dakota has no voter registra-

---

16. *Federal Election Commission v. National Conservative PAC,* 84 L. Ed. 2d 455 (1985).

17. Though now somewhat dated, the most thorough study of voter turnout in America is that by Raymond E. Wolfinger and Steven J. Rosenstone, *Who Votes?* (New Haven, Conn.: Yale University Press, 1980).

18. Samuel C. Patterson and Gregory A. Caldeira, "Getting Out the Vote: Participation in Gubernatorial Elections," *American Political Science Review* 77 (September 1983): 675–689; and Gregory A. Caldeira, Samuel C. Patterson, and Gregory A. Markko, "The Mobilization of Voters in Congressional Elections," *Journal of Politics* 47 (May 1985): 498–509.

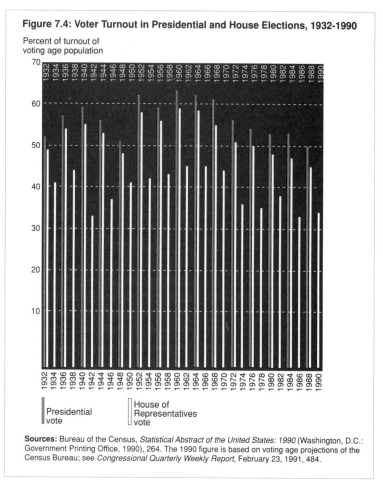

Figure 7.4: Voter Turnout in Presidential and House Elections, 1932-1990

Percent of turnout of voting age population

Presidential vote

House of Representatives vote

Sources: Bureau of the Census, *Statistical Abstract of the United States: 1990* (Washington, D.C.: Government Printing Office, 1990), 264. The 1990 figure is based on voting age projections of the Census Bureau; see *Congressional Quarterly Weekly Report,* February 23, 1991, 484.

tion; Maine, Minnesota, and Wisconsin permit election day registration at the polls; and several states have "motor voter" programs that allow people to register automatically to vote when they renew or apply for a driver's license. Most states, however, require advance in-person registration, which can depress turnout. The third factor affecting state voter turnout is the *composition of a state's electorate.* The character of the electorate varies from state to state. Characteristics associated with high levels of turnout are a high income, a high-status occupation, educational achievement, and being middle-aged, Jewish or Catholic, and white.

Who Votes? Personal Characteristics of Voters and Nonvoters

Age and *education* are the two personal characteristics most closely related to voter turnout. Young people tend to have the lowest

Figure 7.5: Where They Voted . . . and Where They Did Not

(1988 presidential election turnout as percent of voting age population)

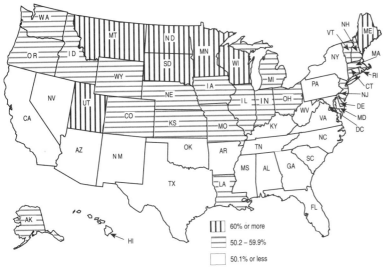

	1988 Turnout Rate (percent of voting age population)	Change, 1984-1988 (percentage points)
NATIONAL	50.1	-3.0
1. Minnesota	66.3	-1.9
2. Montana	62.4	-2.7
3. Maine	62.2	-2.6
4. Wisconsin	62.0	-1.5
5. North Dakota	61.5	-1.2
South Dakota	61.5	-1.0
7. Utah	60.0	-1.6
8. Iowa	59.3	-2.9
9. Vermont	59.1	-0.7
10. Oregon	58.6	-3.2
11. Idaho	58.3	-1.6
12. Massachusetts	58.1	+0.5
13. Connecticut	57.9	-3.2
14. Nebraska	56.8	+1.2
15. Colorado	55.1	0.0
Ohio	55.1	-2.9
17. Missouri	54.8	-2.5
18. New Hampshire	54.7	+1.7
19. Washington	54.6	-3.8
20. Kansas	54.3	-2.5
21. Michigan	54.0	-3.9
22. Illinois	53.3	-3.8
Indiana	53.3	-2.6
24. Rhode Island	53.0	-2.8
25. New Jersey	52.1	-4.5
26. Alaska	51.7	-7.5
27. Louisiana	51.3	-3.2
28. Delaware	51.0	-4.4
29. Wyoming	50.3	-3.0
30. Pennsylvania	50.1	-3.9
31. Mississippi	49.9	-2.3
32. Maryland	49.1	-2.3
33. Oklahoma	48.7	-3.4
34. Kentucky	48.2	-2.6
Virginia	48.2	-2.5
36. New York	48.1	-3.1
37. California	47.4	-2.2
38. New Mexico	47.3	-4.0
39. Arkansas	47.0	-4.8
40. West Virginia	46.7	-5.0
41. Alabama	45.8	-4.1
42. Arizona	45.0	-0.2
43. Nevada	44.9	+3.4
44. Florida	44.7	-3.5
Tennessee	44.7	-4.4
46. Texas	44.2	-3.0
47. North Carolina	43.4	-4.0
48. Hawaii	43.0	-1.3
49. District of Columbia	39.4	-3.8
50. South Carolina	38.9	-1.8
51. Georgia	38.8	-3.2

Legend: ⫾⫾⫾ 60% or more; 50.2 – 59.9%; 50.1% or less

Source: *Congressional Quarterly Weekly Report*, January 21, 1989, 136.

rates of turnout (see Table 7.1). In 1988, 36.7 percent of eighteen-to twenty-one-year-olds reported that they had voted, compared with 69.3 percent of those between ages forty-five and sixty-four. The unsettled character of young people's lives affects their election day participation. Registration requirements, attending college away from home, military service, and residential mobility all create obstacles to political participation by the young.

Although the turnout rates of various age groups differ significantly, by age thirty-five most people vote at least occasionally. Only a small proportion of the middle-aged population are habitual nonvoters, and, of the total electorate, less than 5 percent almost never vote.[19]

Education is the most important personal characteristic affecting turnout: the higher one's level of education, the greater the likelihood of voting. Better-educated people are likely to recognize how politics affects their lives and the things they care about, to be interested in politics, and to be skilled in dealing with registration requirements. Higher levels of education also are associated with

19. William H. Flanigan and Nancy H. Zingale, *Political Behavior of the American Electorate,* 7th ed. (Washington, D.C.: CQ Press, 1991), 18–20.

Table 7.1 Voter Participation in 1988

	% Who Reported Voting
White	59.1
Black	51.5
Hispanic	28.8
Male	56.4
Female	58.8
Age	
18–20	36.7
21–24	38.3
25–34	48.0
35–44	61.3
45–64	69.3
65 and older	68.8
Employed	58.4
Unemployed	38.6
Not in labor force	57.3
School years completed	
8 years or less	36.7
4 years of high school	54.7
1–3 years of college	64.5
4 years or more of college	77.6

SOURCE: Bureau of the Census, *Statistical Abstract of the United States: 1990* (Washington, D.C.: Government Printing Office, 1990), 262.

Is Nonvoting a Social Disease?

higher incomes and greater social prestige. When education is held constant, however, income has little impact on voter turnout.

Racial groups also differ in their turnout rates. Blacks have lower turnout levels than whites, but blacks vote more frequently than Hispanics. These turnout rates tend to reflect the generally lower levels of education of these minorities. Turnout rates among blacks have risen steadily as discriminatory barriers to their voting have been outlawed and determined efforts to mobilize black voters have continued. As a result, the black vote has become a critical factor in determining the outcome of some elections. In 1986, for example, overwhelming black support for Democratic candidates in four highly competitive Senate races contributed to Democratic victories.

In the past, women had lower rates of turnout than men because until 1920 and ratification of the Nineteenth Amendment giving them the vote, their participation in politics had been neither widely accepted nor encouraged. Today, however, women report slightly higher rates of turnout than men.

Partisan Implications of Turnout Patterns

Because people who rank relatively high in socioeconomic status and educational attainment, who are middle-aged, and who are white have the highest turnout rates, more Republicans are likely to go to the polls than Democrats. Is it surprising then that get-out-the-vote campaigns and efforts to increase turnout through easing of registration requirements have been a standard Democratic electoral strategy? Increased voter turnout does not necessarily benefit the Democrats, however. In the 1988 presidential election, nonvoters probably held down Bush's margin in the popular vote. A 1989 *New York Times*/CBS survey showed that nonvoters preferred Bush by a 50–34 margin. This information as well as Republican successes among first-time voters in the Reagan elections of 1980 and 1984 indicate that the conventional wisdom that high turnout helps the Democrats is open to question.[20]

Nonvoting is not primarily a matter of voter registration holding down turnout. Rather, it is caused by personal attitudes—a lack of interest, a low sense of civic duty, a feeling that elections are not important, and weak attachments to a political party (see Table 7.2).

20. *New York Times*/CBS poll, reported in *Congressional Quarterly Weekly Report*, January 21, 1989, 138. Also see James DeNardo, "Turnout and the Vote: The Joke's on the Democrats," *American Political Science Review* 74 (June 1980): 406–420; and Abramson et al., *Change and Continuity*, 108–113.

Table 7.2 Personal Attitudes and Voter Turnout (percent agreeing)

Attitude	Likely Voters	People Who Do Not Vote Regularly
I'm aligned with a political party.	88	54
There are important differences between the parties.	85	65
I'd feel guilty if I didn't vote.	71	31
Politics and government are so complicated that I can't understand them.	50	77
People like me have no say in what government does.	32	57
It's a waste of time to vote.	12	41

SOURCE: Jeff Alderman, ABC News Poll, Survey 0080, June 29–July 13, 1983.

With a voter turnout rate at just over 50 percent, well below that of most Western democracies, is the American Republic healthy? Any comparison with other democratic systems, however, must take into account how most nations compute their turnout rates: based on the percentage of registered voters who actually cast ballots on election day. In the United States, which does not have uniform national registration requirements and where the government does not assume responsibility for registering voters, turnout rates are normally based on the percentage of the voting age population. These different methods of calculation mean that other nations consistently show much higher turnout rates than the United States. Although it must be recognized that a higher proportion of the citizens of other democracies are registered, a quite respectable 87 percent of registered Americans turn out to vote.[21]

An even more disturbing question is: Do Americans' relatively low turnout rates distort the will of the people? To date, there is no convincing evidence that turnout rates are distorting the public's policy and candidate preferences in elections. In general, nonvoters have

21. David Glass, Pevrill Squire, and Raymond Wolfinger, "Voter Turnout: An International Comparison," *Public Opinion,* December/January 1984, 52. For a more complete comparative analysis of voter turnout, see Ivor Crewe, "Electoral Participation," in *Democracy at the Polls,* ed. David Butler, Howard R. Penniman, and Austin Ranney (Washington, D.C.: American Enterprise Institute, 1981), 216–262.

candidate preferences much like those of voters.[22] After analyzing turnout in the 1988 election, political scientist Paul Abramson and his colleagues concluded that "there is no reasonable scenario under which increased turnout would have altered the outcome of the presidential election . . . [as] the problem for the Democrats is not low turnout but low levels of support." They found that even if two groups who voted heavily Democratic—blacks and Hispanics—had turned out at the same rate as whites, Dukakis would have received 2.6 million additional votes, far fewer than Bush's 7-million-vote victory margin. Yet the conditions likely to stimulate higher turnout among blacks and Hispanics would in all probability also cause higher turnout among whites.[23]

Voter turnout rates provide only a limited perspective on the electoral and more general political participation within a society. As noted in Chapter 5, there is more to political participation than casting a ballot, and Americans tend to have higher rates of nonvoting participation in politics than do citizens of most democracies. Nor do turnout rates reflect the amount of electing—frequency of elections, the range of offices, and type of electoral decisions—that can occur within a country. Thus, although Americans have a turnout rate below those of most other democracies, they do not necessarily do less voting than other citizens; in fact, they probably do more. Americans' relatively low rates of turnout also may reflect general satisfaction with the political order and a belief that the next election will not bring major and threatening changes since both the Republican and Democratic parties espouse essentially middle-of-the-road policies.

Although nonvoting in America is perhaps less worrisome than it might appear at first glance, reasons for concern still exist. With the educated, more well-to-do, and influential having the highest turnout rates, universal suffrage does not provide the kind of counterweight to power and wealth once envisioned by the advocates of universal suffrage.[24]

22. See John R. Petrocik, "Voter Turnout and Electoral Preference: The Anomalous Reagan Elections," in *Elections in America,* ed. Kay Schlozman (Boston: Unwin Hyman, 1987), 261–292.

23. Abramson et al., *Change and Continuity,* 111. Also see Ruy Teixeira, "Registration and Turnout," *Public Opinion,* January/February 1989, 12–13, 56–58; and Austin Ranney, "Non-Voting Is Not a Social Disease," *Public Opinion,* October/November 1983, 16–19.

24. See Crewe, "Electoral Participation," 261–262.

The Impact of Partisanship

Voters' choices on election day reflect their long-held attitudes and beliefs as well as such short-term transitory influences as current issues and **candidate images**. The impacts of these long- and short-term influences on the voter vary from election to election.

The most important and enduring influence on voters' choices is their *party identification*—a feeling of attachment and sympathy toward a political party.[25] Party identification is considered a long-term, stable influence on voter choice because it is not normally subject to sudden shifts from one election to the next.[26]

Political scientists measure party identification by surveying voters with such questions as "Generally speaking, do you think of yourself as a Republican, Democrat, or independent?" The strength of voters' commitments to a party and the party leanings of independents have been probed as well. These surveys were the basis for the development of a seven-point scale of partisanship, ranging from strong Democrats through independents to strong Republicans. From 1952 to 1988, between two-thirds and three-fourths of the electorate identified with either the Republican or Democratic parties (Table 7.3), but Democrats have held a consistent advantage over Republicans in terms of party identification. This advantage declined, however, during the 1980s and after the Persian Gulf War some polls even showed the GOP with a narrow edge over the Democrats.[27]

For strong partisans, the pull of their commitment to the Republican or Democratic party is substantial, and their rate of defection to the opposition is low. Strong Republicans in particular show a high level of party loyalty in presidential elections. For those with weaker partisan commitments, short-term influences such as issues and candidate appeal take on greater importance and can cause a substantial proportion of such voters to defect from their party on election day. In 1980, 1984, and 1988, for example, at least 30 percent of weak Democrats failed to support their party's presidential

25. A classic explanation of the concept of party identification is found in Angus Campbell et al., *The American Voter* (New York: Wiley, 1960), 121–128.
26. For a summary of research on the stability of party identification, see Herbert B. Asher, *Presidential Elections and American Politics: Voters, Candidates and Issues since 1952*, 4th ed. (Chicago: Dorsey, 1988), 70–75.
27. ABC/*Washington Post* poll, reported in *Washington Post*, March 7, 1991, A4.

Table 7.3 Party Identification in the United States, 1952–1988 *(percent)*

	1952	1956	1960	1964	1968	1972	1976	1980	1982	1984	1988
Strong Democrats	22	21	20	27	20	15	15	18	20	17	17
Weak Democrats	25	23	25	25	25	26	25	23	24	20	18
Independent (leaning) Democrats	10	6	6	9	10	11	12	11	11	11	12
Independent	5	9	10	8	11	13	15	13	11	11	11
Independent (leaning) Republicans	7	8	7	6	9	11	10	10	8	12	13
Weak Republicans	14	14	14	14	15	13	14	14	14	15	14
Strong Republicans	14	15	16	11	10	10	9	9	10	12	14
Apolitical	3	4	3	1	1	1	1	2	2	2	2
Total	100	100	100	100	100	100	100	100	100	100	100

SOURCE: National Elections Study surveys.

candidate,[28] making it possible for Republicans to win recent presidential elections even though they have fewer party identifiers than the Democrats. Most partisans, however, do vote for their party's presidential candidates. In 1988, a *New York Times*/CBS exit poll reported that 91 percent of all Republicans and 82 percent of all Democrats voted for their parties' presidential tickets.[29]

The tendency of both strong and weak partisans to support their parties' nominees is more pronounced in elections below the presidential level. At the presidential level, weakly committed voters, bombarded with saturation news coverage and an avalanche of campaign advertising, may be influenced to defect from their party by a particularly salient issue or appealing candidate. But at the level of House races, with their relative lack of publicity and low-visibility campaigns, weak partisans are more likely to vote in accord with their party identification because less information is available to them.

More Independents. One of the most notable changes in the partisanship of the electorate has been the increase in the proportion of voters labeling themselves **independents**. This trend was especially strong from the 1960s through the mid-1970s and was most noticeable among young voters who did not align themselves with a

28. For data on defection rates by strong and weak partisan identifiers as well as those leaning toward one or the other of the parties, see Asher, *Presidential Elections and American Politics*, 87–89; and Michael M. Gant and Norman R. Luttbeg, *American Electoral Behavior* (Itaska, Ill.: Peacock, 1991), 41.

29. *New York Times,* Nov. 10, 1988, 18Y, National edition.

party as quickly as older generations had. Thus, the increased proportion of independents in the electorate has stemmed mainly from a large influx of new voters—so-called baby boomers who came of voting age in the 1960s and 1970s—and not from partisans adopting the independent label.[30] The tendency of voters to declare themselves independents leveled off after the mid-1970s, and in the 1980s partisanship showed a modest resurgence among voters. Even so, the current number of independents is high compared with the number found in the 1950s.

Independents have shown a capacity to switch back and forth between the Republican and Democratic candidates in post-World War II presidential elections. They were overwhelmingly Republican in the Eisenhower elections of the 1950s; almost 2–1 Democratic in the 1964 Johnson landslide; and Republican by the same proportion in 1984. With independents constituting approximately one-third of the electorate and capable of great swings in party preference from one election to the next, they constitute a critical voting bloc for both parties. The tendency of independents since 1952 to favor Republican over Democratic presidential candidates in every election but the Democratic landslide of 1964 has been a critical element in Republican dominance of the presidency.

Declining Influence of Partisanship. Although studies of voting behavior have consistently demonstrated that party identification is the single most important determinant of voter choice,[31] the influence of partisanship on voter choice has weakened in recent decades. Increasing proportions of the electorate now engage in *ticket splitting*—voting for candidates of different parties instead of voting a straight party line ballot. Voters' tendencies to split their tickets are evident in the high percentage of congressional districts carried by different parties in presidential and congressional elections. In 1988, for example, 34 percent of the congressional districts yielded split outcomes between presidential and House contests. Earlier in this century, ticket splitting was much rarer—in 1920, for example, only 3.2 percent of the congressional districts had split outcomes.[32]

The decline of the influence of party identification on voter choice

30. Warren E. Miller and Teresa E. Levitin, *Leadership and Change: Presidential Elections from 1952–1976* (Boston: Winthrop, 1976), 250–251.

31. See Campbell et al., *American Voter.*

32. For data on ticket splitting since 1900, see Norman J. Ornstein, Thomas E. Mann, and Michael Malbin, *Vital Statistics on Congress, 1989–90* (Washington, D.C.: CQ Press, 1989), 62; for 1988 data, see Rhodes Cook, "Key to Survival for Democrats Lies in Split-Ticket Voting," *Congressional Quarterly Weekly Report,* July 8, 1989, 1711.

reflects a view among voters that parties are less relevant than they were in the past. Indeed, people are increasingly neutral in their attitudes toward political parties.[33] The trend in this century has been away from party-centered campaigns in which the party organizations controlled nominations, ran campaigns, and appealed to the voters on the basis of partisanship. Modern-day campaigns—especially presidential ones—tend to be candidate centered and media oriented. Today's candidates are no longer dependent on the organizational resources of their parties. Television provides a means of establishing contact with voters without relying on party organizations. In addition, candidates need not depend on their parties to staff their campaigns. They can create personal campaign organizations by hiring consultants who specialize in all the techniques—direct mail, polling, placement of television commercials, appeals to various voter groups—of modern campaigning. With a personal organization and through extensive use of the media, particularly television, candidates can sell themselves, not their parties, to the voters. They can even de-emphasize their party ties when it is advantageous. Such candidate-centered campaigning reinforces attitudes about the candidates, but it does little to reinforce partisan commitments among the electors and renders party affiliation a less powerful influence on many voters. Voters do see differences between the Republican and Democratic parties, but issues and evaluations of the candidates themselves are looming larger in their decisions.

The Role of Candidate Image

A candidate's image—personality, physical appearance, style, and background—figure heavily in the media coverage accompanying presidential campaigns. Candidates with a favorable public image can contribute significantly to their party's vote on election day. Dwight Eisenhower, whose personal appeal transcended partisanship, was a classic example of a candidate whose image added substantially to his total vote. His status as a hero of World War II and his personal qualities—sincerity, sense of duty, commitment to family, religious devotion, and sheer likeableness—all of which were captured in the slogan "I like Ike," caused heavy Democratic defections to the Republican party in 1952 and again in 1956. Candidate images also played a significant role in the 1988 election. Through hardline stands on crime and national defense as well as aggressive attacks on Dukakis for being a far-out liberal, Bush was able to over-

33. Martin P. Wattenberg, *The Decline of American Political Parties, 1952–1988,* 2d ed. (Cambridge, Mass.: Harvard University Press, 1990), 50–72.

come the "wimp factor," an image that had plagued his campaign for the GOP nomination. Bush also benefited from the voters' perceptions of him as both experienced and competent—the two most frequent answers given when a CNN/*Los Angeles Times* poll asked people why they voted for a presidential candidate. Dukakis's most positive characteristic was the perception that he "cares about people like me."[34]

Voters also are influenced by negative perceptions of candidates. In both 1984 and 1988, Democratic nominees were hurt by such perceptions. In 1984, for example, Ronald Reagan benefited from public perceptions of the Democratic nominee, Walter Mondale, as "a weak leader," "a big spender," and "tied to special interests."[35] When asked as they left the polls in 1988 what they liked least about the candidates, Bush voters most often said that Dukakis was too liberal, indicating that the Bush campaign's efforts to define Dukakis in ideological terms were successful. Interestingly, in response to the same question Dukakis supporters said that Bush ran a dirty campaign.[36]

With the exception of the 1964 contest between Lyndon Johnson and Barry Goldwater, the Republicans have been helped more than the Democrats by the public's evaluation of their presidential candidates. In the 1980 election between President Jimmy Carter and Ronald Reagan, however, there was a general lack of enthusiasm for both candidates, and candidate images had a negligible effect on the election.[37]

The Impact of Issues

Classical democratic theory assigns issues a prominent role in voter decisions; nevertheless, they normally follow party identification and candidate image in importance of influence on the voter. Early systematic research in the 1940s and 1950s found that issues had scant influence on how voters arrived at a decision.[38] But these findings have been questioned by more recent research, which used improved methodologies and took into account the relatively calm politics of the 1950s compared to the more turbulent and divisive decades of the sixties, seventies, and eighties. According to this research, issues are now a more important basis for determining voters'

34. Poll results reported in *National Journal*, November 12, 1988, 2854.
35. ABC News poll, year-end wrap-up, 1984.
36. *National Journal*, November 12, 1988, 2854.
37. Asher, *Presidential Elections and American Politics*, 184.
38. See Bernard Berlson, Paul Lazarsfeld, and William McPhee, *Voting* (Chicago: University of Chicago Press, 1954); and Campbell et al., *American Voter.*

BLOOM COUNTY

by Berke Breathed

choices than in the 1950s.[39] Some aspects of human behavior, however, work to reduce the impact of issues.

The widespread ignorance of voters about issues and candidates' positions on them works against issue-based voting. This is especially true of foreign policy matters, which voters often find little related to their own lives. So-called issue voting is further diminished by some voters projecting their personal issue positions onto their preferred candidates, regardless of those candidates' actual issue positions. In 1968, for example, both hawks and doves on America's military involvement in Vietnam were found among the supporters of Richard Nixon and his Democratic opponent Hubert Humphrey. Since the candidates were less than explicit about their Vietnam policies, voters who saw a difference between them on this issue were responding to their own wishes and not engaging in issue voting.[40] It is also possible for voters to adopt issue positions because their preferred candidate has taken that position.

An issue has an impact on voter choice only when (1) voters are informed and concerned about the issue; (2) candidates take distinguishable stands on the issue; and (3) voters perceive how the candidate stands in relation to their own concerns. In the 1972 presidential contest between Republican Richard Nixon and Dem-

39. For a summary of research on the extent of issue influence on voter choice, see Asher, *Presidential Elections and American Politics*, chap. 4. An important study in demonstrating the heightened significance of issues was Norman Nie, Sidney Verba, and John R. Petrocik, *The Changing American Voter* (Cambridge, Mass.: Harvard University Press, 1976).

40. Benjamin I. Page and Richard A. Brody, "Policy Voting and the Electoral Process: The Vietnam Issue," *American Political Science Review* 66 (September 1972): 987.

ocrat George McGovern, issues clearly had an impact. On eleven of fourteen issues studied, the voters felt closer to Nixon than to McGovern, and there was a close correlation between people's perceptions of where the candidates stood on the issues and the candidate for whom they voted. Only on issues related to the environment and urban unrest did McGovern appear to be closer to citizens' positions, whereas Nixon was viewed as closer to voters' preferences on such issues as the Vietnam War, marijuana, desegregation, and campus unrest.[41]

To base their voting on issues, voters must have information about candidates' policy positions. Such information is available quickly and easily when candidates and parties take distinct positions on issues and campaign on the basis of those positions. The candidates and parties, however, do not always offer clear-cut policy alternatives the way they did in the Nixon-McGovern contest. With most voters tending to be moderate or centrist in their orientations and with each party composed of people with diverse viewpoints, there may be little incentive for candidates to take strongly opposing stands. They may, therefore, straddle issues and make issue-based voting difficult for the average citizen.

Voters' decisions are made easier when an incumbent is seeking reelection. Having had a substantial opportunity to judge the candidate's performance, voters can render a verdict on his or her behavior in office. This process of electoral decision making is called **retrospective voting**.[42] In the 1980 and 1984 elections, voters issued their verdicts about the performance of incumbent presidents. In 1980, amid rising inflation, unemployment, and interest rates, voters rendered a negative judgment on President Jimmy Carter's performance. But in 1984, with most voters believing that the economy was in better shape than it had been four years earlier, they evaluated Ronald Reagan's record in office more favorably. And in 1988, even though no incumbent was on the ballot, Vice President Bush clearly benefited from the public perception that President Reagan had performed well and that Bush would stay the course. Nonetheless, evaluations of the Reagan presidency were less favorable than in 1984, and the vote was therefore closer.[43]

41. Arthur H. Miller et al., "A Majority Party in Disarray: Policy Polarization in the 1972 Election," *American Political Science Review* 70 (September 1976): 753–778.
42. See Morris P. Fiorina, *Retrospective Voting in America* (New Haven, Conn.: Yale University Press, 1981).
43. Abramson et al., *Change and Continuity*, 195.

The Meaning of Elections

Elections do make a difference. Not only do they periodically change the government's leadership, but they also can result in significant changes in public policy. For example, the 1964 Democratic landslide that extended Lyndon Johnson's White House tenure and greatly strengthened Democratic majorities in the House and Senate enabled the president to gain congressional approval for a wide range of social welfare legislation including Medicare, Medicaid, and the War on Poverty. Similarly, Ronald Reagan's election in 1980 resulted in a reordering of governmental priorities as the share of funds allocated to the military was increased, the rate of growth in domestic social spending was restricted, income tax rates were reduced, the budget deficit was allowed to grow, the government embarked on a policy of deregulating the economy, and the Supreme Court became more conservative as a result of three Reagan appointees.[44]

Elections are also important because through them the rank-and-file citizens can have an influence on their government. Since most presidents seek to keep their campaign commitments to the voters who elected them,[45] elections often are seen as the process through which voters register their policy preferences and direct the course of government. But do election results really reveal the policy preferences of the voters? Do elections provide the winners with clear-cut mandates for specific policy decisions? Our consideration of the forces influencing voter choice certainly suggests that there are limits to the extent to which elections reflect the voters' views on specific issues. For many, the decision in the voting booth is determined by party identification and generalized notions that one party or the other is best for peace or jobs. Still others vote on the basis of candidate image, and many render a general retrospective judgment on an incumbent party's performance in office. Only a minority engage in issue- or policy-based voting.

Thus, elections are rarely mandates from the voters on specific issues, and often the message conveyed by the voters is quite murky.[46]

44. The Reagan presidency's impact on domestic and foreign policy is summarized in *The Reagan Legacy: Promise and Performance*, ed. Charles O. Jones (Chatham, N.J.: Chatham House, 1988), chaps. 7 and 8.

45. See Gerald M. Pomper and Susan S. Lederman, *Election in America: Control and Influence in Democratic Politics*, 2d ed. (New York: Longman, 1980); and Jeff Fishel, *Presidents and Promises: From Campaign Pledge to Presidential Performance* (Washington, D.C.: CQ Press, 1985).

46. For a more detailed consideration of why elections are seldom mandates to public officials, see Polsby and Wildavsky, *Presidential Elections*, 290–295. The

This was certainly the case in 1988. Republican George Bush won a comfortable presidential victory, but the Democrats retained control of the Congress and even gained seats in both the House and Senate. And after the election, the Republican president and Democratic congressional leaders argued about the nature of the 1988 election mandate and quickly fell into disagreement about such issues as the minimum wage, affirmative action, child care, capital gains taxes, and the budget.

Other factors over and above the increasing tendency of the voters to grant control of the presidency and Congress to different parties make discernment of clear policy mandates from elections difficult. For example, with so many issues and so many different voter groups involved in a presidential election, candidates tend to collect voters for different, and even conflicting, reasons. Furthermore, candidates do not always indicate clearly what their policies will be once elected. John Kennedy's promise to "get the country going again," for example, was vague enough to cover a wide range of voters' hopes and gave little indication of the policies he intended to follow to achieve economic growth.

Even when candidates are clear about their intentions, the voters may base their decisions on other grounds. Thus in 1980, Reagan was forthcoming with specific proposals in the fields of taxation, government expenditures, and national security policy. Public opinion surveys, however, revealed that the voters did not base their decisions on the conservative policies advocated by candidate Reagan. Rather, the election was primarily a referendum on the performance of the Carter administration, particularly his handling of the economy.

American elections are seldom referendums on specific issues; they decide which of two competing political parties will control government institutions. The relationship between election outcomes and public policy is, therefore, subtle and indirect. Political scientists Nelson Polsby and Aaron Wildavsky have described the electoral process in the following manner:

Two teams of politicians, one in office, the other seeking office, both attempt to get enough votes to win elections. In order to win, they go to various groups of voters and, by offering to pursue policies favored by these groups, or by suggesting policies they might come to favor, hope to attract their votes. If there were only one office-seeking team, their incentive to respond to the policy preferences of the groups in the population would diminish;

Polsby and Wildavsky argument is similar to that found in Robert A. Dahl, *A Preface to Democratic Theory* (Chicago: University of Chicago Press, 1956).

if there were many such teams, the chances that any one of them could achieve a sufficient number of backers to govern would diminish. Hence the two-party system is . . . a kind of compromise between the goals of responsiveness and effectiveness.[47]

The ballot thus guides and constrains elected officials. They are relatively free to act within rather broad limits, subject to their anticipation of the voters' responses to their actions. The existence of electoral competition and the real possibility that the voters might choose new leaders at the next election are incentives for political leaders to stay in touch with the voters.

For Review

1. Elections are regulated by both the federal and state governments. The federal government is engaged primarily in protecting people from discrimination in their exercise of the right to vote, regulating campaign finance in elections for federal office, and setting uniform dates for federal elections. The states regulate voter registration and the administration of elections.

2. To be elected president, a candidate must receive a majority of the electoral college vote. A state's electoral votes are allocated to candidates on a winner-take-all basis in which the candidate who gains a plurality of the popular vote receives the state's full complement of electoral votes. Because of the winner-take-all feature, candidates concentrate their campaign efforts on states with large blocs of electoral votes and on states where the race is tightly contested.

3. The Federal Election Campaign Act provides public funding for presidential candidates who agree to accept no private contributions to their campaigns. The law's expenditure limits have been breached, however, by both parties channeling funds to state and local party committees for use in party-building activities that aid presidential campaigns.

4. The turnout of eligible voters is approximately 50 percent in presidential elections and normally less than 40 percent in midterm elections. Voter turnout is affected by such social characteristics as age and education, registration requirements, the amount of publicity a campaign receives, the competitiveness of the election, and personal attitudes such as party identification.

5. Voter choice on election day is influenced by the interaction of

47. Polsby and Wildavsky, *Presidential Elections*, 290.

party identification, a long-term influence, and more short-term forces such as issues and candidate image.

For Further Reading

Abramson, Paul R., John H. Aldrich, and David W. Rohde. *Change and Continuity in the 1988 Elections*. Rev. ed. Washington, D.C.: CQ Press, 1991. An analysis of the 1988 and 1990 elections demonstrating the interaction of partisanship, candidates, issues, and presidential performance on voter choice.

Asher, Herbert B. *Presidential Elections and American Politics: Voters, Candidates and Issues Since 1952*. Chicago: Dorsey, 1988. An analysis of presidential elections between 1952 and 1984.

Flanigan, William H., and Nancy H. Zingale. *Political Behavior of the American Electorate*. 7th ed. Washington, D.C.: CQ Press, 1991. A concise consideration of voter turnout, determinants of voter choice, and the social bases of partisanship.

Guide to U.S. Elections. 2d ed. Washington, D.C.: Congressional Quarterly Inc., 1985. An authoritative compendium of statistics on presidential, congressional, and gubernatorial elections, along with brief accounts of American electoral history.

Kessel, John H. *Presidential Campaign Politics*. 4th ed. Pacific Grove, Calif.: Brooks/Cole, 1992. An analysis of presidential campaign organizations, strategies, and the determinants of citizen choice.

Polsby, Nelson W., and Aaron Wildavsky, *Presidential Elections: Contemporary Strategies of American Electoral Politics*. 7th ed. New York: Free Press, 1988. An insightful and provocative consideration of presidential electoral politics and proposals for reform.

Sorauf, Frank J. *Money in American Elections*. Glenview, Ill.: Scott, Foresman, 1988. The most current and comprehensive analysis of campaign finance available.

Wattenberg, Martin P. *The Decline of American Political Parties, 1952–1988*. 2d ed. Cambridge, Mass.: Harvard University Press, 1990. An analysis of the declining influence of party identification on the electoral decisions of Americans.

8. Interest Groups

F EW ASPECTS of American politics arouse more suspicion and righteous indignation than the activities of interest groups and their agents—so-called **lobbyists**. These "special interests" are perceived as having a self-serving, sometimes corrupt disregard for the interest of the general public. *Time* magazine captured this sentiment in a cover story, "Influence Peddling: Lobbyists Swarm over Capitol Hill."

The hallway is known as Gucci Gulch after the expensive Italian shoes they wear. At tax-writing time, the Washington lobbyists line up by the hundreds in the corridor outside the House Ways and Means Committee room, ever vigilant against the attempt of lawmakers to close their prized loopholes. Over near the House and Senate chambers, Congressmen must run a gauntlet of lobbyists who sometimes express their views on legislation by pointing their thumbs up or down. . . . Senator John Danforth . . . could be seen on the Capitol steps trying to wrench his hand from the grip of a lobbyist. . . . The Senator, an ordained Episcopal minister, rolled his eyes heavenward and mumbled, "Save me from these people."[1]

Although Americans are suspicious of interest groups, they also are world-class organizers of such groups. This tendency was noted as far back as the 1830s by Alexis de Tocqueville, the astute French observer who wrote *Democracy in America,* a classic commentary on our society in its formative years.[2] Even de Tocqueville probably would be amazed at the extent of interest group proliferation in present-day Washington. Indeed, Congressional Quarterly's *Washington Information Directory* uses up almost five hundred pages just listing major government offices and the organizations concerned with their policies.

The widespread public disapproval and fear of group activities that exist side by side with broad public participation in interest groups reflect the public's ambivalence toward interest groups in general. Many people object to some groups' policy goals, fearing that through such groups the well-connected, well-organized, and well-off will exert undue influence over government institutions. Yet at the same time, people can be firm, fervent supporters of the groups to which they themselves belong. The self-described citizens' orga-

---

1. *Time,* March 3, 1986, 26.
2. Alexis de Tocqueville, *Democracy in America,* ed. Richard D. Heffner (New York: New American Library, 1956), 102. For evidence of extensive group affiliations by Americans, see Frank R. Baumgartner and Jack L. Walker, "Survey Research and Membership in Voluntary Associations," *American Journal of Political Science* 32 (November 1988): 908–928.

nization Common Cause exemplifies this ambivalence. This organization has pushed aggressively for measures that would reduce the role of interest groups in the government process. Yet Common Cause itself is an influential participant in the interest group system with thousands of members and a professional staff in Washington. Whether condemned as special interests or cherished as a special way in which citizens can have their say in politics, interest groups are an integral part of the American political process. This chapter examines the nature and scope of interest groups in America, the determinants of a group's clout, the techniques groups use to exert influence, and the issues raised by the prominent role they play in the American system.

What Are Interest Groups?

"An **interest group** is an organized body of individuals who share some goals and who try to influence public policy."[3] The key elements of this definition are "organized" and "influence public policy." Thus, the National Association of Manufacturers (NAM), the National Association for the Advancement of Colored People (NAACP), and the American Farm Bureau Federation (AFBF) are organized groups seeking to influence government policy. But manufacturers, blacks, workers, and farmers are not interest groups. Being unorganized, they are interests and potential interest groups. Not all interest group activity is carried on by such huge groups as the AFL-CIO or AFBF. Some organizations consist merely of a small staff backed by financial patrons. For example, the Media Access Project is a public interest law firm concerned about the public's access to government information. In addition, there are the so-called hired guns—Washington lawyers, public relations consultants, and lobbyists—who, for a fee, try to influence government policy for their clients.

As the opening quotation from *Time* suggests, much of the media coverage of interest group activities is critical in nature. Yet it is important not to lose sight of the essential functions these groups perform: they are one way in which people who share the same attitudes or interests can be represented informally. Specialized interests in society are drawn to such organizations as the American Council for the Blind, the Flight Attendants Association, and the National Association of Securities Dealers. Because such groups often deal with issues that affect too few people to attract the attention of the

3. Jeffrey M. Berry, *The Interest Group Society* (Boston: Little, Brown, 1984), 3.

political parties, or with issues too specialized and technical to attract media attention, it can be said that the group system of informal representation supplements the formal system of geographic area representation used in Congress. In their representational roles, interest groups provide policy makers with specialized information that otherwise might not be readily available. Interest groups also are an avenue for more effective political participation than is likely to be achieved by a lone individual picketing on the sidewalk in front of the White House.

The Diversity of Organized Interests

One glance at the building directory of one of the office buildings that line K or M streets in Northwest Washington just a few blocks from the White House gives a vivid sense of the wide range of organized interests that are riding herd on national politics. The thousands of organizations, corporations, law firms, and political consultants listed in such directories reflect the incredible diversity of American interests.

Groups with a direct economic stake in government policy (such as the National Association of Broadcasters) as well as organizations not motivated by material gain (such as the Children's Defense Fund) operate in a permanent state of mobilization on the scene in Washington, poised to advance or defend their organization's interests. According to political scientist David Truman, organized groups become involved in politics and inevitably gravitate toward Washington and the federal government when they find their own resources inadequate to deal with a problem.[4] Government assistance in solving their problems or achieving their objectives is their goal. Even business organizations, which often espouse a philosophy of minimal government interference in economic markets, troop to Washington for assistance when times are difficult. Thus when faced with bankruptcy in the late 1970s, Chrysler Corporation put on an all-out lobbying drive to win government-guaranteed loans as a means of staying in business.

But organized interests do not reserve their big guns just for the federal government; on occasion, they also react (mostly negatively) to the objectives of another interest group. Indeed, one group's actions to advance its interests are likely to trigger a defensive response

4. The concept of interest groups inevitably gravitating toward the government is developed in one of the classic books in the field, David B. Truman's *The Governmental Process* (New York: Knopf, 1951), chap. 3.

Lobbying organizations, which seek to influence government decision makers, are concentrated at the corner of 16th and K Streets, N.W., a few blocks north of the White House.

Economic Interests

from those who would be disadvantaged by the new policy, causing a spiraling level of interest group activity. For example, in the 1980s, when unions pressed for adoption of a legislative agenda that included raising the minimum wage, requiring advance notice of plant closings, granting job leaves to new parents, and mandating health insurance coverage for part-time workers, the U.S. Chamber of Commerce, which saw these measures as threatening its interests, mounted a major counterattack that at least temporarily stymied the unions. The Chamber was supported in its attack by its member state and local chambers of commerce, companies, and business associations, as well as its staff of 1,400 and its budget in excess of $65 million.

Since the 1960s, there has been a virtual explosion in the number and diversity of interest groups operating in Washington. As the scope of government activities has grown, more and more groups have recognized the benefits of having a presence in the nation's capital. The composition of the interest group system has changed as well. The traditional farm, union, professional, and business groups must now compete with a vast array of citizens' groups organized around an idea or cause and having no occupational basis for membership. In addition, individual corporations, states, cities, counties, and universities have gravitated toward Washington to advance or protect interests that can be dramatically affected by government policy. But, all this being said, business, union, and professional groups—organizations based on economic self-interest—are among the most prominent and durable of the interests seeking to influence government policy.

Business-oriented groups dominate the interest group universe. The largest of these are the so-called peak business organizations that seek to represent general business interests. These include the U.S. Chamber of Commerce, the National Association of Manufacturers, and the Business Roundtable. NAM is composed of large manufacturing concerns, and the Business Roundtable comprises approximately two hundred of the nation's largest companies—for example, IBM, General Motors, GTE, and Shell Oil.

The more specialized business groups are called trade associations, composed of companies in the same line of business. Trade associations range from the American Bankers Association with its thirteen thousand member banks to the much smaller American Institute of Nail and Tack Manufacturers and the Chain Link Fence Manufacturers Institute.

Rankings of the Sixteen Most Influential and Active Interests in the Fifty States

Ranking	Interest	Number[a]
1	Schoolteachers' organizations	43
2	General business organizations	31
3	Bankers' associations	28
4	Manufacturers	23
5	Traditional labor organizations (AFL-CIO)	23
6	Utility companies	20
7	Individual banks and financial institutions	20
8	State and local government employee associations	16
9	Lawyer associations	15
10	Local government associations	15
11	Doctors	14
12	Insurance companies and associations	13
13	Individual traditional labor unions (teamsters, auto workers)	13
14	Realtors' associations	12
15	General farm organizations (farm bureaus)	11
16	K-12 educational interests (other than teachers)	10

Source: Allan J. Cigler and Burdett A. Loomis, eds., *Interest Group Politics,* 3d ed. (Washington, D.C.: CQ Press, 1991), 68. Based on data published in Clive S. Thomas and Ronald J. Hrebenar, "Interest Groups in the States," in *Politics in the American States,* 5th ed., ed. Virginia Gray, Herbert Jacob, and Robert B. Albritton (Glenview, Ill.: Scott, Foresman/Little, Brown, 1990), 123-158.

[a] Number of states in which the interest was ranked in the "most effective interest" category.

Individual corporations also try to influence policy making. Over six hundred have Washington offices, and those without an office frequently hire a law firm or lobbyist to look out for their interests.[5] In a sense, corporations have multiple representation in Washington: their own corporate representation as well as the resources of such groups as the U.S. Chamber of Commerce and the trade associations to which they belong. In fact, large corporations engaged in several lines of businesses can belong to over twenty lobbying organizations.

Labor unions have a larger base of individual members than do business organizations. The largest and most influential union is the

5. A listing of corporate offices in Washington is found in the *National Journal*'s annual publication *The Capital Source: The Who's Who, What, Where in Washington* (Washington, D.C.: National Journal, 1990).

Partial Listing of Organizations to Which General Electric Belongs

- *Peak business associations:* U.S. Chamber of Commerce, National Association of Manufacturers, Business Roundtable

- *Export trade associations:* Council of the Americas, Business Group on the Export Administration Act, Coalition for Employment through Exports

- *Nuclear power trade associations:* American Nuclear Energy Council, Atomic Industrial Forum, American Nuclear Society, U.S. Committee for Energy Awareness

- *Taxes and finance groups and trade associations:* The Carlton Group, American Council for Capital Formation, Tax Foundation, American Financial Services Association, American Equipment Leasing Association

- *Medical equipment and electronics trade associations:* National Electrical Manufacturers Association, Health Industries Manufacturers Association, Electronics Industries Association, American Electronics Association

- *Defense and aircraft trade associations:* Aerospace Industries Asso-ciation of America, American Helicopter Society, American Defense Pre-paredness Association, National Security Industries Association

Source: "Organizations to Which General Electric Belongs," *Washington Post,* April 13, 1985, A12. Copyright © 1985 by the *Washington Post.*

AFL-CIO, a confederation of such operating unions as the United Steel Workers, United Auto Workers, and United Brotherhood of Carpenters and Joiners of America. (Not all unions are affiliated with the AFL-CIO; the highly politicized National Education Association, a union of teachers, operates independently of the AFL-CIO, as do various railroad employee unions.) The AFL-CIO's political involvement extends beyond such bread-and-butter union issues as the minimum wage and occupational safety and health to include what the federation considers to be the social justice concerns of working people—civil rights, health care, and Social Security. Member unions are likely to focus their political activities on issues dear to their members. The postal workers' union, for example, is primarily concerned with wages, work rules, and retirement benefits for government workers.

As the industrial sector of the economy has declined since the 1950s, the longtime AFL-CIO unions representing industrial and building trades workers have seen their memberships decline as well. Whereas in the 1950s the auto workers', steel workers', and carpenters' unions were the nation's largest, they have been replaced today by such white-collar and service sector unions as the Teamsters and the American Federation of State, County, and Municipal Employees.

The agricultural sector, another economic interest, is organized to reflect general farm interests as well as those of specific commodity producers. The largest of the general farm interest groups is the American Farm Bureau Federation, composed of state farm bureau federations representing approximately three million farm families. AFBF tends to represent the larger, more efficient producers and to support a relatively conservative political agenda. On many issues, it is opposed by the politically weaker National Farmers Organization and National Farmers Union, who represent the dwindling number of small producers. Major powers in agriculture policy making are the organizations that promote the interests of specific commodity growers and processors—for example, the National Peanut Council, Tobacco Institute, National Association of Wheat Growers, and such agribusiness corporations as Ralston Purina and Cargill.

Finally, professional associations represent many of the individuals whose occupations demand technical training and expertise. Political involvement is greatest among those professional groups heavily regulated by government or dependent on government for financing. Examples of such groups are the American Bar Association and the American Medical Association.

Unlike private sector groups that advance the interests of those engaged in profit-making enterprises or have occupational prerequisites for membership, nonprofit organizations represent the interests of people not as wage earners, stockholders, or producers, but as citizens, consumers, and taxpayers, or as the elderly, disadvantaged, handicapped, or minorities.[6] Membership in these organizations is open to all regardless of professional or organizational affiliations. Many of these organizations—particularly advocates for consumers, the environment, minorities, and the poor—are commonly called **public interest groups**, although their "public interest" label has stirred the resentment of those who oppose them and have a different conception of public interest.[7]

The range of interests spanned by nonprofit groups is extremely broad. Some groups voice the concerns of citizens, consumers, women, minorities, and environmentalists; others crusade for single issues such as the right to life and gun control; and still others are ideologues of the Left and Right. One of the most prominent and influential of the public interest groups is Common Cause. It has called for government reforms in such areas as campaign finance, lobbying, government ethics, congressional organization, and voter registration.[8] Public interest groups also have taken up the causes of the environment (Sierra Club and National Wildlife Federation), women's rights (National Organization for Women), civil rights (NAACP), and those unable to present their own case to the government such as children (Children's Defense Fund). The broad ideological concerns of liberals and conservatives also have found outlets in the interest group system. For those with a liberal policy orientation, there is the Americans for Democratic Action, and for conservatives, there is the American Conservative Union.

Religious organizations have long played a prominent role in politics. In earlier eras, Protestant groups led the struggle for the abolition of slavery and for Prohibition. More recently, church organizations have been in the forefront of the civil rights and anti-Vietnam War movements. The National Council of Churches and its

6. A typology of interest groups is provided by Jack L. Walker, "Origins and Maintenance of Interest Groups in America," *American Political Science Review* 77 (June 1983): 392–394.

7. For a comprehensive and insightful study of public interest groups, see Jeffrey M. Berry, *Lobbying for the People: The Political Behavior of Public Interest Groups* (Princeton, N.J.: Princeton University Press, 1977).

8. For a detailed analysis of Common Cause, see Andrew S. McFarland, *Common Cause: Lobbying in the Public Interest* (Chatham, N.J.: Chatham House, 1984).

mainline Protestant denominations, such as the Methodists, Presbyterians, and Episcopalians, have generally adopted liberal policy positions. Opposing them have been fundamentalist Christian groups, led by such evangelists as the Reverend Jerry Falwell. The National Council of Churches and right-wing Christians, for example, clashed over the nomination of Judge Robert Bork, an outspoken conservative, to the Supreme Court in 1987.

The principal Catholic organizations that lobby the government are the U.S. Catholic Conference and the National Conference of Bishops. These organizations strongly oppose abortion but have taken generally more liberal stands on such issues as welfare, civil rights, regulating business, and arms control. The policy clashes among the wide array of church organizations have led one analyst of these politically active groups to note that they were speaking with "dissonant voices" and "not praying together."[9]

Government Interests

Because the federal government is a critical source of funds for state and local governments, as well as their major regulator, these governments have been no less eager than other groups to have organized representation in Washington. Thus, nearly all of the states have federal liaison offices, and many cities, counties, and state universities as well have their own Washington offices or law firms or lobbyists representing them. Major associations representing the government sector include the National Governors Association, the National Association of Counties, and the U.S. Conference of Mayors.

Given America's prominent role in world affairs, even foreign governments have joined the fray of interest group politics in an effort to influence U.S. public policy. Some of this activity is carried out by foreign ambassadors and their staffs, but, increasingly, high-priced Washington lobbyists and law firms are acting on behalf of their foreign government clients. This is a highly controversial practice, however, because critics claim that these representatives of foreign interests are using their skills for purposes that may run counter to the interests of the United States.[10] Not all interest group activity in behalf of foreign countries is initiated by their governments or hired agents in Washington. Some nations have home-grown support organizations. For example, Israel has benefited from having

9. Kirk Victor, "Not Praying Together," *National Journal,* October 10, 1987, 2546.
10. See Kirk Victor, "Risky Representation," *National Journal,* December 12, 1987, 3132–3137.

an aggressive, politically savvy, and well-financed organization of Americans interested in protecting its interests, the American Israel Public Affairs Committee.

Diversity, Conflicts, and Alliances among Groups

The sweeping range of interests making up the interest group system is suggested by the preceding categories of groups. What is less apparent from such descriptions is the lack of unity among groups that on the surface seem to represent similar interests. It is, for example, frequently impossible to cite a business position on a particular issue because within the organizations representing business interests substantial diversity exists, possibly leading to intergroup conflicts. In one such instance, by calling for a major overhaul of the tax code, the 1986 tax reform act caused a sharp split among business interests (Table 8.1). With major corporations found on both sides of the issue, depending on how the new tax code would affect their operations, business was unable to present a united front and maximize its influence in shaping the legislation. Even though they are both giants in the auto industry, Ford and General Motors were on opposite sides of the issue. Ford believed that the overall effect of lowering individual income tax rates would stimulate auto sales and improve the company's bottom line, but General Motors was more concerned about how changes in the tax code might affect corporate taxes.

Similarly, organized medicine does not speak with one voice. The American Medical Association (AMA), with 292,000 physician members, has seen its influence undermined by rivalries among medical specialists. For example, when in 1989 Congress debated a revision of the Medicare payment system to doctors, the plan was supported by the AMA, the American Society of Internal Medicine, and the American Academy of Family Physicians, but opposed by the American College of Surgeons, who feared a loss of income.

The level of intergroup conflict depends on the policy issue at stake. For example, the role of government in agriculture tends to create a high level of conflict among the major farm interest groups as the Farm Bureau tries to limit government involvement in the agriculture sector, while the Farmers Union promotes government regulation and assistance. Energy and health care issues, however, are somewhat less likely to generate conflicts among business groups operating in these fields. As for labor unions, they tend to stick together and generally develop supportive relationships.[11]

11. Robert H. Salisbury, et al., "Who Works with Whom? Interest Group Alli-

Table 8.1 Divided They Stand: A Sampling of Positions Taken by Business Groups on the 1986 Tax Reform Bill

For Tax Reform Bill

American Bankers Association
American Mining Congress
American Petroleum Institute
Business Roundtable
National Association of Home Builders
National Association of Manufacturers
National Machine Tool Builders Association
U.S. Chamber of Commerce
Aluminum Co. of America
AT&T
Bank of America
Caterpillar Tractor
Chase Manhattan
Dow Chemical
Duke Power
DuPont
Exxon
Ford Motor
GTE
Inland Steel
Mobil
Rockwell International
Texas Instruments
Weyerhaeuser

Against Tax Reform Bill

American Apparel Manufacturers Association
American Electronics Association
American Trucking Association
Food Marketing Institute
Grocery Manufacturers of America
National Association of Wholesaler-
    Distributors
National Federation of Independent Business
National Retail Merchants Association
Beatrice
Dart & Kraft
Digital Equipment
Federated Department Stores
General Mills
General Motors
IBM
Levi Strauss
PepsiCo
Philip Morris
Procter & Gamble
R.J. Reynolds Industries
Sara Lee
3M

SOURCE: Jeffrey H. Birnham, "Business's Schism over Tax Overhaul Reflects the Divide-and-Conquer Strategy of Proponents," *Wall Street Journal*, Dec. 5, 1985, 64. Reprinted by permission of the *Wall Street Journal*, © 1985 Dow Jones & Company Inc. All rights reserved worldwide.

In their efforts to influence government policy, groups frequently form alliances and work cooperatively on selected issues. One of the oldest and most prominent alliances is the Leadership Conference on Civil Rights, composed of approximately 150 black, labor, religious, Hispanic, Asian-American, women's, and senior citizens' organizations. Since its founding in 1950, this group has been at the forefront of issues involving minorities, women, the handicapped, and the poor. Other coalitions are more short-lived and dissolve when the issue of immediate concern is resolved. For example, the Tax Reform Action Coalition, comprised of business organizations, formed to mobilize support for the 1986 tax reform bill, but it did not become a permanent organization.

Why Interest Groups Organize

Interest groups form around people's shared attitudes and interests. One compelling basis for organization is a common economic interest such as those shared by farmers, teachers, manufacturers, doctors, factory workers, and realtors. Other bases for organizing include a common ethnic heritage, race, religion, recreational interest, ideology, or concern about a specific issue such as gun control, environmental protection, abortion, hunger, or civil rights. People frequently resort to creating a formal organization and trying to influence the government when they find their positions threatened or their goals unfulfilled. Thus, farmers organized in the face of agricultural depressions; workers formed unions to achieve decent wages and working conditions; businesses organized in the earliest days of the Republic to gain the protection of tariffs; and veterans formed groups like the Society of Cincinnati, Grand Army of the Republic, and the American Legion to secure government benefits to compensate for the hardships caused by serving the nation in time of war. Even independent-minded college students have periodically organized to oppose hikes in tuition.

America's society, culture, Constitution, and party system have all created a favorable climate for the proliferation of interest groups.[12] For groups to develop, there must be substantial differences and disagreements among society's citizens. And since this nation's birth, these conditions for interest group development have abounded. In the post-Revolution period, for example, conflicts

ances and Opposition," *American Political Science Review* 81 (December 1987): 1217–1234.

12. Allan J. Cigler and Burdett A. Loomis, *Interest Group Politics,* 2d ed. (Washington, D.C.: CQ Press, 1986), 5–6.

arose between debtor and creditor classes and between northern commercial interests and agrarian interests in the South. As the nation expanded from ocean to ocean, sources of division and conflict were introduced: immigrants from diverse racial, ethnic, and religious backgrounds had to be accommodated, an industrialized economy became the rule, and massive metropolitan areas began to dot the landscape.

By providing a way for people to advance their own interests or the causes in which they believe, interest groups help Americans satisfy their need for personal achievement and the value they attach to individualism. Likewise, by guaranteeing freedom of speech, association, and the right to petition the government for redress of grievances, the U.S. Constitution has made its contribution to a favorable environment for interest group formation. The structure of the governmental system has encouraged group proliferation as well. With our highly decentralized government produced by the principles of separation of powers and federalism, groups must be capable of influencing the three branches of the federal government as well as state and local governments.[13] And the large number of points—especially local ones—at which citizens can influence public policy probably contributes to Americans' sense of political effectiveness and proclivity to join groups.[14]

The decentralized and undisciplined nature of the American political party system also has proven a favorable setting for interest group activity. The inability of the parties to control their own elected officials creates a power vacuum in the decision-making process into which interest groups have readily moved.

Effects of Societal Complexity and Disturbances

David Truman has concluded that interest groups develop and proliferate naturally as society becomes more diverse and economic specialization emerges.[15] Farm organizations, for example, developed only after the Civil War when agriculture became commercialized and farmers began increasingly to specialize in growing particular commodities.[16] The interests of the various commodity producers then began to vary as well—among wheat, cotton, beef, corn, hog, sugar, and tobacco producers.

13. See Truman, *Governmental Process,* 519.
14. See Gabriel Almond and Sidney Verba, *The Civic Culture* (Boston: Little, Brown, 1976), chaps. 8 and 10.
15. Truman, *The Governmental Process,* chap. 3.
16. Robert H. Salisbury, "An Exchange Theory of Interest Groups," *Midwest Journal of Political Science* 13 (February 1969): 3–4.

Falling prices for farm commodities provoked angry farmers to form the American Agriculture Movement. In 1979, its members drove their tractors to Washington—and tied up traffic—to draw lawmakers' attention to their plight.

It also has been suggested that interest groups develop when disturbances threaten certain interests or provide them with opportunities to improve their positions. The American Agriculture Movement, for example, whose tractorcades of angry farmers tied up traffic in downtown Washington, D.C., in 1979, was the response of small farmers to low farm prices in the 1970s. The National Association of Manufacturers was formed to take advantage of opportunities for developing foreign trade, but it grew and prospered by responding to the emergence of organized labor as a political force. The interest group system is thus believed to go through waves of group mobilization and countermobilization.[17]

Personal Motivations

While there are many examples of groups forming because of individuals' shared and specialized interests, there also are examples of groups not forming even though circumstances would seem to require it. The poor, for example, are not organized into interest groups even though they share a common plight. Nor have racial and gender discrimination led most blacks and women to join interest groups. Political scientists have begun to believe, therefore, that any explanations of group development require attention to personal motivations.

According to political scientist Mancur Olson, the **free-rider**

17. Truman, *Governmental Process*, chap. 3.

problem is a major barrier to people joining groups that serve their interests.[18] Olson has contended that rational people (or the so-called free riders) recognize that the "collective" benefits (safer cars, cleaner air, improved Social Security benefits, and such) of an interest group's activities are available to both group members and non-members alike. Nonmembers can receive the benefits of a group's activities without paying the costs (dues, time, effort) of formal group membership. Thus, the efforts of the American Lung Association to pass tougher clean air legislation in 1990 made the benefits of cleaner air available to all Americans even though most did nothing to assist the association.

To overcome the free-rider problem, many groups provide their members with "selective" benefits—benefits available only to group members. The country's largest interest group in terms of membership, the American Association of Retired Persons (AARP), provides members with such selective benefits as low-cost prescription drugs, discount travel fares, health insurance, and its slick monthly magazine, *Modern Maturity*.

Three incentives or motivations are usually behind an individual's decision to actually join a group: material, solidary, and expressive.[19] **Material incentives** are tangible rewards that have economic value. Thus, an important basis for joining a union, business group, professional association, or farm organization is the promise of economic benefits—better prices for corn, job benefits, and such—that will flow from the group's activities.

Not everyone joins a group to gain material rewards; there also are **solidary incentives**—the rewards of companionship, fraternity, status, and pleasure that come from associating with people with whom one shares a common bond. One of the benefits of the American Legion, for example, is the fellowship derived from sharing common wartime and other military experiences. Nationality, racial, and religious organizations all provide their members with solidary benefits.

Expressive (also known as **purposive**) **incentives** also induce people to join groups. These incentives are the intangible rewards that come from working for a cause that is thought to be right and just, even though no personal gain is to be had from it. Members of en-

18. Mancur Olson, *The Logic of Collective Action* (Cambridge, Mass.: Harvard University Press, 1965).
19. See Peter Clark and James Q. Wilson, "Incentive Systems: A Theory of Organizations," *Administrative Science Quarterly* 6 (September 1961): 126–166; and James Q. Wilson, *Political Organizations* (New York: Basic Books, 1973).

vironmental groups, such as the Wilderness Society or Sierra Club, gain such benefits from their organizations, as do members of the League of Women Voters, Planned Parenthood, and Common Cause. Such ideological groups as the liberal People for the American Way or the right-leaning Young Americans for Freedom also have memberships based on expressive incentives.

Material, solidary, and expressive incentives should not be viewed as mutually exclusive; membership in a group may indeed produce all three types of benefits. For example, members of the American Legion may enjoy the comradeship of fellow veterans, gain the legion's assistance in securing benefits from the Department of Veterans Affairs, and derive satisfaction from belonging to an organization that lobbies for a strong national defense.

Organizational Entrepreneurs

Examples abound of leaders who felt strongly about issues or a cause and were willing to risk investing their time and personal resources in the formation of an interest group.[20] Cesar Chavez, the dedicated leader of the United Farm Workers Union, worked tirelessly against great odds and eventually succeeded in forming a union. Similarly, Common Cause owes its existence to the vision and determination of its founder, former secretary of health, education, and welfare John Gardner. Ralph Nader, the consumer advocate who heads a number of consumer, health, and environmental organizations, is a particularly striking case of individual commitment and organizational entrepreneurship. With the over $300,000 he received from General Motors in settlement of his infringement of privacy charge against the company for hiring private detectives to dig up information about him, Nader was able to form a series of consumer rights organizations that gave impetus to the consumer movement in the 1970s.

Entrepreneurs like Nader and Gardner have been aided in their organizational efforts by advances in communications technology such as computerized direct-mail solicitation. Using such technology, group leaders can reach large target audiences with appeals designed to enlist members and financial contributions.

Sponsors

The National Council on Aging, a group founded to champion the expansion of senior citizens centers across the country, relied in its early years primarily on Ford and other private foundation grants for funding. And the militant National Welfare Rights Organization,

20. See Salisbury, "An Exchange Theory of Interest Groups."

which flourished briefly in the 1970s, received large contributions from Singer and Sears Roebuck heirs. Organization and maintenance of an interest group often require a patron or sponsors who will provide financial backing. An early 1980s survey by Jack Walker revealed that 34 percent of occupational groups and 89 percent of citizens' groups used financial aid from outside sources to start their operations.[21] Indeed, some organizations unable to overcome the free-rider problem have had to rely on sponsors—individuals, foundations, government in the form of grants, and other interest groups—rather than a membership to sustain them. A 1970s study of public interest groups showed that 30 percent had no members at all.[22] Rather, they were staff operations working out of a Washington headquarters.

The government itself can be an important force in the creation of interest groups. Early in this century, the federal and state governments promoted the development of the American Farm Bureau Federation and provided encouragement and financial support for local Farm Bureau organizations so that they could help county extension agents in their work with farm families. Interest groups also form when major new legislation creates a clientele for government services. For example, more than half of the groups representing the elderly were formed after 1965, the year in which Medicare and the Older Americans Act were passed by Congress. Similarly, the numbers of education, transportation, environmental, and women's[23] groups have ballooned as a result of government action or support. In providing this assistance to groups, the federal government is seeking their help in publicizing and supporting its programs.[24] Thus, interest groups may be the offshoots as well as the roots of public policy.

Determinants of Group Influence

Interest groups can affect government policy by providing public officials what they need to keep their jobs: public support, election campaign assistance, and information. With their abilities to mobilize people, groups can help supply (or withhold) the votes a legislator needs to gain and stay in office. Groups also can provide

21. Walker, "The Origins and Maintenance of Interest Groups," 397.
22. Berry, *Lobbying for the People*, 28.
23. For information on how government resources were used to help build the women's movement, see Georgia Duerst-Lahti, "The Government's Role in Building the Women's Movement," *Political Science Quarterly* 104 (Summer 1989): 249–268.
24. Walker, "The Origins and Maintenance of Interest Groups," 401–403.

campaign contributions, as well as the reliable information public officials need to make informed decisions. Although interest groups are not decision makers' only sources of information, members of Congress, for example, are reluctant to act without at least having the perspectives of the groups affected on an issue. Thus, when considering changes in banking regulatory statutes during the 1980s, Congress eagerly sought the views of various segments of the banking industry. And during the periodic debates on renewing the Clean Air Act, Congress has consistently solicited information from the auto industry about its ability to manufacture cars at a reasonable price that meet the government-mandated standards for auto exhaust emissions.

But interest groups are not equal in their abilities to influence government policy. While it is extremely difficult to measure group influence, it is possible to identify the factors that affect the potential power of a group. These factors include both group characteristics such as membership and financial resources and the various effects of how the government itself is organized.

Membership

The advantages of being a huge organization—such as the American Association of Retired Persons (twenty-eight million elderly members; its Washington headquarters even has its own ZIP Code), the National Education Association (two million teachers), or the National Rifle Association (three million gun owners)—are likewise huge. Representatives and senators are unlikely to ignore the views of a group that has millions of informed, interested members back in their home districts or states. Moreover, a large dues-paying membership can provide the financial resources often required to sway government policy making.

But a large membership has a disadvantage as well: internal unity problems. A group whose members are split on an issue is not apt to be an effective force. A perfect example of such unity problems is the American Bankers Association (ABA). Disagreements between the big banks, which pay for most of ABA's expenses, and the small, independent banks, which provide the ABA with grass-roots influence, have substantially weakened the group's clout. Presenting a unified front on issues has been an acute problem as well for the giant U.S. Chamber of Commerce. As one business lobbyist noted, "With its breadth of members, the Chamber has trouble finding consensus on anything except labor-management issues."[25]

25. Burt Solomon, "Measuring Clout," *National Journal,* July 4, 1987, 1711.

When the members of an organization are fervently committed to that organization and its objectives, its capacity to exert influence is enhanced. As members of Congress know, people who feel intensely about an issue are likely to cast their votes and mobilize other voters based on the way their representatives and senators dealt with that issue. Thus, legislators frequently seek to avoid antagonizing such fervent groups. This helps explain how a group like the National Rifle Association, which is fiercely opposed to gun control, manages to block such legislation even though polls show a majority of the public favors restricting handguns. A similar intensity of commitment has made the Independent Insurance Agents of America an effective force. Individual agents have shown a willingness to travel to Washington and aggressively lobby representatives and senators. In a colorful and disapproving description of the group in action, the leader of a rival organization recounted how these agents "regularly swarm Capitol Hill. They can almost be like rabid dogs."[26]

When a group's membership tends to be concentrated in particular districts or states (for example, the concentrations of dairy farmers in Wisconsin, Minnesota, Vermont, and upstate New York), the members of Congress representing those constituencies are usually particularly sensitive to these groups' interests. A membership dispersed across many states and congressional districts can be advantageous as well. When a group's membership blankets virtually every state and district in the nation and is, moreover, politically assertive, representatives and senators sit up and listen. Such groups include the National Education Association (NEA), the National Rifle Association, and the National Association of Realtors.

The prestige and status of a group's members also affect its ability to influence government policy makers. Groups whose members belong to prestigious professions or have achieved status in their chosen professions normally gain **access** to decision makers—that is, a hearing for their point of view in a nonhostile environment—with relative ease. Physicians, attorneys, and bankers, for example, can expect at least an opportunity to state their positions before government officials. But for such groups as students or migrant workers, access may be more difficult.

Financial and Leadership Resources

The tools of governmental influence—experienced lobbyists, up-to-date communications equipment, a research staff—do not come

26. Ibid., 1707.

free.[27] They cost money, giving those groups with substantial resources a hefty advantage over poorer groups. Such groups as the U.S. Chamber of Commerce, AFL-CIO, and NEA are financially very well off and even have their own office buildings near either the Capitol or White House. Groups with adequate funding can hire the most skilled, best-connected Washington operatives, conduct sophisticated research, undertake public relations and media campaigns, contribute financially to campaigns, and stir up blizzards of mail from constituents, all to fall on the desks of government decision makers.

Although it is always better to have plenty of financial resources than be without them, lack of money is not necessarily a fatal liability for interest groups. Skill in generating publicity, a dedicated staff, effective research, and intense commitment, for example, have made Ralph Nader's organizations highly effective in spite of their having only modest revenues. Even poorly financed, low-status groups, if clever enough, can grab the public's attention for a cause. The late Mitch Snyder, an advocate for the homeless, used demonstrations—including encampments in Lafayette Park across from the White House—to dramatize the plight of people living on the streets and thereby succeeded in attracting the attention of Congress.

Indeed, no small part of some groups' clout has been attributed to shrewd leadership. Jack Valenti, head of the Washington outpost of the Motion Picture Association of America (MPAA) for over twenty-one years, uses his organization's best asset—Hollywood glamour—to influence members of Congress: "He arranges Hollywood fundraisers, lends celebrities to Members' campaigns and invites Members and spouses to the MPAA's plush little theater in Washington to watch films before they are released."[28]

In addition to using a group's resources skillfully to influence the powers that be, a group leader must be able to maintain the organization—gain and hold members, raise money, and fire up member commitment to the group's goals. Group leaders spend a great deal of their time, therefore, just trying to keep the group afloat and avoiding internal rifts.

27. The sources of group funds and the differences among groups in their funding sources is described in Mark A. Peterson and Jack L. Walker, "Interest Group Responses to a Partisan Change," in Cigler and Loomis, *Interest Group Politics,* 162–182.

28. Solomon, "Measuring Clout," 1708.

Governmental structures, procedures, and rules are not neutral in their impacts on interest groups. Some groups benefit and others suffer from the way in which the government is structured and decisions are made.[29] The lengthy, complicated process involved in getting a bill approved by the Congress, with its many opportunities for delay and obstruction, works to the defensive advantage of groups opposed to policy changes. The congressional committee system also has its advantages for selected interests. The House and Senate agriculture committees, for example, tend to be composed of members from commodity-producing regions. They are therefore more responsive to producer interests than to the more general consumer interests.

The constitutional mandate that each state shall have two senators has important consequences for interest group access. Agricultural and mining interests, which are concentrated in the sparsely populated Plains and Mountain states, derive an advantage from having the same number of senators responsive to their concerns as the more thickly populated states like California. Federalism also has implications for group access. Groups with minimal influence at the federal level may find state governments more responsive. For example, with Republicans controlling the White House and the Senate for six of the eight years of the Reagan administration, organized labor had few policy victories at the national level in the 1980s. But with Democrats in control of most governorships and state legislatures, it had notable successes at the state level on such issues as raising the state minimum wage.

It is because changes in governmental rules and procedures could help some interests and damage some others that the battles over rules changes are often so intense. Maritime interests, for example, waged a fierce battle in the 1970s to prevent a House reform committee from abolishing the Merchant Marine and Fisheries Committee, the membership of which was drawn from coastal constituencies and was supportive of the maritime industry.

The Tactics of Influence

Interest groups have at their disposal an arsenal of tactics and techniques for use in pressuring representatives, senators, bureau-

29. For a classic statement of the impact of governmental structure on group access, see Truman, *Governmental Process,* 322–332.

Lobbying by representatives of special interest groups is not a new phenomenon. This reproduction from Harpers Weekly *portrays lobbyists outside the House of Representatives seeking to influence House action on the Civil Rights Act of 1866.*

crats, and presidents. The technique or combination of methods selected depends largely on the nature of the group, its resources, which branch or level of government is making the decision, and whether the group is seeking to initiate a policy change or defend an existing policy.

Lobbying

A *lobbyist* acts as an agent of an interest to influence legislative or administrative government decisions. The term goes back to the early 1800s when favor-seekers jammed the lobbies, cloakrooms, and hallways of legislatures. Initially, these individuals were called "lobby agents," which was shortened to lobbyists in the 1830s. Although the term **lobbying** was not yet in vogue when the Constitution was written, the right to lobby was made explicit by its First Amendment, which provides that "Congress shall make no law . . . abridging . . . the right of the people . . . to petition the Government for a redress of grievances."

About three-quarters of the over ten thousand lobbyists in Washington work as officers and other employees of interest groups. The rest are attorneys or consultants, who represent clients and in return receive a fee or retainer.

Lobbying Congress. In *direct lobbying*, interest group representatives meet personally with government officials to inform them about and persuade them to accept their groups' positions. This method of exerting influence is most readily available to groups that have sufficient status and political standing to gain access to policy makers, as well as the financial resources to hire skilled Washington insiders who understand the inner workings of Congress and the executive branch.

Members of Congress are usually willing to meet with lobbyists because the interest groups they represent often have the expertise and specialized knowledge members need to make informed decisions on legislative issues. This information is presented formally at congressional committee hearings or informally (and usually more effectively) in private meetings with legislators and their staffs. Normally missing from lobbyist-legislator meetings are such threats as "If you don't support us on this bill, we'll see that you're defeated in the next election!" To the contrary, lobbyists try to maintain good relations even when members of Congress oppose them on a key issue. Interest group representatives understand that politics is an ongoing process; the member whose support they cannot win today may be supportive tomorrow on a different issue.[30]

It is just because most interest groups are interested in influencing representatives and senators on a range of issues over an extended period of time that lobbyists guard their reputations as providers of reliable, specialized information. It may be possible to peddle misleading information while seeking to influence a congressional decision and even have some impact, but such a technique is not a passport to long-term influence in Washington. Career politicians have long memories when it comes to those who caused them political embarrassment.

Lobbyists tend to work primarily with members of Congress who are friendly and supportive and to avoid those who are known opponents. Often the relationship between lobbyist and legislator is that of allies working cooperatively to achieve a legislative objective important to both. Interest groups can help draft bills and amendments and line up support and provide strategic advice as well. Members, in turn, often have indispensable insider information on the political situation within Congress. Representatives and senators may even lobby interest groups to take up an issue, a situation described in the following statement by a Democratic House member:

I find myself arguing with an interest group . . . to get them turned on to go to work on some other members. I had a couple of people in my office

---

30. For an informed consideration of how the ongoing nature of the political process in Congress affects interest group politics, see Raymond A. Bauer, Ithiel de Sola Pool, and Lewis A. Dexter, *American Business and Public Policy* (New York: Atherton, 1963), part V.

this afternoon. They're involved in something that's key in my committee, and they were of the opinion that a couple of Democratic colleagues on that committee were with them on this issue. I knew the guys had taken a walk [not voted] on a key vote, and we lost by two votes. . . . I told them that and laid out for them the record of what had happened and urged them to go focus on what I thought ought to be an appropriate target. You do get into that occasionally . . . so they'll go to work where they're going to be effective. They can be an ally.[31]

Because elected officials ignore the sentiments of the voters at their own peril, an effective lobbying technique called *grass-roots lobbying*—mobilizing constituents to contact their representative and senators—is often used in conjunction with direct in-person lobbying. With its strategy of calling on constituents to bury their legislators under an avalanche of mail, telegrams, faxes, and phone calls, grass-roots lobbying is not a new technique, but it has become feasible for more groups (as well as more efficient and economical) with the development of advanced computer and communications technologies. It is now possible for an interest group to send out a "legislative alert" to its members across the country advising them of a crucial vote in Congress and asking them to contact their representative or senators immediately. The result can be a flood of mail to Capitol Hill. But not all groups can use grass-roots lobbying; it requires a sizable membership concerned enough about an issue to contact their representatives, as well as the funds to finance a mass mailing to the membership.

Members of the House have even attested to the effectiveness of constituency pressures mobilized by interest groups:

[The] most effective lobbyists are the ones back home. I think hospital cost containment got beat not by anybody here in Washington lobbying heavily. It got beat by people who were on boards of directors of various community hospitals back home who personally wrote you a letter or called you on the phone or stopped by to see you.

The Chrysler bailout bill [was] . . . a classic piece of work in terms of mobilizing local support. . . . I just got hammered on that one. . . . When a Chrysler dealer walks in from your home town area and says, "If I go down, it involves this number of mechanics, this number of local people, and these jobs"—that has a real impact. . . . That's a radically different quality of information [than that] from a $300,000-a-year lawyer sitting in your office.[32]

---

31. John F. Bibby, ed., *Congress Off the Record: The Candid Analyses of Seven Members* (Washington, D.C.: American Enterprise Institute, 1983), 35.
  32. Ibid., 34.

Members of Congress, of course, recognize mail inspired by an interest group, but their responses are not always the ones a grass-roots campaign is looking for. This does not mean, however, that grass-roots lobbying is not without an impact. It tells legislators that an interest group feels strongly enough about an issue to mount a major constituent contact operation. They should, therefore, give that issue their thoughtful consideration so that they can account to their constituents for their final decision. Grass-roots lobbying does not necessarily tell members of Congress what to do, but it does tell them they will have to take some action on the issue.

Lobbying the Executive. Most discussions of lobbying emphasize interest group efforts to influence Congress. Indeed, efforts to lobby the legislative branch are highly visible. A tourist to Washington need not be particularly sophisticated to observe lobbyists testifying before congressional committees, patrolling the hallways outside the House chamber, or cornering a senator for an informal talk outside a committee room. The visibility of congressional lobbying, however, should not obscure the fact that the executive branch (indeed, any place in government where policy decisions are made) also is a target for lobbyists—executive branch operations may be less visible, but they are not less important.

Even the White House is not out of reach of the long arms of interest groups. Numerous groups, particularly those that supported the president in the last election, seek to influence appointments to executive posts as well as policy decisions through their contacts with key White House staffers. Because interest groups are such important players in Washington politics, specific White House personnel maintain contact with interest group leaders and keep the president and senior presidential aides advised of their concerns and activities. Like members of Congress, the White House also tries to mobilize interest groups to support its policies. During the Ford administration, the interest group contact function was formally recognized through creation of the Office of Public Liaison within the White House.[33]

One means of gaining access to Washington policy makers is to hire as lobbyists former officers of the executive and legislative branches who have insider knowledge of how a department or agency

33. For an account of White House-interest group relations, see Martha Joynt Kumar and Michael Baruch Grossman, "The President and Interest Groups," in *The Presidency and the Political System,* ed. Michael Nelson (Washington, D.C.: CQ Press, 1984), chap. 11; and Joseph A. Pika, "Opening Doors for Kindred Souls: The White House Office of Public Liaison," in *Interest Group Politics,* ed. Allan J. Cigler and Burdett A. Loomis, 3d ed. (Washington, D.C.: CQ Press, 1991), chap. 13.

operates as well as personal ties with its personnel. Former executive branch officials often find highly lucrative employment as lobbyists after leaving government service. (Critics refer to this practice of trading on insider knowledge and personal contacts as *influence peddling*.) One of the most prominent examples of such lobbyists was Michael Deaver, President Reagan's deputy chief of staff during his first term. Until questions about the propriety of his exploiting his access to the White House created a storm of adverse publicity and he was charged with perjuring himself before a congressional committee, Deaver's lobbying firm had picked up six-figure retainers from such major clients as CBS, TWA, and the governments of Singapore and Canada.

It is commonplace for defense contractors to hire as their Washington operatives former officials of the Department of Defense, and for industries regulated by the Federal Trade Commission, Securities and Exchange Commission, and Federal Communications Commission to hire former agency staff personnel. Although the impact of this "revolving door" system is impossible to assess accurately, fears that it can affect policy making have led to legislation restricting former government employees from lobbying their former agencies for a year after leaving government service. Many critics contend, however, that this restriction is not effective and should be strengthened.

Political Action Committees

Because elected officials cannot wage credible election campaigns without money, interest groups are often willing to provide campaign cash. The chosen vehicle for these financial contributions is the **political action committee** or PAC. The Federal Election Campaign Act (FECA) amendments of 1971 and 1974 allow a political committee created by an interest group to solicit funds for distribution to candidates. According to the act, corporate PACs are exempt from the general rule against campaign expenditures by corporations or federally insured financial institutions such as banks and savings and loan associations. These PACs can use corporate funds to offset the cost of setting up a PAC and can solicit voluntary contributions from stockholders, administrative personnel, and their families. Labor unions and trade associations also are given the right by the FECA to solicit campaign funds from their members. Independent PACs abound as well, composed of like-minded people interested in promoting a particular ideology or policy position. Ideological PACs include the National Conservative Political Action Committee and the liberal Committee for an Effective Congress. PACs must comply with federal regulations calling for regular re-

Table 8.2 PAC Contributions to Winning House and Senate Campaigns, 1975–1990

Election Cycle	Senate Campaigns		House Campaigns	
	Amount (millions of dollars)	% of Total Receipts	Amount (millions of dollars)	% of Total Receipts
1975–1976	3.1	14.8	10.9	25.6
1977–1978	6.0	14.0	17.0	28.3
1979–1980	10.2	24.5	27.0	31.4
1981–1982	15.6	22.0	42.7	34.7
1983–1984	20.0	19.8	59.5	41.1
1985–1986	28.4	26.6	72.8	42.2
1987–1988	31.8	26.1	86.1	45.1
1989–1990	31.1	25.6	91.6	46.4

SOURCE: Federal Election Commission.

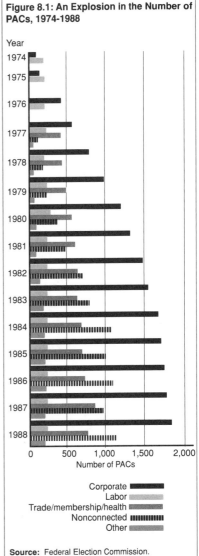

Figure 8.1: An Explosion in the Number of PACs, 1974-1988

Year

0   500   1,000   1,500   2,000
Number of PACs

Corporate
Labor
Trade/membership/health
Nonconnected
Other

Source: Federal Election Commission.
Note: For the years 1974–1976, numbers are not available for nonconnected PACs, trade/membership/health PACs, or PACs in the "Other" category. The "Other" category consists of PACs formed by corporations without capital stock and incorporated cooperatives.

ports of receipts and with expenditure limits on contributions to candidates of $5,000 per election.

Before the 1960s, PACs were largely a labor union phenomenon led by the AFL-CIO's Committee on Political Education (COPE), although the American Medical Association and National Association of Manufacturers also operated PACs. The 1970s changes in the FECA resulted in a massive increase in the number of PACs, especially those sponsored by corporations and trade associations (see Figure 8.1). As the number of PACs has increased, their role in funding election campaigns has expanded as well (Table 8.2). Individuals are still the largest source of campaign money, but PACs constituted 45.1 percent of the total receipts of House candidates in 1987–1988 and over a quarter of total Senate campaign funds.

In their allocations of funds, PACs show a strong preference for incumbents. In fact, more than three-quarters of PAC contributions to House and Senate candidates in the 1989–1990 election cycle went to incumbents, and only about 10 percent was given to candidates challenging incumbents—the balance went to open-seat campaigns in which no incumbent was running (Table 8.3). Incumbency also affects the shares of PAC money received by Republican and Democratic candidates. In 1989–1990, the Democrats, with more congressional incumbents than the Republicans, received $92.5 million—or 62 percent of all PAC contributions—compared with $57.3 million for the Republicans (Table 8.3).

Table 8.3 PAC Contributions to House and Senate Candidates, 1989–1990 Election Cycle

PAC Contributions to	Amount (millions of dollars)	% of Total PAC Contributions
All incumbents	117.2	78.2
All challengers	15.5	10.4
All open-seat candidates	17.1	11.4
Total	149.8	100.0
Republicans		
House candidates	36.3	24.2
Senate candidates	21.0	14.0
Total	57.3	38.2
Democrats		
House candidates	72.3	48.3
Senate candidates	20.2	13.5
Total	92.5	61.8

SOURCE: Federal Election Commission.
NOTE: Minor parties not included.

PACs representing different interests show distinctive contribution patterns. Labor PACs give almost exclusively to Democrats (93.4 percent of their 1989–1990 contributions), and business PACs, although often thought to favor Republicans, follow a strategy of giving to incumbents. Thus, in the 1989–1990 election cycle, Democrats received 55 percent of business PAC money. Because ideological PACs want to influence the policy orientation of the Congress as a whole, they frequently contribute to challengers and open-seat races.

Even with the significant exceptions such as the labor PACs, most PACs are *not* trying to shape election outcomes by following a strategy of, first, contributing only to candidates who support their groups' issue positions and, second, of intervening only when the race is close enough to be affected by an infusion of additional cash. Rather, by contributing primarily to incumbents, most of whom have strong reelection prospects, PACs tend to follow a strategy designed to win them access to Congress. They operate on the belief, borne of practical experience, that campaign contributions "grease the skids" and help their lobbyists in presenting their groups' positions to congressional decision makers. The impact of their access gained from PAC contributions, however, tends to vary, depending on the nature of the issue.

PAC contributions and follow-up lobbying by an interest group are apt to have their greatest impacts on issues that are highly technical and attract little public attention, such as amendments to the tax code. But when issues generate media attention, competing forces—ideological concerns, party and White House pressures, and constituency interests—impinge upon legislators and weaken the impacts of interest groups and their PACs. The impact of PAC contributions on public policy making is a matter of intense public debate. Some journalists and public interest groups believe PAC contributions have a pervasive influence, which is creating what one PAC critic has called "the best Congress money can buy."[34] Common Cause and other public interest groups have sought to ban PAC contributions altogether. The analyses of political scientists, however, find much less evidence of PAC contributions affecting congressional votes than many journalists and public interest groups believe.[35]

Electioneering

Campaign funds are not the only kind of campaign assistance interest groups make available to candidates; mass membership organizations can even mobilize their members to vote for and work in behalf of preferred candidates. Organized labor, for example, operates phone banks during election campaigns, contacting union households to get out the vote for union-endorsed candidates (almost exclusively Democrats). But efforts by group leaders to mobilize their memberships to support a particular candidate may meet with only limited success. Group members often have other commitments and beliefs that conflict with those of the group, and they may, therefore, not vote in accordance with the official position of their leaders. Indeed, in spite of organized labor's vigorous support of Democratic presidential nominee Michael Dukakis in 1988, 42 percent of voters in union households cast their ballots instead for his Republican opponent, George Bush.

Few groups have the resources or personnel to operate phone

34. See Philip M. Stern, *The Best Congress Money Can Buy* (New York: Pantheon Books, 1988).

35. For a discussion of the PAC vote-buying controversy, see Larry J. Sabato, *PAC Power: Inside the World of Political Action Committees* (New York: Norton, 1984), 132–140; John R. Wright, "PACs, Contributions, and Roll Calls," *American Political Science Review* 79 (June 1985): 400–414; Janet M. Grenzke, "PACs and the Congressional Supermarket: The Currency Is Complex," *American Journal of Political Science* 33 (February 1989): 1–24; and John R. Wright, "Contributions, Lobbying, and Committee Voting in the U.S. House of Representatives," *American Political Science Review* 84 (June 1990): 417–438.

banks like those of the AFL-CIO, but all organizations are themselves communications systems that can be used to help preferred candidates. Informal communications channels within firms can pass the word from senior to junior executives that the leadership is supporting a particular candidate or party. Newsletters and other publications can shower candidates with favorable publicity and make their mailing lists available to campaign organizations. Invitations to speak at group meetings and conventions may be forthcoming as well for favored candidates.

Interest groups may even take the more extreme measure of reaching beyond their membership and publicizing the record—often in a negative manner—of a public official. Environmental Action, for example, periodically announces the names of its "Dirty Dozen," incumbent members of Congress who, in its view, have the worst records on environmental issues. And the National Conservative Political Action Committee has used independent expenditures to pay for massive media advertising campaigns against senators it considers vulnerable to charges of being ultraliberal.

Shaping Public Opinion

Few can doubt that public support adds strength to an interest group's lobbying and other efforts to influence government policy. Corporations, unions, and nonprofit sector groups often supplement their lobbying and PAC activities with media advertising. This technique is especially evident when an interest group believes its political influence as well as its public image could benefit from a little polishing. Perhaps no group is better at this than the National Rifle Association, which tries to offset criticism of its intense opposition to gun control legislation by using the likes of gun-toting movie stars in television spots and former presidents like Franklin Roosevelt with a rifle in hand in newspaper ads.

Citizens' organizations reliant on broad public support resort to media advertising as well. Planned Parenthood, for example, fearing that the appointment of Reagan nominee Robert Bork to the Supreme Court would result in the Court overturning its *Roe v. Wade* decision protecting women's rights to abortions, waged in 1987 a major advertising campaign designed to turn public opinion against the nomination. The televised struggle in the Senate over Bork's nomination worked to heighten even further public awareness of the significance of the nomination.

Advertising campaigns have their limits, however. Because they are expensive and only a small fraction of the population is likely to even view or read the advertisements, they are an option only for such well-established, well-heeled groups as corporations, trade associations, and unions.

Direct mail—targeting past and potential supporters with an appeal to contact public officials and contribute money to a group—is another means of mobilizing mass support for a cause. One large-scale practitioner of this method is right-wing organizer Richard Viguerie, who claims to have the addresses of millions of conservative voters on file in his northern Virginia office.

Not all techniques for shaping public opinion to affect public policy are costly. For example, "outsider" organizations that lack close ties with friendly members of Congress and administrative agencies often simply release information calculated to raise eyebrows and rate a story on the evening news. A skilled user of this technique is Ralph Nader. His exposés of government and corporate insensitivity to threatened public health and safety have helped build support for stronger consumer, workplace safety, and environmental protection legislation. Nader and other leading nonestablishment organizations have found the revelations leaked to them by so-called **whistle-blowers** particularly helpful. Acting either out of sympathy for a group's goals or disillusionment with the actions of an agency, whistle-blowers are employees of the government or private sector who reveal inside information. For example, advocates of reduced military spending and procurement reform have periodically publicized leaks from within the Pentagon about cost overruns—such as $1,000 toilet seats—to dramatize their arguments. This information is then used by an interest group to generate publicity for its position on an issue.

Former White House press secretary James Brady, who was severely wounded in a 1981 assassination attempt on President Ronald Reagan, makes his way to the Capitol in April 1991 to lobby for the "Brady bill." It called for a seven-day waiting period for the purchase of handguns. Despite heavy opposition spearheaded by the National Rifle Association, the legislation passed.

When the more conventional techniques for exerting group influence do not produce the desired results or are not available to a group because of limited resources or lack of access to public officials, groups may resort to demonstrations and protests—such as picketing and marching—to express their frustration and outrage over government policy and to attract public and media attention. For example, after the Supreme Court's highly controversial 1989 decision in *Webster v. Reproductive Health Services,* which permitted state regulation of abortion, a Washington protest march coordinated by the National Organization for Women (NOW) attracted 300,000 protesters and extensive media coverage. Similarly, anti-abortion rights groups have periodically demonstrated—including attempts to block and close down abortion clinics—in attempts to dramatize their opposition to abortion and attract publicity for their cause.

Not all demonstrations and protests are orchestrated and planned by organizing groups; they may arise spontaneously out of frustration. This was certainly the situation in the South during the 1960s with the early civil rights demonstrations. In one case, a handful of young black men initiated lunch-counter sit-ins, and in Montgomery, Alabama, a bus boycott started when Rosa Parks refused to accept racial discrimination and sit in the back of a bus. These acts of protest were then used by the Reverend Martin Luther King, Jr., and such civil rights groups as the NAACP to mobilize public support for the cause of racial equality.

The use of demonstrations and protests as a tool for exerting influence has a major drawback, however: they are hard to sustain over an extended period of time. Yet a prolonged effort is normally required to affect government policy because the policy-making process is lengthy and complicated, with most policy changes occurring in increments. One of the remarkable features of the civil rights movement of the 1960s was its ability to sustain a high level of activity and public visibility. Only through this accomplishment was it able to achieve in turn such major legislation as the Voting Rights Act of 1965 and the Civil Rights Act of 1968.

Going to Court

With its vast powers to interpret and enforce the Constitution and laws, the judicial branch, like the Congress and executive, has been used by interest groups to shape policies to their liking. One of their favorite techniques is litigation—bringing test cases to the courts—aimed at challenging existing laws or government practices. This important avenue for advancing the goals of public interest groups is favored particularly by groups who have been unsuccessful in their efforts to influence either Congress or the executive branch. But such litigation requires, of course, access to capable attorneys either through in-house counsel or the assistance of outside lawyers.[36] To use the courts to affect government policy, a group must also select test cases with care so that, first, the chances of winning a favorable decision are enhanced and, second, the courts will have to rule on the specific question of law the group is contesting.

One of the most important and far-reaching instances in which a group used litigation to promote its interests involved the National

36. Berry, *Lobbying for the People,* 225.

Association for the Advancement of Colored People. The NAACP and its legal staff supported the lawsuit, *Brown v. Board of Education of Topeka* (1954), that resulted in the Supreme Court declaring school segregation unconstitutional. Public interest groups—including environmental, women's, and consumer organizations—also have successfully used court cases to affect policy.

Court decisions can be influenced in indirect ways as well, such as by trying to influence the selection of judges. These indirect techniques of influence over court policy are described in Chapter 13, which describes the politics of the judiciary.

Policy Making, Group Representation, and Regulation

Although interest group activities have received more media attention in recent years, lobbyists are hardly a new phenomenon in the nation's capital. The number and diversity of interests represented have increased greatly, however, since the 1960s. Well-established economic interests—business, farm, labor, and professional groups—must now compete not only among themselves but also with newly mobilized nonprofit organizations representing minority, consumer, women's, environmental, disadvantaged, and citizens' interests.

This has meant that policy making is less dominated now than in the early 1960s and before by tight little subgovernments or **iron triangles**, composed of cooperating and allied interest groups, congressional committees, and executive agency bureaus. During the earlier era, a subgovernment could virtually control specific areas of public policy such as sugar import quotas, milk marketing, water projects, and public works projects. Today, with the proliferation of nonprofit groups, the notion of policy making through cozy arrangements among a few select interest groups, congressional committees, and agency bureaus fails to capture the complexity of the process. Policy making increasingly involves not so much iron triangles as it does loose, highly flexible, and web-like **issue networks**, composed of varied and competing interest groups (both profit- and nonprofit-oriented), policy experts, academicians, consultants, executive department personnel, and members of Congress and their staffs.[37]

Almost nowhere has the breakup of the cozy iron triangle and its

37. On issue networks, see Hugh Helco, "Issue Networks and the Executive Establishment," in *The New American Political System*, ed. Anthony King (Washington, D.C.: American Enterprise Institute, 1978), chap. 3.

replacement by a more complex issue network been more evident than in the field of agriculture—a policy domain once dominated by a small cadre of farm state legislators, Department of Agriculture officials, and major farm interest group representatives. This tripartite alliance was so powerful that agriculture policy was portrayed as being outside the control of or intervention by the Congress or White House. But as the components of food and fiber production have become more fragmented and specialized, farms have become larger and more capital-intensive, and agriculture has been forced to operate in an international competitive market affected by food surpluses, government trade policies, and budget deficits, the interests concerned with agriculture policy have become much more complex and conflictual. The old iron triangle has been supplemented by specific commodity producer and processor organizations, which have proliferated and become as active as such general organizations as the American Farm Bureau Federation, huge agribusiness organizations, protest groups asserting the anxieties of smaller producers, and consumer and environmental groups, among others. The executive branch agencies vitally interested in agriculture policy also have expanded beyond the Department of Agriculture to include the White House, Office of Management and Budget, and the Office of the U.S. Trade Representative. The cozy iron triangle that once dominated farm policy has ceased to exist, and policy is now shaped by a much broader array of forces.[38]

The emergence of issue networks such as the one operating in the field of agriculture has made policy making much more complicated and less predictable than in the past. It also has heightened the level of conflict in American politics because of the ideological differences between commercial interests and the newly developed citizens' groups attempting to achieve broad policy objectives.[39]

How Representative Is the Interest Group System?

The increased diversity of interest groups, the expanded role of public interest groups, and the diminished capacity of iron triangles to dominate selected areas of policy have not resolved the concern many feel about the representativeness of the interest group system. Participation in group politics has its costs: time away from work,

38. For an account of the development of the agriculture policy issue network, see William B. Browne, "Policy and Interests: Instability and Change in a Classic Issue Subsystem," in Cigler and Loomis, *Interest Group Politics*, 2d ed., chap. 10.

39. Thomas I. Gais, Mark A. Peterson, and Jack L. Walker, "Interest Groups, Iron Triangles and Representative Institutions in American National Government," *British Journal of Political Science* 14 (April 1984): 161–185.

Table 8.4 Interest Group Representation in Washington

	% of Total Groups Having a Washington Office	% of Total Groups Retaining a Lobbyist or Having a Washington Office
Corporation	20.6	45.7
Trade association	30.6	17.9
Foreign business	0.5	6.5
Professional association	14.8	6.9
Union	3.3	1.7
Citizens' group	8.7	4.1
Civil rights, minorities	1.7	1.3
Social welfare and poor	1.3	0.6
Elderly, women, handicapped	2.5	1.1
Government units	1.4	4.2
Others	14.6	8.2
Total	100.0	100.0
	(N = 2,810)	(N = 6,601)

SOURCE: Adapted from *Organized Interests and American Democracy* by Kay Lehman Scholzman and John T. Tierney. Copyright © 1986 by Kay Lehman Scholzman and John T. Tierney. Reprinted by permission of Harper Collins Publishers.

family, and recreation, and the expense of attending meetings, contacting government officials, and communicating with group members. Not everyone, therefore, is able to participate equally in the interest group system. Unsurprisingly, studies show that interest group participation is more prevalent among better-educated and up-scale Americans than among the less well-to-do.[40] Because data on interest groups with Washington offices or representatives show a heavy preponderance of economic groups (Table 8.4), it has been suggested that the interest group "chorus sings with a strong upper-class accent."[41]

This apparent class bias of the interest group system is counterbalanced in part by the existence and increasing activity of groups that act as advocates for the poor or for more general interests—consumers, taxpayers, and environmentalists. But many issues do not pit the rich against the poor—for example, most foreign policy issues or the struggles over water rights between California and its

40. Kay Lehman Schlozman and John T. Tierney, *Organized Interests and American Democracy* (New York: Harper and Row, 1986), chap. 4.
41. E. E. Schattschneider, *The Semi-Sovereign People* (New York: Holt, Rinehart and Winston, 1960), 35.

neighboring states. Nor are all elements of the poor in agreement—for example, the young poor have scant interest in Medicare and Social Security, but these are prime concerns of the elderly poor. It is even possible for powerful economic interests to benefit from and support programs designed to help the poor. Agribusiness benefits from the food stamp program; health care professionals and hospitals benefit from Medicare and Medicaid. The influence of major economic interests may be diminished, however, by disagreements among them. Such is the case with the continuing battles over government regulatory policy, which pit banks against savings and loan associations.

Although there are limits on the effectiveness of economic interest groups and advocates for the disadvantaged do exist, the fact remains that groups anchored in economic self-interest do have certain advantages. They are relatively permanent, have substantial resources, and normally can develop working relationships with policy makers. Public interest groups must rely more heavily on their ability to mobilize and sustain public support and interest—more difficult tasks than using insider lobbying techniques and making campaign contributions. In politics, as in other aspects of life, it is still better to be well off than poor. The group struggle in America, however, is a process open to all who wish to participate.

Regulation

Concern about the undue influence of special interest groups on the political process has led Congress to enact regulatory legislation. Regulation of interest groups, however, is limited by their protection under the Constitution's First Amendment guarantees of freedom of speech, press, assembly, and the right to petition the government for redress of grievances.

Under the Federal Regulation of Lobbying Act passed in 1946, groups and individuals seeking to influence legislation are required to register with the clerk of the House and the secretary of the Senate and to file quarterly financial statements. As it has been interpreted, however, the act has little practical impact. The Supreme Court has held that the law applies only to groups or individuals involved in direct lobbying and whose "principal purpose" is lobbying. As a result, not all groups register, and grass-roots lobbying is not covered by the law. In addition, it does not apply to attempts to influence the executive branch.

There is broad support for the notion that the public is entitled to more information than the current law permits about the activities of interest groups. But proposals to strengthen reporting and disclosure provisions of the law have raised serious issues. Disclosure of groups' contributors has been opposed by consumer, environmental, and civil rights groups on the grounds that such information could expose these individuals to intimidation. It also has been recommended that interest groups file detailed reports on their activities and contacts with public officials. These proposals would impose particularly heavy burdens on small and modestly financed groups, which have claimed that their effectiveness would be impaired because they would be mired in red tape.

Interest Groups, Government, and the Public Interest

Interest groups are a natural development in a free society characterized by socioeconomic diversity, and they gravitate toward the government because its power enables them to achieve goals that they cannot secure with their own resources. Because groups supplement the geographic representation system of Congress and are a means of mobilizing citizens to influence their government, they are essential linkages between the people and the government and their activities are constitutionally protected. But intergroup competition, lack of internal unity, and the competition of other political forces such as political parties and the mass media limit the capacity of interest groups to gain all their policy objectives.

For all their contributions to the political system, however, interest groups continue to stir unease in Americans. Even though interest group membership is widespread, there is concern that the public interest is being trampled by the stampede of interest groups to Washington. Most question whether the net effect of interest group pulling and hauling necessarily results in what is best for the nation as a whole. There is also worry about the inherent biases in the interest group system because not all interests have the same capacities for influencing the government; middle- and upper-class interests appear to have an advantage. It is for this reason that political scientists stress the role of political parties as America's most broadly based counterweight to interest group influence. Another force that can limit interest group influence is the mass media with their capacity to sway mass opinion. The media are the subject of the next chapter.

For Review

1. An interest group is an organized body of individuals with shared goals who try to influence government policy. Interest group activity is protected by the Constitution.

2. American society contains a vast array of interest groups which have grown dramatically in number since the 1960s. With their growth has come a change in the composition of the interest group universe. Traditional occupational groups have been supplemented by an increase in citizens' (public) interest groups and lobbying operations sponsored by corporations and state and local government bodies. Moreover, policy making now takes place in an often more complex and conflictual group environment than in the recent past.

3. The influence of individual interest groups depends on such factors as the nature of a group's membership, its financial and leadership resources, its prestige and status, and government structure, rules, and procedures.

4. Groups try to influence any branch or level of government that they believe will respond to their concerns. The tactics used by interest groups to influence government policy include direct and grass-roots lobbying, PAC contributions and other forms of electoral support, efforts to shape public opinion, and demonstrations and protests.

5. The interest group system supplements the formal and geographic system of congressional representation by providing citizens with an informal means of influencing government. Not all Americans are equally represented, however, by the interest group system. Although every American is free to organize and participate in interest group activity, the people most likely to participate are the better educated and those with financial resources.

For Further Reading

Berry, Jeffrey M. *The Interest Group Society.* 2d ed. Glenview, Ill.: Scott, Foresman, 1989. An overview of the formation and maintenance of groups as well as their activities in the political arena.

———. *Lobbying for the People: The Political Behavior of Public Interest Groups.* Princeton, N.J.: Princeton University Press, 1977. A study of public interest groups, including case studies of peace and animal rights organizations.

Cigler, Allan J., and Burdett A. Loomis, eds. *Interest Group Politics.* 3d ed. Washington, D.C.: CQ Press, 1991. A collection of original studies detailing the tactics of groups.

McFarland, Andrew S. *Common Cause: Lobbying in the Public Interest.* Chatham, N.J.: Chatham House, 1984. The most thoroughgoing analysis of the internal politics and lobbying tactics of a unique and influential public interest group.

Moe, Terry M. *The Organization of Interests: Incentives and the Internal Dynamics of Political Interest Groups.* Chicago: University of Chicago Press, 1980. An analysis of the internal dynamics of farm and business organizations.

Olson, Mancur, Jr. *The Logic of Collective Action.* New York: Schocken, 1968. An analysis of the free-rider problem and how shared interests are not sufficient for groups to organize and maintain themselves.

Schlozman, Kay Lehman, and John T. Tierney. *Organized Interests and American Democracy.* New York: Harper and Row, 1986. An analysis of group formation, internal dynamics, and strategies of influence.

Truman, David B. *The Governmental Process.* New York: Knopf, 1951. A classic treatment of the group basis of politics.

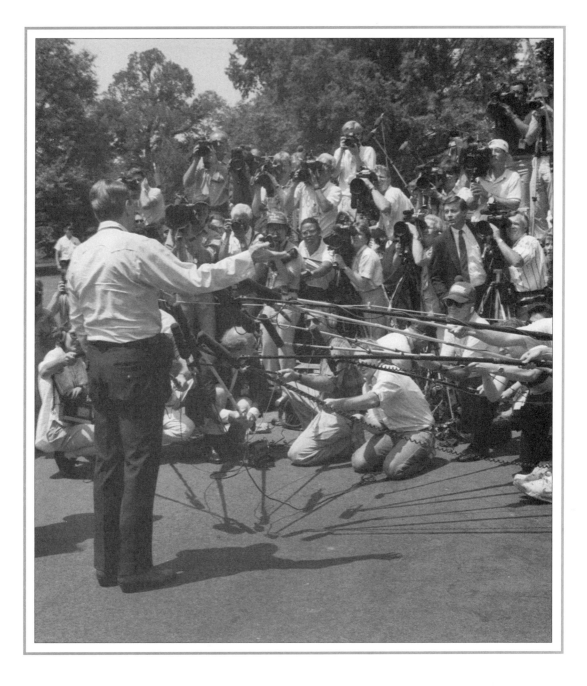

9. The Mass Media

I N THE 1988 presidential election campaign, only a tiny fraction of the voters actually met or saw the Republican and Democratic nominees, George Bush and Michael Dukakis. Most of what people knew about these men was absorbed from watching television or reading about them in newspapers and news magazines. In fact, news stories from all of these sources are an important part of how Americans perceive what is happening politically in the world around them, whether it be presidential debates, battles in the Persian Gulf, or congressional investigations. These shared political experiences constitute a basis for public opinion and the coming together of people for political action.[1]

The term **news media** refers to the diverse array of national and local newspapers, weekly and monthly news magazines, television networks and stations, and radio stations. Within this broad complex of news outlets, there are the more narrowly defined and influential national media consisting of the major television networks, the Public Broadcasting Service (PBS), and the three newspapers specializing in national political news—the *New York Times,* the *Washington Post,* and the *Wall Street Journal.* These national media are especially influential because they are watched and read by the country's political leaders, as well as by journalists themselves. This chapter deals primarily with this powerful national segment of the news media.

The news media act as intermediaries between the people and their government institutions. And like political parties and interest groups and their members, the media can mobilize their viewers and readers to take political action that will affect the inner workings of the government. Although the extent of the media's influence has not been determined conclusively, it is widely accepted that they played a significant role in shaping public opinion about the Vietnam War and even swayed the Vietnam policies of news-obsessive president Lyndon Johnson.[2] Public support for American military involvement fell after intense, ongoing television coverage, which featured graphic pictures of the deaths, atrocities, and destruction caused by the war. Television also helped antiwar leaders win respectability by simply giving them coverage. President Johnson attached so much importance to the role of the media that he concluded there was no hope

1. Doris A. Graber, *Mass Media and American Politics,* 3d ed. (Washington, D.C.: CQ Press, 1989), 3.
2. Ibid., 240–241.

of regaining public support for the war after trusted and respected CBS anchorman Walter Cronkite editorialized against Johnson's Vietnam policy. This led *New York Times* reporter David Halberstam to observe, "It was the first time in history a war had been declared over by an anchorman."[3]

Unlike in the Vietnam days, media coverage also can increase public support for government policy. The steady flow of almost exclusively positive news accounts of the Persian Gulf War—Patriot missiles downing Iraqi Scud missiles, smart bombs hitting their targets, well-trained military personnel performing their missions cooperatively, and a charismatic commander, Gen. Norman Schwartzkopf, providing televised briefings—moved a nation initially divided about going to war to give its overwhelming support to President Bush's decision to use force to drive Iraqi invaders from Kuwait.

Because they recognize the importance of the media's effects on public opinion, political leaders constantly seek to influence the content of news coverage. The media, however, are able to raise issues that political leaders would prefer to keep out of the limelight. It was the enterprising journalism of two *Washington Post* reporters, for example, that played a critical role in revealing President Richard Nixon's role in covering up the 1972 break-in at the Democratic National Headquarters in the Watergate complex and led to his eventual resignation from the presidency. And it was the *Miami Herald* that broke the story of Sen. Gary Hart's extramarital affair aboard the yacht *Monkey Business* that effectively ended his bid for the 1988 Democratic presidential nomination.

In these days in which the average high school student spends more time in front of a television screen than in school, and adults are spending almost half their leisure time watching television or reading newspapers and magazines, the potential political influence of the media is obviously substantial. This chapter, then, probes the nature of the media and their influence on public opinion, elections, and government institutions. The starting point for this analysis is a look at the media's evolution as well as the government's regulatory policies.

The Coming of Age of the Mass Media

Today's multidimensional print and electronic media are vastly different from the highly partisan, exclusively print media that

3. David Halberstam, *The Powers That Be* (New York: Knopf, 1979), 514.

existed when the government under the Constitution began. The character of the twentieth-century media reflects the interaction of social changes, technological advances, government policies, and the attitudes of Americans toward both the media and government.

In the early days of the Republic, political factions and later political parties founded and controlled newspapers to convey their own interpretations of political events to the reading public. The *Gazette of the United States* gave the Federalist view of public affairs, and the opposing Jeffersonian interpretation was found in the *National Gazette*. Party leaders even used public funds to subsidize their papers. Indeed, when he became president, Thomas Jefferson began to help support the *National Intelligencer,* his administration's party organ, by awarding it contracts to print government documents.

Perhaps more than any other single event, the Civil War brought about major changes in journalism. The war created a popular appetite for news, which editors scurried to fill. In the North alone, over five hundred correspondents covered the war, with the *New York Herald* having sixty reporters in the field and spending more than $1 million on coverage. Although war coverage was hampered by erratic mail and telegraph service, government censorship, and inexperienced correspondents, the war established war correspondence as an essential brand of reporting and significantly expanded journalism's horizons.

By the mid-1880s, technological advances and societal changes made it possible for newspaper publishers to establish profitable enterprises based on mass readership. Industrialization, immigration, and urbanization, as well as rising literacy rates, created mass audiences for newspapers in America's cities. Mass readership, in turn, attracted advertising that paid the cost of printing and enabled publishers to turn a profit. Later, technological advances such as high-speed presses made it possible to print thousands of papers and sell them at low cost—often only a penny a copy. The invention of the telegraph in 1844 meant that national news could be cabled immediately from Washington to all parts of the country.

The popular press that emerged in the nineteenth century was often highly partisan, but its partisanship stemmed from the orientations of its publishers and not from its sponsorship by various political parties. The papers of the late 1800s and early 1900s often engaged in sensationalism, vulgarity, and sleazy reporting—also called **yellow journalism** for the Yellow Kid, a comic-strip character in the *New York World*. One of the most notorious examples of sensationalism occurred when William Randolph Hearst's *New York Journal* found itself locked in a circulation battle with Joseph Pulitzer's *New York World*. Both papers sent reporters and illustrators to Cuba in 1897 with orders to provide lurid details of Spanish atrocities against the Cuban people. When Frederic Remington, the noted artist and illustrator, sent a cable to Hearst in New York requesting permission to return to the United States because "everything is quiet. . . . There will be no war," Hearst responded, "Please remain. You furnish the pictures and I'll furnish the war." The newsmen obliged—frequently with only casual regard for accuracy—and provided American readers with a steady stream of stories depicting Spanish mistreatment of Cubans. Yellow journalism of this character stoked the fires of public indignation against Spain and provided public support for the Spanish-American War of 1898.

It also was during this era that mass-circulation magazines of opinion—*Collier's, McClure's, Scribner's,* and *Cosmopolitan*—emerged. Their investigative reporting, which President Theodore Roosevelt called **muckraking**, exposed the seamy side of American government and business—corrupt urban political machines, special-interest influence in the Senate, and corporate misconduct that threatened public health and safety. The muckraking tradition and its accompanying suspicion of politicians are still very much alive today in American journalism as CBS's popular and long-running investigative program "60 Minutes" demonstrates.

The Media in the Twentieth Century

The communications industry has changed dramatically in this century. Yellow journalism has been largely replaced by more professional news-gathering standards, and the mass media now encompass a staggering assortment of both print and electronic outlets: over 9,100 newspapers (of which 18 percent are published on a daily basis), 11,000 periodicals, 10,000 radio stations, 1,200 television stations, and 7,800 cable systems. But while Americans are served by a wide array of news sources, the communications industry has become increasingly centralized in terms of ownership and control. This trend is largely the result of economic forces. Because worldwide news gathering and program production for television are extremely expensive (on average each story broadcast on the "NBC Nightly News" costs $63,000!),[4] only large-scale enterprises are able

4. Graber, *Mass Media and American Politics,* 49.

to generate the revenue required to provide Americans with the range and quality of media fare they have come to expect.

Journalistic Professionalism. Also in the twentieth century, journalists began to adhere to professional norms calling for factual accuracy and objectivity. This movement toward professionalism was aided by the establishment of university schools of journalism. Journalistic independence took root in this heightened professionalism as well; reporters believed themselves independent of politicians, whose actions were to be reported accurately, fully, and fairly, and of their colleagues on the business side of the media, whose interference with news content was not to be tolerated.

Newspapers. Newspapers, like most other forms of media, are profit-making enterprises whose ownership is increasingly concentrated in the hands of large chains such as Gannett, Cox, Scripps Howard, Knight-Ridder, Times Mirror, and the Tribune Company. Although more than sixteen hundred papers publish on a daily basis, 68 percent of these papers (boasting 78 percent of total circulation) are controlled by national and regional chains. Thus, with the ten largest chains accounting for nearly half (63 million papers) of the total daily newspaper circulation in the United States, a large share of the news read by Americans each day is screened by the people who work for these giant firms. These chains do permit their individual papers to enjoy editorial page autonomy, but they tend to be more uniform in their political endorsements than the independently owned papers.[5] The trend toward concentration within the industry has been exacerbated by the decline in the number of daily papers. Intense competition and rising costs have forced smaller papers to cease operation and left many cities such as Cleveland and Columbus with only one daily newspaper.

Even though ownership and control of the industry have become increasingly concentrated, individual papers still have a strong local orientation—after all, newspaper readers want to know what their state and local governments are up to, and it is impossible for the national media to cover state and local politics. Most papers therefore devote a large proportion of their news space to state and local politics. Even the Washington bureaus of the newspaper chains and the large city dailies have a local orientation. The job of the reporters for such papers as the *Denver Post* or *Milwaukee Journal* is to get the local or state angle on Washington events. It is not their job to cover the big national news stories. That task is left up to the national-

5. Ibid., 45.

circulation papers as well as the Associated Press (AP) and United Press International (UPI) wire services.

National-circulation papers that are not primarily local or regional in their orientation include the *New York Times, Washington Post, Wall Street Journal, Los Angeles Times,* and *USA Today.* These papers are important sources of information not just for ordinary citizens but also for Washington decision makers. Political leaders even communicate with each other by making statements and taking actions that are reported in the national press. Other segments of the news industry rely on these papers as well. Reporters, editors, and producers in local newsrooms and editorial offices across the country read the national press to identify newsworthy events and trends. Television news executives, in particular, having only limited air time available to them, use the national newspapers to help them decide what to cover. The impact of the national press, therefore, is much more substantial than their circulation numbers might suggest.

Periodicals. Periodicals are an important part of the print media. The mass-circulation news weeklies—*Time, Newsweek,* and *U.S. News and World Report*—tend to provide a more interpretative slant on the news than newspapers and may reflect the opinions of reporters and editors. More clearly journals of opinion are such periodicals as the conservative *National Review* and the liberal *Nation* and *New Republic.* Periodical publishing also includes highly specialized publications for trade and professional associations as well as for people with particular lifestyles, ethnic and religious backgrounds, and recreational interests. The American Association of Retired Persons, for example, sends *Modern Maturity* and other publications to 27 million households updating its members on government policies affecting the elderly, and *Golf Digest* keeps its readers apprised of how changes in the tax code will affect country club members.

Rise of the Electronic Media. The mass communications industry was transformed from an exclusively print medium into a more complex print and electronic enterprise with the advent of radio in the 1920s and television after World War II. Radio and then television made possible instantaneous coverage of public affairs and gave political leaders unprecedented opportunities to speak directly to the American people. One of the first to utilize radio skillfully was President Franklin Roosevelt, whose "fireside chats" from the White House hearth to the living rooms of millions demonstrated radio's potential for swaying public opinion.

Radio's potential for mobilizing public support for presidential policies was demonstrated by President Franklin Roosevelt, who is shown delivering one of his "fireside chats" to the American people during the Great Depression.

Television added a visual dimension to the electronic media that enhanced their impact. With 98 percent of American homes having a television set, which is on in the average home about seven hours a day, television has become the public's primary source of news. According to the Roper Organization, television is the most important source of news for 65 percent of the public. Exposure to television is not related to one's social class or educational level, although the less educated are more likely to rely on television as their sole source of political information. Better-educated segments of the population tend to rely on the print media for information as well.

Not only is television the public's principal news source, but it also is the source that Americans trust most. More than any other medium, television has close-up, intimate qualities. Confirming this, a 1988 survey found that in a case of conflicting news reports, 49 percent of those surveyed said they would believe the television report; in contrast, the believability score for newspapers was 21 percent; magazines, 7 percent; and radio, 6 percent.[6]

Because of the high cost of television technology and personnel, television is even more centralized than newspaper publishing. In fact, the industry is dominated by three major commercial net-

6. Survey by the Roper Organization for the Television Information Office, November 1988, reported in *American Enterprise*, July/August 1990, 96.

works—ABC, CBS, and NBC. Only about one-third of the 982 commercial stations operating in 1986 were not affiliated with a major network. The drawing power of the commercial networks is enormous—approximately thirty million households tune into one of the three network evening news programs during weekdays. The networks not only produce the bulk of the programming seen on local stations, but also own stations in the nation's largest media markets—New York, Los Angeles, and Chicago—as well as in Washington, D.C., Philadelphia, Detroit, St. Louis, and San Francisco.

But the television networks' dominance of the market is far from complete. In the 1980s, their share of the viewing market declined as new technologies diversified the video industry. The networks must now compete not only among themselves, but also with the over 300 public television stations as well as cable systems and videocassette recorders (VCRs). The Public Broadcasting Act of 1967 established the Corporation for Public Broadcasting, which provides programming and financial assistance to local noncommercial stations. These local public television stations also receive funding through contributions from state and local governments, businesses, foundations, and individuals. The Cable News Network (CNN) has built a sizable audience with its all-news format and was a particularly important news source during the early days of the Persian Gulf War in 1991. Other new technologies—minicams and satellite transmissions—are making local television stations less dependent on the network news organizations. These days, even some of the major national news stories, such as the New Hampshire presidential primary or the national nominating conventions, are within the reaches of local broadcasters.

All these developments mean that America is moving away from the broadcast era in which television signals were transmitted over the air to the wireless home receivers of a massive, heterogeneous audience. Rather, the television industry is rapidly entering an age of "narrowcasting" in which television signals are transmitted by air or direct wires to people's homes and aimed at smaller, more narrowly defined, and more homogeneous audiences. Some viewers, then, can push their remote-control buttons and choose from over sixty programming options to find the one compatible with their interests and political tastes. Some choose programming devoid of political content such as ESPN sports coverage or an old movie on a VCR; others select a channel that stresses a particular point of view such as one of the Christian broadcasting channels; and still others choose public affairs programming on CNN or C-SPAN (Cable-Sat-

Since 1979, C-SPAN (the Cable-Satellite Public Affairs Network) has made gavel-to-gavel coverage of proceedings in the House of Representatives available to some 43 million households in fifty states. C-SPAN also provides coverage of the Senate.

ellite Public Affairs Network, which relays the proceedings of both the House and Senate) or a "white paper" investigation on NBC. Media analyst Austin Ranney has speculated about the consequences of this new type of communications cafeteria:

In the era of narrowcasting, people who are already highly politicized are likely to become even more so. . . . A certain amount of channel hopping will yield an even higher proportion than formerly of the kind of politics they find congenial. . . . People who are not very politicized—which is most Americans—. . . are likely to become even less so. This . . . is likely to make political interest groups even less inclined and less able to make coalitions, and to make mass publics even less concerned about whether they do.[7]

Wire Services. Newspapers and radio and television news depend heavily on wire services for a huge share of all but their local news stories. Ninety-two percent of the daily news sources in the United States utilize the services of the two largest wire services, AP and UPI.[8] Major national newspapers such as the *New York Times, Washington Post, Los Angeles Times,* and *Chicago Tribune* also op-

7. Austin Ranney, "Broadcasting, Narrowcasting, and Politics," in *The New American Political System,* 2d ed., ed. Anthony King (Washington, D.C.: American Enterprise Institute, 1990), 201.
8. Graber, *Mass Media and American Politics,* 46.

erate wire services. Wire service news stories often are used verbatim or are rewritten by client papers and radio and television stations.

Ownership and Regulation of the Media

In the United States, most forms of media are privately owned, profit-making businesses. As such, they operate under less government control than the media in, for example, France, Israel, and Sweden, where the national governments own and operate the major television channels. As we just noted, however, the American media are increasingly controlled by large corporate enterprises, which have taken several forms: *multiple ownership of several media of the same type*—ownership of a number of newspapers or radio stations or television stations; *media conglomerates*—ownership of a combination of different types of media (Capital Cities/ABC, for example, owns in addition to ABC a cable network, seven television stations, nineteen radio stations, nine daily newspapers, forty weekly newspapers, and a number of magazines);[9] and *cross-industry conglomerates*—ownership of media and other enterprises unrelated to communications (General Electric, for example, owns NBC in addition to its various manufacturing and service enterprises).[10]

FCC Regulation of the Electronic Media

Because the concentration of print media ownership has generally stopped short of violating antitrust laws, the print media are largely unregulated. Government regulation impinges much more directly, however, on the operation of the radio and television industries. The airwaves are a national resource, and only a limited number of radio and television frequencies are available. To avoid chaos, therefore, the Federal Communications Commission (FCC) licenses stations. FCC regulations fall into three categories: (1) rules limiting the number of stations controlled by a single organization; (2) rules calling for examination of the goals and performances of stations as part of their periodic licensing; and (3) rules guaranteeing fair treatment of individuals.[11]

By using its licensing power to limit the number of television stations owned by a single organization, the FCC is able to prevent high

---

9. Ibid.

10. Ronald Berkman and Laura W. Kitch, *Politics in the Media Age* (New York: McGraw-Hill, 1986), 42.

11. The categories of FCC regulations are adapted from Graber, *Mass Media and American Politics*, 53.

concentrations of ownership and assure the public of diverse sources of information. Thus, FCC rules state that no owner can acquire more than one AM and FM radio station or more than one television station within the same media market. Limits are also placed on the total number of stations one owner may hold: not more than twelve AM radio stations, twelve FM radio stations, and twelve television stations. In actual practice, the FCC rarely uses its power to refuse a station's license renewal application in an effort to reduce ownership concentration.

Radio and television stations are required by law to "serve the public interest, convenience, and necessity." This rather vague standard gives the FCC little guidance in determining whether to renew a station's license other than to review the mix of programs presented, the proportion of public service offerings, and the inclusion of programs for selected groups. But the agency does not try to scrutinize the contents of programs in any detail. With its limited staff, the FCC has been neither inclined nor able to rigorously define and enforce rules regarding programming for the public interest.

To ensure that the airwaves are used fairly by broadcasters, the FCC implements equal time and right-of-rebuttal rules. Under the **equal time rule**, a station that gives or sells time to one candidate for a specific office must make the same opportunity available to other candidates for the same office. But the rule does not apply to regular news programs, most talk shows, and debates between candidates. The *right-of-rebuttal* rule requires stations to make their facilities available to individuals who have been assailed on radio or television for purposes of rebutting the criticism.

Until 1987, radio and television stations were required to comply with the **fairness doctrine**, which required stations to give opposing views reasonable time if a controversial public issue was discussed on the air. This rule had a long history of controversy and litigation. Broadcasters were highly critical of the fairness doctrine, claiming that it actually worked against presentation of different viewpoints on issues of public policy. Indeed, they pointed out that the fairness doctrine actually encouraged stations to avoid controversial programming for fear of having to give free air time to opposing viewpoints. There also was evidence that under the fairness doctrine the media, wishing to comply with the doctrine and not risk nonrenewal of their licenses, assumed that every political issue had two sides and only two sides—a rather dubious assumption. In answer to this interpretation, CBS correspondent Bill Plante observed, "If you have somebody who's calling the president an idiot, you then almost have to have somebody who's saying, 'Well, no, he's not, he's a great statesman.'"[12] In the atmosphere of deregulation that characterized the Reagan administration, such arguments received a sympathetic hearing and the FCC abandoned the fairness doctrine. When in 1987 the Democratic-controlled Congress passed legislation reinstating the doctrine, President Reagan vetoed the bill. The media, then, legally control the array of viewpoints aired by their own radio and television stations. Congressional pressures and potential litigation, however, have encouraged broadcasters to permit the airing of opposing viewpoints, and the broadcasting of rebuttals after presidential, gubernatorial, and mayoral addresses dealing with major public issues is now commonplace.[13]

Generally, the FCC regulates the electronic media with a light hand. With its vague statutory mandate and small staff, as well as its constant buffeting by conflicting industry, congressional, and administration pressures, the agency has earned the reputation of a benign regulator. Even so, the broadcasting industry is vulnerable to government pressures in a way that the print industry is not. Radio and TV station licenses are not granted on a permanent basis and must be renewed every five years. Although nonrenewal is rare, the absence of a clear standard for determining whether a station has used the airwaves in a responsible manner makes the industry extremely uneasy and sensitive to the political winds blowing through the FCC and Congress.

Access to Government Information

As we saw in Chapter 4, the First Amendment's guarantee of freedom of the press has been interpreted as a virtual ban on government acts of prior censorship. Freedom of the press, however, is of limited value if the press does not have access to information about how the government is going about its business. In gaining such access, the press has been strengthened by the 1966 Freedom of Information Act, which gives the media a strong legal basis for forcing government officials to release documents that they might prefer to keep under wraps. To prevent the release of government documents, the government is required by law to demonstrate that public access to them will be harmful to the country—such as by damaging national security. The impact of the act has been limited, however, because

12. Quoted by Michael J. Robinson and Margaret A. Sheehan, *Over the Wire and on TV: CBS and UPI in Campaign '80* (New York: Russell Sage Foundation, 1983), 61. Also see Austin Ranney, *Channels of Power: The Impact of Television on American Politics* (New York: Basic Books, 1983), 48–50.
13. Graber, *Mass Media and American Politics*, 117.

application procedures are burdensome, and most reporters tend to cover current events rather than dig into government files to report on past government actions. Nevertheless, the act has revealed some newsworthy happenings such as American troops' involvement in the 1968 My Lai massacre of civilians in Vietnam, Central Intelligence Agency (CIA) involvement in the overthrow of Chilean president Salvador Allende in 1973, and government failure to protect the public from unsafe nuclear reactors, contaminated drinking water, and ineffective drugs.

Disagreements over just where the government should draw the line in providing the media with information almost always arise during military operations and when national security is a concern. For example, during the 1983 invasion of the small Caribbean island of Grenada where a Cuban-backed government was in control, the Reagan administration restricted the media's access to the island. Then-secretary of state George Shultz justified the restriction, recalling that

[during World War II] reporters were involved [in military operations] all along. And on the whole, they were on our side. These days, in the adversary journalism that's been developed, it seems as though the reporters are always against us and so they're always seeking to report something that's going to screw things up. And when you're trying to conduct a military operation, you don't need that.[14]

The working press was so enraged by the Pentagon's restrictions on news coverage of the Grenada invasion that later a new set of guidelines for press coverage of military actions was developed by the Department of Defense. In 1991, the controversy flared anew, however, during the early stages of the war against Iraq in the Persian Gulf. The U.S. military exercised tight control by withholding information about the extent and impact of coalition bombing, limiting press access to combat areas, and restricting interviews with troops and returning pilots. Some journalists complained that these restrictions prevented accurate reporting of the war and left the public without adequate information to assess its progress. But the military justified its actions on the grounds that they were essential to prevent the inadvertent disclosure of battle plans to the enemy and to protect the lives of combat personnel.

All this being said, government leaders are generally sensitive to the issue of media access because they rely on the media for public

14. Quoted by David S. Broder, *Behind the Front Page: A Candid Look at How the News Is Made* (New York: Simon and Schuster, 1987), 305.

visibility. They then are reluctant to stir up alienation among the press corps.

The Issue of Media Bias

The media are constantly under fire about their designations of what is and is not newsworthy and their fairness and objectivity in reporting the news. News reporters are subject to two kinds of bias. The first is political bias—unbalanced or slanted news coverage of issues, candidates, or political parties stemming from a reporter's personal attitudes. The second is structural bias—an orientation toward news coverage and content that stems from the nature of the communications industry and the news-gathering process.[15]

Thunder on the Right and Thunder on the Left: Political Bias

Conservatives often accuse the media of having a liberal bias. In a blistering attack in 1969, former vice president Spiro Agnew singled out "the effete Eastern liberal press"—a "tiny and enclosed fraternity of privileged men, elected by no one"—for undermining public support for the Nixon administration and its policies.[16] The political Right's continuing concern about liberal bias was reflected as well in the 1980s campaign by Sen. Jesse Helms (R-N.C.) to have conservatives gain control of CBS by buying up its stock.

Conservatives and Republicans are not the only ones to question the objectivity of the media. The political Left has voiced its doubts as well. President Jimmy Carter's press secretary, Jody Powell, argued that reporters are harder on Democratic presidents than on Republican presidents.[17] Other media-watchers have charged that the media are biased against liberal and radical leaders and their causes. According to this argument, because the media are owned by profit-motivated businesspeople, they use their influence to maintain the status quo. It is charged therefore that the media fail to report antiestablishment ideas and movements and use entertainment—sitcoms, cop shows, and sports—to prevent the public from questioning and challenging mainstream politics.[18]

Journalists' Personal Attitudes. Conservatives often base their

15. Ranney, *Channels of Power*, 35–36.
16. Quoted by Ranney, ibid., 32.
17. Jody Powell, *The Other Side of the Story: An Insider's View of the Carter Administration* (New York: William Morrow, 1984).
18. The leftist critique of the media is summarized by Ranney, *Channels of Power*, 39–42. Also see Robert Cirino, *Don't Blame the People* (New York: Random House, 1972); and Nicholas Johnson, *How to Talk to Your Television Set* (Boston: Atlantic-Little, Brown, 1970).

Table 9.1 Political Attitudes of Journalists, the Public, and College-educated Professionals: A Comparison *(percent)*

Issue	Journalists	Public	College-educated Professionals
Consider self			
Liberal	55	23	38
Conservative	17	29	30
The way President Reagan is handling his job			
Favor	30	56	57
Oppose	60	27	33
Government regulation of business			
Favor	49	22	26
Oppose	41	50	57
Increased defense spending			
Favor	15	38	32
Oppose	80	51	63
Abortion rights			
Favor	82	49	68
Oppose	14	44	28
Prayer in public schools			
Favor	25	74	58
Oppose	67	19	36

SOURCE: *Los Angeles Times* poll, February 1985; reprinted in *Public Opinion,* August/September 1985, 7. Reprinted with the permission of The American Enterprise Institute for Public Policy Research, Washington, D.C.

charges of media bias on surveys that consistently reveal that journalists are more liberal in their attitudes than the general public or other college-educated professionals. Journalists are most markedly liberal on social issues such as abortion and prayer in the public schools (Table 9.1). Surveys conducted since 1964 also have shown that a substantial majority of journalists prefer Democratic presidential candidates. While revealing the political orientation of people in the news business, these data do not prove that newspeople are guilty of biased reporting. To prove bias, it must be demonstrated that journalists act in accordance with their ideological or partisan orientations.

Do the Media Give a Partisan or Ideological Slant to the News? The most thorough studies of possible media bias have been analyses of television coverage of presidential campaigns. Media researcher Michael Robinson and his associates concluded after an exhaustive study of television's coverage of presidential campaigns that there was no continuing or consistent partisan or candidate bias. Nor did the selection of stories to be covered reveal a consistent bias.[19]

A variety of forces work against political bias in the media. One counterforce against potential liberal bias stemming from reporters' political views is the generally more conservative political orientation of the owners, managers, and editors who direct the flow of the news by deciding which events will be covered and how stories will be handled.[20]

Both the economics and professional norms of the industry also work against political bias by either management or reporters. Unlike the media owners of an earlier era, today's owners and managers generally believe that it is their responsibility to provide their readers or viewers with information, not indoctrinate them. But there are other compelling reasons why they do not dictate news content and tone of coverage to their correspondents. Media owners are interested in the profits produced when there is a large audience for their product. They do not want to alienate readers or viewers by offering them biased news coverage.

The increasing level of professionalism among newsroom personnel reduces publisher/owner-induced bias as well. Professional reporters tend to be independent-minded and unlikely to accept owners' political dictates. For example, David Broder, respected columnist and reporter for the *Washington Post,* has observed that had his paper's management bowed to pressure from the Nixon administration to call off the investigation of the 1972 Watergate scandal, "it would have caused a newsroom rebellion that might have damaged the *Post*'s credibility far more than any political or commercial pressure from the administration."[21]

Journalism's professional norms also have a disciplinary impact on reporters. One moves up in the profession by demonstrating reporting skills, not ideological purity. To climb to a prominent position with a television network or national newspaper, a reporter

19. Michael J. Robinson, "Just How Liberal Is the News: 1980 Revisited," *Public Opinion,* February/March 1983, 55–66; also see Robinson and Sheehan, *Over the Wire and on TV.* A study of the 1972 campaign also found an absence of ideological and partisan bias. See C. Richard Hoffstetter, *Bias in the News* (Columbus: Ohio State University Press, 1976).
20. William Schneider and I. A. Lewis, "Views on the News," *Public Opinion,* August/September 1985, 8.
21. Broder, *Behind the Front Page,* 325.

must undergo a long and demanding process of peer assessment and screening. As Michael Robinson has observed, "If you show much ideological bias in network journalism . . . you're going to be out of a job because there are bigger questions here to be resolved at the network level than whether you can as a journalist express your point of view."[22]

The Antipolitician Bias. Most social scientists and journalists reject the charge that the media exhibit ideological or partisan bias in news coverage. Media analysts, however, believe that reporters have a skeptical and even cynical attitude toward politics and politicians and that these feelings are reflected in their news coverage.

Reporters tend to view politics as a game in which one side wins and the other loses, not as a process for resolving conflicts or distributing values within society. Politicians are viewed as players whose basic motives are simple enough: to win elections and to hold power.[23] The muckraking tradition is still strong among journalists; they are suspicious of the powerful and anxious to ferret out wrongdoing, strip politicians of their disguises, and pierce their rhetoric. The media's skeptical and often adversarial attitude toward politicians has been defended on the grounds that it serves the public interest by keeping people informed about what is really happening, by raising troublesome issues that politicians might prefer to ignore, and by preventing abuses of power. The media serve as the public's watchdog, it is claimed. Some political scientists, however, see potential adverse consequences stemming from the media's generally antipolitician orientation. Since the 1960s, for example, public trust in government institutions has declined. This decline has multiple sources—such as the divisiveness of the Vietnam War, the Watergate scandal, and double-digit inflation during the 1970s; the Iran-contra affair of the 1980s; and the revelations of House members bouncing checks and not paying their House restaurant tabs in the 1990s. Austin Ranney believes that television's portrayal of politics also has been a contributing factor.[24]

Structural Bias

The nature of the communications industry and the processes of news gathering have introduced a number of well-verified structural biases into news coverage.

22. Michael J. Robinson, quoted from an interview taped by the Department of Governmental Affairs, University of Wisconsin-Madison, July 1987.

23. See Ranney, *Channels of Power,* 58–61; and Edward Jay Epstein, *The News from Nowhere* (New York: Random House, 1973), 215.

24. Ranney, *Channels of Power,* 74–79. Also see Michael J. Robinson, "American Political Legitimacy in an Era of Electronic Journalism," in *Television as a Social Force,* ed. Douglass Cater and Richard Adler (New York: Praeger, 1975), 113–114.

Deciding What Is News. The *New York Times* masthead proclaims that the paper contains "All the News That's Fit to Print." But even as complete a paper as the *Times* cannot fulfill this goal. There is too much happening in the world, and more stories are filed by reporters than can be carried in either the print or electronic media. Thus, within all news organizations there are *gatekeepers*—city editors, national news editors, editors-in-chief, film editors, executive producers—who decide what is printed in the papers and aired on television and radio. Their decisions about what is news determine to a significant extent the pictures of reality that we carry around in our heads.

The primary criterion used by newspeople in selecting news stories is *audience appeal*—not their political impact, educational value, or social purpose. Other criteria are whether the story concerns *violence, conflict, disaster, or scandal*; whether it involves a *familiar person or situation* (one reason the Kennedy family has provided much fodder for news stories); whether it is a story *close to home* (newspapers and local television and radio stations devote roughly three-fourths of their coverage to local events); and whether it is *timely and novel* (while over five hundred apparently honest members of Congress are not news, it was news when a handful of members were caught taking bribes from phony Arab sheiks in the Abscam investigation—a 1980 FBI "sting" operation).[25]

The news business is just that, a business. Moreover, because it is one that relies on an audience to make a profit, the amount and kind of coverage a story receives are not necessarily commensurate with its political or social significance at the time of publication or broadcast. As media analyst Doris Graber has pointed out, a particularly heinous crime may focus attention on crime stories and lead to an increase in the number and prominence of such stories at the very time the crime rate is actually declining. In addition, an important event that in the past received substantial coverage and is becoming more important each day may not receive prime-time coverage if the audience is getting bored with such stories. An example of such a discrepancy between the frequency of newsworthy events and the extent of news coverage was the coverage accorded racially charged urban riots in the 1960s which caused widespread destruction and looting in such cities as Washington, Detroit, and Los Angeles. The peak year for urban riots was 1968, but the peak year for

25. These criteria were identified by Graber, *Mass Media and American Politics,* 78–79.

Table 9.2 Network Television News Characteristics

Story Length (seconds)	%	Picture Exposure (seconds)	%	Number of Pictures	%
Less than 60	29	1–10	47	1–4	38
60–179	47	11–20	29	5–10	13
180–299	16	21–30	12	11–20	26
300+	8	31+	13	21–54	23

SOURCE: Doris A. Graber, *Mass Media and American Politics*, 3d ed. (Washington, D.C.: CQ Press, 1989), 175. Author's research based on a sample of 149 news stories from early evening newscasts on ABC, CBS, and NBC.

riot stories was 1967. The ratio of riots to riot stories in 1967 was 4:1, but in 1968 it was 12:1.[26]

With the criteria just described being used to select news stories, it is inevitable that the media are giving the public a world view that is incomplete, simplified, and a bit distorted. But this is not the result of some conscious plot or conspiracy on the part of the media gate-keepers or reporters. Rather, distortion is introduced in the effort to create a sizable audience for the media's product.

Time and Space Constraints. The totality and complexity of the human experience, and of politics in particular, just cannot be captured in a half-hour telecast or a page of national news. For television, the public's most important news source, time limitations have meant that it tends to be, in the words of Walter Cronkite, a "head-line service," providing something equivalent to the headline and first and second paragraphs of a newspaper story.[27]

Because television must present its news in short "bites," thereby precluding in-depth analysis, television programmers have recognized the benefits of presenting news stories as part of a larger, on-going story (see Table 9.2). In the early 1980s, such a continuity theme was the Reagan revolution, whereas later in the same decade it was the weakening of the Reagan presidency. And in the 1990s it has been the legacy of problems created by 1980s policies.

An extremely important part of television production is therefore the selecting, editing, and interpreting of material so that thirty-second and two-minute time bites will make sense to the viewer.

26. Ibid., 84–85; and G. Ray Funkhouser, "Trends in Media Coverage of the Issues of the '60s," *Journalism Quarterly* 50 (Fall 1973): 523–538.
27. Ranney, *Channels of Power*, 46.

Unless continuity and meaning can be established quickly, viewer interest may be lost.[28]

The print media, of course, must undertake the same process, but they are not subject to the same tight time/space constraints as television and can cover a wider range of events and give more play to their context. But even in the newspaper business, a tremendous pressure is on to be concise and give only bare-bones coverage to public affairs. The successful national daily *USA Today* illustrates this pattern.

Reliance on Politicians as News Sources. Whenever the media must depend heavily on political leaders for information, the content and tone of news stories are bound to be affected. Reporters are naturally reluctant to alienate the powerful news sources with whom they must deal on a day-to-day basis. They also are vulnerable to manipulation by political leaders, who may try to co-opt them through exclusive stories, background briefings, regular access, or friendly gestures.

Politicians also try to shape the flow of news. For example, after President Reagan and Soviet general secretary Mikhail Gorbachev were unable to reach an arms reduction agreement at their 1986 Iceland summit meeting, the president and senior administration officials made a well-coordinated series of public appearances to present their side of the summit story. The result was extensive coverage of the administration's point of view. What at first appeared to be a failure in diplomacy was presented as the president's firm stand in negotiations. Administration officials may even go as far as limiting subordinates' contacts with the media for fear that their comments will conflict with the administration's official line. Other manipulations of the press may take the form of scheduling newsworthy events for slow news days or staging television spectaculars such as President Carter's televised citizen call-in program moderated by Walter Cronkite, and presidential trips to Saudi Arabia, Moscow, and China.[29]

Is There Media Bias?

Although the issue of media bias is normally posed in partisan or ideological terms, social science studies provide little support for a consistent pattern of media bias favoring particular parties, candidates, or issues. There is, in other words, no conspiracy afoot to manipulate public opinion to bring it into conformity with that of

28. Ibid., 46–47.
29. Graber, *Mass Media and American Politics,* 247–249.

the professionals who work for the media. There are, however, structural forces inherent in the communications industry and in news gathering that substantially affect the news content. Decisions by the media about what constitutes news, for example, determine in part what information reaches the public. But as we will see in the next section, it is important to keep in mind that the media play a larger role in conveying information than they do in shaping attitudes and opinions. Many who gain information from the media use it as a point of departure for formulating their own opinions. And some readers and viewers either reject or ignore any opinions and attitudes conveyed explicitly or implicitly by the media.[30]

The Impact of the Media on Politics

Although it is widely accepted that the media profoundly affect people's attitudes and the operation of the political system, establishing a direct link between media coverage and people's attitudes and government action has proven difficult and controversial. Two presidential commissions, for example, have produced contradictory conclusions about the impact of sexual stimuli in the media on the incidence of deviant behavior such as rape or child abuse. The assessment of the media's impact that follows examines its influence on public opinion, the public agenda, and the electoral process.

Do the Media Affect Public Attitudes?

The media are a major source of information and news for Americans, yet in spite of heavy exposure to the media, people remain relatively uninformed about political events.[31] In March 1984, for example, the evening news programs of the major television networks carried forty-three stories (including eight leadoff stories) about the ethical and policy controversies surrounding President Reagan's attorney general-designate, Edwin Meese. In spite of this generous coverage, which amounted to 51,000 seconds of air time, one-quarter of the respondents in a national survey could not remember anything about Meese (although one person falsely identified him as a "vicious killer"!), and another 10 percent knew only that he had been nominated to be attorney general.[32] How can public

30. Ibid., 153–154; and Doris A. Graber, *Processing the News: How People Tame the Information Tide*, 2d ed. (New York: Longman, 1988), 90–93.
31. L. Harmon Zeigler and William Haltom, "More Bad News about the News," *Public Opinion*, May/June 1989, 50–52.
32. Michael Robinson and Maura Clancey, "Teflon Politics," *Public Opinion*, April 1984, 15–16.

ignorance of politics continue to thrive with such widespread coverage? Is it possible that the media have no influence on the public and politics?

The impact of television, radio, newspapers, and the like on public attitudes is limited by people's selective exposure and attention to them. People tend to avoid information that upsets their peace of mind, offends their political and social tastes, or conflicts with information, attitudes, and feelings they already have. In addition, many people watch the television news, for example, while doing other things such as making dinner, caring for children—or even reading the newspaper! These distractions can diminish the media's impact. An individual's lack of interest in politics also may limit the media's capacity to influence his or her opinion as does the distrust of the media that exists among some elements of society. Some white ethnics, police, and union members view the media with a jaundiced eye because they believe the media improperly cast the police as oppressors of the disadvantaged and unions as corrupt and barriers to economic progress.

How the media present the news can diminish its impact as well. Television news programs bombard viewers with fifteen to eighteen news stories—unconnected snippets of three minutes or less—in half an hour. The public is thus given more news than it can handle. Furthermore, much of the news is touted as being important, but it actually may be quite trivial. The net effect can be numbness and boredom.[33]

Even with these limitations, however, the media are capable of moving public opinion. For example, public approval of the president is highly volatile and has been found to be related to whether the news media are reporting stories that are favorable or unfavorable to the president.[34] In a study that compared changes in public opinion on eighty domestic and foreign issues with the positions taken by a variety of information sources—television news commentators, interest groups, the president, and political parties—researchers found that television news commentators were capable of moving public opinion by as much as four percentage points.[35]

Finally, the way in which the media present issues also can affect

33. Graber, *Mass Media and American Politics*, 160–162, 173–176.
34. Richard A. Brody and Benjamin I. Page, "The Impact of Events on Presidential Popularity: The Johnson and Nixon Administrations," in *Perspectives on the Presidency*, ed. Aaron Wildavsky (Boston: Little, Brown, 1975), 136–148.
35. Benjamin I. Page, Robert Y. Shapiro, and Glenn R. Dempsey, "What Moves Public Opinion?" *American Political Science Review* 81 (March 1987): 23–43.

people's thinking. People's explanations for the causes of such national problems as poverty, unemployment, and terrorism have been shown to be related to how these issues were presented on television. Moreover, people's explanations for these problems affect their assessments of presidential performance. Those who attributed poverty to the poor being insufficiently motivated are more likely to give a favorable assessment of presidential performance than those who viewed the primary cause of the problem as government policies or societal trends.[36]

The Media as Agenda Setter

According to some political scientists, the media play a particularly strong role in determining which issues are put on the **public agenda**—the issues of concern to the public and worthy of government attention. By covering some events, problems, and issues and ignoring others, the news media help determine the priority Americans give to various issues.[37] The importance the media attach to a story is communicated through such cues as banner headlines, front page placement, lead story placement on television, and frequent, repeated coverage. For example, repetitious and often lead story coverage of the American hostages in Iran during the last year of the Carter administration helped keep the hostage issue on the public agenda.

Political leaders follow the news closely, especially that provided by the major television networks and such national papers as the *New York Times, Washington Post,* and *Wall Street Journal.* Indeed, the president and senior White House aides receive a daily summary of the news and how it was covered by the major media outlets. Issues worthy of the attention of these outlets often find their way onto the public agenda. For example, over the last few years the media have covered extensively charges of ethical misconduct filed against several former Reagan aides and former House Speaker Jim Wright (D-Texas), honorariums paid to members of Congress by corporations and interest groups, and the role of political action committees in financing political campaigns. As a result, ethics in government has climbed onto the political agenda and helped prompt President George Bush, congressional leaders, and interest groups to propose reforms.

36. Shanto Iyengar, "Television News and Citizens' Explanations of National Affairs," *American Political Science Review* 81 (September 1987): 815–831.

37. See Graber, *Mass Media and American Politics,* 163–164; and Shanto Iyengar and Donald R. Kinder, *News That Matters: TV and American Opinion* (Chicago: University of Chicago Press, 1987).

But while the media may set a policy agenda, the public does not necessarily follow it in a slavish manner. Past and current experiences, discussions with friends and family, and independent reasoning also have an impact on people's political priorities. Media guidance tends to apply most to issues not yet subject to widespread discussion or to issues beyond people's personal experiences.

Media Coverage of Elections

Because media coverage is essential in a campaign for major office, campaigns are structured to generate maximum media visibility and present the candidate in a positive light (also see Chapter 7, Elections, Campaigns, and Voters). National nominating conventions are now programmed for national television and their sessions scheduled for broadcast during prime evening viewing hours. Political parties use their ready access to the media during the conventions to showcase their candidates and kick off the general election campaigns. After the conventions, media events are staged regularly to gain media attention and get a minute or two on evening news programs. President Ronald Reagan's campaign managers in 1984 were particularly adept at creating settings for campaign events that evoked positive images of the president. Lesley Stahl of CBS News reported that after the network aired a piece in which she gave a particularly biting commentary about Reagan avoiding serious discussion of issues, she actually got a call from Michael Deaver, Reagan's media adviser, saying he loved the piece. A surprised Stahl asked how he could love such a critical news story. Deaver replied, "Haven't you figured it out yet? The public doesn't pay attention to what you say. They just look at the pictures." Later, when Stahl replayed the tapes with the sound turned off, she realized that she had prepared a "magnificent montage of Reagan in a series of wonderful, upbeat scenes, with flags, balloons, children, and adoring supporters—virtually an unpaid commercial."[38] In addition to television's quest for "good visuals," other patterns characterize media coverage of elections, such as emphasizing slogans, the "horse race," and "campaign issues." The rhetoric of candidates is filled with references to substantive domestic and foreign policy issues. In 1988, for example, Michael Dukakis campaigned on themes of economic fairness and competent leadership, while George Bush stressed continuing the Reagan policy agenda, albeit in a "kinder and gentler" manner. Their stump speeches were finely tuned to embody policy positions. Reporters, however, do not view policy statements by the

38. Broder, *Behind the Front Page*, 181–182.

candidates as particularly newsworthy. They prefer clear-cut issues that neatly divide the candidates, provoke controversy, seem to rest on principle, and can be stated in simple terms. It has been argued, for example, that a turning point in the 1988 presidential campaign occurred when Bush recognized that serious discussion would not carry him far in news coverage and that a dramatic phrase like "Read my lips—no new taxes!" was needed. As this example indicates, candidates' issue positions tend to become newsworthy only after they have assumed a stylized form.[39]

Emphasis also is given to the "horse race" aspects of the campaign, and election coverage tends to be similar to that used for sporting events. This stress on who's ahead, who's behind, who's gaining, whose campaign is lagging, and candidate strategies reflects the public's relatively low level of interest in issues, offset by the media's efforts to provide drama and generate interest in and an audience for their product.

The media focus as well on "campaign issues"—concerns about how the campaigns are being run, the performances of the candidates and their staffs, and the personal qualities of the candidates. In 1976, for example, the media heavily played up President Gerald Ford's gaffe about the existence of political freedom in Eastern Europe and what this remark indicated about his competence. In 1984, 40 percent of television news coverage focused on campaign issues: Reagan's age, his lack of availability to the press, his ties to fundamentalist preachers, and Democratic vice-presidential candidate Geraldine Ferraro's family finances.[40] In the 1988 presidential campaign, the media dwelled extensively on the role of the negative campaign ads used by the Bush campaign in its effort to define Michael Dukakis as an out-of-the-mainstream liberal. Media critics contend that such emphases on the "horse race" and "campaign issues," especially by television, tend to trivialize elections.

Covering the front-runners—the candidates leading in the polls and somewhat familiar to the public—is standard election fare. In the early stages of the contest for the 1984 Democratic presidential nomination when there were eight candidates in the race, the media threw most of their spotlights on the two candidates who ranked highest in the polls, former vice president Walter Mondale and Sen.

39. Thomas E. Patterson, "The Press and Its Missed Assignment," in *The Elections of 1988*, ed. Michael Nelson (Washington, D.C.: CQ Press, 1989), 101–102.
40. Maura Clancey and Michael J. Robinson, "General Election Coverage: Part I," in *The Mass Media in Campaign '84*, ed. Michael J. Robinson and Austin Ranney (Washington, D.C.: American Enterprise Institute, 1985), 29–30.

Figure 9.1: Good Press versus Bad Press: Television News Commentary during the 1984 Presidential Campaign

News seconds

Total Reagan / Bush =   730 good press seconds
                     8,740 bad press seconds

Total Mondale / Ferraro =1,970 good press seconds
                        1,450 bad press seconds

*Bush had 0 good press seconds.

Source: Maura Clancey and Michael J. Robinson, "General Election Coverage: Part I," in *The Mass Media in Campaign '84,* ed. Michael J. Robinson and Austin Ranney (Washington, D.C.: American Enterprise Institute, 1985), 28. Reprinted with the permission of the American Enterprise Institute for Public Policy Research, Washington, D.C.

John Glenn (D-Ohio).[41] In 1988, front-running candidates George Bush and Sen. Bob Dole (R-Kan.) garnered the bulk of the coverage in the six-candidate field of Republican candidates. Former senator Gary Hart, the early leader in the polls, was the beneficiary of heavy press coverage on the Democratic side, as was the Reverend Jesse Jackson.

But being a front-running candidate carries some risks in terms of media coverage. Leading candidates' performances in presidential primaries are measured against a media-defined standard of whether or not they did as well as they were expected to do. In 1988, Vice President George Bush was the early favorite to win the Republican nomination, but after he finished a weak third behind Senator Dole and television evangelist Pat Robertson in the Iowa caucuses, the media began to write off Bush's chances of ever becoming the nominee. The Iowa winner, Senator Dole, was then given heavy media attention and considered on the verge of knocking Bush out of the race. Eight days after the Iowa caucuses, however, Bush staged a come-from-behind victory in the New Hampshire primary and, by doing far better than expected, reestablished himself as the front-runner. Doing less well than expected had devastating consequences for Dole's standings in the polls and his ability to raise money and campaign support.

In the general election campaigns, front-runners risk receiving a lot of negative campaign coverage. Reporters covering presidential candidates often add a "spin" to their stories—giving the story a tone or embellishing the facts. An exhaustive analysis of ABC, CBS, and NBC evening newscasts in the 1984 presidential campaign revealed lots of "spin" in correspondents' reports of the campaign—decidedly more negative for the Republican ticket of Reagan and Bush than for Democrats Mondale and Ferraro (Figure 9.1). In the opinion of media experts Maura Clancey and Michael Robinson, this was not caused by partisan or ideological bias. Rather, it reflected correspondents' desires to see a competitive election—a real horse race—as well as a tendency to hold incumbents and front-runners to a higher standard of performance than challengers and underdogs.[42]

In 1988, the media's "spin" favored the Republican candidate. Analyses of *Time* and *Newsweek* election coverage revealed that the coverage of George Bush was initially negative (a *Newsweek* cover

41. William C. Adams, "Media Coverage of Campaign '84: A Preliminary Report," in Robinson and Ranney, *Mass Media in Campaign '84,* 10.
42. Clancey and Robinson, "General Election Coverage: Part I," 31–33.

story even featured his alleged "wimp" image) and then became positive after he emerged from President Reagan's shadow at the Republican convention. By contrast, Michael Dukakis's early press coverage was generally positive. But it took a negative turn as news reports zeroed in on his icy personality and his problems in becoming a credible candidate when his popularity began to dip and he fell behind Bush in the polls (see Figure 9.2). The changing nature of candidate coverage in 1988 raises the intriguing, but as yet unresolved, question of whether journalists' evaluations of candidates reflect voters' assessments or actually influence voters' perceptions.[43]

Impact of the Media on the Voters

In the 1940s, before the introduction of television into political campaigning, the media apparently had little impact on voter decisions. Researchers believed that the media mainly *reinforced* the partisan loyalties or predispositions of voters. Although the capacity of the media to reinforce people's attitudes is important, reinforcement implies that there were initial predispositions to be strengthened and that these predispositions were often partisan loyalties.[44] As we saw in Chapter 7, however, partisan considerations are less important in guiding voter choices today than in the 1940s and 1950s, presenting fewer opportunities for the media, through its coverage of candidates and campaigns, to reinforce voters' partisan inclinations. With voters now showing weaker attachments to parties, the media may instead have greater potential to affect voter choice.

On the whole, however, contemporary research, like the classic studies of the 1940s, has found that the media have little effect on voter preference. In particular, studies have demonstrated that regular viewing of network news has no effect on voters' awareness of candidates, yet viewing political commercials is associated with higher voter awareness of candidates' issue stances. The simple explanation for the difference in issue awareness associated with viewing network news versus paid advertisements is that political commercials contain more information about the issues than nightly news programs.[45]

The tendency noted in Chapter 7 of approximately two-thirds of

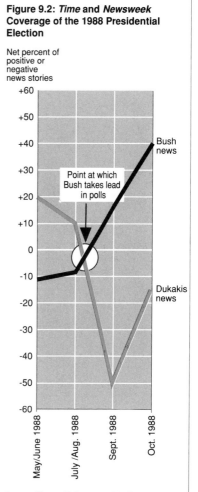

Figure 9.2: *Time* and *Newsweek* **Coverage of the 1988 Presidential Election**

Net percent of positive or negative news stories

Source: Thomas E. Patterson, "The Press and Its Missed Assignment," in *The Elections of 1988,* ed. Michael Nelson (Washington, D.C.: CQ Press, 1989), 107.

Note: "Bush news" and "Dukakis news" figures are the differences between the percentage of positive and percentage of negative news references to Bush and Dukakis, respectively, for the time period indicated.

43. Patterson, "The Press and Its Missed Assignment," 105–106.
44. See Bernard Berelson, Paul Lazarsfeld, and William McPhee, *Voting* (Chicago: University of Chicago Press, 1954).
45. Research on the impact of the media on voter choice is ably summarized by Herbert B. Asher, *Presidential Elections and American Politics,* 4th ed. (Chicago: Dorsey, 1987), 260–268; and by Graber, *Mass Media and American Politics,* 216–223.

voters to decide on their choice for president by the close of the national conventions and before the general election campaign officially
begins limits the impact of media coverage of the general election on
voter choice. In close elections, however, media coverage that sways
even a small percentage of voters can be crucial. During the period
between elections, the media may make its impact known as well by
providing voters with information about and images of the candidates that later become the basis for voters' choices. In 1984, for
example, Democratic presidential nominee Walter Mondale was hurt
by preconvention news stories conveying images of his domination
by special interests.[46]

Paid Media

Following the 1968 presidential campaign, Joe McGinnis published a best-seller, *The Selling of the President,* based on the thesis
that it was possible to buy the presidency with television ads—after
all, he claimed, winner Richard Nixon had fooled the public through
slick advertising. The McGinnis thesis rapidly found its fans, especially among supporters of losing presidential candidates. Many
Democrats, for example, were willing to accept the theory that
Bush's hard-hitting television ads led to Dukakis's defeat in 1988.
Political scientists, however, have not uncovered any convincing evidence that paid media advertising has a significant effect on voter
choice in presidential elections. Nor does the level of spending for
commercials appear to affect voters in presidential elections. In a
study of the 1988 presidential campaign, media expert Michael Robinson and his associates compared the Bush campaign's week-by-
week paid media buys with the candidate's standing in the polls and
found no significant correlations.[47]

The ability of the paid media to raise the visibility of a candidate
and permit relatively unknown candidates to build support among
the electorate is not relevant in a presidential election where both
candidates receive extensive news media coverage. But in elections
that receive little press attention, paid media can be important. Media expenditures by challengers for House seats, for example, enable
them to be better known and to compete with the generally more
visible and familiar congressional incumbents. Indeed, such expenditures, the largest share of which goes for advertising, are related to
the percentage of the vote received by House challengers. Thus, as challengers' expenditures increase, their share of the vote also goes up.

46. Asher, *Presidential Elections and American Politics,* 262.
47. Michael Robinson, Clyde Wilcox, and Paul Marshall, "The Presidency: Not
for Sale," *Public Opinion,* March/April 1989, 49–53.

Interestingly, paid advertising seems to be most effective in campaigns for and against ballot propositions—lawmaking by popular referendums, which is permitted in some states (most noticeably California). When party identification is not a factor, no candidates are on hand to provide a human embodiment of policy directions, and public knowledge of the issues is at its usual low level, political advertising can have a maximum influence. In these circumstances, ads can effectively portray the nature and consequences of the proposition and help crystallize public opinion.[48]

The Media and Government Institutions

The news media cover more aspects of politics than just electoral campaigns; government institutions, public officials, and the processes of decision making are fair game as well. No matter which branch of the government the media happen to be covering, tension inevitably arises between public officials and reporters. Reporters are out to get the real story on what is going on in the government, but political leaders frequently find that reporters' quests for stories serve neither their career interests nor the causes they support. Conflict also arises when public officials try to use or manipulate the media to gain the public support needed to stay in office and implement many policies. The media, however, see themselves as an independent force and not as a willing helpmate of politicians.

Conflicts between public officials and reporters intensified after the events of the 1960s and 1970s. During the Vietnam War and the Watergate crisis, reporters felt that they had been misled and lied to by Presidents Johnson and Nixon. This led to a breakdown of trust between reporters and public officials, with the result that the media challenged the statements, explanations, and actions of public officials more vigorously than in the past, and public officials became distrustful of reporters and reluctant to provide the media with access to information.

Although tension in the media-public official relationship is greater now than in the pre-Vietnam War/Watergate era, reporters and public officials find that they have to cooperate. Reporters need access to public officials if they are to get the information necessary to produce news stories. At the same time, public officials need the media if they are to get their messages out to the public. Neither media personnel nor politicians, however, want to feel used or abused by the other.

48. Graber, *Mass Media and American Politics,* 226.

The Media and the Presidency

Although presidents are at the center of the government, they cannot know fully what is happening within their administrations, the nation, or the world without the media. Thus, in fulfilling one of their critical functions, the media help keep the chief executive informed of current events. The role of the media also extends to providing information about the major concerns of the public, helping convey presidential messages to the country, and maintaining public visibility for presidents.

The president's personal image, the nature and effectiveness of administration policies, and presidential behavior are all heavily influenced by the saturation media coverage the president inevitably receives as head of the executive branch and the nation's most powerful public official. Indeed, the power of the White House has been enhanced by the unremitting attention the media give its occupant. Everything the president does, from meeting with world leaders to vacationing in Kennebunkport, Maine, is covered extensively. Media coverage, however, tends to emphasize not the substantive issues with which the president is dealing or the consequences of presidential decisions but rather the politics of a situation: the battles among contending forces or the president's ability to handle a delicate situation. For example, press coverage of the Reagan administration's economic policy decisions in 1981 were depicted as grudge matches between the executive and Congress and among opposing camps within the administration.[49]

Former White House staffer James Fallows has attributed reporters' tendencies to focus on the politics of the White House rather than on the substance of decisions to the fact that reporters feel more comfortable and competent dealing with political conflicts than with policy. He notes that White House reporters are particularly attracted to scandal, internal White House dissension, political blunders or gaffes, and the business of winning elections and gaining points in opinion polls.[50]

In a similar vein, Austin Ranney has observed that

no television correspondent or anchorman has ever received an Emmy or Peabody or even a promotion for a series of broadcasts focusing on what a marvelous job a president (or any other elected official) is doing. Those re-

49. James Fallows, "The Presidency and the Press," in *The Presidency and the Political System*, ed. Michael Nelson (Washington, D.C.: CQ Press, 1988), 296. On president-press relations, also see Berkman and Kitch, *Politics in the Media Age*, chap. 7.

50. Fallows, "The Presidency and the Press," 301–307.

The Presidency, the Press, and News Management

EACH PRESIDENT has had his troubles with the press.... We have a photograph of FDR in our press room which is inscribed to the White House reporters from their "devoted victim." "When the press stops abusing me, I'll know I'm in the wrong pew," said Truman. "Reading more and enjoying it less," said Kennedy. What LBJ said is unprintable.... Once when the press walked in the Cabinet room for a picture taking, Nixon looked up at the press and said, "It's only coincidental that we're talking about pollution when the press walks in." Carter always seemed to be saying, "Lord, forgive them for they know not what they do." As for Reagan, well, it's like being in those silent movies. He thinks we should be seen and not heard.

Helen Thomas, senior White House reporter, United Press International

THE WHOLE business is so influenced by network television.... 100 million people across this country get all their news from network television. So the visual is expremely important.... That visual is as critical as what we're saying....

If you only get your message across in 30 or 40 seconds on the evening news, then it's important that you restate that message in as many ways as you can.... We plot out a decent story or theme for every day....

Michael Deaver, White House deputy chief of staff, 1981–1985

THEY DON'T need us as long as they capture our cameras.

Sam Donaldson, ABC News White House correspondent

FROM THE Eisenhower administration to Ronald Reagan's, the White House propaganda machine has become an increasingly effective instrument of presidential will and presidential purpose.... It has enhanced the power of the Communicator-in-chief as against that of other institutions of government....

Managing the news and public opinion was recognized by the ... administration as such a central part of running the presidency that it had to become a major part of the workday of senior policy aides.

David S. Broder, *Washington Post* reporter and columnist

Source: David S. Broder, *Behind the Front Page: A Candid Look at How the News Is Made* (New York: Simon and Schuster, 1987), 178–195. Helen Thomas quote was originally printed in Kenneth W. Thompson, *The White House Press on the Presidency* (Lanham, Md.: University Press of America, 1983), 41.

wards go to newspeople who expose moral lapses, lies, and policy failures of public officials, and the president is the biggest game of all in the perennial hunt.[51]

Presidents and their staffs try to overcome these tendencies of the media by "managing the news"—staging media events, controlling the flow of information, and communicating directly with the public via televised speeches, interviews, and press conferences from the White House. Using one of its more controversial techniques, the Reagan White House restricted media access to the president by rarely holding press conferences and forcing reporters to shout their questions over the roar of helicopter motors on the South Lawn of the White House. By contrast, President Bush has used the opposite

51. Ranney, *Channels of Power,* 141.

Frequent and impromptu presidential meetings with reporters have been a standard technique of the Bush White House. During the Reagan presidency, by contrast, presidential contact with journalists was limited and occurred under more structured circumstances like televised news conferences in the East Room of the White House.

technique—frequent news conferences and informal and spontaneous meetings with reporters (even on the golf course). No administration, however, can completely manage the news. Reporters have too many alternative sources of information; their goals and those of an administration are not necessarily the same; and the norms of the profession dictate that reporters keep some distance between themselves and the subjects they cover. Thus in spite of President Bush's efforts during his first two years in office to replace acrimony with access and build relationships with the media, television news evaluations of his performance for that period were only 44 percent positive and assessments of his policies were 2:1 negative. Public approval of the president's performance went up, however, when he received high visibility while dealing with several world crises.[52]

Through its media management strategies, the White House can have a major impact on which news stories make it onto the evening news programs. But the tone of the coverage is likely to reflect the media's interest in the politics of the situation and their desire not to appear as propaganda agents for the president. Media coverage also can bring to the public's attention issues that administrations would rather keep out of the limelight. Media probing and prodding into the 1972 Watergate scandal, for example, played a major role in forcing President Nixon's resignation. Likewise, in 1986–1987 the media's thirst for more details on the Iran-contra affair (so-called because the administration used surreptitious arms sales to Iran and other means to support the Nicaraguan contras) caused the Reagan administration severe embarrassment. And critical coverage of the White House handling of its 1990 budget struggle with Congress caused President Bush's public approval ratings to fall dramatically.

As we will see in Chapter 11, public support is critical to a strong and successful presidency. Direct appeals for public support via television can help a president build that support, but this approach is seldom enough to sustain support. Perceptions of a presidency are affected by media coverage that cannot be controlled by any president. Successful administrations, then, must be able to explain and defend their actions to sensible people in the media. When they have difficulty doing so, the president is likely to suffer a severe setback as President Reagan found after the media revealed the Iran-contra affair in 1986.

The Media and Congress

Media coverage of the executive branch has a focal point—the president. But Congress, with its 535 members, hundreds of committees and subcommittees, platoons of leaders, and lengthy and complicated decision-making processes, has no such focal point. Except for the final stages of decision making on the floors of the House and Senate or an unusually dramatic congressional hearing, congressional proceedings are not very interesting television fare. Yet, even though the president often seems to dominate the news, Congress and the president are accorded roughly equal coverage. Probably to Congress's dismay, however, congressional activity in shaping public policy is often treated as if it is part of the work of the executive branch.

The nature of the reporting on Congress depends in part on whether the national or the local and regional media are involved. The national media tend to cover the big, dramatic stories of national importance such as a resolution authorizing military action against Iraq, Senate confirmation of Supreme Court nominees, conflicts between the president and Congress, investigations, and scandals. These media, especially television, are particularly attracted to congressional hearings and investigations like the 1991 Senate hearings into Professor Anita Hill's charges of sexual harassment against Supreme Court nominee Clarence Thomas because they provide drama and confrontation. The "nuts and bolts" work of Congress—such as shepherding bills through the Senate and House and negotiating complicated compromises—is largely ignored by the national media. National media correspondents tend to treat Congress in a tough, skeptical, hard-nosed, and frequently cynical manner. Veteran television broadcaster David Brinkley, for example, once remarked during an evening newscast that "it was widely believed that it would take Congress 30 days to make instant coffee." One consequence of this type of coverage is a generally negative image of Congress as an institution.[53]

In a more positive vein, national media publicity can catapult a member of Congress into prominence and contention for a presidential nomination as it did for Senators Hubert Humphrey, John Kennedy, Lyndon Johnson, and Robert Dole. The media also provide senators and representatives with a means of mobilizing national constituencies to back legislation they are supporting. For example, Sen. Jesse Helms (R-N.C.) has used media attention to create a personal following for a series of conservative policies, and Sen. Bill Bradley (D-N.J.) gained national attention for his role in the sweeping reform of the tax code during the 1980s.

For members not trying to use national publicity as a springboard to the presidency or for legislative purposes, the local and regional media are more important. Reporters for local and regional media outlets do not cover the big national news stories or Congress as an institution. Rather, they concentrate on their home state's congressional delegation. Because these delegations are an essential part of these local and regional reporters' beats in getting the local angle on Washington events, coverage of them is normally rather "soft" and seldom as critical in tone as the coverage accorded Congress by the national media.

With the national media dealing with Congress in a generally harsh manner and the local and regional media treating congressional incumbents relatively well, the net media effect is one of conveying a negative impression of the institution while presenting its individual members in a favorable light to their constituents. This dual pattern of congressional coverage helps explain why Americans seem to like their representatives in Congress and consistently reelect them but do not hold Congress as an institution in high regard.[54]

53. Michael J. Robinson, "Three Faces of Congressional Media," in *The New Congress*, ed. Thomas E. Mann and Norman J. Ornstein (Washington, D.C.: American Enterprise Institute, 1981), 73–75; and Berkman and Kitch, *Politics in the Media Age*, 215–230.

54. Robinson, "Three Faces," 93.

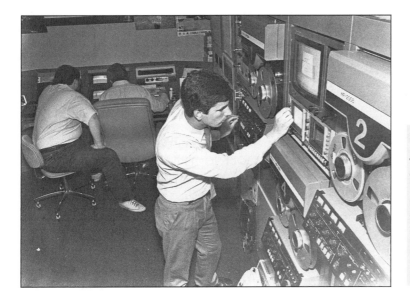

The Republican and Democratic congressional campaign committees provide House members with the latest in electronic technology to assist in maintaining contact with constituents. This television recording studio on Capitol Hill is operated by the National Republican Campaign Committee.

Also handy for strengthening the positions of individual members of Congress with their constituents are the in-house congressional media. Using their franking privilege (free mailings) and computerized printing, members of Congress can run sophisticated direct-mail operations to maintain contact with the people back home. Members also are provided with the personnel and facilities needed to produce broadcast and print material for use by the media. Finally, each member has at least one press aide responsible for media relations and for supervising the preparation and release of materials to the media. Indeed, recording studios are available for members who wish to produce radio and videotapes for distribution to media outlets in their constituencies. Some senators and representatives even produce television shows that are aired regularly on local stations.

The Media and the Judiciary

Media coverage of the Supreme Court is usually limited to informing the public and government officials about selected newsworthy decisions. The Court in turn uses the media to gauge the public's reaction to and acceptance of its decisions. Of the three branches of government, however, the judiciary gets the least (and the most superficial) coverage.[55] Supreme Court justices receive sub-

55. Graber, *Mass Media and American Politics*, 265–269. Also see Berkman and Kitch, *Politics in the Media Age*, chap. 8.

stantial publicity at the time of their appointments, but little personal publicity is forthcoming after they go on the bench. Justices rarely grant press interviews, and they keep conventional politics at arm's length.

Information about the Court is largely restricted to the formal decisions handed down by the justices, who conduct their business in an atmosphere cloaked in secrecy, tradition, legalese, and solemnity. These practices tend to insulate the Court from the day-to-day hassle of politics and protect judicial independence and influence. Media coverage of the Court, therefore, focuses almost entirely on major controversial decisions such as those about school prayer, abortion, affirmative action, or legislative redistricting. Other decisions tend to receive only cursory media attention or are ignored altogether.

Although decisions like the 1954 school desegregation case of *Brown v. Board of Education of Topeka* can have consequences that reverberate through the political system for decades, a variety of factors hold down extensive media coverage of the Supreme Court. These include the Court's ability to control the flow of information to the media about its internal operations; the complexity of the subject matter, which does not lend itself to exciting sound bites or headlines; the large volume of cases decided each year; the understaffed Supreme Court beat; and the need for reporters covering the Court to have more specialized training than reporters covering the Congress or White House. The job of covering the Supreme Court is further complicated by the fact that reporters receive little assistance from the Court in interpreting the meaning and significance of decisions. Justices do not grant interviews to discuss their decisions, nor do they indulge in the practice of leaking confidential information to the media. Moreover, there is no Court press office to assist correspondents. This contrasts sharply with the executive and legislative branches where officials are usually anxious to provide reporters with background information and the rationales for their actions. Because news about the Court is gathered under such conditions, coverage of its decisions may be not only limited but also inaccurate and misleading.

The Media and Governing

The media link citizens to their government by helping shape public opinion, by giving public officials a channel of communication to citizens, and by influencing the behavior of political leaders. In providing common experiences and depicting common concerns, the media also help unite Americans, but they divide Americans as well by bringing into the nation's living rooms the controversies that abound in society.

The media can have a profound influence on public perceptions of government institutions and leaders. But because television news tends to be negative and to focus on the problems and shortcomings of government, it may distance citizens from their government instead of bringing them closer to it. Indeed, public trust in government has declined during the television age.

Austin Ranney has suggested several additional consequences that the mass media, particularly television, might have for the governing process.[56] First, through its instantaneous coverage of events and preference for neat, clear-cut decisions and fast results, television tends to compress the time elected officials have to install programs and get results in dealing with societal problems. Because of their expectations of fast results and their tendencies to treat politics like a sporting event, newscasters keep score and dramatize short-term changes in such things as inflation and unemployment rates.

Second, the media may reduce the policy options available to leaders by giving publicity to proposals in the early stages of consideration. When the spotlight of news coverage focuses on a policy option in the early stages of its development, this publicity may raise a storm of controversy that effectively precludes further consideration of the policy option.

And third, by highlighting the activities of politicians who offer simple solutions and take extreme and uncompromising stands, the media weaken the coalition builders who make governmental action possible. Governance involves negotiation, compromise, and the knitting together of coalitions of diverse interests. These processes are complicated, it is thought, by the media's tendency to cover those who offer dramatic and controversial proposals and assume a confrontational stance toward their opponents.

Political science research has not produced definitive conclusions about the impact of the media on the governmental process. But informed suggestions about that impact, such as those just noted, serve as a reminder that the messages received each day from the media constantly affect how the political system operates.

56. Ranney, *Channels of Power*, 124–147.

For Review

1. As a major source of political information, the media, particularly television, help shape the public's perceptions of reality. These perceptions, in turn, constitute a basis for the public's political activity. As intermediaries between the people and their government, the media are then able to mobilize citizens to take political action and influence the behavior of government officials.

2. The various kinds of print and electronic media approach public affairs in different ways. The American people rely on and trust television more than the other kinds of media, but the dominance and influence of the major television networks have been reduced by cable networks, videocassette recorders, and other technological advances.

3. Among the most important decisions journalists make is what constitutes news. What should be aired on television and printed in the papers? The standards for newsworthiness include audience appeal and impact, uniqueness, and timeliness. The nature of media coverage also is affected by time and space constraints and the accessibility of news sources.

4. The media have a strong voice in deciding which issues will be placed on the public agenda, but when the media cover election campaigns, they tend to focus on the "horse race" aspects of the contest and not on substantive issues.

5. Political leaders and newspeople are mutually dependent. Politicians rely on the media to provide them with information and to convey their messages to the public. The media in turn rely heavily on public officials for the information on which to base their reporting. The relationship is characterized by tension, however, as politicians seek to use the media to achieve their objectives and the media seek to perform their news-gathering functions.

For Further Reading

Berkman, Ronald, and Laura W. Kitch. *Politics in the Media Age.* New York: McGraw-Hill, 1986. A survey of the mass media and their impact on the political process.

Broder, David S. *Behind the Front Page: A Candid Look at How the News Is Made.* New York: Simon and Schuster, 1987. A description and critique of how reporters cover political news by one of journalism's most respected and insightful reporters.

Graber, Doris A. *Mass Media and American Politics.* 3d ed. Washington, D.C.: CQ Press, 1989. A thorough account of how the media cover political events and their impact.

Hess, Stephen. *The Washington Reporter*. Washington, D.C.: Brookings, 1981. A description of the people, work, and views of reporters, based on an extensive survey of the Washington press corps.

Ranney, Austin. *Channels of Power: The Impact of Television on American Politics*. New York: Basic Books, 1983. An analysis of how the media do their jobs and their impact on the public, elections, and the governing process.

Robinson, Michael J., and Margaret A. Sheehan. *Over the Wire and on TV*. New York: Russell Sage Foundation, 1983. An analysis of television and wire service coverage of the 1980 presidential campaign.

Robinson, Michael J., and Austin Ranney, eds. *The Mass Media in Campaign '84*. Washington, D.C.: American Enterprise Institute, 1985. A collection of articles originally published in *Public Opinion* by leading analysts assessing the media's role in the nomination and election processes.

PART III

Governmental Institutions

Politics along the Potomac

Washington, D.C., is the center of national policy making and a magnet for all those who wish to influence, have a say in, or report on that process. It is a city that mirrors the American people and their politics. Yet it is also unique among American cities; in no other are politics so all-consuming, the political stakes so high, or the players more skilled. With a professional political community that numbers in the thousands, Washington has a special impact on our political system.

Congress created the District of Columbia in 1790 from land along the Potomac River that was given to the United States by the states of Maryland and Virginia. The Virginia portion of the District (Arlington County and the city of Alexandria) was ceded back to Virginia in 1846.

A Federal City with Its Roots in a Maryland-Virginia Wilderness

District of Columbia, 1791

POTOMAC RIVER

ROCK CREEK

MARYLAND

WASHINGTON COUNTY

Georgetown

White House (built later)
The Capitol (built later)
WASHINGTON

EASTERN BRANCH (ANACOSTIA RIVER)

VIRGINIA

POTOMAC RIVER

Alexandria

Present D.C. Area

0 1 2 3
Miles

Unlike all other American cities, Washington is not located within state boundaries and is not subject to state laws and regulations. Rather, the District of Columbia, on the banks of the Potomac River, is a *federal city,* carved out of the surrounding states of Maryland and Virginia (see map of the District of Columbia). As a federal city, the district falls under the jurisdiction of Congress, which created its system of local government. The federal government is the district's largest landowner, but, in lieu of paying property taxes, Congress appropriates substantial sums (in excess of $500 million annually) to help fund the city government's activities.

The district's status as a federal city is not without controversy, however. Since it is not a state of the Union, Washington residents lack voting representation in Congress, although they do have an official nonvoting delegate to the House of Representatives. In fact, advocates of statehood for the district assert that Washington is America's "last colony." In an effort to advance the cause of statehood, the district recently elected two "shadow senators," the Reverend Jesse Jackson and Florence Pendleton, to lobby for statehood from those unofficial posts. Proponents of retaining the district's current federal city status stress that since Washington is the seat of government for all the people of the United States, it requires congressional supervision.

Unlike such world-famous European capitals as Paris, London, and Rome, whose political preeminence evolved from their positions as centers of commerce and culture, America's seat of

Georgetown, home of some of Washington's most well-known residents and glitziest boutiques, was a bustling port when this photo was taken in 1863.

government was created where there was no existing metropolis. Georgetown (now a chic shopping and residential section of Washington) was a small port city just below the falls of the Potomac; the National Mall area between what is now the Capitol and the Washington Monument was a swamp drained by Tiber Creek; and Jenkins Hill (now Capitol Hill) was undeveloped.

In 1791, President George Washington, himself a former surveyor, commissioned visionary French engineer and architect Pierre Charles L'Enfant to plan the city. L'Enfant dreamed of transforming this wilderness plot into a monumental city of grand avenues and stately buildings. In keeping with the Constitution's separation of powers principle, however, L'Enfant and Washington proposed a city with no central focus of activity; the legislative, executive, and judicial branches were to be separated by considerable distances to avoid confrontation and yet to share routes of communication and be "seemingly connected," in L'Enfant's words.[1] Although battered by land speculators and al-tered by generations of political leaders, L'Enfant's basic plan for the city has been retained to this day.

With its massive government buildings, green expanses of the Mall and Rock Creek Park, memorials to the famous (and not so famous), wide thoroughfares like Pennsylvania and Constitution avenues, traffic circles with tiny

1. Quoted by James Sterling Young, *The Washington Community, 1800-1828* (New York: Harcourt, Brace and World, 1966), 3. Young provides one of the most complete and insightful studies of the Washington community in the formative days of the Republic.

parks at their centers, and a regulation forbidding any building higher than the Capitol, the Washington of today has a distinguished and appealing character. Also adding to Washington's uniqueness is L'Enfant's quadrant system—NE, SE, SW, NW—and street grid (alphabetical streets run east-west and numbered streets run north-south).

One important change in L'Enfant's plan is particularly noteworthy because it speaks volumes about how the capital city's geography and architecture reflect American values. In his original plan, L'Enfant included a "great church of national purpose" to be built on a site near the Capitol. Proponents of church-state separation, however, found another location for the Washington Cathedral (the world's only Gothic cathedral to be completed in the twentieth century) in Northwest Washington on Mount St. Alban, the highest point in the city, miles from the Capitol.[2]

Washington, which was named such to honor the first president, was for most of its history a rather sleepy southern city. Although it is not well known, the District of Columbia is located sixty miles south of the Mason-Dixon line and, like the rest of the South, practiced racial segregation until the 1950s. Even into the early twentieth century, sheep manicured the White House lawn. And before air conditioning and ready cures for malaria, Washington was considered a hardship post by foreign diplomats.

Today, however, the Washington area is a booming metropolis of over 3.9 million people, about 626,000 of whom actually live in the District of Columbia. The area's phenomenal growth, prosperity, and international prominence have coincided with the federal government's increased responsibilities for social services and economic regulation, as well as America's assumption of a leadership role

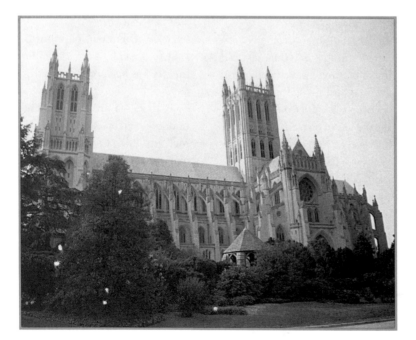

The spires of Washington Cathedral rise above the city on Mount St. Alban in Washington's northwest quadrant.

2. Ari L. Goldman, "For the Capital Cathedral, A Slow Finishing Touch," *New York Times,* Jan. 14, 1990, 12Y, National edition.

Before the malaria-infested swamps were drained and air conditioning provided relief from the humid heat of summer, Washington was considered a hardship post by foreign diplomats. In 1865 cattle could be found grazing amid the swamps within sight of the Capitol.

Worldwide prominence and burgeoning growth now characterize Washington. But for much of its history, it was a quiet and segregated southern city where sheep groomed the White House lawn.

in world affairs. In the process, Washington has become the world capital for news and information, politics, and diplomacy. It also has developed a vibrant cultural life and is becoming a commercial center.

This sprawling metropolitan area revolves around the action occurring in the major geographic sectors of the city (identified in the map of central Washington).

Capitol Hill

The Capitol, with its imposing landmark dome, reflects the checks and balances devised by the drafters of the Constitution.

The House and Senate occupy separate wings of the building. Surrounding the Capitol (which has no "behind"—only two "fronts," East and West) are the massive House and Senate office buildings named for three famous Speakers of the House—Joseph Cannon (R-Ill.), Nicholas Longworth (R-Ohio), and Sam Rayburn (D-Texas)—and three respected senators—Richard Russell (D-Ga.), Everett Dirksen (R-Ill.), and Philip Hart (D-Mich.). Also nearby are the Botanic Garden, Library of Congress, Supreme Court, a smattering of offices for lobbyists and "think tanks" (nonprofit public

policy research centers), and an increasingly gentrified residential area of townhouses.

The Mall

Extending westward from the Capitol all the way to the Potomac River is the Mall, a green parkway on which are located two of the city's most famous landmarks, the Lincoln and Washington memorials. Between these landmarks in a tastefully landscaped grove of trees is the simple but stirring Vietnam Veterans Memorial—a low wall of black marble on which are inscribed the names of all the American men and women who are missing

Linked by Pennsylvania Avenue, the Capitol and the White House are the focal points of central Washington, D.C.

The Lincoln Memorial contains thirty-six columns, the number of states in the Union at the time Lincoln was assassinated.

The Washington Monument stands tall amid cherry trees, which were a gift from the city of Tokyo and planted in 1912.

The names of the men and women who are missing in action or who lost their lives in Southeast Asia are memorialized at the Vietnam Veterans Memorial on the Mall.

The memorial to Thomas Jefferson—author of the Declaration of Independence and third president of the United States—is situated along the south bank of the Tidal Basin.

The Library of Congress, originally located in the U.S. Capitol, was overflowing with books by 1880 (left). The three current Library of Congress buildings—named for presidents Jefferson, Adams, and Madison—contain 535 miles of bookshelves. At right is the Great Hall of the Jefferson Building.

in action or who died in that conflict. The Mall is also home to a series of museums, including the Smithsonian Institution's Air and Space Museum and Museum of American History. These attractions make the Mall a mecca for tourists, particularly during the spring, when the Japanese cherry trees that line the Tidal Basin adjacent to the Mall are in bloom.

The Federal Triangle

Bounded on the north by Pennsylvania Avenue, the east by Sixth Street, the south by Constitution Avenue, and the west by the Ellipse behind the White House, the

Federal Triangle is the site of thirteen limestone buildings that include the Departments of Commerce and Justice, Federal Bureau of Investigation, Federal Trade Commission, Internal Revenue Service, and National Archives. Close by on Pennsylvania Avenue amid government buildings stands the new and architecturally distinct Canadian embassy, our neighbor to the north's bid for prominence in Washington. The Federal Triangle is also home to the beautifully restored Old Post Office Pavilion, which houses a few federal agencies such as the National Endowment for the Arts

From the steps of the U.S. Capitol the distinctive architecture of the buildings on the Mall is clearly evident. On the left is the "Castle" of the Smithsonian Institution, completed in 1855; at center are the Washington Monument and the Grecian temple-like Lincoln Memorial; and on the right is the Smithsonian's Museum of Natural History.

and a collection of boutiques and restaurants.

Independence Avenue Area

Across the Mall from the Federal Triangle is another complex of executive agencies that includes the National Aeronautics and Space Administration, U.S. Information Agency, U.S. Postal Service, as well as Departments of Agriculture, Energy, Health and Human Services, Housing and Urban Development, and Transportation.

Downtown

The White House, an attractive but not overly elegant dwelling appropriate for an elected chief executive, is this section's focal point. Next door is the magnificent, but inefficient, Old Executive Office Building, a French Second Empire structure, which accommodates many of the president's key aides. In the immediate neighborhood are found the Departments of the Treasury and Interior, the World Bank, the American National Red Cross, and the offices of trade associations, unions, and all manner of interest groups, lobbyists, consultants, law firms, and think tanks. Indeed, the high-rent area around K and M streets in downtown

Pictured here is the Greek embassy on Embassy Row.

Arlington Cemetery is the final resting place for more than two hundred thousand veterans representing every war the United States has fought.

Washington is so crammed with the offices of lobbyists, lawyers, and consultants that it is sometimes referred to as "Lobby, Inc."

Embassy Row

Northwest of downtown along Massachusetts and Connecticut avenues and the adjoining tree-lined streets are the frequently lavish embassies of foreign governments.

Foggy Bottom

The Department of State, a massive building with a commanding view of the Potomac, is located in what was once a low-lying, swampy, and often foggy section of the city. Each summer, foreign diplomats are invited to the State Department's elegant, antique-filled, top-floor reception areas to view the massive July Fourth fireworks display at the Tidal Basin and Mall.

The Pentagon, Arlington National Cemetery, and National Airport

Across the Potomac in Virginia lies Arlington National Cemetery with its precise rows of memorials to bravery and sacrifice. In addition to offering panoramic views of the nation's capital, the cemetery is the site of the family home of Confederate general Robert E. Lee. Adjacent to Arlington National Cemetery is the focal point of the country's defense establishment, the massive five-sided Pentagon building—headquarters of the Department of Defense. To provide busy politicians with ready access to air transportation, National Airport (with its reserved parking spaces for members of Congress, Supreme Court justices, and diplomats) is located on the Potomac just a short drive from the White House and the Capitol.

The Pentagon, said to be the world's largest office building, is the only U.S. government departmental headquarters outside the District of Columbia.

Away from the monumental buildings, broad tree-lined avenues, plush office buildings, and stately embassies is the "Other Washington," where the inhabitants do not share in the general affluence of the nation's capital.

The Other Washington

The sections of Washington just described are the ones frequented by tourists and the ones that serve as the backdrop for the events and people making the news. But in this city of movers and shakers, monumental buildings, and stately homes, there is another Washington. Largely out of the public eye, it provides disquieting examples of the problems afflicting inner cities across the country: poverty, drug abuse, high crime rates, substandard housing, and inadequate schools.

President Jimmy Carter and his aides, even after four years in Washington, considered themselves outsiders. Carter's successor, Ronald Reagan, also raised political capital by railing against "the Washington establishment." In this photo, Carter is chatting with his closest advisers and fellow Georgians Jody Powell (left) and Hamilton Jordan (right).

A One-Industry Town

L ike any city, Washington has many faces, and the face one sees is to a large degree in the eye of the beholder. The casual tourist mainly sees the awesome government buildings and monuments. But *Washington Post* columnist Haynes Johnson sees Washington as a reflection of the nation. According to this over thirty-year veteran of the city, "Washington *is* America, quintessentially, indisputably a mirror of all the country's strengths and weaknesses."[3] But other observers see it as a city atypical of America.

They note Washington's affluence—it has the highest per capita household income of any metropolitan area in the country. Moreover, the Washington area is almost recession proof because the federal government and related interests maintain such high employment levels. Washington-area residents as a group also are better educated than the inhabitants of other metropolitan areas. But above all, its residents are more politicized and attuned to national politics than other Americans. In a nationally tele-

vised address, President Jimmy Carter, who remained a Washington outsider even after his election, called Washington an island, cut off and isolated from the concerns of ordinary Americans. His successor was no less critical. Ronald Reagan complained about the "puzzle palaces along the Potomac" of "Disneyland East," and just before leaving office he assailed the alliances of members of Congress, the media, and spe-

3. Haynes Johnson, "The Capital of Success," *Washington Post Magazine,* February 2, 1986, 44.

cial interests for thwarting his policies, which he claimed the public supported.[4]

There is, however, one aspect of the city few would dispute. It is a one-industry town and that industry is politics. Washington is not America's economic or cultural center, but it is the political center of the nation. The manifestations of the city's obsession with things political are everywhere.

The office walls of Washington's political community are covered with row after row of "power pictures"—autographed photographs of the office's occupant with prominent politicians. These "walls of fame" are collected over the years and are adjusted to mirror shifting loyalties and changes in the balance of power within Congress and the administration. The significance of this Washington tradition has been described by an insider:

> It's an anthropological signal to your visitors of who you are and what your station in life is. . . . It's a sign of what fires you've walked through . . . and what potentates you've touched. It's a way of letting your visitors know who you are, establishing a parentage and a peerage much more interesting than the Green Book [Washington's social registry] or Burke's peerage.[5]

Social standing in Washington is not based on wealth or good bloodlines; it is based on political standing. The nature of the social life for the political community has been captured by *New York* *Times* correspondent Lynn Roselli:

Looks, charm, wealth, intellect—they alone count for little in Washington. Power is all. What really matters is: Whom do you know? What have you done? And what can you do for me? Guests don't get invited out in Washington because they've got twinkly blue eyes. . . . Nobody among the 2,500 men and women who make up the inner village of political-social Washington goes anywhere just for fun. "It's really a continuation of a day's work," says Lorraine Cooper, a veteran hostess and wife of the late Senator John Sherman Cooper.[6]

With social standing dependent on one's political position, election to the Senate or appointment to a key White House post can elevate one's status overnight. But politics is as uncertain as ever, and in Washington a fall

Posing in his Washington office — adorned with photographs of friends in high places—is Paul A. Equale, lobbyist for the Independent Insurance Agents of America.

4. Bill McAllister, "Reagan Assails `Washington Colony' as Out of Touch," *Washington Post,* Dec. 14, 1988, A4.
5. Elizabeth Kastor, "The Walls of Fame," *Washington Post,* Aug. 18, 1987, D1.
6. Lynn Roselli, "A Capital Game of Power," *New York Times Magazine,* January 4, 1981, 18.

Dinner parties, like this one at the Austrian embassy, are considered part of the job for Washington's political leadership—a place to make contacts, gather political intelligence, discuss business informally, and even practice the art of persuasion.

On Pennsylvania Avenue between the Capitol and the White House, Canada has erected a distinctive new embassy in an effort to gain stature among the foreign governments seeking to influence American policy makers.

from social grace can be just as rapid.

The sheer number of politically motivated social events to which public officials are invited is staggering—up to one hundred or more a week for White House officials and members of Congress. Every evening between 5:30 and 8:00, dozens of receptions are held in hotels and office buildings to which members of Congress, lobbyists, and administration officials are invited. Most of these events are sponsored by businesses or interest groups.

With social events frequently having a primarily political/business function, Washingtonians develop strategies for holding and attending events. In fact, the intimidating number of nightly receptions has spawned a bizarre ritual called the "drop by": "In just 20 minutes, a skilled Congressman can arrive, seek out a few key individuals [such as home state constituents, interest group leaders, or administration officials], pump their hands and then depart, perhaps even grabbing a snack on the way out."[7] And a thirty-year-old rising public relations man hires a driver so he can make it to three receptions a night. Without a driver, such an attendance rate would be impossible because parking in down-

7. Lynn Roselli, "Good Eating and Good Politicking (in 20 Minutes)," *New York Times,* Aug. 17, 1981.

Sunday interview shows are consumed and analyzed by Washingtonians while beyond the Beltway most Americans enjoy a day of rest and relaxation. The Democratic chairmen of the Senate and House Armed Services Committees, Sen. Sam Nunn of Georgia (left) and Rep. Les Aspin of Wisconsin (right), are shown here discussing national security policy on "This Week with David Brinkley."

town Washington is rarely available between 5:30 and 8:00 P.M.[8]

On the diplomatic circuit, the British ambassador, Anthony Acland, is known for giving "closely focused" dinners at his residence and for not "wasting taxpayers' money on unusable guests."[9] Sondra Gotlieb, the somewhat irreverent wife of a recent Canadian ambassador noted for her glamorous parties and skill in promoting her country's interests, operated using a similarly utilitarian social code: "We invite *jobs* [persons holding influential positions], not individuals. Our purpose is to promote our country. We don't spend the taxpayers' money for the neighbors."[10]

For Washington's political leadership, social life is an extension of business as people relate to each other in terms of position and title and exchange implicit *quid pro quos.* Hedrick Smith, an insightful chronicler of life "inside the Beltway" (the interstate highway encircling the city), has noted that at dinners and informal gatherings

journalists turn to officials and politicians for stories; politicians trade for favorable mention. Lobbyists need politicians for legislation, and the politicians need lobbyists for money and votes. Of course, there are times of levity and humor, but the underlying transactions of the political bazaar sap most occasions of serendipity.[11]

And in the same vein, diplomatic hostess Sondra Gotlieb wrote, "People will go to an embassy party if they think they might see

8. See Walt Harrington, "The Education of David Carmen," *Washington Post Magazine,* February 28, 1988, 13-19, 35-37.

9. "Washington: The Silk Tie and Hairy Chest," *Economist,* December 24, 1988, 19.

10. Quoted by Sandra McElwaine, "Take 'My Wife of'—Please," *Regardie's,* October 1985, 42.

11. Hedrick Smith, *The Power Game: How Washington Works* (New York: Random House, 1988), 110.

The Washington community's hunger for news is demonstrated by this phalanx of newspaper vending machines on a downtown street corner.

someone they have missed during the day. . . . Powerful Jobs come to parties to trade information with other Powerful Jobs they hadn't made contact with during the day."[12]

In this environment, it is small wonder that the cynics enjoy quoting President Harry Truman, who said, "If you want a friend in Washington, buy a dog." Similarly, Hedrick Smith, after years of observing the capital's political culture, concluded that despite their back-slapping gregariousness, Washington politicians tend to be "a lonely crowd, making few deep friendships because almost every relationship is tainted by the calculus of pow-

er. How will this help me?"[13]

Although Washington's political community finds the contacts made and the information gathered at social events helpful in their continuing struggle for influence and advancement, the social pressures do take their toll. The highly politicized nature of Washington life means that there is almost no respite from one's political work. Family life can be particularly hard hit by the pressures of the Washington environment.[14]

Washington's preoccupation with politics is also reflected in its hunger for news. Information is power, and Washingtonians are anxious for the latest news. In no

other city does a single corner (Connecticut Avenue and K Street, N.W.) have twenty-five newspaper vending machines. As the *New Yorker*'s Elizabeth Drew noted:

Washingtonians do not live like other people. On Sunday, when other people are hiking, sailing or doing nothing, many Washingtonians are earnestly going through their thick Sunday papers and watching "Meet the Press" and "Face the Nation."

12. Sondra Gotlieb, *Wife of . . .* (Washington, D.C.: Acropolis Books, 1985), 28.

13. Smith, *Power Game,* 92.

14. For an informed account of the impact of Washington on politicians' marriages, see Myra MacPherson, *The Power Lovers: An Intimate Look at Politicians and Their Marriages* (New York: Putnam, 1975).

Washingtonians do this even when there is little going on.[15]

The Sunday process of soaking up the news shows now goes on for hours. Viewers tape the competing network programs on their VCRs and watch them back to back.

Washington's preoccupation with politics also has made it a mecca for think tanks. In 1991, the *Capital Source,* a reliable Washington directory, listed eighty-five think tanks. These competing and politically savvy public policy research centers reflect a wide variety of policy interests and ideological perspectives. For example, the conservative Heritage Foundation claims to have provided the Reagan administration with its policy agenda, and the more moderately conservative American Enterprise Institute provided policy initiatives and key personnel for the Reagan and Bush administrations as well. The scholarly Brookings Institution is generally perceived as having a liberal tilt (its critics sometimes call it a "government in exile" waiting to staff the next Democratic administration), and the Institute for Policy Studies provides a clearly left-of-center perspective on issues. The existence of over three score think tanks in Washington reflects the tremendous market among the political leadership for alternative public policy ideas, critiques of existing policy, and insights into future events.[16]

---

15. Elizabeth Drew, *Washington Journal* (New York: Random House, 1975), 23.

16. For an informed discussion of think tanks, see R. Kent Weaver, "The Changing World of Think Tanks," *PS,* September 1989, 563-578.

Just as the Washington community accords automatic status to out-of-towners who take high offices, so it revokes that status when they leave office. Former Speaker of the House Jim Wright, D-Texas, once one of the most powerful people in Washington, "vanished to Texas" when he resigned his speakership in June 1989. Accompanied by his wife, Betty, he returned to Washington for the first time in July 1990 for the unveiling of his official portrait at the Capitol.

In June 1991 President George Bush and Secretary of State James Baker (left) announced that they were bringing Robert Strauss (center), a highly respected Democrat and one of Washington's most influential insiders, back into government service by nominating him to be U.S. ambassador to the Soviet Union.

Just Who Makes Up Washington's Political Community?

Although Washington is not your normal American city, it is hardly an island unto itself. The leadership of the Washington community consists mainly of people who hail from someplace else. Even middle-aged residents who raised their children in Washington often do not think of themselves as Washingtonians. They view themselves, instead, as transplanted Texans, Wisconsinites, Kansans, and Californians. Unlike other cities, this highly permeable community "regularly accords automatic, immediate, and unshakeable top status to someone from out of town, even if that someone's [Jimmy Carter's or Ronald Reagan's] public conversation consists mainly of unpleasant statements about the community and attacks on its oldest inhabitants."[17]

Washington's political community is a large collection of people who came to Washington specifically to practice politics—presidents and their staffs, members of Congress and their aides, people who direct the major government departments and agencies, the upper levels of the permanent bureaucracy, career military personnel, judges and their clerks and assistants, foreign diplomats, interest group representatives, think tank associates, media personnel, and politically oriented

17. Nelson W. Polsby, "The Washington Community," in *The New Congress,* ed. Thomas E. Mann and Norman J. Ornstein (Washington, D.C.: American Enterprise Institute, 1981), 8.

Prose along the Potomac

All large organizations, government bureaucracies included, develop their own jargon for describing the work they do and the environment in which they do it. In "bureaucratese," traffic lights become "electronically adjusted, color-coded vehicular-flow control mechanisms," and waves, "sea-air interface climatic disturbances."[1]

One government agency well known for its use of jargon is the Department of Defense (DoD). DoD does not purchase steel nuts at the local hardware store; it submits purchase orders for "hexiform rotatable surface compression units." Paratroops do not use parachutes; they use "individual aerial deceleration mechanisms." And the infantry dig "foxholes" with "combat emplacement evacuators" (shovels) and live in "frame-supported tension structures" (tents).[2] Although absurd, the use of such phrases for everyday items is harmless.

Sometimes, however, similar obfuscations are used to hide the meaning of some unpleasant or embarrassing fact. For example, the near-meltdown at the Three Mile Island nuclear plant in 1979 was dubbed an "abnormal evolution," and the explosion of the space shuttle *Challenger* in 1986 was an "anomaly." And beginning in 1984 the State Department replaced the word "killing" with "unlawful or arbitrary deprivation of life" in its annual reviews of human rights around the world.[3]

Technical language, when coupled with excess verbiage, can compound communication problems. One NASA spokesperson, in the aftermath of the *Challenger* catastrophe, offered the following explanation of the preflight preparations:

The normal process during the countdown is that the countdown proceeds, assuming we are in a 'go' posture, and at various points during the countdown we tag up the operational loops and face to face in the firing room to ascertain the facts that project elements that are monitoring the data and that are understanding the situation as we proceed are still in the 'go' direction.[4]

Although these examples of the tortuous use of the English language have ranged from the light-hearted to the plainly disheartening, the consequences of such convoluted phraseology should not be overlooked. Statements that "make the bad seem good, the negative appear positive, [and] the disastrous seem tolerable" undermine the relationship between the government and the governed.[5]

---

1. Quoted in Bill McAllister, "Gobbledygook Is Short-Time at VA," *Washington Post,* June 21, 1990, A17.
2. Ibid.; and "NASA Wins 'Doublespeak' Award," *Washington Post,* Nov. 23, 1986, A5.
3. Press release, National Council of Teachers of English.
4. "NASA Wins 'Doublespeak' Award," A5.
5. Press release, National Council of Teachers of English.

lawyers. With every election, a new group of outsiders, in Nelson Polsby's words, "floats into Washington on the political tide and is deposited in one or another organization . . . most of which contain strata from previous administrations."[18] Washington can, therefore, be viewed geologically. It contains strata of people who came to town around the same time and remained to build up networks of friendship, alliance, and enmity dating back to the Eisenhower, Kennedy, Johnson, Nixon, Ford, Carter, or Reagan years. Indeed, many of these people caught "Potomac Fever"—an addiction to wielding power, being close to power, or feeling that one is at the center of things. When their president departed the White House, they were defeated for reelection, or their patron lost his or her position of power, most stayed on in Washington. They became lobbyists, lawyers, and consultants, seeking to remain part of the action. These geological networks, then, interconnect with networks of people who must deal with each other because they share a common policy interest (for example, health, trade, housing, urban transit, or national security policy), though not necessarily a common point of view. There also are political networks based on people's states of origin.

Providing an element of continuity in the Washington political

community are the so-called in-and-outers. When the political leaders with whom they are affiliated are in office, then they are in; they help staff the White House and key departmental posts. But when those to whom they have access are out of office, then they too are out and they return to their law firms, consultantships, think tanks, interest groups, and congressional staff positions.

Washington also has its sages. These are the senior members of the community who over the years have earned its respect—people such as columnist David Broder of the *Washington Post;* lawyers Robert Strauss, Clark Clifford, Lloyd Cutler, Harry McPherson, and William Rogers; former defense secretary Melvin Laird; lobbyist Charles Walker; pollster Peter Hart; and former presidential economic advisers Herbert Stein and Charles Schultze. These elders are known for their straight talk and sound advice. Their analyses of complex problems, assessments of political leaders, and views about which issues are worthy of attention find outlets among the media and political leaders.[19] They are not a monolithic group with a common point of view, but they can affect how the public and political leaders perceive issues and even the substance of government policy.

Among the most dramatic changes in the Washington community since the 1950s has been

the explosive growth in the number and diversity of interest groups, businesses, consultants, law firms, and think tanks involved in the policy process.[20] Particularly noteworthy has been the proliferation of so-called public interest lobby groups concerned with civil rights, the environment, health, women's issues, and poverty issues. Also swelling the ranks of the Washington community have been the representatives of the intergovernmental lobby (agents for states, local governments, and universities), the "hired gun" lobbyists who work on behalf of foreign governments, and representatives of corporations. In the 1960s, as the government's role expanded when President Lyndon Johnson's Great Society programs leapt onto the policy agenda, "firms sprang up designed to hook the bureaucracies into their client groups, to discover needs, to monitor the performance of the public sector in relation to needs," and to monitor the private sector responses to government interventions.[21]

18. Ibid., 9.
19. See the account of Washington insider Robert Strauss's activities by Steven V. Roberts, "Out of Texas, the Capital's Leading Wise Man," *New York Times,* Dec. 20, 1987, 10, National edition.
20. For an insightful and concise account of how the Washington community changed between the 1950s and 1980s, see Barbara Sinclair, *The Transformation of the U.S. Senate* (Baltimore: Johns Hopkins University Press, 1989), chap. 4.
21. Ibid., 10.

This proliferating array of interests operating within the Washington community reflects the country's expanded and conflictual issue agenda. During the Eisenhower era of the 1950s, the issue agenda was quite limited and lacking in intense conflict. Foreign policy conflicts subsided with the ending of the Korean War, and domestic issues heated up only modestly when dealing with such questions as aid to depressed areas. The 1990s are quite different. With its civil rights revolution, women's and environmental movements, expanded governmental responsibilities, increased salience of such social issues as abortion, end of the Cold War, Persian Gulf War, and massive federal budget deficit, Washington's issue agenda has become more crowded and highly conflictual. In turn, decision making has become more complex and difficult for the occupants of formal positions of power within the Congress, White House, bureaucracy, and courts.

Residents of the District of Columbia share the roads with foreign diplomats, whose U.S. State Department-issued license plates identify their native country. The "FC" identifies this as a Soviet diplomat's tag.

Working within the Washington Community

It is not possible to come to Washington as president, a presidential assistant, cabinet officer, or member of Congress, and remain aloof from the city's political community. Governing involves more than communicating directly with the American people via television or face-to-face negotiations with senators and representatives. Personnel must be recruited to staff an administration or congressional office, policy initiatives developed and meshed with existing policies, and various interests within and outside government either accommodated or overcome—all while maintaining public support. In this, the involvement of the Washington political community is inevitable.

The importance of the Washington community has not been

During her December 1987 visit to the United States, Raisa Gorbachev, wife of the Soviet leader, demonstrated a shrewd understanding of the importance of establishing contact with leaders of the Washington community. She is seen here with a prominent Democratic insider, Pamela Harriman.

lost on such foreign visitors as Raisa Gorbachev, wife of the Soviet leader. Schooled by the wily former Soviet ambassador Anatoly Dobrynin before her visit to the United States in 1987, Mrs. Gorbachev asked Pamela Harriman, the socially prominent and politically connected widow of governor and ambassador Averell Harriman, to host a small luncheon where she could meet influential women leaders.

Presidential scholar Richard Neustadt, after reviewing five transitions from one president to another, has concluded that future presidents and their administrations will find it increasingly difficult to adjust to the Washington community. He sees the maze of issues, interests, institutions, and individuals with which presidents must deal growing thicker, more complex, more interactive, more entrenched, and harder to understand.[22] As a result, administrations need more time now than in the past to learn how to cope with the Washington environment. During this learning process, however, presidents are in constant danger of the Washington community rendering negative and possibly fatal judgments about their leadership abilities and their administrations' policies. In this, the Washington community's role is similar to that of Broadway's drama critics, who cannot through their reviews guarantee a smash hit but who can guarantee that a show will have a short run. The Washington community's reactions to the nation's political leaders are transmitted to the public via television newscasts, talk shows, and

22. Richard E. Neustadt, *Presidential Power: The Politics of Leadership from FDR to Carter* (New York: Wiley, 1980), 232.

the print media, and their impact on the public can be profound.

Even though some claim that the Washington community is cut off from reality and the rest of America, it is permeated with leadership from throughout the nation, and it is not monolithic in its viewpoint. It is splintered among various interests and specializations, conflicting ideological and partisan loyalties, home state ties, and geological strata. Yet despite its connections to all sectors of society, Washington's political community does share

"frames of reference, life styles, media, customs, and language."[23] Where else but in Washington can people, in the jargon of the locals, just "disappear" because they have taken up residence some place in the world out beyond the Beltway?[24] People interested in politics can, of course, live far from Washington, but from one election and from one administration to the next, the Washington political community acts as an ever-present force in the corridors of power affecting the actions of Congress, the pres-

idency, the bureaucracy, and the Supreme Court. Indeed, a now-accepted piece of lore, even among political observers outside the Beltway, is that national political leadership requires an ability "to work with or otherwise win over the Washington community."[25]

23. Ibid., 240.
24. Polsby, "The Washington Community," 13.
25. See Fred I. Greenstein, ed., *Leadership in the Modern Presidency* (Cambridge, Mass.: Harvard University Press, 1988). Also see the comments on this book by David Broder, "The Qualities of a President," *Washington Post,* March 25, 1988, C7.

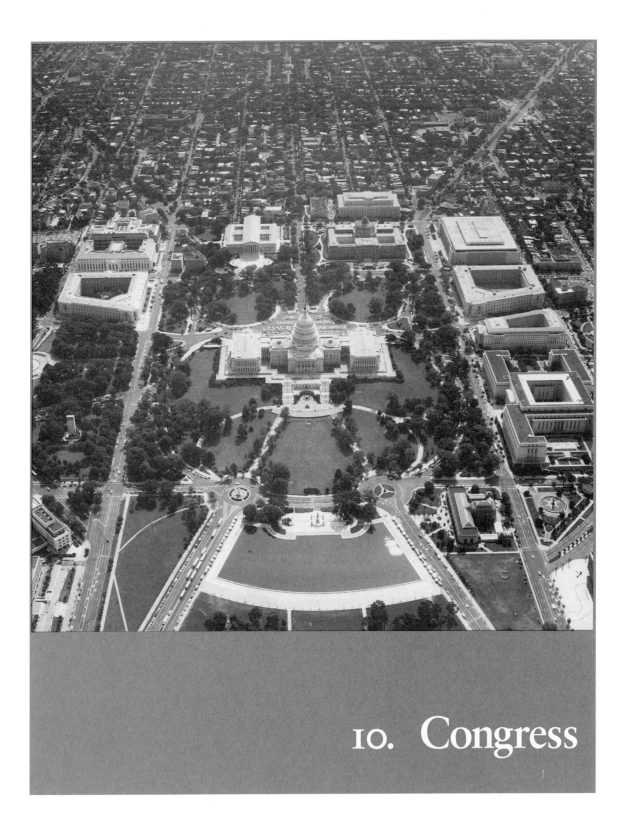

10. Congress

THE CONGRESS of the United States is a highly unusual legislative institution. Most of the world's national legislatures are primarily arenas for debate where decisions of the executive or national political parties are ratified and some oversight of the executive is carried out. They are not places where important policy decisions are made. The U.S. Congress, however, is decidedly different. It does make important decisions that significantly shape domestic and foreign policy, and its actions affect the politics of the nation.[1] The centrality of Congress in the policy-making process has been aptly summarized by congressional scholar Ralph Huitt, who observed: "Whoever tries to weave the seamless web of American policy . . . will find soon enough that all threads lead ultimately to Congress."[2]

This chapter describes the organization and operation of the Congress and explains why Congress has retained a prominent policy-making role, why the institution and its members function and behave as they do, and what the consequences of those behavior patterns have been. The starting point for this exploration of congressional politics is the process through which members of Congress are selected.

The Electoral Connection

A closer look at the Congress quickly reveals the connection between how Congress functions and the processes used to choose its members. The composition of Congress is determined by constitutional and statutory rules that govern eligibility to serve and apportionment of representation among the states, as well as by the processes used to recruit and nominate candidates. The behavior of the legislators themselves also is affected by the general electoral process because it gives individual candidates—not party organizations—the primary responsibility for securing election and reelection. Members of the House and Senate, therefore, enter Congress

---

1. See Kenneth A. Shepsle, "Representation and Governance: The Great Legislative Trade-Off," *Political Science Quarterly* 103 (Fall 1988): 653.

2. Ralph K. Huitt, "Congressional Organization and Operations in the Field of Money and Credit," in *Fiscal and Debt Management Policies,* ed. Commission on Money and Credit (Englewood Cliffs, N.J.: Prentice-Hall, 1963), 408. Also see reporter David Broder's comments on how Congress is the best vantage point from which to cover Washington and national politics in his *Behind the Front Page: A Candid Look at How the News Is Made* (New York: Simon and Schuster, 1987), 208–212.

with a substantial degree of independence and a sense of personal responsibility for winning a seat there.

Eligibility and Length of Terms

The Constitution imposes only minimal requirements for holding congressional office: *age*—twenty-five years for House members and thirty years for senators; *citizenship*—seven years for representatives and nine years for senators; and *residency*—officeholders must reside in the state they represent. Even though House candidates are not required constitutionally to reside in the district they represent, voters expect them to do just that. Residency even occasionally becomes a campaign issue—Americans seem to be always on the move. Sen. Frank Lautenberg (D-N.J.), for example, effectively accused his 1988 opponent, Pete Dawkins (Heisman Trophy winner, Rhodes scholar, army general, and Wall Street banker), of being a celebrity in search of a state in which to run. Well-known candidates, however, can occasionally overcome "carpetbagging" charges as did New York Democratic senators Robert Kennedy (1965–1968) and Daniel Patrick Moynihan (1977–   ), both of whom had out-of-state residences before becoming candidates.

House members serve two-year terms, with the entire House up for election in even-numbered years. When a vacancy occurs through death or retirement, the governor of the state in which the vacancy exists may call a special election to choose a successor to fill out the balance of the unexpired term. Governors may not fill House vacancies through appointments.

Senators too are elected in even-numbered years, but they serve six-year terms; one-third of the Senate stands for election every two years. Senate vacancies can be filled either by gubernatorial appointment or by special election, depending on state law.

Apportionment and Redistricting

Under the Constitution, representation in the House is based on each state's population, with every state entitled to at least one representative. Each state is also automatically allotted two senators.

To ensure that apportionment of the 435 House seats reflects shifts in the nation's population, Congress is required to reapportion the seats after every decennial census. When that **reapportionment** occurs, states experiencing population growth gain additional congressional representation at the expense of states with lower rates of growth or population losses. The big gainers from the 1990 census were the Sun Belt states of California, Florida, and Texas; the Middle-Atlantic and midwestern states sustained the greatest seat losses (Figure 10.1).

Figure 10.1: Reapportionment of the House of Representatives after the 1990 Census: Gainers and Losers

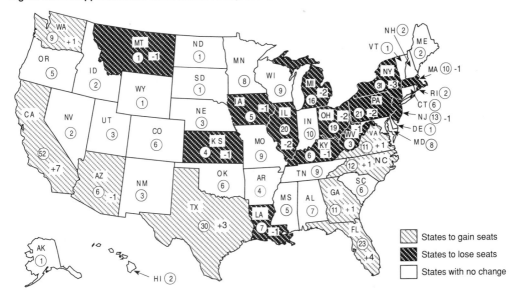

Note: Total number of House seats after reapportionment is encircled. Plus (+) or minus (-) denotes gain or loss of House seats resulting from 1990 census.

House members are elected from districts whose boundaries are drawn by the various state legislatures. To ensure that all districts within a state are as equal as possible in population, congressional district boundaries are redrawn or *redistricted* after each decennial census. The political stakes in **redistricting** are high. The political careers of incumbents and challengers, party control of congressional seats, and interest group access to representatives can all hinge on how district lines are drawn. Indeed, in most states redistricting is an intensely partisan matter, with both parties trying to create districts that will maximize their control of House seats. With the next election in mind, incumbents and potential challengers look for ways as well to have district lines drawn to their advantage.

Drawing district lines to gain political advantage—so-called *gerrymandering*—originated in 1812 when Gov. Eldridge Gerry engineered an unusually blatant manipulation of district lines by the Massachusetts legislature. Gerrymandering for partisan advantage can be achieved by (1) concentrating blocs of opposition party voters in a single or small number of districts while creating safe majorities for one's own party in the remaining districts; or (2) spreading blocs of opposition party voters across a number of districts in a manner that precludes the opposition from gaining district-level majorities. An ingenious partisan gerrymander was pulled off in California after the 1980 census that added two seats to the state's House delegation. The redistricting plan devised by the Democratic-controlled state legislature resulted in the congressional delegation changing from twenty-two Democrats and twenty-one Republicans to twenty-eight Democrats and seventeen Republicans.

Since 1962, the Supreme Court has required that legislative districts within a state be substantially equal in population. In enforcing the Court's "one person, one vote" doctrine, the federal courts have invalidated state redistricting schemes for failing to meet strict standards for equality among a state's districts. The courts also have redrawn district lines themselves when a state legislature either failed to act or passed a plan that did not meet the "one person, one vote" standard.[3]

The already substantial involvement of the courts in redistricting disputes is apt to intensify in the 1990s. In a 1986 case challenging a Republican gerrymander in Indiana, the Supreme Court stated that in the future it would review instances of partisan gerrymandering to determine whether voters' constitutional guarantee of protection of the laws had been violated.[4] Since virtually all redistricting legislation is tinged with partisanship, this decision will likely generate a spate of litigation that will prolong the redistricting struggles within the states.

Candidate Recruitment and Nomination

Important influences on the nature of campaigns and their outcomes are the decisions that incumbents make about whether to seek reelection and the decisions that potential challengers and open-seat candidates make about whether to run.[5] In most races, the incumbent will seek reelection. If the incumbent is considered electorally

3. For an insightful analysis of the redistricting politics in the 1980s and the role of the courts, see Alan Ehrenhalt, "Reapportionment and Redistricting," in *The American Elections of 1982*, ed. Thomas E. Mann and Norman J. Ornstein (Washington, D.C.: American Enterprise Institute, 1983), 44–71.
4. *Davis v. Bandemer*, 478 U.S. 109 (1986).
5. For an insightful analysis of the factors influencing candidates' decisions to enter House contests, see Linda Fowler and Robert D. McClure, *Political Ambition: Who Decides to Run for Congress* (New Haven, Conn.: Yale University Press, 1989).

secure, meaningful opposition is unlikely to be encountered in either the primary or general election. But when the incumbent is considered vulnerable or there is an open seat (the incumbent is not seeking reelection), potentially strong candidates—people with experience in public office or standing in their communities—are likely to emerge. Quality candidates normally can attract the publicity, supporters, and financing essential to a hard-fought, competitive campaign.

Candidates emerge in a variety of ways. Most are self-starters or self-selected. They decide, after weighing their chances and talking with advisers and potential supporters, whether or not the time is right to make a run for the House or Senate. Some candidates are recruited by local and state party leaders. In recent years, the national party campaign committees in the House and Senate have played a bigger role in recruiting candidates and in seeking to smooth the way to the nomination for these potential candidates by providing financial support and discouraging rival candidates.

It is, however, an unusual party organization that can guarantee a preferred candidate a House or Senate nomination. As was noted in Chapter 6, in nearly every instance congressional candidates are nominated via primary elections by the voters; party organizations have a limited influence over nominations. In a few areas of the country, however, that is not the case. A prominent example of a party organization that continues to dominate the nomination process is the Nassau County (Long Island, New York) GOP organization. Its leaders select the party's congressional candidates from a pool of party workers who have earned the right to run through lengthy, loyal service to the organization. For most candidates, however, winning a House or Senate nomination through a primary election is a do-it-yourself process, which requires building and financing a personal campaign organization to contest the primary.

Because the recruitment and nomination process is highly fragmented, decentralized, and not controlled by party organizational hierarchies, senators and representatives are able to operate with a substantial measure of independence. The strongest, most experienced candidates tend to emerge from the ranks of state and local officeholders—legislators, district attorneys, governors, mayors. Because Democrats predominate in these lower steppingstones to Congress, the Democratic party has been more successful in recruiting strong candidates than the Republican party. This is one of the factors contributing to continuing Democratic control of the House.[6]

6. Gary C. Jacobson, "Congress: A Singular Continuity," in *The Elections of 1988,* ed. Michael Nelson (Washington, D.C.: CQ Press, 1989), 146.

Campaign Finance

A critical element of electoral success is having enough money to run a competitive campaign. Costs, however, have been escalating steadily as campaigns have come to rely more heavily on sophisticated technology, television advertising, and professional consultants. Unlike presidential elections, congressional races receive no public funding and have no limits on campaign expenditures. In 1990, the mean expenditure by a Senate incumbent was $3.8 million, and the mean expenditure by a House incumbent was $378,811, with 125 candidates spending in excess of $500,000. Indeed, the million-dollar House campaign is no longer unusual. In California, the 1988 expenditures of seven candidates exceeded $1 million, led by Republican representative Robert Dornan with $1.7 million.

Campaign finance in congressional races is governed by the 1971 Federal Election Campaign Act (FECA), which was amended significantly in 1974, 1976, and 1979. It provides for the following limits on contributions *per election* (the primary and general elections are considered to be separate): (1) individuals, $1,000; (2) political action committees (PACs), $5,000; and (3) political party committees, $5,000 to House candidates and $17,500 to Senate candidates. Party committees also are authorized to make coordinated expenditures (for polling, media advertising, consultants, voter mobilization) to support House and Senate candidates.[7] Coordinated expenditures are particularly important in closely contested Senate races. In the 1988 California battle between Republican senator Pete Wilson and Democratic challenger Leo McCarthy, the Republican and Democratic parties each spent $1.9 million in support of their candidates. Because the national Republican organizations have been more effective in raising party funds, the GOP plays a more significant role in financing congressional campaigns than the Democratic party.

As was noted in Chapter 7, a major consequence of the 1974 amendments to the FECA has been the formation of PACs, an increasingly important source of campaign funds. The obvious willingness of PACs to contribute to incumbents (74 percent of PAC funds in 1987–1988 went to incumbents) is a source of incumbent advantage over their challengers.

As would be expected, the two parties' views of campaign finance

7. For a detailed analysis of national party committee involvement in House and Senate elections, see Paul S. Herrnson, *Party Campaigning in the 1980s* (Cambridge, Mass.: Harvard University Press, 1988).

reform proposals are heavily influenced by their respective fund-raising abilities. Congressional Democrats are wary of President George Bush's proposals to severely limit PAC contributions because they raise more money from PACs than Republicans. Democrats also oppose Republican proposals to increase the amount spent by party organizations because of the GOP's advantage in party fund-raising. As the minority party in Congress, the Republicans generally reject any proposals for public funding of campaigns because such pro-posals also impose ceilings on campaign expenditures. These limits would work to the disadvantage of challengers who normally must pull out all the financial stops to have a chance of unseating an in-cumbent.[8]

House Elections

The normal pattern of outcomes in House elections is easily summed up: *"Incumbents win!"* In the 1980s, House incumbents had a 94.5 percent reelection rate. Not only are incumbents winning, but they are winning by wider margins. Indeed, the average vote received by challengers and the share of incumbents getting less than 60 percent of the vote reached postwar lows in the 1980s (Figure 10.2).

Incumbents generally win because they are able to publicize their activities through franked (paid with public funds) mailings to their constituents, press releases and radio and videotapes sent to con-stituency news outlets, frequent trips back to their districts, and the work of their official staffs. Incumbents also benefit from the ten-dencies of PACs to give primarily to incumbents. With these publicity and resource advantages, incumbents have been able to build per-sonal followings among their constituents at a time when voters have been paying less attention to partisan considerations in making their election day choices. Finally, strong challengers are increasingly re-luctant to enter what often appear to be contests they are sure to lose.

The Democrats have maintained uninterrupted control of the House since 1954 in spite of GOP successes in winning the presi-dency. This Democratic dominance of the House has been aided not only by incumbency advantages but also by the party's success in winning open-seat contests (those in which the incumbent does not seek reelection). For example, in the thirty open-seat contests of 1990, the Democrats achieved a net gain of six.

8. See Gary C. Jacobson, "The Effect of Campaign Spending in Congressional Elections," *American Political Science Review* 72 (June 1978): 469–491.

Figure 10.2: Incumbency Advantage in House Elections

Average House challenger's share of the major party vote, 1946–1988

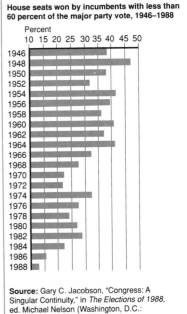

House seats won by incumbents with less than 60 percent of the major party vote, 1946–1988

Source: Gary C. Jacobson, "Congress: A Singular Continuity," in *The Elections of 1988*, ed. Michael Nelson (Washington, D.C.: CQ Press, 1989), 132–133.

Senate Elections

While most House incumbents coast to relatively lopsided victories, a significant share of Senate elections in recent years has been vigorously contested, and control of the Senate has hinged on a small proportion of the total vote cast. Thus, a shift of just 35,000 votes in 1982 would have returned the chamber to Democratic control, and a switch of just 55,000 votes in 1986, properly distributed among various candidates, would have left the Senate in Republican hands.

Senate elections are more often sharply contested than House elections because of the attractiveness of the office and the fact that Senate constituencies, which are statewide, tend to be more evenly balanced between Democratic and Republican voters than is the case in most House districts. These factors increase the likelihood that potentially strong candidates will enter Senate contests because they believe they have a decent chance of winning. Although incumbency is an advantage in Senate elections (83 percent of incumbents seeking reelection between 1980 and 1990 were victorious), senators find it more difficult than House members to develop reputations of electoral invincibility that will scare off strong challengers. Senate races, therefore, tend to attract more electable candidates, who in turn are able to attract the resources—money and workers—needed to mount full-scale campaign efforts.

Congressional elections analyst Gary Jacobson has summarized the differences between House and Senate elections:

Competition breeds competition. Senate contests are more often competitive than House elections because Senate challengers are more often experienced, high-quality candidates who are able to raise adequate funds. Superior candidates run because the record shows that Senate challengers have a decent chance of winning. The same dynamic that inhibits competition in House elections encourages it in Senate elections.[9]

Candidate-centered Campaigns

Whether the race is for the Senate or House, competitive or noncompetitive, congressional elections share certain common characteristics. Candidates are largely on their own and can normally rely on only moderate levels of support from their party organizations. They build their own campaign organizations, collect their own financial contributions, and stress their own records. Most have been able through highly personalized campaigning to insulate themselves

9. Jacobson, "Congress: A Singular Continuity," 136.

from national swings of electoral sentiment. As a result, **presidential coattails** (when popular presidential candidates are able to transfer their popularity to their party's House and Senate candidates) have worn extremely thin in recent elections. In 1988, for example, Republican Senate candidates won only eleven of twenty-four Senate races (44 percent) in states carried by George Bush, while winning three contests in the eight states having Senate contests that were carried by Democrat Michael Dukakis.

What sort of legislator emerges from Congress's decentralized and highly personalized electoral environment? Most members of the Senate and House consider themselves loyal party members and generally vote with their party leadership on roll-call votes. But they also recognize that it was their own campaign efforts and the image they conveyed to their constituents—not their parties'—that got them elected. They further understand a basic reality of political survival: reelection ultimately depends on their own ability to satisfy constituents and not on loyalty to their party's or president's policy positions. Neither the president nor a party organization is capable of saving a member whose constituents are disenchanted.

The electoral process has profound implications for the way Congress operates. Given the independence encouraged by the electoral process, today's senators and representatives could be described as *independent political entrepreneurs*—free enterprisers in politics. The men and women elected are responsible for sustaining a personal political enterprise and for achieving their personal goals within the legislative arena. Thus, although we speak frequently of "the Congress," "the Senate," or "the House," such general images give a false sense of unity to these institutions. Congress is actually 535 separate political enterprises, all being run simultaneously. Not a paradigm of orderliness, to be sure, but that is Congress—a highly individualized and decentralized institution. It is an institution in which individuals with diverse objectives—reelection, power in the chamber, policy leadership, service to constituents, and even presidential aspirations—pursue their goals, sometimes in conflict with colleagues, sometimes with the acquiescence of colleagues, and sometimes with the cooperation and assistance of colleagues.

Congressional Functions

Congress is first and foremost a legislative body, but its activities and functions within the political system extend beyond lawmaking and include overseeing the administration, educating the

The Composition of Congress: 102d Congress, 1991–1993

Although Congress functions as a representative body for all Americans, its membership is hardly representative of the social and economic characteristics of the population. Like most leadership groups, it is predominantly white, middle-aged, male, and middle to upper middle class. To maintain the legitimacy of the institution as well as electoral support for themselves, representatives and senators must therefore develop relationships of trust between themselves and broad segments of their constituencies.

	House	Senate
Republicans	167	44
Democrats	267	56
Independents	1	0
Average years of tenure	12.4	11.1
Average age	53.0	57.3
Men	407	98
Women	29 [a]	2
Whites	397	98
Blacks	26 [a]	0
Hispanics, Asians, Pacific Islanders	17 [b]	2
Religion [c]		
Protestants (traditional) [d]	243	55
Catholics	122	20
Jews	33	8
Others [e]	66	17
Prior occupations (major categories)		
Law	183	61
Business or banking	157	31
Public service/politics	61	4
Education	57	10
Journalism	25	10
Agriculture	20	8
Engineering	7	0
Medicine	5	0
Professional sports	3	1

[a] Includes nonvoting delegate from the District of Columbia.
[b] Includes nonvoting delegates from American Samoa, Guam, Puerto Rico, and Virgin Islands.
[c] Includes all nonvoting delegates.
[d] Includes Baptists, Episcopalians, Lutherans, Methodists, Presbyterians, United Church of Christ/Congregational, and unspecified Protestant.
[e] Includes nontraditional Protestant, Mormon, Unitarian, Seventh-Day Adventist, Greek Orthodox, and unspecified.
Source: Congressional Quarterly.

public, and representing its constituents. Congress should not be viewed as some kind of bill and resolution factory, where the members are graded on a piecework basis.[10]

Lawmaking is the principal legal function of the Congress—a function that has taken on massive proportions as the role of government and the complexity of the issues to be resolved have increased. Approximately ten thousand bills are introduced during the two years between congressional elections, with each senator introducing an average of thirty-three bills and each House member averaging fourteen bills. Eight thousand committee meetings are held to review these measures, and the House and Senate are normally in session approximately 285 days.[11]

In spite of all this activity, only a small share of the bills introduced ever reaches the president's desk for signature. This high mortality rate reflects the difficulties encountered in developing sufficient support for a bill as well as the fact that not all legislation is introduced with the expectation that it will be passed. Often bills are introduced with the objective of beginning a long process of building public, interest group, administration, and congressional support for the measure. For example, many of the New Frontier and Great Society measures of the Kennedy and Johnson administrations—including the Peace Corps and Medicare—had incubated in the Congress in the 1950s until momentum developed for their passage in the early 1960s. Similarly, the Reagan administration's 1981 tax reduction bill had its roots in proposals made in the 1970s by Rep. Jack Kemp (R-N.Y.) and Sen. William Roth, Jr. (R-Del.). Legislation also may be introduced to satisfy the demands of interest groups or to apply pressure to administrators to change the implementation of an existing law. In the 1980s, the number of bills passed by Congress declined; as part of a government awash in a huge budget deficit, Congress found its ability to initiate new or expanded spending programs restricted. And although the number of bills being passed has declined in recent years, the length of those enacted has gone up. The cause is the increasing complexity of the problems—drug abuse, foreign trade deficits, tax reform—with which Congress must wrestle

10. See Ralph K. Huitt, "The Outsider in the Senate: An Alternative Role," *American Political Science Review* 55 (September 1961): 566–575.

11. Norman J. Ornstein, Thomas E. Mann, and Michael J. Malbin, eds., *Vital Statistics on Congress, 1989–1990* (Washington, D.C.: CQ Press, 1989), 155–156.

and statutory requirements to pass comprehensive budget legislation (the congressional budget process is described later in this chapter).

In seeking to pass bills, members of Congress stick to one overriding strategy: attract majority support while making as few concessions as possible to opponents. Compromise and accommodation with potential supporters as well as opponents are inevitable, however, because lawmaking requires finding a majority that will support a bill. Not surprisingly, then, few bills emerge from the House and Senate chambers in the same form in which they were introduced. In fashioning legislative compromises that a majority finds satisfactory, Congress plays a major role in resolving and managing the conflicts that exist in American society.

Oversight of Administration

After legislation has been enacted, the responsibility for its implementation falls to the bureaucracy. In carrying out congressional mandates, the bureaucracy inevitably has a great deal of discretion. The Environmental Protection Agency, for example, can enforce antipollution laws aggressively or look for more accommodating solutions for those industries and communities threatening the environment. And the Justice Department through litigation can seek to broaden or restrict the reach of affirmative action legislation. Because of the profound policy consequences of administrative actions, Congress actively engages in **oversight** and review of administrative actions. Administrators are all too aware of such reviews because Congress is able to enact legislation altering the structures, budgets, and authority of government agencies.

The focal point for oversight of administration is congressional committees. During committee hearings on proposed bills, administrators are constantly asked to account for past decisions and to assess the effectiveness of the programs they administer. Controversial administration actions or scandals, such as the 1987 Iran-contra affair or the influence peddling revealed in 1989 within the Department of Housing and Urban Development, can provoke highly publicized congressional investigations. The pain and unpleasantness administrators must endure during lengthy, hostile questioning by senators or representatives at committee hearings often renders them quite compliant when pressed for changes in administrative policy. Just the threat of congressional criticism can cause administrators to adjust their policies to avoid hostile reactions from Capitol Hill.

Oversight occurs not just in committee meetings; individual legislators and their staffs constantly check on administrative actions as they assist constituents having difficulties with the bureaucracy (also called **casework**). Examples include helping the elderly secure Social Security benefits, helping veterans obtain medical assistance, or speeding up the processing of a community's application for a grant for new sewer construction. Recognizing Congress's legislative power and access to publicity, the bureaucracy is responsive to congressional intervention in behalf of constituents. Members devote a substantial share of their staff resources to casework because (1) it provides the assistance that ordinary citizens so badly need when confronting a vast federal bureaucracy, and (2) a reputation for responsiveness to constituency interests is definitely an asset at reelection time.[12]

Public Education

The activities of Congress and its members are prime subjects for coverage by both the national and local and regional media. This ability to generate publicity has put Congress in the public education business of informing citizens about current issues. Debates in the House and Senate chambers, committee hearings, interviews with representatives and senators, and press releases cover virtually every aspect of government activity. Often, congressionally generated publicity has helped crystallize public opinion on issues and facilitate passage of new legislation and changes in administration policy. During the 1960s and 1970s, for example, persistent criticism of America's Vietnam War policy before the Senate Foreign Relations Committee swayed public opinion and government policy on this divisive issue. More recently, in 1991 Congress helped make clear the stakes and consequences of authorizing military action against Iraq. Members of Congress also have been able to dramatize the problems created by drug abuse, rising medical costs, military procurement fraud, homelessness, and nuclear wastes. Congress is thus more than an object of public opinion; it is also a mover and shaker of public opinion, stimulating public interest in issues and influencing public thinking.

Representation

Legislators go to great lengths to stay in touch with their constituents, making grueling schedules the rule for most members. For members, a typical week includes three to four days in Washington, each of which often starts with breakfast meetings with administra-

12. For consideration of the electoral benefits of effective casework for members of Congress, see Morris P. Fiorina, *Congress: Keystone of the Washington Establishment* (New Haven, Conn.: Yale University Press, 1977); and Bruce Cain, John Ferjohn, and Morris Fiorina, *The Personal Vote* (Cambridge, Mass.: Harvard University Press, 1988).

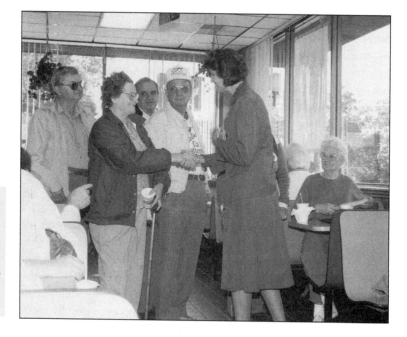

Maintaining close ties with the folks back home is essential to reelection and representation. As a result, most members of Congress spend at least one-third of the year in their districts. Democratic representative Liz Patterson meets informally with constituents in a South Carolina restaurant.

tors, interest group representatives, or constituents, and ends with a series of evening receptions and fund-raisers. After tending to legislative business in Washington, most members board planes and spend the balance of the week back in their districts or states with constituents—holding town meetings and office hours, appearing on local television programs, speaking to community groups, cutting ribbons, and marching in local parades. In the process, they develop a **home style**—a way of presenting themselves and explaining their actions to constituents—which helps build a sense of trust among the "home folks."[13]

Representation is a complex phenomenon. Some legislators view themselves primarily as *delegates* from their constituencies. They carry to Washington the views and interests of the voters who elected them. Legislators who adopt a delegate style of representation do not try to exercise independent judgment in casting their votes on the floor of the House or Senate. Rather, they vote their constituency's interests. The personalized nature of campaigning in the United States and the weakness of the parties in compelling members

13. See Richard F. Fenno, Jr., *Home Style: House Members in Their Districts* (Boston: Little, Brown, 1978), especially 151–169.

to vote a party line encourage members to adopt a local or district orientation toward issues.

But even if members of Congress adopt a delegate style of representation, their behavior is also influenced by how they perceive their constituencies and by which interests within their constituencies they feel deserve their representation and support. Democrat Daniel Patrick Moynihan and Republican Alphonse D'Amato, for example, both represent the same geographic area—the state of New York—in the Senate. Yet they represent their state quite differently. Moynihan has compiled a liberal voting record and D'Amato a conservative one because in part they perceive New York quite differently.

Unlike delegate-type legislators who try to mirror the views of their constituents in making legislative decisions, legislators adopting a *trustee* style of representation do not feel bound to follow the dictates of their constituents. Rather, when they believe their constituents are wrong, they feel free to follow their own judgments about what is or is not wise public policy. Interestingly, members of Congress often have more freedom from constituency pressures in deciding how to vote than is commonly believed. In his study of members' behavior in their districts, Richard Fenno discovered that a home style that successfully builds a sense of trust among constituents is also one that often frees members to vote as they see fit in Washington. He concluded that voters are seeking more than representation of their policy views in Congress; they are also seeking representation by individuals they consider accessible and trustworthy.[14]

The Committee System

Responsible lawmaking requires specialized knowledge and expertise. Since its earliest days, Congress has relied on committees to collect the information needed to make informed decisions and to draft and refine legislative proposals. Initially, temporary committees were created to refine each bill developed on the floors of the House and Senate. By 1816, however, Congress had recognized that ad hoc committees were just not up to the task of developing complex legislative proposals. For the Congress to compete for influence with the executive branch and interest groups, it needed permanent committees with subject matter expertise. By the mid-1800s, permanent or **standing committees** with specific subject matter jurisdictions and composed of member specialists were being

14. Ibid.

used to develop and recommend legislation for the full House and Senate.[15] Indeed, the influence of committees on the legislative process had become so dominant by the late 1800s that Woodrow Wilson, in his classic treatise *Congressional Government,* stated that "Congress in session is Congress on display, but Congress in committee is Congress at work."[16]

Today committees continue to play a major role in shaping legislation. Virtually all legislation that reaches the floors of the House and Senate for consideration has first been reviewed and frequently revised by a committee.

Types of Committees

The most important congressional committees are the standing committees—twenty-two in the House and sixteen in the Senate (Tables 10.1 and 10.2). They continue to operate in each succeeding congressional session (hence the term *standing committee*) and have fixed subject matter jurisdictions. The House Ways and Means Committee, for example, has jurisdiction over taxes and trade legislation, while the bailiwick of the House Banking, Finance, and Urban Affairs Committee is housing, community development, financial institutions, and international lending agencies. Standing committees have the power to report bills to the full House and Senate.

Of the four basic types of standing committees, the most numerous are the *authorizing committees.* These bodies develop legislation spelling out the substance or content of policy and empowering the government to act—for example, the House Education and Labor Committee drafts legislation governing education policy and authorizing government agencies to carry out that policy. *Appropriations committees* control the actual appropriation of money from the federal Treasury to pay for programs recommended by the authorizing committees. Jurisdiction over revenue-raising measures is exercised by the *taxing committees*—the Senate Finance Committee and the House Ways and Means Committee. And the *Budget committees* in both chambers coordinate expenditures and revenues.

The size of committees and the ratio of Democrats to Republicans on standing committees are determined through bargaining between the two parties' leaders after each election. These party ratios, which normally reflect party strength in the two chambers, can dramatically

15. For an insightful account of the development of congressional committees and the consequences of recent changes in the committee system, see Shepsle, "Representation and Governance," 461–484.

16. Woodrow Wilson, *Congressional Government* (Baltimore: Johns Hopkins University Press, 1980), 79 (first published in 1885).

Table 10.1 Standing Committees of the House, 102d Congress (1991–1993)

Standing Committee	Party Ratio	Number of Subcommittees
Agriculture	27D : 18R (60.0% D)	8
Appropriations	37D : 22R (62.7% D)	13
Armed Services	31D : 21R (59.6% D)	7
Banking, Finance, and Urban Affairs	31D : 20R (60.8% D)	8
Budget	23D : 14R (62.2% D)	6
District of Columbia	7D : 4R (63.6% D)	3
Education and Labor	23D : 14R (62.2% D)	8
Energy and Commerce	27D : 16R (62.8% D)	6
Foreign Affairs	26D : 17R (60.5% D)	9
Government Operations	25D : 15R (62.5% D)	7
House Administration	15D : 9R (62.6% D)	7
Interior and Insular Affairs	26D : 16R (61.9% D)	6
Judiciary	21D : 13R (61.8% D)	7
Merchant Marine and Fisheries	28D : 17R (62.2% D)	6
Post Office and Civil Service	14D : 8R (63.6% D)	7
Public Works and Transportation	34D : 21R (61.8% D)	6
Rules	9D : 4R (69.2% D)	2
Science, Space, and Technology	32D : 19R (62.7% D)	6
Small Business	27D : 17R (61.4% D)	6
Standards of Official Conduct	7D : 7R (50.0% D)	0
Veterans' Affairs	21D : 13R (62.8% D)	5
Ways and Means	23D : 13R (63.9% D)	6

Table 10.2 Standing Committees of the Senate, 102d Congress (1991–1993)

Standing Committee	Party Ratio	Number of Subcommittees
Agriculture, Nutrition, and Forestry	10D : 8R (55.6% D)	7
Appropriations	16D : 13R (55.2% D)	13
Armed Services	11D : 9R (55.0% D)	6
Banking, Housing, and Urban Affairs	12D : 9R (57.1% D)	4
Budget	12D : 9R (57.1% D)	0
Commerce, Science, and Transportation	11D : 9R (55.0% D)	8
Energy and Natural Resources	11D : 9R (55.0% D)	5
Environment and Public Works	9D : 7R (56.3% D)	5
Finance	11D : 9R (55.0% D)	8
Foreign Relations	10D : 8R (55.5% D)	7
Governmental Affairs	8D : 6R (57.1% D)	5
Judiciary	8D : 6R (57.1% D)	7
Labor and Human Resources	10D : 7R (58.8% D)	6
Rules and Administration	9D : 7R (56.3% D)	0
Small Business	10D : 8R (55.5% D)	6
Veterans' Affairs	7D : 5R (58.3% D)	0

SOURCE: *Congressional Quarterly Weekly Report*, May 4, 1991, 12–75.

affect the outcomes of committee decisions on legislation. To exert maximum party influence on important legislation, the majority party has customarily insisted on extraordinary majorities on such key committees as the tax-writing House Ways and Means Committee (23D:13R) and the House Rules Committee (9D:4R), which controls the procedures under which bills are considered on the House floor.

In both the House and Senate, **select committees** study and investigate specific problems and issues. Unlike the standing committees, select committees are not generally considered permanent bodies, and they do not have authority to report bills to the full House and Senate for consideration. Select committees have been used to educate the Congress and the public about such problems as drug abuse, hunger, and the elderly, and to make legislative recommendations. These committees also enable members of Congress to become personally identified with a particular issue or cause. The late Claude Pepper (D-Fla.), for example, gained national attention as a champion of the elderly through his work as chairman of the House Select Committee on Aging.

Joint committees are composed of both senators and representatives, with chairmanships rotating between the chambers at the beginning of each newly elected Congress. These committees perform studies, investigations, oversight of the executive, as well as administrative tasks. The Joint Economic Committee, for example, conducts hearings on and studies of a wide range of economic issues, and the Joint Committee on Printing oversees the Government Printing Office.

Before legislation can be sent to the president, it must pass both the House and Senate in identical form. But since the two chambers often pass different versions of a bill, reconciliation of these differences is a must. This task usually falls to a **conference committee** comprised of representatives and senators. Conference committees negotiate compromises between the House and Senate and then report the results of their negotiations back to the full House and Senate, which must approve the compromise bill before it can be sent to the president (for a more detailed discussion of conference committees, see "The Legislative Process: How a Bill Becomes a Law" in this chapter).

Committee Assignments

Because committees often play a crucial role in shaping legislation, members wage fierce campaigns to land desirable committee assignments. In both the House and Senate, the Republican and Democratic parties have committees on committees which handle the delicate task of members' assignments. Committee assignments are particularly important in the House, where the large membership and procedural rules restrict individual members' opportunities to exert influence when bills are being considered by the full House. Senators, by contrast, are less concerned about their committee assignments because the chamber's rules give individual members ample opportunities to shape bills after they have been reported from committee and are being considered on the Senate floor (see "The Legislative Process: How a Bill Becomes a Law" in this chapter for a look at the differences in House and Senate floor procedures).

The committee assignments sought by members depend on their personal goals. Those interested in wielding power over a wide range of issues often aim for a seat on the money committees such as the House and Senate Appropriations or Budget committees. Other committees serve members' reelection needs by giving them a chance to assist constituents and influential interest groups. Thus, legislators from farm areas often gravitate toward the agriculture committees, big city members toward the banking committees (housing and urban development), and westerners toward the interior committee (public lands policy). Members also may seek assignments in which they can have a say in policy of special concern to them. Senators with an interest in foreign policy, for example, may seek slots on the Foreign Relations Committee.

The tendency of members to be attracted by committees that will help them achieve their career goals means that committees are not necessarily representative of their parent chambers. They are apt to contain members with the same particular constituency interests or policy orientations. Indeed, the House Agriculture Committee is composed exclusively of members from agricultural constituencies. Consumers in Brooklyn, Chicago, or Los Angeles simply have no voice on this committee.

The makeup of a committee affects, of course, its decisions on policy matters. And because members normally retain their committee assignments for the duration of their congressional careers, the impact of committee assignments on policy can be long term. Is it any wonder then that party leaders, senior committee members, and interest groups seek to "stack" committees to favor particular policy outcomes? According to Rep. Henry Waxman (D-Calif.), who has skillfully worked to achieve majorities on the Energy and Commerce Committee favoring tougher environmental protection and expanded health care legislation, "There are enormous policy implications in the committee assignment process. . . . A number of issues on the Energy and Commerce Committee were decided by one or two votes. Millions, if not billions, of dollars are at stake for major industries in this country."[17]

Committee chairmen are always members of the majority party. From early in this century until the 1970s, these leaders were selected automatically via the **seniority system,**[18] under which the member of the majority party with the longest continuous service on a committee automatically became its chairman. Awarding chairmanships on the basis of seniority tends to restrict committee leadership to members from electorally safe constituencies since these are the members who pile up seniority. Under the seniority system, chairmen also may be unrepresentative of their party's regional composition and policy orientation. This was particularly true for the House Democrats in the 1960s and 1970s, when their party's committee chairmen were disproportionately southern conservatives. Some of these conservative Democrats used their procedural powers to call meetings, appoint subcommittees, and hire staff to stymie liberal legislation. Frustrated with these maneuvers, younger liberal Democrats successfully pressed for a change in the method of selecting committee chairmen that would make them more accountable to the members of their party.

As a result of their efforts, since 1975 House Democratic committee chairmen have been elected by the party **caucus** (the full party membership in the House) at the beginning of each new Congress. Although normally the caucus has followed seniority in choosing chairmen, between 1975 and 1991 six elderly chairmen were deposed. In recent years, this system of election has reduced the independence of the chairmen in leading their committees because reelection by their colleagues, not automatic retention of their posts based on seniority, is the rule. In 1987, for example, Les Aspin (D-Wis.) nearly lost his Armed Services Committee chairmanship because he voted in favor of the MX missile and aid to the Nicaraguan contras—positions that put him at odds with a majority of his Democratic colleagues.

The influence of committee chairmen also has been restricted, particularly in the House, by the rise of **subcommittee government**

Committee Leadership Selection: A Modified Seniority System

---

17. Quoted by Steven V. Roberts, "Committee Selection: Art and Science," *New York Times,* Jan. 13, 1983, 10Y, National edition.

18. The development of the seniority system in the House is described in Nelson W. Polsby, Miriam Gallaher, and Barry S. Rundquist, "The Growth of the Seniority System in the U.S. House of Representatives," *American Political Science Review* 63 (September 1969): 787–807.

since the 1970s. Nearly every standing committee now has subcommittees that consider most legislation (see Table 10.1 and Table 10.2). In the past, subcommittees were subject to control by the full committee chairmen who appointed subcommittee members, controlled the size of their staffs, and managed their budgets. Through a series of 1970s reforms, however, House subcommittees now function as relatively autonomous power centers within the Congress. They have specific subject matter jurisdictions, elect their own chairmen, and control their budgets and staffs.

With full committee chairmen dependent on their party colleagues for reelection and subcommittees playing a larger role in congressional policy making, committee chairmen have lost the dominating power they exerted in the 1950s and 1960s. Nevertheless, through the sheer force of their personalities and well-honed political skills, these chairmen still have substantial clout over their committees. During most of the 1980s, for example, Chairman John ("Iron Man") Dingell, Jr. (D-Mich.), of the House Energy and Commerce Committee managed to prevent passage of clean air legislation that ran counter to the interests of his Michigan constituents, the auto industry, and the United Auto Workers.

In the Senate, committee chairmen also are subject to election by their party colleagues, but the seniority system in that chamber has engendered much less controversy than that in the House, and the chamber adheres much more strictly to seniority in selecting committee leaders. Committee chairmanships, however, are not as important in the Senate because (1) the Senate tends to resolve more issues on its floor rather than rely on its committees to shape legislation, and (2) in the smaller Senate it is possible for every senator of the majority party to serve as a committee or subcommittee chairman.

Decentralizing Power
within Congress

The standing committee system, with its twenty-two House and sixteen Senate committees, as well as its over two hundred subcommittees, creates multiple power centers within Congress based on subject matter jurisdiction and expertise. But such fragmented power has its benefits—it is extremely difficult for anyone either inside or outside Congress to dominate that body; there are just too many centers of power and too many influential leaders. This fragmentation of power also contributes to Congress's autonomy from national political parties, presidents, and interest groups, as well as its vitality. In this decentralized environment, members of Congress have many outlets for their initiatives.

But for all its contributions toward maintaining the autonomy and vitality of Congress, the committee system does create problems. With policy making scattered among numerous committees and subcommittees, it becomes difficult for Congress to develop consistent, coordinated policies. For example, the following House committees have a significant role in the field of foreign policy, but each operates independently of the others.

Committee	Foreign Policy Jurisdiction
Foreign Affairs	Foreign aid, State Department
Appropriations	Funds for Departments of Defense and State and for other agencies
Banking, Finance, and Urban Affairs	International lending agencies
Budget	Spending for foreign policy and national security
Energy and Commerce	Foreign commerce, aviation, communications
Intelligence (select committee)	Oversight of Central Intelligence Agency
Judiciary	Immigration
Merchant Marine and Fisheries	Merchant marine and fisheries
Science, Space, and Technology	International scientific cooperation
Ways and Means	Trade

Unsurprisingly, with this array of House committees, as well as a similar collection of Senate committees, decisive, timely, and coordinated foreign policy making is extremely difficult to achieve.

Congressional Parties and Leadership

Counterbalancing both the individualism of members of Congress who find themselves responsible for their own reelection and the fragmentation of the decision-making process stemming from the committee system are the political parties in Congress. It is the parties that select congressional leaders, organize both the House and Senate, determine the schedule of business, and play a major role in determining the content of legislation.

A Partisan Environment

Almost all representatives and senators gain office by securing party nominations and running as Republicans and Democrats.

Then, in the heat of campaigning partisan commitments are forged, and most members enter Congress with a sense of loyalty to their party and a desire to advance its policies. This sense of partisanship is often reinforced by Congress's organizational and social environment.

Congress is organized on a partisan basis. Party leaders are elected by their fellow party members in caucus or conference. Only members of the majority party hold the powerful positions of Speaker of the House and Senate majority leader and the chairmanships of committees and subcommittees. It is the parties that assign members to committees, and in rare instances parties discipline maverick members by removing them from committees. For example, after leading a battle to enact President Ronald Reagan's budget and tax measures, Rep. Phil Gramm (D-Texas) was removed by the Democratic Steering and Policy Committee from the influential Budget Committee for what his colleagues considered political treason. He then resigned his seat and was subsequently elected as a Republican. Domination of chamber leadership positions and committees gives the majority party control over the schedule, policy agenda, and procedures of Congress. This procedural power aids majority party members in passing legislation and often leaves members of the minority party frustrated.

The physical setting and the social life of Congress contribute to the partisanship that pervades the institution as well. The Senate and House chambers each have a center aisle with Republicans on one side and Democrats on the other. A similar seating arrangement is used in committee meetings. As a result, information, political gossip, and pleasantries are shared with fellow partisans. This segregation even extends to the cloakrooms off the House and Senate chambers, where members can relax, chat, make a phone call, or get a cup of coffee.

Party Leadership in the House

The **Speaker of the House** is the chamber's most influential leader.[19] This post combines the duties of presiding officer with those of leading the majority party. Although modern Speakers lack the formal powers wielded by those legendary Speakers Thomas ("Czar") Reed (R-Maine, 1889–1891 and 1895–1899) and Joseph ("Uncle Joe") Cannon (R-Ill., 1903–1911), they can exert substantial influence over the House's schedule and policy decisions. The Speaker

19. For a thorough analysis of the Speaker and majority party leadership in the House, see Barbara Sinclair, *Majority Party Leadership in the U.S. House* (Baltimore: Johns Hopkins University Press, 1983).

A Legendary Speaker: Thomas Brackett Reed, Czar of the House

Before 1890, legislative business in the House could be stalled because the rules permitted members to engage in a variety of delaying actions, including use of the "disappearing quorum"—members present in the House chamber would refuse to vote when their names were called, resulting in lack of the quorum needed to conduct business. Frustrated by the House's seeming inability to act, Speaker Thomas B. Reed (R-Maine) led a reform effort in 1890 which put the majority in firm control of House business. He declared that the "object of a parliamentary body is action, and not stoppage of action." And when confronted with a "disappearing quorum," he ordered that the clerk of the House count as present all members who had refused to vote. Under Reed's guidance, the House adopted the so-called Reed Rules, which facilitated the passage of legislation by severely weakening the ability of a minority to delay or prevent House action.

First elected to the House in 1876, Reed served in the chamber for almost a quarter century and as its Speaker from 1889 to 1891 and from 1895 to 1899. He was an intimidating figure, standing over six feet two inches, weighing over 300 pounds, with a drooping mustache and a booming voice. But more intimidating than his size was his formidable intellect. Reed also was renowned for his biting wit.

He exercised power in a bold and often brazen manner that earned him the nickname "Czar." When challenged and asked about the rights of the minority in the House, Reed replied, "The right of the minority is to draw its salaries and its function is to make a quorum." And after having decided upon a parliamentary procedure to advance legislation he favored, he would announce with grim sarcasm, "Gentlemen, we have decided to perpetrate the following outrage."

Of two House colleagues, he once said, "They never open their mouths without subtracting from the sum of human knowledge." And it was Reed who coined the classic definition of a statesman—"a successful politician who is dead." Reed's retort to a House colleague who said that like Henry Clay he would rather be right than president was, "The gentleman need not be disturbed, he never will be either." And when asked to attend the funeral of a longtime political foe, he declined with the comment, "but that does not mean to say I do not heartily approve of it."

Present-day Speakers do not have the czar-like power exercised by Reed. They must constantly consult, negotiate, and persuade their independent-minded colleagues. But the Speaker's positions as majority party leader and arbiter of House procedures, the schedule of business, and committee assignments for party colleagues make the Speakership the crucial power center of the chamber.

(1) refers bills to committee, (2) influences members' committee assignments, (3) coordinates the work of committees, (4) influences the procedures under which bills will be considered on the House floor, and (5) presides at House sessions. From the presiding officer position, the Speaker also recognizes members who wish to speak and applies the chamber's complex and voluminous rules (often in a manner beneficial to the majority party). The Speaker serves as well as the public spokesperson for the majority party. The influence that Speakers can bring to bear on their colleagues depends heavily on their skills in persuasion, negotiation, and bargaining. Each occupant of the office brings to it a different style of leadership. The current Speaker, Thomas Foley (D-Wash.), is noted for his accommodating, collegial, and low-key manner, in contrast to the often highly partisan, confrontational, and frequently lone-wolf style of his predecessor, Jim Wright (D-Texas).

The second-ranking leadership position is that of the *majority leader*, who schedules bills, handles party strategy, and serves as party spokesperson on the House floor. Assisting the majority leader is the **whip** organization, composed of a chief whip and deputy whips (the term *whip* originated with the English hunt; it was the job of the whip to keep the dogs together). The whip organization notifies members when key votes will occur, conducts head counts of member sentiment on controversial issues, and attempts to "whip up" support for the party position on important roll-call votes.

The **minority leader** is the highest-ranking figure in the minority party and acts as its principal spokesperson and strategist. When the minority party controls the White House, as it has since Robert Michel of Illinois became the House Republican leader in 1981, the minority leader serves as the president's principal advocate within the House and carries major responsibility for guiding the president's legislative program through the chamber. Like the majority party, the minority has a whip organization to assist its leader.

As a large body of 435 members, the House has developed a relatively complicated set of rules that put the majority party firmly in control of its proceedings and impose restrictions on the abilities of individual members to delay and obstruct legislative action. The willingness of the Democratic party's majority to use its procedural powers to dominate the House and the Republicans' frustration at their minority status since 1954 combined during the 1980s to create an often highly charged partisan atmosphere in the House of Representatives.[20]

20. For a discussion of the increasingly powerful role played by majority leaders

Senate majority leader Lyndon Johnson (1955–1961) exercises his persuasive powers by giving Sen. Theodore Green (D-R.I.) "the treatment."

Party Leadership in the Senate

The Senate with its only one hundred members, who expect substantial deference, operates with more relaxed rules and in a more informal manner than the House. Party leaders, therefore, have fewer formal powers under the rules and must rely primarily on their skills of persuasion and negotiation to lead their colleagues.

There is no position comparable to the Speaker of the House in the Senate; the presiding officer there is not an influential leader. The vice president, who is not a member of the Senate, is constitutionally empowered to preside over the chamber but seldom performs this duty. Nor does the **president pro tempore** often preside. This strictly honorific post is given to the member of the majority party with the longest continuous service in the chamber. Rather, the duty of presiding falls to freshmen senators as a way for them to learn the rules and ways of Senate life.

The most important leaders of the Senate are the majority and minority leaders and their assistants, the party whips. The majority leader is responsible for scheduling Senate business, a procedural prerogative that gives this leader some bargaining leverage in dealing with colleagues. The majority leader also serves as the party's chief spokesperson and legislative tactician. Lacking the formal powers of

and the intensified partisanship of the modern House, see Lawrence C. Dodd and Bruce I. Oppenheimer, eds., *Congress Reconsidered*, 4th ed. (Washington, D.C.: CQ Press, 1989), 50–60.

Figure 10.3: Proportion of Partisan Roll Calls

House ━━━ Senate ━━━

Source: *Congressional Quarterly Weekly Report,* December 22, 1990, 4188.
 Note: The figure portrays the percentage of recorded votes from 1954 to 1990 in the House and Senate in which a majority of Democrats opposed a majority of Republicans.

the Speaker of the House, the current Democratic majority leader in the Senate, George Mitchell (Maine), operates in a highly collegial manner, engaging in wide-ranging consultations and consensus-seeking as he leads his party. With the GOP controlling the presidency and the Democrats in the majority within the Senate, the major responsibility for leading the president's supporters and working out compromises with the Democrats in the Senate falls to the Republican minority leader, Robert Dole (Kan.).

In his classic analysis of the Senate majority leader, congressional expert Ralph Huitt observed that such leaders, having no patronage and no power to discipline or fire other senators, must rely heavily on their skills of persuasion and their abilities to help individual senators achieve their personal goals in the Senate. Huitt also noted that Lyndon Johnson, an unusually successful Democratic majority leader (1955–1961), "never forgot the basic skill of politicians, the ability to divide by two and add one . . . and the need to find a ground on which a majority could stand. . . ."[21]

*Party Influence on
Decision Making*

Party unity on roll-call votes in the Senate and House stems not only from the efforts of party leaders, but also from the common

21. Ralph K. Huitt, "Democratic Party Leadership in the Senate," *American Political Science Review* 55 (June 1961): 337.

ideological orientations, similar constituencies, and shared ties to interest groups of party members (see Figure 10.3, which charts for 1954–1990 the percentage of times a majority of Republicans aligned themselves against a majority of Democrats on House and Senate roll-call votes). Although party-line votes only recently once again exceeded 50 percent of total roll calls, the extent of partisanship is impressive, especially when it is remembered that each chamber holds eight hundred to one thousand roll calls during the two-year life of each Congress and that a large number of bills are minor and noncontroversial.

The sharp increase in party-line votes, especially in the House, in the 1980s reflects the divisiveness of such issues as the budget, defense versus social program spending, affirmative action, aid to the Nicaraguan contras, and the so-called "Star Wars" or Strategic Defense Initiative (Figure 10.3). These and other issues pitted Democrats in Congress against a Republican president and his congressional partisans. Intensified partisan conflict also mirrors the changing composition of the two parties in the Congress. As a partisan realignment has occurred among southern voters, Republicans have won an increasingly larger share of the region's House and Senate seats. Thus, the Republican congressional membership has become more southern and more conservative and the Democratic membership less southern and less conservative. Further contributing to heightened partisanship is the growing number of Republicans from generally conservative western state constituencies. The net effects of these membership changes have sharpened partisan divisions within Congress and strengthened party unity.

Neither party in Congress is monolithic in terms of its policy orientation. The Republican party includes such far-right figures as Sen. Jesse Helms (N.C.) and such moderates as Sen. John Chafee (R.I.). Within the Democratic ranks reside the likes of such conservatives as Sen. Howell Heflin (Ala.), as well as of such staunch liberals as Ted Kennedy (Mass.). Despite such internal diversity, the Republicans and Democrats have a relatively high degree of internal unity. During the 101st Congress (1989–1991), for example, 86 percent of House Democrats on average aligned themselves against 77 percent of the Republicans on those roll-call votes sufficiently controversial to stimulate such blatant partisanship (see Table 10.3).

Democrats and Republicans Really Are Different

Congressional Democrats and Republicans have substantial policy and ideological differences. On economic, social, and foreign pol-

Table 10.3 Congressional Party Unity, 1980–1990 *(percent)*

	House	
Year	Democrats	Republicans
1980	78	79
1981	75	80
1982	77	76
1983	82	80
1984	81	77
1985	86	80
1986	86	76
1987	88	79
1988	88	80
1989	86	75
1990	86	78

	Senate	
Year	Democrats	Republicans
1980	76	74
1981	77	85
1982	76	80
1983	76	79
1984	75	83
1985	79	81
1986	74	80
1987	85	78
1988	85	74
1989	80	74
1990	82	77

SOURCES: Harold W. Stanley and Richard G. Niemi, *Vital Statistics on American Politics* (Washington, D.C.: CQ Press, 1989), 193; and *Congressional Quarterly Weekly Report,* December 22, 1990, 4212.

NOTE: The data in each column show the percentage of members voting with a majority of their party members on roll-call votes in which a majority of Democrats voted against a majority of Republicans. These party unity scores reveal a relatively high level of agreement on controversial issues within both the Democratic and Republican congressional parties.

Table 10.4 Democrats and Republicans Are Different! Ideological Profiles of the Congressional Parties, 1990

Party/Region	On average are more liberal than . . . % of their House colleagues	On average are more conservative than . . . % of their House colleagues
Western Democrats	77	19
Eastern Democrats	74	22
Midwestern Democrats	71	26
Southern Democrats	52	47
Eastern Republicans	35	62
Midwestern Republicans	20	77
Western Republicans	16	79
Southern Republicans	13	81

Party/Region	On average are more liberal than . . . % of their Senate colleagues	On average are more conservative than . . . % of their Senate colleagues
Eastern Democrats	79	12
Western Democrats	71	23
Midwestern Democrats	66	28
Southern Democrats	57	39
Eastern Republicans	38	58
Midwestern Republicans	22	75
Western Republicans	19	76
Southern Republicans	12	82

SOURCE: Richard E. Cohen and William Schneider, "Partisan Patterns," *National Journal,* January 19, 1991, 137, 139. Copyright 1990 by National Journal, Inc. All rights reserved. Reprinted by permission.

icy issues, Democrats take a vastly more liberal policy stance than Republicans (Table 10.4). Indeed, even the most conservative element of the Democratic party, southern senators and representatives, are more liberal than the most liberal group in the GOP, the eastern Republicans. Some Democrats are, of course, conservatives, and some Republicans are moderate to liberal. The center of gravity for the Democrats, however, is distinctly on the liberal side of the political spectrum, while the Republicans tend toward the conservative side. The conclusion? Clearly, the frequently laid charge that the Democrats and Republicans are as little different as Tweedledum and Tweedledee has almost no basis in fact.

When most Americans think of a bureaucracy, reams of paper-work, red tape, and civil servants toiling in anonymity may come to mind. Although Congress is thought to be anything but a bureaucracy, a vast staff bureaucracy has grown up nevertheless—particularly during the 1970s—around its 100 senators and 435 representatives. Numbering approximately eighteen thousand, the House and Senate staffs are large enough to populate a small city. When the entire support staff of the Congress is included, the congressional bureaucracy numbers in excess of 31,000 employees.

Every senator and representative has a personal staff, divided between personnel working in Washington and those working in the member's state or district. The size of senators' staffs depends on their state's population and can be as large as seventy. House members usually have staffs of about seventeen. Much of the staff work involves constituent relations—answering correspondence, doing casework, handling press relations, and arranging meetings with constituents.

The legislative assistants on members' staffs analyze legislation being considered in committee or on the floor, prepare bills and amendments, write speeches, go to meetings that members cannot attend, and represent members in meetings with lobbyists and administration officials.

Each committee and subcommittee also has a professional staff to assist its members in their deliberations on legislation. Much of the staff work is organized along party lines. Committee staffs primarily serve the senior members of committees and subcommittees, although all senators have staff assistance on their major committees.

To give it specialized advice and information, Congress has created a series of support agencies staffed by professionals. These include the *Congressional Budget Office,* which evaluates presidential budget proposals; the *General Accounting Office,* a congressional watchdog agency that audits and investigates government agencies and programs; the *Congressional Research Service,* whose specialists respond to requests for research and information; and the *Office of Technology Assessment,* an agency created to inform Congress about the impacts of scientific and technological advances.

Congress could not function without staff assistance. Many observers, however, worry that these "unelected representatives" are wielding too much power. As the workload of Congress has expanded and members have become busier, they find it increasingly necessary to rely on their staffs for the information needed to make decisions and to maintain communication with the administration, interest groups, the media, and even other members. This is particularly true in the Senate, where members have more committee assignments, larger constituencies, more interest groups with which to deal, and greater media exposure than is true of representatives. In fact, some key congressional staffers have become almost surrogate senators and representatives.

There is no easy answer to the question of what role staff should play in the congressional process. Most observers believe that representatives and senators, to do their jobs and to maintain a strong and independent Congress, must depend heavily on their staffs. But this does not diminish the need to monitor continually the role of staff, who do not have to face the voters at election time and whose interests may not be quite the same as those of their members.[22]

The Legislative Process: How a Bill Becomes a Law

Passing a bill is a lengthy, complicated, and frequently conflict-ridden struggle that involves building majorities at each stage of the process (see Figure 10.4). Because of the different systems of election, memberships, and procedural rules in the House and Senate, the requirements for building a majority in the House are quite unlike those for passing a bill in the Senate. Then, when all the congressional hurdles to passage have been cleared, a bill must still receive presidential approval or at least acquiescence to become a law.[23]

Introduction and Committee Consideration

Only representatives and senators can introduce bills, although the legislative proposals they introduce may have been developed by the administration, interest groups, concerned citizens, or congressional staff. After a bill has been introduced, it is referred to the standing committee that has jurisdiction over the subject matter of the legislation. Thus, aid-to-education bills fall within the jurisdiction of the House Education and Labor Committee, and measures

22. For an informed analysis of the role of congressional staff, see Michael J. Malbin, *Unelected Representatives: Congressional Staff and the Future of Representative Government* (New York: Basic Books, 1979).

23. For a detailed account of the procedures and strategies used in the legislative process in Congress, see Walter J. Oleszek, *Congressional Procedures and the Policy Process*, 3d ed. (Washington, D.C.: CQ Press, 1989).

dealing with the licensing of radio and television stations are within the purview of the House Energy and Commerce Committee.

Strategic considerations enter into the introduction and referral process. Because committees differ in their composition and policy preferences, and because some committees' jurisdictions overlap, proponents of bills try to draft those bills in a way that will land them on the table of a friendly committee. When legislation falls within the jurisdiction of more than one standing committee because it is multifaceted and comprehensive, it may be referred to several standing committees. Or in the House, a special ad hoc committee may be appointed by the Speaker to consider legislation. In 1977, for example, Speaker Thomas ("Tip") O'Neill (D-Mass.) used this power to create ad hoc committees that would expedite President Jimmy Carter's energy reform legislation.

Another strategic consideration is deciding whether a bill's chances will be enhanced by having the House or the Senate give first approval to the legislation. Proponents normally seek action first in the chamber they believe to be most sympathetic, in the hope that passage in one house will create pressure to pass the bill in the more resistant chamber. While the Senate was in Republican hands between 1981 and 1986, for example, the Reagan administration often pressed its advantage there as a way to influence the decisions of the Democratic House.

After a bill has been sent to committee, it is normally referred to a subcommittee specializing in the subject matter of the legislation. Most legislation dies at this stage because of insufficient interest or support from committee members. But those bills that are deemed important or have substantial member support are scheduled for hearings, usually before the subcommittee. At congressional hearings, witnesses testify and are questioned by committee members about the consequences of proposed bills. Hearings are usually characterized as fact-gathering operations designed to give members the information they need to develop effective legislation and to aid them in deciding how to vote on a bill. But because Congress is an arena of conflict, hearings involve more than neutral fact-gathering. They also provide an opportunity to generate publicity for and against the bill as each side in a controversy seeks to build a case that will bolster its cause later in the decision process. Thus during the 1989 hearings on President George Bush's proposal to lower the capital gains tax (a tax on the sale of assets that have increased in value), proponents argued that the reduced tax would stimulate investment and create

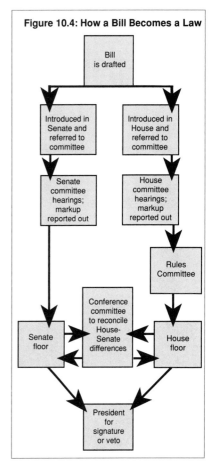

Figure 10.4: How a Bill Becomes a Law

jobs, and opponents claimed the proposal was a tax break for the wealthy.

After the hearings have been completed, the subcommittee schedules *markup* sessions. During markup, the subcommittee goes through the bill section by section—amending, deleting, and sometimes engaging in wholesale rewriting. Markup is a critical stage in the process because it determines the form in which the bill will emerge from the subcommittee.

If the subcommittee approves the bill, it is then reported to the full committee for consideration. Because the membership of a full committee differs from that of a subcommittee, the full committee may repeat the subcommittee procedures, including hearings and another markup (perhaps introducing substantial changes), or it may simply approve the bill and vote to report it to the full House or Senate.

Committee and subcommittee procedures are similar in both chambers, although in the Senate the markup is usually undertaken by the full committee. But after bills have been reported from committee, the procedures for scheduling and considering legislation in the House and Senate are quite different.

Scheduling Bills for Floor Consideration

Because Congress must consider many bills in a limited amount of time, both chambers of Congress have adopted procedures for scheduling floor consideration of legislation. In the House, scheduling is tightly controlled by the majority party leadership, and individual representatives have little influence over the floor schedule. By contrast, in the Senate individual senators have such leverage under the rules.

Most bills reach the House floor after being recommended for scheduling by the House Rules Committee. This committee has special powers, including the right to introduce a resolution—normally called a rule—that brings a bill up for immediate House consideration. The rule also sets the conditions under which the House will consider a bill: (1) the length of time allotted for debate; (2) whether amendments can be considered, which amendments can be considered, and how voting on amendments will be conducted; and (3) whether certain House procedural rules can be waived during consideration of the pending bill. If the rule recommended by the Rules Committee is approved by the full House, the bill is brought before the House for consideration.

Because of its power to control the flow of legislation to the House floor and its ability to influence legislative outcomes by controlling the conditions under which legislation is considered, the Rules Committee is a crucial seat of power in the House. Indeed, it is so important to the majority Democratic party in the House that it has allocated itself nine of the thirteen positions on the committee. Selected by the Speaker, the committee's Democratic majority works closely with the Speaker to construct rules that will help the party achieve its legislative goals.[24] For example, during House consideration of a bill to give nonlethal aid to the Nicaraguan contras in 1988, the rule devised by the Democrats on the Rules Committee in close consultation with the Speaker did not guarantee the Republicans that they would ever get a separate House vote on their contra aid proposal. Under the rule's provisions, the Democratic alternative would be voted on first, and, if passed, no vote would be held on the GOP alternative. This rule virtually assured passage of the Democratic leadership's proposal. With the Democrats utilizing the Rules Committee to assert firm procedural control and to prevent what they consider GOP obstructionism, the minority Republicans are frequently at a substantial disadvantage and often in a state of frustration.[25]

No Senate committee has scheduling powers comparable to those of the House Rules Committee. In the Senate, the majority leader schedules legislation, most of it through a unanimous consent procedure in which the floor leader asks members of the Senate for unanimous consent to bring a bill up for floor action. If there is an objection to this request, a motion to the same effect requiring majority approval is needed. This is harder than it appears because individual senators wishing to block a bill can engage in prolonged debate—a **filibuster**—to prevent a bill from being considered. Breaking a filibuster is difficult, however, because an extraordinary three-fifths majority of the Senate membership (sixty votes) is required under Senate rules to invoke **cloture**—or to cut off debate. As a result, individual senators have the power—if they wish to use it—to delay Senate consideration of legislation, to gain assurances that the majority leader's **unanimous consent agreement** will enable them to offer certain amendments to a bill, or to wring concessions from a bill's proponents by objecting or reserving the right to object

24. For a thorough look at the use of special rules to influence the outcome of House decisions, see Stanley Bach and Steven S. Smith, *Managing Uncertainty in the House of Representatives: Adaption and Innovation in Special Rules* (Washington, D.C.: Brookings, 1988).

25. See the comments of former Rep. Dick Cheney (R-Wyo.) in "An Unruly House: A Republican View," *Public Opinion*, January/February 1989, 41–44.

to unanimous consent requests. This means that the majority party leadership does not control the Senate's schedule as firmly as is the case in the House. Rather, the leader must constantly cope with senators whose individualism is backed up by Senate rules. As Senate majority leader George Mitchell observed, "We have 100 equal Senators. I am constantly reminded of the limitations on my authority on a daily basis."[26]

Floor Consideration
of Legislation

Floor consideration of legislation in the House proceeds in accordance with the rule proposed by the Rules Committee and adopted by the full House. This means that there is a fixed time limit on debate, and procedures are frequently in place to give an advantage to the majority party leaders.

House rules permit members to speak for only five minutes when debating an amendment, apt to be the most important floor action on a bill. Floor amendments give the House an opportunity to work its will on legislation as reported from standing committees. Proposing amendments also provides even junior members with an opportunity to influence the content of bills not handled by their committees and to gain national visibility. For example, Rep. Henry Hyde (R-Ill.), as a freshman member of the House, began his fight against public funding of abortions by offering his now-famous "Hyde amendments" to a variety of funding bills.

Amendments take many forms. *Sweetener amendments* make legislation more attractive to members by, for example, providing for construction of dams, highways, and airports, and other grants to various congressional districts. *Saving amendments* are compromises that, if adopted, enhance the prospects for passage of a bill. By contrast, *killer amendments* deliberately strengthen a bill too much and turn a majority against it. For example, adoption of an amendment to include primary elections in a bill providing public funding of congressional campaigns would be likely to kill the legislation because House members from safe one-party districts oppose any measure that would assist party challengers.[27]

As a general rule, the House tends to accept committee legislation involving technical issues, minor modifications of existing government programs, and issues without strong partisan and ideological

26. Quoted by Robin Toner, "Beset by Critics Hungry for a Dynamic Leader, Dogged Mitchell Lashes Back," *New York Times*, Oct. 17, 1989, 9Y, National edition.
27. Oleszek, *Congressional Procedures*, 162.

overtones. Any issues arising in such legislation are usually resolved in committee before they reach the House floor. But highly visible, partisan, ideological issues—such as military action in the Persian Gulf, savings and loan bailouts, funding of abortions, MX missiles, taxes, minimum wage rates, federal budget priorities—tend to be fought out on the floor.

While the House extends considerable deference to the decisions of its committees when acting on legislation, the Senate is more reluctant to do so, preferring instead to resolve issues on the floor. Operating under rules that permit wide latitude to individual members, senators freely offer floor amendments to bills that did not originate in committees on which they serve.

A further difference between the chambers is the degree to which the majority or minority is advantaged by procedural rules. Under House procedures, which utilize rules proposed by the Rules Committee, the majority is in control and the minority's ability to engage in lengthy delaying tactics is severely limited. In the Senate, the situation is just the reverse. As former Democratic leader Robert Byrd (D-W.Va.) noted: "[Senate rules] were meant to favor the minority and prevent the majority from running over the minority. That is why there is a Senate. That is why this Senate ought to remain a Senate and not become a second House of Representatives."[28]

The principal reason for the minority's strong position in the Senate is the chamber's cloture rule requiring sixty votes to bring speechmaking to an involuntary end. Since it is frequently difficult to muster the votes necessary to invoke cloture, the filibuster can be used to block passage of a bill or to force concessions from a bill's proponents, especially toward the end of a session when little time for consideration of bills is available. Once, filibusters were primarily used by conservative southern Democrats to block civil rights bills. In 1957, for example, Sen. Strom Thurmond (R-S.C.), then a Democrat, set the Senate filibuster record by holding the floor for twenty-four hours and eighteen minutes. Today, filibusters are used by liberals and conservatives against a wide range of bills about which they feel strongly. In a chamber in which the two parties have been so closely divided during the 1980s and 1990s, it has been particularly difficult for the majority party leaders to muster the votes necessary to cut off debate. Minority party filibusters or threats of filibusters have then resulted in the majority party making concessions to the minority or the death of legislation. In 1987, for example, the Re-

28. Quoted by Oleszek, ibid., 286.

Using Floor Amendments to Build Majorities (AKA Softening Up the Membership)

Time's congressional correspondent Neil MacNeil provided the following account of how the amending process is used to build support for legislation in the House of Representatives.

[In attempting] to pass a farm bill, Harold Cooley of North Carolina, chairman of the Agriculture Committee and floor manager of the bill, desperately and openly bargained for votes for the bill by accepting amendments, and he made no pretense at hiding his intent. . . . At one point, William Avery of Kansas challenged Cooley to explain why he was willing to accept a particular amendment. Cooley answered candidly. "The membership probably might be softened up by this amendment," Cooley replied.

Avery was startled. "What was that?" he asked. "Will the gentleman restate that?"

Cooley began to reply. "Do you want me to tell you the truth?" he asked. Cooley, however, did not get the chance to explain. Frank Chelf of Kentucky, one of the Representatives who had demanded the amendment, interrupted him. "It is because he needs fellows like me to vote for the bill," Chelf said bluntly. "That is why. I cannot vote for it unless you adopt this amendment."

"That," said Avery, having made his point, "clears that up."

Source: Neil MacNeil, *Forge of Democracy: The House of Representatives* (New York: David McKay, 1963), 346-347.

Flanked by their staffs, Senate Agriculture Committee members meet in a conference committee with their House counterparts to hammer out a compromise agreement on the 1990 farm bill.

publicans were able to scuttle a bill to overhaul campaign finance laws after the Democratic leadership failed seven times to get the Senate to invoke cloture against a GOP filibuster.

Resolving House-Senate Differences: The Conference Committee

Normally, a bill passes the House and Senate in different forms. For a bill to become law, however, it must pass both chambers in identical form. The task of reconciliation is usually left to a joint House-Senate conference committee.

Conference committees are composed of representatives and senators appointed by the presiding officers of the House and Senate. The conferees' jobs are to hammer out a compromise between the House and Senate versions of a bill. Conference committee members are usually selected from among the senior members of the committee in each chamber that had initial jurisdiction over the legislation. As a result, the impact of the congressional committee system is felt strongly not just in the initial consideration of a bill but also in the critical final stages of the legislative process.

Conference committees are arenas of hard bargaining and negotiations between representatives of the two chambers, perhaps leading to substantial rewriting of the House and Senate versions of a bill. In conference, both proponents and opponents of legislation have another chance to influence the legislative product. A majority of both House and Senate conferees must agree to any compromises that are worked out in conference.

If a conference committee succeeds in resolving House-Senate differences on a bill, the compromise legislation still needs full House and Senate approval. In both the House and Senate, conference committee reports are considered privileged legislation and are quickly scheduled for floor action. When both chambers have approved the conference committee bill, it is sent to the president for either a signature or veto.

The Congressional Labyrinth

The tortuous path bills must travel to become law demonstrates that the congressional process is not geared to speedy action. Much more is needed to pass legislation than a majority on the House and Senate floors; majorities are required at each stage in the process—in the subcommittee, full committee, and House Rules Committee; on the floor; and in the conference committee. At each stage, a small band of representatives or senators can either delay, severely weaken, or even kill a bill. To muster the votes necessary to move a bill to the next stage in the process, it is normally necessary to bargain, negotiate, and compromise—all of which will probably substantially change the legislation. As a result, the bills that emerge from Congress are seldom as strong as their original supporters had envisioned, nor are they as objectionable as their opponents had initially feared. Enacted legislation reflects the price that had to be paid to gain approval at each stage in the process.

Critics complain that congressional processes make prompt, decisive action difficult. Indeed, because it is so difficult to navigate this process, those advocating policy changes normally operate at a disadvantage and the defenders of the status quo happily relish their advantage. Defenders of the congressional policy-making process make no boasts about the system's efficiency. They argue instead that Congress, because of its procedures and fragmented power, effectively compromises competing interests and resolves differences. The products that emerge from Congress may be less bold and decisive than some might wish, but congressional bargaining and compromising usually result in laws that are widely accepted by the public and competing interests in society.

*The Congressional
Budget Process*

Until the mid-1970s, Congress dealt with budgetary issues through a series of separate bills—over a dozen measures that appropriated money from the Treasury and several that raised revenues. This fragmentation of budgetary decisions meant that Congress seldom had to confront the overall fiscal consequences of its actions. Indeed, Congress was encouraged to indulge in its preference for spending money over raising taxes, a problem further complicated by the growth of entitlement programs in the 1960s and 1970s. These programs—such as Social Security, food stamps, and Medicare—transfer funds to individuals who qualify for, or are entitled to, federal payments.

As federal budget deficits mounted in the late 1960s and early 1970s, President Richard Nixon criticized Congress for overspending and then *impounded* (refused to spend) congressionally appropriated funds. In response, Congress enacted in 1974 the Budget and Impoundment Control Act. This act created procedures under which Congress could fix overall federal spending and revenue levels and review and rescind presidential impoundments. In addition, two new standing committees were created—the House and Senate Budget committees—together with the Congressional Budget Office, designed to provide technical expertise to Congress as it deliberated on the budget. To keep track of its revenues and expenditures, the federal government has established a twelve-month period known as a **fiscal year** (FY). Under the 1974 budget act, the government's fiscal year begins on October 1.

As federal budget deficits ballooned in the 1980s and early 1990s, budget legislation took center stage and dominated congressional decision making. In 1990, for example, congressional leaders and the president were involved in extended and often intense maneuvering, recriminations, negotiations, and bargaining from spring through October before an agreement on budget legislation was reached. In the process, President George Bush was forced to go back on his campaign pledge of "No new taxes" as Congress and the president wrangled over issues of tax rates for the middle class and wealthy and spending priorities for military and domestic programs.

In taking the first step in the budget process, the president submits budget recommendations to Congress in early February for the following fiscal year. The Budget committees in each chamber then draw up their own budget resolutions, specifying overall government spending, revenue, and debt levels. These budget resolutions also break down spending among functional areas of government activity (for example, defense, health, and income security). The full House and Senate are required to pass one agreed-on budget resolution by April 15. Once passed, the budget resolution guides Congress as it acts on separate appropriations and other measures that provide the actual authority for spending on federal programs.

To impose tighter fiscal discipline on this process, Congress enacted in late 1985 the Gramm-Rudman-Hollings law (usually referred to simply as Gramm-Rudman), sponsored by Senators Phil Gramm (R-Texas), Warren Rudman (R-N.H.), and Ernest Hollings (D-S.C.). This bill was designed to force the president and Congress to arrive at spending and taxing decisions that would steadily reduce the budget deficit to zero by 1991. Gramm-Rudman's most publicized provision specified that if deficit-reduction targets in the law were not met, automatic budget cuts were to go into effect (so-called **sequestration**). Gramm-Rudman did not succeed in bringing the budget deficit down to zero because 70 percent of federal expenditures were exempt from its sequester provisions, a number of political difficulties were involved in either reducing spending or raising taxes, and periodic adjustments were required in the law's provisions. One of the consequences of the prolonged struggle over the budget for FY 1991, however, was an overhaul of the Gramm-Rudman law. The FY 1991 budget law called for caps on future spending and for sequestration to go into effect if Congress exceeded those spending limits.

As the failed history of Gramm-Rudman and the prolonged maneuvering over the budget for FY 1991 have shown, Congress has a long way to go to make the budget process work effectively. Delays in meeting deadlines have been common, and budgetary gimmickry, including accounting tricks (sometimes called "smoke and mirrors"), have been used to meet budget targets. Setting budgetary priorities in a period of huge federal budget deficits has meant that finding money to expand existing programs or to create new ones (for example, for day care or a war on drugs) requires either cutting existing programs or raising taxes. Neither alternative is appealing to elected officials. Further complicating the difficult task of passing a federal budget has been the inevitable partisan maneuvering created by having a Republican president and a Democratic Congress—each with different spending priorities. For all its problems, however, the new congressional budget process has forced Congress to deal with fiscal issues in a way that it never did in the past—from a total federal budget perspective.

An additional consequence of the new congressional budget process has been the introduction of an element of centralization into congressional decision making. The budget resolutions rank among the most important pieces of legislation passed each year because they affect the levels of spending on virtually all federal programs and activities. As a result, those representatives and senators in a position to have a say on the content of these critical measures have seen their influence enhanced. Among the major beneficiaries have been the members of the House and Senate Budget committees. But at the same time, because budget resolutions impose limits on how much money other standing committees can propose for programs within their jurisdictions, the influence of the standing committees has been severely restricted. Party leaders also have gained influence through the new budget process because budget resolutions normally involve major battles on the floors of the House and Senate. At the floor consideration stage of the legislative struggle, party leaders often are in a position to exert substantial influence on the process.

Congress and the Web of American Policy Making

Old Washington hands find that Congress is one of the best vantage points from which to watch and gain insights into American politics. Many of the strands of the political system come together on Capitol Hill. Representatives and senators are sensitive to the shifting tides of public opinion because their survival depends on being able to spot those shifts. The White House and its occupants are part of the view from the Capitol as well. In fact, information flows constantly between "the Hill" and "downtown." The reputations of presidents, their top aides, and agency heads "are made and broken on Capitol Hill."[29] Finally, there is even a back channel of information that flows between the career civil servants in the various executive agencies and members of Congress and their staffs. Anyone tapping into this channel will better understand the workings of the executive agencies.

Congress is at the center of this political universe, but its role has shifted over time. During some periods, it has clearly dominated policy making—such as the post-Civil War era when the Radical Republicans were riding high in Congress, the post-World War I period of Normalcy in the 1920s, and Gerald Ford's post-Watergate administration in the mid-1970s. But there also have been times when Congress has been completely dominated by popular presidents whose agendas coincided with the public's desire for a change of policy—during the first years of Franklin Roosevelt's New Deal in the 1930s, Lyndon Johnson's Great Society days in the mid-1960s, and Ronald Reagan's one-year honeymoon with Congress in 1981.

29. Broder, *Behind the Front Page,* 209.

At other times, the balance of power between the branches has been shared more evenly—as during the presidencies of Dwight Eisenhower, John Kennedy, and George Bush. As these examples suggest, Congress's role in policy making has been one of neither steady decline nor ascendancy.

But whether dominant, dominated, or coequal, Congress brings to the policy-making process a special perspective: that of its constituency. Electoral realities create incentives for members of Congress to look at issues from the perspectives of the voters who sent them to Washington. Members understand that the cloak of statesmanship cannot be worn by those defeated and out of office. Ever mindful of this, politicians over the years have made sure that Congress conducts its business in ways that enhance their chances for reelection. Through their personal staffs, members maintain contact with their constituents; committees permit members to shape the policies important to their constituencies and interest groups active in election campaigns; and the party organizations in Congress are tolerant of their members' needs to deviate periodically from the party position on an issue in order to maintain electoral support back home.

Reelection is never far from the minds of this nation's representatives and senators, especially when they pursue other goals such as advancing the national interest and maintaining a strong, independent Congress. To be sure, excessive attention to reelection can undermine Congress's capacity as an institution to maintain its influence and to make responsible decisions. It is hardly surprising, then, that Congress is constantly trying to strike a balance between actions that meet the reelection needs of its members and the need to maintain the decision-making capacity of the institution.[30] But all this being said, members' reelection goals have a significant impact on congressional policy making.[31] For example:

- Congress tends to shape legislation in a way that distributes its benefits widely among the congressional districts and states. In other words, Congress likes bills in which nearly every member's constituency wins and few folks lose. Wrapping bills up in this kind of package, of course, helps build congressional majorities for legisla-

30. For insightful consideration of the tension between members' reelection needs and the needs of Congress as an institution, see Gary C. Jacobson, *The Politics of Congressional Elections*, 3d ed. (Glenview, Ill.: Harper Collins, 1992), chap. 7.

31. The following list of policy consequences flowing from Congress's electoral connection is taken from David R. Mayhew, *Congress: The Electoral Connection* (New Haven, Conn.: Yale University Press, 1974), chap. 2.

tion, but it may result in watered-down legislation that fails to target the areas in greatest need of federal action.

• When issues create clear losers and winners (bills that do not distribute benefits widely), Congress tends to service those interests that are well organized and have electoral clout.

• When the alternative policies available to Congress all involve unpleasant consequences for constituents (taxes) and interest groups (cuts in services or tighter regulation), Congress tends to delay action for as long as possible. One example of this that stands head and shoulders above others is Congress's difficulty in coming to terms with the huge federal budget deficit.

• Symbolic action is common because the public frequently responds to righteous position taking, even when it has little practical impact.

These tendencies in congressional policy making have provoked criticism of the institution, yet they are the natural consequences of an electoral and party system with which most Americans feel comfortable. Americans want their senators and representatives to be responsive to and dependent on their constituencies and citizens' concerns. They prefer weak parties incapable of controlling nominations and disciplining dissident legislators. Their admiration normally goes out to those independent-minded politicians who do not follow the party line once elected. Congress's approach to national issues, therefore, is not likely to change unless Americans also change their preferences about the nature of the electoral process and party system.

But is Congress's approach to policy making as harmful as it appears at first blush? The institution's defenders readily admit to the policy-making tendencies just identified. They would argue that Congress also should be judged by such considerations as its capacity to (1) compromise societal conflicts; (2) reflect the concerns of a diverse people; (3) protect the interests of specific persons, communities, and interests; and (4) act as a check on presidential power. Judged by these criteria, Congress's performance is cast in a more favorable light.

Given its reelection orientation, its often local perspective, and its fragmented power structure, Congress does find it difficult to approach societal problems from a truly national perspective and to develop genuinely comprehensive and coherent policies. To a considerable degree, however, the national orientation and the comprehensive, coherent approach to policy making that Congress finds so difficult to achieve may be found in the presidency and executive branch. Under the American constitutional system, Congress and the executive must share policy-making responsibility. In the process, they tend to counterbalance each other's approaches to decision making.

For Review

1. To reflect shifts in population, seats in the House are reapportioned among the states after every decennial census. Since the 1960s, this process has caused a major shift of seats from the Northeast and Midwest to the Sun Belt states. Under the Supreme Court's "one person, one vote" rule, every congressional district must be as equal in population as possible. To meet this judicially mandated standard, state legislatures must redraw (redistrict) congressional district lines after every census. The redistricting process inevitably involves maneuvering for partisan advantage.

2. Because senators and representatives are ultimately responsible for their own electoral survival, they develop their own campaign organizations to run their candidate-centered campaigns. A prominent pattern in congressional elections: incumbents win.

3. The functions of Congress within the political system extend beyond lawmaking to include oversight of administration, public education, and representation.

4. Committees are major and specialized power centers within Congress that frame legislation for consideration by the full House and Senate. Committees have the power to block and delay legislation as well as the power to develop and refine bills. The committee and subcommittee systems tend to decentralize power within Congress. Committee chairmen are still chosen primarily on the basis of seniority, but they must now be more responsive to their party colleagues because they are elected to their posts.

5. Congress is organized on a partisan basis, and party affiliation is a major predictor of how members will vote. The political parties in Congress exhibit different policy and ideological orientations on roll-call votes. Party leaders in Congress have limited formal powers and must rely heavily on more informal, collegial techniques.

6. The lengthy, complex legislative process of Congress requires building majorities at each stage. As a result, proponents of legislation must often bargain and compromise to secure its passage.

7. Because of the huge federal budget deficit, the budget process has assumed a central position in congressional decision making. The congressional budget process tends to centralize decision making and strengthen the role of party leaders.

For Further Reading

Congressional Directory. An invaluable official directory of Congress containing biographical information, statistical data, and listings of committees, congressional staff, and executive officials.

Congressional Quarterly publishes a series of periodicals and volumes of authoritative and up-to-date information on the Congress: *Congressional Quarterly Weekly Report,* a newsletter of congressional and national politics; *Congressional Quarterly Almanac,* an annual compendium of data on congressional activities; *Guide to Congress,* a complete reference guide to the Congress; and *Politics in America,* a reference guide to the individual members of Congress—their constituencies, backgrounds, electoral histories, and voting records.

Dodd, Lawrence C., and Bruce I. Oppenheimer, eds. *Congress Reconsidered.* 4th ed. Washington, D.C.: CQ Press, 1989. An up-to-date and insightful series of essays on various aspects of congressional life—elections, committees, parties, and policy making—by leading scholars.

Fenno, Richard F., Jr. *Home Style: House Members in Their Districts.* Boston: Little, Brown, 1978. An analysis by the preeminent congressional scholar of House members in their constituencies and how "home style" affects members' behavior in Washington.

Jacobson, Gary C. *The Politics of Congressional Elections.* 3d ed. Glenview, Ill.: Harper Collins, 1992. The most complete analysis of congressional elections available.

Mayhew, David R. *Congress: The Electoral Connection.* New Haven, Conn.: Yale University Press, 1974. An extremely insightful examination of how legislators' reelection sights affect the organization and functioning of Congress.

Oleszek, Walter J. *Congressional Procedures and the Policy Process.* 3d ed. Washington, D.C.: CQ Press, 1989. A guide to congressional procedures and legislative strategies.

Ornstein, Norman J., Thomas E. Mann, and Michael J. Malbin, eds. *Vital Statistics on Congress, 1989–1990.* Washington, D.C.: CQ Press, 1989. A compendium of statistics on major aspects of Congress (such as elections, staffing, committees, parties, workload, and activities) as well as interpretive essays. This publication is updated every two years.

Polsby, Nelson W. *Congress and the Presidency.* 4th ed. Englewood Cliffs, N.J.: Prentice-Hall, 1986. A perceptive analysis of the distribution of power within the House and Senate along with consideration of the budget process and congressional-presidential relations.

Smith, Steven S., and Christopher J. Deering. *Committees in Congress.* 2d ed. Washington, D.C.: CQ Press, 1990. An analysis of the committee system which takes into account the changes of the 1970s.

II. The Presidency

As the nation's most prominent and powerful political leader, the president can take actions that have profound consequences. Examples abound: Abraham Lincoln's decisions to defend the Union and free the slaves; Franklin Roosevelt's use of federal government resources to combat the depression; Harry Truman's commitment to containment of post-World War II Soviet expansionism; Lyndon Johnson's support of civil rights legislation as well as his escalation of the war in Vietnam; Ronald Reagan's efforts to scale back the role of government; and George Bush's decision to use military force against Iraq after its invasion of Kuwait.

Unlike members of the House and Senate, the president is known countrywide and is, in fact, a national symbol. This visibility is a potent tool when the president needs the public's support. Preeminence, however, carries risks. Americans have high expectations of their presidents. The chief executive is expected to maintain prosperity, hold inflation in check, and protect American interests in world affairs. Presidents whose governing performances are found wanting in these areas are apt to be rejected at the polls as were Gerald Ford (1976) and Jimmy Carter (1980), and those viewed as relatively successful are reelected—Franklin Roosevelt (three times!), Dwight Eisenhower, and Ronald Reagan found themselves happily in this category.

Because presidents have different goals, party affiliations, personalities, political allies, and styles of leadership, the presidency will always have a highly personal dimension. But the presidency has an often impersonal side to it as well: the many layers of bureaucracy surrounding the occupant of the Oval Office. This chapter examines the role of the president in American politics, the powers and organizational structure of the office, and the relationships between the president and the White House staff, the public, the media, Congress, and the executive branch.

The President and the Constitution

The nature and powers of the presidency were among the most difficult problems confronting the writers of the Constitution. Most were convinced of the need for stronger executive leadership because of their post-Revolution experiences under the Articles of Confederation with all-powerful legislatures and weak governors at

BORN TO COMMAND.

OF VETO MEMORY.

HAD I BEEN CONSULTED.

KING ANDREW THE FIRST.

By vetoing bills simply because he had policy disagreements with Congress, President Andrew Jackson set a critical precedent that strengthened the presidency. His opponents depicted him as a tyrant, as in this 1832 cartoon, trampling on the Constitution, a ledger of Court decisions, and the watchwords virtue, liberty, *and* independence.

the state level and with a national government that had no chief executive. But at the same time, with the memory of arbitrary rule by colonial governors and the British Crown still fresh in their minds, they did not want to create a monarchical regime or conditions conducive to executive abuse of power. One of the foremost advocates of a strengthened executive was Alexander Hamilton, who believed that "energy in the executive" was a "leading character in the definition of good government" (*Federalist* No. 70). A majority of the delegates to the Constitutional Convention, including James Madison, also favored a strengthened executive to prevent congressional abuses of power, but they wanted the president's power to be circumscribed by checks and balances.

Checks and Balances with an Ambiguous Grant of Power

Convention delegates solved the problem of presidential power by fashioning a constitutional arrangement that both checked presidential power and yet left room for the expansion of presidential power if need be. Under the separation of powers and checks and balances system, presidents are required to share with the Congress power over taxing, spending, war making, and appointments within the executive branch. The president cannot govern without Congress, and governmental action requires executive-legislative cooperation.

A second element in the constitutional arrangement devised by the Founders was the broad and somewhat ambiguous language used to list presidential powers. This language imposed few specific limitations, and it ensured that the executive would have sufficient power to cope with future contingencies. Thus, Article II of the Constitution states that "the executive Power shall be vested in a President. . . . The President shall be Commander in Chief of the Army and the Navy. . . . [H]e shall take Care that the Laws be faithfully executed."

These constitutional phrases have been subjected to sweeping interpretations that have vastly expanded the legal basis for the exercise of presidential power. The president's position as commander in chief of the military, for example, has been used as a constitutional justification for sending American forces into action abroad without a formal declaration of war by Congress. And the president's command of the military, along with the power to execute the laws faithfully, has provided legal authority for the use of federal troops and marshals to enforce the integration of public schools, quell domestic disorders, and maintain such government services as mail delivery.

The Founders' formula of shared power with the other branches and presidential grants of authority stated in broad, ambiguous language guaranteed that over the years the issue of presidential power would remain the subject of periodic squabbling as future presidents interpreted and tested the limits of their powers and succeeding generations evaluated the office in light of their own experiences. From the 1930s to the 1950s, most scholars and commentators believed the president needed additional power to move the nation out of the depression, win World War II, fight the Cold War, and advance social justice at home.[1] By the mid-1960s and 1970s, however, presidential decisions to intervene in the Vietnam conflict and revelations of abuses of power at home had created fears that a dangerous "imperial presidency" was emerging.[2] Those fears eased in the 1980s, although the issue of presidential power continued to rest on the front burner as President Reagan ordered an invasion of the Caribbean island of Grenada and an air attack on Libya in retaliation for alleged Libyan support of terrorists. The issue of whether the president could initiate a major military action without a congressional declaration of war gained new urgency in August 1990 when President Bush vowed that Iraq's conquest of Kuwait would not go unchallenged. This controversy was temporarily resolved, but not finally settled, when Congress voted in early 1991 to authorize military action to enforce United Nations resolutions calling for Iraq to withdraw from Kuwait.

The Constitution imposes only minimal restrictions on who can serve as president. The president must be thirty-five years of age, a native-born citizen, and a resident of the United States for at least fourteen years. The informal requirements for the office, however, are much more demanding. The president must be capable of winning a Republican or Democratic national convention nomination by contesting primaries and caucuses across the nation. This requirement tends to limit the field of potential presidential candidates to the holders of high elective office—senators, governors, or vice presidents—or to people with national prominence such as Gen. Dwight Eisenhower, the commander of Allied Forces in Europe during World War II.

1. See Thomas E. Cronin, *The State of the Presidency,* 2d ed. (Boston: Little, Brown, 1980), chap. 3.
2. See Arthur M. Schlesinger, Jr., *The Imperial Presidency* (Boston: Houghton Mifflin, 1989); George Reedy, *The Twilight of the Presidency* (New York: New American Library, 1970); and Cronin, *State of the Presidency.*

To date, all presidents have been white males, and, with the exception of John Kennedy, all have been Protestants. Most were born into relatively prosperous families and were well educated. Many practiced law before entering politics.[3]

While certain social characteristics do tend to dominate the backgrounds of presidents, these social backgrounds are not prerequisites for becoming president. Six presidents—Andrew Johnson, James Garfield, Herbert Hoover, Dwight Eisenhower, Richard Nixon, and Ronald Reagan—emerged from working-class families. Hoover was an engineer, Carter a peanut farmer, and Reagan an actor. Truman never attended college. The backgrounds of recent presidents differ from those of their predecessors. For example, the only president to practice law from Truman through Bush was Nixon. And, as members of such traditionally disadvantaged groups as blacks, women, and descendants of immigrants from eastern and southern Europe, Latin America, and Asia rise through the political ranks, the backgrounds of presidents will change even more.

Presidential Succession and Disability

The Constitution provides that the vice president shall serve as president if the president dies, resigns, is impeached and convicted, or is unable to discharge the duties of the office. The succession of vice presidents to the presidency has gone smoothly in the eight instances that it has occurred because of death or resignation.

A more difficult problem is presidential disability. The Twenty-fifth Amendment provides that the vice president shall become *acting president* if (1) the president informs Congress in writing that he or she is incapable of performing the duties of the office, or (2) the vice president and a majority of the cabinet, or another body created by Congress, decide that the president is unable to discharge his or her duties. The president may reassume office by a written declaration to Congress that no inability exists, unless the vice president and a majority of the cabinet or other body believe that the president is still unable to perform the duties of that office. In the latter instance, the vice president would continue as acting president if backed by a two-thirds vote of both houses of Congress.

Since it was ratified in 1967, the disability provisions of the Twenty-fifth Amendment have never been formally invoked, although there were two instances of presidential hospitalization dur-

3. The social backgrounds of presidents are summarized by Richard A. Watson and Norman C. Thomas, *The Politics of the Presidency,* 2d ed. (Washington, D.C.: CQ Press, 1988), 125–133.

ing the Reagan administration. In 1981, President Reagan was wounded in an assassination attempt and was rushed into surgery. White House aides monitored events, and Vice President Bush hurried back to the White House from a speaking engagement. The president, however, recovered quickly, and the amendment was not invoked. In 1985, when Reagan underwent cancer surgery, he transferred power temporarily (for eight hours) to Bush but without invoking the amendment.

The Twenty-fifth Amendment also provides for filling a vacancy in the office of vice president through presidential nomination, confirmed by a majority vote in both houses of Congress. This provision has been invoked twice: first, in 1973 when President Nixon nominated Gerald Ford to replace Vice President Spiro Agnew, who had resigned amid scandal, and again a year later when New York governor Nelson Rockefeller was appointed vice president by Ford, who had moved up to the presidency following Nixon's resignation.

Impeachment

Because of their worries about possible executive abuse of power, the writers of the Constitution included an **impeachment** clause as the ultimate congressional check on the president. For the removal of a president from office to occur through impeachment, he must be (1) charged by the House of Representatives with "Treason, Bribery, or other high Crimes and Misdemeanors," (2) then tried before the Senate with the chief justice of the Supreme Court presiding, and (3) convicted by a two-thirds vote of the Senate. No president has ever been removed from office in this manner, but in two instances impeachment proceedings were advanced in Congress. In 1868, impeachment charges were voted against Andrew Johnson by the House, but he was not convicted by the Senate. In 1974, following a 1972 break-in at the Democratic National Committee's Watergate headquarters and subsequent presidential complicity in a coverup of the affair, impeachment proceedings were begun in the House against President Richard Nixon. But before the full House could bring impeachment charges against him, Nixon resigned. He is the only president ever to be forced from office by impeachment proceedings initiated in the House of Representatives.

The Evolution of the Presidency

The modern presidency is the product of an evolutionary process in which the power advantage has shifted periodically between

Line of Succession

On March 30, 1981, President Ronald Reagan was shot by assassin John Hinckley outside a Washington hotel and rushed to an area hospital for surgery. In the meantime, Vice President George Bush was on a plane returning to Washington from Texas. Presidential aides and cabinet members gathered at the White House, where questions arose among them and the press corps about who was "in charge."[1] Secretary of State Alexander M. Haig, Jr., rushed to the press briefing room and, before an audience of reporters and live television cameras, said, "As of now, I am in control here in the White House, pending the return of the vice president.... Constitutionally, gentlemen, you have the president, the vice president, and the secretary of state."

Haig was, as many gleeful critics subsequently pointed out, wrong. The Constitution says nothing about who follows the vice president in the line of succession. The Succession Act of 1947 (later modified to reflect the creation of new departments) established which congressional leaders and heads of the departments (in the order the departments were created) would fill the line of succession that follows the vice president.

The line of succession is:

- vice president
- Speaker of the House of Representatives
- president pro tempore of the Senate
- secretary of state
- secretary of the Treasury
- secretary of defense
- attorney general
- secretary of the interior
- secretary of agriculture
- secretary of commerce
- secretary of labor
- secretary of health and human services
- secretary of housing and urban development
- secretary of transportation
- secretary of energy
- secretary of education
- secretary of veterans affairs

1. "Confusion over Who Was in Charge Arose Following Reagan Shooting," *Wall Street Journal*, April 1, 1981.

the president and Congress. The long-term trend, however, has been toward a stronger, more influential presidency.

Washington, Jackson, and the Pre-Civil War Presidents

As the nation's first president, George Washington (1789–1797) made a major contribution to the office by establishing the legitimacy of the presidency. He lent his prestige to the position, kept the powers and trappings of the office modest, and sought to stay above the fray of political conflict. Washington cast but two **vetoes** and then only because he believed the legislation to be unconstitutional. His relations with Congress were correct but somewhat distant as Congress asserted its independence. When in 1789 he went to the Senate in person for "advice and consent" on a treaty, he was rebuffed in an embarrassing incident in which senators made it clear that they preferred to consider treaties in private.

The presidency of Andrew Jackson (1829–1837) shifted the balance of power between the president and Congress toward the president. He took a more expansive view of his powers than did his predecessors, and he did not shrink from open sparring with Congress. His twelve vetoes were more than all those of his predecessors, and he used them not only against bills he considered unconstitutional but also against those he viewed as just bad policy. Because of his personal popularity with the expanding electorate, none of his vetoes was overridden. Jackson provided a glimpse into the future of the presidency by demonstrating the power potential of a president capable of generating broad public support.

After the Jackson administration and through the pre-Civil War period, the government wrestled unsuccessfully with the problems of slavery and sectional rivalries. The pre-Civil War era was a period of congressional dominance and little-known presidents—Zachary Taylor, Millard Fillmore, Franklin Pierce, and James Buchanan. It was not until the crisis of the Civil War that a president acted in a manner that significantly expanded the powers of the office.

Lincoln and Congressional Government after the Civil War

After a divisive election campaign in 1860, Abraham Lincoln (1861–1865) assumed office in the midst of a secession crisis. He then used the broad language of the Constitution designating him commander in chief and charging him to "take Care that the Laws be faithfully executed" to justify a series of unprecedented actions to suppress the Confederate rebellion. Among other things, Lincoln activated state militia, suspended the writ of *habeas corpus* (a court

President Abraham Lincoln, as commander in chief, was deeply involved in Civil War battlefield strategy and occasionally issued direct orders to his generals regarding troop movements. Here he confers with Gen. George McClellan after the battle of Antietam.

order directing an official holding a person in custody to show cause for his or her detention) in militarily insecure areas, blockaded southern ports, spent appropriations for unauthorized purposes, and issued the Emancipation Proclamation without congressional approval. The Supreme Court failed to overturn any of these actions and set a precedent for supporting presidential actions in time of war.[4]

Lincoln's post-Civil War successors were dominated by an assertive Congress that imposed Reconstruction on the South and dominated American politics for the balance of the nineteenth century. The basic character of American government in the latter part of the century was captured in Woodrow Wilson's phrase "congressional government."[5] Except for the presidencies of Theodore Roosevelt (1901–1909) and Woodrow Wilson (1913–1921), congressional dominance of the federal government continued into this century. Both Roosevelt and Wilson used the high visibility of the presidency to mobilize public support for their policies. They also sought to lead Congress by developing legislative programs and pressing aggressively for their adoption. Congressional government, however,

4. Ibid., 459.
5. Woodrow Wilson, *Congressional Government* (New York: Meridian Books, 1956), originally published in 1885.

reestablished itself in the 1920s and continued until national emergencies—the depression of the 1930s and the world war that followed—combined with the actions of Franklin Roosevelt to transform and enlarge the powers of the office.

The Modern Presidency

The modern presidency really begins with that of Franklin Roosevelt (1933–1945). His administration formulated and aggressively pressed for congressional approval of massive government programs to cope with the depression and turn the economy around. As the Jacksonian experience had foretold, a president capable of garnering public support can in turn use that support to successfully wring concessions out of a reluctant Congress. In winning public support, Roosevelt was a master with his buoyant and optimistic manner, flare for the dramatic, and communications skills (the first president to effectively use radio to appeal to the public).

And like Lincoln before him, Roosevelt freely used his powers as commander in chief and the nation's chief diplomat. For example, in spite of strong isolationist sentiment in Congress, he provided U.S. support for the Allies before America's entry into World War II. In one such instance, through an **executive agreement**, which did not have to be ratified by the Senate, he traded fifty over-age destroyers to Britain in return for a lease to British bases in the Caribbean, Bermuda, and Newfoundland. After the United States entered the war, Roosevelt continued to use his war powers freely to direct the war effort at home and negotiate strategy and postwar occupation arrangements with the Allies.

Roosevelt's successors have continued to take an expansive view of the president's war powers and have committed American troops to combat—Truman in Korea, Johnson and Nixon in Vietnam, Carter in Iran (an unsuccessful attempt to rescue American hostages), Reagan in Grenada and in an air strike against Libya, Bush in Panama and the Persian Gulf—all without declarations of war. Much of the growth of presidential power has been accomplished with congressional support or acquiescence, as during the depression of the 1930s and World War II. Indeed, Congress has periodically delegated to the president politically difficult decisions such as the authority to implement wage and price controls or ration petroleum.

The relationship between the president and Congress has not, however, been one of steady presidential aggrandizement. Just as the strong Lincoln presidency was followed by an era of "congressional government," continued assertions of presidential power in the 1960s and 1970s brought a congressional reaction. Johnson's and

Nixon's use of their war powers to prosecute the war in Vietnam, Nixon's attempt to restrict or close down social programs by impounding (refusing to spend) congressionally appropriated funds, and the Watergate scandal resulted in Congress asserting its might through a series of measures designed to limit presidential power. One of the most important was the **War Powers Resolution of 1973.** This act requires the president to notify Congress promptly of the use of military forces abroad and to terminate military action if congressional approval is not given within sixty days. Congress is authorized to terminate military action through House and Senate passage of a resolution. Presidents have consistently asserted, however, that the War Powers Resolution is unconstitutional. A second important measure was the *Budget and Impoundment Control Act of 1974.* According to this act, congressional approval of presidential impoundments must be obtained within forty-five days or the impoundment is rescinded. If the president tries to defer congressionally approved expenditures, these deferrals can be overruled by Congress. In addition, Congress strengthened its own capacity to handle budget issues by creating specialized budget committees in both chambers and a Congressional Budget Office.

After a period of diminished presidential influence during the Ford and Carter administrations, the Reagan presidency (1981–1989) seemed to signal a shift in the balance of power back toward the president. Reagan engineered a major shift in government policy in 1981 by gaining congressional approval of a program of tax cuts, reduced growth in domestic spending, and a military buildup. Reagan also demonstrated that it was possible for a president to circumvent the provisions of the War Powers Resolution and commit American troops to action without gaining congressional approval. Perhaps most important, President Reagan, like Franklin Roosevelt, was able to make his policy agenda the basis for American political discourse. He showed that it was possible for the American people to entertain a more modest view of what the government should do.[6] And unlike his immediate predecessors—Johnson, Nixon, Ford, and Carter—he was able to win reelection, serve two complete terms, and leave office with a high level of public support.

Why Have Presidents Become So Influential?

As this brief historical survey has shown, the broad, general language of the Constitution has permitted presidents, frequently with

6. James W. Ceaser, "The Reagan Presidency and American Public Opinion," in *The Reagan Legacy: Promise and Performance,* ed. Charles O. Jones (Chatham, N.J.: Chatham House, 1988), 206.

judicial approval and congressional support or acquiescence, to establish precedents that have expanded the powers of their office. The language of the Constitution by itself, however, does not explain why these grants of authority have been used to parlay the presidency into such a prominent position in the American system. A combination of historical and institutional forces provides at least a partial explanation.[7]

As America has emerged as an economic, political, and military superpower, the scope of presidential responsibilities and influence has grown. The president's power to recognize foreign governments by sending and receiving ambassadors, to negotiate treaties and agreements with foreign governments, and to command the army and navy place the presidency in a preeminent position to determine the nation's foreign policy. The president can, for example, suspend diplomatic relations with a hostile country, as Carter did with Iran after the 1979 seizure of the U.S. embassy, or open relations with a former enemy, as Nixon did in 1972 with China; make agreements with foreign nations, as Roosevelt did with the Allied powers regarding the occupation of Germany at the end of World War II; negotiate arms control treaties with the Soviet Union, as Reagan did in the 1980s for medium-range missiles; and mobilize and lead an alliance of nations in war, as Bush did in 1991 against Iraq. In a world that has been shrunk by technological advances and economic interdependence, the public expects and constitutional powers provide the means for the president to act to protect the prosperity, tranquillity, and safety of the United States.

The president's potential for influence also has grown as the responsibilities of the federal government have expanded since the New Deal era of the 1930s. The long arm of the federal government has now stretched to managing the economy, protecting the environment, and providing for the public's health, welfare, and safety—all requiring, of course, a bigger, more powerful executive branch with the president at its head. As we will see later in this chapter, controlling the massive bureaucracy of the executive branch is difficult for all presidents. But through presidential appointments of cabinet and subcabinet officers and overall budget and policy decisions, the president can substantially influence executive agency decisions. Whether enforcement of environmental protection, antitrust, or an-

7. For a concise and insightful consideration of the historical and institutional bases for the expanded role of the president, see Nelson W. Polsby, *Congress and the Presidency,* 4th ed. (Englewood Cliffs, N.J.: Prentice-Hall, 1986), 15–17.

tidiscrimination statutes is vigorous or lax, for example, often depends on the policies adopted by the president.

Yet another basis for increased presidential influence is the changed relationship between the president and the media. In the early days of the Republic, the media did not adhere to the professional norms of objectivity now associated with good journalism. The press was openly partisan, and the president was given coverage heavily laced with vituperation and name-calling. Today, however, in a period of more responsible and objective journalism, the media expect the president to play a less partisan or more impartial role as "a kind of guardian of national morale, a focus for affectionate emotions, an animate symbol of American sovereignty."[8] Presidents have found that by donning this mantle of nonpartisanship fashioned for them by the press, they appear to be above politics. This is of great value when trying to win the support of a public suspicious of political parties and politicians.

George Bush, like presidents before him, has also benefited from coverage of his every move—from chowing down with U.S. soldiers stationed in Saudi Arabia during the Persian Gulf War to cart-side interviews during a round of golf in Kennebunkport, Maine. No one can compete with the president when it comes to news coverage. Presidential news coverage is intense, automatic, and instantaneous. First radio and now television have made it possible to forge direct links between the president and the American people, and by skillful manipulation of this coverage, the president can gain political leverage. Often this involves mixing pictures of the president as family member (playing with grandchildren and the family dog) and as ceremonial head of state (greeting foreign leaders) with the White House presentation of domestic and foreign policy initiatives.

The Presidential Establishment

The president is expected to play many roles—head of state, commander in chief, manager of the economy, legislative leader, chief diplomat, head administrator, and world leader. Although the presidency combines all these roles in one person, the president is not a factotum—these jobs are too much for just one person. Recognizing this, the Committee on Administrative Management appointed by Franklin Roosevelt concluded in 1936 that "the president needs help." Thus, in 1939 the Executive Office of the President

8. Ibid., 16.

(EOP) was created to supply this help. Originally, the EOP was composed of the White House staff (the immediate assistants to the president) and the Bureau of the Budget (now called the Office of Management and Budget—OMB), a budget-making and review agency. Since then, as the responsibilities of the federal government and the president have burgeoned, the EOP has grown into a large bureaucracy with over fifteen hundred employees[9] molded by individual presidents to suit their own particular style of leadership. The flow of influence between the president and EOP, however, is reciprocal. Not only does the president affect the functioning of the EOP, but this bureaucracy exerts a powerful influence on presidential decision making.

The White House Staff

Because members of the White House staff are the president's closest associates, more often than not they have been chosen for their posts because of their personal loyalty to the president. Former campaign aides and supporters are no exceptions; they frequently occupy White House offices. Former New Hampshire governor John Sununu, for example, committed his personal prestige and campaign organization to supporting candidate George Bush in the critical New Hampshire primary in 1988. Bush rewarded him by making him his chief of staff.

Because of their proximity, both personally and spatially, to the president, senior White House staff personnel are among the most powerful figures in the government. They are quite literally the president's eyes and ears, arms and legs—providing the information on which presidential decisions will be made; evaluating policy proposals submitted by cabinet secretaries; monitoring the activities of the executive branch; controlling access to the president; and maintaining liaison with Congress, interest groups, party leaders, and the media. Among the most important White House staff members are the chief of staff, national security adviser, press secretary, communications advisers and speechwriters, legal counsel, domestic policy adviser, chairman of the Council of Economic Advisers, and special assistants to handle relations with Congress, interest groups, the party organization, and state and local government officials.

In any organization there is a constant contest for influence. At the White House, this struggle is particularly intense because so

9. For an account of the development of the Executive Office of the President, see John Hart, *The Presidential Branch* (New York: Pergamon Press, 1987), 1–132.

The Old Executive Office Building

Once characterized by President Harry Truman as "the greatest monstrosity in America," the Old Executive Office Building, adjacent to the West Wing of the White House, is filled to capacity with aides to the president. It stands today not only as a monument of French Second Empire architecture that was saved from the wrecker's ball by First Lady Jacqueline Kennedy, but also as a monument to the growth of the president's staff. Before World War II, this building was called the State, War, and Navy Building and housed the modern-day equivalents of the Departments of Defense and State. Today, however, it is not even large enough to hold all the aides to the president, who constitute the Executive Office of the President.

Eleanor Roosevelt

The First Lady:
A Demanding Public and Political Role

The president's spouse is better known than members of Congress, cabinet officers, and often even the vice president. The modern first lady's roles have been varied and demanding—White House manager and hostess, political activist, and supporter of social causes on behalf of the administration. Yet she has held no official position—the Constitution does not mention her—and she has earned no salary. Her responsibilities have been so central to the functioning of the modern presidency, however, that she has operated with a permanent staff that has included a chief of staff, scheduling director, personal assistant, projects director, correspondence director, advance arrangements personnel, and three press secretaries.

The early first ladies were not expected to play any political role at all. Their official responsibilities were restricted to acting as hostesses at White House functions. But, as the nation's attitudes toward women in public life changed and the mass media made presidents' wives celebrities, the public and political dimensions of their jobs expanded.

The increasing attention of the media, changing attitudes toward women's roles, and the development of the first lady's office came together with *Eleanor Roosevelt,* who from 1933 to 1945 redefined the role of the first lady. She was constantly in motion—visiting the rural poor, miners, soldiers, hospitals, and New Deal social program sites. To an unprecedented degree, she was active politically, openly pushing for an end to racial segregation and equality for women and drawing attention to the plight of the slum dwellers, the unemployed, and World War I veterans without pensions. She scrutinized New Deal programs and offered suggestions when possible. In an effort to push her programs, she frequently pressured the president (some-

times to such an extent that he would leave the room), and her political clout was thought to be extensive. By the time she left the White House, the role of the first lady had changed drastically. She established it as something separate from the presidency and, with her outspokenness, activity, and visibility, made it independent from, although linked to, the Oval Office. Mrs. Roosevelt also changed public expectations. After her, the public would begin to look for an active woman in the White House. The days of the passive, retiring first lady were gone for good.

Young, cosmopolitan *Jacqueline Kennedy* (1961–1963) brought even greater visibility and a touch of glamour to the position. Not interested in politics, she focused on art and culture, bringing historical antiques to the White House and entertaining with a style that included opera and classical music.

Lady Bird Johnson (1963–1969), unlike Jacqueline Kennedy, was interested in politics and used her position to press for policy goals about which she cared deeply. She traveled the country supporting her beautification program and personally lobbied Congress in behalf of the Highway Beautification Act of 1965. She also was an active campaigner for her husband and an unofficial presidential aide whom White House staffers frequently used as a channel to influence the president.

The somewhat liberal views of *Betty Ford* (1974–1977) on social issues supplemented the more traditional ones of her moderately conservative spouse, and she was active in a variety of social causes. She became perhaps the most visible spokesperson for women's rights and the Equal Rights Amendment. Among the most candid of the first ladies, Betty Ford was willing to discuss such controversial issues as abortion, premarital sex, and even personal problems including her bout with breast cancer.

Rosalynn Carter (1977–1981) was distinguished by her political involvement. She testified before a congressional committee to promote mental health legislation, sat in on cabinet meetings, met heads of state as her husband's representative, and held regular working luncheons with the president. As essentially an equal partner in her husband's presidency, she functioned effectively as a presidential adviser, and her influence with the president was openly acknowledged by both. It has been argued that she took the position further than the public was willing to see it go.

Nancy Reagan (1981–1989) was much less public in her political involvement, but her behind-the-scenes influence was extensive. Reportedly, she played a leading role in cashiering Chief of Staff Donald Regan and in pressing the president to move forward on an arms control agreement with the Soviet Union. She was interested in restoring elegance to the White House, and she adopted as a social cause the fight against drug abuse.

Barbara Bush (1989–) is also considered an important behind-the-scenes influence in the White House. She campaigned actively for her husband's election and has undertaken a campaign to promote literacy.

much is at stake—billion-dollar policies that affect the lives of millions of people, personal careers, ideological principles, and personalities. White House personnel have been described as "young, highly intelligent, . . . unashamedly on the make,"[10] hard driving, and highly skilled in bureaucratic infighting. As Bradley Patterson, a former White House staffer, has observed, "Policy differences, piled on top of personality clashes, multiplied by time pressures, and heated by sometimes vindictive news leaks, can add up to an incandescent plasma of high-voltage conflict."[11]

What ultimately matters in the White House is whether one has access to the president or to the people who have that access. Symbols of access and status are particularly important—such as one's position on the organizational chart, an office (however small and windowless) in the West Wing of the White House rather than next door in the Old Executive Office Building, or luncheon privileges in the White House Mess, which is nestled in the West Wing basement. At the White House, the struggle for influence and power never stops.

Each president has organized the White House staff somewhat differently to serve his interests as he defined them. Presidents Franklin Roosevelt, John Kennedy, and Lyndon Johnson operated with a relatively loose organizational structure that permitted a number of key aides and cabinet officers to have regular access to the president. In this way, these presidents were privy to information from a variety of sources and perspectives when weighing their various policy options. By contrast, Presidents Eisenhower, Nixon, Reagan, and now Bush preferred a more hierarchical staff arrangement with a chief of staff in charge of running the White House. Former top presidential aides largely agree that the White House functions best under a chief of staff system if the organizational needs of the presidency are to be met. These include using the president's time efficiently, achieving orderly and careful consideration of policy options, and having the administration speak with a reasonably united voice. Gerald Ford, who inherited a highly centralized staff structure from President Nixon, has observed:

I initially felt that what I perceived as the Johnson organization was preferable, with seven or eight different people within the White House reporting directly to the President. But I must say, that after six months I did find that a President needs one person who at least coordinates people such as the President's assistant for national security affairs, head of the Domestic [Pol-

10. Patrick Anderson, *The President's Men* (New York: Doubleday, 1969), 469.
11. Bradley Patterson, "The Buck Still Stops at 1600 Pennsylvania Avenue," *Washingtonian,* December 1980, 205.

The Bush White House:
Who's Down the Hall from the President?

Source: Diagram by Jo Ellen Murphy, *Washington Post*, Jan. 23, 1989, A17, national edition. Copyright © 1989 by the *Washington Post*. Reprinted by permission.
  Note: Diagram is schematic and not to scale.

icy] Council, and the Economic Policy Board, et cetera. Somebody had to organize the day's schedule and the flow of paperwork.[12]

Ford's successor, Jimmy Carter, came to a similar conclusion. Midway through his term he abandoned a collegial organizational structure in which staff members were supposed to work as a team and installed fellow Georgian Hamilton Jordan as chief of staff.

Responsible for the president's schedule, as well as for controlling access to the Oval Office and the flow of information to the president, the chief of staff is in a position to exercise tremendous influence. This has been demonstrated by President Bush's strong-willed and often combative chief of staff, John Sununu. When someone like Reagan chief of staff James Baker (later President Bush's secretary of state), an experienced and skilled politician and a knowledgeable Washington insider, is at the helm of the White House organization, the likelihood of a forward-moving, successful administration is enhanced. But when the position is occupied by a less experienced and less skillful person, the chances for presidential embarrassment increase.

The weighty responsibilities that fall upon the chief of staff were noted by the so-called Tower Commission (for former senator John Tower, R-Texas), which investigated White House operations during the Iran-contra affair of the mid-1980s. In this affair, presidential aides made unauthorized arms sales to Iran in an attempt to gain release of American hostages in Lebanon. Profits from these sales were then illegally diverted to support contra rebels fighting the Sandinista government of Nicaragua. In addition to criticizing Reagan for his detached leadership style and noting the errors in judgment of senior administration officials, the commission laid much of the blame for this fiasco on the shoulders of President Reagan's chief of staff, Donald Regan. Regan was faulted for failing to insist that prescribed, orderly policy-making processes be followed in the White House.

Although the president requires extensive staff assistance to perform the duties of the office, serious problems have developed as the size and power of the White House staff have grown. Indeed, maintaining control over the large presidential bureaucracy has become a presidential-size headache. Too solicitous a staff can cut the president off from reality—from hearing unpleasant news and critical assessments of the administration. Overly zealous, inexperienced, or

12. *A Discussion with Gerald Ford: The American Presidency* (Washington, D.C.: American Enterprise Institute, 1977), 4.

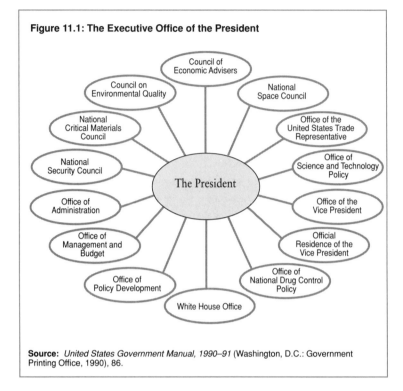

Figure 11.1: The Executive Office of the President

Source: *United States Government Manual, 1990–91* (Washington, D.C.: Government Printing Office, 1990), 86.

misguided White House aides may act without full presidential approval or in ways that contradict established policy and even violate the law.

The Iran-contra affair is a clear example of White House staff exceeding their authority and acting in ways contrary to established policy. It also illustrates how a president's personal style (in this case, a detached management style) can magnify the difficulties of controlling the White House bureaucracy. The net result of this incident was a major foreign policy embarrassment for the United States and damage to the president's standing at home.

An efficient and politically sensitive White House staff is therefore an essential ingredient in any president's success. But keeping these unelected, often intensely committed, ambitious, and powerful officials under the presidential thumb is one of the continuing problems of the American presidential system.

The Executive Office of
the President

The White House staff is but a part of the much larger presidential bureaucracy, the Executive Office of the President (Figure 11.1). The agencies making up EOP provide the president with specialized information and help coordinate government policy related to the budget, the economy, trade, drug abuse, science and technology, and the environment. The Office of Management and Budget, National Security Council staff, the Office of Economic and Domestic Policy, and the Council of Economic Advisers are the main units of EOP.

The large (approximately six hundred employees), politically sensitive, and highly professional *Office of Management and Budget (OMB)* is primarily responsible for preparing the federal budget. Federal agencies submit their budget requests to OMB, which reviews them—often making substantial cuts—and then in accord with presidential guidelines puts together a composite budget for the entire government. The president reviews the OMB budget before submitting the administration's final budget recommendations to Congress. All requests by federal agencies for money from Congress must go through a central clearance process at OMB. Since the budget constitutes a comprehensive statement of administration policy and a means of exerting control over the far-flung executive branch, OMB is one of the most important power centers in any administration.

The role of OMB has been heightened in recent years. The omnipresent massive budget deficit has forced Washington decision makers, whether in the executive branch or in Congress, to heed the budgetary implications of their decisions. As the president, cabinet officers, and Congress seek to make decisions while swimming in this sea of budgetary red ink, the director of OMB has become the key policy maker and administration strategist in negotiations with Congress.

The *National Security Council (NSC)* is a cabinet-like body composed by statute of the president, vice president, and secretaries of state and defense, with the chairman of the Joint Chiefs of Staff and director of the Central Intelligence Agency as statutory advisers. This body makes formal decisions about foreign and military affairs—such as the 1991 decision to go to war in the Persian Gulf. The NSC staff of approximately sixty persons is headed by the national security adviser to the president, a position filled by Brent Scowcroft in the Bush administration. The staff operates as a kind of miniature State/Defense department within the White House, providing information to the president and helping coordinate national security policy. Because of their daily contact with the president, national security advisers have exerted a weighty influence on foreign policy. This was particularly true during the administration of Richard Nixon, who used his NSC adviser, Henry Kissinger, rather than the State Department to conduct foreign policy.

The domestic policy counterpart to the NSC staff is the *Office of Economic and Domestic Policy*. It helps the president develop domestic policy proposals, evaluates recommendations for cabinet departments, and assists in the coordination of administration policy.

Because the actions of the government have such profound consequences for the economy (and because voters tend to hold the president accountable for the state of the economy), the president needs the expert economic advice provided by the *Council of Economic Advisers (CEA)*. The CEA consists of three professional economists and a small staff. Economic advisers are not always popular within the White House because what they consider sound economic policies may be viewed as politically damaging. For example, Martin Feldstein, President Reagan's CEA chairman and a Harvard professor, resigned his post after his advisory role was diminished because he insisted on warning publicly about the consequences of the budget deficit.

The Cabinet

By tradition, the cabinet is composed of the heads of the major departments of the executive branch. Since Dwight Eisenhower's administration, presidents at their discretion have elevated other senior members of their administrations to cabinet rank. President Bush, for example, included in his cabinet White House Chief of Staff John Sununu, OMB Director Richard Darman, and U.S. Trade Representative Carla Hills.

Cabinet officers are chosen for a variety of reasons: to provide subject matter expertise and administrative competence, to build support among diverse elements of the president's party and electoral coalition, to win the backing of key interest groups, and to achieve geographic, racial, gender, and religious representation. As a result, a cabinet is unlikely to be composed of people with close personal ties to the president. It is not then surprising that presidents rarely use cabinet meetings to make important decisions. Also working against use of the cabinet as a decision-making mechanism is the tendency of the White House to view departmental secretaries as representatives of their departments' bureaucracies and clienteles (interests served by the departments) and not necessarily as advocates of the president's priorities (a phenomenon called "going native").

As administrators responsible for government programs in such specific areas as defense, health, education, veterans' affairs, or transportation, cabinet secretaries are not well equipped to give advice outside their agencies' fields of jurisdiction. Presidents, then, tend not to work with the cabinet as a group but with individual department secretaries or groups of cabinet officers responsible for related areas of policy. President Bush, for example, places heavy reliance on his secretary of state, James Baker, with whom he has a close working relationship.

Bush has tended to give substantial leeway to his cabinet officers in developing major policy initiatives—such as Treasury Secretary Nicholas Brady's plan for dealing with Third World debt. Over the long term, however, the White House staff has gained influence at the expense of cabinet officers.[13] Members of the cabinet labor under a number of disadvantages: (1) they lack the proximity and relatively easy access to the Oval Office enjoyed by senior White House staff; (2) some had little or no contact with the president before being appointed; and (3) they are subject to the pressures exerted by the departmental bureaucracies, clientele groups, and congressional committees with which they must work. White House staff operate from a uniquely presidential perspective.

Recent presidents, especially since the Kennedy administration, have expanded the policy advisory and executive branch monitoring responsibilities of their White House staffs. But this expanded role has frequently produced policy conflicts and power rivalries between department heads and presidential aides. The Nixon administration in particular was characterized by White House staff-cabinet friction because Nixon employed his staff to keep an unusually tight rein on cabinet officers (the president's role as chief executive and the president's relations with the executive branch departments and the federal bureaucracy are considered in more detail in Chapter 12, The Federal Bureaucracy).[14]

The Vice President

Of the forty men who have served as president, nine succeeded to the office while serving as vice president (see Table 11.1). Despite the fairly strong odds of a vice president becoming president, the vice presidency has been the object of ridicule since its inception. The nation's first holder of the office, John Adams, described it as "the most insignificant office that ever the invention of man con-

13. For a survey of how recent presidents have utilized and sought to control their cabinet officers, see James P. Pfiffner, *The Strategic Presidency: Hitting the Ground Running* (Chicago: Dorsey Press, 1988), 41–67.

14. An informative account of cabinet-White House relations during the Nixon and Reagan administrations is contained in Richard Nathan, *The Administrative Presidency* (New York: Wiley, 1983).

Table 11.1 The Vice Presidency as a Steppingstone to the Presidency, 1789–1990

Total number of presidents		40
Total number of vice presidents		43
Vice presidents who have become president		13
Upon death of the president	8	
Upon resignation of the president	1	
Elected after serving as vice president	4	
Vice presidents who ran unsuccessfully for president because they		8
Failed to gain party nomination	4	
Were nominated by a major party but defeated in general election	3	
Were nominated by a third party but defeated in general election	1	

SOURCE: *Guide to U.S. Elections,* 2d ed. (Washington, D.C.: Congressional Quarterly, 1985), 252, 383.

trived or his imagination conceived." In the 1930s, the delightful musical comedy *Of Thee I Sing* had as one of its characters Vice President Throttlebottom, an inept political hack who took tours of the Capitol along with the tourists. Adams's frustration and that of his successors reflect the fact that the role of a vice president in any administration is largely determined by the president.

Since vice-presidential candidates normally have been selected with an eye toward strengthening a party's presidential ticket, vice presidents have seldom been close associates of the president. Indeed, often they have been the president's opponents for the nomination or members of a different party faction and treated with indifference or largely ignored by the president. As vice president, Harry Truman saw President Franklin Roosevelt mainly at ceremonial affairs. Thus, when he was forced to assume the presidency upon Roosevelt's death, he was not fully informed about the conduct of World War II, including the existence of the atomic bomb and postwar planning.

Because of this experience, Truman and his successors have tried to keep their vice presidents well informed. Two recent vice presidents, Walter Mondale and George Bush, played more active roles than their predecessors—advising the president, taking on special administrative assignments to develop and coordinate policies, acting as presidential emissaries to foreign governments, and serving as the point men in rebutting administration critics. Even though the vice presidency grew in stature under Mondale and Bush, it is still the president who determines the role of the vice president, and it would be an exaggeration to say that any vice president, including Bush's own, Dan Quayle, has yet achieved the status of being the number two person in the White House in terms of influence.

The Importance of One Individual

Governmental institutions are affected by the basic beliefs, personalities, and skills of the people who run them. This is particularly true of the executive branch, which is headed by one individual, the president. The chief executive's actions count for more in our system than do those of anyone else. Since every president is a unique individual, there are as many ways of being president as there are presidents. Each president, therefore, shapes the presidency in accord with a personal theory of how the office should function. The Washington community in turn adapts its operations to the president's personality and style of operation.

The President's Basic Political Beliefs

Presidential behavior is affected by a variety of forces, but probably none is more important than the basic political beliefs of the person behind the desk in the Oval Office. Herbert Hoover's opposition to relief programs during the Great Depression, for example, was based on his belief that such government programs were inconsistent with a free-enterprise economy and constitutional principles. His successor, Franklin Roosevelt, saw government's responsibilities quite differently and initiated a massive expansion of the federal government's role in regulating the economy and providing social services. Domestic social welfare programs were augmented significantly in the 1960s because of the prodding of President Lyndon Johnson, an FDR protegé, who also believed in an activist government. More recently, Ronald Reagan's conservative ideology had a major impact on government policy as he pressed for lower taxes, increased military expenditures, and restraints on domestic spending. George Bush's less ideological approach has meant that his administration's policy thrust is less focused than his predecessor's. Since presidents' "world views" affect their behavior in office, it behooves voters to listen carefully to presidential candidates for indications of just what their beliefs are.

Presidents' views on how government policy making should be conducted also can profoundly affect their behavior in office.[15] Pres-

15. For a discussion of how a president's conception of the president's and Con-

ident Jimmy Carter, who had never served in the federal government before his election, had experiences with the Georgia legislature that left him apprehensive about legislative politics. He believed that presidents had a responsibility to analyze problems carefully and develop policies designed to meet societal needs. Congress should then accept those policies because they had been developed with the best interests of the country in mind. But what he saw up on Capitol Hill—Congress's tendencies to cater to special interests, to make decisions based on electoral considerations, and to compromise—made him reluctant to negotiate and bargain with members of Congress to gain approval of his policies. Not surprisingly, this approach to relations with an institution that thrives on representation and identification with special interests was largely unsuccessful.[16]

President Richard Nixon also questioned Congress's competence to make major policy decisions. Moreover, he questioned its legitimacy because in his mind the president was the only true representative of all the American people. Thus being the president, he was accountable to his electoral majority, not to Congress. Nixon then sought to run the government without Congress by impounding funds, deferring spending, and shifting money from one purpose to another. By contrast, Presidents Johnson and Ford, who had served as party leaders in Congress, as well as President Bush, an experienced Washington insider, readily accepted sharing power with Congress and were comfortable in bargaining directly with its members.

Presidential Character

According to presidential scholar James David Barber, presidential character is of prime importance in explaining the behavior of presidents. In his research, Barber analyzed two features of presidential character: (1) whether presidents were "active" or "passive" (invested a lot or little energy in political activity), and (2) whether they were "positive" or "negative" (enjoyed their activities or engaged in them out of sense of compulsion and obligation). Barber believes that these character traits develop early in childhood and can be identified before an individual is elected president. Using Nixon and Johnson as examples, Barber warns against "active-

gress's role in policy making affected the presidency of Jimmy Carter, see Charles O. Jones, *The Trusteeship Presidency: Jimmy Carter and the United States Congress* (Baton Rouge: Louisiana State University Press, 1988). Also see his analysis of Carter and Nixon in "Congress and the Presidency," in *The New Congress,* ed. Thomas E. Mann and Norman J. Ornstein (Washington, D.C.: American Enterprise Institute, 1981), 223–249.

16. Charles O. Jones, "Carter and Congress: From the Outside In," *British Journal of Political Science* 15 (July 1985): 271.

negative" politicians taking on the presidency. They are, he believes, driven personalities—"ambitious, striving upward, and power-seeking"—apt to behave too aggressively and to view the world with which they must deal as excessively hostile.[17]

Although few presidential observers would dispute that character has an impact on presidential behavior, many scholars are less confident than Barber that enough is known about political psychology to predict how presidential candidates will act once in office. Indeed, Barber's predictions about the types of presidents that Ford, Carter, and Reagan would become have been shown to be of doubtful validity by students of the presidency. In addition, if Barber's preference for "active-positive" character types had been used as a criterion for determining who was fit to serve as president, the list of eligibles would have not included the often moody and depressed Abraham Lincoln. There is also the possibility that a person's character may change while in the White House.[18]

Leadership Skills and the Power to Persuade

In his classic study of the presidency, Richard Neustadt argued that the president is too often portrayed as a person possessed of great formal authority—the power to command. Presidents, however, do not govern the nation by command;[19] the Constitution requires that they share power, particularly with Congress. Moreover, to achieve their goals, presidents have to persuade others to support their policies. Some of the powers presidents do have can act as significant bargaining chips when dealing with other politicians. When played skillfully, these chips can advance presidential causes. Presidents are in a position, for example, to affect the careers and goals of most political leaders in the United States. Presidents draw up the budget, exercise significant (though not complete) control over the vast executive branch, make appointments to the executive and courts, and enjoy special advantages in appealing to the public.

President Lyndon Johnson's hard-nosed approach to bargaining with opponents was legendary. When seeking congressional support for Medicare, he once told a senator that he understood the senator's problems with Medicare but that much worse might befall him if he

17. James David Barber, *Presidential Character*, 3d ed. (Englewood Cliffs, N.J.: Prentice-Hall, 1985), 9.
18. For a concise discussion of presidential character and a critique of the Barber theory, see Michael Nelson, "The Psychological Presidency," in *The Presidency and the Political System*, 3d ed., ed. Michael Nelson (Washington, D.C.: CQ Press, 1990), 189–212; and Watson and Thomas, *Politics of the Presidency*, 495–500.
19. See Richard E. Neustadt, *Presidential Power* (New York: Free Press, 1990).

did not see things the president's way. At White House state dinners, cooperative senators like Republican minority leader Everett Dirksen (Ill.) were seated at the head table with the president and visiting heads of state, but those who opposed the president, including fellow Democrats, were assigned to side tables or were not invited at all. And when vexed by an Idaho senator's opposition to his Vietnam policy, Johnson remarked, "The next time Frank Church wants a dam, let him build it."[20]

Ronald Reagan favored a subtler approach. A southern Democrat has described how he succumbed to Reagan's persuasion in the Oval Office:

I wasn't there more than a couple of minutes, but I didn't feel rushed and I'm not quite sure how I was shown the door. A photographer shot the usual roll of pictures; the president gave me a firm, friendly handshake. He patted me on the back and told me how much he needed and appreciated my support. He said I should call if I need help on anything. And that was it.

The same representative painted quite a different picture of President Carter's method of Oval Office persuasion with members of Congress:

I came in with other members to discuss a bill we were working on in committee. We had hardly got seated and Carter started lecturing us about the problems he had with one of the sections of the bill. He knew the details better than most of us, but somehow that caused more resentment than if he had left the specifics to us.[21]

The ability of presidents to persuade other political leaders to back their policies is not exclusively a matter of interpersonal skills or manipulation of presidential favors. Presidents also need a reputation for political competence and for an ability to use their powers skillfully and willingly. Such a reputation will cause representatives, senators, governors, cabinet officers, senior civil servants, and foreign diplomats to sit up and take notice of the advantages of working with the president and the potential adverse consequences of not cooperating. Finally, presidents who can create and sustain popular support will find warmer receptions when they begin courting members of Congress for their votes (a subject covered more thoroughly later in this chapter).

20. Quoted by George C. Edwards, III, *Presidential Influence in Congress* (San Francisco: Freeman, 1980), 140.
21. Quoted by Allen Schick, "How the Budget Was Won and Lost," in *The President and Congress: Assessing Reagan's First Year,* ed. Norman J. Ornstein (Washington, D.C.: American Enterprise Institute, 1982), 23–24.

Most studies of the presidency have stressed the impact of individual presidents on the presidency and how they have used the office to achieve their goals. But influence can flow in the other direction as well; the presidency can leave its mark on the occupant of the Oval Office.

The problems, crises, powers, responsibilities, and deference that go along with the office can transform its occupants in different ways. Harry Truman, for example, changed from a quiet, unassuming senator into a confident, forceful, farsighted executive. Lyndon Johnson and Richard Nixon isolated themselves and adopted a bunker mentality when faced with mounting criticisms of their policies and leadership styles. As president, Gerald Ford, a former House minority leader from Michigan, shed much of his midwestern conservatism, adapted easily to international diplomacy, and demonstrated unusual skill in restoring public confidence in the integrity of the presidency. And George Bush, who was criticized for being excessively passive as vice president, demonstrated forcefulness and determination in seeking to roll back Iraq's 1990 invasion of Kuwait.

Reporters and commentators watch every move a president makes and assess its significance, even to the extent of questioning competence because a president bumps his head on the doorway to *Air Force One* (Ford) or fails to show emotion when commenting on the dismantling of the Berlin Wall (Bush). The psychological strain that this incessant coverage, commentary, and criticism imposes on a president is considerable and helps explain the defensiveness and obsession with press leaks that frequently characterize the White House when things are not going well for the president.

Close observers of the presidency have expressed fears about the royal court-type environment in which presidents often must operate—deferential aides anxious to please and ease presidential burdens, high levels of public respect for the office, and isolation from ordinary citizens and the political hurly-burly of give-and-take with peers. Indeed, because presidents have no real peers or equals in the American system, some believe they are in danger of losing touch with reality, too enamored with their own importance and power, and apt to make imprudent decisions. President Johnson's press secretary, George Reedy, observed:

The atmosphere of the White House is a heady one . . . calculated to instill in any man a sense of destiny. He literally walks in the footsteps of hallowed figures—of Jefferson, of Jackson, of Lincoln. The almost sanctified relics of the distant, semimythical past surround him as ordinary household objects to be used by his family. From the moment he entered the halls he is made aware that he has become enshrined in a pantheon of semidivine mortals who have shaken the world, and that he has taken from their hands the heritage of American dreams and aspirations.[22]

Such an atmosphere not only may cause the pursuit of unwise policies, but also may help explain the periodic escapades of White House personnel that go beyond the law.

The President and the Public

The ability of presidents to lead the nation depends heavily on their standing with the American public. An important ingredient of presidential efforts to stir up the support of members of Congress and other political leaders for administration policies is popular support from the American people. The public's steady backing, however, is not something on which presidents can rely. Over the course of an administration, there are peaks and valleys of public support, and, unfortunately for most presidents, the trend is normally downward. Popular support, which cannot be turned up on command, is affected by international and domestic conditions and events often beyond the president's capacity to control.

The Shifting Tides of Presidential Popularity

Presidential popularity is generally measured in public opinion surveys by asking voters for a job approval rating. The Gallup poll periodically asks: "Do you approve of the way _____ is handling his job as president?" The percentage of respondents approving of the president's performance is used as a measure of presidential support or popularity.

Most administrations begin with a "honeymoon" period; the public shows its goodwill toward the president and a willingness to give the new leader a chance. In this relatively noncritical environment, high public expectations envelop the president. Also early in their terms, presidents benefit from not yet having made any controversial decisions that cost them support.

The media generally adopt a similar stance toward the new administration. Reporters refrain from sharp criticism and provide abundant human interest-type coverage of the new White House residents. Thus, Millie, the Bush family dog, generated more television

22. George E. Reedy, *The Twilight of the Presidency* (New York: Mentor Books, 1970), 27.

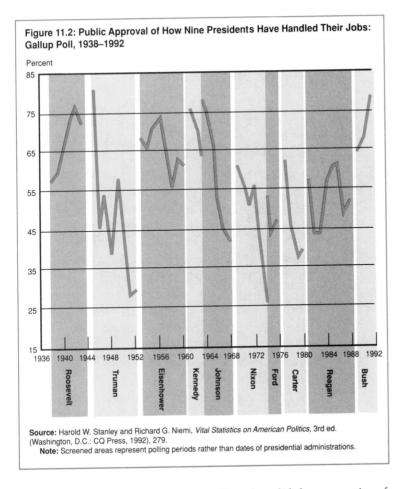

Figure 11.2: Public Approval of How Nine Presidents Have Handled Their Jobs:
Gallup Poll, 1938–1992

Source: Harold W. Stanley and Richard G. Niemi, *Vital Statistics on American Politics,* 3rd ed.
(Washington, D.C.: CQ Press, 1992), 279.
Note: Screened areas represent polling periods rather than dates of presidential administrations.

stories in 1989, Bush's first year in office, than did the secretaries of
education, agriculture, or veterans affairs.[23]

But this honeymoon atmosphere does not last. Presidents Truman, Johnson, Nixon, Ford, and Carter all left office substantially
less popular than when they entered (Figure 11.2). But Reagan did
not suffer as dramatic a fall in public support as his predecessors;
indeed, he showed remarkable recuperative powers from adverse
economic conditions and foreign policy setbacks. Nevertheless, his
administration experienced an overall downward trend in public
support (see Figure 11.2).

The problems with which the president must deal—budget and
trade deficits, drug abuse, terrorism, uncooperative foreign governments—are not ones that will show improvement overnight. Most,

23. Ann Devroy, "Bush Less a TV President than Reagan, Study Shows," *Washington Post,* Dec. 16, 1989, A2.

Rallying 'Round the President

Reagan 68% Johnson 80% Kennedy 83% Roosevelt 84% Truman 87% Bush 89%

Major military events, glorious or ig-nominious, have often propelled pres-idents to their peaks in popular ap-proval. The Persian Gulf victory lifted George Bush to an 89 percent approval rating in the Gallup poll released March 5, 1991, the highest rating since Gallup began measuring presidential approval in 1938. Shown here are the personal highs in the Gallup survey for those presidents who have reached 80 per-cent approval, as well as the high mark for Bush's predecessor, Ronald Reagan.

George Bush (89%), March 1991. After liberation of Kuwait in Persian Gulf War.
Harry Truman (87%), May-June 1945. After surrender of Nazi Germany.
Franklin Roosevelt (84%), January 1942. After Japanese attack on Pearl Harbor.
John Kennedy (83%), April-May 1961. After abortive Bay of Pigs invasion.
Lyndon Johnson (80%), January 1964. In aftermath of the Kennedy assassina-tion.
Ronald Reagan (68%), May 1981. After assassination attempt. Reagan dupli-cated this peak in May 1986.

Source: *Congressional Quarterly Weekly Report*, March 9, 1991, 585.

in fact, have proven to be relatively intractable. When solutions to such problems are not forthcoming, high public expectations go un-fulfilled, and some voters are alienated by the controversial decisions that presidents inevitably must make. President Gerald Ford, for ex-ample, took office in 1974 with substantial public support after the prolonged period of divisiveness and the Watergate scandal that had caused President Nixon's job rating to plummet (see Figure 11.2). But after his pardon of former president Nixon, Ford's popular sup-port went into a nose dive, and an extended period of presidential-congressional wrangling ensued.

The news media tend to file a higher proportion of critical stories as an administration ages. Although news organizations do produce more favorable than unfavorable stories about presidents, a content analysis of media coverage between 1953 and 1978 showed that fa-vorable stories declined by more than 20 percent from the first to last years of the Eisenhower, Truman, and Nixon administrations. At the same time, the percentage of unfavorable stories increased nearly 10 percent for Eisenhower and Johnson and 30 percent for Nixon.[24]

Because people usually hold the president responsible for the state of the Union, presidential popularity is closely linked with the well-being of the economy. America's economic problems in the late 1970s eroded President Jimmy Carter's popularity and played a crit-ical role in his reelection defeat in 1980. After defeating Carter, Ron-ald Reagan saw his public support also fall victim to a sagging economy between 1981 and 1983. By the midterm elections of 1982, his approval rating for that point in an administration stood lower than that of any other president since Truman, and by winter of 1983 only 35 percent of the American public gave him a favorable job rating. Later, when the economy improved, so did the president's popularity. Indeed, by 1984 the Gallup poll reported that voters cited his handling of the economy as their main reason for voting for him.[25] The state of the economy also has affected the public's assessment of Bush's performance. As the nation moved into a reces-sion in mid-1990, his previously high approval rating dipped.

Presidential popularity also reflects the state of America's foreign relations. In times of international tension—when the peace or American interests are threatened—Americans tend to rally around

24. Michael Baruch Grossman and Martha Joynt Kumar, *Portraying the Presi-dent* (Baltimore: Johns Hopkins University Press, 1981), 262, figs. 4 and 5.
25. Ceaser, "The Reagan Presidency," 194. Ceaser provides an in-depth analysis of Reagan's changing levels of public approval.

the president, who is the symbol of the nation. In fact, they respond with support whether the president's policy was a success or less than successful. Thus, the Gallup poll showed President Kennedy's popularity moving from 73 percent before the disastrous 1961 Bay of Pigs invasion of Cuba to 83 percent after the crisis, and from 61 percent before the Cuban missile crisis to 73 percent after the Soviets backed down on placing missiles within ninety miles of Florida.[26] Similarly, George Bush's approval rating soared to 89 percent in March 1991 after the U.S.-led alliance defeated Iraq with only minimal casualties.

The public assessment of the president's persona or character is yet another factor in determining presidential support. When presidents meet public expectations for integrity, strength, and competence, their public standings are enhanced. For example, analyses of Reagan's popularity indicate that he benefited from an image of decisiveness and toughness as a leader, a dedication to his basic political convictions, and a "common touch"—openness, likability, and absence of pomposity.[27] But public assessments of Reagan's character declined and with them his popularity when the Iran-contra affair was publicized in 1986–1987. For the first time in his presidency, questions were raised about his honesty. Had he really not known about the illegal transfer of profits from arms sales to the contra rebels in Nicaragua? And he looked weak and unaware of what was going on in his administration. The greatest asset of the Reagan persona—his strength as a leader, his "Rambo" image—was challenged. When public interest in the Iran-contra affair faded in late 1987 during a period of improved relations with the Soviet Union and continued economic expansion at home, Reagan's popularity partially recovered. "Real world" conditions and the president's record in office do thus color the public's assessments of a president's character.

Going Public

In the American constitutional system of shared powers, presidents must inevitably win the support of other political leaders to achieve their policy goals. The Washington political community, however, is complex and highly fragmented. It is populated by independent-minded representatives and senators, proliferating interest group representatives, issue specialists, insiders, aggressive journalists, and senior bureaucrats. As a result, presidents have

26. Evidence of the American people rallying to support the president in times of international crisis has been compiled by Polsby, *Congress and the Presidency,* 73.
27. Ceaser, "The Reagan Presidency," 183, 197.

found it more and more difficult to persuade and bargain with the leaders whose support they need. In their dealings with Congress, for example, modern presidents have found that party leaders and committee chairmen often have insufficient clout to deliver their colleagues' votes in support of a deal they might cut with the president. Members of the Washington political community, however, are hesitant about opposing a president backed by the weight of public opinion. Indeed, congressional support for the president's legislative program is related to the president's public approval rating.[28]

Faced with all these difficulties, presidents have increasingly "gone public" in an attempt to achieve administration objectives.[29] "Going public" takes a variety of forms—televised speeches from the Oval Office, ceremonial functions in the White House Rose Garden, media events abroad or outside Washington, informal talks with visiting interest group leaders, off-the-cuff comments to reporters, and leaks of inside information by White House staff. The informal techniques are impossible to quantify, but the more formal methods of sending messages to the public—such as public addresses and public appearances—can be analyzed quantitatively. These measures of "going public" reveal that modern presidents are much more into public relations than were their predecessors thirty or forty years ago.[30]

Sophisticated attempts to manage the news go back at least to Eisenhower's press secretary, James Hagerty. According to *Washington Post* political reporter David Broder, the Reagan administration built on the techniques developed by Hagerty and his successors. It explicitly recognized "managing the news and public opinion . . . is such a central part of running the presidency" that it constitutes "a major part of the work day of senior policy aides."[31] In the Reagan White House presidential assistants met regularly to plan a communications strategy. With a general strategy in place, a daily 8:15 A.M. senior staff meeting was held to finalize each day's White House program with an eye toward dominating that night's network news programs and the next morning's newspaper headlines. The Bush administration has been much less explicit and programmed in its approach. It has tended to rely more on impromptu news confer-

28. See Edwards, *Presidential Influence in Congress*, chap. 4.

29. Samuel Kernell, *Going Public: New Strategies of Presidential Leadership* (Washington, D.C.: CQ Press, 1986), chap. 2.

30. Data on the extent of going public by presidents are derived from Kernell, ibid., 85–97.

31. David S. Broder, *Behind the Front Page: A Candid Look at How the News Is Made* (New York: Simon and Schuster, 1987), 180.

ences, although it too tries to stage presidential events that provide good visuals and sound bites for television.

As presidents and their staffs have sought to manage the news and, in the case of news conferences, to use the press as "one of the props,"[32] the relationship between the president and the media has become increasingly adversarial. White House reporters tend to seek out and pounce on the facts behind a president's statement or press release and take pleasure in uncovering mistakes and highlighting what they perceive to be failures and contradictions in administration policy.[33] A senior Washington journalist has remarked, "The White House reporter has one accepted role—to report the news—and several self-appointed roles. . . . I feel I'm there, in part, to compel the government to explain and justify what it's doing. A lot of people don't like that, but I feel we're the permanent in-house critics of the government."[34] White House reporters are also sensitive to the charge, leveled at them early in the Reagan administration, that they are giving the president "a free ride." All this adds up to a future in which adversarial relations between the White House and media are apt to be the norm.

The President as Chief Legislator

The Constitution thrusts presidents into the legislative process by giving them the power to recommend legislation, call Congress into special session, and veto laws passed by Congress. Their own interest in having a say in the direction of American policy pushes them into the legislative arena as well. And not to be forgotten, the public and the media now expect the president to lead the Congress. Although they have no power to introduce bills, speak during debate, or vote on the floor, presidents leave a substantial imprint on congressional decision making.

Setting the Legislative Policy Agenda

With their high public visibility, national constituency, and unrivaled political resources, presidents are able to play a major role in

32. Reporter Peter Lisagor quoted by Kernell, *Going Public*, 76.
33. Michael Grossman, Martha Joynt Kumar, and Frances E. Rourke, "Second-Term Presidencies: The Aging of Administrations," in *The Presidency and the Political System*, 2d ed., ed. Michael Nelson (Washington, D.C.: CQ Press, 1988), 218.
34. James Deakin quoted by Kernell, *Going Public*, 76.

determining which issues come up on the government's agenda for action. Among other things, presidential speeches and messages to Congress help determine exactly which of the many issues fighting for space on the policy agenda will receive top priority. Charles Jones, a close observer of White House-congressional relations, has described the president's role in setting the government's policy agenda as a "certifying function."[35] By giving an issue priority (certifying its place on the policy agenda), the president normally triggers the development of policy proposals that become the focus of public and congressional attention. After his election in 1980, for example, President Reagan had a clear-cut policy agenda—reduced domestic spending, tax cuts, and a buildup of military strength. His program then became the central concern of the Congress.

But as much as they would like to be, presidents are not in complete control of the government's policy agenda; events in the "real world" impinge on the president's agenda-setting power. The democratic revolutions that swept Eastern Europe, changes in the Soviet Union, and Iraq's invasion of Kuwait, for example, have forced President Bush and Congress to confront complicated, unforeseen national security/international relations issues. Similarly, the legacy of large budget deficits from the Reagan years means that whether President Bush wishes it or not, fiscal issues will be a major congressional concern.

The president's agenda-setting power is strengthened by Congress's decentralized power structure and its members' proclivities toward political independence. Congress needs a presidential agenda for action. The president's budget, for example, is the usual starting point for congressional deliberations on fiscal policy, even though Congress may elect to set aside much of what the president has recommended.

Sources of Conflict between the President and Congress

As the Founders envisioned, the separation of powers system has resulted in continual sparring matches between presidents and members of the Congress. They constantly complain about each other. About this situation, Abraham Lincoln reportedly said, "I have been told I was on the road to Hell, but I had no idea that it was just a mile down the road with a dome on it." As we will learn here, pres-

35. Charles O. Jones, "Presidents and Agenda Politics: Sustaining the Power of the Office" (Paper delivered at the annual meeting of the American Political Science Association, Atlanta, August 30–September 3, 1989), 13.

idential-congressional conflicts have deep electoral and institutional roots.

The principal basis for executive-legislative conflict is that the president and members of Congress have different constituencies—states or districts for senators and representatives, a national constituency for the president. It is not surprising then that the president and members of Congress bring to their offices quite dissimilar perspectives. Members of Congress worry about how proposed policies will affect the folks back home, while the president looks at issues from a more national perspective. In trade policy, for example, many legislators support more protection for American industries and workers threatened by foreign imports. The White House, however, opposes restrictive trade measures, believing they would damage the overall economy.

Differences between the White House and Congress are further exacerbated by the presidential, Senate, and House election schedules—no two the same. With the entire House up for reelection midway through a president's term and two-thirds of the Senate elected at a different time than the president, legislators and the president are likely to see their electoral mandates quite disparately.

As we saw in Chapter 7, different constituencies and staggered terms mean that it is possible for different parties to control the presidency and the Congress. Indeed, this has become commonplace in the post-World War II era. Divided party control of the presidency and Congress leads inevitably to conflict, maneuvering for partisan advantage, and difficulties for presidents in securing passage of their legislative programs.

As for institutional sources of conflict between the president and Congress, the Constitution interweaves executive and legislative functions, giving the president such legislative powers as the veto and Congress the authority to confirm major presidential appointments and ratify treaties. Under such conditions, struggles for influence between these two coequal branches of government are bound to erupt.

The president and members of Congress also approach their work from different time perspectives. Members of Congress view their congressional careers as open-ended and potentially lifetime. As a result, among their main concerns are achieving power within the chamber, getting reelected, helping out constituents, and enacting their own policy goals. Serving presidential ends is not their first priority. Presidents, by contrast, have only a fixed period of time in which to achieve their objectives and establish their niches in history.

Although presidential conflicts with the Congress are inevitable, presidents are able to claim victory on a relatively high percentage of congressional roll-call votes. Thus, cooperation between the two branches is possible as well.

The most important basis for cooperation between the president and Congress is partisan loyalty. Studies of congressional roll-call votes have consistently shown that presidents can expect at least two-thirds of their party's members to support their legislative proposals, and frequently 80 percent or more. Because no Republican president since Eisenhower has served with a Congress controlled by his party (1953–1955), recent Democratic presidents (Johnson, Kennedy, and Carter) have generally fared better with Congress than GOP presidents (Table 11.2).

When party unity in Congress breaks down, as it does frequently, the president cannot necessarily depend on party loyalty to prevail in the end. It is just in such situations that the benefits of keeping the lines of communication open to members of the opposition party become apparent. But cutting deals with the opposition party to achieve legislative victories has its risks, including resentment among members of the president's party. Presidents must, therefore, constantly seek to balance the interests of their own party's members against their needs for bipartisan support to achieve their policy goals.

The ability of the White House to win victories in Congress has varied substantially during presidential terms, as well as among presidents (Table 11.2). Presidential support in Congress is thus affected by factors other than party control of the chamber. One such factor is the tie between a president's victories in Congress and high public approval ratings (Figure 11.3). That relationship is not always direct and immediate, but it certainly appears to be one of the reasons that two Democratic presidents, Kennedy and Johnson (especially early in his administration), had greater success than fellow Democrat Jimmy Carter with Democratic-controlled Congresses.

Because both the president and members of Congress have an interest in maintaining government programs and initiating new ones to meet social problems—neither achievable if a policy deadlock occurs because of presidential-congressional conflicts—they do cooperate to make certain that basic services and programs are maintained. At the end of the 1990 session of Congress, for example, Republican President Bush and Democratic congressional leaders achieved a compromise on the FY 1991 budget and spending levels

Table 11.2 Presidential Victories on Votes in Congress, 1953–1990

Years	President (Party)	Presidential Roll-call Victories, House and Senate[a] (%)	Party in Control of Congress House	Party in Control of Congress Senate	Same or Divided Party Control of Presidency and Congress
1953–1954	Eisenhower (Rep.)	86.0	Rep.	Rep.	Same
1955–1956	Eisenhower (Rep.)	72.5	Dem.	Dem.	Divided
1957–1958	Eisenhower (Rep.)	72.1	Dem.	Dem.	"
1959–1960	Eisenhower (Rep.)	58.6	Dem.	Dem.	"
1961–1962	Kennedy (Dem.)	83.5	Dem.	Dem.	Same
1963	Kennedy (Dem.)	87.1	Dem.	Dem.	"
1964	Johnson (Dem.)	87.9	Dem.	Dem.	Same
1965–1966	Johnson (Dem.)	86.0	Dem.	Dem.	"
1967–1968	Johnson (Dem.)	76.7	Dem.	Dem.	"
1969–1970	Nixon (Rep.)	75.9	Dem.	Dem.	Divided
1971–1972	Nixon (Rep.)	70.6	Dem.	Dem.	"
1973–1974	Nixon (Rep.)	55.1	Dem.	Dem.	"
1974	Ford (Rep.)	58.1	Dem.	Dem.	Divided
1975–1976	Ford (Rep.)	57.4	Dem.	Dem.	"
1977–1978	Carter (Dem.)	76.9	Dem.	Dem.	Same
1979–1980	Carter (Dem.)	76.0	Dem.	Dem.	"
1981–1982	Reagan (Rep.)	77.4	Dem.	Rep.	Divided
1983–1984	Reagan (Rep.)	66.5	Dem.	Rep.	"
1985–1986	Reagan (Rep.)	58.2	Dem.	Rep.	"
1987–1988	Reagan (Rep.)	45.5	Dem.	Dem.	"
1989–1990	Bush (Rep.)	54.7	Dem.	Dem.	"

SOURCE: Norman J. Ornstein, Thomas E. Mann, and Michael J. Malbin, *Vital Statistics on Congress, 1989–1990* (Washington, D.C.: CQ Press, 1989), 193–194; and *Congressional Quarterly Weekly Report*, December 22, 1990, 4208.

[a] Average percentage approval for time period.

for the next five years after much highly televised wrangling. It was not popular with Republicans or Democrats, but neither side was prepared to permit the government to shut its doors because of a stalemate over funding.

Influencing Congress

All presidents have a variety of resources at their disposal to influence Congress. In this work, they are assisted by the White House

Figure 11.3: Presidential Victories on Congressional Roll-call Votes and Public Support, 1953–1990

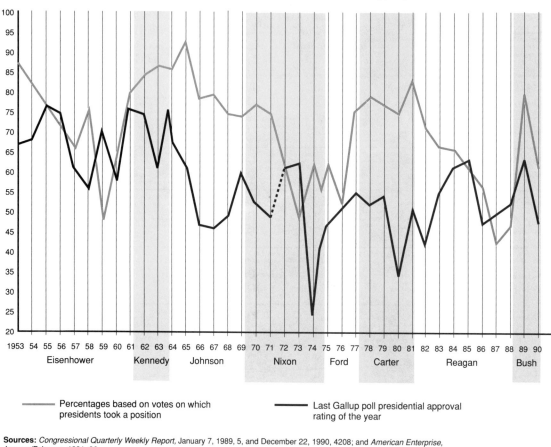

———— Percentages based on votes on which presidents took a position

———— Last Gallup poll presidential approval rating of the year

Sources: *Congressional Quarterly Weekly Report,* January 7, 1989, 5, and December 22, 1990, 4208; and *American Enterprise,* January/February, 1991, 96.
   Note: Kennedy was assassinated on November 22, 1963. Nixon resigned on August 9, 1974.

congressional relations office (their personal lobbyists), the congressional relations personnel of the various executive departments, and the White House interest group liaison staff (Office of Public Liaison).

Every member of the Congress needs *administration assistance* at some point. Perhaps it is a promise of presidential campaign assistance, support for a public works project for the member's constituency, appointment of a supporter to a federal position, public endorsement of a member's policy proposal, adjustment of an administrative decision affecting a member's constituents, or an invitation to a White House state dinner. Because presidents head the vast executive branch and have more influence than any other American politician, they are in a position to advance the interests of members of Congress. Skillful presidents have used this bargaining position to build support for their legislative proposals. Thus, in an unusually candid moment, Rep. John Breaux (D-La.) once remarked after striking a deal with the Reagan White House that his vote could not be bought but that "it could be rented."

Members of Congress want to make rational decisions that will advance their policy and political goals, but to do this, they must have *sound information*. In the nation's capital, information is power, and those with the best and most up-to-date information are at an advantage. With its ability to draw on the entire executive branch, the administration frequently has an information edge over Congress. This is particularly the case in national security matters where the president is able to call on the resources of the Departments of State and Defense, the Central Intelligence Agency, and the National Security Council.

When President Lyndon Johnson once told members of Congress, "I'm the only president you've got," he was reminding them of the importance of maintaining the *prestige of the office of president* even though the incumbent might not be held in high regard. The respect that legislators, like other Americans, have for the office is another basis for presidential influence. Appeals for support made in a one-on-one conversation with the president in the White House are difficult to resist. In the Oval Office, the president is surrounded by the trappings of the office—the presidential flag, the massive desk, and the military aide nearby with the "presidential emergency satchel" containing the authentication codes to be used in the event of war. A presidential appeal for support in this setting can be compelling, even for hardened congressional veterans.

The veto and the threat of a veto is another source of presidential clout over Congress. When a bill has been passed by Congress, the president has four options:

1. Sign the bill into law.
2. Allow the bill to become law without a signature by holding the bill for more than ten days (a little-used procedure reserved for bills the president dislikes but prefers not to veto).
3. Veto the bill. It becomes law only if the veto is overridden by a two-thirds vote of both the House and Senate.
4. Veto the bill by failing to sign it within ten days (**pocket veto**). This is possible only when Congress has adjourned, and the president

Table 11.3 Presidential Vetoes, 1945–1990

Years	President (Party)	Party Control of Congress	Regular Vetoes	Overridden		Pocket Vetoes	Total Vetoes
				Number	%		
1945–1953	Truman (Dem.)	Dem. 1945–1946 Rep. 1947–1948 Dem. 1949–1953	180	12	6.7	70	250
1953–1961	Eisenhower (Rep.)	Rep. 1953–1954 Dem. 1955–1961	73	2	2.7	108	181
1961–1963	Kennedy (Dem.)	Dem.	12	0	0.0	9	21
1963–1969	Johnson (Dem.)	Dem.	16	0	0.0	14	30
1969–1974	Nixon (Rep.)	Dem.	26	7	26.9	17	43
1974–1977	Ford (Rep.)	Dem.	48	12	25.0	18	66
1977–1981	Carter (Dem.)	Dem.	13	2	15.4	18	31
1981–1989	Reagan (Rep.)	House: Dem. Senate: Rep. 1981–1986 Dem. 1987–1989	39	9	23.1	39	78
1989–1990	Bush (Rep.)	Dem.	15	0	0.0	6	21
Totals			422	44	10.4	299	721

SOURCE: Senate Library, *Presidential Vetoes, 1798–1984*; updates provided by Senate Library.

is therefore unable to return the bill to that body for a possible veto override.

The veto is the president's ultimate weapon. It is a rare presidential veto that is overridden because to defeat an override attempt, the president needs the support of only one-third plus one of the members of either the House or Senate. By relying on party loyalty, the chief executive can usually muster the votes needed to sustain a veto (see Table 11.3).

Because it is so difficult to override presidential vetoes, the threat of a veto can have a substantial impact on congressional decision making. Faced with a threatened veto, senators and representatives frequently seek compromises with the White House rather than risk total defeat of their legislative proposals.

When the White House and Congress are controlled by different parties, vetoes and override attempts tend to occur more frequently than when the same party controls both branches. Presidential popularity also affects veto politics. When the president's popularity is low, Congress is frequently emboldened to pass bills over the president's objections. This provokes presidential vetoes and ensuing override attempts. By contrast, when presidential popularity is high, Congress is less likely to pass bills to which the president objects, thereby reducing the number of presidential vetoes and congressional override attempts.[36]

The White House may even resort to *appeal to interest groups and the public* to gain support in Congress. Because senators and representatives must stand for reelection, White House staff often work in harness with supportive interest groups to exert pressure on wavering members of Congress. Presidents also may make dramatic television appeals for public support. Several popular presidents have used this technique effectively. In the 1950s, for example, President Eisenhower appealed to voters in a television address to support his call for labor reform legislation. The result was an outpouring of public support that caused a reluctant Congress to pass the Landrum-Griffin Act. But public appeals should not be made too frequently lest they lose their unique character and effectiveness. And there is also a risk in presidential appeals to the public over the head of Congress. Should such an appeal fail to arouse public support, as Reagan's appeal for support of contra aid did in the 1980s, Congress then finds it much easier to oppose the president.

The president's constant quest for congressional support, the ups and downs of presidential influence with Congress, and the seemingly never-ending controversies between the branches are a reminder of the wisdom of Edwin Corwin, a constitutional scholar, who observed that "the Constitution is an invitation to struggle for the privilege of directing American . . . policy."[37]

The President as Commander in Chief and Chief Diplomat

In the foreign policy arena, as in other policy fields, the presidents must share power with Congress. Even so, the Constitution gives the president an impressive array of powers: to act as commander in

36. For an analysis of the circumstances that produce vetoes, override attempts, and successful overrides, see David W. Rohde and Dennis M. Simon, "Presidential Vetoes and Congressional Response," *American Journal of Political Science* 29 (1985): 397–427. There is evidence that recent presidents have found it necessary to use the veto power more frequently on major bills than their predecessors. See David McKay, "Presidential Strategy and the Veto Power: A Reappraisal," *Political Science Quarterly* 104 (Fall 1989): 447–461.
37. Edwin S. Corwin, *The President: Office and Powers*, 4th ed. (New York: New York University Press, 1957), 171.

chief of the military, to bestow (and withdraw) formal diplomatic recognition on foreign governments, and to negotiate treaties.

Because Congress is not equipped to undertake comprehensive strategic military planning, make timely foreign or national security decisions (including decisions about the deployment of troops and the use of nuclear weapons), or conduct relations with other governments on a day-to-day basis, foreign policy leadership tends to reside with the president. The president's preeminent role in foreign policy was demonstrated dramatically in December 1989. In that one month, President Bush held a mini-summit/get-acquainted meeting at Malta with President Mikhail Gorbachev of the Soviet Union; met with the heads of state of the North Atlantic Treaty Organization (NATO); authorized American military jets to fly over Manila during a coup attempt to demonstrate support for Philippine president Corazon Aquino; sent a high-level secret mission to China; recognized new governments in Eastern Europe and granted some special trade concessions; and ordered an American invasion of Panama to remove President Manuel Noriega from power. All of this was accomplished without any formal action on the part of the Congress, which had adjourned until January 1990.

The President's War Powers

As several of these examples indicate, an important source of the president's foreign policy authority is derived from the war powers that go with the office—the constitutional designation of commander in chief of the military. Although this constitutional provision was designed to ensure civilian supremacy over the military, the president's war powers extend beyond purely military operations. Abraham Lincoln, for example, issued the Emancipation Proclamation as a war measure, and at the beginning of World War II President Franklin Roosevelt authorized the army to create "defense zones" on the West Coast and by executive order, supported by an act of Congress, forcibly moved people of Japanese ancestry to relocation centers.

The president shares authority over the military with Congress, which must vote the money to support the armed forces and can enact regulations governing the military. Although Congress has the power to declare war, presidential conduct of foreign relations and orders to the military may lead to hostilities. Numerous examples of this situation are found throughout American history: in 1846 President James K. Polk sent troops into disputed territory in Texas, thereby precipitating the Mexican War; President Harry Truman ordered American troops to resist the 1950 invasion of South Korea

Summit conferences with world leaders are now a standard tool of presidential diplomacy, along with the more conventional private channels of contact. Soviet leader Mikhail Gorbachev and President George Bush demonstrate their political skills on the streets of downtown Washington, D.C., and take advantage of the intense media coverage that accompanied their June 1990 summit meeting.

by North Korea; and in 1965 President Lyndon Johnson used American troops to intervene in the Dominican Republic. Presidents Eisenhower, Kennedy, and Johnson ordered troops into Vietnam before Johnson secured congressional support in 1964 for escalating American involvement. And in more recent years, in the Mideast, President Reagan used the navy to escort oil tankers through the Persian Gulf during the last two years of the Iran-Iraq War (1980–1988), and President Bush ordered American forces to the Persian Gulf after Iraq invaded Kuwait in 1990.

Congress has the authority to resist such actions by refusing to grant funds for military uses or putting conditions on the use of the funds it does grant. But it has rarely used these powers to limit presidential war powers in a significant way. The problems faced by Congress when the president has sent American armed forces abroad had a humorous outcome in 1907 when President Theodore Roosevelt sent the U.S. Navy halfway around the world to demonstrate that the United States had become a major world power. Congress threatened to withhold the money for this adventure but was then faced with the choice of either providing the funds to get the fleet back to the United States or leaving it stranded in the Pacific. It voted the money.

More recently, however, Congress has taken actions to restrict presidential discretion in military matters. In 1970 Congress reacted to growing domestic opposition to the Vietnam War by imposing an unprecedented restraint on the president's discretion as commander in chief: it stipulated that no funds could be used to send ground troops into Laos or Cambodia. When opposition to presidential policies in Vietnam continued, Congress passed in 1973 the War Powers Resolution over President Nixon's veto. The act required the president to notify Congress within forty-eight hours of the commitment of American troops abroad and provided that the troop commitment would be terminated within sixty days if Congress did not give its approval. An additional thirty days was allowed if the president certified to Congress that an unavoidable military necessity required continued use of American troops. Congress also was authorized to terminate a deployment of troops at any time.

Although the War Powers Resolution was designed by Congress to limit the president's war powers, it has in fact imposed few limits on the president and has been implemented only twice (in 1975 when marines were sent to rescue a merchant vessel captured by Cambodia, and in 1982 when marines were sent to Lebanon). Since the War Powers Resolution was enacted, presidents have opposed it as an unwise and undue restriction on presidential foreign policy prerogatives. And not only have presidents opposed it, but they also have not implemented it. Without invoking the War Powers Resolution, President Reagan invaded Grenada in 1983 and bombed Libya in 1986, and President Bush invaded Panama in 1989 and sent troops to the Persian Gulf in 1990. Some members of Congress have complained, but Congress itself has been reluctant to implement the resolution for fear of endangering military missions and causing the United States to appear less than resolute in its dealing with hostile governments.

Probably more important than the War Powers Resolution are the political constraints on the president. The American experiences in the Korean and Vietnam wars show that presidential popularity can quickly erode and cause electoral defeat if military actions lead to high U.S. casualty counts, drag on without victory, and evoke extensive public and congressional opposition.

Chief Diplomat

The president is responsible for conducting day-to-day relations with foreign governments. As chief diplomat, he is assisted by the Department of State, which maintains embassies around the globe, as well as by a large bureaucracy in Washington. Included in the president's responsibilities are the sending and receiving of ambassadors, through which the United States extends official diplomatic recognition to foreign governments. Disapproval of a foreign government is expressed by withdrawing the U.S. ambassador as was the case for Cuba's Castro government. Presidents also convey their views of foreign governments and events through public statements—for example, President Bush's statements of support for the Aquino government of the Philippines when it was threatened by a military coup in 1989.

In addition to public and formal actions, presidents also maintain informal contact with foreign heads of state. President Bush, for example, as a part of his itinerary for a 1989 Malta meeting also met privately with Prime Minister Margaret Thatcher of Britain and Chancellor Helmut Kohl of West Germany.

Traditionally, treaty negotiations have been an important part of American foreign policy making. Treaty-signing ceremonies, like that held in 1988 when Presidents Reagan and Gorbachev affixed their signatures to the Intermediate Nuclear Forces (INF) Treaty, are preceded by extensive negotiations between presidential envoys and representatives of foreign governments. Treaties must be ratified by a two-thirds vote of the Senate before they become part of the "law of the land." But for treaties to be operative, the president must take steps to implement them, often requiring congressional appropriations or legislation.

In addition to their treaty-making powers, presidents have the power to enter into executive agreements with foreign governments. Executive agreements are much like treaties except that they do not require Senate ratification to go into effect. Unless countermanded by Congress, executive agreements, like treaties, become law. They are even used frequently in major negotiations—for example, the Yalta (1944) and the Potsdam (1945) agreements among the World War II Allies have governed the occupation of Germany and the future of Europe. In most years, five times more executive agreements have been negotiated than formal treaties ratified.[38]

Other foreign policy tools are economic and military aid to foreign governments. In 1989, the new, democratically elected government of Poland received economic aid as a show of U.S. support. Similarly, a key element of American policy in the Middle East has been steady support for Israel through high levels of economic and military aid. But just as foreign aid can be used as a sign of support, its withdrawal can be used to signal American disapproval of a for-

38. J. W. Peltason, *Understanding the Constitution,* 11th ed. (New York: Holt, Rinehart, and Winston, 1988), 95.

eign government's actions. Thus, the Bush administration reduced aid to Jordan after it tilted toward Iraq in the Persian Gulf conflict of 1991.

Control over foreign aid policy is shared by the president, who administers the aid, and the Congress, which provides the funds and spells out general guidelines for their distribution. In their efforts to use aid to gain maximum influence with foreign governments, presidents naturally seek wide discretionary authority in administering foreign aid. In recent years, however, Congress has sought to play a more active role in foreign policy making by attaching restrictions to the granting of American aid. For example, aid to El Salvador is conditional on the president's certifying that the Salvadoran government is making progress in protecting human rights. Such attempts by Congress to influence policy by imposing restrictions on how the president administers foreign aid have kept the White House and Congress in continual conflict since the 1970s.

The Presidency: A Continuing American Dilemma

The presidency brings to American government qualities not found in either the Congress or the judiciary. Unlike Congress, the president provides a national rather than local perspective for national and international problems as well as a capacity to develop comprehensive and consistent policy proposals. The presidency is a symbol around which the citizenry can rally when the nation faces a crisis. And unlike the judiciary, which is an appointed institution lacking the democratic legitimacy derived from a popular election, the president is selected by the voters.

As America has become a world power over this century and the government's role has grown, the power of the office of president has expanded tremendously. Yet for all this presidential power, there are times when presidents appear hemmed in and incapable of decisive action. Presidential scholar Fred Greenstein believes that the modern presidency has developed a "double-edged" quality. Presidents have greater formal and informal powers than ever in history, but they are also subject to greater potential for backlash. Presidents, he observed,

serve as the chief agenda setters for the nation, but in the process they create expectations that they can rarely fulfill; preside over a huge White House bureaucracy, which is necessary to achieve presidential goals, but which can also become a liability by distorting information and abusing power in the president's name; and are the most visible actors in American politics, which carries the danger of being made scapegoats for national disappointments.[39]

Presidents also must labor under the limitations imposed by deadlines, conduct routine business, and share power with Congress and the courts. They have to deal with difficult allies and cope with hostile foreign and domestic opponents while trying to resolve thorny, seemingly unsolvable problems. Often decisions must be made when the correct course of action is by no means clear.

Under these circumstances, does the president have too much power? Compared to other participants in the political system, the president has enormous power. But when presidential powers are stacked up against the problems to be solved, they appear less substantial. The presidency is now, as it was for the Founders, a dilemma. How can it be made strong enough to serve the nation's leadership needs without becoming too powerful and a threat to democracy itself?

For Review

1. The Constitution both grants power to and limits the power of the president, who must share power with the other branches of government. Because the constitutional powers of the president are stated in broad terms, it has been possible to interpret them in ways that have permitted a vast expansion of presidential influence.

2. A combination of historical and institutional forces provides at least a partial explanation for the increased prominence and power of the president in the twentieth century. These include America's expanded role in world affairs, the expansion of government responsibilities in domestic affairs and the accompanying growth of the executive branch, and the changed relationship between the president and the public stemming from the growth of the electronic media.

3. The presidency itself encompasses a sizable bureaucracy—the Executive Office of the President. Presidents mold this bureaucracy to fit their particular leadership styles and objectives. The presidential bureaucracy, particularly the White House staff, exercises great influence over administration policy making. Effectively utilizing and controlling this presidential bureaucracy are two major prob-

39. Greenstein's notion of a "double-edged" presidency is summarized by Dom Bonafede, "Presidential Focus: What's a Leader?" *National Journal*, April 18, 1987, 972.

lems modern presidents have had to confront. The White House staff is frequently the center of intense power and policy struggles.

4. Presidential power depends heavily on public support—a fragile commodity that is subject to sharp fluctuations depending on economic and world conditions. After an early "honeymoon" period, most presidents see their public approval ratings fall, although the public normally rallies to support the president in the midst of international crises.

5. The president plays a major role in establishing the congressional policy agenda. But presidential success with Congress is strongly affected by whether or not the president's party controls Congress and by the president's level of public support.

6. Presidents exert preeminent influence on foreign policy, but even in this area they must share power with Congress, which can restrict presidential initiatives through its legislative and funding powers.

For Further Reading

Cronin, Thomas E. *The State of the Presidency.* 2d ed. Boston: Little, Brown, 1980. An analysis of presidential leadership with particular attention on the sources and limits of presidential influence.

Edwards, George C., III. *At the Margins: Presidential Leadership of Congress.* New Haven, Conn.: Yale University Press, 1989. An analysis of the sources and conditions for presidential leadership of Congress.

Jones, Charles O., ed. *The Reagan Legacy: Promise and Performance.* Chatham, N.J.: Chatham House, 1988. A collection of essays by leading scholars assessing the impact of the Reagan presidency on American politics.

———. *The Trusteeship Presidency: Jimmy Carter and the United States Congress.* Baton Rouge: Louisiana State University Press, 1988. A penetrating analysis of Carter's difficult relationship with the Congress.

Kernell, Samuel. *Going Public: New Strategies of Presidential Leadership.* Washington, D.C.: CQ Press, 1986. A consideration of how presidents increasingly rely on public relations to build support for their programs in Washington.

King, Gary, and Lyn Ragsdale. *The Elusive Executive: Discovering Statistical Patterns in the Presidency.* Washington, D.C.: CQ Press, 1988. A compendium of statistical information on the presidency, supplemented with interpretive essays.

Mayhew, David R. *Divided We Govern: Party Control, Lawmaking, and Investigations, 1946–1990.* New Haven: Yale University Press, 1991. An analysis that challenges the conventional wisdom about the adverse consequences of divided party control of government.

Nelson, Michael, ed. *The Presidency and the Political System.* 3d ed. Washington, D.C.: CQ Press, 1990. An excellent collection of essays analyzing such topics as presidential power; presidential relations with the press, interest groups, Congress, the bureaucracy, and the judiciary; and domestic and foreign policy leadership.

Neustadt, Richard E. *Presidential Power and the Modern Presidents: The Politics of Leadership from Roosevelt to Reagan.* New York: Free Press, 1990. A classic analysis of how presidents acquire and maintain power.

Polsby, Nelson W. *Congress and the Presidency.* 4th ed. Englewood Cliffs, N.J.: Prentice-Hall, 1986. Contains lively and concise accounts of presidential leadership styles, insightful evaluations of modern presidents, and an analysis of congressional-presidential relations.

Watson, Richard A., and Norman C. Thomas. *The Politics of the Presidency.* 2d ed. Washington, D.C.: CQ Press, 1988. A comprehensive text on the modern presidency.

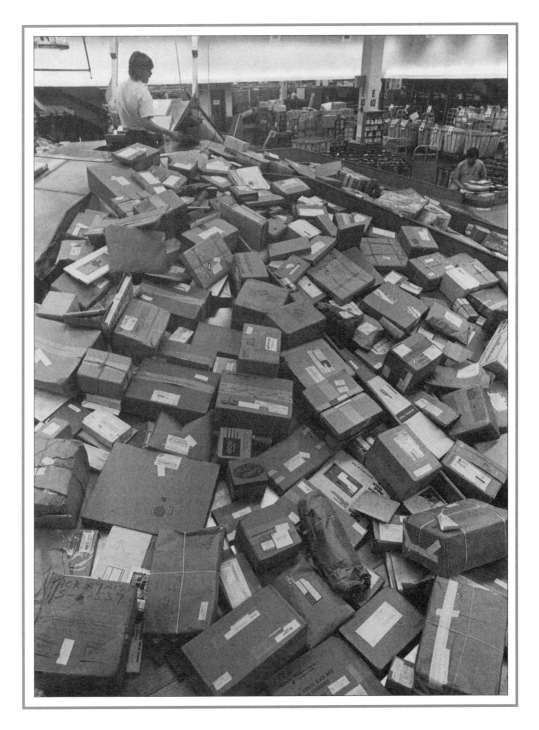

12. The Federal Bureaucracy

PRESIDENT Jimmy Carter probably voiced the thoughts of many Americans when he once said, "Before I became president, I realized and was warned that dealing with the federal bureaucracy would be one of the worst problems I would have to face. It has been worse than anticipated." Indeed, for better or worse, the tentacles of the massive federal **bureaucracy** reach into Americans' lives in many ways. Among other things, the Internal Revenue Service (IRS) collects their taxes, federal air traffic controllers oversee their otherwise hazardous skyways, government-paid health care professionals care for their military veterans, Federal Bureau of Investigation (FBI) agents chase their lawbreakers, and Social Security Administration employees provide their retirement checks and Medicare benefits when they get older. Because without all these government employees Congress and the president would be unable to carry out the policies they have authorized, the bureaucracy is an essential element of the governing process.

The term *bureaucracy* refers to the complex of agencies that administers government programs and policies. The men and women who work for these government agencies are often called **bureaucrats**. Most bureaucracies are structured hierarchically with clear lines of authority running from the department or agency head to subordinates. Within each organization, there is a substantial division of labor organized around specialized subunits. Bureaucracy is not just a governmental phenomenon. Massive bureaucracies also flourish within the private sector, especially in large corporations. Moreover, bureaucracies run unions, churches, universities, foundations, and health care institutions.

As the government's role in providing services and regulating the economy has expanded over the last sixty years, the bureaucracy has expanded as well. In fact, each new government function spawns a new bureaucracy. In the 1970s, for example, the energy bureaucracy ballooned in the wake of the Arab oil embargo as the government became a bigger player in the energy field and concerns surfaced about the effects of nuclear energy on the environment. Initially, the responsibility for energy matters was given to the existing Office of Emergency Preparedness. But when this small agency, which had been operating in the backwaters of government policy making, proved inadequate to the task, two new agencies were created in 1974—the Federal Energy Office (FEA) in the Executive Office of the President and the Energy Research and Development Administration (ERDA). In 1977 FEA and ERDA became components of the cabinet-level Department of Energy.

Most government bureaucracies develop a survival instinct along with powerful allies who enable them to resist dismantlement. For example, although newly created in 1977, the Department of Energy was able to resist President Ronald Reagan's 1980 campaign pledge to oversee its demise because Congress and interest groups rallied to its defense. Today, the department is firmly established with seventeen thousand employees and annual expenditures of over $20 billion.

The growth of the bureaucracy is more than simply a matter of expanding agencies, staffs, and budgets. Its impact on people's daily lives has grown by leaps and bounds as well. The food on the breakfast table is certified by the U.S. Department of Agriculture; the cost of long-distance calls to relatives is regulated by federal and state agencies; exhaust emissions on cars are controlled by catalytic converters required by the Environmental Protection Agency; all the advertisements heard on car radios are subject to Federal Trade Commission (FTC) regulations, while the radio stations themselves are licensed by the Federal Communications Commission; and workplaces are subject to standards imposed by the Occupational Safety and Health Review Commission.[1]

The recent history of the Federal Trade Commission is a good example of just how broad the implications of such government agency activities and policy making are for citizens everywhere. For much of its existence, the FTC was a rather quiescent agency, but after congressional criticism and a critical exposé by consumer advocate Ralph Nader in 1969, President Richard Nixon appointed Casper Weinberger to chair the commission. Weinberger reorganized the FTC, fired one-third of its employees, and recruited young, aggressive, consumer-oriented lawyers for its staff. The result was heightened regulatory activity through the 1970s, which included antitrust suits filed against major oil companies and cereal makers; attacks on doctors, accountants, and lawyers for prohibiting advertising and other forms of competition; rules to prevent anticompetitive practices in the eyeglass industry; and investigations of the insurance industry, children's television shows, used-car marketing, and funeral homes. Although Congress initially encouraged these activities, the specific policies were developed by the FTC itself.

1. On the growth and impact of the bureaucracy, see Kenneth J. Meier, *Politics and Bureaucracy: Policymaking in the Fourth Branch of Government,* 2d ed. (Monterey, Calif.: Brooks/Cole, 1987), 1–3.

Not surprisingly, the FTC's aggressive consumer protection activities provoked howls of protest from many of the industries and professions affected, who demanded that Congress pass legislation to restrict the FTC. But in spite of threats from some in Congress to either restrict or even abolish the agency, the commission continued its aggressive, consumer-oriented policies during the Carter administration. When President Reagan appointed a new FTC chairman following the 1980 election, its policies finally changed: the commission switched its focus from the consumer to the market and became a strong advocate of market-oriented solutions to consumer problems. Now, however, with the appointment of Janet Steiger as FTC chairman by the Bush administration, the commission has resumed its more activist role in consumer protection, antitrust, and misleading advertising issues.[2]

The knowledge and expertise bureaucrats develop in the course of carrying out their duties produce the essential information needed for congressional and presidential decision making. When developing tax policies, for example, both the president and Congress must depend heavily on the IRS to provide data on the impacts of existing tax laws and proposed changes. Without the bureaucracy, the government could not enforce the law or provide the services its citizens have come to expect. Even so, the term *bureaucracy* for many Americans implies endless delays, arbitrary decisions, confusion, inefficiency, and inflexibility. And, as the controversy over FTC policy illustrates, the bureaucracy is also criticized for not being sufficiently accountable to elected officials. Indeed, the bureaucracy is sometimes called the "fourth branch" of government—a vast army of nonelected administrators whose power to make administrative decisions threatens to usurp the policy-making powers of the Congress and the president. It is thus ironic that while the knowledge and skills bureaucrats bring to policy development and implementation are indispensable, many Americans tend to view the bureaucracy as somewhat illegitimate.[3] This chapter reviews the constitutional position of the bureaucracy, gives an account of its growth and structure, and,

2. For an account of FTC politics by a former commission chairman, see Michael Pertschuk, *Revolt against Regulation* (Berkeley: University of California Press, 1982). Also see Barry Weingast and Mark J. Moran, "Bureaucratic Discretion or Congressional Control? Regulatory Policymaking by the Federal Trade Commission," *Journal of Political Economy* 91 (May 1983): 765–800; Meier, *Politics and Bureaucracy*, 12–13; and W. John Moore, "Stoking the FTC," *National Journal*, May 19, 1990, 1217–1221.

3. Francis E. Rourke, "Bureaucracy in the American Constitutional Order," *Political Science Quarterly* 102 (Summer 1987): 232.

most important, analyzes the bureaucracy's participation in the policy-making process.

The Constitutional Setting for the Bureaucracy

Because the writers of the Constitution were more concerned about the balance of power among the legislative, executive, and judicial branches than about the administration of government policies, the Constitution gives the structure of the executive branch only indirect attention. Yet this inattention to administration is hardly surprising given the few functions the government carried out in the late eighteenth century. It was expected to defend the shores, maintain order, deliver the mail, assist with a few public works projects, and little else.

The Founders did envision that Congress would create executive departments and delegate to them the power to carry out national policies (departments are mentioned in Article I). Moreover, in Article II Congress was empowered to give the president, courts, and department heads the authority to appoint government officials. This article also cleared the way for the president to request written opinions from the "principal Officer in each of the executive Departments."

But what the Constitution does not spell out clearly is who is responsible for the exercise of administrative power—the Congress or the president? As a result, the years have seen an ongoing tug of war between the two branches to control the bureaucracy. A recent example of this struggle was the 1989 battle between President George Bush and the Democratic-controlled Senate over who would lead the Department of Defense. The Senate, in a highly charged atmosphere, rejected the president's nominee for secretary of defense, former senator John Tower (R-Texas), thereby forcing the president to submit a new nominee, Rep. Dick Cheney (R-Wyo.), who was acceptable to a majority of the senators.

Whatever the ambiguities of the Constitution on who would control the administration of policy, two points were made clear by the nation's Founders. First, in Article I, section 6, of the Constitution, members of Congress are explicitly forbidden to hold concurrently a federal executive office. This reflected the Constitution writers' aversion to the practice in the British parliamentary system of appointing cabinet and lesser executive officers from the ranks of Parliament. Second, the president's power to remove executive branch officials whose original appointments had been confirmed by the Senate was recognized in the 1789 statute that created the first executive department. Presidents can therefore hold administrators accountable for their actions and prevent them from becoming independent of the chief executive.

The Constitution has left its mark on the American bureaucracy in other ways as well. Under its separation of powers principle, both the president and Congress exercise authority over the bureaucracy. Congressional statutes create government agencies, determine their powers and functions, and set their organizational structures. Committees of the Congress can use their investigative authority to review administrative performance and exert pressure on administrators. In addition, the Senate confirms presidential appointments to major policy-making posts within agencies. But, at the same time, executive power is "vested in a President," who is charged with seeing that the laws are "faithfully executed." Bureaucrats in America thus serve two masters—the Congress and the president. In the process, they often play one off against the other to gain a measure of independence. In countries with parliamentary systems, by contrast, the lines of authority are more clearly drawn, and the prime minister and the cabinet exercise greater control over the bureaucracy.

The constitutional principle of federalism, which assures the states of a prominent role in the governmental system, also has had profound effects on the administration of government programs. Many major government programs and policies are administered jointly by federal government agencies and state and local governments—for example, Aid to Families with Dependent Children (welfare), food stamps, unemployment compensation, mass transit, housing, and educational programs (see Chapter 3, Federalism). Unlike in governments organized on a unitary (nonfederal) basis, only a limited number of U.S. federal government agencies—such as the IRS, FBI, Postal Service, National Park Service, Social Security Administration, and Bureau of Indian Affairs—deal directly with the American people.

The Federal Trade Commission has assumed a more activist role on consumer protection issues under the leadership of Janet Steiger, who was appointed chairman by President Bush in 1989.

The Development of the Bureaucratic State

The bureaucratic state, with its sprawling organizational structure, complex procedures, service and regulatory activities, and millions of civilian employees, is a twentieth-century phenomenon in America. This vast administrative apparatus, however, had modest beginnings.[4]

The Executive Branch in Its Infancy: 1789 to the Civil War

In 1789, the first year of the government under the Constitution, Congress authorized three executive departments—State, War, and Treasury—and the offices of the attorney general and the postmaster general. The U.S. Post Office was actually created in 1792 and the Department of the Navy in 1798. By the time the Federalists left office after the election of 1800, the government had only three thousand civilian employees. The State Department had a staff of nine plus a messenger boy, and the attorney general was expected to earn his living in private practice. The Jeffersonians retained the administrative structure inherited from the Federalists and did not add substantially to the federal bureaucracy. From 1830 until the Civil War, only one new department—Interior—was created, and the government's administrative apparatus remained "small, unpretentious and limited to a few essential functions."[5] Much of the increase in employment during this period was accounted for by the growth of the Post Office.

Growth of the Bureaucracy, 1861–1930

With the onset of the Civil War, the ranks of the federal government began to swell significantly. After the war, economic and social changes—industrialization, development of an urban working class, the emergence of corporations and monopolistic trusts, the building of transcontinental railroads, farm recessions, waves of immigration, and the rise of large, impersonal cities—created new pressures for government services and for economic regulatory activity to protect the consumer. Between 1881 and 1910, the number of civilians working for the federal government increased fourfold—from 100,000 to 400,000. The Departments of Agriculture and of Labor and Commerce were created to provide services to important sectors of the economy. In addition, the government embarked on its first serious steps toward regulating the economy with the creation of the Interstate Commerce Commission in 1887 to regulate the railroads, passage of the Sherman Anti-Trust Act in 1890 (enforced by the Justice

4. For concise accounts of the development of the American administrative state, see Lawrence C. Dodd and Richard L. Schott, *Congress and the Administrative State* (New York: Wiley, 1979), 16–57; and James Q. Wilson, "The Rise of the Bureaucratic State," *Public Interest* 41 (Fall 1975): 77–103.
5. Dodd and Schott, *Congress and the Administrative State,* 20.

Department), and establishment of the Federal Reserve System (1913), the Federal Trade Commission (1914), and the Federal Power Commission (1920). The Pure Food and Drug and Meat Inspection acts of 1906 created agencies to help protect the food supply. World War I further spurred the development of the federal bureaucracy as new agencies were created to coordinate the war effort.

After World War I, most of the wartime agencies were abolished and the number of government employees shrank, but not back to prewar levels. The 1920s saw only modest growth in government programs—regulation of some farm products and radio stations, additions to the national park and forest systems, and credit assistance to farmers.

Replacing the Spoils System
with a Merit System

Although the government was small during the early years of the Republic, the struggles over who would be appointed to government posts were often bitter and intense. Beginning with the administration of Andrew Jackson (1829–1837), the practice of awarding jobs in the federal executive branch to presidential supporters and friends became entrenched. Under this practice, known as the **spoils system** (derived from the expression "to the victor belong the spoils"), winning presidential candidates and parties dismissed many of the government employees of the previous administration and installed their own loyalists instead. By the time the Civil War had begun, the system was a way of life in Washington—so much so, in fact, that on assuming the presidency, Abraham Lincoln turned 90 percent of federal employees out of office and replaced them with loyal party supporters. He even reportedly wrote a letter dunning a patronage employee for his failure to pay the usual assessment on his salary to the party.[6]

One rationale for this system was that government would remain responsive to the people by circulating ordinary citizens through its ranks. Furthermore, it was claimed that the patronage system assured the president that subordinates would be reasonably supportive of his policies. Finally, the spoils system was justified as a means of nurturing political party organizations by providing their supporters with government employment.

Although the spoils system had its benefits, it brought in its wake

6. Paul Van Riper, *History of the U.S. Civil Service* (New York: Harper and Row, 1958), 43–47.

Charles Guiteau, a disgruntled federal job seeker, is arrested on July 2, 1881, after shooting President James Garfield. Guiteau's bullet killed Garfield and gave birth to a reform movement that helped eliminate the federal spoils system.

substantial graft and corruption. The sale of government jobs and kickbacks to party officials were commonplace. Instead of keeping government close to the people, the unsavory aspects of the spoils system undermined public trust in the government, and civil service reform became a prominent issue after the Civil War. The spoils system also imposed overwhelming burdens on newly elected presidents who were besieged by federal job seekers. President James Garfield, for example, complained, "The stream of callers . . . became a torrent and swept away my day. . . . I felt like crying out in the agony of my soul against the greed for office and its consumption of my time."[7] The final, but tragic, impetus for civil service reform was Garfield's assassination in 1881, just a few months after he took office, at the hand of a disappointed job seeker.

The Pendleton Act of 1883 created a Civil Service Commission and introduced hiring based on competence (not political connections), normally determined by open, competitive examinations. The basic principles of the civil service system are (1) selection of subordinate government officials on the basis of merit—the ability to perform the work—rather than partisan or personal favoritism; (2) job tenure for those hired regardless of any political changes at the top of the government organization; and (3) "willing responsiveness

7. Leonard D. White, *The Republican Era* (New York: Macmillan, 1958), 94.

to political leaders of the day" on the part of government employees in return for guarantees of job security.[8]

Passage of the Pendleton Act coincided with the beginning of substantial growth in the number of federal employees as the government expanded its functions. It thus began a process of transforming executive branch personnel from patronage appointees closely tied to elected politicians into an independent career civil service. Particularly important in this process were the efforts of two Progressive era presidents, Theodore Roosevelt (1901–1909) and Woodrow Wilson (1913–1921). Roosevelt was instrumental in creating the Commerce and Labor departments, the Forest Service, and the Food and Drug Administration. In keeping with the Progressive philosophy, he insisted that these agencies be professionally staffed. Wilson led the movement for a nonpartisan Federal Reserve System to regulate the currency and banks and for an independent Federal Trade Commission to enforce antitrust legislation.

Gradually, the merit system was extended so that by 1930, 80 percent of federal employees were covered. A further effort to depoliticize the bureaucracy came with the 1939 passage of the Hatch Act, which severely restricted the extent to which government employees could participate in partisan politics.

A major effect of the introduction of the merit system was the creation of a governmental work force separate from both the Congress and president. With its emphasis on merit as the basis for appointment, expertise, and permanence in office, the federal civil service has achieved substantial insulation from direct control by the president or Congress. Yet because it leads an existence balanced between the president and Congress, it also must be sensitive to the political forces operating within both institutions.

The Impact of the New Deal and World War II

The bureaucratic state as we know it today is largely the product of the depression of the 1930s and World War II. These crises changed public attitudes about the role of government in American society. The public accepted an activist government staffed by technical experts as a means of coping with the depression and the external threat posed by Nazi Germany and Imperial Japan. President Franklin Roosevelt's New Deal policies to combat the depression led to an explosion in the size of the federal bureaucracy as existing

8. Hugh Heclo, *A Government of Strangers: Executive Politics in Washington* (Washington, D.C.: Brookings, 1977), 20.

government programs were expanded, additional economic regulations were imposed, and new social services were provided. Among the welter of new agencies created were the Tennessee Valley Authority, Securities and Exchange Commission, Social Security Administration, Export-Import Bank, Federal Deposit Insurance Corporation, and the National Labor Relations Board. In mobilizing for World War II, government involvement in the economy reached unprecedented levels as the War Production Board mobilized industry and the Office of Price Administration regulated prices and rationed scarce consumer goods. To fund the war effort and the government's domestic programs, the federal government dramatically increased individual and corporate income taxes. With this lucrative source of revenue, the federal government was able to support its expanded role.

During the war years, scientific and technological advances caused the bureaucracy to grow in ways unimaginable earlier. The development of atomic energy necessitated creation of a government bureaucracy to regulate its use for military and peaceful purposes. Advances in rocket technology provided the basis for the creation of the National Aeronautics and Space Administration (NASA) after the war. And the growth of the airline industry, which had benefited from military research and development, spawned a system of federal regulation currently administered by the Federal Aviation Administration.

Further Expansion of Government Activity since World War II

The 1950s through the 1970s brought forth new government initiatives in health, civil rights, education, housing, income maintenance, transportation, and urban development. Particularly notable for their contributions to the growth of the federal government in the 1960s were President Lyndon Johnson's Great Society programs aimed at eliminating the causes of poverty. Among the additional federal departments and agencies created from the 1950s through the 1970s were the Departments of Health and Human Services (originally named Health, Education, and Welfare), Housing and Urban Development, Transportation, Education, and Energy, as well as the Environmental Protection Agency, Occupational Safety and Health Administration, Consumer Product Safety Commission, Equal Employment Opportunity Commission, and the Peace Corps.

Unlike previous periods of growth in government activity, the era since the 1950s has not been accompanied by significant increases in federal government employment. The growth in federal government spending from 1960 into the 1980s was dramatic (see Figure 3.1 in Chapter 3, Federalism), but, interestingly, during this expansion in government activity federal employment remained relatively stable. This paradox reflects higher costs for such existing programs as Social Security as well as increases in federal payments to state and local governments and to government contractors and consultants. Although the number of federal employees has remained relatively stable since the 1960s, employment in state and local governments implementing federal policies with grants-in-aid has increased substantially. Under the federal system, growing federal government budgets and activities do not necessarily translate into a corresponding surge in the number of federal employees. The employment impact of increased federal spending is often at the state and local levels where the programs are administered.

The executive branch has almost three million civilian employees of which only about 354,000 work in the Washington, D.C., area. The rest work in the fifty states, the territories, and around the world. To provide work space for these employees, the federal government owns or leases 412,000 buildings with 2.7 million square feet of floor space (see Figure 12.1, an organization chart of the sprawling executive establishment, for a more complete indication of the size of the bureaucracy and the scope of its activities). In terms of civilian employees, the Department of Defense ranks first with over 951,000 workers (32 percent of the federal civilian work force), followed by the U.S. Postal Service (28 percent), the Department of Veterans Affairs (8 percent), and the Department of Health and Human Services (4 percent).

The Organization of the Federal Bureaucracy

The federal government is composed of a bewildering array of agencies with diverse histories, statutory authorities, activities, and bases of political support. Government organization charts convey something of the scope of the bureaucracy (see Figure 12.1) but not the power struggles involved in creating an agency, ensuring its survival, determining where it will be located within the executive branch, or deciding on its budgets and policies.

The rise and fall of the Office of Economic Opportunity (OEO), the centerpiece of President Lyndon Johnson's War on Poverty, demonstrates the importance of organizational structure and political support in the functioning of a government agency and its programs.

Figure 12.1: Organization of the Executive Branch

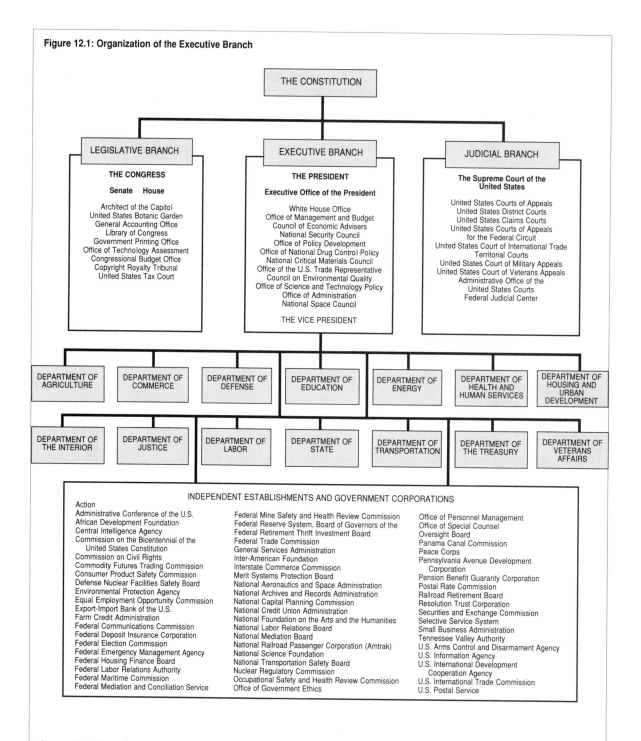

THE CONSTITUTION

LEGISLATIVE BRANCH

THE CONGRESS

Senate   House

Architect of the Capitol
United States Botanic Garden
General Accounting Office
Library of Congress
Government Printing Office
Office of Technology Assessment
Congressional Budget Office
Copyright Royalty Tribunal
United States Tax Court

EXECUTIVE BRANCH

THE PRESIDENT

Executive Office of the President

White House Office
Office of Management and Budget
Council of Economic Advisers
National Security Council
Office of Policy Development
Office of National Drug Control Policy
National Critical Materials Council
Office of the U.S. Trade Representative
Council on Environmental Quality
Office of Science and Technology Policy
Office of Administration
National Space Council

THE VICE PRESIDENT

JUDICIAL BRANCH

The Supreme Court of the United States

United States Courts of Appeals
United States District Courts
United States Claims Courts
United States Courts of Appeals
for the Federal Circuit
United States Court of International Trade
Territorial Courts
United States Court of Military Appeals
United States Court of Veterans Appeals
Administrative Office of the
United States Courts
Federal Judicial Center

DEPARTMENT OF AGRICULTURE

DEPARTMENT OF COMMERCE

DEPARTMENT OF DEFENSE

DEPARTMENT OF EDUCATION

DEPARTMENT OF ENERGY

DEPARTMENT OF HEALTH AND HUMAN SERVICES

DEPARTMENT OF HOUSING AND URBAN DEVELOPMENT

DEPARTMENT OF THE INTERIOR

DEPARTMENT OF JUSTICE

DEPARTMENT OF LABOR

DEPARTMENT OF STATE

DEPARTMENT OF TRANSPORTATION

DEPARTMENT OF THE TREASURY

DEPARTMENT OF VETERANS AFFAIRS

INDEPENDENT ESTABLISHMENTS AND GOVERNMENT CORPORATIONS

Action
Administrative Conference of the U.S.
African Development Foundation
Central Intelligence Agency
Commission on the Bicentennial of the
    United States Constitution
Commission on Civil Rights
Commodity Futures Trading Commission
Consumer Product Safety Commission
Defense Nuclear Facilities Safety Board
Environmental Protection Agency
Equal Employment Opportunity Commission
Export-Import Bank of the U.S.
Farm Credit Administration
Federal Communications Commission
Federal Deposit Insurance Corporation
Federal Election Commission
Federal Emergency Management Agency
Federal Housing Finance Board
Federal Labor Relations Authority
Federal Maritime Commission
Federal Mediation and Conciliation Service

Federal Mine Safety and Health Review Commission
Federal Reserve System, Board of Governors of the
Federal Retirement Thrift Investment Board
Federal Trade Commission
General Services Administration
Inter-American Foundation
Interstate Commerce Commission
Merit Systems Protection Board
National Aeronautics and Space Administration
National Archives and Records Administration
National Capital Planning Commission
National Credit Union Administration
National Foundation on the Arts and the Humanities
National Labor Relations Board
National Mediation Board
National Railroad Passenger Corporation (Amtrak)
National Science Foundation
National Transportation Safety Board
Nuclear Regulatory Commission
Occupational Safety and Health Review Commission
Office of Government Ethics

Office of Personnel Management
Office of Special Counsel
Oversight Board
Panama Canal Commission
Peace Corps
Pennsylvania Avenue Development
    Corporation
Pension Benefit Guaranty Corporation
Postal Rate Commission
Railroad Retirement Board
Resolution Trust Corporation
Securities and Exchange Commission
Selective Service System
Small Business Administration
Tennessee Valley Authority
U.S. Arms Control and Disarmament Agency
U.S. Information Agency
U.S. International Development
    Cooperation Agency
U.S. International Trade Commission
U.S. Postal Service

Source: *United States Government Manual, 1990–91* (Washington, D.C.: Government Printing Office, 1990), 21.

OEO was created by the Economic Opportunity Act of 1964 to serve as the lead agency in coordinating the government-wide War on Poverty. In addition, OEO was to administer the most innovative and controversial aspect of the act: a program of direct grants to community action agencies in which the poor were to take an active part in developing and carrying out antipoverty initiatives. To give his War on Poverty visibility and White House backing, President Johnson lodged OEO in the Executive Office of the President. With his active support, the agency thrived during the mid-1960s, but the succeeding Nixon and Ford administrations were not OEO backers, and the agency was downgraded administratively. The agency was then dismantled, and what remained of its programs were transferred to a new independent agency, the Community Services Administration (CSA) and to existing departments such as Health, Education, and Welfare. In its new form as CSA, the agency lacked its former prestige and political muscle as a presidential agency in the Executive Office of the President. The administrative downgrading of the agency continued under President Ronald Reagan. In 1981, CSA was abolished and its functions transferred to the Office of Community Services within the massive Department of Health and Human Services (HHS). Whereas OEO had once been a prestigious and influential agency with programs receiving vigorous presidential support, it was now a bureau almost lost within the sprawling HHS bureaucracy. Most agencies are able to defend themselves more successfully than OEO, but all face recurring efforts to either expand or restrict their effectiveness, prominence, and power through changes in organizational structure.

Cabinet-level Departments

The fourteen departments of the federal executive branch are headed by a secretary or by the attorney general in the case of the Department of Justice (see Table 12.1). The heads of these departments make up the president's cabinet.[9] Because an agency's importance within the executive branch is affirmed when it receives departmental or cabinet status, supporters of programs administered by agencies lacking cabinet rank lobby from time to time for their pet agencies to become departments as a means of raising their visibility and budgets. In 1988, for example, veterans' organizations and their administrative and congressional allies succeeded in having

---

9. The president may designate other officials to be members of the cabinet. Frequently included are the White House chief of staff, the director of the Office of Management and Budget, the U.S. trade representative, and the ambassador to the United Nations.

Table 12.1 Cabinet-level Departments of the Federal Government

Department	Year Established	Historical Development
State	1789	Originally named Department of Foreign Affairs but redesignated Department of State in 1789
Treasury	1789	Expanded through a subsequent series of statutes
Interior	1849	Created by the merger of the General Land Office, Bureau of Indian Affairs, Pension Office, and Patent Office
Agriculture	1862	Originally administered by a commissioner, the department saw its powers expand in 1889.
Justice	1870	Before 1870 the attorney general was a cabinet officer but not head of a department
Labor	1913	Originally a bureau within the Department of Interior, it became an independent department in 1913.
Commerce	1913	Designated a department when the Department of Commerce and Labor, created in 1903, was reorganized
Defense	1949	After several reorganizations, the original Departments of War (1789) and Navy (1798) were merged into the Department of Defense.
Health and Human Services	1953	Established as the Department of Health, Education, and Welfare but redesignated Health and Human Services when Education was made a separate department in 1979
Housing and Urban Development	1965	Created by combining agencies responsible for housing, including the Housing and Home Finance Agency, with those involved in urban development
Transportation	1966	Created out of eight existing agencies
Energy	1977	Created by transferring existing energy agencies and bureaus to the new department
Education	1979	Originally the Office of Education in the Department of Health, Education, and Welfare
Veterans Affairs	1988	Created by elevating the Veterans Administration to cabinet-level status

SOURCE: *United States Government Manual, 1989–90* (Washington, D.C.: Government Printing Office, 1989).

the Veterans Administration elevated to cabinet status for these reasons. Likewise, some members of Congress have sought to raise the Environmental Protection Agency to cabinet status so that its voice will be heard more forcefully on major policy issues.

Within each department, a chain of command runs from the secretary to the various units of the organization, normally designated as bureaus, administrations, offices, or divisions. Each is responsible for carrying out a congressionally mandated function of the department. The secretary is responsible for the entire agency. Under secretaries and assistant secretaries, who report to the secretary, control various segments of the department's activities. In the Department of Commerce, for example, the under secretary for economic affairs is responsible for the Bureau of the Census, Bureau of Economic Analysis, and Office of the Chief Economist (Figure 12.2). Although the secretary sets general policy, the actual implementation of policy occurs at the bureau level, where the permanent civil service personnel have a major influence over the program's operation. For example, a major responsibility of the Commerce Department is conducting the decennial census, an extremely technical operation designed and implemented by the professional staff of the Bureau of the Census. But even so technical an activity as the census has major policy implications. In conducting the 1990 census, for example, the bureau became embroiled in a controversy over the extent to which people living in the nation's largest cities had been undercounted. This issue was of critical importance because population determines the apportionment of congressional representation among the states and figures in the amount of federal aid states and cities receive.

Independent Agencies

Independent agencies are headed by presidential appointees, but they operate outside the jurisdiction of departments. In spite of their lack of cabinet status, independent agencies can have major policy-making roles. Examples of such agencies are the Central Intelligence Agency (CIA), Environmental Protection Agency (EPA), and NASA.

The extent of independent agencies' autonomy from presidential direction varies from agency to agency, depending on the statute that created them. Such agencies as the CIA, EPA, NASA, United States Information Agency, and Small Business Administration are subordinate to the president just as any department would be. The U.S. Postal Service, however, operates quite independently of the president. It is governed by an eleven-member board appointed by the president for overlapping terms. The board appoints the postmaster general, who is responsible to the board, not the president.

Figure 12.2: Department of Commerce

Source: *United States Government Manual, 1990–91* (Washington, D.C.: Government Printing Office, 1990), 148.

A special category of independent agency is the independent regulatory commission. These commissions regulate major sectors of the economy and are empowered to hold hearings, investigate business practices, and make rulings that affect both individual firms and whole industries. Members of regulatory commissions are appointed by the president with the consent of the Senate. But unlike departments, commissions are headed by several commissioners (often five) instead of a single administrator. To insulate them from partisan and presidential pressures, commissioners are required by statute to be from both parties and are appointed for fixed, overlapping terms of at least five years. In addition, commission members may not be removed by the White House because the president disagrees with their policies.

Examples of major independent regulatory agencies include the Interstate Commerce Commission (ICC), created in 1887 to regulate railroads, bus lines, water carriers, trucking companies, and coal slurry pipelines, and the Federal Trade Commission (FTC), established in 1914 to promote competition and prevent restraints on trade, prevent false advertising and discriminatory pricing, and ensure truthful labeling of products and disclosure of credit charges. The Federal Communications Commission (FCC) was created in 1934 to regulate radio and television broadcasting, as well as telephone, telegraph, cable television, and satellite communications. And the National Labor Relations Board (NLRB), established in 1935, is responsible for preventing and remedying unfair labor practices by employers and unions and conducting collective bargaining elections.

Although the regulatory commissions were designed to be insulated from political pressures, they are not, in reality, immune from such influences. Regulatory commission decisions have far-reaching consequences for both the regulated industries and the public. For example, the ICC can rule against railroad mergers; the FCC can either grant or deny the renewal of a television station's license worth millions of dollars; and the FTC can rule that a cereal company is guilty of false and misleading advertising for its leading product. These kinds of impacts cause affected interests, particularly regulated industries and more recently public interest groups, to seek influence over commission policy.

The potential for interest group influence is enhanced by the organizational structures of the independent regulatory agencies which limit direct presidential and congressional control of agency policy. This lack of control can increase agencies' dependence on the interests they regulate for support, leading in some instances to their "capture" by regulated interests. Indeed, after the initial reform fervor favoring regulation has subsided, agencies may find that the expertise, interest, and dependable political support they need to sustain themselves rests mainly in the regulated industry. The regulator and regulated, therefore, tend to develop a relationship of mutual support, the kind found, for example, between the ICC and the railroads or the Federal Energy Regulatory Commission and the natural gas producers.[10] Not all regulatory agencies are "captured," however. The Environmental Protection Agency and the Occupational Safety and Health Review Commission, for example, have been less vulnerable to "capture" because, among other things, the statutes they administer contain strict guidelines and, in the case of EPA, the timetables for compliance leave limited discretion to administrators. They also regulate an array of industries and do not have to confront a single, united opposition. Finally, these agencies have been supported by activist public interest groups and the media.

Although their direct influence is limited, neither the president nor Congress is without weapons to influence regulatory commissions. A president can affect agency policy through commission appointments. Presidents Nixon and Carter, for example, appointed consumer-oriented chairmen to the FTC; Reagan, in contrast, appointed nonactivist commissioners. Congress can influence policy by changing the regulatory statutes the agencies enforce, passing legislation to reorganize the agencies, reducing or increasing agency budgets, and lobbying the White House on appointments. But the critics of such measures point out that things can quickly get out of hand. They charge, for example, that Congress bears some responsibility for the massive savings and loan association collapse of the 1980s that cost taxpayers billions because it relaxed regulatory statutes, limited funds available to the Federal Savings and Loan Insurance Corporation, and intervened in the regulatory process to assist constituents.[11]

10. For a discussion of "capture," see Carl Van Horn, Donald C. Baumer, and William T. Gormley, Jr., *Politics and Public Policy* (Washington, D.C.: CQ Press, 1989), 111–112. For an alternate view, see Paul J. Quirk, *Industry Influence in Federal Regulatory Agencies* (Princeton, N.J.: Princeton University Press, 1981).

11. Thomas Romer and Barry R. Weingast, "Political Foundations of the Thrift Debacle," in *Politics and Economics of the 1980s,* ed. Alberto Alesina and Geoffrey Carliner (Chicago: University of Chicago Press, 1991).

*Government Institutes
and Foundations*

To promote science, scholarship, and the arts, Congress created a series of independent institutes and foundations, each with its own board of directors responsible for its operations. The oldest is the Smithsonian Institution, which operates museums, art galleries, the John F. Kennedy Center for the Performing Arts, and a zoo in the District of Columbia. Medical research institutes include the National Institutes of Health, National Cancer Institute, and the National Heart Institute. Among the foundations established to promote scholarship and the arts are the National Science Foundation, a major funding source for scientific research, and the National Foundation on the Arts and the Humanities.

Government Corporations

Government corporations, which are chartered by congressional statute, operate much like private corporations except that the president, not stockholders, selects the board of directors. Some of these corporations provide consumer services, such as the National Railroad Passenger Corporation (Amtrak, the intercity passenger train service), and COMSAT, the communications satellite system. Other government corporations provide insurance; the Federal Deposit Insurance Corporation, which insures bank depositors' savings, and the Federal Crop Insurance Corporation for farmers are two examples. Some government corporations function as a unit within a regular department—for example, the Department of Agriculture's Commodity Credit Corporation. Others, like the Export-Import Bank and Pension Benefit Guaranty Corporation, operate as independent agencies.

The Federal Service

The men and women who staff the federal government are a diverse lot. They range from the presidential appointees who handle delicate relations with other nations, to the doctors in the U.S. Public Health Service, to the forest rangers, astronauts, nurses, painters, secretaries, lawyers, accountants, and cooks who labor in the other far corners of the government. They work in sharply contrasting bureaucratic cultures—the rather staid, tradition-bound professionalism of the Bureau of the Census or Department of the Treasury; the protocol-laden, cautious, procedure-conscious atmosphere of the State Department; the socially activist milieu of the Department of Housing and Urban Development; the pressure-

Surgeon General Antonia Novello, shown here in the official uniform of the Public Health Service, helps direct the work of thousands of health care professionals in the massive Department of Health and Human Services.

Political Appointees

packed environment of the Federal Aviation Administration's air-traffic controllers.

The federal service is not composed of people cut from the same cloth. Because of the wide variety of jobs within the federal government, the federal work force is quite representative of the American population in terms of such social characteristics as region of origin, occupation, education, income, social background, and race.[12] Although women (49.8 percent of total civilian employment in 1988) and minorities (blacks, 16.3 percent, and Hispanics, 4.8 percent) are substantially represented, they tend to be concentrated in the lower pay grades (Table 12.2). The upper levels of the civil service are composed mainly of highly educated, white, male, urban-dwelling professionals from middle-class backgrounds.[13]

Merit System Employees

Ninety percent of federal civilian employees are selected through a merit system. Of these, over 60 percent are hired after completing competitive examinations administered by the government's principal personnel agency, the Office of Personnel Management (OPM). In addition, some professional and managerial personnel are appointed on the basis of their job qualifications (much like in the private sector), as specified by the OPM. Several agencies have their own merit hiring systems, which operate outside the jurisdiction of OPM. These include the State Department (for its Foreign Service employees), CIA, FBI, U.S. Postal Service, Department of Veterans Affairs, and the Public Health Service (for its physicians). Personnel exempt from OPM control constitute almost 40 percent of the federal work force.

Also exempt from the civil service merit system are the approximately 3,900 presidential appointees who serve at the pleasure of the president. Through these appointments, presidents are able to install their own people in policy-making positions and in slots that involve confidential relationships with policy makers. With this system of hiring, however, a substantial turnover in the federal service occurs whenever a new administration takes office. By contrast, in Britain only a small number of senior civil service positions change hands when a new prime minister is chosen. All remaining personnel are expected to assist the new cabinet and implement its policies.

In the United States, among the top-level policy-making positions

12. Kenneth J. Meier and Lloyd G. Nigro, "Representative Bureaucracy and Policy Preferences," *Public Administration Review* 36 (July/August 1976): 458–469.

13. Meier, *Politics and Bureaucracy,* 182.

Table 12.2 Composition of the Federal Service by Salary Level, Racial/Ethnic Group, and Sex: 1988

The lower ranks of the federal service are filled by a substantial proportion of minority and female employees. Even with government affirmative action programs, the upper levels of the federal service are composed predominantly of white males.

Government Service (GS) Salary Level		Total Number	Percent Black	Percent Hispanic	Percent Female
GS-01	$ 9,811–12,275	6,255	39.0	9.9	75.0
GS-02	$11,032–13,883	16,792	35.9	8.2	71.4
GS-03	$12,038–15,647	71,557	28.6	6.9	73.9
GS-04	$13,513–17,563	172,407	26.6	6.2	76.4
GS-05	$15,118–19,654	215,092	22.8	5.8	72.2
GS-06	$16,851–21,909	101,956	23.6	5.0	76.7
GS-07	$18,726–24,342	155,423	18.8	5.5	61.2
GS-08	$20,739–26,958	33,827	22.8	4.0	57.9
GS-09	$22,907–29,783	172,189	13.1	5.5	46.3
GS-10	$25,226–32,795	30,139	12.9	5.5	48.0
GS-11	$27,716–36,032	212,102	11.1	4.5	37.6
GS-12	$33,218–43,181	203,468	9.1	3.5	26.0
GS-13	$39,501–51,354	133,032	6.9	2.6	18.5
GS-14	$46,679–60,683	72,932	5.2	2.1	13.8
GS-15	$54,907–71,377	41,662	3.8	2.2	11.4
Total, all pay plans		2,125,148	16.5	5.2	42.2
Total, GS and equivalent		1,638,833	16.3	4.8	49.8

SOURCE: Harold W. Stanley and Richard G. Niemi, eds., *Vital Statistics on American Politics,* 3d ed. (Washington, D.C.: CQ Press, 1992), table 12-20.

subject to presidential control are the over five hundred cabinet secretaries and subcabinet officers (including under, deputy, and assistant secretaries; top-level independent agency personnel; ambassadors; U.S. attorneys; and members of various commissions and boards). In addition to these are the so-called Schedule C appointees, who are entrusted with policy-determining responsibilities or who have a confidential relationship with key decision makers. As presidents have sought to exert more influence over the executive branch, the number of high-level political appointees has increased dramatically, from 500 in 1977 to 986 in 1988.[14]

14. Judith Havemann, "Program Would Lure Talented Students to Civil Service with Fellowships," *Washington Post,* June 9, 1988, A17.

The Senior Executive Service (SES)

The Civil Service Reform Act of 1978, by creating a Senior Executive Service, gave presidents and their appointees even more flexibility in managing the federal bureaucracy. The reformers behind this act recognized that career civil service executives had important policy-making responsibilities but that their primary loyalty was normally to their agency, not necessarily to the administration's objectives. Indeed, according to the reformers, these career bureaucrats were excessively insulated from the legitimate control of their politically appointed superiors. To rectify this situation, the act created an 8,500-member Senior Executive Service. Unlike regular civil service personnel, SES members can be transferred from one agency to another and to different positions within an agency. They also can be dismissed for ineffectiveness more readily than regular members of the civil service. Both President Jimmy Carter, who had pressed for enactment of the Civil Service Reform Act, and President Ronald Reagan took advantage of the flexibility the act provided to restructure the senior bureaucracy. Indeed, Reagan reassigned 520 SES members in his first year in office, slightly fewer than those reassigned by Carter.

The initial response to SES within the bureaucracy was highly favorable, and 98 percent of the senior managers eligible to join did so. Within two to three years, however, disillusionment set in as Congress and the Office of Management and Budget slashed the number of SES personnel eligible for cash bonuses. Complaints were made that bonuses went to people with good political connections and that the SES system was being used to politicize the bureaucracy. Moreover, bureaucrats with a liberal Democratic orientation reacted bitterly to having to carry out the conservative policies of the Reagan administration. It was thus no great surprise that 40 percent of SES officials left government service between 1979 and 1983.[15]

The high turnover at the top is but one manifestation of a much deeper problem of low morale within the civil service generally. A 1987 survey showed that more than 60 percent of federal managers would not recommend a career in the federal government to young people.[16] These morale problems appear to stem from pay scales below those of the private sector, budget cutbacks imposed by Congress and OMB, reductions in force during the Reagan administra-

15. William T. Gormley, *Taming the Bureaucracy: Muscles, Prayers, and Other Strategies* (Princeton, N.J.: Princeton University Press, 1989), 131.
16. John Schachter, "Volker's Target: A Flagging Federal Service," *Congressional Quarterly Weekly Report,* November 26, 1988, 3405.

tion, and the increased politicization of the Office of Personnel Management.[17] Because the government must be able to recruit and retain high-quality personnel if it is to perform its functions, the status of the federal service is an issue that will probably receive even more attention in the 1990s.

The Political Outlook of the Bureaucracy

Because the bureaucracy is in a position to influence the direction of departmental and agency policy, political activists and scholars worry about how well the bureaucracy represents the public's political outlook. A related issue is the extent to which the personnel of various agencies differ in their policy orientations and what impact those differences may have.

Representativeness and Interagency Differences

Surveys show that when upper-level civil servants are viewed in the aggregate, they appear to have policy views quite similar to those of the total U.S. population. Though somewhat more liberal than the public as a whole, the bureaucracy is not a hotbed of radicalism as some conservative critics have charged.[18] Bureaucrats are not disaffected by American values. Indeed, their views are more supportive of American society than those of the leading journalists, public interest group activists, or Hollywood elites (TV writers, producers, and directors).[19] The most significant way in which the civil service and the public differ is partisanship. Government employment is more likely to appeal to Democrats than to Republicans, whose commitment to smaller government makes private sector employment more attractive.[20]

The roughly representative nature of upper-level civil servants' policy views should not obscure the fact that employees' political outlooks vary from agency to agency. Certain types of agencies tend to attract people with particular policy orientations; indeed, departments and bureaus often recruit employees from among the clienteles they serve. Thus, the Department of Agriculture recruits heavily from farm interests and state land-grant universities, and the Department of Housing and Urban Development recruits from ur-

17. Gormley, *Taming the Bureaucracy*, 132–133.
18. Meier, *Politics and Bureaucracy*, 183.
19. Stanley Rothman and S. Robert Lichter, "How Liberal Are Bureaucrats? *Regulation* 7 (December 1983): 17–18.
20. Meier, *Politics and Bureaucracy*, 35.

ban dwellers and minorities. In addition, bureaus within departments are quite successful in socializing their personnel to the values and roles prescribed by the agency.[21]

The relationship between the type of agency a bureaucrat works for and his or her political viewpoint is evident in a comparison of the attitudes of employees in activist and traditional agencies (Table 12.3). Employees of such activist agencies as the Environmental Protection Agency, Federal Trade Commission, Consumer Product Safety Commission, Equal Employment Opportunity Commission, and the civil rights division of the Justice Department are more apt to be liberals than members of such traditional departments as Agriculture, Commerce, and Treasury, or the Bureau of Prisons in the Department of Justice.[22]

But the extent to which personal ideology actually affects bureaucratic behavior is complicated by a variety of other forces impinging upon government workers. Civil servants must carry out policies contained in the federal statutes, some of which may be categorized as liberal and others as conservative. Government employees also must be sensitive to the wishes of influential members of Congress, their politically appointed superiors, the clienteles that they serve, and their coworkers. In addition, most senior bureaucrats are professionally trained—as, for example, lawyers, doctors, engineers, administrators, accountants, economists—and they are therefore affected by the norms and ways of thinking that characterize their professions.

Bureaucratic Conflict

Bureaucratic power struggles and conflicts among agencies over policy are an enduring feature of the governmental process. Each department and agency was created by its own statutes, has its own programs to administer, serves a particular clientele, and, of course, has its own permanent staff. As a result, distinctive traditions, ways of thinking, policy orientations, and modes of operation are found within government agencies. Such differences can lead to interagency conflicts.

Because almost all bureaucratic personnel are highly protective of their particular missions and programs, they usually try to prevent other agencies from encroaching on their activities. Thus, "turf"

21. For a discussion of the impact of agency socialization processes and social backgrounds on top-level administrators' political attitudes, see Meier and Nigro, "Representative Bureaucracy and Policy Preferences"; and Joel D. Aberbach and Bert A. Rockman, "Clashing Beliefs within the Executive Branch: The Nixon Administration," *American Political Science Review* 70 (June 1976): 456–468.

22. Rothman and Lichter, "How Liberal Are Bureaucrats?" 21.

Table 12.3 Political Orientation of Senior Bureaucrats

Attitude/Behavior	Percent of Bureaucrats Agreeing from		
	Traditional Agencies[a]	Activist Agencies[b]	Combined
Liberal	48	63	56
Voted for Carter (1980)	34	55	45
Voted for Reagan (1980)	48	27	36
Government should substantially redistribute income.	49	55	52
Government should guarantee a good standard of living.	41	46	43
A woman has a right to an abortion.	80	82	81
U.S. institutions need complete overhaul.	25	16	20
U.S. should move toward socialism.	14	14	14
CIA overthrows are sometimes necessary.	57	63	60
Adultery is wrong.	69	65	67
Homosexuality is wrong.	54	40	47
In America hard work leads to financial security.	72	63	67

SOURCE: Stanley Rothman and S. Robert Lichter, "How Liberal Are Bureaucrats?" *Regulation* 7 (December 1983): 18. Reprinted with the permission of the American Enterprise Institute for Public Policy Research, Washington, D.C.

[a]Traditional agency administrators consisted of a sample of ninety-eight persons in the Departments of Agriculture, Commerce, and Treasury, and the Bureau of Prisons in the Department of Justice.

[b]Activist agency administrators consisted of a sample of 102 persons in the Environmental Protection Agency, Federal Trade Commission, Consumer Product Safety Commission, Equal Employment Opportunity Commission, Food and Drug Administration of the Department of Health and Human Services, Department of Housing and Urban Development, and Justice Department's civil rights division.

battles over control of programs, policy, budgets, and personnel are an additional source of interagency conflict. For example, as President Bush mounted his war on drugs, intense, behind-the-scenes struggles for control of policy and administration took place between the Justice Department (the principal law enforcement agency of the federal government) and the new drug policy director's office in the Executive Office of the President.[23]

23. Ruth Marcus, "Goodwill for Thornburgh Erodes," *Washington Post,* Jan. 6, 1990, A1, A8.

One of the most prominent examples of the continuing pattern of interagency maneuvering and conflict has been the relationship among the Department of State, Department of Defense, and the National Security Council (NSC) staff at the White House. Each agency has a different mission and orientation. The State Department's mission is to seek diplomatic accommodation, sometimes through the selective use of military force. The Pentagon is interested in maintaining force levels and improving its technology. Not surprisingly, it has been skeptical about reforms in the Soviet Union and often has been reluctant to commit its forces to further diplomatic objectives. The NSC staff at the White House is concerned with presidential policy priorities as well as with the president's political standing.

Conflicts among these foreign policy institutions frequently dominate Washington's bureaucratic landscape. During the Reagan presidency, for example, State and Defense clashed over such arms control issues as whether to abide by the provisions of the unratified SALT II agreement with the Soviets. There were also differences over sending marines on a peace-keeping mission to Lebanon. State favored deployment; Defense opposed it. A related incident in November 1983 proved to be a dramatic example of the State-Defense conflict. Following the October 1983 terrorist bombing that killed 241 marines and 59 French paratroopers in Beirut, Lebanon, the United States planned a joint air strike with the French against the Shiite militiamen believed by the CIA to be responsible for the bombing. At the appointed hour, however, the French jets took off alone; the final go-ahead order had not been given by the Pentagon. The Defense Department had opposed the operation, which was championed by the State Department and the National Security Council staff, who had secured the president's approval. Secretary of Defense Casper Weinberger explained the Pentagon's failure to order the planes into action by saying that the navy needed more time to plan and execute the mission.[24]

The military and the State Department also differed on how to deal with Panamanian dictator Manuel Noriega, who had been accused of running drugs in the United States. In 1988 and 1989, the military indicated its substantial reluctance to confront Noriega, despite being urged to do so by the Department of State. Thus, the December 1989 invasion of Panama occurred only after the White

24. Hedrick Smith, *The Power Game: How Washington Works* (New York: Random House, 1988), 583.

House asserted its authority.[25] Since that time, however, the institutional rivalries that were so prominent during the Reagan administration seem to have subsided over the life of the Bush administration. For example, apparently no major interdepartmental conflicts arose over America's response to Iraq's invasion of Kuwait in 1990. But, as the foreign policy disputes within the Reagan administration illustrate, the executive branch is anything but monolithic, and interagency conflicts are a recurring feature of the governing process.

The Political Environment of Bureaucratic Policy Making

When administering the laws passed by Congress, the bureaucracy must apply the laws to specific circumstances in a manner consistent with the intent and statutory guidelines set by Congress. Congress, however, is frequently vague about both the intent of a new law and how it should operate—usually a side effect of the delicate negotiations and compromises required to muster congressional majorities for passage of a bill and the inability of Congress to anticipate all the circumstances administrators will face in implementing the law. To offset this ambiguity, the bureaucracy is given substantial administrative discretion in implementing the statutes. For example, after the massive tax reform act of 1986, which ran almost a thousand pages, was passed, it was up to the Internal Revenue Service to develop the intricate rules needed to apply the act to individuals and an array of different types of businesses. Similarly, the Environmental Protection Agency is responsible for implementing the 1990 Clean Air Act by developing administrative policies designed to limit the amount of pollutants released into the air by autos, power plants, and factories.

Rule Making and Regulations

In exercising administrative discretion, the bureaucracy engages in **rule making**, aimed at developing a set of **regulations** (rules) to govern the functioning of a government program. The procedures for rule making are set forth in the Administrative Procedures Act of 1946, which was designed to ensure that rule making occurs openly and systematically so that all the interested parties can be heard. Proposed regulations are published in the *Federal Register,* an official document which also publishes finalized government regulations. The public is then given an opportunity to comment on the

25. Joe Pichirallo and Patrick E. Tyler, "Long Road to the Invasion of Panama," *Washington Post,* Jan. 14, 1990, A1, A20.

proposed regulations (which may include public hearings) before administrators decide on their final form. Administrative regulations have the force of law because they are authorized by congressional statutes.

In exercising administrative discretion and its rule-making powers, the bureaucracy is an integral part of the political or policy-making process. Indeed, administrative processes are in no way separate and distinct from politics—interests who lost in the policy-making struggles in the Congress frequently try to recoup some of their losses by influencing the administrative process, while those who were successful in Congress find that they must protect victories at the implementation stage of policy making.

Iron Triangles: Mutual
Support Environments

The Washington political environment is highly charged, competitive, and combative. And making things worse, the leadership on Capitol Hill and at 1600 Pennsylvania Avenue is subject to change with each election; when this happens the thrust of government policy can shift as well. In this uncertain atmosphere and because inevitably their actions arouse controversy and opposition, agency bureaucracies seek the constancy of stable, long-term relationships with both their supporters in government and their clientele groups outside government. In addition, agencies must constantly fight for a share of the government's limited budgetary resources, defend their "turf" (policy jurisdictions and missions) from poachers in other agencies, and fend off critics seeking agency dismantlement.

One possible source of support is the White House, but presidents and their staffs come and go. Moreover, presidents may not be particularly supportive of an agency's activities, as President Richard Nixon's policies toward the Office of Economic Opportunity demonstrated. Some agencies, however, are able to develop relationships of mutual support with members of the congressional committees having jurisdiction over them and with the interest groups they serve. As we saw in Chapter 8, these mutually advantageous and durable three-sided alliances of the bureaucracy, congressional committees, and clientele groups have been described as *iron triangles* or *subgovernments.*[26] Such alliances permit agency personnel to gain support for their programs, interested senators and representatives to pro-

---

26. For a discussion of iron triangles or subgovernments, see Douglas Cater, *Power in Washington* (New York: Random House, 1964), 26–50; Roger Davidson, "Breaking Up Those 'Cozy Triangles': An Impossible Dream," in *Legislative Reform and Public Policy,* ed. Susan Welch and J. G. Peters (New York: Praeger, 1977).

mote policies in which they believe (and in the process pick up electoral backing from interest groups and constituents), and clientele groups to derive benefits from agency programs. Although this description makes iron triangles appear self-serving for their members, most participants sincerely believe in the merits of the government programs in which they are involved. For members of the bureaucracy, their agency and its programs are their life's work; for members of Congress, agency programs can be a way of promoting their conception of the public interest and their constituents' interests (legislators frequently see them as one and the same!); and for an agency's clientele, the agency programs from which they benefit are sound policy.

One stable and powerful subgovernment is composed of the Department of Veterans Affairs, the Veterans Affairs committees of the House and Senate, and veterans' organizations. All these groups cooperate to maintain and expand the programs of the department. Another example of a subgovernment is the alliance of the Federal Maritime Commission, the House Merchant Marine and Fisheries Committee, and the maritime industry and its unions. This subgovernment promotes Maritime Commission programs, which subsidize shipbuilding and ocean-going transportation. In promoting these interests, the maritime industry and unions have been particularly aggressive in lobbying and making campaign contributions to their congressional allies.

With alliances such as these, it is often difficult to alter agency policies substantially or to eliminate government agencies. Once in operation, most government domestic programs build a cadre of supporters within Congress, among benefiting groups and individuals, and, of course, among the agency's staff. Although Ronald Reagan retained a high level of popularity throughout most of his presidency, he was consistently thwarted by these three-way alliances in his efforts to eliminate what he considered unnecessary agencies and programs. In fact, he failed to ax forty-three of the forty-five programs on his hit list.

Iron triangles tend to occur in policy fields that are not highly visible or conflictual. For example, neither the media nor the public pay much attention to veterans or maritime policy, and neither area produces much controversy. Not every agency, however, operates in such a cozy, calm environment.

For an iron triangle to exist, an agency normally must have clientele groups that do not have conflicting goals. The Environmental Protection Agency, for example, finds itself constantly being praised or attacked by such diverse interests as industry, public health interest groups, and environmentalists as it implements controversial clean air and water statutes. Even members of Congress, acting for one of these interests, may exert pressure on the agency—all of which, of course, makes the life of the top EPA administrator unenviable. He or she cannot benefit from a tight, supportive alliance composed of the agency, the appropriate congressional committees, and clientele groups.

Issue Networks: Open,
Conflictual Environments

Many agencies, like EPA, operate in environments inhabited by interests with different goals and levels of political activity and clout. Called *issue networks,* these diverse and often conflicting configurations of interests can be composed of interest groups, members of Congress and their staffs, bureaucrats, experts from academe and think tanks, concerned individuals, Washington insiders, and journalists.[27] Whereas iron triangles and subgovernments suggest a stable set of participants who coalesce to control a narrow area of policy from which they derive benefits, issue networks convey a strikingly different image. Fluid, ever-changing participation by individuals or groups with often sharp differences of opinion and the absence of a tight agency-congressional committee-clientele group controlling policy characterize issue networks.

The emergence of issue networks stems from the proliferation of interest groups (described in Chapter 8) and the expanded role of government in providing services and regulating the economy.[28] In the current political environment of Washington, some policy areas once dominated by iron triangles are now multidimensional: the number of participants has increased along with the frequency of conflict. Perhaps nowhere is this more evident than in the rivers and harbors improvement program of the U.S. Army Corps of Engineers—once a textbook example of an iron triangle. In those days, the corps built dams, levees, and harbors for the benefit of local business interests in representatives' and senators' constituencies in accordance with legislation drafted by the congressional Public Works committees. But what was once a small, close-knit policy community

27. The concept of issue networks has been developed by Hugh Heclo, "Issue Networks and the Executive Establishment," in *The New American Political System,* ed. Anthony King (Washington, D.C.: American Enterprise Institute, 1978), 87–124.

28. For a description of how an expanded issue agenda, the growth of and change in interest groups, and an increased role for the media have transformed the Washington political community, see Barbara Sinclair, *The Transformation of the U.S. Senate* (Baltimore: Johns Hopkins University Press, 1989), chap. 4.

controlling operations stemming from **pork-barrel legislation** (pet projects of less critical need for legislators' constituencies) had to cave in to today's major environmental concerns. Abandoned by its iron triangle which operated in relative anonymity and without open conflict, rivers and harbors policy is now made within the context of a larger, less stable, and conflictual issue network.

With the proliferation of issue networks, a broader array of concerns and interests are being brought to bear on the decisions of the executive branch and the Congress. But at the same time, policy making within an issue network environment is extremely complex and time-consuming.

Coping with the Bureaucracy: Presidential, Congressional, and Judicial Strategies

In spite of people's dependence on it for cradle-to-the-grave services, the bureaucracy finds few champions in America. Indeed, hostility to the bureaucracy has been bipartisan. "Bureaucracy-bashing" was a common and compelling theme of the presidential campaigns of Republican Richard Nixon and American Independent George Wallace in 1968 (Wallace complained of "pointy headed bureaucrats that couldn't park their bicycles straight"), Democrat Jimmy Carter in 1976, and Republican Ronald Reagan in 1980. As the bureaucracy has grown, some observers fret that it poses a threat to our constitutional order and to its institutions—the presidency, the Congress, and the courts.

The President and the Executive Branch

Although the Constitution charges the president with the responsibility for taking "Care that the Laws be faithfully executed," presidents cannot, of course, personally supervise the vast federal executive apparatus. But they do have the means to significantly influence administrative decision making. Presidents have the power to appoint high-level administrators, draw up the federal budget, and give policy direction to administrators.

Ronald Reagan, for example, had a profound impact on federal regulatory policy. Whereas his predecessor, Jimmy Carter, had appointed pro-regulation officials to head up the federal regulatory agencies, Reagan advocated a policy of deregulation and appointed individuals who were not strong advocates of regulation to such agencies as the National Highway Traffic Safety Administration (NHTSA), Occupational Safety and Health Review Commission

(OSHRC), Environmental Protection Agency (EPA), Federal Trade Commission (FTC), and Consumer Product Safety Commission (CPSC). The Reagan appointees were supported by a White House order that subjected all regulations to an exacting cost-benefit analysis. The impact of the administration's policies and appointees was substantial: NHTSA repealed twenty-four rules to assist the auto industry; OSHRC emphasized voluntary compliance instead of agency enforcement; EPA became a battleground between political appointees and civil service employees over environmental policy; the FTC became a free-market advocate; and CPSC became an inactive industry regulator.[29] As Bush appointees replaced Reagan personnel, there were further policy changes. At the Department of Labor, which had been relatively inactive, for example, Secretary Elizabeth Dole (1989–1990) initiated consultations with leaders of organized labor, investigated eight major corporations to determine if an invisible barrier—a "glass ceiling"—was impeding the progress of women and minorities up the corporate ladder, tightened OSHRC enforcement of safety and health regulations, and sought settlements of the bitter Appalachian miners' strike against the Pittston Coal Company.[30]

The Problem of Presidential Control. Although presidential influence over government policy stems from the president's position as head of the executive branch, over the years presidents have had their hands full in trying to control the massive executive establishment. In theory, the nonelected personnel of the executive branch are accountable to and take their marching orders from the president, who is ultimately responsible to the American people. But because the president has limited time and energy and is able to participate personally in only a small fraction of the government's activities, it is up to the president's appointees to carry forward administration policies.

The problem of maintaining presidential control over the executive branch is further complicated by the multiple constituencies that the heads of federal agencies must serve. Presidents fear that the people they have appointed to high-level executive positions will "go native"—that is, they will adopt the orientations of their agency's career employees, of the clientele groups served by the agency, and of the congressional committees with which the agency must deal. To do their jobs, cabinet and subcabinet appointees of the president

29. Meier, *Politics and Bureaucracy,* 156.
30. Kirk Victor, "Changeover at Labor," *National Journal,* November 3, 1990, 2660–2663.

President Bush meets with his cabinet in the White House.

must work with staffs of all these groups. But the need to accommodate these constituencies often causes department heads to see issues from a perspective different from that of the occupant of the Oval Office. It is hard to imagine, for example, a secretary of agriculture being effective without cordial relations with at least some of the major farm interest groups and key members of the Agriculture committees on Capitol Hill.

This tendency for cabinet officers to see the president as only one of several constituencies they must serve led Charles Dawes, Calvin Coolidge's vice president and holder of a variety of high executive posts, to remark that "the members of the Cabinet are the President's natural enemies."[31] Although Dawes's use of the word "enemies" may have been a bit strong, his comment does convey presidents' recurring worries about the extent of cabinet commitment to presidential priorities. President Lyndon Johnson lamented,

When I looked out at the heads of the departments, I realized that while all had been appointed by me, not a single one was really mine. I could never fully depend on them to put my priorities first. All too often, they responded to their constituencies instead of mine.[32]

After the 1980 election, the transition team of Reagan loyalists planning for his administration were so concerned about this problem

31. Quoted by Richard E. Neustadt, *Presidential Power: The Politics of Leadership* (New York: Wiley, 1960), 39.
32. Doris Kerns, *Lyndon Johnson and the American Dream* (New York: Harper and Row, 1976), 253.

that they seriously considered housing the cabinet secretaries in the Old Executive Office Building next door to the White House instead of in the various departmental office buildings.[33]

But the president's difficulties in controlling the executive departments stem not just from problems with department heads. The permanent bureaucracy may seek to thwart presidential policies because of genuine policy disagreements with the president or in an effort to protect the budget, personnel, and programs of their agencies. Presidential appointees within departments and agencies serve on average only about two years, but key committee and subcommittee chairmen in Congress are apt to be around for a long time. Thus, according to David Broder of the *Washington Post,* senior civil servants give their formal

allegiance to their executive superiors and their knowledge to their old pals on Capitol Hill. The bureaucrat can say "Yes, sir," when an assistant secretary directs him to do something [with which he disagrees] . . . , and then make certain that the memorandum he had written protesting the order falls into the hands of the right congressman or staff member. It happens everyday. And the congressman or staff member, instead of confronting the assistant secretary, often leaks the memorandum to a Capitol Hill reporter and, when the story is published, declares solemnly that the issue deserves investigation.[34]

Bureaucratic sabotage such as this again demonstrates that administration and politics are inseparable.[35]

Presidential Strategies to Achieve Control. Faced with a massive bureaucracy beyond the scope of one person to supervise personally and the tendency of department heads to have multiple loyalties, presidents have tended to rely on their White House staffs to assess policy recommendations coming from the departments and to supervise departmental activities. In contrast to agency personnel, White House staff have only one constituency—the president—and their influence depends on their relationship with the occupant of the Oval Office.

The rise of the White House staff, however, has created its own problems. It has caused tension and conflict between department heads and the White House and has meant that the president has a

33. Hugh Heclo, "One Executive Branch or Many?" in *Both Ends of the Avenue,* ed. Anthony King (Washington, D.C.: American Enterprise Institute, 1983), 46.
34. David S. Broder, *Behind the Front Page: A Candid Look at How the News Is Made* (New York: Simon and Schuster, 1987), 210.
35. For a discussion of bureaucratic sabotage and political executives' responses, see Heclo, *Government of Strangers,* 224–232.

new control problem—supervising the large and sometimes overly active White House staff.

While all modern presidents have worried about gaining control over the executive branch, probably no president has gone to the lengths that Richard Nixon did to corral what he considered to be a hostile executive establishment. In 1971, he proposed the creation of a "supercabinet," which would have merged the eight existing domestic departments into four new superagencies—natural resources, human resources, economic affairs, and community development. Congress, however, rejected the idea. Nixon also sought to appoint emissaries—some have called them "spies"—within each department to work with the White House staff in controlling the departments. But his attempt to gain presidential control over the executive branch was cut short by the Watergate scandal and his forced resignation from the presidency. Like his predecessors and his successors, then, Nixon left office dissatisfied with his ability to direct the executive branch.[36]

President Reagan's approach to the problem of presidential control over the executive branch was quite different than Nixon's. He entered office with clearly defined policy goals that departmental appointees were expected to implement. Heavy emphasis was placed on appointing people loyal to the president and his positions on issues. But where Presidents Nixon and Carter had given their cabinet officers a relatively free hand in appointing subordinates, the Reagan White House scrutinized and cleared appointees for compatibility with the Reagan philosophy. The Reagan administration also centralized the development of legislative strategy in the White House so that departmental officials had little power to negotiate with Congress on their own. Centralized policy planning was encouraged as well by the use of cabinet councils—cabinet subgroups with responsibility for developing coordinated policies in various areas of governmental activity such as economic policy. These cabinet councils were kept on a short leash by having their work coordinated and reviewed by White House staff.[37] Although the Bush administration has tended to give department heads more leeway in developing pol-

---

36. For an account of the Nixon strategy for controlling the executive branch, see Richard P. Nathan, *The Administrative Presidency* (New York: Wiley, 1983), chaps. 3 and 4.

37. Heclo, "One Executive Branch or Many?" 43–47; and Peter M. Benda and Charles H. Levine, "Reagan and the Bureaucracy," in *The Reagan Legacy: Promise and Performance,* ed. Charles O. Jones (Chatham, N.J.: Chatham House, 1988), chap. 4.

icy and appointing subordinates, many of the control mechanisms employed by the Reagan White House remain in place.

Responsible Government or a "Fourth Branch"? Democratic theory would seem to dictate that since presidents are constitutionally responsible for the actions of the executive branch and are held politically accountable for them, they also should have the power needed to control the executive agencies. It is, after all, the president who is elected, not the personnel staffing the agencies. Acting on this theory, reformers have traditionally advocated giving presidents more authority and staff to carry out their administrative responsibilities.

An alternative argument, however, is that the bureaucracy should be an independent force within the government—a "fourth branch of government" to check on potential abuses of power by any president bent on centralizing power in the White House. This perspective sees the executive establishment as a representative institution, reflecting the concerns of a wide variety of societal interests, some of which lack the normal bases for political power like large formal memberships, lobbyists, and money. The bureaucracy also has been viewed as a source of rationality in decision making—a place where decisions are based on analyses of the relevant information to achieve identifiable objectives.[38] In addition, some argue that attempts to centralize power in the White House tend to create cumbersome and inflexible decisional structures that inhibit effective management.

These alternative theories of presidential responsibility and representative bureaucracy reflect a continuing dilemma of American democracy: how to achieve a government staffed by competent, professional civil servants who are responsive and accountable to the public through elected officials, while preventing any one of those officials from becoming too powerful.

Congress and the Bureaucracy

Not just the president is concerned with controlling the bureaucracy; Congress also has a stake in how the bureaucracy performs (see Chapter 10). After all, Congress passes the laws that the bureaucracy administers, and those administrative actions can affect the general direction of public policy, powerful interest groups, and legislators' constituents. As Congress has delegated more and more authority to the bureaucracy, it has sought to maintain its policy influence by engaging in *oversight of administration*.

38. See Norton E. Long, "Bureaucracy and Constitutionalism," *American Political Science Review* 46 (September 1952): 808. Also see Peter Woll, *The American Bureaucracy* (New York: Norton, 1963), 3.

Most oversight is conducted by congressional committees and subcommittees that have jurisdiction over executive departments and agencies. During hearings on proposed legislation, for example, bureaucrats and witnesses are called before committees to discuss, explain, and defend past administrative decisions and justify budget requests.

But much of the responsibility for oversight rests with the committee staff who monitor agency performance, delve into the backgrounds of presidential appointees seeking Senate confirmation, and do the background work for committee hearings. Congressional staff members also maintain informal information networks within the bureaucracy and among interest group representatives.

The ultimate source of congressional committee influence over bureaucrats is Congress's lawmaking power. Using this power, Congress can alter, expand, or reduce the functions of an agency; reorganize an agency; or cut its budget and the size of its staff. Is it any wonder then that bureaucrats tend to develop a strategic sensitivity to a committee leader's concerns? Committee oversight, however, is rarely systematic and ongoing. Rather, it tends to be episodic and irregular, usually occurring when members of Congress realize that oversight may produce some political benefits. The political incentives for legislators to invest their scarce time, energy, and staff resources in oversight activity may surface when a powerful interest group is complaining about the adverse effects of bureaucratic decisions; partisan advantage can be gained from a critical investigation into the opposition party's administration of an agency; or a legislator may gain extensive media coverage by holding hearings on a controversial administrative decision.[39]

In addition to committees, congressional oversight is carried out by those individual representatives and senators trying to help out constituents having problems with the bureaucracy (casework).

A dramatic instance of congressional oversight occurred in 1987 when a special House-Senate investigating committee called former White House aide Lt. Col. Oliver North to testify about his role in the Iran-contra affair. This scandal involved the secret sale of weapons by the United States to Iran and the use of profits from the sale to support contra rebels fighting the Sandinista government of Nicaragua.

The Judiciary and the Bureaucracy

The judiciary's role in the political system, like those of the presidency and Congress, also has been affected by the growth of the bureaucracy. The statutes creating a vast regulatory bureaucracy contain provisions that give private parties opportunities to challenge the decisions of executive agencies. With the proliferation of

39. On congressional oversight, see Dodd and Schott, *Congress and the Administrative State*; and Matthew D. McCubbins and Thomas Schwartz, "Congressional Oversight Overlooked: Police Patrols versus Fire Alarms," *American Journal of Political Science* 28 (February 1984): 165–179.

these lawsuits, the courts have increasingly found themselves thrust into the process of bureaucratic decision making. The judiciary generally applies two standards when considering the legality of bureaucratic actions. The first concerns whether or not an agency's action is consistent with congressional intent. When it can be demonstrated that an agency has overstepped congressional intent, the courts may overrule the agency decision. In reviewing an agency's implementation of congressional legislation, the courts also may prod agencies into more aggressive regulatory activity. For example, the judiciary pushed the EPA into requiring tougher clean air standards than it had originally planned and helped persuade the Equal Employment Opportunity Commission to take stronger action to protect women in the workplace.[40] It is, however, often difficult to clearly identify congressional intent. Advocates of a bill frequently have conflicting goals, and mustering congressional majorities may require that bills contain compromise and ambiguous language capable of various interpretations.

The second standard used by the courts in overruling an executive agency is agency adherence to proper procedures. Environmental groups, for example, have instituted hundreds of court challenges to government construction projects on the grounds that the agencies involved failed to comply with the National Environmental Protection Act of 1969, which requires government agencies to file environmental impact statements. Using such suits, environmental groups have been able to delay a number of federal construction projects. Lawsuits can be used as well to force government agencies to meet congressionally mandated timetables for implementation of legislation.

Although the courts periodically impose significant restraints on the bureaucracy, judicially imposed controls have limited effectiveness. As a general rule, the courts have been quite willing to permit Congress to delegate to the bureaucracy wide discretion in implementing statutes. Furthermore, the costs of litigation are high and beyond the resources of many would-be challengers of administrative decisions. In addition, judicial remedies for alleged bureaucratic injustices are time-consuming and often characterized by lengthy delays. Thus, while the courts provide one avenue for influencing bureaucratic decisions, those who choose this route are by no means assured of success.[41]

40. Rourke, "Bureaucracy," 227.
41. Meier, *Politics and Bureaucracy,* 150–154.

The Essential but Ambiguous
Place of the Bureaucracy
in the American System

As was noted earlier in this chapter, practically all government policies depend on some bureaucratic organization for their implementation and enforcement. In fact, the modern, Western-style democracy itself, with its multiplicity of citizen services as well as its regulatory functions, could not function without the bureaucracy. Yet in spite of this demonstrable need, the bureaucracy lacks legitimacy in the American political culture. Indeed, since the 1960s campaigning against bureaucracy has been a winning presidential campaign strategy. And members of Congress, through their extensive casework activities, have exploited the inefficiencies and red tape of the bureaucracy for electoral gain.[42]

Unlike the presidency, the Congress, and the judiciary, the bureaucracy has a rather ambiguous constitutional status. The Constitution does not speak directly about the administrative aspects of the state. The legitimacy of the bureaucracy is further diminished by its appointed character; unlike the president and the Congress, it is not chosen by the people, making its responsiveness to elected officials a matter for ongoing concern. At the same time, however, too much presidential or congressional control over the bureaucracy could cause excessive concentrations of power and damage to the professionalism and integrity of bureaucratic decision making. Contributing further to the legitimacy problems of the bureaucracy is its lack of the dignity and honored traditions characteristic of the judiciary. Thus, as distinguished scholar of the bureaucracy Francis Rourke has pointed out, one of the paradoxes of American government is that the bureaucracy is "at one and the same time altogether indispensable, and, at least in the eyes of many citizens, somewhat illegitimate."[43]

Although the bureaucracy may be suspect in many quarters and a ready target for government's critics, one fact stands out: the bureaucracy is a major player in the policy-making process—a coparticipant and competitor for influence with the White House, Congress, and interest groups.

42. See Morris P. Fiorina, *Congress: Keystone of the Washington Establishment* (New Haven, Conn.: Yale University Press, 1977). Also see Rourke, "Bureaucracy," 226–227.
43. Rourke, "Bureaucracy," 232.

For Review

1. The bureaucracy is the complex of agencies that administers government programs and policies. It is an essential part of the governmental system, but it lacks the legitimacy accorded the presidency, the Congress, and the courts.

2. The process of interpreting and implementing the laws passed by Congress and the executive orders of the president is inevitably political in character because these administrative acts of the bureaucracy have consequences for individuals and groups in society.

3. The organizational elements of the federal bureaucracy include departments, independent agencies, independent regulatory agencies, and government institutes, foundations, and corporations. The vast majority of bureaucrats are selected on the basis of merit, with only a small percentage appointed at the discretion of the president.

4. Each government agency operates in a separate political environment affected by its statutory base, unique subject matter and functions, clientele groups, departmental traditions and norms, White House relations, and ties to Congress.

5. One of the unresolved issues of the bureaucracy is how to achieve accountability to elected officials without giving those officials excessive power or causing the bureaucracy to become so overly politicized that it loses its professionalism and integrity.

For Further Reading

Dodd, Lawrence C., and Richard L. Schott. *Congress and the Administrative State.* New York: Wiley, 1979. An analysis of the complicated relationship between the administrative agencies and Congress.

Gormley, William T. *Taming the Bureaucracy: Muscles, Prayers, and Other Strategies.* Princeton, N.J.: Princeton University Press, 1989. An analysis of strategies to control the bureaucracy and their consequences.

Heclo, Hugh. *A Government of Strangers: Executive Politics in Washington.* Washington, D.C.: Brookings, 1977. An examination of the relationship between the career federal service and political appointees.

Kaufman, Herbert. *The Administrative Behavior of Federal Bureau Chiefs.* Washington, D.C.: Brookings, 1981. A description of what federal bureau chiefs do and an explanation of how they exercise their power.

Kettl, Donald F. *Government by Proxy: (Mis?)Managing Federal Programs.* Washington, D.C.: CQ Press, 1988. An analysis of the consequences of using private companies, individuals, and state and local governments to carry out federal policy.

Meier, Kenneth J. *Politics and Bureaucracy: Policymaking in the Fourth*

Branch of Government. 2d ed. Monterey, Calif.: Brooks/Cole, 1987. A text stressing and critically examining the policy-making role of the bureaucracy.

Seidman, Harold, and Robert Gilmour. *Politics, Position, and Power: From Positive to Regulatory State.* 4th ed. New York: Oxford University Press, 1986. A perceptive account of bureaucratic politics by a former Washington insider.

13. The Judiciary

M OST AMERICANS look upon the courts as institutions that are, or at least should be, nonpolitical. But it is impossible to take the judiciary out of politics. Because the courts are an integral part of government, they are, by their very nature, political institutions. Most federal judges, in fact, were active in party politics before their appointment to the bench, and their personal values, experiences, and perceptions of the political climate in the country at large and within the Congress and White House affect their actions while on the bench.

Although the judiciary, like the Congress, presidency, and bureaucracy, is a political institution that makes important policy decisions, it is also quite different from the legislative or executive branches: judges must make their decisions within the framework of the existing law. Court decisions are matters of legal interpretation, and judges are restricted to interpreting the meaning of the Constitution and laws (statutes) enacted by Congress. Thus, whereas legislators are free to advocate publicly and propose new laws, judges are confined to interpreting laws. Presidents, too, may campaign for changes in the law and seek public and congressional support for constitutional and statutory changes.

Judges also are expected to adhere to the norms of the legal profession; they are not free to decide cases based exclusively on their personal views of what constitutes sound policy. One of the most important of these norms is the doctrine of **stare decisis** ("let the decision stand")—abiding by the principles of law set forth in prior decisions of one's own court or of higher courts. Under *stare decisis,* citizens know before entering court their rights and obligations because this norm encourages consistent, predictable application of legal rules. But the doctrine of *stare decisis* is not as restrictive as it first appears. Conflicting precedents in some areas of the law can provide a judge with substantial discretion in making a decision. In the field of constitutional law, the Supreme Court has periodically reversed past decisions when it thought those decisions were in error or no longer appropriate. It was a reversal of precedent, for example, that enabled the Court to declare segregated school systems unconstitutional in 1954.

Public expectations that the courts will operate in a nonpolitical manner also provide judges with a bit of cover from the more routine political pressures. It is, for example, considered improper for a judge to engage in partisan activity—such as endorsing a presidential or congressional candidate—or for interest groups to informally discuss a pending case with a judge over lunch or cocktails. Interest groups can, however, use more formal means of trying to influence judicial decisions such as filing legal briefs and making formal arguments before the courts.

Although as legal institutions the courts operate in a political atmosphere different from those of the other branches of government, their policy-making role is no less important. Early in the history of the Republic, French observer Alexis de Tocqueville noted, "Scarcely any political question arises in the United States that is not resolved, sooner or later, into a judicial question."[1] De Tocqueville's observation remains valid in the 1990s. This chapter, therefore, analyzes the judiciary as a policy-making institution deeply enmeshed in today's political process.[2]

Judicial Policy Making

Courts make policy in the course of deciding legal conflicts brought before them as cases—disputes between two or more litigants (individuals, organizations, or governments) who are asserting their rights under the law. The millions of cases that are filed each year fall into two broad categories. **Civil cases** are disputes between individuals, groups, or governments about rights and responsibilities. Disputes over contracts, business relations, domestic relations, and personal injuries fall into this category. If involved in a civil suit, the government may be either a **defendant** (person being sued) or a **plaintiff** (person bringing suit).

Criminal cases concern violations of state or federal law that are punishable by fines or imprisonment. A defendant in a state criminal case might be charged with a theft or drug offense (the most common) or with a felony such as murder, rape, armed robbery, assault and battery, or manslaughter. Congress has specified certain crimes as federal offenses—for example, attempting to murder the president, transporting stolen property across state lines, and kidnapping. In criminal cases, either the state or federal government is always the prosecutor (plaintiff).

Policy Making by Interpreting the Constitution and the Laws

In the course of deciding both civil and criminal cases by interpreting the Constitution and laws passed by Congress, courts influ-

1. Alexis de Tocqueville, *Democracy in America* (New York: Knopf, 1945), 280.
2. For an overview of the Supreme Court in American politics, see Lawrence Baum, *The Supreme Court,* 3d ed. (Washington, D.C.: CQ Press, 1989), 2–5.

ence the law as surely as do legislatures (see Chapter 2, The Constitution). This has been true since the early days of the Republic when Chief Justice John Marshall (1801–1835) led the Supreme Court in establishing the principle of judicial review (*Marbury v. Madison,* 1803), stating the doctrine of implied powers for the national government (*McCulloch v. Maryland,* 1819), and upholding federal supremacy over interstate commerce in the face of state government intrusions (*Gibbons v. Ogden,* 1824).[3] No less significant were the decisions made in the early 1930s by conservative justices who declared New Deal legislation recommended by a popular president and endorsed by Congress to be unconstitutional. Nevertheless, the Court's narrow view of the government's power to regulate the economy and to take steps to lift the nation out of the Great Depression was reversed in 1938 when two justices changed their interpretation of the Constitution to form a Court majority in support of the federal government exercising broad powers over the economy. Just as the so-called Judicial Revolution of 1938 changed the direction of government policy in the 1930s, the Court since the 1950s has created new legal doctrines that have been both far-reaching in their implications and controversial.

In the area of *racial equality,* it was the Supreme Court, particularly in *Brown v. Board of Education of Topeka* (1954), that initiated a government policy designed to achieve racial equality (see Chapter 4, Civil Liberties and Civil Rights). One of the most controversial racial issues the Court was asked to decide in recent years was the constitutionality of affirmative action programs designed to assure minorities access to jobs, government contracts, and admission to universities. In 1989, the Court sided with those who charged that these programs can constitute reverse discrimination when it declared unconstitutional a Richmond, Virginia, ordinance requiring that 33 percent of city contracts be set aside for minorities.

In addressing the *reapportionment* issue, the Supreme Court announced in 1962 (*Baker v. Carr*) that henceforth the judiciary would interject itself into the process of drawing legislative district lines to ensure that districts were equal in size and followed the "one person, one vote" principle (see Chapter 10, Congress). This decision dramatically changed how Americans were represented in their state legislatures and Congress. In 1986, the Court took a step further into this politically charged area when it stated that in the future it

3. *Marbury v. Madison,* 1 Cr. 137 (1803); *McCulloch v. Maryland,* 4 Wheat. 316 (1819); and *Gibbons v. Ogden,* 9 Wheat. 1 (1824).

would review the constitutionality of partisan gerrymandering in legislative redistricting.

Through a series of decisions beginning in the 1920s, and resulting in *nationalization of the Bill of Rights,* the Court has protected people's basic First Amendment rights from infringement by the states as well as by the federal government. And in the 1960s and 1970s, it took dramatic steps to extend the Bill of Rights protections afforded defendants in federal courts to the people accused of crimes in state courts. These actions caused wholesale changes in state criminal justice systems—the provision of attorneys for the poor, requirements that people in custody be advised of their constitutional rights, and the exclusion from trials of evidence taken illegally by the police (see Chapter 4).

And in taking on the highly volatile issue of *abortion* the Supreme Court declared in *Roe v. Wade* (1973) that states may not interfere with a woman's right to an abortion during the first three months of pregnancy. This decision, as well as a 1989 decision that indicated that the Court would permit greater state regulation of abortions (*Webster v. Reproductive Health Services*), set off a firestorm of controversy, which continues to swirl around all three branches of government at the national and state levels as pro-choice groups battle to protect the *Roe* decision and pro-life groups fight to overturn it (see Chapter 4 for more on both of these decisions).

Judicial Activism versus
Judicial Restraint

When the Supreme Court has demonstrated a willingness to make significant changes in public policy—in particular, policies established by the legislative and executive branches—it is said to be engaged in **judicial activism**. An activist judiciary inevitably spawns debate not just about the substance of the judicial decisions but also about the proper role of the judiciary. An independent judiciary is the keystone of a free society and a key feature of the American constitutional system. But, unlike the president and the Congress, the federal judiciary is not popularly elected. Its members are nominated by the president and confirmed by the Senate. Moreover, they have life tenure and cannot be removed except in extraordinary circumstances through impeachment.

Supporters of judicial activism believe it is legitimate for appointed judges to act as a check upon the unwise and arbitrary acts of elected legislatures and executives. They particularly endorse judicial activism and court leadership when the elected branches of government have failed, in their view, to protect vigorously civil

Thurgood Marshall (fourth from the right), counsel for the Legal and Education Defense Fund of the National Association for the Advancement of Colored People, and other members of the legal team leave the Supreme Court building after arguing the landmark desegregation case of Brown v. Board of Education *(1954). In 1967, Marshall became the first African American to serve on the Supreme Court.*

rights and civil liberties. But advocates of **judicial restraint** argue that it is not proper for nonelected officials to take over from elected officials the responsibility for major policy decisions. According to these observers of the judicial system, the courts should defer to the decisions of elected executives and legislators and not impose their own views of what is desirable government policy on the public.[4]

Of course, whether people stand with the advocates of judicial activism or those of judicial restraint depends to some degree on whether they support or disagree with the content of Court decisions. Activists on the Court, it must be remembered, hail from either the liberal or conservative schools of political thinking. For example, in the early 1930s liberal Court watchers argued for judicial restraint when a conservative Court attacked government regulation of the economy. But in the 1960s, they became supporters of the Warren Court activism, particularly its emphasis on civil rights and civil liberties. By contrast, conservatives defended the activist Court in the early 1930s. Yet during the 1960s and 1970s they argued for judicial restraint and frequently urged justices to confine themselves to determining the true intent of the drafters of the Constitution.

In 1986, Associate Justice William Rehnquist, an articulate conservative, was elevated to the position of chief justice upon the retirement of Chief Justice Warren Burger. The Rehnquist promotion, as well as the appointment by President Ronald Reagan of two con-

4. See the discussion of judicial activism and judicial restraint in David F. Forte, ed., *The Supreme Court in American Politics: Judicial Activism versus Judicial Restraint* (Lexington, Mass.: D.C. Heath, 1972); and Stephen C. Halpern and Charles M. Lamb, eds., *Supreme Court Activism and Restraint* (Lexington, Mass.: Lexington Books, 1982), especially chapter 15 by Bradley C. Canon, which analyzes the six dimensions of judicial activism.

servative justices, Antonin Scalia (1986) and Anthony Kennedy (1988), created expectations (hope among conservatives and fear among liberals) that the Rehnquist Court would pursue an activist conservative policy. But the highest hopes of conservatives and greatest fears of liberals have not been realized to date. The Rehnquist Court has tended, however, toward conservative policies—for example, its ruling against the Richmond affirmative action program; its approval of drug testing for selected types of transportation and federal employees; its permitting exceptions to the exclusionary rule, which bars the use of evidence gathered illegally in criminal trials; and its willingness to permit state restrictions on a woman's right to an abortion.[5]

The debate over the role of an appointed judiciary in a democracy deals with fundamental issues of governance. It is unlikely, however, that the controversy over judicial activism versus judicial restraint will ever be finally resolved. In a free society with an independent judiciary, individuals and groups will continue to use litigation as a means of achieving their policy goals. The courts, therefore, will be constantly thrust into the political arena and forced to decide vital issues of public policy.

A Dual Judicial System: Federal Courts and State Courts Side by Side

The Constitution created a federal system of government in which both the national and state governments exercise significant powers (see Chapter 3, Federalism). Thus, in the United States, fifty state judicial systems operate side by side with the federal court system. Each system has its own personnel and jurisdiction, and each interprets and enforces its own constitution and laws. But while the two court systems are separate and distinct, they do overlap: the constitutional principle of federal supremacy enables the federal courts to throw out state actions that they deem to be in violation of the U.S. Constitution or acts of Congress.

Both the federal and state systems have **trial courts** and **appellate courts**. Trial courts are the tribunals in which a case is first heard—that is, they are courts of **original jurisdiction**. Cases in trial courts may be heard before a jury, or a judge may render the verdict. Appellate courts hear cases on appeal from lower courts. But appellate

5. Linda Greenhouse, "The Year the Court Turned Right," *New York Times,* July 7, 1989, Y1, Y11, National edition.

courts have no juries; all cases are decided by a panel of judges. These courts are concerned primarily with whether lower courts correctly interpreted the applicable laws and followed proper judicial procedures in deciding a case. Appellate courts normally do not consider new factual evidence since the record of the lower court constitutes the basis for judgment.

Whether a case is tried in federal or state court depends on which court has **jurisdiction**—the authority to hear the case. The rules of federal court jurisdiction are contained in the Constitution and federal statutes, and only if a case meets specific jurisdictional tests can it be heard in a federal court. It is not enough to believe one's case is important enough to be a "federal case." Access to the federal court system is determined by (1) the *nature of the subject matter* and (2) the *nature of the parties or litigants in the suit*. Subject matter that falls within the jurisdiction of the federal courts would be conflicts arising under the Constitution, federal laws, or treaties, and admiralty and maritime law. In addition, federal courts can exercise jurisdiction over cases in which the United States is a party to the dispute, or in which there are conflicts between states or between citizens of different states.

The U.S. Supreme Court is the only federal court with the authority to review the decisions of state courts. The Supreme Court, therefore, acts as umpire of the federal system by enforcing the federal supremacy clause of the Constitution, which requires that state laws conform to the Constitution, federal laws, and treaties. If the Court did not have the power to review state laws, chaos would reign as fifty different state courts determined whether their laws conformed to the U.S. Constitution and laws. Thus, the Supreme Court is the final arbiter of the federal system.

The Structure of the Federal Judiciary

The judicial article of the Constitution, Article III, calls for the creation of only one court—the Supreme Court—and empowers Congress to establish inferior federal courts. The First Congress, then, was faced with the task of creating a federal judicial system. But it was not to be an easy task. Disagreements immediately broke out between the Antifederalists and Federalists in the Congress over the power and extent of the federal judiciary. Fearful that a strong federal judiciary would impinge upon the power of the states, the Antifederalists tried to derail the creation of lower federal courts. The majority prevailed, however, and in passing the Judiciary Act of

1789 Congress set up the Supreme Court (then composed of a chief justice and five associate justices) and a series of lower federal district courts in each of the states and in the territories of Maine and Kentucky.[6]

Courts created by Congress under its authority in Article III are called **constitutional courts**. These courts handle the bulk of the caseload within the federal judicial system. Congress also used the legislative powers granted to it in Article I to create a series of **legislative courts**. These courts, which handle specialized and technical types of cases, relieve the caseload burden on the regular constitutional courts. For example, the U.S. Court of Military Appeals was created under Congress's Article I authority "to make rules for the government and regulation of the land and naval forces." Other legislative courts include the U.S. Tax Court, a court that decides disputes between taxpayers and the Internal Revenue Service, and the U.S. Claims Court, which hears cases in which claims are brought against the U.S. government.

The federal court system, then, is a three-tiered structure of constitutional courts: federal district courts, courts of appeals, and the Supreme Court. In addition, there are several legislative courts with limited jurisdictions (see Figure 13.1).

U.S. District Courts

U.S. district courts are the principal trial courts—courts of original jurisdiction—of the federal judiciary. They are the busiest of the federal courts, handling approximately 200,000 civil and criminal cases a year, plus over 300,000 bankruptcy proceedings. Most federal cases begin and end in these courts. There is at least one federal district court in each state, but some states have as many as four. In California, for example, there are federal district courts for the northern, southern, central, and eastern regions (see Figure 13.2, which shows the boundaries of federal district courts). Altogether the fifty states have eighty-nine district courts, the Virgin Islands have three, and there is one each for the District of Columbia, Puerto Rico, Guam, and the Northern Mariana Islands.

The number of judges assigned to a district court varies from one to twenty-seven (in the Southern District of New York), depending on the caseload in the district. Most cases are heard with a single

6. For a brief account of the creation of the federal judiciary, see Carl B. Swisher, *American Constitutional Development,* 2d ed. (Boston: Houghton Mifflin, 1954), 56–61. Also see Charles Warren, "History of the Judiciary Act of 1789," *Harvard Law Review* 37 (November 1923): 49–123.

Figure 13.1: The Federal Court System

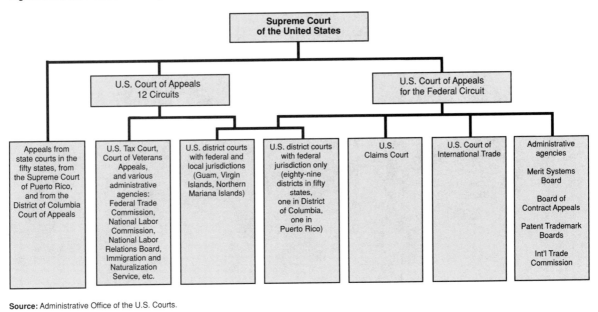

Source: Administrative Office of the U.S. Courts.

judge presiding, but for certain kinds of cases a panel of three judges may decide.

U.S. Courts of Appeals

The U.S. courts of appeals, which are exclusively appellate in jurisdiction, hear appeals from the decisions of the federal district courts, the Tax Court, some District of Columbia courts, and some federal regulatory agencies such as the Federal Trade Commission. Cases being appealed from the highest state courts bypass both the district courts and the U.S. courts of appeals. Rather, these cases go directly to the Supreme Court, provided it agrees to accept jurisdiction.

Because they are appellate courts, the courts of appeals do not conduct jury trials. Rather, all cases are heard before a panel of normally three judges. Cases are decided by a majority vote of the judges participating. Each court of appeals is headed technically by a Supreme Court justice, who, while not actively involved in court business, can act upon petitions for extraordinary procedures such as pleas for a stay of execution in death sentence cases. Most of the approximately seven thousand cases appealed annually from the federal district courts are finally adjudicated by the U.S. courts of ap-

Figure 13.2: Boundaries of the Thirteen Federal Judicial Circuits and the Ninety-four U.S. District Courts

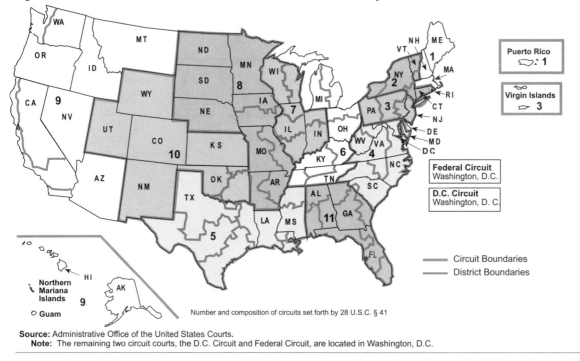

Source: Administrative Office of the United States Courts.
Note: The remaining two circuit courts, the D.C. Circuit and Federal Circuit, are located in Washington, D.C.

peals. In selected instances, however, cases decided by the courts of appeals and highest state courts are appealed to the U.S. Supreme Court, the nation's highest court.

The nation is divided geographically into twelve judicial circuits, each of which has a court of appeals (also known as circuit courts); each state and territory is assigned to a circuit. The District of Columbia also has a court of appeals, a particularly important court because it is located in the seat of the government (see Figure 13.2). The Court of Appeals for the Federal Circuit, located in Washington as well, hears only cases dealing with specific subject matter (for example, appeals from the U.S. Claims Court, the U.S. Court of International Trade, regulatory agencies, and trademark, patent, and copyright cases from federal district courts).

The 168 judges within the courts of appeals are assigned to a particular court according to the volume of judicial business within the circuit. For example, the Ninth Circuit (which includes California) has twenty-eight judges, while only six are assigned to the First Circuit in New England.

The U.S. Supreme Court: How Cases Reach the Court

The nation's highest tribunal, the Supreme Court, is composed of a chief justice and eight associate justices, each of whom is appointed by the president and confirmed by the Senate. Justices "hold their Offices during good Behavior" (Article III, section 1). The Supreme Court has both original jurisdiction and appellate jurisdiction but acts almost exclusively as an appellate court.

The Court's original jurisdiction includes some cases in which a state is a party (for example, disputes between states or between a state and the federal government) and cases involving foreign diplomatic personnel. Cases heard in the Court's original jurisdiction, such as a dispute between California and Arizona over water rights,[7] are rare—there have been only about 150 in the entire history of the Court.[8]

In its appellate jurisdiction, the Court hears cases brought by parties dissatisfied with the decisions of U.S. courts of appeals and specialized federal appellate courts. The Court also hears cases appealed from special three-judge federal district courts that Congress has created to adjudicate a narrow category of cases. For example, because questions were raised about the constitutionality of the 1985 Gramm-Rudman-Hollings budget-deficit control act, Congress included in the law a provision calling for challenges to the law to be heard before a special three-judge federal district court with the appeal process to be expedited by permitting direct appeal to the Supreme Court.

The Supreme Court also hears cases appealing the decisions of the highest state courts when issues of federal or constitutional law are involved. An issue of federal law could be raised in state court proceedings when, for example, an individual charged with violating a state murder statute claims that during the course of his arrest and trial in the state courts his constitutional rights (such as through an illegal search or interrogation) were violated. In such a circumstance, a constitutional issue is raised, and the case could be brought to the Supreme Court. If the Supreme Court heard such a case, it would confine itself to determining whether the defendant's constitutional

7. *Arizona v. California*, 373 U.S. 546 (1963).
8. Henry J. Abraham, *The Judiciary*, 7th ed. (Boston: Allyn and Bacon, 1987), 25.

rights had been violated and would not seek to decide questions of state law or whether the defendant actually committed a crime.

Practically all cases brought to the Supreme Court are heard under the Court's discretionary jurisdiction. The Constitution gives Congress the power to determine the appellate jurisdiction of the Supreme Court, but in exercising this power, Congress has granted the Court broad discretion in determining which cases it wishes to consider. As a result, nearly all cases brought to the Supreme Court are there because the Court has chosen to hear them. The Court exercises its discretion over its review of cases primarily through a **writ of certiorari** ("to make more certain")—an order from a higher court to a lower court to deliver up the records of a case so that the higher court may review the lower-court decision.

People seeking to have the Supreme Court review their cases in its appellate jurisdiction must request or petition for such a review. If four justices (one less than a majority—the so-called rule of four) vote to grant the petition, the Court will review the decision of the lower court. The extent of discretion exercised by the justices in deciding which cases they will review is demonstrated by the following statistics. More than 90 percent of the more than four thousand requests for certiorari are denied,[9] and, on average, the Court hears oral arguments on about 175 cases each year.

A particularly important figure in determining which cases that involve the U.S. government reach the Supreme Court is the **solicitor general**. As the third-ranking official in the Justice Department, the solicitor general is responsible for (1) deciding which cases the government will try to have reviewed by the Supreme Court, (2) reviewing briefs filed by the government, and (3) presenting oral arguments before the Court (wearing, by the way, the traditional tails and striped trousers). This is an extremely sensitive post because it influences the extent to which an administration engages in litigation to advance its policy goals. Traditionally, the solicitor general has functioned with a moderate amount of independence from the normal political pressures within an administration. Because of this tradition and his position as the government's lawyer, the solicitor's arguments have had special significance before the Court. For example, the solicitor general is more successful than most private attorneys in getting the Court to accept petitions for certiorari, doing so at a rate of 70 percent.[10]

9. Ibid., 33.
10. Stephen L. Wasby, *The Supreme Court in the Federal Judicial System,* 2d ed.

In determining which cases it will review, the Court is doing more than just managing a heavy caseload; its choice of cases sets the substantive policy agenda of the Court as well. For example, a Court majority led by Chief Justice Earl Warren (1953–1969) used its discretionary power over the Court agenda to advance liberal policies. Thus, the Court of the 1960s heard a large number of cases involving the rights of persons accused of crimes and used these cases to extend the guarantees of the Bill of Rights to individuals in the state as well as federal courts. The composition of the Court, however, became more conservative under Chief Justice Warren Burger (1969–1986) and William Rehnquist (1986–   ) in the 1970s through the 1990s when new justices were appointed by Presidents Nixon, Reagan, and Bush. Unlike the Warren Court, the Burger and Rehnquist Courts have been generally hostile to considering cases brought by indigent defendants challenging government actions. Indeed, through its selection of cases, the Burger and Rehnquist Courts have adjusted somewhat the direction of constitutional law espoused by the Warren Court. For example, the requirement that police act only on the basis of search and arrest warrants has been limited, and government affirmative action programs that provided for automatic or quota-like educational, employment, and contracting opportunities for minorities have been thrown out.[11] Because of the "rule of four," the bloc of generally conservative justices (Chief Justice Rehnquist and Justices Kennedy, Sandra Day O'Connor, David Souter, Antonin Scalia, and Byron White) is currently in a position to influence substantially the agenda of the Court. This conservative bloc was potentially strengthened by President Bush's nomination in July 1991 of Clarence Thomas to replace the retiring liberal justice Thurgood Marshall.

How the Supreme Court Does Its Work

With the words "Equal Justice Under Law" carved above the massive bronze doors at its entrance, the Supreme Court's five-story, white marble building is an imposing monument to the

---

(New York: Holt, Rinehart, and Winston, 1984), 106–107. On the role of the solicitor general in the Reagan and Bush administrations, see Joan Biskupic, "Starr Takes Moderate Line as U.S. Solicitor General," *Congressional Quarterly Weekly Report,* May 5, 1990, 1349–1351.

11. For discussions of the different policy orientations of the Supreme Court since the 1950s, see David M. O'Brien, "The Supreme Court: From Warren to Burger to Rehnquist," *PS* 12 (Winter 1987): 12–20; and Martin Shapiro, "The Supreme Court from Burger to Rehnquist," in *The New American Political System,* 2d ed., ed. Anthony King (Washington, D.C.: AEI Press, 1990), 47–86.

law. It occupies a square block across from the East Front of the Capitol. On days when the Court is in open session, the justices, led by the chief justice, enter from behind purple drapes. The audience rises, and a marshal makes the traditional announcement: "Oyez, Oyez, Oyez! All persons having business before the Honorable, the Supreme Court of the United States, are admonished to draw near and give their attention, for the Court is now sitting. God save the United States and this Honorable Court." The black-robed justices then take their seats behind the high judicial bench, with the chief justice in the center and the associate justices seated to his right and left alternately in declining order of seniority. The atmosphere is one of legal ritual, dignity, solemnity, and respect for the law.

Near the courtroom are the conference room, where the Court meets to decide cases, and the chambers that contain the offices of the justices and their staffs. The chief justice has five law clerks and each associate justice has four to assist them in researching cases and preparing opinions. The justices' law clerks are recent graduates of the nation's most prestigious law schools who ranked at the top of their classes.

The Court is normally in session for thirty-six weeks annually from the first Monday in October through June. A Court term is divided into *sittings*—about two weeks in length—during which the Court meets in open session and holds private conferences. The Court then goes into recess so that the justices can work behind closed doors considering cases and writing decisions.

Filing Briefs and Oral Arguments

For the approximately 170 cases that receive detailed review each year, the process begins with the filing of printed briefs (detailed legal arguments and supporting material) prepared by the attorneys in the case. **Amicus curiae** ("friend of the court") briefs also may be filed by individuals, interest groups, and governments seeking to influence the Court's decision. Department of Justice amicus curiae briefs are particularly important because through them the government can express a point of view on a case even though it is not a party to the lawsuit. The briefs of the litigants and the friends of the court are reviewed by the justices and their clerks before oral arguments are presented to the entire Court.

During oral arguments, which are conducted on Mondays through Wednesdays during sittings, attorneys for both sides have the opportunity to supplement the material in their briefs. Often, attorneys are subjected to interruptions and sharp questioning from justices seeking to influence their colleagues' perceptions of the case. Justices

Members of the U.S. Supreme Court, 1992

Justice	Year Appointed	Appointing President	Prior Party Affiliation	Age When Appointed
Byron R. White	1962	Kennedy	Democrat	45
Harry A. Blackmun	1970	Nixon	Republican	61
William H. Rehnquist [a]	1971	Nixon	Republican	48
John Paul Stevens	1975	Ford	Republican	55
Sandra Day O'Connor	1981	Reagan	Republican	50
Antonin Scalia	1986	Reagan	Republican	50
Anthony M. Kennedy	1988	Reagan	Republican	51
David H. Souter	1990	Bush	Republican	50
Clarence Thomas	1991	Bush	Republican	43

[a]Became chief justice on September 26, 1986, after being nominated by President Reagan.

Rehnquist, O'Connor, and John Paul Stevens are particularly aggressive in their questioning, and Justice Scalia frequently consumes large segments of the strict time allotments made to attorneys with his questions.

The Conference and Opinion Writing

On Wednesday afternoons and Fridays, the justices discuss cases behind locked doors in the conference room. The chief justice presides during conferences, speaks first, and is followed by the other justices in order of seniority. As each justice speaks, he or she indicates his or her vote on the case as the justices keep informal track of the voting.

During the conference, justices use a variety of strategies to influence the outcome of a case. Chief Justice Earl Warren, determined to have a unanimous Court strike down school segregation as unconstitutional in the landmark case of *Brown v. Board of Education of Topeka*,[12] postponed the voting until he could persuade the entire Court to support his position. At times, a justice will vote with the others if they appear to have a majority even though he or she may disagree with the majority's decision. That justice will then bargain

12. *Brown v. Board of Education of Topeka*, 347 U.S. 483 (1954).

with other members of the majority in order to influence the content of the majority's written opinion and thereby limit what he or she perceives as the damage of the Court's decision. Justices also may threaten to file a **dissenting opinion** in order to influence the final decision.[13]

The assignment of opinion-writing responsibility is particularly important because skillful drafting of an opinion may be required to maintain a Court majority. Moreover, the written opinion formally expresses the Court's interpretation of federal law and sets a precedent that will be followed in the future. The impact of a decision is thus likely to be affected by how the opinion is drafted. If the chief justice has voted with the majority of the Court, he assigns responsibility for writing the opinion to either himself or another justice. When the chief justice is in the minority, the most senior justice in the majority makes the assignment. While Warren Burger was chief justice, opinion-writing assignments were extremely contentious. At times, Burger would switch his vote to the majority side in an effort to prevent such liberal justices as William Brennan and William O. Douglas from controlling opinion assignments.[14]

A written opinion states the facts of the case, the legal issues at stake, the decision of the Court, and, most important, the reasoning of the Court in making its decision. In this way, the Court advises lower-court judges on how to decide similar cases in the future.

The justice finally assigned responsibility for writing an opinion circulates a draft to his or her colleagues. The drafter of an opinion normally tries to maintain the support of the majority and win over justices who initially voted in the minority. Negotiations among the justices occur, and wording may be changed to gain support for the opinion.

In most cases, a majority of the Court will support a single opinion—the **majority opinion**. But justices who disagree with the outcome of the case may file dissenting opinions. Sometimes a justice will agree with the decision of the Court but will disagree with the rationale used in reaching the decision. In these circumstances, justices may file a **concurring opinion** to explain the legal reasoning they followed in arriving at a decision. Concurring opinions do not count as a vote against the opinion of the majority, but they may

13. David M. O'Brien, *Storm Center: The Supreme Court in American Politics* (New York: Norton, 1986), 232–240.
14. Bob Woodward and Scott Armstrong, *The Brethren: Inside the Supreme Court* (New York: Simon and Schuster, 1979), 210–213.

introduce an element of ambiguity into the rule of law being enunciated by the decision.

A variety of forces influence and constrain judicial decision making. These include the constraints of the legal system and governmental structure, the personal values and ideologies of the justices, the group life of the Court, and the forces within the larger political system such as public opinion and interest groups.

The *constraints of the legal system and of the governmental structure* are many. For example, justices are limited to ruling on just those cases that fall within the Court's jurisdiction and for which litigants have legal standing to enter the judicial process. The discretion of justices in deciding cases is restricted by the expectation that they will follow recognized modes of legal interpretation. They are normally expected, as we noted previously, to follow past precedents of the Court in making decisions.

There are also practical limits on the Court's decision-making powers stemming from the nature of the governmental structure. The Court must rely on the executive branch to *enforce* its decisions since it has no police force or army of its own. Indeed, in the end, the Court must depend on the other branches of government and the American people to *obey* its rulings. And, as we shall see later in this chapter, the Court also is limited by the fact that the other branches of government have powers they can use against it. Congress controls the Court's budget and can regulate its jurisdiction, and the president can refuse to enforce Court decisions, can rally public opinion against Court decisions, and can even pardon people convicted of violating Court rulings.

The role of values and ideology in judicial decision making was a concern in 1971 when William Rehnquist was testifying before the Senate Judiciary Committee at his confirmation hearing. He stated, "My fundamental commitment, if I am confirmed, will be to totally disregard my own personal belief."[15] This assertion that a justice's personal policy preferences are not relevant to the judicial decision-making process does not appear to be consistent with the actual behavior of judges. Granted, there are legal and practical constraints on judges in making their decisions, but there is also ample opportunity for personal attitudes and values to influence decisions.

Indeed, at times the Court has adopted major legal doctrines that appeared to have little basis in recognized modes of legal interpre-

15. Quoted by Baum, *Supreme Court*, 136.

tation and instead seemed to have been dictated by the personal views of the justices. For example, in *Griswold v. Connecticut* (1965),[16] the Court, while striking down a state statute limiting the availability of contraceptives, declared that people have the constitutional right to privacy. The inability of the seven justices who adopted this view to agree on the constitutional provisions that provided the basis for this liberty led judicial scholar Lawrence Baum to conclude that the justices "reached their conclusion first and then searched for a supporting rationale."[17]

Justices' personal attitudes derive from their life experiences—political socialization by their families, educational backgrounds, and career experiences. The influence of background is suggested by Justice Sandra Day O'Connor's dissent against the Court's failure to hear a sex discrimination case (she is the Court's only female member) and by Justice Lewis Powell's statements that his experience as a college trustee influenced his decision on an affirmative action admissions case. The link between background and judicial attitude, however, is complex. In fact, justices with similar backgrounds often vote differently.[18] Former chief justice Burger and Justice Harry Blackmun went to the same Minnesota high school, for example, but frequently opposed each other on the Court.

Students of judicial behavior have demonstrated, however, that most justices establish quite consistent positions on an ideological spectrum that spans a broad range of issues. This is particularly true of the justices at the ends of the liberal-conservative spectrum. For example, Court watchers have had no trouble identifying Chief Justice Rehnquist and Justice Scalia as conservatives and former justice Marshall as a liberal. In recent years, the Court's most consistent conservatives have been Chief Justice Rehnquist and Justices Scalia, O'Connor, Kennedy, and White. Since joining the Court in 1990, Justice Souter also has tended to vote with the conservatives. Until his retirement in 1991 the Court's most liberal member, Justice Marshall, frequently had been joined by Justices Blackmun and Stevens.

Although the group life of the Supreme Court is very much evident, members of the Court work for the most part as individuals or as nine separate law firms staffed with bright, young clerks who assist the justices in researching legal issues, developing positions, and writing opinions. The decisional process of the Court, however, is affected by the group setting of oral arguments and the conference.

16. *Griswold v. Connecticut*, 381 U.S. 479 (1965).
17. Baum, *Supreme Court*, 126.
18. Ibid., 137.

The justices of the Supreme Court pose informally after a symbolic investiture of Justice Clarence Thomas in the courtroom where they hear oral arguments. From left, Thomas, Byron White, David Souter, Antonin Scalia, John Paul Stevens, Harry Blackmun, Anthony Kennedy, Sandra Day O'Connor, and Chief Justice William Rehnquist.

To secure a majority decision on each case, the justices must interact, often leading to competition among them to persuade colleagues to accept their viewpoints and win votes in cases in which the Court is narrowly divided.

Lawrence Baum has described the Court as a "quasi-collegial body, one in which group interaction plays a limited but significant role in the decisionmaking process."[19] Because decisions are shaped by negotiations between the justice assigned to write an opinion and other members of the Court, these negotiations may result in a final opinion that is quite different than the one initially drafted by the assigned justice. While these negotiations are under way, justices demonstrate considerable "fluidity of judicial choice" and may shift their votes in response to arguments presented by their colleagues.[20]

19. Ibid., 149.
20. J. Woodward Howard, "On the Fluidity of Judicial Choice," *American Political Science Review* 62 (March 1968): 43–56.

While the small-group atmosphere of the Court does affect decisions, the impact of these interactions should not be overstated. After justices have developed a position on a case, or on an issue that runs through a series of cases over time, a colleague is apt to find it difficult to dislodge them from their positions, and many votes are quite predictable.

Although justices, unlike the president and members of Congress, do not stand for election, the Supreme Court does not operate in a political vacuum. Indeed, even the so-called High Nine are not immune from *the influence of public opinion and interest groups*. The Court's decisions affect people and organized interests prepared to use their political resources to influence judicial decisions. The Court also is subject to pressures from the elected branches of government—the executive, which often is responsible for enforcing Court orders, and the legislature, which through legislation can affect the size, jurisdiction, and budget of the Court. It should not be surprising, therefore, that Court decisions reflect a sensitivity to public opinion. For example, in supporting minority rights by throwing out state laws that mandated segregated schools, banned interracial marriage, restricted women's rights, and prohibited abortions, the Court has been shown to have acted in a manner consistent with trends in public opinion. But the Court has been reluctant to rule in favor of minority rights on those issues—busing, legalization of marijuana, and legalization of homosexual activity—that did not enjoy majority support.[21] These examples of Court sensitivity to public opinion are not meant to suggest that justices slavishly follow the Gallup poll when making their decisions. They do, however, indicate that the oft-stated notion that the Court is an antimajoritarian institution is an overstatement.

The Court's sensitivity to external political forces is also seen in its decisions to grant writs of certiorari, thereby bringing specific cases before the Court for consideration. Researchers have found that the Court is more likely to grant certiorari when organized interests, including the government, file amicus curiae briefs either favoring or opposing a grant of certiorari.[22]

21. David G. Barnum, "The Supreme Court and Public Opinion: Decision Making in the Post-New Deal Era," *Journal of Politics* 47 (May 1985): 652–666.

22 Gregory A. Caldeira and John R. Wright, "Organized Interests and Agenda Setting in the U.S. Supreme Court," *American Political Science Review* 82 (December 1988): 1109–1127.

Using the power of judicial review, the courts are able to declare acts of Congress, orders of the executive branch, or state laws unconstitutional—that is, they cannot be put into effect. As the ultimate authority on interpretation of the Constitution, the Supreme Court is a crucial power center in the American political system. Court decisions about the meaning of the Constitution can be changed only through a later reinterpretation of the Constitution by the Court or through the difficult and time-consuming process of amending the Constitution.

Incorporating Judicial Review
into the Constitution

Judicial review is one of the basic principles of the American constitutional system, but, surprisingly, this power is not mentioned in the Constitution. Rather, the power of judicial review was asserted by the Court in the case of *Marbury v. Madison* (1803).

The case arose on the heels of the election of 1800. After losing the election, President John Adams late in the same year appointed a series of federal judges in an effort to control the judiciary after his successor, Thomas Jefferson, took office. One of these appointees, William Marbury, was designated justice of the peace for the District of Columbia, a minor judicial post. Before leaving office, however, the Adams administration neglected to give Marbury his commission to office, and the new secretary of state, James Madison, refused to do so. Marbury then brought suit in the Supreme Court in its *original jurisdiction* asking that Madison be required to give him his commission. Suits such as Marbury's in the original jurisdiction of the Supreme Court were permitted under the Judiciary Act of 1789.

Chief Justice John Marshall, a former official in the Federalist administration of John Adams, was confronted with a delicate problem in deciding the case. If the Court ordered Madison to give Marbury his commission, Madison, with the backing of President Jefferson, was expected to ignore the Court order. The prestige and power of the fledgling Court would then suffer a heavy blow. But if Madison was not ordered to give Marbury the commission, the Jeffersonians would achieve a political triumph over the Federalists, the party of John Marshall.

To solve this dilemma, Marshall's opinion for the Court stated that Marbury was indeed entitled to his commission and that Madison had been in error in denying it to him. The Court ruled, however, that it lacked the power to order Madison to give Marbury his commission because the Court did not have jurisdiction over the case. According to Marshall, the provisions in the Judiciary Act of 1789 giving the Supreme Court jurisdiction over cases such as Marbury's were an unconstitutional extension by Congress of the Court's original jurisdiction, which had already been provided for in Article III, section 2. In asserting its power of judicial review, Marshall wrote that

the particular phraseology of the constitution of the United States confirmed and strengthens the principle, supposed to be essential to all written constitutions, that a law repugnant to the constitution is void; and that *courts,* as well as other departments [branches of government] are bound by that instrument.[23]

As we noted earlier, the Court's power of judicial review also extends to state government interpretations of the Constitution. In such instances, the principle of federal supremacy governs and enables the Court to strike down state actions that it deems to be violations of the Constitution, federal laws, or treaties. Thus in a dramatic confrontation between Arkansas and the federal courts over integration of Central High School in Little Rock in 1958, the Supreme Court upheld the power of the federal district courts to supervise the integration of the school over the state's objections.[24]

Exercising the Power of
Judicial Review

Judicial review is not a power that the Court has used frequently. Indeed, after *Marbury v. Madison* it was fifty-four years before another act of Congress was declared unconstitutional. This occurred in the case of *Dred Scott v. Sandford* (1857) in which a slave claimed to be free when his master took him to a territory where slavery was banned.[25] The Court, however, ruled that the Missouri Compromise of 1820, which outlawed slavery in the northern territories, was unconstitutional because it took the slaveowner's property without due process of law. In declaring that free Negroes were not citizens and without constitutional rights, the Court in the *Dred Scott* case created a public furor and helped precipitate the Civil War.

Since it asserted its power of judicial review, the Supreme Court has declared state laws or provisions of state constitutions uncon-

23. *Marbury v. Madison,* 1 Cr. 137 (1803).
24. *Cooper v. Aaron,* 358 U.S. 1 (1958).
25. *Dred Scott v. Sandford,* 19 How. 393 (1857).

stitutional over a thousand times and, through 1989, federal enactments unconstitutional in 120 instances (approximately 80 percent of which occurred in this century).[26] The most conflictual period between the Court and Congress was between 1933 and 1936 when the Court struck down important New Deal legislation in a frontal attack on the policies of the Franklin Roosevelt administration. Since the late 1930s, when the Court retreated from its opposition to the New Deal, the most frequent instances of declaring federal laws unconstitutional have involved findings that laws violated the personal rights and liberties guaranteed by the Constitution.

When judicial review is viewed in historical perspective, it is clear that by striking down a number of important government decisions, the Supreme Court has established itself as a major participant in the policy-making process. The Court, however, has been selective in exercising its power, and the great majority of government policies—particularly in the case of foreign policy—have operated without Court interference. Thus, while judicial review has helped the Court play a major role in the policy process, it has not made the Court the dominant participant.[27]

Judicial Selection

Federal judges are nominated by the president and confirmed by a majority vote of the Senate. Judgeships are lifetime appointments, although judges, like all other civil officers of the government, can be removed for "high Crimes and Misdemeanors" through impeachment procedures in which the House of Representatives brings impeachment charges against a judge and the Senate then votes to impeach. With the prospects of lengthy tenure in office, federal judges, particularly Supreme Court justices, can have a long-term impact on judicial policy making. It is not greatly surprising, then, that Supreme Court appointments often engender intense controversy because determining the composition of the courts is one of the most important ways of influencing judicial policy making.

In contrast to the federal government where all judges are appointed by the president, the states use a variety of selection procedures, depending on state constitutions and statutes. Both appointment and election are used. Almost half the states follow a mixed appointment and election process, such as the Missouri plan, in which the governor appoints judges from a list of candidates ap-

---

26. Baum, *Supreme Court,* 177.
27. Ibid., 181.

proved by a judicial commission, and a referendum is held on each appointee's performance at the next general election.

U.S. District Court and Court
of Appeals Judges

In appointing federal district and court of appeals judges, presidents are forced to share power with their party's senators. The practice of **senatorial courtesy** enables the senior senators of the president's party to block federal appointments within their own states when they disapprove of a nominee. As a result, these senators do much of the screening of lower-federal court judges. Many, in fact, have set up judicial selection committees in their states to assist them in picking well-qualified judicial nominees to propose to the Department of Justice and president for nomination. Also involved in the selection process is the American Bar Association (ABA), which evaluates the qualifications of judicial nominees. A "not qualified" rating by the ABA makes it extremely difficult to secure Senate confirmation for a nominee, and presidents, therefore, rarely nominate people whom they believe cannot pass muster before the ABA screening panel.

Because federal judicial appointments have a significant policy-making impact and are among the most prized patronage plums at the disposal of the president and the Senate, there is a great deal of jockeying for influence among home state senators of the president's party, White House staff, the Department of Justice, and interest groups. The ultimate decision on which name will be submitted to the Senate for confirmation is a presidential one. During the Reagan and Bush administrations, periodic clashes between the Justice Department and GOP senators over federal district court nominations prompted delays in the president's submission of judicial nominees to the Senate for confirmation.

For appointments within states where there is no senator of the president's party, the president usually consults with state party leaders. During the Kennedy and Johnson administrations, for example, the legendary leader of the Cook County Democratic organization, Chicago mayor Richard Daley, personally approved every federal judge appointed to the Northern District of Illinois.[28]

The impact of the appointing process on the federal judiciary can be profound (see box, Imprints on the Bench). Approximately 90 percent of judicial appointees come from the ranks of the president's

---

28. Robert A. Carp and Ronald Stidman, *Judicial Process in America* (Washington, D.C.: CQ Press, 1990), 219.

Imprints on the Bench

By the end of his presidency, Franklin Roosevelt had appointed an estimated 75 percent of the judge ships authorized at that time for the federal courts. As of 1992, President George Bush and former President Ronald Reagan together may have come close to that figure.

This chart shows the impact of presidents Roosevelt to Bush on the federal bench. But these figures do not present a precise picture. The total number of life-tenured judgeships reflects all appointments made during a term, including those to replace deceased, retiring, or elevated judges who the same president had appointed earlier. No numbers are readily available for all ten presidents that would eliminate those duplications, which are generally believed to be proportionately few. For example, although Reagan appointed 51 percent of all positions available over the eight years of his term, his legacy of the entire judiciary in 1988 generally has been calculated at 47 percent. (The longer presidents are in office, the more likely they are to fill the same spot twice, thus slightly inflating the percentage.)

"Total judgeships" represents the number of positions authorized in a president's last year in office; the two most recent bills creating judgeships were passed in 1984 and 1990. Because the latter took effect after Congress had adjourned, Bush was unable to fill any of the eighty-five positions created by it.

Appeals court judges include members of all twelve circuits. The appeals court for the Federal Circuit, created in 1982, is not included because, unlike the other circuits, it has limited jurisdiction. The district courts include those in each state and in each of the four territories.

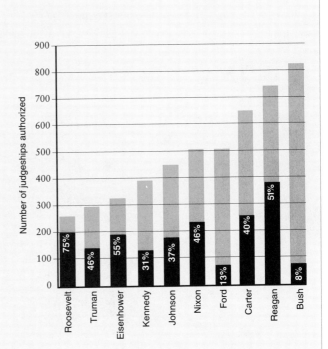

President	Supreme Court	Courts of Appeals	District Courts	Total Judges Appointed	Total Judgeships Authorized
Roosevelt (1933–45)	9	52	136	197	262
Truman (1945–53)	4	27	102	133	292
Eisenhower (1953–61)	5	45	127	177	322
Kennedy (1961–63)	2	20	102	124	395
Johnson (1963–69)	2	41	125	168	449
Nixon (1969–74)	4	45	182	231	504
Ford (1974–77)	1	12	52	65	504
Carter (1977–81)	0	56	206	262	657
Reagan (1981–89)	3	83	292	378	740
Bush (1989–90)	1	18	48	67	825

Source: Administrative Office of the U.S. Courts. Reprinted in *Congressional Quarterly Weekly Report*, January 19, 1991, 173.

Table 13.1 Political Party Backgrounds of Federal District Court and Court of Appeals Nominees, Presidents Johnson to Bush *(percent)*

| | Nominees of Presidents | | | | | |
	Johnson	Nixon	Ford	Carter	Reagan	Bush[a]
District Courts						
Democrat	94.3	7.3	21.2	92.6	4.8	4.2
Republican	5.7	92.7	78.8	4.4	93.4	93.8
Independent	0.0	0.0	0.0	2.9	1.7	2.1
Active in party politics	49.2	48.6	50.0	60.9	58.6	62.5
Courts of Appeals						
Democrat	95.0	6.7	8.3	82.1	0.0	0.0
Republican	5.0	93.3	91.7	7.1	97.4	94.4
Independent	0.0	0.0	0.0	10.7	1.3	5.6
Other	0.0	0.0	0.0	0.0	1.3	0.0
Active in party politics	57.5	60.0	58.3	73.2	69.2	66.7

SOURCE: Harold W. Stanley and Richard G. Niemi, eds., *Vital Statistics on American Politics,* 3d ed. (Washington, D.C.: CQ Press, 1992), 288–289.
[a] Appointees through December 1990.

own party (see Table 13.1), and it is common for the president and Department of Justice to seek appointees who share the president's political and judicial philosophies. During his eight years in office, Ronald Reagan was able to transform the federal bench from a predominantly Democratic institution into one with a Republican majority. Because of the unusually high level of concern shown by the Reagan administration for appointing judges who shared the president's ideology, it is likely that a conservative Republican bench will be one of the lasting legacies of his presidency.[29] His successor, George Bush, has continued to appoint conservatives to federal judicial posts.[30]

Both Democratic and Republican court appointees have tended to be white males educated at a top university and with prior judicial experience or membership in a medium- to large-sized law firm. The percentage of appointees drawn from the ranks of women and minorities increased significantly during the Carter administration, de-

29. For an account of the Reagan administration's judicial selection practices and their impact, see David M. O'Brien, "The Reagan Judges: His Most Enduring Legacy?" in *The Reagan Legacy: Promise and Performance,* ed. Charles O. Jones (Chatham, N.J.: Chatham House, 1988), 60–101.

30. Neil Lewis, "Bush Travels Reagan's Course in Naming Judges," *New York Times,* April 10, 1990, C19, National edition.

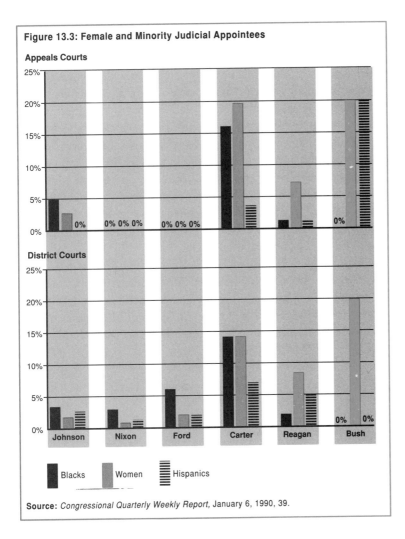

Figure 13.3: Female and Minority Judicial Appointees

Appeals Courts

District Courts

Johnson   Nixon   Ford   Carter   Reagan   Bush

■ Blacks   ▦ Women   ☰ Hispanics

Source: *Congressional Quarterly Weekly Report,* January 6, 1990, 39.

clined under Reagan, and for women and Hispanics rose again during the first year of the Bush presidency (see Figure 13.3).

U.S. Supreme Court Justices

Between 1789 and 1991, only 105 men and one woman served on the nation's highest tribunal, the Supreme Court. Because this select group has tremendous power to influence the direction of public policy, the resignation, death, or infirmity of a justice is an immediate cause for speculation and maneuvering about a successor.

In making Supreme Court nominations, presidents consider professional competence and integrity, party affiliation and service, political ideology and judicial philosophy, and matters of race, gender, ethnic background, religion, and geography. President Lyndon

Johnson, for example, appointed longtime adviser, friend, and liberal Jewish Democrat Abe Fortas. He also appointed Thurgood Marshall to be the Court's first black justice, an act that the president recognized had great symbolic significance and political benefits for his party.[31] President Reagan's appointees shared his conservative ideology: William Rehnquist, the Court's most conservative justice, was elevated to the position of chief justice; conservative Sandra Day O'Connor, who had served as GOP leader in the Arizona State Senate, was the fulfillment of a 1980 campaign promise to appoint a woman to the Court; and Antonin Scalia (the Court's first Italian-American justice) and Anthony Kennedy strengthened the Court's conservative bloc and served as recognition of the importance of Catholics in Reagan's electoral coalition.

Most presidential choices for the federal judiciary are confirmed easily by the Senate. But, because appointments to the Supreme Court carry the potential for changing the direction of judicial policy over an extended period of time, major controversies arise periodically over presidential nominees. Intense confirmation battles tend to occur when (1) the Court is closely divided between Republican and Democratic appointees; (2) the nominee is perceived as not being moderate in ideology; (3) questions are raised about the qualifications of the nominee; (4) the president is politically weak; or (5) different parties control the presidency and Senate.[32] Some or all of these conditions have been present since the 1970s as a divided Court has wrestled such divisive issues as criminal defendants' rights, abortion, and affirmative action. Since 1789, twenty-nine of 145 nominations to the Supreme Court failed to gain Senate confirmation, including six since 1968 (see Table 13.2). Twelve were rejected outright by the Senate, and the others were either withdrawn or allowed to lapse in the face of opposition.

The public policy implications of Supreme Court appointments were dramatically displayed in 1987 when the Senate rejected President Reagan's nomination of court of appeals judge Robert Bork to replace retiring justice Lewis Powell. Bork was an outspoken conservative intellectual, who as a Yale law professor had harshly criticized liberal Court decisions of the 1960s and 1970s. With the Court narrowly divided between its liberal and conservative wings,

31. O'Brien, *Storm Center*, 63–64.

32. See Charles M. Cameron, Albert D. Cover, and Jeffrey A. Segal, "Senate Voting on Supreme Court Nominees: A Neoinstitutional Model," *American Political Science Review* 84 (June 1990): 525–534; and Peter H. Lemieux and Charles H. Stewart, III, "Senate Confirmation of Supreme Court Nominations from Washington to Reagan," Working Paper Series, Hoover Institution, Stanford University, 1990.

Table 13.2 Supreme Court Nominations That Failed to Gain
Senate Confirmation

Nominee	Year	President	Action
William Paterson	1793	Washington	Withdrawn
John Rutledge	1795	Washington	Rejected, 10–14
Alexander Wolcott	1811	Madison	Rejected, 9–24
John Crittenden	1828	J. Q. Adams	Postponed[d]
Roger B. Taney[a]	1835	Jackson	Postponed[d]
John Spencer	1844	Tyler	Rejected, 21–26
R. Walworth	1844	Tyler	Withdrawn
Edward King	1844	Tyler	Withdrawn
Edward King	1844	Tyler	Withdrawn
John Read	1845	Tyler	Postponed[d]
G. Woodward	1846	Polk	Rejected, 20–29
Edward Bradford	1852	Fillmore	Postponed[d]
George Badger	1853	Fillmore	Postponed[d]
William Micou	1853	Fillmore	Postponed[d]
Jeremiah Black	1861	Buchanan	Rejected, 25–26
Henry Stanbery	1866	A. Johnson	Postponed[d]
Ebenezer Hoar	1870	Grant	Rejected, 24–33
George Williams	1874	Grant	Withdrawn
Caleb Cushing	1874	Grant	Withdrawn
Stanley Matthews[b]	1881	Hayes	Postponed[d]
W. B. Hornblower	1894	Cleveland	Rejected, 24–30
Wheeler H. Peckham	1894	Cleveland	Rejected, 32–41
John J. Parker	1930	Hoover	Rejected, 39–41
Abe Fortas[c]	1968	L. Johnson	Withdrawn
Homer Thornberry	1968	L. Johnson	Withdrawn
C. Haynsworth	1969	Nixon	Rejected, 45–55
G. H. Carswell	1970	Nixon	Rejected, 45–51
Robert Bork	1987	Reagan	Rejected, 42–58
Douglas Ginsburg	1987	Reagan	Not submitted[e]

SOURCE: Harold W. Stanley and Richard G. Niemi, eds., *Vital Statistics on American Politics,* 2d ed. (Washington, D.C.: CQ Press, 1990), 269.
Note: Twenty-nine of 145 presidential nominations to the Court have failed to obtain Senate confirmation. Five nominees, however, declined appointment after having been nominated (Harrison, 1789; W. Cushing, 1796; Jay, 1800; Lincoln, 1811; Adams, 1811) and two withdrew after being confirmed (W. Smith, 1837; Conkling, 1882).
[a]Later nominated for chief justice and confirmed.
[b]Later nominated and confirmed.
[c]In 1968, Fortas, an associate justice, was nominated chief justice.
[d]Senate either postponed or failed to act on nomination.
[e]Publicly announced but withdrawn before the president formally submitted his nomination to the Senate.

the Bork nomination became an all-out battle over the future of the judicial policy. On one side were the Reagan administration and its allies and on the other a Democratic-controlled Senate and such liberal interest groups as Planned Parenthood, organized labor, and civil rights organizations. Although Bork was rejected by a 42–58 Senate vote, President Reagan was able to strengthen the Court's conservative bloc when he later nominated and gained confirmation for Judge Anthony Kennedy, a less well-known and less politically vulnerable conservative, as a replacement for Powell.

In 1990, Justice William Brennan (1956–1990), the leader of the Court's liberal wing, resigned, giving President Bush an opportunity to strengthen the bloc of conservative justices. His nominee to replace Brennan was David Souter, a New Hampshire Supreme Court justice whom the president described as a conservative who would not "legislate from the bench." This nomination reflected the president's desire to avoid the type of ideological and partisan controversy that had torpedoed the Bork nomination three years earlier. Unlike Bork, Souter had left no extensive "paper trail" of court decisions or scholarly writings outlining his views on contentious legal issues. This lack of a written record of his views made him a difficult target for liberal senators and interest groups. His folksy New England manner, seemingly moderate philosophy, and deft responses to senators' inquiries at the confirmation hearings also helped him secure Senate approval. On the Court, Souter has been a reliable vote for the conservative bloc of justices.

The relative calm that characterized the Souter confirmation process was breached in 1991 when President Bush nominated a controversial and outspoken black conservative, Court of Appeals Judge Clarence Thomas, to replace Justice Thurgood Marshall. Thomas's conservative views aroused both fervent support and opposition. But when accusations were leaked to the media that he had sexually harassed former coworker Anita Hill while serving as chairman of the Equal Employment Opportunity Commission, an extraordinary political drama unfolded. The Senate postponed its scheduled confirmation vote, and the Senate Judiciary Committee conducted hearings into Hill's accusations that mesmerized massive television audiences over an October weekend. While the hearings were often tense and dramatic, they were also inconclusive. And when they were over, a handful of mainly southern Democratic senators joined with Republicans to provide Thomas with a narrow confirmation victory that strengthened the conservative bloc on the Court.

Influencing Judicial
Policy Making

The politics of influencing judicial decisions is different than that of influencing Congress or the executive branch. Judges and justices cannot be buttonholed in the corridors, nor is it deemed ethical to meet privately with them in their chambers or take them to lunch to discuss a pending case. Grass-roots lobbying—such as mass letter-writing campaigns orchestrated by interest groups—which can be so effective in dealing with Congress are not thought to be appropriate in the case of the judiciary. The tactics of influence must, therefore, be more indirect and sometimes subtle. One tactic is to influence the composition of the federal judiciary. Other techniques include shaping opinion in the legal community, sponsoring litigation or test cases, and filing amicus curiae briefs.[33]

Court Packing: Influencing Policy through Appointments

Presidential appointments do affect judicial policy making. Indeed, presidents have largely succeeded in gaining supportive Supreme Court decisions on the issues most important to them from the justices they appointed. Scholarly studies, moreover, have shown that judges appointed by Reagan, Ford, and Nixon, for example, have decided cases in a more conservative manner than Kennedy, Johnson, and Carter appointees. Furthermore, Reagan appointees have been more likely to render conservative decisions than either Ford- or Nixon-appointed judges.[34] Based on this, judicial selection expert Sheldon Goldman concluded, "When we elect a president, we're electing a judiciary."[35]

Although presidents often consciously pack the Supreme Court with ideological soul mates and longtime political associates, they have at times been disappointed by their appointees. For example, after two justices he had appointed voted to strike down his assertion of broad executive authority to seize steel mills during the Korean War, President Harry Truman lamented that "packing the Supreme

33. The following discussion of techniques for influencing the judiciary relies heavily on Kay Lehman Schlozman and John T. Tierney, *Organized Interests and American Democracy* (New York: Harper and Row, 1986), chap. 14.

34. For a summary of studies assessing the impact of presidential appointees on judicial policy, see Sheldon Goldman, "Reagan's Second Term Judicial Appointments: The Battle at Midway," *Judicature* 70 (April–May 1987): 335–338.

35. Quoted by Howard Kurtz, "Reagan Transforms the Federal Judiciary," *Washington Post*, March 31, 1985, A4.

President Franklin Roosevelt's proposal to "pack" the Supreme Court created a furor, as this historical cartoon demonstrates. Though his Court-packing plan failed, Roosevelt and recent presidents Ronald Reagan and George Bush have succeeded in influencing Court policy through their appointments.

Court simply can't be done. I've tried it and it won't work."[36] Truman's successor, Dwight Eisenhower, suffered from similar misgivings. He called his appointment of Earl Warren as chief justice "the biggest damn-fooled mistake"[37] he ever made. Once justices are on the Court, their perspective on controversial issues may change. In addition, new issues arise. Chief Justice Rehnquist has observed,

History teaches us . . . that even a "strong" president determined to leave his mark on the Court, like Lincoln or Franklin Roosevelt, is apt to be only partly successful. . . . Neither the President nor his appointees can foresee what issues will come before the Court during the tenure of the appointees, and it may be that none had thought very much about these issues. Even though they agree as to the proper resolution of current issues, they may well disagree as to future cases involving other questions.[38]

Presidents also have been frustrated when elderly justices have stayed on the Court rather than retire and let a president with whom they disagreed appoint their successor. Thus in 1987, seventy-nine-year-old liberal justice Thurgood Marshall, whose health was declining, vowed to stay on the Court until after conservative Ronald Reagan left office, saying, "Don't worry, I'm going to outlive those bastards."[39]

Perhaps the most blatant attempt at "Court packing" was Franklin Roosevelt's attempt to expand the size of the Court in 1937. Roosevelt was confronted with a Court that blocked his New Deal policies by regularly declaring major legislative enactments unconstitutional, usually by narrow 5–4 votes. It was Roosevelt's further misfortune that during his first term no vacancies developed, and he was denied the opportunity to make a Court appointment. To cope with a hostile Court, the president proposed that the maximum size of the Court be set at fifteen and that when a justice reached age seventy, the president would be authorized to appoint an additional justice. This proposal to pack the Court set off a firestorm of controversy. With the Court's independence apparently threatened, one of the conservative justices announced his retirement, and two other justices changed their views on the meaning of the Constitution and voted to sustain New Deal legislation. With this "switch in time that

36. Quoted by Henry J. Abraham, *Justices and Presidents* (New York: Oxford University Press, 1985), 70.
37. O'Brien, *Storm Center*, 81.
38. Quoted by Stuart Taylor, Jr., "Re: Shaping the Court," *New York Times,* July 2, 1988, 1, 9, National edition.
39. Stephen Labaton, "Justice Marshall Tells Critics He Is Going to Outlive Them," *New York Times,* Oct. 18, 1987, Y17, National edition.

Table 13.3 Shaping the Supreme Court through Appointments: Presidential Opportunities Vary Greatly

President	Party	Period in Office	Number of Nominees Confirmed	Number of Nominees Not Confirmed or Withdrawn
Hoover	Rep.	1929–1933	3	1
Roosevelt	Dem.	1933–1945	9	0
Truman	Dem.	1945–1953	4	0
Eisenhower	Rep.	1953–1961	5	0
Kennedy	Dem.	1961–1963	2	0
Johnson	Dem.	1963–1969	2	2
Nixon	Rep.	1969–1974	4	2
Ford	Rep.	1974–1977	1	0
Carter	Dem.	1977–1981	0	0
Reagan	Rep.	1981–1989	4	2
Bush	Rep.	1989–1991	2	0

saved nine," the Court-packing plan became unnecessary, and it was allowed to lapse in Congress.

The extent to which presidents can actually exercise their appointive powers and shape Court policy varies greatly from president to president. But the fact is, a president can only make appointments when there is a vacancy. Luck, therefore, counts. Some presidents— like Jimmy Carter and Franklin Roosevelt in his first term—never get a chance to make a Supreme Court appointment. But others can reshape the Court—for example, Reagan and Nixon each made four appointments, and Roosevelt appointed nine justices in his over twelve years in office (see Table 13.3).

Changing the Judicial Structure and Jurisdiction

Congress can exert influence over judicial decision making through its powers to control the organizational structure, size, and jurisdiction of the federal courts. For example, after Woodrow Wilson's election in 1912, Democrats and progressive Republicans in Congress passed a bill abolishing the Commerce Court, which they believed had treated the railroads too favorably.

Even the Supreme Court's jurisdiction has been the object of congressional tampering. The most famous instance occurred in 1869 when Congress passed a law removing from the Court's jurisdiction a case that involved the constitutionality of post-Civil War Reconstruction legislation. More recently, opponents of Court policies on abortion, school prayer, and school busing have introduced bills to withdraw these kinds of cases from the Court's jurisdiction. These efforts, however, have gained little support in Congress.

Shaping Opinion in the Legal Community

Organized interests may seek to influence the thinking of judges, lawyers, and legal scholars by preparing articles supporting a particular point of view for law reviews and other professional journals read by members of the legal fraternity—so-called law review lobbying. Well-placed articles advocating a particular line of judicial reasoning written by experts can change the opinions of judges, their clerks, and attorneys on key issues in the legal community and can be used by lawyers in preparing their briefs and cited by judges in their written opinions. The National Association for the Advancement of Colored People (NAACP) has used this technique effectively to alter legal opinion about government policies that the NAACP believed discriminated in an unconstitutional manner against blacks. Women's rights groups also have sought to advance their goals by shaping opinion among members of the legal community.

Engaging in Litigation

The NAACP and women's rights groups—as well as environmentalists, consumer groups, corporations, and, recently, conservative legal foundations—have found bringing a lawsuit an important avenue for advancing policy objectives. Although the benefits of winning an important lawsuit can be awesome—for example, the NAACP's victory in the famous school desegregation case of *Brown v. Board of Education of Topeka* (1954)—the consequences of losing a major case can be no less so. Litigation carries substantial risks because losing a case means that an adverse legal precedent for the future has been created.

When organized interests bring test cases seeking to overturn existing court policy, they carefully choose the strongest case possible for their purposes. For example, in 1935 the National Association of Manufacturers used the case of a small kosher butcher in Brooklyn, New York, in challenging the constitutionality of a major and controversial piece of New Deal legislation, the National Recovery Act (NRA). As a result, the NRA was debated before the courts in terms of its impact on a small merchant who claimed to be involved merely in intrastate commerce rather than in interstate commerce where the federal government would have regulatory power.[40] Under

40. *Schechter Poultry Corporation v. United States*, 295 U.S. 485 (1935).

these circumstances, the anti-NRA forces, who succeeded in getting the Court to declare the NRA unconstitutional, had a much more persuasive case than they would have had if such giant interstate enterprises as railroads or auto makers had been parties to the suit.

Filing Amicus Curiae Briefs

Amicus curiae, or "friend of the court," briefs filed by interests that are not parties to a suit are a way in which organized groups can present their organization's views on an issue to the Court. These briefs present information and arguments favoring a group's point of view. For example, in the Supreme Court's 1973 landmark *Roe v. Wade* case denying states the power to interfere with a woman's right to an abortion,[41] amicus briefs were filed by such pro-choice organizations as Planned Parenthood, the National Organization for Women (NOW), and the American College of Obstetrics and Gynecologists. Right-to-life groups filed amicus briefs as well.

The federal government also seeks to advance its policy agenda by filing amicus briefs in cases in which the United States is not a party to the suit. The filing of such briefs by the Department of Justice on behalf of the administration is particularly important because it advises the Court of the government's position on important issues.

Role of Other Government Institutions in the Implementation of Federal Court Decisions

Supreme Court decisions are not self-enforcing. The Court, which has no enforcement machinery of its own, must rely on others to implement its decisions. Compliance with Court decisions depends on the clarity, quality, and unanimity of the Court's decision; the kind of issue at stake; and the number of institutions, groups, and individuals affected by the decision. When the issue is clear-cut and only one person is ordered by the Court to act in a prescribed manner, compliance is prompt. This was the case when President Nixon was ordered in 1974 to turn over taped Oval Office conversations about the Watergate coverup to a lower federal court. But when the issue is complicated and many people and government units are affected, implementation is more difficult and drawn out. The Court's 1963 decision in *Gideon v. Wainwright,* for example, that the states must provide attorneys for poor defendants in felony

41. *Roe v. Wade,* 410 U.S. 113 (1973).

trials affected state governments, lower courts, attorneys, and tax-payers.[42] As a result, implementation was slow and involved. Like-wise, the Court's 1962 decision declaring prayer in public schools unconstitutional did not result in immediate compliance across the country.[43] Prayers continued to be recited in school districts where people supported school prayer and where no one brought suit to prevent the practice. Noncompliance with Court decisions is, how-ever, not the norm, and eventually the existence of legally enforceable Court rulings tends to bring individuals, private organizations, and government units into compliance with the law.

Chief Justice Charles Evans Hughes once commented that the "Constitution is what the Supreme Court says it is." Certainly the Court plays a critical role in constitutional as well as statutory in-terpretation, but as this brief look at the implementation of court decisions will indicate, the policy struggle does not end with the an-nouncement of a Court decision. Contending forces seek to influence how the decision will be implemented, and those who are dissatisfied with the decision, especially Congress and the president, may even seek to overturn the action of the Court.

The Lower Federal Courts

Lower-court federal judges are particularly important in carrying out Supreme Court decisions. In performing this function, they dem-onstrate considerable independence and discretion; they do not func-tion as mere bureaucratic arms of the Supreme Court. Their independence is encouraged by life tenure, traditions of running their courts as they see fit, an absence of disciplinary measures, and vir-tually no fear of impeachment.[44] The discretion of lower-court judges also may be the product of the language of the Supreme Court's de-cision. For example, in its landmark school desegregation decision, the Supreme Court required public school systems to make a prompt and reasonable start toward desegregation and to proceed with "all deliberate speed" to bring about desegregation. The Court did not specify what constituted promptness, reasonableness, or all delib-erate speed. As a consequence, lower-district court judges used sub-stantial discretion when confronted with community opinion op-posed to desegregation and with school districts that were dragging their feet on integration while claiming that they were proceeding with all deliberate speed.

42. *Gideon v. Wainwright*, 372 U.S. 335 (1963).
43. *Engel v. Vitale*, 370 U.S. 421 (1962).
44. Robert A. Carp and Ronald Stidham, *The Federal Courts* (Washington, D.C.: CQ Press, 1985), 200.

After the judiciary has made a decision, Congress can respond in ways that either facilitate implementation of the decision or hinder it. Where Congress disapproves of a judicial decision, it has a variety of legislative weapons available to it for use against the courts. For example, the courts are regularly required to engage in *statutory interpretation*—interpreting the meaning of laws passed by Congress and applying them to specific cases. But when a court interprets a congressional statute in a manner of which Congress disapproves, Congress can pass a new statute that in effect overturns the Court's decision. A notable example occurred in 1988 when Congress overturned the Supreme Court's 1984 decision in *Grove City College v. Bell,* a case involving a small Pennsylvania college.[45] The Court interpreted Title IX of the 1972 Education Act amendments, which forbids sex discrimination, to apply only to the specific program receiving federal funds. As a result, the college's financial aid office alone was affected by the law instead of the entire college. Congress responded to this decision by passing the Civil Rights Restoration Act of 1988, which stated that if one part of a college receives federal funds, the entire institution is covered by the Title IX antidiscrimination provisions. Such actions by Congress, however, are relatively rare, and the vast majority of federal judicial decisions are not challenged by Congress.[46]

In addition to interpreting statutes, the Supreme Court also interprets the Constitution. Here, too, Congress may act legislatively either to reverse a decision or to alter its effects. For example, after the Court in 1973 struck down government prohibitions on abortions as unconstitutional, Congress responded in 1976 with the Hyde Amendment and other statutes restricting the use of federal funds for elective or therapeutic abortions. These congressional actions were upheld by the Court.[47] Or Congress can take another avenue if it disapproves of—and wants to reverse—a Court decision: a constitutional amendment. For example, the Thirteenth Amendment (1865) reversed a decision dealing with the legality of slavery, and the Sixteenth Amendment (1913) overturned a Court decision invalidating a federal income tax. Amending the Constitution is, of course, a difficult and time-consuming process. It requires a two-thirds vote of both houses of Congress and ratification by three-fourths of the states.

45. *Grove City College v. Bell,* 465 U.S. 555 (1984).
46. Carp and Stidham, *Judicial Process in America,* 207–208.
47. *Harris v. McRae,* 448 U.S. 297 (1980).

Other legislative weapons available to Congress for use against the courts are the previously noted "Court packing" in which Congress attempts to change the composition of the Supreme Court by expanding its size; altering the Supreme Court's appellate jurisdiction; or exercising budgetary control over the federal courts, although the Constitution prohibits reducing judges' salaries. While individual members of Congress have occasionally tried to pressure the Supreme Court through budgetary measures, the Congress itself has refrained from engaging in such actions.

More informal congressional or individual member responses to disfavored Supreme Court decisions may take the form of attack, usually verbal, on the Court or specific justices. One representative in 1956, for example, even asserted that the Court was a "greater threat to this Union than the entire confines of Soviet Russia."[48] While such attacks may weaken the Court by undermining public confidence in the institution, the actual impact is difficult to assess.

The ultimate weapon against all federal judges that Congress has at its disposal is its power to impeach and remove them from office. Although this power is seldom used, its use against three lower-federal court judges in the 1980s is a reminder that Congress does have this power in its arsenal.

The reluctance of Congress to use its powers to pressure the Court reflects the influence of several factors. First, a substantial number of members of Congress usually agree with Court decisions and will resist attempts to undermine those decisions. Second, legislative assaults on the Court are frequently perceived by the public as lacking in legitimacy. The public tends to believe that the Court should be independent from the other branches of government. And, third, the Court has often retreated from positions that would provide the impetus for congressional intervention.[49]

The President

Presidents, too, can affect the implementation of judicial decisions. For example, when a Supreme Court decision meets open opposition, the president must decide whether and with what degree of force the power of the federal government will be used to support that decision. In these matters, the president has considerable discretion. President Andrew Jackson purportedly said, after the Marshall Court rendered a decision of which he heartily disapproved, "John Marshall has made his decision; now let him enforce it." This

48. Quoted by Baum, *Supreme Court,* 227.
49. Ibid., 229.

oft-quoted statement aptly captures the Court's dependence on the executive branch for assistance in enforcing its decisions.

At times, presidents have used the most coercive powers of the government to gain compliance with Court decisions. In 1957, for example, federal troops under the command of President Dwight Eisenhower ultimately forced the governor of Arkansas to comply with the court-ordered integration of Little Rock Central High School. And in 1963 federal marshals under the command of the Kennedy administration's Justice Department compelled Gov. George Wallace of Alabama to admit blacks to the University of Alabama.

Through their public statements or failure to speak out in support of Court decisions, presidents are thought to be able to affect the level of compliance as well. Some observers, for example, believe that had President Eisenhower spoken more forcefully in support of the 1954 school desegregation decision, southern officials would have made fewer attempts to circumvent the Supreme Court decision banning segregated public school systems.

Because public expectations for compliance with Court decisions are so strong, presidents normally respond promptly to Supreme Court decisions even when the Court has ruled against a presidential action. Presidents do, however, have weapons for use in influencing Court policy. They may, for example, propose legislation or constitutional amendments aimed at retaliating against the Court—Franklin Roosevelt's "Court-packing" plan was a dramatic example. President Ronald Reagan sought to use the constitutional amendment approach. He vigorously, though unsuccessfully, supported amendments designed to overturn the Court's ban on school prayer.

Where Does the Judiciary Fit in the American Political Process?

Although the popular image of the federal courts is one of an apolitical third branch of government, it is clear from our look at the courts in this chapter that this image does not conform to reality. The members of the judiciary gain their positions through a highly politicized process of presidential appointment and Senate confirmation. Most were active in partisan politics before their appointments, and they do not suddenly shed attitudes and approaches to issues the moment they put on judicial robes. Once on the judicial bench, judges are confronted with some of the most controversial issues facing society—abortion, the rights of the accused, powers of the president to use military force, and affirmative action. In shaping public policy on such issues, the courts are not immune from political pressures from litigants, interest groups, public opinion, political parties, Congress, and the executive branch.

As it decides cases and resolves societal conflicts, the Supreme Court gains strength and independence from the discretion it exercises over its caseload and the types of cases that it will consider. The Court's stature with the public has meant that other political leaders, even the president, are expected to comply with Court orders. The Supreme Court also benefits from public expectations that it should be independent of the Congress and the president and insulated from such direct pressures as lobbying. These public expectations constrain the Congress and the president from aggressively using their full array of powers to attack the actions of the Supreme Court.

The Court, too, operates under constraints. As a legal institution, it is required to follow legal procedures in making its decisions. Thus there is the expectation that normally it will follow past precedents in making its rulings. Then too, the Court can only deal with those issues that arise from the cases that are brought before it. Unlike the president and Congress, justices are limited in their ability to initiate government action; they must wait for a case to come before them before making policy. Supreme Court justices are also heavily dependent on the willingness of the American people to comply with their decisions. Moreover, the Court is dependent on the executive branch to enforce its policies if those policies meet with open opposition.

The position of the federal courts in the American political system is a unique one. They operate in an environment that provides them with a degree of independence and insulation not enjoyed by the other branches. The judiciary, however, is not immune from attempts to exert influence on its decision-making processes because the courts are major policy makers in the American system.

For Review

1. Although commonly considered apolitical, the federal judiciary plays a central and prominent policy-making role along with the president or Congress. Many of the most important issues facing Americans eventually find their way to the courts.

2. The United States has a dual judicial system, with federal and state courts operating with their own personnel and jurisdictions.

Each interprets and enforces its own constitution and laws. But overlap exists between the two as well, with the federal judiciary able to declare state actions unconstitutional.

3. The federal judicial system is composed of federal district courts (trial courts), courts of appeal (intermediate appellate courts), and the Supreme Court (which has discretion over the cases it chooses to hear and decide). A series of legislative courts hears specialized types of cases.

4. In the case of *Marbury v. Madison,* the Supreme Court read into the Constitution the power of the federal courts to declare acts of Congress unconstitutional. The federal judiciary has used its power of judicial review sparingly against acts of Congress but has frequently asserted this power to strike down state laws.

5. Federal judges are appointed by the president, must be confirmed by the Senate, and have lifetime appointments. Presidents normally appoint members of their own parties to the federal bench and, particularly in the case of the Supreme Court, seek to appoint individuals who share their views on important matters of public policy. The policy orientation of the Court can be altered by presidential appointments.

6. Although the Supreme Court with its appointed justices is often considered an antimajoritarian institution, Court decisions tend to be in accord with trends in public opinion.

7. Among the techniques used to influence judicial decisions are: changing the composition and size of the judiciary, seeking to shape public opinion within the legal community, bringing test cases to the courts, and filing "friend of the court" briefs.

For Further Reading

Abraham, Henry J. *The Judiciary.* 7th ed. Boston: Allyn and Bacon, 1987. A description of the operation of the American judiciary, with special emphasis on the Supreme Court as policy maker in the area of fundamental freedoms.

———. *The Judicial Process.* 5th ed. New York: Oxford University Press, 1986. A comprehensive description of the functioning of the American judicial system with comparisons to the judicial processes in other countries.

Baum, Lawrence. *The Supreme Court.* 3d ed. Washington, D.C.: CQ Press, 1989. An account of how the Supreme Court functions, forces that influence judicial decisions, and the Court's policy impact.

Carp, Robert A., and Ronald Stidham. *The Federal Courts.* 2d ed. Washington, D.C.: CQ Press, 1991. A description of the federal court system and its decision-making process and impact.

Gates, John B., and Charles A. Johnson, eds. *The American Courts: A Crit-*

ical Assessment. Washington, D.C.: CQ Press, 1991. A collection of essays by leading scholars analyzing the role of the courts in America.

O'Brien, David M. *Storm Center: The Supreme Court in American Politics.* 2d ed. New York: Norton, 1990. Both a scholarly and a readable account of the Court's role in politics.

Woodward, Bob, and Scott Armstrong. *The Brethren: Inside the Supreme Court.* New York: Simon and Schuster, 1979. A behind-the-scenes look at Supreme Court decision making.

PART IV

Politics and Public Policy

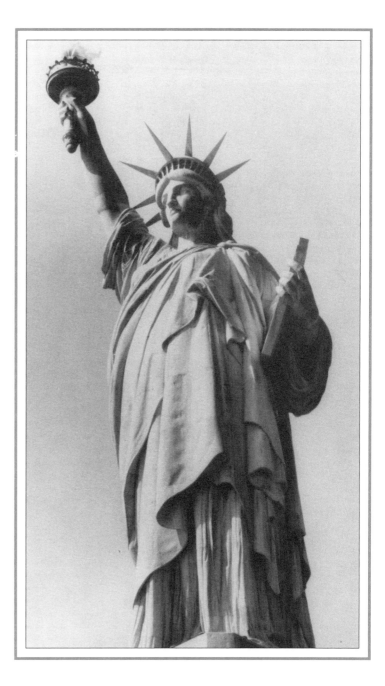

14. Public Policy, Politics, and
Democracy in America

THE CONGRESS, the presidency, the bureaucracy, and the courts—what ultimately makes these institutions so important? The answer: their *policy* decisions affect people both in the United States and around the world. Thus, it follows that as students of American politics we would be concerned about the inner workings of *public policy,* which is whatever the government chooses to do or not to do about perceived problems, and *policy making,* which is how the government decides what will and will not be done about perceived problems.[1]

These definitions of public policy and policy making recognize that government inaction can have just as great an impact on society as government action. The failure of the government earlier in this century to rid the public schools of racial segregation and to prevent denials of the right to vote to all voting-age people had momentous consequences for America, just as government action in these same areas since the 1950s has dramatically changed American society.

American public policy is, of course, affected by the constitutional framework, societal characteristics, political processes, and governmental institutions discussed in previous chapters. A combination of these forces constitutes the unique context for American policy making.

Policy Making in the American Context

Those early Americans who crafted the Constitution primarily were concerned about how to create a government capable of maintaining public order and yet at the same time protecting personal liberty. In their efforts to restrain government, they sought to fragment the government's power by separating powers at the national level and creating a federal system. Three separate branches of government were created—each with the power to check the other two. The national government was strengthened, but it still had to share power with the states. These features of the Constitution have had a lasting effect on the policy-making process. Indeed, the Constitution writers devised a system that makes it difficult to adopt new policies or change existing policies. Legislation, for example, must

---

1. These definitions are derived from Thomas R. Dye, *Understanding Public Policy,* 6th ed. (Englewood Cliffs, N.J.: Prentice-Hall, 1987), 3; and Randall B. Ripley and Grace A. Franklin, *Congress, the Bureaucracy, and Public Policy,* 5th ed. (Pacific Grove, Calif.: Brooks/Cole, 1991), 1.

be approved by the House, Senate, and president; implemented by the bureaucracy; and accepted by the courts.

The Constitution, however, is an incomplete guide to American policy making because America has more than just the three formal branches of government specified in that document. There also are the hybrid government organizations that have significant policy-making authority such as the independent regulatory agencies, government corporations, and foundations. Some, like the regulatory commissions, even combine judicial, administrative, and legislative functions. The actions of government decision makers are also swayed by interested citizens, public opinion, elections, political parties, interest groups, and the media. In fact, some informed observers have found nongovernmental organizations such as interest groups to be so prominent and permanent a feature of government decision making that they have called these organizations the fourth branch of government—a title others reserve for the bureaucracy. But in reality, many different political interests, processes, and institutions join together to make policy. Moreover, as we will see later in this chapter, the kinds of decisional processes used and the types of institutions playing the chief roles will depend on the nature of the issue being considered.

Although the constitutional order often makes government action more easily talked about than done, the federal government has become quite the activist in the twentieth century. This is in contrast to its relative passivity in the early days of the Republic when it simply delivered the mail, defended the shores, levied tariffs and regulated foreign commerce, and built a few public works projects. The government was not involved in the lives of its citizens to any significant degree. But even if it had wanted to, the Constitution and restrictive Supreme Court definitions of the national government's authority would have severely limited its activities. Moreover, there was little in the way of public demand for services from the national government, and those that sought them often lacked the political clout needed to get them. The government's policy agenda was, therefore, limited.

In the depression of the 1930s and during World War II, the government saw its role expand tremendously. The Supreme Court stopped adhering to restrictive definitions of the federal government's power, people began to demand government services and regulation of the economy, and even those who before had lacked the political resources needed to obtain services developed them through such organizations as labor unions.

The 1960s and 1970s were a particularly turbulent period in the nation's history. Blacks and women demanded equality; young people, in particular, protested America's military involvement in Vietnam; and environmental, consumer, health care, poverty, and energy concerns took on new urgency. To accommodate these public concerns, the number and variety of interest groups operating in Washington exploded between the 1960s and 1980s. In response to these pressures, the government's role in society again expanded.

The number of issues on the policy agenda of the 1990s is almost endless. The range is suggested by the major categories of policy on the government's front burner. *Economic policy* includes government taxing and spending, trade, regulation and promotion of business, monetary (money supply) policy, and agriculture. Under *social policy* fall income security (Social Security, Aid to Families with Dependent Children, food stamps), housing, health care, and education. *Civil rights and civil liberties policy* is geared toward safeguarding basic liberties, preventing discrimination, addressing affirmative action and abortion issues, protecting the rights of the accused, and ensuring voting rights. *Natural resources and environmental policy,* which has come of age in this century, revolves around clean air and water, protection of wilderness areas, wildlife protection, national parks, public lands, and water resources. Finally, *foreign and national security policy* covers such wide-ranging areas as weapons systems, troop levels, military alliances, intelligence activities, treaties, foreign aid, trade, immigration, and relations with foreign governments.

Given the wide-ranging, complicated nature of these policy areas, analysis and understanding of policy making can appear staggering to even the most sophisticated analyst. But the job is made easier and the policy process more comprehensible if we begin by examining the stages of the policy-making process and the different types of public policy.

Stages in the Policy-making Process

The government's policy is contained in its official statements of goals and projected activities. The most important of these policy statements are found in the laws passed by Congress and in the executive orders of the president. Government policies also arise from bureaucratic regulations designed to implement congressional and presidential actions and from court decisions. But if these policies are to have any real impact, they must be implemented through

Figure 14.1: Stages in the Policy-Making Process

Stage and Activities   Product

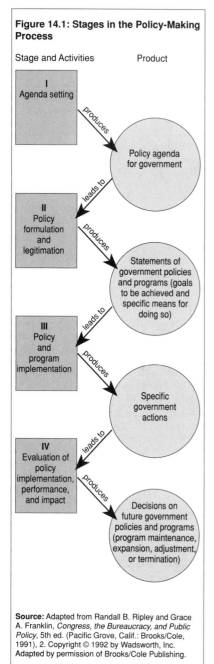

Source: Adapted from Randall B. Ripley and Grace A. Franklin, *Congress, the Bureaucracy, and Public Policy*, 5th ed. (Pacific Grove, Calif.: Brooks/Cole, 1991), 2. Copyright © 1992 by Wadsworth, Inc. Adapted by permission of Brooks/Cole Publishing.

concrete actions. Thus, when Congress passed the landmark Clean Air Act of 1990, mandating cleaner air for America, the actual impact of the act depended on the effectiveness of the Environmental Protection Agency's enforcement actions.

The actual process of making public policy can be broken down into four main stages: (1) setting the agenda, (2) formulating and legitimating a policy, (3) implementing a policy, and (4) evaluating policy implementation, performance, and impact (see Figure 14.1).[2]

Stage One: Agenda Setting

Agenda setting is a process in which decision makers perceive that a problem exists, leading them to adopt broad goals to cope with the problem. In the current era of government activism, the government's agenda is full—controlling the federal budget deficit, dealing with instability and conflict in the Middle East, combating drugs, eliminating the trade deficit, adapting to the collapse of communism in Eastern Europe, coping with the spread of AIDS, combating terrorism, and dealing with the problems of the homeless, environmental pollution, airline safety, housing, family farmers, gender and racial discrimination, and the list goes on. Agenda space is limited because government decision makers can pay attention only to so many things.

Problems find space on the government's policy agenda when existing conditions arouse the concern of the citizens and their leaders. The greater the number of people who perceive that a problem exists, the greater is the likelihood that it will move onto the government's policy agenda. For example, foreign trade is an extremely complicated field to which few Americans or members of Congress have paid much attention. But that changed when America's trade deficit with foreign nations reached unprecedented levels in the 1980s and manufacturing industries closed their factories and laid off workers because they found it difficult to compete in the world market. In this atmosphere, with some communities ravaged by unemployment and even employed people frightened about their future, trade became a highly salient issue in terms of media attention, interest group agitation, and congressional and administration maneuvering. The result was congressional passage of a major revision of American trade policy in 1988.

Even a specific event can push an issue onto the public policy agenda. The Iraqi invasion of Kuwait in August 1990, for example,

2. The stages discussed are derived from the conceptual framework developed by Randall B. Ripley, *Policy Analysis in Political Science* (Chicago: Nelson-Hall, 1985); and Ripley and Franklin, *Congress, the Bureaucracy, and Public Policy.*

The tide of Japanese products flooding the U.S. marketplace, like these Nissan automobiles, has helped put foreign trade policy on the public agenda.

prompted the dispatch of a massive U.S. military force to the Persian Gulf to defend Saudi Arabia and the formation of a U.S.-led alliance which launched a war to remove Iraq from Kuwait. Earlier, in 1957, the Soviet launching of the first satellite, *Sputnik,* spurred the United States to activate its space program.

And the aim of interest groups, of course, is to focus the attention of government officials and help push issues onto the government's policy agenda. Organized labor, for example, has exerted pressure on Congress to consider trade, minimum wage, plant closing, child care, and parental leave legislation during the administrations of Presidents Ronald Reagan and George Bush.

Political leaders can have an impact on the public agenda as well. The president is a particularly important agenda setter. When he became president, President Reagan cited such priorities as lower taxes, cuts in domestic spending, higher expenditures for defense, and deregulation of business. His agenda became to a large degree the government's agenda.

Stage Two: Formulating and Legitimating Policies

Once it has been acknowledged that a problem deserves the government's attention, the government must decide what to do about the problem and what goals must be met to achieve the solution. As the discussion in Chapter 10 on lawmaking in Congress demonstrated, this can be a long, tortuous process. *Policy formulation* involves developing alternative proposals and collecting, analyzing, and disseminating the information needed to assess the alternatives and persuade people to support one proposal or another. Next, specific policies have to be adopted, but in a way that uses procedures widely accepted by society. This is the *legitimation* process—adopting government policies in a manner that conforms to the public's expectations about what is the proper and correct way to do things. A common method of legitimation is passage of a law by Congress, but Supreme Court decisions and White House executive orders also give legitimacy to government policies. Legitimation is extremely important because without it public acceptance of a policy is easily undermined.

Policy formulation normally has its strategic implications—that is, information is assembled, arguments developed, and alternatives shaped with an eye toward winning the approval of official decision makers. When Congress is the legitimating agent, the rule of the day is coalition building—shaping policy in such a way that it will attract a majority. In the House of Representatives, for example, passage of legislation is facilitated when a proposed program will distribute benefits widely among a large number of congressional districts.[3] Thus, federal highway, rivers and harbors, and water reclamation project legislation is usually a shoo-in. Knitting together a congressional majority normally involves extensive negotiation, bargaining, and compromise.

Although the formal decisions on public policy are made by government officials, they are not the only participants in policy making. As we observed in Chapter 7, interest groups can have a profound impact, as can ordinary citizens when they are mobilized. For example, in 1988 Congress responded to pressure from the multimillion-member American Association of Retired Persons and passed the Medicare Catastrophic Coverage Act, which provided the elderly with catastrophic illness benefits but also imposed an increase in Medicare taxes. Only seventeen months after passage of the law, it was repealed by a Congress that was feeling the heat from its elderly constituents. Outraged senior citizens, objecting to increased Medicare taxes ($800 per person in 1989 and a projected $1,050

3. See David R. Mayhew, *Congress: The Electoral Connection* (New Haven, Conn.: Yale University Press, 1974), 127–130.

in 1993) formed grass-roots organizations and deluged their senators and representatives with angry demands for the law's repeal. Congress responded.

But not all policy decisions take the form of positive government action. Government decision makers also may decline to act, and that too is a policy decision. Strongly organized opposition within and outside the government, for example, blocked legislation on key elements of President Reagan's social agenda—permitting prayer in the public schools and banning abortions.

Stage Three:
Policy Implementation

Few government policies are self-implementing. Once a policy has been proclaimed officially through passage of legislation, issuance of an executive order by the president, or the announcement of a court decision, it must be implemented. Even the most brilliantly conceived policy will fail to achieve its designers' goals if it is poorly implemented.[4]

Implementation is "those activities directed toward putting a program into effect."[5] One of the three major activities required for implementation is *interpretation*—translation of the program language into acceptable and feasible administrative directives.[6] Administrators must be able to discern Congress's intent when it passes a law creating a new government program. Legislation often sets lofty goals—achieving clean air or declaring war on poverty and drugs—but it is left to the administrators to fill in the details about how the goals will be accomplished. Frequently, laws purposely are left vague to avoid offending key lawmakers whose votes were needed to enact a bill. In these circumstances, the implementers of the legislation have a great deal of leeway in determining how the new program will actually operate.

The second major activity needed for implementation is *organization*—establishing administrative units and methods for putting a program into effect. Resources, in the form of money, buildings, equipment, and information, must be acquired and a staff hired and trained.

For the third activity, *application*, services and benefits are routinely provided (for example, mailing out Social Security checks,

4. George C. Edwards, III, *Implementing Public Policy* (Washington, D.C.: CQ Press, 1980), 1.
5. Charles O. Jones, *An Introduction to Public Policy*, 2d ed. (North Scituate, Mass.: Duxbury Press, 1977), 139.
6. See Jones's consideration of implementation activities, ibid., chap. 7.

Coast Guard personnel implement the government's policy of interdicting and seizing shipments of illegal drugs bound for U.S. ports and the streets of America's cities.

providing health care for veterans) and sanctions and regulations are imposed (for example, enforcing Occupational Safety and Health Review Commission regulations and criminal statutes).

As described here, interpretation, organization, and application may appear rather dull and routine. But, in fact, the manner in which these activities are carried out can dramatically affect the extent to which policy goals are achieved. A striking example is the National Health Service Corps, a program designed by Congress in 1970 to encourage doctors to practice in areas lacking adequate health care. The brief four-page law gave the Health Services Administration (designated the Health Resources and Services Administration in a 1982 reorganization) little in the way of guidance about implementation. But the intent of the law was clear: to place physicians in areas that could support them economically. In implementing the law, HSA administrators defined an area lacking physicians loosely and allowed exceptions to the "shortage"-of-doctors requirement if an area had low utilization of health services. They then placed physicians in urban sites where HSA-sponsored group practices were already operating. Thus, rather than providing doctors for rural areas, the implementation process funneled substantial numbers of physicians into inner-city areas, and rather than fighting the geographic barriers inhibiting health care availability, the HSA sought to fight the economic barriers. The HSA used its administrative discretion to implement the program in a way that was consistent with the agency's traditional emphasis on delivering health care to the poor rather than, as Congress had intended, establishing physicians in private practice. The implementation process, then, transformed the National Health Service Corps into a program more consistent with the goals of the administering agency than with those of Congress. But by 1990, budget cuts had reduced the number of doctors participating in the program and had forced administrators to alter their implementation policy. In an effort to cover as many areas of the country as possible, the agency shifted family practitioners out of urban areas into poverty-stricken rural ones. As might be expected, this policy shift stimulated complaints from urban clients and members of Congress.[7]

7. For a more detailed account, see Frank J. Thompson, "Bureaucratic Discretion and the National Health Service Corps," *Political Science Quarterly* 97 (Fall 1982): 427–445; and Josh Barbanel, "U.S. Orders Family Doctors from Cities to Country," *New York Times,* June 24, 1990, 1Y, 17Y, National edition.

*Stage Four: Evaluation of
Policy Implementation,
Performance, and Impact*

After a government policy has been put into effect, it is evaluated to determine how well it was implemented, whether its goals were achieved, and what its impact was. The results of these assessments can result in a program being maintained, expanded, changed, or even terminated. In effect, after the results of the evaluation stage are in, an existing policy may go back on government's policy agenda.

Some government programs do achieve their desired goals. The Voting Rights Act of 1965, for example, substantially increased the percentage of eligible blacks exercising their right to vote. Other programs, however, fall short of their objectives. In the 1960s, for example, President Lyndon Johnson's War on Poverty did not end poverty, although such programs as Head Start (preschool education for disadvantaged children) won widespread praise. And the Safe Streets Act of 1968 did not cause people to feel safe in our cities. Indeed, Washington's great, and at times exaggerated, expectations of the programs it has conceived can be dashed because of implementation problems out in the field. Political scientists Jeffrey Pressman and Aaron Wildavsky found, for example, that an Economic Development Administration program implemented in the late 1960s to dramatically expand minority employment in Oakland, California, produced relatively few minority jobs, generated large fees for architects, and involved a construction project hampered by extensive delays.[8] Programs also may fail to achieve their goals because inadequate resources have been allocated to deal with a problem. For example, the federal government has been sharply criticized for failing to commit adequate resources to coping with drug abuse, environmental pollution, and problems of education.

One of the major difficulties in achieving federal program objectives is the fact that a large share of government programs is implemented not by the federal government but by third parties. This occurs when (1) the federal government contracts with the private sector for a wide array of goods and services (for example, weapons for the Department of Defense or concession stands for national parks); (2) through federal grants, state and local governments build

8. Jeffrey L. Pressman and Aaron B. Wildavsky, *Implementation: How Great Expectations in Washington Are Dashed in Oakland* (Berkeley: University of California Press, 1974).

highways, construct public housing, administer welfare programs, or operate mass transit systems (see Chapter 3); (3) tax incentives (sometimes called tax breaks or loopholes) encourage selected types of behavior, such as taking tax deductions for home ownership and charitable contributions; (4) the federal government makes or assists with billions of dollars in loans to make credit available where private money markets might not—for example, for student loans, home mortgages, and small business investments; and (5) federal government rules and regulations determine the cost and availability of many private sector goods and services such as interest rates and the availability of bank loans and govern the safety of such consumer products as food, drugs, and cars. Political scientist Donald Kettl has described these practices as "government by proxy." He also has noted that when implementation of federal programs is turned over to third parties, the government loses control of the programs because the goals of third-party administrators are apt to be different than those of the federal government.[9]

Some government policies, such as the amendments to the 1974 Federal Election Campaign Act (FECA), have unintended consequences. Intended to restrict the role of money in campaigns by strictly limiting contributions by individuals, interest groups, and parties, the amendments also facilitated the formation of political action committees (PACs), thereby stimulating the almost immediate creation of thousands of primarily business-oriented PACs. Contrary to the hopes of the campaign finance reformers, then, money did not lose its significance for elections. Indeed, campaign funds from organized interests increased substantially. And even more dismaying for the liberal advocates of campaign finance reform was the realization that they had helped create the conditions that encouraged the development of business-oriented PACs, to the detriment of their supporters in politically active labor unions.

Because the verdicts rendered on a program's implementation, performance, and impact can influence whether that program is continued, expanded, changed, or terminated, the policy evaluation process can be highly controversial. When most people think of policy evaluation, they tend to think in terms of objective social science analyses. In truth, this may be part of the process, but in the world of practical politics policy evaluation has a much broader meaning. For that world, it is a process in which many different types of peo-

9. See Donald F. Kettl, *Government by Proxy: (Mis?)Managing Federal Programs* (Washington, D.C.: CQ Press, 1988).

ple—bureaucrats, members of Congress, interest group representatives, academicians, White House staffers, and ordinary citizens—assess a policy based on their own unique sets of criteria and experiences with government programs. It is not surprising, then, that their evaluations are apt to differ. For example, Republican and Democratic members of Congress have entirely different ideas about the problems associated with the Federal Election Campaign Act and thus divergent reform agendas. According to Republicans, FECA-encouraged PACs are giving large and disproportionate shares of their contributions to incumbent Democrats. GOP lawmakers believe that electoral reform should make it possible to channel more money to congressional challengers, thereby overcoming the advantages of incumbents (who are mostly Democrats). The Republican reform agenda, then, calls for tight restrictions or even bans on PAC contributions, higher contribution limits for parties, and opposition to expenditure limits on candidates.

The Democrats, however, define the problem as too much money being spent on elections and members of Congress having to spend inordinate amounts of time chasing campaign contributions. Their reform proposals place limits on expenditures and call for some form of public funding for elections. Since the two parties define the problems with the existing law so differently, it is small wonder that campaign finance reform has been such a contentious issue in the 1990s.

Another example of the controversy that can surround the implementation and impact of government policy concerns the effects of government transfer payments under the Aid to Families with Dependent Children (AFDC) program. Some argue that this welfare program, which gives aid to families headed by single mothers, has deprived recipients of incentives for self-improvement and self-sufficiency. It is further charged that AFDC has encouraged fathers to be absent from their families because aid goes only to households headed by a single woman. Others hotly dispute these contentions and see the program primarily as an essential safety net for the nation's most disadvantaged citizens.

As these examples demonstrate, policy making is a difficult, often controversial process. But by looking only at the stages in this process, we do not have a well-rounded view of public policy in America. That requires a look at the different types of policies on our national agenda.

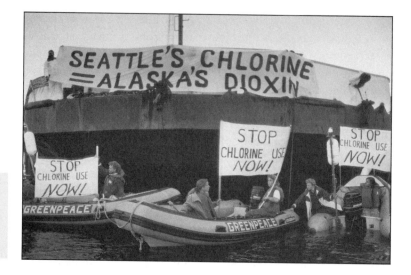

Activists from Greenpeace use unconventional and aggressive tactics to pressure the government into strengthening environmental protection regulations.

Types of Public Policies

The nature of the policy-making process varies tremendously from one issue area to another. Decisions in 1991 regarding whether to go to war with Iraq and how the war would be conducted, for example, were made by the president and his national security and foreign policy advisers. Once it had authorized the president to take military action, Congress was not a major policy maker, nor were interest groups highly visible or influential. By contrast, the major participants in the enactment and subsequent repeal of the 1988 Medicare Catastrophic Coverage Act were, as we have already noted, the Congress and interest groups representing the elderly. Other less visible policy issues—such as those involving the protection of copyrights and patents—may be left to the bureaucracy or committees of the Congress to resolve.

To understand the policy-making process in a way that moves beyond examining such isolated examples, it is helpful to think in terms of types of government policies (see Figure 14.2). Using these types, it is then possible to identify the different patterns of government decision making that occur across a range of government policies.[10]

10. The following consideration of different types of public policy relies heavily on the conceptualization and analysis in Ripley, *Policy Analysis in Political Science*, and in Ripley and Franklin, *Congress, the Bureaucracy, and Public Policy*.

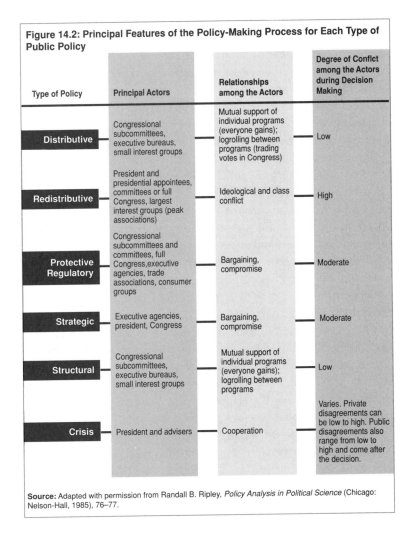

Figure 14.2: Principal Features of the Policy-Making Process for Each Type of Public Policy

Type of Policy	Principal Actors	Relationships among the Actors	Degree of Conflct among the Actors during Decision Making
Distributive	Congressional subcommittees, executive bureaus, small interest groups	Mutual support of individual programs (everyone gains); logrolling between programs (trading votes in Congress)	Low
Redistributive	President and presidential appointees, committees or full Congress, largest interest groups (peak associations)	Ideological and class conflict	High
Protective Regulatory	Congressional subcommittees and committees, full Congress, executive agencies, trade associations, consumer groups	Bargaining, compromise	Moderate
Strategic	Executive agencies, president, Congress	Bargaining, compromise	Moderate
Structural	Congressional subcommittees, executive bureaus, small interest groups	Mutual support of individual programs (everyone gains); logrolling between programs	Low
Crisis	President and advisers	Cooperation	Varies. Private disagreements can be low to high. Public disagreements also range from low to high and come after the decision.

Source: Adapted with permission from Randall B. Ripley, *Policy Analysis in Political Science* (Chicago: Nelson-Hall, 1985), 76–77.

Domestic Policies

Within the domestic policy sphere, there are four types of policies: distributive, redistributive, competitive regulatory, and protective regulatory. Each has its own particular pattern of decision making.

Distributive policies are intended to promote desirable private activities in need of government assistance. Subsidies are provided (not necessarily in the form of cash) to encourage the desired activity. The examples of government subsidy programs are legion and include (1) loans and loan guarantees to home buyers, college students, owners of small and some large businesses, and farmers; (2) grants to farmers in the form of price supports, universities for scientific research, and state and local governments for housing, community development, education, mass transit, airports, highways, environmental protection, libraries, and health care; (3) income tax deductions for interest paid on home mortgages, local property taxes, and charitable contributions; (4) permits to encourage utilization of public resources for cutting timber, mining, and grazing on public lands at rates below those determined on the open market; and (5) tariffs to protect American products from foreign competition.

Typically distributive policies are enacted with a minimum of controversy because for such policies there appear to be only winners, no losers. It is a matter of distributing benefits widely while not inflicting any readily apparent harm on others. Thus, when the federal government provides the states with highway grants, all the states (as well as car owners and manufacturers, road contractors, and concrete suppliers) benefit, and the costs are hardly noticeable to the individual taxpayers who ultimately foot the bill.

Subsidy programs tend to develop a strong base of support among their beneficiaries, program administrators, and interested members of Congress. These mutually beneficial three-sided alliances have been dubbed "iron triangles" or "subgovernments" (see Chapter 12, The Bureaucracy). One powerful subgovernment dominating veterans policy includes veterans groups (American Legion and Veterans of Foreign Wars), the Department of Veterans Affairs, and the members of the House Veterans Affairs Committee. Subgovernments tend to dominate policy making for each subsidy program, as major issues are normally resolved among the interested parties at the congressional subcommittee level. The president and the full House and Senate do not usually play an active role in distributive issues.

Redistributive policies are designed to shift wealth, property rights, or other values (access to education, jobs, and government services) among social classes and groups (including racial groups) in society, and especially to those perceived to be disadvantaged. Unlike distributive policies, redistributive policies have clear winners and losers, and, as a result, they tend to be highly controversial. Examples of these policies are (1) progressive income taxes (where the wealthy pay a higher percentage of their incomes in taxes than the poor); (2) food stamps, public housing, welfare, medical care, legal services, and job training for the poor; (3) prohibitions against racial discrimination in housing, education, and public accommodation, and requirements for affirmative action in employment; and (4) health care for the elderly.

The debate on redistributive issues tends to take on an ideological and class conflict cast, with liberals generally supportive of such programs and conservatives either opposed or giving reluctant assent. Whereas distributive policies are likely to arouse only low-level conflicts that can be resolved in congressional subcommittees, redistributive policies tend to be highly visible, ideological, and partisan. As a result, strong presidential leadership is usually needed to resolve such issues (for example, President Johnson's enthusiastic support for a war on poverty and medical care for the elderly). Redistributive issues also normally receive the attention of the full House and Senate, the executive agencies, and the major interest groups in society.

Since the 1930s and the administration of Franklin Roosevelt, presidents have tended to take the lead in pressing for the redistribution of resources to aid the relatively disadvantaged. But, after the explosion of often controversial redistributive programs in the 1960s and early 1970s, interest and support for such programs ebbed. In the 1980s, the Reagan administration, especially in its tax and budget policies, pursued a course that was distinctly nonredistributive.[11]

Whether the Reagan legacy is permanent or temporary, it is useful to remember that American public policy overall has not been strongly redistributive in character. This reflects the absence of a genuine working-class party in the United States, a relative lack of economic-class consciousness and militancy among Americans, and a continuing public belief in progress, self-reliance, free enterprise, and limited government. Moreover, because most Americans are not poor, redistributive policies require, then, the support of middle-class voters.

A significant aspect of redistributive policy making in the United States is that once such programs are proposed or put into effect, there is pressure to extend the benefits to people who are not deprived. The histories of the Economic Development and Model Cities programs illustrate this pattern. The Economic Development program was designed to assist economically deprived areas, but eventually the definition of such areas was expanded so that four-fifths of the country was eligible for assistance. The Johnson administration's Model Cities program was designed to target the most deprived neighborhoods in a limited number of cities for federal aid. It was, however, altered by Congress to permit aid to less-deprived neighborhoods in 150 cities, including small ones.

Competitive regulatory policies and programs limit the number of people or organizations within the economy that can supply a

11. Ripley and Franklin, *Congress, the Bureaucracy, and Public Policy,* 122–123.

particular good or service. More specifically, such policy sets the framework through which the government determines who will have the right to provide a good or service. Competitive regulatory policies often allocate scarce resources when it has been determined that free access to the marketplace would be impossible or unworkable. To prevent chaos in the broadcasting industry, for example, the Federal Communications Commission (FCC) allocates the limited number of highly valued radio frequencies and television channels. But in return for obtaining their broadcast licenses, radio and television stations are required to meet standards of public service. In another area, before the deregulation movement of the 1970s and 1980s, such regulatory agencies as the Interstate Commerce Commission (ICC) and the Civil Aeronautics Board (CAB) were heavily involved in determining which transportation companies would and would not have access to the marketplace. This effort to ensure approved standards of service was carried out by allocating routes to airlines, railroads, barge lines, and truckers.

Because of its technical, complicated nature, decision making in competitive regulatory policy tends to be delegated to such independent regulatory agencies as the FCC. Representatives and senators, however, sometimes intervene to influence individual decisions, and interest groups representing regulated industries are extremely active in this field.

After regulatory policies that substantially restricted access and competition, particularly in transportation and telecommunications, were criticized for hiking prices, distorting the marketplace, and being cumbersome and ineffective, a movement for deregulation took hold in the late 1970s and 1980s. The amount of regulation in the transportation field was then reduced, most notably for the airlines. With the abolition of the CAB and the deregulation of routes and prices, airlines now wage fierce price wars and provide other incentives (such as frequent flyer programs) to win passengers.

Deregulation in most modes of transportation and some aspects of communications has meant that positive policy formulation in these areas has diminished in recent years. Rising dissatisfaction with quality of service, especially by the airlines, however, may trigger renewed interest in limited forms of competitive regulatory policy.

Protective regulatory policies are designed to protect the public by specifying the conditions under which various private as well as government activities can take place. When it follows its normal pattern, Congress legislates broad policy goals (protecting patient rights in nursing homes, bans on unfair methods of competition or on false and misleading advertising) but gives few details. It then establishes a regulatory commission or some other agency in the bureaucracy to develop and administer the necessary details. Thus, the Department of Health and Human Services is responsible for enforcing the 1987 law setting requirements to improve patient care in nursing homes, and the Federal Trade Commission polices business trade and advertising practices. Examples of protective regulatory policy are requirements that banks, savings and loans, credit card companies, and department stores disclose their interest rate charges; high "sin" taxes on such goods as tobacco and alcohol; prohibitions against unfair labor and business practices; penalties for auto manufacturers whose cars do not meet clean air standards; inspection of food processing; safety standards for pharmaceuticals; minimum wage and occupational safety standards; and requirements that government agencies comply with Freedom of Information rules and publish proposed administrative rule changes in advance.

Conflicts over protective regulatory policies are frequent and often bitter because regulations can impose costs on the regulated businesses and restrict their activities. The tobacco industry, for example, has consistently fought against a series of protective regulations, including warning messages on cigarette packages and bans on smoking on domestic airline flights. Not to be outdone, coal strip-mine operators have sought to prevent regulation of their operations and requirements that they restore land after mining it.

Protective regulatory conflicts are rarely resolved at the level of congressional subcommittees and agency bureaus. Negotiations and bargaining are normally required at a higher level. Passage of clean air legislation in 1990, for example, required extensive, high-level negotiations among the White House, executive agencies, congressional party and committee leaders, and organized interests.

Foreign and National Security Policies

When a nation's interests or very existence are threatened, there is no international police force waiting in the wings to offer its protection. Nations must look after their own security and interests in the international system. American foreign policy, then, provides for this nation's security and protects American interests around the globe. It also advances causes to which the United States is committed such as human rights, remedies for disease and poverty, environmental protection, and economic development. Like domestic policy, foreign and national security policies can be broken down into different types, each with its own distinctive policy-making process.

Strategic policies and programs assert and provide for the implementation of the basic foreign and military stances of the United States toward other nations. Strategic policies deal with, among other things, arms control (the mix of weapons systems and forces to be deployed at home and around the world); alliances (for example, the U.S.-led alliance to enforce U.N. resolutions calling for an end to Iraq's invasion of Kuwait, or the status of the North Atlantic Treaty Organization alliance as the threat of Soviet military aggression recedes); America's position toward countries with records of human rights abuses (such as South Africa and the People's Republic of China); foreign trade (tariffs, import quotas, and export policy); immigration; and foreign aid—who will receive how much of what kind of aid (foreign and military).

Decisions on strategic policy tend to be dominated by the president and executive agencies, especially the Departments of Defense and State. When dealing with strategic issues, Congress has either supported the administration's requests (such as when it acceded to President Reagan's wishes by providing funds for weapons development, including the B-1 bomber, Strategic Defense Initiative research, and the MX missile, and when it authorized President Bush to use military means to remove Iraq from Kuwait), or has sought to register a competing point of view without completely depriving the administration of its flexibility.[12] While usually willing to give at least grudging support to most administration strategic policy recommendations, Congress can attach conditions to its support, which can have a substantial impact. In 1974, for example, through the Jackson-Vanik amendment Congress tied expansion of American trade with the Soviet Union to freer emigration policies for Russian Jews. As the Cold War thawed in the late 1980s and President Bush looked for ways in 1989 to integrate the Soviet Union into the world economy, this law delayed granting the Soviet Union most favored-nation trade status. Further evidence of Congress interjecting itself into strategic policy making has been a requirement in foreign aid legislation that the president certify improvements in human rights policies in El Salvador before permitting that Central American nation to receive aid.

On occasion, Congress has come into direct conflict with the ad-

12. For an informed series of analyses of presidential-congressional relations in foreign policy making, see Thomas E. Mann, ed., *A Question of Balance: The President, the Congress, and Foreign Policy* (Washington, D.C.: Brookings, 1990).

Military procurement policies, such as production of the B-2 bomber, have a major impact on employment and local economies and, therefore, are the subject of intense lobbying within the executive branch and Congress.

ministration on strategic issues. One dramatic example was the Boland amendments of the 1980s banning military aid to the anti-Sandinista insurgents (contras) in Nicaragua. Attempts by the White House staff during the Reagan administration to circumvent the Boland amendments led to a major administration embarrassment—the Iran-contra affair—and to the criminal conviction (later overturned on appeal) of the president's national security adviser, John Poindexter, for lying to Congress.

Structural policies are those concerned primarily with the procurement, deployment, and organization of military personnel and materiel, as well as the organization and maintenance of civilian foreign affairs operations such as the State Department, Agency for International Development, and the U.S. Information Agency. Structural policies cover such matters as defense procurement of weapons systems and supplies, as well as the specific suppliers to be used; the creation (including their location and size) and closing of military installations; the size, composition, and location of reserve forces; the staffing and compensation for the Departments of Defense and

State; and programs to distribute surplus American agricultural products.

Structural policies clearly affect important economic interests within the United States—major defense industry corporations and their unions, localities dependent on defense contracts and military installations for jobs, and farmers whose incomes are affected by whether surplus farm products are distributed abroad.[13] Such policies have their distributive aspects and often call for subsidies. Like domestic distributive policies, structural defense policies are heavily influenced by subgovernments. Defense procurement decisions, for example, tend to be dominated by policy subgovernments composed of Pentagon procurement officials, private sector contractors, subcommittees of the congressional Armed Services and Appropriations committees, and senators and representatives whose states and districts benefit from defense contracts. Reserve forces policy is heavily influenced by the close relationship that exists among the Reserve Officers Association, congressional Armed Services committees, members of Congress who are themselves members of the reserves or have an interest in them, and interested members of the executive branch. This subgovernment has been largely successful in attaining its goals of retaining a large reserve force, generous pay, retirement income, and other benefits.[14]

Crisis policies are made in response to immediate problems that are viewed as serious and demand prompt action. Examples of crisis policies are the U.S. government's responses to the Japanese attack on Pearl Harbor in 1941, the Soviet imposition of the Berlin blockade in 1949, the erection of the Berlin Wall in 1961, the placement of Soviet offensive missiles in Cuba in 1962, the Iranian seizure of the U.S. embassy in Tehran in 1979, terrorists' seizure of the cruise ship *Achille Lauro* and a TWA airliner in the Middle East in 1985, and Iraq's 1990 invasion of Kuwait. In such crises, the principal decision makers are the president and high-level officials of the executive branch, who function with a minimum of publicized conflict. Congressional involvement, in most cases, is limited to briefings by officers of the executive branch and gestures of symbolic support for administration policies.

Policy Types and Patterns of Policy Making

The types of public policy just described are not airtight compartments; a government policy can contain elements of more than

13. Ripley, *Policy Analysis in Political Science*, 72–73.
14. Ripley and Franklin, *Congress, the Bureaucracy, and Public Policy*, 163–164.

one type. Military procurement, for example, not only is a structural foreign policy but also has its domestic distributive policy dimensions. These policy types are of value, however, when trying to understand the various policy-making patterns that exist within the political system.

Key to these patterns, of course, are the people who are influential in shaping a policy and who vary from one policy type to another. As we saw earlier, close-knit subgovernments—congressional subcommittees, agency bureaus, and program beneficiaries—dominate most domestic distributive and structural foreign policy decisions, which are made in an atmosphere largely free of ideological conflict. Because the benefits of governmental largess are distributed widely, there are no apparent losers in these policy processes.

By contrast, redistributive policies are made in an atmosphere charged with intense ideological and partisan conflict—conflicts that cannot be resolved at the subcommittee level in Congress but must be fought out at a higher level by the president, the full Congress, the heads of executive departments, and the major interest groups.

Competitive regulatory policy, which is highly technical and complicated, tends to be delegated to regulatory agencies, which are subject to pressure from affected interest groups, whereas protective regulatory policy making is characterized by high levels of conflict and requires the involvement of congressional and executive branch leaders, along with interest groups.

In strategic, and particularly crisis, foreign policy making, the president and executive branch leaders are the dominant participants.

Assessing the American Political System

Any assessment of the American policy-making system depends in part on which of the variety of evaluative criteria available are being used. Should the American system be judged in terms of how "democratic" it is? In other words, does it permit relatively open participation? Is it responsive to societal concerns? Do citizens have a relatively high degree of control over their leaders? Or should the main concern be whether the policy-making process effectively manages conflict within society and maintains political stability—change without violence? Another basis for evaluation relates to the adequacy of the public policies the system produces—do they adequately provide for freedom, national security, educational opportunities, and economic well-being?

Salient Features of the American
Policy-making Process

Before considering these issues, it will be useful to recall the features of the political process identified in previous chapters. The American system is characterized by fragmented power. The Constitution's principles of separation of powers and federalism have created numerous power centers within the government. Thus, to formulate, enact, and implement policies, the various branches and levels of government must share power. This fragmentation of power is further encouraged by weak political parties, the procedures and practices of the House and Senate, and the proliferation of organized interest groups. As a result, policy making in the American system is an exercise in coalition politics—building coalitions within and across party lines to pass legislation, building coalitions among interest groups to exert influence on decision makers, and building coalitions between members of the executive and legislative branches of government. Coalition building, of course, takes time and inevitably involves bargaining, negotiation, and compromise before a majority can be created for a new policy. It was, for example, only after months of tortuous and delicate negotiations among a Republican president, senior administration officials, Democratic and Republican congressional party leaders, and influential congressional committee members, that it was possible for the Congress to pass budget legislation for fiscal year 1991.

With power so fragmented, it is possible for interests in control of a critical juncture in the policy process (such as a congressional committee or an agency bureau responsible for carrying out a policy) to virtually veto policy changes until their concerns have been at least partially satisfied. The policies that then emerge from this process, because they are generally compromises forged through coalition building, rarely constitute dramatic changes of direction. Rather, policy change in the United States is usually incremental in character. And because so many officials and interests must either agree or acquiesce before a policy change can occur, delay is commonplace.

The Issue of
Public Policy Adequacy

The adequacy of American public policies is, of course, a favorite target for criticism. Some critics stress the apparent incapacity of the government to confront and cope with today's problems and injustices. This is a serious matter because certain major problems do stand out like festering sores on the body politic. Liberal and conservative critics alike have complained about the halting steps being

Bush administration officials and the Democratic and Republican congressional leadership negotiate late into the night of October 24, 1990, to forge a compromise agreement on the fiscal 1991 budget. From bottom left are Rep. Leon Panetta (D-Calif.), chairman of the House Budget Committee; Sen. Jim Sasser (D-Tenn.), chairman of the Senate Budget Committee; Rep. Richard Gephardt (D-Mo.), House majority leader; Secretary of the Treasury Nicholas Brady; Rep. Robert Michel (R-Ill.), House minority leader; Sen. Pete Domenici (R-N.M.), ranking GOP member of the Senate Budget Committee; Richard Darman, director of the Office of Management and Budget; Sen. George Mitchell (D-Maine), Senate majority leader; and Sen. Robert Dole (R-Kan.), Senate minority leader.

taken to deal with the massive federal budget deficit, and the government's seeming inability to cope with a wave of violent crime that is terrorizing many neighborhoods. Liberals, especially, tend to criticize the political process for not developing the social programs needed to deal with homelessness, inadequate housing and education, high rates of unemployment among minority youth, and a health care crisis characterized by spiraling costs and millions of Americans without access to care. Many conservatives also complain about the inadequacy of government responses to what they see as the salient problems and have advocated stepped-up government activity to ban abortions, curb obscenity, permit prayer in public schools, maintain law and order, and protect traditional values.

But while some critics fault the political system for its failure to act and would favor steps making it easier for government to act more decisively, others criticize the government for trying to do too much, interfering unduly in the economic marketplace, and providing services and benefits to virtually every group in society—students, farmers, educators, veterans, the elderly, the poor, industry, homeowners, and environmentalists. It is claimed that the result is "Big Government" and a heavy burden on the taxpayer. Big government, they assert, is virtually impossible to manage; it does little well and is thus ineffective, burdensome, and expensive. These generally conservative critics support measures that they believe would restrain politicians' tendencies to provide benefits to key constituency groups. Among these measures are constitutional amendments to require a balanced federal budget each year and to grant the president a line-item veto—the power to veto specific items in a bill instead of having to either accept or veto the entire bill.

These two evaluations of American policy making—one pointing to the government's lack of responsiveness to major societal problems and the other citing the government's overextension—reflect these two groups' different philosophies about the role of government and their distinctly different views about the government's capacity to deal with societal problems. These philosophies and viewpoints are not easily reconciled.

In balancing the costs and benefits of policies achieved through bargaining and compromise, the issue of public policy adequacy also can be approached from a less philosophical perspective. The delays inevitably involved in the coalition building needed to enact government programs, it is argued, are costly. Indeed, the delays encountered in enacting programs to provide improved and less expensive health care or to rebuild America's aging infrastructure of roads, bridges, and water and sewer systems, prevent the nation from profiting from these investments. Even worse, these delays, which are inherent in the system, may cause such problems as urban decay to worsen and therefore become more expensive to remedy.

There is the danger as well that the policies and programs that do emerge from our system of bargaining and compromise will end up being "too little, too late." Yet the patchwork of policies that manage to survive the American process of bargaining, negotiation, and bargaining stand a good chance of remaining in force and being accepted by the public because of the broad coalitions required to adopt them in the first place. The American process—even with its delays and patchwork character—does seem to contribute to policy stability. Contrast the stability of policies in the United States with that of policies in Great Britain where dramatic policy reversals occur regularly, depending on whether the Conservative or Labour parties control the government.[15] For example, the steel industry was nationalized by a Labour government after World War II, denationalized by a Conservative government in 1953, nationalized again by Labour in 1963, and substantially denationalized and restructured by the Conservative government of former prime minister Margaret Thatcher which took office in 1977. Under Thatcher, the Conser-

15. Fred I. Greenstein and Frank B. Feigert, *The American Party System and the American People*, 3d ed. (Englewood Cliffs, N.J.: Prentice-Hall, 1985), 155–156.

vatives transformed government policy related to taxation, local government, education, and organized labor. Should Labour replace the Conservatives as the ruling party in the near future, it is expected to undo much that Thatcher's Conservatives did in these areas. By contrast, the American policy process is characterized by greater policy stability. The Republican administration of Dwight Eisenhower (1953–1961), for example, did not repeal the New Deal of the Roosevelt era, nor did the Reagan administration (1981–1989) repeal—although it did modify and in some instances cut back—the major programs of Lyndon Johnson's Great Society. Once a program is enacted in the United States, it tends to become part of a national consensus.

Another possible benefit of the American policy-making process is its ability to manage conflict. With the major exception of the Civil War, political conflict in the United States has been kept within tolerable levels. It is essential, then, that government policies not only respond to society's problems but also be made in a way that does not tear the political system apart. The American governmental system, with its many power centers that together shape policy, does this by allowing competing interests to find supporters within the government, resulting in policies borne of bargaining and compromise. Those that do emerge are rarely all that their sponsors sought, nor are they as threatening as their opponents originally feared. Both sides usually can live with the outcome even though they are not satisfied. And both sides have the option of seeking to change the policy at a later date.

Thus, the American policy process is seldom speedy, and its products are rarely clear-cut, final solutions to problems. Rather, as laws passed by Congress illustrate, today's policies are verbal formulae that a majority of the members of Congress "find adequate as a basis for their continuing policy struggle."[16]

Is the Process Democratic?

Most Americans would probably accept the notion that they live under a democratic political order. But there are also those who believe that saying America is a democracy implies a sort of smug satisfaction with the status quo that does not take into account our government's apparent incapacity to cope with serious problems and injustices. Certainly the overview in this chapter of different types of policies has suggested that redistributive policies, designed to shift

16. Raymond A. Bauer, Ithiel de Sola Pool, and Lewis Anthony Dexter, *American Business and Public Policy* (New York: Atherton, 1963), 426.

wealth and opportunity to the relatively disadvantaged in society, are much more difficult to enact than distributive policies, which bestow government subsidies and largess widely within the country. Indeed, there is even a tendency for those redistributive policies that we do have to be gradually converted into distributive programs. While acknowledging that injustices do exist and public policies are not necessarily responsive to societal needs, one could still make a strong argument that the American political process is more democratic than many political systems because, in political scientist Nelson Polsby's words, it (1) permits "relatively (but not perfectly) open participation by those possessing requisite skills and interests," (2) it is "relatively (but not perfectly) responsive to the demands of a variety of participants," and (3) it is "run (but not flawlessly) according to a relatively stable and equitable set of rules."[17]

Application of these relativist standards, however, still leaves open the question of the extent to which the system actually meets such standards as the ideal of majority rule. As the chapters dealing with the Constitution, public opinion, interest groups, and Congress have shown, it would be inaccurate to suggest that the majority always decides issues of policy in the United States. But would Americans really want pure majority rule if it resulted in the majority being able to permanently disenfranchise a minority? Or if the winning party in an election rolled up huge majorities but no opposition was tolerated? Or if a majority, which did not really care about an issue, still voted down a proposal that a minority supported fervently? Such a majoritarian system would be viewed as "less open, less responsive, less stable, less equitable, and therefore less democratic" than most Americans would find acceptable.[18]

The American federal government, then, does operate in ways that can thwart majority rule.

• The electoral college system for electing presidents does not give equal weight to each person's vote. Because state electoral votes are allocated among candidates on a winner-take-all basis, a vote in California is worth more than a vote in Wyoming (a vote in California helps determine the disposition of fifty-four electoral votes, but a vote in Wyoming affects only three electoral votes).

• Equal representation of the states in the Senate also works to thwart majority rule. Because each state, irrespective of its population, has two senators, the senators from the nine least populous

17. Nelson W. Polsby, *Congress and the Presidency*, 4th ed. (Englewood Cliffs, N.J.: Prentice-Hall, 1986), 6–7. This discussion relies heavily on Polsby's insights.
18. Ibid., 7.

states (containing less than 3 percent of the nation's population) can cancel out the votes of the senators from the nine most populous states (containing over 50 percent of the nation's people).

• Congressional procedures also may prevent the majority from exercising its will. In the Senate, a determined minority using the filibuster can prevent the majority from working its will on legislation. In both chambers, committees unrepresentative of the total membership may bottle up legislation and prevent it from reaching the floor for a vote. Furthermore, the modified seniority system used to select committee chairmen can elevate to positions of power people who are out of step with both a majority of their party and congressional colleagues.

• An unelected Supreme Court whose members are appointed for life has the power to interpret the laws passed by Congress and even declare the actions of an elected Congress and president unconstitutional.

• Unelected bureaucrats engage in major policy making as they implement laws enacted by the people's representatives in Congress sometimes in ways that are at odds with congressional intent.

These majority-thwarting institutions are at least in part responsible for the openness, responsiveness, and stability of the American political system and, therefore, may actually contribute to democracy. But what makes the American system democratic is more complicated than having a few majority-thwarting devices built into the Constitution and government practices. The American system's fragmented power also stems from federalism, separation of powers, a far-flung bureaucracy, multiple centers of congressional power, thousands of organized interests, and decentralized political parties. Fragmented political power has contributed to democracy because "each center of special power is for various reasons responsive to different segments of society."[19] Thus, because many power centers must share in the making of policy, public policies are likely to reflect a variety of societal interests and to constitute compromises among competing power centers that must share in decision making.

What ultimately makes these power centers responsive to various interests, as well as willing to make alliances and admit new participants, are the uncertainties introduced by frequent elections. Although most incumbents win reelection, elections conducted within the context of a competitive party system mean that politicians cannot take their tenure in office for granted. They must be concerned

19. Ibid., 9.

about developing and maintaining an electoral base of support. This requires sensitivity to shifting tides of opinion, the activities of other politicians, and changes in the makeup of one's constituency. Elections may not tell us precisely what the voters want in terms of public policy, but by electing politicians responsive to different segments of society, they do contribute to democracy by keeping the system open and responsive.

Reform the System?

Some political observers recognize the contributions that a policy-making system characterized by extensive negotiation, bargaining and compromise makes to managing societal conflict, political stability, and democracy, yet they continue to believe that major institutional reforms are required. A group of distinguished and experienced Washington hands, led by President Jimmy Carter's senior White House aide Lloyd Cutler and former undersecretary of state and secretary of the Treasury Douglas Dillon, has come to the conclusion that power in the American system is too fragmented and that our government, especially the president, cannot assemble enough power to carry out the policies needed in these difficult times.[20] This concern was particularly strong in the last days of the Carter administration because of the president's inability to secure congressional approval of his energy program and the SALT II treaty with the Soviets. Their solution to what they see to be insufficient presidential power is the adoption of some version of a parliamentary system so that presidents can muster automatic congressional majorities for what they consider to be desirable, albeit controversial, policies. Of course, constitutional change so far-reaching in character is not likely to occur in the foreseeable future. The issue of whether decision makers can aggregate sufficient power to lead the government and shape its policies is, however, a serious and legitimate question that deserves thoughtful consideration, especially in an era when the thrust of many reform proposals has been to weaken the institutional power bases of party leaders, presidents, and congressional leaders by making the government and party processes more open and participatory.

Maintenance of a democratic government requires constantly reassessing how the system is functioning. But that assessment must be an informed one. It must reflect an understanding of how the

20. Lloyd N. Cutler, "To Form a Government," *Foreign Affairs* (Fall 1980): 126–130.

governmental system actually operates, attention to its constantly changing nature, and clarity about the criteria being used for evaluation. In observing the world of politics, one must probe deeply. Indeed, in doing so one might do well to remember the lines from Gilbert and Sullivan's *H.M.S. Pinafore,*

Things are seldom what they seem,
Skim milk masquerades as cream.

For Review

1. *Public policy* is whatever the government chooses to do or not to do about perceived problems, and *policy making* is how the government decides what will be done about perceived problems.

2. The policy-making process involves a series of stages: agenda setting, formulation and legitimation of policies, policy implementation, and evaluation of policy implementation, performance, and impact.

3. For analytic purposes, public policies can be classified by types. Domestic policies are either distributive, redistributive, competitive regulatory, or protective regulatory, and foreign and national security policies are either strategic, structural, or crisis.

4. Each type of policy is characterized by a particular set of principal participants, distinctive relationships among the participants, and certain levels of conflict during decision making.

5. Because power within the American political system is fragmented, policy making normally is an exercise in coalition building, which involves negotiation, bargaining, and compromise. As a result, in the United States public policy is relatively stable, and policy change is normally incremental.

For Further Reading

Birnbaum, Jeffrey H., and Alan S. Murray. *Showdown at Gucci Gulch.* New York: Random House, 1987. A lively, fascinating account of the passage of the Tax Reform Act of 1986 by two reporters who covered the action.

Dye, Thomas R. *Understanding Public Policy.* 6th ed. Englewood Cliffs, N.J.: Prentice-Hall, 1987. An introduction to public policy analysis that seeks to explain both domestic and foreign policy development.

Jones, Charles O. *An Introduction to the Study of Public Policy.* 3d ed. Monterey, Calif.: Brooks/Cole, 1984. A concise, insightful consideration of the forces shaping the development of public policy.

Kennedy, Robert F. *Thirteen Days: A Memoir of the Cuban Missile Crisis.* New York: Norton, 1969. An insider's account of a dramatic instance of foreign policy making in a crisis.

Kettl, Donald F. *Government by Proxy: (Mis?)Managing Federal Programs.* Washington, D.C.: CQ Press, 1988. A probing analysis of the consequences of using third parties to implement federal programs.

Kingdon, John W. *Agendas, Alternatives, and Public Policies.* Boston: Little, Brown, 1984. An analysis of how issues find their way onto the public agenda.

Mann, Thomas E., ed. *A Question of Balance: The President, the Congress, and Foreign Policy.* Washington, D.C.: Brookings, 1990. A series of analyses focusing on balancing presidential and congressional influence in foreign decision making.

Pressman, Jeffrey L., and Aaron B. Wildavsky. *Implementation: How Great Expectations in Washington Are Dashed in Oakland.* Berkeley: University of California Press, 1974. A case study of the difficulties involved in implementing national policies at the grass-roots level.

Ripley, Randall B., and Grace A. Franklin. *Congress, the Bureaucracy, and Public Policy.* 5th ed. Pacific Grove, Calif.: Brooks/Cole, 1991. An analysis of how public policy is made in different policy arenas.

Schick, Allen, ed. *Making Economic Policy in Congress.* Washington, D.C.: American Enterprise Institute, 1983. A series of insightful analyses of congressional economic policy making.

Spanier, John W. *American Foreign Policy since World War II.* 12th ed. Washington, D.C.: CQ Press, 1991. A historical survey of American foreign policy making since 1945.

White, Joseph, and Aaron Wildavsky. *The Deficit and the Public Interest: The Search for Responsive Budgeting in the 1980s.* Berkeley: University of California Press/Russell Sage Foundation, 1990. An informed analysis of fiscal policy which argues that the budget deficit is high because reducing it would have adverse consequences for most citizens and thus for the country as a whole.

REFERENCE MATERIAL

Appendix
Glossary
Index
Acknowledgments

❧ Appendix

Declaration of Independence

In Congress, July 4, 1776

The Unanimous Declaration of the Thirteen United States of America

When in the Course of human events, it becomes necessary for one people to dissolve the political bands which have connected them with another, and to assume among the Powers of the earth, the separate and equal station to which the Laws of Nature and of Nature's God entitle them, a decent respect to the opinions of mankind requires that they should declare the causes which impel them to the separation. We hold these truths to be self-evident, that all men are created equal, that they are endowed by their Creator with certain unalienable Rights, that among these are Life, Liberty and the pursuit of Happiness. That to secure these rights, Governments are instituted among Men, deriving their just powers from the consent of the governed. That whenever any form of Government becomes destructive of these ends, it is the Right of the People to alter or to abolish it, and to institute new Government, laying its foundation on such principles and organizing its powers in such form, as to them shall seem most likely to effect their Safety and Happiness. Prudence, indeed, will dictate that Government long established should not be changed for light and transient causes; and accordingly all experience hath shown, that mankind are more disposed to suffer, while evils are sufferable, than to right themselves by abolishing the forms to which they are accustomed. But when a long train of abuses and usurpations, pursuing invariably the same Object evinces a design to reduce them under absolute Despotism, it is their right, it is their duty, to throw off such Government, and to provide new Guards for their future security.—Such has been the patient sufferance of these Colonies; and such is now the necessity which constrains them to alter their former Systems of Government. The history of the present King of Great Britain is a history of repeated injuries and usurpations, all having in direct object the establishment of an absolute Tyranny over these States. To prove this, let Facts be submitted to a candid world. He has refused his Assent to Laws, the most wholesome and necessary for the public good. He has forbidden his Governors to pass Laws of immediate and pressing importance, unless suspended in their operation till his Assent should be obtained; and when so suspended, he has utterly neglected to attend to them.

He has refused to pass other Laws for the accommodation of large districts of people, unless those people would relinquish the right of Representation in the Legislature, a right inestimable to them and formidable to tyrants only.

He has called together legislative bodies at places unusual, uncomfortable, and distant from the depository of their Public Records, for the sole purpose of fatiguing them into compliance with his measures.

He has dissolved Representative Houses repeatedly, for opposing with manly firmness his invasions on the rights of the people.

He has refused for a long time, after such dissolutions, to cause others to be elected; whereby the Legislative Powers, incapable of Annihilation, have returned to the People at large for their exercise; the State remaining in the mean time exposed to all the dangers of invasion from without, and convulsions within.

He has endeavored to prevent the population of these States; for that purpose obstructing the Laws of Naturalization of Foreigners; refusing to pass others to encourage their migration hither, and raising the conditions of new Appropriations of Lands.

He has obstructed the Administration of Justice, by refusing his Assent to Laws for establishing Judiciary Powers.

He has made Judges dependent on his Will alone, for the tenure of their offices, and the amount and payment of their salaries.

He has erected a multitude of New Offices, and sent hither swarms of Officers to harass our People, and eat out their substance.

He has kept among us, in times of peace, Standing Armies without the Consent of our legislature.

He has affected to render the Military independent of and superior to the Civil Power.

He has combined with others to subject us to a jurisdiction foreign to our constitution, and unacknowledged by our laws; giving his Assent to their acts of pretended legislation:

For quartering large bodies of armed troops among us:

For protecting them, by a mock Trial, from Punishment for any Murders which they should commit on the Inhabitants of these States:

For cutting off our Trade with all parts of the world:

For imposing taxes on us without our Consent:

For depriving us in many cases, of the benefits of Trial by Jury:

For transporting us beyond Seas to be tried for pretended offences:

For abolishing the free System of English Laws in a neighbouring Province, establishing therein an Arbitrary government, and enlarging its Boundaries so as to render it at once an example and fit instrument for introducing the same absolute rule into these Colonies:

For taking away our Charters, abolishing our most valuable Laws, and altering fundamentally the Forms of our Governments:

For suspending our own Legislature, and declaring themselves invested with Power to legislate for us in all cases whatsoever.

He has abdicated Government here, by declaring us out of his Protection and waging War against us.

He has plundered our seas, ravaged our Coasts, burnt our towns, and destroyed the lives of our people.

He is at this time transporting large armies of foreign mercenaries to compleat the works of death, desolation and tyranny, already begun with circumstances of Cruelty & perfidy scarcely paralleled in the most barbarous ages, and totally unworthy the Head of a civilized nation.

He has constrained our fellow Citizens taken Captive on the high Seas to bear Arms against their Country, to become the executioners of their friends and Brethren, or to fall themselves by their Hands.

He has excited domestic insurrections amongst us, and has endeavoured to bring on the inhabitants of our frontiers, the merciless Indian Savages, whose known rule of warfare, is an undistinguished destruction of all ages, sexes and conditions.

In every stage of these Oppressions We have Petitioned for Redress in the most humble terms: Our repeated Petitions have been answered only by repeated injury. A Prince, whose character is thus marked by every act which may define a Tyrant, is unfit to be the ruler of a free People.

Nor have We been wanting in attention to our British brethren. We have warned them from time to time of attempts by their legislature to extend an unwarrantable jurisdiction over us. We have reminded them of the circumstances of our emigration and settlement here. We have appealed to their native justice and magnanimity, and we have conjured them by the ties of our common kindred to disavow these usurpations, which would inevitably interrupt our connections and correspondence. They too have been deaf to the voice of justice and of consanguinity. We must, therefore, acquiesce in the necessity, which denounces our Separation, and hold them, as we hold the rest of mankind, Enemies in War, in Peace Friends.

We, therefore, the Representatives of the United States of America, in General Congress, Assembled, appealing to the Supreme Judge of the world for the rectitude of our intentions, do, in the Name, and by Authority of the good People of these Colonies, solemnly publish and declare, That these United Colonies are, and of Right ought to be Free and Independent States; that they are Absolved from all Allegiance to the British Crown, and that all political connection between them and the State of Great Britain, is and ought to be totally dissolved; and that as Free and Independent States, they have full Power to levy War, conclude Peace, contract Alliances, establish Commerce, and to do all other Acts and Things which Independent States may of right do. And for the support of this Declaration, with a firm reliance on the Protection of Divine Providence, we mutually pledge to each other our Lives, our Fortunes and our sacred Honor.

John Hancock

New Hampshire:
Josiah Bartlett,
William Whipple,
Matthew Thornton.

Massachusetts-Bay:
Samuel Adams,
John Adams,
Robert Treat Paine,
Elbridge Gerry.

Rhode Island:
Stephen Hopkins,
William Ellery.

Connecticut:
Roger Sherman,
Samuel Huntington,
William Williams,
Oliver Wolcott.

New York:
William Floyd,
Philip Livingston,
Francis Lewis,
Lewis Morris.

Pennsylvania:
Robert Morris,
Benjamin Harris,
Benjamin Franklin,
John Morton,
George Clymer,
James Smith,
George Taylor,
James Wilson,
George Ross.

Delaware:
Caesar Rodney,
George Read,
Thomas McKean.

Georgia:
Button Gwinnett,
Lyman Hall,
George Walton.

Maryland:
Samuel Chase,
William Paca,
Thomas Stone,
Charles Carroll
of Carrollton.

Virginia:
George Wythe,
Richard Henry Lee,
Thomas Jefferson,
Benjamin Harrison,
Thomas Nelson Jr.,
Francis Lightfoot Lee,
Carter Braxton.

North Carolina:
William Hooper,
Joseph Hewes,
John Penn.

South Carolina:
Edward Rutledge,
Thomas Heyward Jr.,
Thomas Lynch Jr.,
Arthur Middleton.

New Jersey:
Richard Stockton,
John Witherspoon,
Francis Hopkinson,
John Hart,
Abraham Clark.

Federalist No. 10

Among the numerous advantages promised by a well-constructed Union, none deserves to be more accurately developed than its tendency to break and control the violence of faction. The friend of popular governments never finds himself so much alarmed for their character and fate, as when he contemplates their propensity to this dangerous vice. He will not fail, therefore, to set a due value on any plan which, without violating the principles to which he is attached, provides a proper cure for it. The instability, injustice, and confusion introduced into the public councils, have, in truth, been the mortal diseases under which popular governments have everywhere perished; as they continue to be the favorite and fruitful topics from which the adversaries to liberty derive their most specious declamations. The valuable improvements made by the American constitutions on the popular models, both ancient and modern, cannot certainly be too much admired; but it would be an unwarrantable partiality, to contend that they have as effectually obviated the danger on this side, as was wished and expected. Complaints are everywhere heard from our most considerate and virtuous citizens, equally the friends of public and private faith, and of public and personal liberty, that our governments are too unstable, that the public good is disregarded in the conflicts of rival parties, and that measures are too often decided, not according to the rules of justice and the rights of the minor party, but by the superior force of an interested and overbearing majority. However anxiously we may wish that these complaints had no foundation, the evidence of known facts will not permit us to deny that they are in some degree true. It will be found, indeed, on a candid review of our situation, that some of the distresses under which we labor have been erroneously charged on the operation of our governments; but it will be found, at the same time, that other causes will not alone account for many of our heaviest misfortunes; and, particularly, for that prevailing and increasing distrust of public engagements, and alarm for private rights, which are echoed from one end of the continent to the other. These must be chiefly, if not wholly, effects of the unsteadiness and injustice with which a factious spirit has tainted our public administrations. By a faction, I understand a number of citizens, whether amounting to a majority or minority of the whole, who are united and actuated by some common impulse of passion, or of interest, adverse to the rights of other citizens, or to the permanent and aggregate interests of the community. There are two methods of curing the mischiefs of faction: the one, by removing its causes; the other, by controlling its effects. There are again two methods of removing the causes of faction: the one, by destroying the liberty which is essential to its existence; the other, by giving to every citizen the same opinions, the same passions, and the same interests. It could never be more truly said than of the first remedy, that it was worse than the disease. Liberty is to faction what air is to fire, an aliment without which it instantly expires. But it could not be less folly to abolish liberty, which is essential to political life, because it nourishes faction, than it would be to wish the annihilation of air, which is essential to animal life, because it imparts to fire its destructive agency.

The second expedient is as impracticable as the first would be unwise. As long as the reason of man continues fallible, and he is at liberty to exercise it, different opinions will be formed. As long as the connection subsists between his reason and his self-love, his opinions and his passions will have a reciprocal influence on each other; and the former will be objects to which the latter will attach themselves. The diversity in the faculties of men, from which the rights of property originate, is not less an insuperable obstacle to a uniformity of interests. The protection of these faculties is the first object of government. From the protection of different and unequal faculties of acquiring property, the possession of different degrees and kinds of property immediately results; and from the influence of these on the sentiments and views of the respective proprietors, ensues a division of the society into different interests and parties.

The latent causes of faction are thus sown in the nature of man; and we see them everywhere brought into different degrees of activity, according to the different circumstances of civil society. A zeal for different opinions concerning religion, concerning government, and many other points, as well of speculation as of practice; an attachment to different leaders ambitiously contending for pre-eminence and power; or to persons of other descriptions whose fortunes have been interesting to the human passions, have, in turn, divided mankind into parties, inflamed them with mutual animosity, and rendered them much more disposed to vex and oppress each other than to co-operate for their common good. So strong is this propensity of mankind to fall into mutual animosities, that where no substantial occasion presents itself, the most frivolous and fanciful distinctions have been sufficient to kindle their unfriendly passions and excite their most violent conflicts. But the most common and durable source of factions has been the various and unequal distribution of property. Those who hold and those who are without property have ever formed distinct interests in society. Those who are creditors, and those who are debtors, fall under a like discrimination. A landed interest, a manufacturing interest, a mercantile interest, a moneyed interest, and many lesser interests, grow up of necessity in civilized nations, and divide them into different classes, actuated by different sentiments and views. The regulation of these various and interfering interests forms the principal task of modern legislation, and involves the spirit of party and faction in the necessary and ordinary operations of the government.

No man is allowed to be a judge in his own cause, because his interest would certainly bias his judgment, and, not improbably, corrupt his integrity. With equal, nay with greater reason, a body of men are unfit to be both judges and parties at the same time; yet what are many of the most important acts of legislation, but so many judicial determinations, not indeed concerning the rights of single persons, but concerning the rights of large bodies of citizens? And what are the different

classes of legislators but advocates and parties to the causes which they determine? Is a law proposed concerning private debts? It is a question to which the creditors are parties on one side and the debtors on the other. Justice ought to hold the balance between them. Yet the parties are, and must be themselves the judges; and the most numerous party, or, in other words, the most powerful faction must be expected to prevail. Shall domestic manufactures be encouraged, and in what degree, by restrictions on foreign manufactures? are questions which would be differently decided by the landed and the manufacturing classes, and probably by neither with a sole regard to justice and the public good. The apportionment of taxes on the various descriptions of property is an act which seems to require the most exact impartiality; yet there is, perhaps, no legislative act in which greater opportunity and temptation are given to a predominant party to trample on the rules of justice. Every shilling with which they overburden the inferior number, is a shilling saved to their own pockets.

It is in vain to say that enlightened statesmen will be able to adjust these clashing interests, and render them all subservient to the public good. Enlightened statesmen will not always be at the helm. Nor, in many cases, can such an adjustment be made at all without taking into view indirect and remote considerations, which will rarely prevail over the immediate interest which one party may find in disregarding the rights of another or the good of the whole.

The inference to which we are brought is, that the *causes* of faction cannot be removed, and that relief is only to be sought in the means of controlling its *effects*.

If a faction consists of less than a majority, relief is supplied by the republican principle, which enables the majority to defeat its sinister views by regular vote. It may clog the administration, it may convulse the society; but it will be unable to execute and mask its violence under the forms of the Constitution. When a majority is included in a faction, the form of popular government, on the other hand, enables it to sacrifice to its ruling passion or interest both the public good and the rights of other citizens. To secure the public good and private rights against the danger of such a faction, and at the same time to preserve the spirit and the form of popular government, is then the great object to which our inquiries are directed. Let me add that it is the great desideratum by which this form of government can be rescued from the opprobrium under which it has so long labored, and be recommended to the esteem and adoption of mankind.

By what means is this object attainable? Evidently by one of two only. Either the existence of the same passion or interest in a majority at the same time must be prevented, or the majority, having such coexistent passion or interest, must be rendered, by their number and local situation, unable to concert and carry into effect schemes of oppression. If the impulse and the opportunity be suffered to coincide, we well know that neither moral nor religious motives can be relied on as an adequate control. They are not found to be such on the injustice and violence of individuals, and lose their efficacy in proportion to the number combined together, that is, in proportion as their efficacy becomes needful.

From this view of the subject it may be concluded that a pure democracy, by which I mean a society consisting of a small number of citizens, who assemble and administer the government in person, can admit of no cure for the mischiefs of faction. A common passion or interest will, in almost every case, be felt by a majority of the whole; a communication and concert result from the form of government itself; and there is nothing to check the inducements to sacrifice the weaker party or an obnoxious individual. Hence it is that such democracies have ever been spectacles of turbulence and contention; have ever been found incompatible with personal security or the rights of property; and have in general been as short in their lives as they have been violent in their deaths. Theoretic politicians, who have patronized this species of government, have erroneously supposed that by reducing mankind to a perfect equality in their political rights, they would, at the same time, be perfectly equalized and assimilated in their possessions, their opinions, and their passions.

A republic, by which I mean a government in which the scheme of representation takes place, opens a different prospect, and promises the cure for which we are seeking. Let us examine the points in which it varies from pure democracy, and we shall comprehend both the nature of the cure and the efficacy which it must derive from the Union.

The two great points of difference between a democracy and a republic are: first, the delegation of the government, in the latter, to a small number of citizens elected by the rest; secondly, the greater number of citizens, and greater sphere of country, over which the latter may be extended.

The effect of the first difference is, on the one hand, to refine and enlarge the public views, by passing them through the medium of a chosen body of citizens, whose wisdom may best discern the true interest of their country, and whose patriotism and love of justice will be least likely to sacrifice it to temporary or partial considerations. Under such a regulation, it may well happen that the public voice, pronounced by the representatives of the people, will be more consonant to the public good than if pronounced by the people themselves, convened for the purpose. On the other hand, the effect may be inverted. Men of fractious tempers, of local prejudices, or of sinister designs, may, by intrigue, by corruption, or by other means, first obtain the suffrages, and then betray the interests, of the people. The question resulting is, whether small or extensive republics are more favorable to the election of proper guardians of the public weal; and it is clearly decided in favor of the latter by two obvious considerations:

In the first place, it is to be remarked that, however small the republic may be, the representatives must be raised to a certain number, in order to guard against the cabals of a few; and that, however large it may be, they must be limited to a certain number, in order to guard against the confusion of a multitude. Hence, the number of representatives in the two cases not being in proportion to that of the two constituents, and being proportionally greater in the small republic, it follows that, if the proportion of fit characters be not less in the large than in the small republic, the former will present a greater option, and consequently a greater probability of a fit choice.

In the next place, as each representative will be chosen by a greater number of citizens in the large than in the small republic, it will be more difficult for unworthy candidates to practise with success the vicious arts by which elections are too often carried; and the suffrages of the people being more free, will be more likely to centre in men who possess the most attractive merit and the most diffusive and established characters.

It must be confessed that in this, as in most other cases, there is a mean, on both sides of which inconveniences will be found to lie. By enlarging too much the number of electors, you render the representatives too little acquainted with all their local circumstances and lesser interests; as by reducing it too much, you render him unduly attached to these, and too little fit to comprehend and pursue great and national objects. This federal Constitution forms a happy combination in this respect; the great and aggregate interests being referred to the national, the local and particular to the State legislatures.

The other point of difference is, the greater number of citizens and extent of territory which may be brought within the compass of republican than of democratic government; and it is this circumstance principally which renders factious combinations less to be dreaded in the former than in the latter. The smaller the society, the fewer probably will be the distinct parties and interests composing it; the fewer the distinct parties and interests, the more frequently will a majority be found of the same party; and the smaller the number of individuals composing a majority, and the smaller the compass within which they are placed, the more easily will they concert and execute their plans of oppression. Extend the sphere, and you take in a greater variety of parties and interests; you make it less probable that a majority of the whole will have a common motive to invade the rights of other citizens; or if such a common motive exists, it will be more difficult for all who feel it to discover their own strength, and to act in unison with each other. Besides other impediments, it may be remarked that, where there is a consciousness of unjust or dishonorable purposes, communication is always checked by distrust in proportion to the number whose concurrence is necessary.

Hence, it clearly appears, that the same advantage which a republic has over a democracy, in controlling the effects of faction, is enjoyed by a large over a small republic,—is enjoyed by the Union over the States composing it. Does the advantage consist in the substitution of representatives whose enlightened views and virtuous sentiments render them superior to local prejudices and to schemes of injustice? It will not be denied that the representation of the Union will be most likely to possess these requisite endowments. Does it consist in the greater security afforded by a greater variety of parties, against the event of any one party being able to outnumber and oppress the rest? In an equal degree does the increased variety of parties comprised within the Union, increase this security. Does it, in fine, consist in the greater obstacles opposed to the concert and accomplishment of the secret wishes of an unjust and interested majority? Here, again, the extent of the Union gives it the most palpable advantage.

The influence of factious leaders may kindle a flame within their particular States, but will be unable to spread a general conflagration through the other States. A religious sect may degenerate into a political faction in a part of the Confederacy; but the variety of sects dispersed over the entire face of it must secure the national councils against any danger from that source. A rage for paper money, for an abolition of debts, for an equal division of property, or for any other improper or wicked project, will be less apt to pervade the whole body of the Union than a particular member of it; in the same proportion as such a malady is more likely to taint a particular country or district, than an entire State.

In the extent and proper structure of the Union, therefore, we behold a republican remedy for the disease most incident to republican government. And according to the degree of pleasure and pride we feel in being republicans, ought to be our zeal in cherishing the spirit and supporting the character of Federalists.

Federalist No. 51

To what expedient, then, shall we finally resort, for maintaining in practice the necessary partition of power among the several departments, as laid down in the Constitution? The only answer that can be given is, that as all these exterior provisions are found to be inadequate, the defect must be supplied, by so contriving the interior structure of the government as that its several constituent parts may, by their mutual relations, be the means of keeping each other in their proper places. Without presuming to undertake a full development of this important idea, I will hazard a few general observations, which may perhaps place it in a clearer light, and enable us to form a more correct judgment of the principles and structure of the government planned by the convention. In order to lay a due foundation for that separate and distinct exercise of the different powers of government, which to a certain extent is admitted on all hands to be essential to the preservation of liberty, it is evident that each department should have a will of its own; and consequently should be so constituted that the members of each should have as little agency as possible in the appointment of the members of the others. Were this principle rigorously adhered to, it would require that all the appointments for the supreme executive, legislative, and judiciary magistracies should be drawn from the same fountain of authority, the people, through channels having no communication whatever with one another. Perhaps such a plan of constructing the several departments would be less difficult in practice than it may in contemplation appear. Some difficulties, however, and some additional expense would attend the execution of it. Some deviations, therefore, from the principle must be admitted. In the constitution of the judiciary department in particular, it might be inexpedient to insist rigorously on the principle: first, because peculiar qualifications being essential in the members, the primary consideration ought to be to select that mode of choice which best secures these qualifications; secondly, because the permanent tenure by which the appointments are held in that department, must soon destroy all sense of dependence on the authority conferring them. It is equally evident, that the members of each department should be as little dependent as possible on those of the others, for the emoluments annexed to their offices. Were the executive magistrate, or the judges, not independent of the legislature in this particular, their independence in every other would be merely nominal. But the great security against a gradual concentration of the several powers in the same department, consists in giving to those who administer each department the necessary constitutional means and personal motives to resist encroachments of the others. The provision for defence must in this, as in all other cases, be made commensurate to the danger of attack. Ambition must be made to counteract ambition. The interest of the man must be connected with the constitutional rights of the place. It may be a reflection on human nature, that such devices should be necessary to control the abuses of government. But what is government itself, but the greatest of all reflections on human nature? If men were angels, no government would be necessary. If angels were to govern men, neither external nor internal controls on government would be necessary. In framing a government which is to be administered by men over men, the great difficulty lies in this: you must first enable the government to control the governed; and in the next place oblige it to control itself. A dependence on the people is, no doubt, the primary control on the government; but experience has taught mankind the necessity of auxiliary precautions.

This policy of supplying, by opposite and rival interests, the defect of better motives, might be traced through the whole system of human affairs, private as well as public. We see it particularly displayed in all the subordinate distributions of power, where the constant aim is to divide and arrange the several offices in such a manner as that each may be a check on the other—that the private interest of every individual may be a sentinel over the public rights. These inventions of prudence cannot be less requisite in the distribution of the supreme powers of the State.

But it is not possible to give to each department an equal power of self-defence. In republican government, the legislative authority necessarily predominates. The remedy for this inconveniency is to divide the legislature into different branches; and to render them, by different modes of election and different principles of action, as little connected with each other as the nature of their common functions and their common dependence on the society will admit. It may even be necessary to guard against dangerous encroachments by still further precautions. As the weight of the legislative authority requires that it should be thus divided, the weakness of the executive may require, on the other hand, that it should be fortified. An absolute negative on the legislature appears, at first view, to be the natural defence with which the executive magistrate should be armed. But perhaps it would be neither altogether safe nor alone sufficient. On ordinary occasions it might not be exerted with the requisite firmness, and on extraordinary occasions it might be perfidiously abused. May not this defect of an absolute negative be supplied by some qualified connection between this weaker department and the weaker branch of the stronger department, by which the latter may be led to support the constitutional rights of the former, without being too much detached from the rights of its own department?

If the principles on which these observations are founded be just, as I persuade myself they are, and they be applied as a criterion to the several State constitutions, and to the federal Constitution, it will be found that if the latter does not perfectly correspond with them, the former are infinitely less able to bear such a test.

There are, moreover, two considerations particularly applicable to the federal system of America, which place that system in a very interesting point of view.

First. In a single republic, all the power surrendered by the people is submitted to the administration of a single government; and the usurpations are guarded against by a division of the government into distinct and separate departments. In the compound republic of America, the power surrendered by the people is first divided between two distinct governments, and then the portion allotted to each subdivided among distinct and separate departments. Hence a double security arises to the rights of the people. The different governments will control each other, at the same time that each will be controlled by itself.

Second. It is of great importance in a republic not only to guard the society against the oppression of its rulers, but to guard one part of the society against the injustice of the other part. Different interests necessarily exist in different classes of citizens. If a majority be united by a common interest, the rights of the minority will be insecure. There are but two methods of providing against this evil: the one by creating a will in the community independent of the majority—that is, of the society itself; the other, by comprehending in the society so many separate descriptions of citizens as will render an unjust combination of a majority of the whole very improbable, if not impracticable. The first method prevails in all governments possessing an hereditary or self-appointed authority. This, at best, is but a precarious security; because a power independent of the society may as well espouse the unjust views of the major, as the rightful interests of the minor party, and may possibly be turned against both parties. The second method will be exemplified in the federal republic of the United States. Whilst all authority in it will be derived from and dependent on the society, the society itself will be broken into so many parts, interests and classes of citizens, that the rights of individuals, or of the minority, will be in little danger from interested combinations of the majority. In a free government the security for civil rights must be the same as that for religious rights. It consists in the one case in the multiplicity of interests, and in the other in the multiplicity of sects. The degree of security in both cases will depend on the number of interests and sects; and this may be presumed to depend on the extent of country and number of people comprehended under the same government. This view of the subject must particularly recommend a proper federal system to all the sincere and considerate friends of republican government, since it shows that in exact proportion as the territory of the Union may be formed into more circumscribed Confederacies, or States, oppressive combinations of a majority will be facilitated; the best security, under the republican forms, for the rights of every class of citizens, will be diminished; and consequently the stability and independence of some member of the government, the only other security, must be proportionally increased. Justice is the end of government. It is the end of civil society. It ever has been and ever will be pursued until it be obtained, or until liberty be lost in the pursuit. In a society under the forms of which the stronger faction can readily unite and oppress the weaker, anarchy may as truly be said to reign as in a state of nature, where the weaker individual is not secured against the violence of the stronger; and as, in the latter state, even the stronger individuals are prompted, by the uncertainty of their condition, to submit to a government which may protect the weak as well as themselves; so, in the former state, will the more powerful factions or parties be gradually induced, by a like motive, to wish for a government which will protect all parties, the weaker as well as the more powerful. It can be little doubted that if the State of Rhode Island was separated from the Confederacy and left to itself, the insecurity of rights under the popular form of government within such narrow limits would be displayed by such reiterated oppressions of factious majorities that some power altogether independent of the people would soon be called for by the voice of the very factions whose misrule had proved the necessity of it. In the extended republic of the United States, and among the great variety of interests, parties, and sects which it embraces, a coalition of a majority of the whole society could seldom take place on any other principles than those of justice and the general good; whilst there being thus less danger to a minor from the will of a major party, there must be less pretext, also, to provide for the security of the former, by introducing into the government a will not dependent on the latter, or, in other words, a will independent of the society itself. It is no less certain than it is important, notwithstanding the contrary opinions which have been entertained, that the larger the society, provided it lie within a practical sphere, the more duly capable it will be of self-government. And happily for the *republican cause,* the practicable sphere may be carried to a very great extent, by a judicious modification and mixture of the *federal principle.*

Constitution of the United States

We the People of the United States, in Order to form a more perfect Union, establish Justice, insure domestic Tranquility, provide for the common defence, promote the general Welfare, and secure the Blessings of Liberty to ourselves and our Posterity, do ordain and establish this Constitution for the United States of America.

Article I

SECTION 1. All legislative Powers herein granted shall be vested in a Congress of the United States, which shall consist of a Senate and House of Representatives.

SECTION 2. The House of Representatives shall be composed of Members chosen every second Year by the People of the several States, and the Electors in each State shall have the Qualifications requisite for Electors of the most numerous Branch of the State Legislature. No Person shall be a Representative who shall not have attained to the age of twenty five Years, and been seven Years a Citizen of the United States, and who shall not, when elected, be an Inhabitant of that State in which he shall be chosen. [Representatives and direct Taxes shall be apportioned among the several States which may be included within this Union, according to their respective Numbers, which shall be determined by adding to the whole Number of free Persons, including those bound to Service for a Term of Years, and excluding Indians not taxed, three fifths of all other Persons.][1] The actual Enumeration shall be made within three Years after the first Meeting of the Congress of the United States, and within every subsequent Term of ten Years, in such Manner as they shall by Law direct. The Number of Representatives shall not exceed one for every thirty Thousand, but each State shall have at Least one Representative; and until such enumeration shall be made, the State of New Hampshire shall be entitled to chuse three, Massachusetts eight, Rhode-Island and Providence Plantations one, Connecticut five, New-York six, New Jersey four, Pennsylvania eight, Delaware one, Maryland six, Virginia ten, North Carolina five, South Carolina five, and Georgia three. When vacancies happen in the Representation from any State, the Executive Authority thereof shall issue Writs of Election to fill such Vacancies. The House of Representatives shall chuse their Speaker and other Officers; and shall have the sole Power of Impeachment.

SECTION 3. The Senate of the United States shall be composed of two Senators from each State, [chosen by the Legislature thereof,][2] for six Years; and each Senator shall have one Vote.

Immediately after they shall be assembled in Consequence of the first Election, they shall be divided as equally as may be into three Classes. The Seats of the Senators of the first Class shall be vacated at the Expiration of the second Year, of the second Class at the Expiration of the fourth Year, and of the third Class at the Expiration of the sixth Year, so that one third may be chosen every second Year; [and if Vacancies happen by Resignation, or otherwise, during the Recess of the Legislature of any State, the Executive thereof may make temporary Appointments until the next Meeting of the Legislature, which shall then fill such Vacancies.][3]

No Person shall be a Senator who shall not have attained to the Age of thirty Years, and been nine Years a Citizen of the United States, and who shall not, when elected, be an Inhabitant of that State for which he shall be chosen.

The Vice President of the United States shall be President of the Senate, but shall have no Vote, unless they be equally divided.

The Senate shall chuse their other Officers, and also a President pro tempore, in the Absence of the Vice President, or when he shall exercise the Office of President of the United States.

The Senate shall have the sole Power to try all Impeachments. When sitting for that Purpose, they shall be on Oath or Affirmation. When the President of the United States is tried the Chief Justice shall preside: And no Person shall be convicted without the Concurrence of two thirds of the Members present.

Judgment in Cases of Impeachment shall not extend further than to removal from Office, and disqualification to hold and enjoy any Office of honor, Trust or Profit under the United States: but the Party convicted shall nevertheless be liable and subject to Indictment, Trial, Judgment and Punishment, according to Law.

SECTION 4. The Times, Places and Manner of holding Elections for Senators and Representatives, shall be prescribed in each State by the Legislature thereof; but the Congress may at any time by Law make or alter such Regulations, except as to the Places of chusing Senators.

The Congress shall assemble at least once in every Year, and such Meeting shall [be on the first Monday in December],[4] unless they shall by Law appoint a different Day.

SECTION 5. Each House shall be the Judge of the Elections, Returns and Qualifications of its own Members, and a Majority of each shall constitute a Quorum to do Business; but a smaller Number may adjourn from day to day, and may be authorized to compel the Attendance of absent Members, in such Manner, and under such Penalties as each House may provide.

Each House may determine the Rules of its Proceedings, punish its Members for disorderly Behaviour, and, with the Concurrence of two thirds, expel a Member.

Each House shall keep a Journal of its Proceedings, and from time to time publish the same, excepting such Parts as may in their Judgment require Secrecy; and the Yeas and Nays of the Members of either House on any question shall, at the Desire of one fifth of those Present, be entered on the Journal.

Neither House, during the Session of Congress, shall, without the Consent of the other, adjourn for more than three days, nor to any other Place than that in which the two Houses shall be sitting.

SECTION 6. The Senators and Representatives shall receive a Compensation for their Services, to be ascertained by Law, and paid out of the Treasury of the United States. They shall in all Cases, except Treason, Felony and Breach of the Peace, be privileged from Arrest during their Attendance at the Session of their respective Houses, and in going to and returning from the same; and for any Speech or Debate in either House, they shall not be questioned in any other Place.

No Senator or Representative shall, during the Time for which he was elected, be appointed to any civil Office under the Authority of the United States, which shall have been created, or the Emoluments whereof shall have been encreased during such time; and no Person holding any Office under the United States, shall be a Member of either House during his Continuance in Office.

SECTION 7. All Bills for raising Revenue shall originate in the House of Representatives; but the Senate may propose or concur with amendments as on other Bills.

Every Bill which shall have passed the House of Representatives and the Senate, shall, before it become a Law, be presented to the President of the United States; If he approve he shall sign it, but if not he shall return it, with his Objections to that House in which it shall have originated, who shall enter the Objections at large on their Journal, and proceed to reconsider it. If after such Reconsideration two thirds of that House shall agree to pass the Bill, it shall be sent, together with the Objections, to the other House, by which it shall likewise be reconsidered, and if approved by two thirds of that House, it shall become a Law. But in all such Cases the Votes of both Houses shall be determined by yeas and Nays, and the Names of the Persons voting for and against the Bill shall be entered on the Journal of each House respectively. If any Bill shall not be returned by the President within ten Days (Sundays excepted) after it shall have been presented to him, the Same shall be a Law, in like Manner as if he had signed it, unless the Congress by their Adjournment prevent its Return, in which Case it shall not be a Law.

Every Order, Resolution, or Vote to which the Concurrence of the Senate and House of Representatives may be necessary (except on a question of Adjournment) shall be presented to the President of the United

States; and before the Same shall take Effect, shall be approved by him, or being disapproved by him, shall be repassed by two thirds of the Senate and House of Representatives, according to the Rules and Limitations prescribed in the Case of a Bill.

SECTION 8. The Congress shall have Power To lay and collect Taxes, Duties, Imposts and Excises, to pay the Debts and provide for the common Defence and general Welfare of the United States; but all Duties, Imposts and Excises shall be uniform throughout the United States;

To borrow Money on the credit of the United States;

To regulate Commerce with foreign Nations, and among the several States, and with the Indian Tribes;

To establish an uniform Rule of Naturalization, and uniform Laws on the subject of Bankruptcies throughout the United States;

To coin Money, regulate the Value thereof, and of foreign Coin, and fix the Standard of Weights and Measures;

To provide for the Punishment of counterfeiting the Securities and current Coin of the United States;

To establish Post Offices and post Roads;

To promote the Progress of Science and useful Arts, by securing for limited Times to Authors and Inventors the exclusive Right to their respective Writings and Discoveries;

To constitute Tribunals inferior to the supreme Court;

To define and punish Piracies and Felonies commited on the high Seas, and Offences against the Law of Nations;

To declare War, grant Letters of Marque and Reprisal, and make Rules concerning Captures on Land and Water;

To raise and support Armies, but no Appropriation of Money to that Use shall be for a longer Term than two Years;

To provide and maintain a Navy;

To make Rules for the Government and Regulation of the land and naval Forces;

To provide for calling forth the Militia to execute the Laws of the Union, suppress Insurrections and repel Invasions;

To provide for organizing, arming, and disciplining, the Militia, and for governing such Part of them as may be employed in the Service of the United States, reserving to the States respectively, the Appointment of the Officers, and the Authority of training the Militia according to the discipline prescribed by Congress;

To exercise exclusive Legislation in all Cases whatsoever, over such District (not exceeding ten Miles square) as may, by Cession of Particular States, and the Acceptance of Congress, become the Seat of the Government of the United States, and to exercise like Authority over all Places purchased by the Consent of the Legislature of the State in which the Same shall be, for the Erection of Forts, Magazines, Arsenals, dock-Yards, and other needful Buildings;—And

To make all Laws which shall be necessary and proper for carrying into Execution the foregoing Powers, and all other Powers vested by this Constitution in the Government of the United States, or in any Department or Officer thereof.

SECTION 9. The Migration or Importation of such Persons as any of the States now existing shall think proper to admit, shall not be prohibited by the Congress prior to the Year one thousand eight hundred and eight, but a Tax or duty may be imposed on such Importation, not exceeding ten dollars for each Person.

The Privilege of the Writ of Habeas Corpus shall not be suspended, unless when in Cases of Rebellion or Invasion the public Safety may require it.

No Bill of Attainder or ex post facto Law shall be passed.

No capitation, or other direct, Tax shall be laid, unless in Proportion to the Census of Enumeration herein before directed to be taken.[5]

No Tax or Duty shall be laid on Articles exported from any State.

No Preference shall be given by any Regulation of Commerce or Revenue to the Ports of one State over those of another; nor shall Vessels bound to, or from, one State, be obliged to enter, clear or pay Duties in another.

No Money shall be drawn from the Treasury, but in Consequence of Appropriations made by Law; and a regular Statement and Account of the Receipts and Expenditures of all public Money shall be published from time to time.

No Title of Nobility shall be granted by the United States: And no Person holding any Office of Profit or Trust under them, shall, without the Consent of the Congress, accept of any present, Emolument, Office, or Title, of any kind whatever, from any King, Prince or foreign State.

SECTION 10. No State shall enter into any Treaty, Alliance, or Confederation; grant Letters of Marque and Reprisal; coin Money; emit Bills of Credit; make any Thing but gold and silver Coin a Tender in Payment of Debts; pass any Bill of Attainder, ex post facto Law, or Law impairing the Obligation of Contracts, or grant any Title of Nobility.

No State shall, without the Consent of the Congress, lay any Imposts or Duties on Imports or Exports, except what may be absolutely necessary for executing its inspection Laws: and the net Produce of all Duties and Imposts, laid by any State on Imports or Exports, shall be for the Use of the Treasury of the United States; and all such Laws shall be subject to the Revision and Controul of the Congress.

No State shall, without the Consent of Congress, lay any Duty of Tonnage, keep Troops, or Ships of War in time of Peace, enter into any Agreement or Compact with another State, or with a foreign Power, or engage in War, unless actually invaded, or in such imminent Danger as will not admit of delay.

Article II

SECTION 1. The executive Power shall be vested in a President of the United States of America. He shall hold his Office during the Term of four Years, and, together with the Vice President, chosen for the same Term, be elected, as follows.

Each State shall appoint, in such Manner as the Legislature thereof may direct, a Number of Electors, equal to the whole Number of Senators and Representatives to which the State may be entitled in the Congress: but no Senator or Representative, or Person holding an Office of Trust or Profit under the United States, shall be appointed an Elector.

[The Electors shall meet in their respective States, and vote by Ballot for two Persons, of whom one at least shall not be an Inhabitant of the same State with themselves. And they shall make a List of all the Persons voted for, and of the Number of Votes for each; which List they shall sign and certify, and transmit sealed to the Seat of the Government of the United States, directed to the President of the Senate. The President of the Senate shall, in the Presence of the Senate and House of Representatives, open all the Certificates, and the Votes shall then be counted. The Person having the greatest Number of Votes shall be the President, if such Number be a Majority of the whole Number of Electors appointed; and if there be more than one who have such Majority, and have an equal Number of Votes, then the House of Representatives shall immediately chuse by Ballot one of them for President; and if no Person have a Majority, then from the five highest on the list the said House shall in like Manner chuse the President. But in chusing the President, the Votes shall be taken by States, the Representation from each State having one Vote; a quorum for this Purpose shall consist of a Member or Members from two thirds of the States, and a Majority of all the States shall be necessary to a Choice. In every Case, after the Choice of the President, the Person having the greatest Number of Votes of the Electors shall be the Vice President. But if there should remain two or more who have equal Votes, the Senate shall chuse from them by Ballot the Vice President.][6]

The Congress may determine the Time of chusing the Electors, and the Day on which they shall give their Votes; which Day shall be the same throughout the United States.

No Person except a natural born Citizen, or a Citizen of the United States, at the time of the Adoption of this Constitution, shall be eligible to the Office of President; neither shall any Person be eligible to that Office who shall not have attained to the Age of thirty five Years, and been fourteen Years a Resident within the United States.

In Case of the Removal of the President from Office, or of his Death, Resignation, or Inability to discharge the Powers and Duties of the said Office,[7] the Same shall devolve on the Vice President, and the Congress may by Law provide for the Case of Removal, Death, Resignation or Inability, both of the President and Vice President, declaring what Officer shall then act as President, and such Officer shall act accordingly, until the Disability be removed, or a President shall be elected.

The President shall, at stated Times, receive for his Services, a Compensation, which shall neither be encreased nor diminished during the Period for which he shall have been elected, and he shall not receive within that Period any other Emolument from the United States, or any of them.

Before he enter on the Execution of his Office, he shall take the following Oath or Affirmation:—"I do solemnly swear (or affirm) that I will faithfully execute the Office of President of the United States, and will to the best of my Ability, preserve, protect and defend the Constitution of the United States."

SECTION 2. The President shall be Commander in Chief of the Army and Navy of the United States, and of the Militia of the several States, when called into the actual Service of the United States; he may require the Opinion, in writing, of the principal Officer in each of the executive Departments, upon any Subject relating to the Duties of their respective Offices, and he shall have Power to grant Reprieves and Pardons for Offenses against the United States, except in Cases of Impeachment.

He shall have Power, by and with the Advice and Consent of the Senate, to make Treaties, provided two thirds of the Senators present concur; and he shall nominate, and by and with the Advice and Consent of the Senate, shall appoint Ambassadors, other public Ministers and Consuls, Judges of the supreme Court, and all other Officers of the United States, whose Appointments are not herein otherwise provided for, and which shall be established by Law: but the Congress may by Law vest the Appointment of such inferior Officers, as they think proper, in the President alone, in the Courts of Law, or in the Heads of Departments.

The President shall have Power to fill up all Vacancies that may happen during the Recess of the Senate, by granting Commissions which shall expire at the End of their next Session.

SECTION 3. He shall from time to time give to the Congress Information of the State of the Union, and recommend to their Consideration such Measures as he shall judge necessary and expedient; he may, on extraordinary Occasions, convene both Houses, or either of them, and in Case of Disagreement between them, with Respect to the Time of Adjournment, he may adjourn them to such Time as he shall think proper; he shall receive Ambassadors and other public Ministers; he shall take Care that the Laws be faithfully executed, and shall Commission all the Officers of the United States.

SECTION 4. The President, Vice President and all Civil Officers of the United States, shall be removed from office on Impeachment for, and Conviction of, Treason, Bribery, or other high Crimes and Misdemeanors.

Article III

SECTION 1. The judicial Power of the United States, shall be vested in one supreme Court, and in such inferior Courts as the Congress may from time to time ordain and establish. The Judges, both of the supreme and inferior Courts, shall hold their Offices during good Behaviour, and shall, at stated Times, receive for their Services, a Compensation, which shall not be diminished during their Continuance in Office.

SECTION 2. The judicial Power shall extend to all Cases, in Law and Equity, arising under this Constitution, the Laws of the United States, and Treaties made, or which shall be made, under their Authority;—to all Cases affecting Ambassadors, other public Ministers and Consuls;—to all Cases of admiralty and maritime Jurisdiction;—to Controversies to which the United States shall be a Party;—to Controversies between two or more States;—between a State and Citizens of another State;[8]—between Citizens of different States;—between Citizens of the same State claiming Lands under Grants of different States, and between a State, or the Citizens thereof, and foreign States, Citizens or Subjects.[8]

In all Cases affecting Ambassadors, other public Ministers and Consuls, and those in which a State shall be Party, the supreme Court shall have original Jurisdiction. In all the other Cases before mentioned, the supreme Court shall have appellate Jurisdiction, both as to Law and Fact, with such Exceptions, and under such Regulations as the Congress shall make.

The Trial of all Crimes, except in cases of Impeachment, shall be by Jury; and such Trial shall be held in the State where the said Crimes shall have been committed; but when not committed within any State, the Trial shall be at such Place or Places as the Congress may by Law have directed.

SECTION 3. Treason against the United States, shall consist only in levying War against them, or in adhering to their Enemies, giving them Aid and Comfort. No Person shall be convicted of Treason unless on the Testimony of two Witnesses to the same overt Act, or on Confession in open Court.

The Congress shall have Power to declare the Punishment of Treason, but no Attainder of Treason shall work Corruption of Blood, or Forfeiture except during the Life of the Person attainted.

Article IV

SECTION 1. Full Faith and Credit shall be given in each State to the public Acts, Records, and judicial Proceedings of every other State. And the Congress may by general Laws prescribe the Manner in which such Acts, Records and Proceedings shall be proved, and the Effect thereof.

SECTION 2. The Citizens of each State shall be entitled to all Privileges and Immunities of Citizens in the several States.

A Person charged in any State with Treason, Felony, or other Crime, who shall flee from Justice, and be found in another State, shall on Demand of the executive Authority of the State from which he fled, be delivered up, to be removed to the State having Jurisdiction of the Crime.

[No Person held to Service or Labour in one State, under the Laws thereof, escaping into another, shall, in Consequence of any Law or Regulation therein, be discharged from such Service or Labour, but shall be delivered up on Claim of the Party to whom such Service or Labour may be due.][9]

SECTION 3. New States may be admitted by the Congress into this Union; but no new State shall be formed or erected within the Jurisdiction of any other State; nor any State be formed by the Junction of two or more States, or Parts of States, without the Consent of the Legislatures of the States concerned as well as of the Congress.

The Congress shall have Power to dispose of and make all needful Rules and Regulations respecting the Territory or other Property belonging to the United States; and nothing in this Constitution shall be so construed as to Prejudice any Claims of the United States, or of any particular State.

SECTION 4. The United States shall guarantee to every State in this Union a Republican Form of Government, and shall protect each of them against Invasion; and on Application of the Legislature, or of the Executive (when the Legislature cannot be convened) against domestic Violence.

Article V

The Congress, whenever two thirds of both Houses shall deem it necessary, shall propose Amendments to this Constitution, or, on the Application of the Legislatures of two thirds of the several States, shall call a Convention for proposing Amendments, which, in either Case, shall be valid to all Intents and Purposes, as Part of this Constitution, when ratified by the Legislatures of three fourths of the several States, or by Conventions in three fourths thereof, as the one or the other Mode of Ratification may be proposed by the Congress; Provided [that no Amendment which may be made prior to the Year One thousand eight hundred and eight shall in any Manner affect the first and fourth Clauses in the Ninth Section of the first Article; and][10] that no State, without its Consent, shall be deprived of its equal Suffrage in the Senate.

Article VI

All Debts contracted and Engagements entered into, before the Adoption of this Constitution, shall be as valid against the United States under this Constitution, as under the Confederation.

This Constitution, and the Laws of the United States which shall be made in Pursuance thereof; and all Treaties made, or which shall be made, under the Authority of the United States, shall be the supreme Law of the Land; and the Judges in every State shall be bound thereby, any Thing in the Constitution or Laws of any State to the Contrary notwithstanding.

The Senators and Representatives before mentioned, and the Members of the several State Legislatures, and all executive and judicial Officers, both of the United States and of the several States, shall be bound by Oath or Affirmation, to support this Constitution; but no religious Test shall ever be required as a Qualification to any Office or public Trust under the United States.

Article VII

The Ratification of the Conventions of nine States, shall be sufficient for the Establishment of this Constitution between the States so ratifying the Same. Done in Convention by the Unanimous Consent of the States present the Seventeenth Day of September in the Year of our Lord one thousand seven hundred and Eighty seven and of the Independence of the United States of America the Twelfth. In witness whereof We have hereunto subscribed our Names, George Washington, President and deputy from Virginia.

New Hampshire:
John Langdon,
Nicholas Gilman.

Massachusetts:
Nathaniel Gorham,
Rufus King.

Connecticut:
William Samuel
Johnson,
Roger Sherman.

New York:
Alexander Hamilton.

New Jersey:
William Livingston,
David Brearley,
William Paterson,
Jonathan Dayton.

Pennsylvania:
Benjamin Franklin,
Thomas Mifflin,
Robert Morris,
George Clymer,
Thomas FitzSimons,
Jared Ingersoll,
James Wilson,
Gouverneur Morris.

Delaware:
George Read,
Gunning Bedford Jr.,
John Dickinson,
Richard Bassett,
Jacob Broom.

Maryland:
James McHenry,
Daniel of St. Thomas
Jenifer,
Daniel Carroll.

Virginia:
John Blair,
James Madison Jr.

North Carolina:
William Blount,
Richard Dobbs
Spaight,
Hugh Williamson.

South Carolina:
John Rutledge,
Charles Cotesworth
Pinckney,
Charles Pinckney,
Pierce Butler.

Georgia:
William Few,
Abraham Baldwin.

[The language of the original Constitution, not including the Amendments, was adopted by a convention of the states on Sept. 17, 1787, and was subsequently ratified by the states on the following dates: Delaware, Dec. 7, 1787; Pennsylvania, Dec. 12, 1787; New Jersey, Dec. 18, 1787; Georgia, Jan. 2, 1788; Connecticut, Jan. 9, 1788; Massachusetts, Feb. 6, 1788; Maryland, April 28, 1788; South Carolina, May 23, 1788; New Hampshire, June 21, 1788.

Ratification was completed on June 21, 1788.

The Constitution subsequently was ratified by Virginia, June 25, 1788; New York, July 26, 1788; North Carolina, Nov. 21, 1789; Rhode Island, May 29, 1790; and Vermont, Jan. 10, 1791.]

Amendments

Amendment 1
(First ten amendments ratified December 15, 1791.)
Congress shall make no law respecting an establish-

ment of religion, or prohibiting the free exercise thereof; or abridging the freedom of speech, or of the press; or the right of the people peaceably to assemble, and to petition the Government for a redress of grievances.

Amendment II

A well regulated Militia, being necessary to the security of a free State, the right of the people to keep and bear Arms, shall not be infringed.

Amendment III

No Soldier shall, in time of peace be quartered in any house, without the consent of the Owner, nor in time of war, but in a manner to be prescribed by law.

Amendment IV

The right of the people to be secure in their persons, houses, papers, and effects, against unreasonable searches and seizures, shall not be violated, and no Warrants shall issue, but upon probable cause, supported by Oath or affirmation, and particularly describing the place to be searched, and the persons or things to be seized.

Amendment V

No person shall be held to answer for a capital, or otherwise infamous crime, unless on a presentment or indictment of a Grand Jury, except in cases arising in the land or naval forces, or in the Militia, when in actual service in time of War or public danger; nor shall any person be subject for the same offence to be twice put in jeopardy of life or limb; nor shall be compelled in any criminal case to be a witness against himself, nor be deprived of life, liberty, or property, without due process of law; nor shall private property be taken for public use, without just compensation.

Amendment VI

In all criminal prosecutions, the accused shall enjoy the right to a speedy and public trial, by an impartial jury of the State and district wherein the crime shall have been committed, which district shall have been previously ascertained by law, and to be informed of the nature and cause of the accusation; to be confronted with the witnesses against him; to have compulsory process for obtaining witnesses in his favor, and to have the Assistance of Counsel for his defence.

Amendment VII

In Suits at common law, where the value in controversy shall exceed twenty dollars, the right of trial by jury shall be preserved, and no fact tried by a jury, shall be otherwise re-examined in any Court of the United States, than according to the rules of the common law.

Amendment VIII

Excessive bail shall not be required, nor excessive fines imposed, nor cruel and unusual punishments inflicted.

Amendment IX

The enumeration in the Constitution, of certain rights, shall not be construed to deny or disparage others retained by the people.

Amendment X

The powers not delegated to the United States by the Constitution, nor prohibited by it to the States, are reserved to the States respectively, or to the people.

Amendment XI (Ratified February 7, 1795)

The Judicial power of the United States shall not be construed to extend to any suit in law or equity, commenced or prosecuted against one of the United States by Citizens of another State, or by Citizens or Subjects of any Foreign State.

Amendment XII (Ratified June 15, 1804)

The Electors shall meet in their respective states and vote by ballot for President and Vice-President, one of whom, at least, shall not be an inhabitant of the same state with themselves; they shall name in their ballots the person voted for as President, and in distinct ballots the person voted for as Vice-President, and they shall make distinct lists of all persons voted for as President, and of all persons voted for as Vice-President, and of the number of votes for each, which lists they shall sign and certify, and transmit sealed to the seat of the government of the United States, directed to the President of the Senate;—The President of the Senate shall, in the presence of the Senate and House of Representatives, open all the certificates and the votes shall then be counted;—The person having the greatest number of votes for President, shall be the President, if such number be a majority of the whole number of Electors appointed; and if no person have such majority, then from the persons having the highest numbers not exceeding three on the list of those voted for as President, the House of Representatives shall choose immediately, by ballot, the President. But in choosing the President, the votes shall be taken by states, the representation from each state having one vote; a quorum for this purpose shall consist of a member or members from two-thirds of the states, and a majority of all the states shall be necessary to a choice. [And if the House of Representatives shall not choose a President whenever the right of choice shall devolve upon them, before the fourth day of March next following, then the Vice-President shall act as President, as in the case of the death or other constitutional disability of the President—][11] The person having the greatest number of votes as Vice-President, shall be the Vice-President, if such number be a majority of the whole number of Electors appointed, and if no person have a majority, then from the two highest numbers on the list, the Senate shall choose the Vice-President; a quorum for the purpose shall consist of two-thirds of the whole number of Senators, and a majority of the whole number shall be necessary to a choice. But no person constitutionally ineligible to the office of President shall be eligible to that of Vice-President of the United States.

Amendment XIII (Ratified December 6, 1865)

SECTION 1. Neither slavery nor involuntary servitude, except as a punishment for crime whereof the party shall have been duly convicted, shall exist within the United States, or any place subject to their jurisdiction.

SECTION 2. Congress shall have power to enforce this article by appropriate legislation.

Amendment XIV (Ratified July 9, 1868)

SECTION 1. All persons born or naturalized in the United States and subject to the jurisdiction thereof, are citizens of the United States and of the State wherein they reside. No State shall make or enforce any law which shall abridge the privileges or immunities of citizens of the United States; nor shall any State deprive any person of life, liberty, or property, without due process of law; nor deny to any person within its jurisdiction the equal protection of the laws.

SECTION 2. Representatives shall be apportioned among the several States according to their respective numbers, counting the whole number of persons in each State, excluding Indians not taxed. But when the right to vote at any election for the choice of electors for President and Vice President of the United States, Representatives in Congress, the Executive and Judicial officers of a State, or the members of the Legislature thereof, is denied to any of the male inhabitants of such State, being twenty-one years of age,[12] and citizens of the United States, or in any way abridged, except for participation in rebellion, or other crime, the basis of representation therein shall be reduced in the proportion which the number of such male citizens shall bear to the whole number of male citizens twenty-one years of age in such State.

SECTION 3. No person shall be a Senator or Representative in Congress, or elector of President and Vice President, or hold any office, civil or military, under the United States, or under any State, who, having previously taken an oath, as a member of Congress, or as an officer of the United States, or as a member of any State legislature, or as an executive or judicial officer of any State, to support the Constitution of the United States, shall have engaged in insurrection or rebellion against the same, or given aid or comfort to the enemies thereof. But Congress may by a vote of two-thirds of each House, remove such disability.

SECTION 4. The validity of the public debt of the United States, authorized by law, including debts incurred for payment of pensions and bounties for services in suppressing insurrection or rebellion, shall not be questioned. But neither the United States nor any State shall assume or pay any debt or obligation incurred in aid of insurrection or rebellion against the United States, or any claim for the loss or emancipation of any slave; but all such debts, obligations and claims shall be held illegal and void.

SECTION 5. The Congress shall have power to enforce, by appropriate legislation, the provisions of this article.

Amendment XV (Ratified February 3, 1870)

SECTION 1. The right of citizens of the United States to vote shall not be denied or abridged by the United States or by any State on account of race, color, or previous condition of servitude.

SECTION 2. The Congress shall have power to enforce this article by appropriate legislation.

Amendment XVI (Ratified February 3, 1913)

The Congress shall have power to lay and collect taxes on incomes, from whatever source derived, without apportionment among the several States, and without regard to any census or enumeration.

Amendment XVII (Ratified April 8, 1913)

The Senate of the United States shall be composed of two Senators from each State, elected by the people thereof, for six years; and each Senator shall have one vote. The electors in each State shall have the qualifications requisite for electors of the most numerous branch of the State legislatures.

When vacancies happen in the representation of any State in the Senate, the executive authority of such State shall issue writs of election to fill such vacancies: *Provided,* That the legislature of any State may empower the executive thereof to make temporary appointments until the people fill the vacancies by election as the legislature may direct.

This amendment shall not be so construed as to affect the election or term of any Senator chosen before it becomes valid as part of the Constitution.

Amendment XVIII (Ratified January 16, 1919)

SECTION 1. After one year from the ratification of this article the manufacture, sale, or transportation of intoxicating liquors within, the importation thereof into, or the exportation thereof from the United States and all territory subject to the jurisdiction thereof for beverage purposes is hereby prohibited.

SECTION 2. The Congress and the several States shall have concurrent power to enforce this article by appropriate legislation.

SECTION 3. This article shall be inoperative unless it shall have been ratified as an amendment to the Constitution by the legislatures of the several States, as provided in the Constitution, within seven years from the date of the submission hereof to the States by the Congress.[13]

Amendment XIX (Ratified August 18, 1920)

The right of citizens of the United States to vote shall not be denied or abridged by the United States or by any State on account of sex.

Congress shall have power to enforce this article by appropriate legislation.

Amendment XX (Ratified January 23, 1933)

SECTION 1. The terms of the President and Vice President shall end at noon on the 20th day of January, and the terms of Senators and Representatives at noon on the 3d day of January, of the years in which such terms would have ended if this article had not been ratified; and the terms of their successors shall then begin.

SECTION 2. The Congress shall assemble at least once in every year, and such meeting shall begin at noon on the 3d day of January, unless they shall by law appoint a different day.

SECTION 3.[14] If, at the time fixed for the beginning of the term of the President, the President elect shall have died, the Vice President elect shall become President. If a President shall not have been chosen before the time fixed for the beginning of his term, or if the President elect shall have failed to qualify, then the Vice President elect shall act as President until a President shall have qualified; and the Congress may by law provide for the case wherein neither a President elect nor a Vice President elect shall have qualified, declaring who shall then act as President, or the manner in which one who is to act shall be selected, and such person shall act accordingly until a President or Vice President shall have qualified.

SECTION 4. The Congress may by law provide for the case of the death of any of the persons from whom the House of Representatives may choose a President whenever the right of choice shall have devolved upon them, and for the case of the death of any of the persons from whom the Senate may choose a Vice President whenever the right of choice shall have devolved upon them.

SECTION 5. Sections 1 and 2 shall take effect on the 15th day of October following the ratification of this article.

SECTION 6. This article shall be inoperative unless it shall have been ratified as an amendment to the Constitution by the legislatures of three-fourths of the several States within seven years from the date of its submission.

Amendment XXI (Ratified December 5, 1933)

SECTION 1. The eighteenth article of amendment to the Constitution of the United States is hereby repealed.

SECTION 2. The transportation or importation into any State, Territory or possession of the United States for delivery or use therein of intoxicating liquors, in violation of the laws thereof, is hereby prohibited.

SECTION 3. This article shall be inoperative unless it shall have been ratified as an amendment to the Constitution by conventions in the several States, as provided in the Constitution, within seven years from the date of the submission hereof to the States by the Congress.

Amendment XXII (Ratified February 27, 1951)

SECTION 1. No person shall be elected to the office of the President more than twice, and no person who has held the office of President, or acted as President, for more than two years of a term to which some other person was elected President shall be elected to the office of the President more than once. But this Article shall not apply to any person holding the office of President when this Article was proposed by the Congress, and shall not prevent any person who may be holding the office of President, or acting as President, during the term within which this Article becomes operative from holding the office of President or acting as President during the remainder of such term.

SECTION 2. This Article shall be inoperative unless it shall have been ratified as an amendment to the Constitution by the legislatures of three-fourths of the several States within seven years from the date of its submission to the States by the Congress.

Amendment XXIII (Ratified March 29, 1961)

SECTION 1. The District constituting the seat of Government of the United States shall appoint in such manner as the Congress may direct:

A number of electors of President and Vice President equal to the whole number of Senators and Representatives in Congress to which the District would be entitled if it were a State, but in no event more than the least populous State; they shall be in addition to those appointed by the States, but they shall be considered, for the purposes of the election of President and Vice President, to be electors appointed by a State; and they shall meet in the District and perform such duties as provided by the twelfth article of amendment.

SECTION 2. The Congress shall have power to enforce this article by appropriate legislation.

Amendment XXIV (Ratified January 23, 1964)

SECTION 1. The right of citizens of the United States to vote in any primary or other election for President or Vice President, for electors for President or Vice President, or for Senator or Representative in Congress, shall not be denied or abridged by the United States or any State by reason of failure to pay any poll tax or other tax.

SECTION 2. The Congress shall have power to enforce this article by appropriate legislation.

Amendment XXV (Ratified February 10, 1967)

SECTION 1. In case of the removal of the President from office or of his death or resignation, the Vice President shall become President.

SECTION 2. Whenever there is a vacancy in the office of the Vice President, the President shall nominate a Vice President who shall take office upon confirmation by a majority vote of both Houses of Congress.

SECTION 3. Whenever the President transmits to the President pro tempore of the Senate and the

Speaker of the House of Representatives his written declaration that he is unable to discharge the powers and duties of his office, and until he transmits to them a written declaration to the contrary, such powers and duties shall be discharged by the Vice President as Acting President.

SECTION 4. Whenever the Vice President and a majority of either the principal officers of the executive departments or of such other body as Congress may by law provide, transmit to the President pro tempore of the Senate and the Speaker of the House of Representatives their written declaration that the President is unable to discharge the powers and duties of his office, the Vice President shall immediately assume the powers and duties of the office as Acting President.

Thereafter, when the President transmits to the President pro tempore of the Senate and the Speaker of the House of Representatives his written declaration that no inability exists, he shall resume the powers and duties of his office unless the Vice President and a majority of either the principal officers of the executive department or of such other body as Congress may by law provide, transmit within four days to the President pro tempore of the Senate and the Speaker of the House of Representatives their written declaration that the President is unable to discharge the powers and duties of his office. Thereupon Congress shall decide the issue, assembling within forty-eight hours for that purpose if not in session. If the Congress, within twenty-one days after receipt of the latter written declaration, or, if Congress is not in session, within twenty-one days after Congress is required to assemble, determines by two-thirds vote of both houses that the President is unable to discharge the powers and duties of his office, the Vice President shall

continue to discharge the same as Acting President; otherwise, the President shall resume the powers and duties of his office.

Amendment XXVI (Ratified July 1, 1971)

SECTION 1. The right of citizens of the United States, who are eighteen years of age or older, to vote shall not be denied or abridged by the United States or by any State on account of age.

SECTION 2. The Congress shall have power to enforce this article by appropriate legislation.

Notes
1. The part in brackets was changed by section 2 of the Fourteenth Amendment.
2. The part in brackets was changed by section 1 of the Seventeenth Amendment.
3. The part in brackets was changed by the second paragraph of the Seventeenth amendment.
4. The part in brackets was changed by section 2 of the Twentieth Amendment.
5. The Sixteenth Amendment gave Congress the power to tax incomes.
6. The material in brackets has been superseded by the Twelfth Amendment.
7. This provision has been affected by the Twenty-fifth Amendment.
8. These clauses were affected by the Eleventh Amendment.
9. This paragraph has been superseded by the Thirteenth Amendment.
10. Obsolete.
11. The part in brackets has been superseded by section 3 of the Twentieth Amendment.
12. See the Twenty-sixth Amendment.
13. This Amendment was repealed by section 1 of the Twenty-first Amendment.
14. See the Twenty-fifth Amendment.

Source: U.S. Congress, House, Committee on the Judiciary, *The Constitution of the United States of America, As Amended Through July 1971,* H. Doc. 93-215, 93rd Cong., 2d sess., 1974.

Tables

TABLE A-I Summary of Presidential Elections, 1952–1988

Year	No. of states	Candidates Dem.	Candidates Rep.	Electoral vote Dem.	Electoral vote Rep.	Popular vote Dem.	Popular vote Rep.
1952	48	Adlai E. Stevenson II John J. Sparkman	Dwight D. Eisenhower Richard M. Nixon	89	442	27,314,649 44.4%	33,936,137 55.1%
1956[a]	48	Adlai E. Stevenson II Estes Kefauver	Dwight D. Eisenhower Richard M. Nixon	73	457	26,030,172 42.0%	35,585,245 57.4%
1960[b]	50	John F. Kennedy Lyndon B. Johnson	Richard M. Nixon Henry Cabot Lodge	303	219	34,221,344 49.7%	34,106,671 49.5%
1964	50*	Lyndon B. Johnson Hubert H. Humphrey	Barry Goldwater William E. Miller	486	52	43,126,584 61.1%	27,177,838 38.5%
1968[c]	50*	Hubert H. Humphrey Edmund S. Muskie	Richard M. Nixon Spiro T. Agnew	191	301	31,274,503 42.7%	31,785,148 43.4%
1972[d]	50*	George McGovern Sargent Shriver	Richard M. Nixon Spiro T. Agnew	17	520	29,171,791 37.5%	47,170,179 60.7%
1976[e]	50*	Jimmy Carter Walter F. Mondale	Gerald R. Ford Robert Dole	297	240	40,830,763 50.1%	39,147,793 48.0%
1980	50*	Jimmy Carter Walter F. Mondale	Ronald Reagan George Bush	49	489	35,483,883 41.0%	43,904,153 50.7%
1984	50*	Walter F. Mondale Geraldine Ferraro	Ronald Reagan George Bush	13	525	37,577,185 40.6%	54,455,075 58.8%
1988[f]	50*	Michael S. Dukakis Lloyd Bentsen	George Bush Dan Quayle	111	426	41,809,083 45.6%	48,886,097 53.4%

Sources: Harold W. Stanley and Richard G. Niemi, *Vital Statistics on American Politics*, 2d ed. (Washington, D.C.: CQ Press, 1990), 102–106; *Guide to U.S. Elections*, 2d ed. (Washington, D.C.: Congressional Quarterly, 1985), 329–366; Federal Election Commission.

Note: Dem.—Democratic; Rep.—Republican.

a. 1956: Walter B. Jones, Democrat, received 1 electoral vote.
b. 1960: Harry Flood Byrd, Democrat, received 15 electoral votes.
c. 1968: George C. Wallace, American Independent party, received 46 electoral votes.
d. 1972: John Hospers, Libertarian party, received 1 electoral vote.
e. 1976: Ronald Reagan, Republican, received 1 electoral vote.
f. 1988: Lloyd Bentsen, the Democratic vice-presidential nominee, received 1 electoral vote for president.
* Fifty states plus District of Columbia.

TABLE A-2 Political Party Affiliations in Congress and the Presidency, 1951–1991

Year	Congress	House			Senate			President
		Majority party	Principal minority party	Other (except vacancies)	Majority party	Principal minority party	Other (except vacancies)	
1991–1993	102nd	D-267	R-167	1	D-56	R-44	—	R (Bush)
1989–1991	101st	D-259	R-174	—	D-55	R-45	—	R (Bush)
1987–1989	100th	D-258	R-177	—	D-55	R-45	—	R (Reagan)
1985–1987	99th	D-252	R-182	—	R-53	D-47	—	R (Reagan)
1983–1985	98th	D-268	R-166	—	R-55	D-45	—	R (Reagan)
1981–1983	97th	D-243	R-192	—	R-53	D-46	1	R (Reagan)
1979–1981	96th	D-276	R-157	—	D-58	R-41	1	D (Carter)
1977–1979	95th	D-292	R-143	—	D-61	R-38	1	D (Carter)
1975–1977	94th	D-291	R-144	—	D-60	R-37	2	R (Ford)
1973–1975	93rd	D-239	R-192	1	D-56	R-42	2	R (Nixon-Ford)
1971–1973	92nd	D-254	R-180	—	D-54	R-44	2	R (Nixon)
1969–1971	91st	D-243	R-192	—	D-57	R-43	—	R (Nixon)
1967–1969	90th	D-247	R-187	—	D-64	R-36	—	D (L. Johnson)
1965–1967	89th	D-295	R-140	—	D-68	R-32	—	D (L. Johnson)
1963–1965	88th	D-258	R-177	—	D-67	R-33	—	D (L. Johnson) D (Kennedy)
1961–1963	87th	D-263	R-174	—	D-65	R-35	—	D (Kennedy)
1959–1961	86th	D-283	R-153	—	D-64	R-34	—	R (Eisenhower)
1957–1959	85th	D-233	R-200	—	D-49	R-47	—	R (Eisenhower)
1955–1957	84th	D-232	R-203	—	D-48	R-47	1	R (Eisenhower)
1953–1955	83rd	R-221	D-211	1	R-48	D-47	1	R (Eisenhower)
1951–1953	82nd	D-234	R-199	1	D-49	R-47	—	D (Truman)

Sources: U.S. Bureau of the Census, *Historical Statistics of the United States, Colonial Times to 1970* (Washington, D.C.: Government Printing Office), 1975; *Congressional Quarterly Weekly Report.*

Note: Figures are for the first session of each Congress. D—Democratic; R—Republican.

TABLE A-3 U.S. Presidents and Vice Presidents

President and political party	Born	Died	President's term of service	Vice president	Vice president's term of service
George Washington (F)	1732	1799	April 30, 1789–March 4, 1793	John Adams	April 30, 1789–March 4, 1793
George Washington (F)			March 4, 1793–March 4, 1797	John Adams	March 4, 1793–March 4, 1797
John Adams (F)	1735	1826	March 4, 1797–March 4, 1801	Thomas Jefferson	March 4, 1797–March 4, 1801
Thomas Jefferson (DR)	1743	1826	March 4, 1801–March 4, 1805	Aaron Burr	March 4, 1801–March 4, 1805
Thomas Jefferson (DR)			March 4, 1805–March 4, 1809	George Clinton	March 4, 1805–March 4, 1809
James Madison (DR)	1751	1836	March 4, 1809–March 4, 1813	George Clinton[a]	March 4, 1809–April 12, 1812
James Madison (DR)			March 4, 1813–March 4, 1817	Elbridge Gerry[a]	March 4, 1813–Nov. 23, 1814
James Monroe (DR)	1758	1831	March 4, 1817–March 4, 1821	Daniel D. Tompkins	March 4, 1817–March 4, 1821
James Monroe (DR)			March 4, 1821–March 4, 1825	Daniel D. Tompkins	March 4, 1821–March 4, 1825
John Q. Adams (DR)	1767	1848	March 4, 1825–March 4, 1829	John C. Calhoun	March 4, 1825–March 4, 1829
Andrew Jackson (DR)	1767	1845	March 4, 1829–March 4, 1833	John C. Calhoun[b]	March 4, 1829–Dec. 28, 1832
Andrew Jackson (D)			March 4, 1833–March 4, 1837	Martin Van Buren	March 4, 1833–March 4, 1837
Martin Van Buren (D)	1782	1862	March 4, 1837–March 4, 1841	Richard M. Johnson	March 4, 1837–March 4, 1841
W. H. Harrison[a] (W)	1773	1841	March 4, 1841–April 4, 1841	John Tyler[c]	March 4, 1841–April 6, 1841
John Tyler (W)	1790	1862	April 6, 1841–March 4, 1845		
James K. Polk (D)	1795	1849	March 4, 1845–March 4, 1849	George M. Dallas	March 4, 1845–March 4, 1849
Zachary Taylor[a] (W)	1784	1850	March 4, 1849–July 9, 1850	Millard Fillmore[c]	March 4, 1849–July 10, 1850
Millard Fillmore (W)	1800	1874	July 10, 1850–March 4, 1853		
Franklin Pierce (D)	1804	1869	March 4, 1853–March 4, 1857	William R. King[a]	March 24, 1853–April 18, 1853
James Buchanan (D)	1791	1868	March 4, 1857–March 4, 1861	John C. Breckinridge	March 4, 1857–March 4, 1861
Abraham Lincoln (R)	1809	1865	March 4, 1861–March 4, 1865	Hannibal Hamlin	March 4, 1861–March 4, 1865
Abraham Lincoln[a] (R)			March 4, 1865–April 15, 1865	Andrew Johnson[c]	March 4, 1865–April 15, 1865
Andrew Johnson (R)	1808	1875	April 15, 1865–March 4, 1869		
Ulysses S. Grant (R)	1822	1885	March 4, 1869–March 4, 1873	Schuyler Colfax	March 4, 1869–March 4, 1873
Ulysses S. Grant (R)			March 4, 1873–March 4, 1877	Henry Wilson[a]	March 4, 1873–Nov. 22, 1875
Rutherford B. Hayes (R)	1822	1893	March 4, 1877–March 4, 1881	William A. Wheeler	March 4, 1877–March 4, 1881
James A. Garfield[a] (R)	1831	1881	March 4, 1881–Sept. 19, 1881	Chester A. Arthur[c]	March 4, 1881–Sept. 20, 1881
Chester A. Arthur (R)	1830	1886	Sept. 20, 1881–March 4, 1885		
Grover Cleveland (D)	1837	1908	March 4, 1885–March 4, 1889	Thomas A. Hendricks[a]	March 4, 1885–Nov. 25, 1885
Benjamin Harrison (R)	1833	1901	March 4, 1889–March 4, 1893	Levi P. Morton	March 4, 1889–March 4, 1893
Grover Cleveland (D)	1837	1908	March 4, 1893–March 4, 1897	Adlai E. Stevenson	March 4, 1893–March 4, 1897
William McKinley (R)	1843	1901	March 4, 1897–March 4, 1901	Garret A. Hobart[a]	March 4, 1897–Nov. 21, 1899
William McKinley[a] (R)			March 4, 1901–Sept. 14, 1901	Theodore Roosevelt[c]	March 4, 1901–Sept. 14, 1901
Theodore Roosevelt (R)	1858	1919	Sept. 14, 1901–March 4, 1905		
Theodore Roosevelt (R)			March 4, 1905–March 4, 1909	Charles W. Fairbanks	March 4, 1905–March 4, 1909
William H. Taft (R)	1857	1930	March 4, 1909–March 4, 1913	James S. Sherman[a]	March 4, 1909–Oct. 30, 1912
Woodrow Wilson (D)	1856	1924	March 4, 1913–March 4, 1917	Thomas R. Marshall	March 4, 1913–March 4, 1917
Woodrow Wilson (D)			March 4, 1917–March 4, 1921	Thomas R. Marshall	March 4, 1917–March 4, 1921
Warren G. Harding[a] (R)	1865	1923	March 4, 1921–Aug. 2, 1923	Calvin Coolidge[c]	March 4, 1921–Aug. 3, 1923
Calvin Coolidge (R)	1872	1933	Aug. 3, 1923–March 4, 1925		
Calvin Coolidge (R)			March 4, 1925–March 4, 1929	Charles G. Dawes	March 4, 1925–March 4, 1929
Herbert Hoover (R)	1874	1964	March 4, 1929–March 4, 1933	Charles Curtis	March 4, 1929–March 4, 1933
Franklin D. Roosevelt (D)	1882	1945	March 4, 1933–Jan. 20, 1937	John N. Garner	March 4, 1933–Jan. 20, 1937
Franklin D. Roosevelt (D)			Jan. 20, 1937–Jan. 20, 1941	John N. Garner	Jan. 20, 1937–Jan. 20, 1941
Franklin D. Roosevelt (D)			Jan. 20, 1941–Jan. 20, 1945	Henry A. Wallace	Jan. 20, 1941–Jan. 20, 1945
Franklin D. Roosevelt[a] (D)			Jan. 20, 1945–April 12, 1945	Harry S Truman[c]	Jan. 20, 1945–April 12, 1945
Harry S Truman (D)	1884	1972	April 12, 1945–Jan. 20, 1949		
Harry S Truman (D)			Jan. 20, 1949–Jan. 20, 1953	Alben W. Barkley	Jan. 20, 1949–Jan. 20, 1953

TABLE A-3 *continued*

President and political party	Born	Died	President's term of service	Vice president	Vice president's term of service
Dwight D. Eisenhower (R)	1890	1969	Jan. 20, 1953–Jan. 20, 1957	Richard Nixon	Jan. 20, 1953—Jan. 20, 1957
Dwight D. Eisenhower (R)			Jan. 20, 1957–Jan. 20, 1961	Richard Nixon	Jan. 20, 1957–Jan. 20, 1961
John F. Kennedy[a] (D)	1917	1963	Jan. 20, 1961–Nov. 22, 1963	Lyndon B. Johnson[c]	Jan. 20, 1961–Nov. 22, 1963
Lyndon B. Johnson (D)	1908	1973	Nov. 22, 1963–Jan. 20, 1965		
Lyndon B. Johnson (D)			Jan. 20, 1965–Jan. 20, 1969	Hubert H. Humphrey	Jan. 20, 1965–Jan. 20, 1969
Richard Nixon (R)	1913		Jan. 20, 1969–Jan. 20, 1973	Spiro T. Agnew	Jan. 20, 1969–Jan. 20, 1973
Richard Nixon[b] (R)			Jan. 20, 1973–Aug. 9, 1974	Spiro T. Agnew[b]	Jan. 20, 1973–Oct. 10, 1973
				Gerald R. Ford[c]	Dec. 6, 1973–Aug. 9, 1974
Gerald R. Ford (R)	1913		Aug. 9, 1974–Jan. 20, 1977	Nelson A. Rockefeller	Dec. 19, 1974–Jan. 20, 1977
Jimmy Carter (D)	1924		Jan. 20, 1977–Jan. 20, 1981	Walter F. Mondale	Jan. 20, 1977–Jan. 20, 1981
Ronald Reagan (R)	1911		Jan. 20, 1981–Jan. 20, 1985	George Bush	Jan. 20, 1981–Jan. 20, 1985
Ronald Reagan (R)			Jan. 20, 1985–Jan. 20, 1989	George Bush	Jan. 20, 1985–Jan. 20, 1989
George Bush (R)	1924		Jan. 20, 1989–	Dan Quayle	Jan. 20, 1989–

Sources: Presidential Elections Since 1789, 4th ed. (Washington, D.C.: Congressional Quarterly, 1987), 4.; Daniel C. Diller, "Biographies of the Vice Presidents," in *Guide to the Presidency*, ed. Michael Nelson (Washington, D.C.: Congressional Quarterly, 1989), 1319–1346.

Note: D—Democrat; DR—Democratic-Republican; F—Federalist; R—Republican; W—Whig.
a. Died in office.
b. Resigned.
c. Succeeded to the presidency.

TABLE A-4 Chief Justices of the United States

Chief Justice	Nominated by President	Date sworn in as Chief Justice	End of term as Chief Justice
John Jay	George Washington	October 19, 1789	June 29, 1795
John Rutledge	George Washington	August 12, 1795	December 15, 1795
Oliver Ellsworth	George Washington	March 8, 1796	December 15, 1800
John Marshall	John Adams	February 4, 1801	July 6, 1835
Roger Brooke Taney	Andrew Jackson	March 28, 1836	October 12, 1864
Salmon Portland Chase	Abraham Lincoln	December 15, 1864	May 7, 1873
Morrison Remick Waite	Ulysses S. Grant	March 4, 1874	March 23, 1888
Melville Weston Fuller	Grover Cleveland	October 8, 1888	July 4, 1910
Edward Douglass White	William Howard Taft	December 19, 1910	May 19, 1921
William Howard Taft	Warren G. Harding	July 11, 1921	February 3, 1930
Charles Evans Hughes	Herbert Hoover	February 24, 1930	July 1, 1941
Harlan Fiske Stone	Franklin D. Roosevelt	July 3, 1941	April 22, 1946
Frederick Moore Vinson	Harry S. Truman	June 24, 1946	September 8, 1953
Earl Warren	Dwight D. Eisenhower	October 5, 1953	June 23, 1969
Warren Earl Burger	Richard Nixon	June 23, 1969	September 26, 1986
William Hubbs Rehnquist	Ronald Reagan	September 26, 1986	

❧ Glossary

access The ability of individuals and groups to gain a hearing for their positions on policy issues before office-holders. *(Ch. 8)*

affirmative action The term applied to programs of hiring and education designed to remedy past acts of discrimination on the basis of race or gender. Such programs may call for either voluntary or mandatory actions to provide equality of opportunity or equality of outcomes. *(Ch. 4)*

amicus curiae brief A "friend of the court" brief submitted by government officials or private groups who are not parties to a lawsuit. *(Ch. 13)*

Antifederalists Opponents of a strong national government and adoption of the U.S. Constitution. *(Ch. 2)*

appellate courts Courts that hear cases on appeal from lower courts. *(Ch. 13)*

Articles of Confederation The first constitution of the United States which took effect in 1781. It created a weak national government and was replaced in 1789 by the Constitution of the United States. *(Ch. 2)*

automatic (super) delegate A delegate to the Democratic national convention who gains delegate status by virtue of holding a party or public office—for example, members of Congress, governors, state party chairs and vice chairs, and members of the Democratic National Committee. *(Ch. 6)*

"bad tendency" test A test no longer used by the Supreme Court to determine the constitutionality of restrictions on speech. It permitted restrictions if the speech was deemed to have a tendency to lead to illegal acts. *(Ch. 4)*

bill of attainder A legislative act declaring an individual guilty of a crime and imposing punishment without a judicial trial. Bills of attainder are banned by Article I of the Constitution. *(Ch. 2)*

Bill of Rights The first ten amendments to the Constitution. Ratified in 1791, these amendments limit gov-

ernmental power and protect the basic rights and liberties of individuals. *(Ch. 2)*

blanket primary A primary election procedure used in Washington State that permits a voter to vote in the primaries of more than one party but for only one candidate per office. *(Ch. 6)*

block grant Grant-in-aid awarded by the federal government to a state for a general area of governmental activity such as crime control, job training, or community development (also see *categorical grant*). *(Ch. 3)*

bureaucracy The organizations that implement government policies. *(Ch. 12)*

bureaucrat An individual who works within the bureaucracy. *(Ch. 12)*

candidate image A voter's perception of the personal attributes of a candidate. *(Ch. 7)*

casework Assistance given by members of Congress to constituents experiencing problems dealing with the federal bureaucracy. *(Ch. 10)*

categorical grant A federal grant-in-aid awarded to a state and certain localities for a specific purpose, normally requiring matching funds and adherence to federal guidelines in spending the funds (also see *block grant*). *(Ch. 3)*

caucus A meeting of political party members to select delegates to national nominating conventions. A meeting of the Democratic membership of the House of Representatives is also called a caucus. *(Ch. 6, 10)*

checks and balances Constitutional mechanisms that authorize each branch of government to share powers with the other branches and thereby check their activities. For example, the president may veto legislation passed by Congress, the Senate must confirm major executive appointments, and the courts may declare acts of Congress unconstitutional. *(Ch. 2)*

civil (law) cases Court cases that involve disputes among individuals, groups, or governments. *(Ch. 13)* "clear and present danger" test A judicial test devised by the Supreme Court to determine whether the government may restrict speech. To be restricted under this test, speech must constitute a "clear and present danger" of bringing about substantive evils which the government has a right to prevent. *(Ch. 4)*

closed primary A type of primary election that restricts voter participation to those who are registered political party members or who publicly declare in which party's primary they wish to vote. *(Ch. 6)*

cloture The process by which a filibuster can be ended in the Senate, other than by unanimous consent. The invocation of cloture in the Senate requires the consent of three-fifths of the Senate membership. *(Ch. 10)*

Commerce and Slave Trade Compromise An agreement reached at the Constitutional Convention of 1787 which granted the national government the power to regulate foreign and interstate commerce, prohibited taxes on U.S. exports, specified that all treaties were to be ratified by a two-thirds vote of the Senate, and prohibited Congress from banning the importation of slaves before 1808. *(Ch. 2)*

concurrent powers Powers that may be exercised by both the federal government and the state governments—for example, levying taxes, borrowing money, and spending for the general welfare. *(Ch. 3)*

concurring opinion An opinion of a Supreme Court justice who agrees with the decision of a majority of the justices but disagrees with their reasons for the decision. *(Ch. 13)*

confederation A league of independent states in which the central government may not make laws applicable to individuals without the approval of the member states. *(Ch. 2)*

conference committee A congressional committee composed of representatives of the House and Senate that reconciles differences between the two houses on provisions of a bill passed by both chambers. *(Ch. 10)*

conservatism A political philosophy favoring limited government involvement in the economy, a strong military, and government action to protect traditional moral values. *(Ch. 5)*

constitutional courts Courts created by Congress by virtue of the powers granted to it in Article III of the Constitution. *(Ch. 13)*

constitutional government A government based on the principle of limited governmental power as specified in a constitution drawn up by the people. *(Ch. 2)*

cooperative federalism A sharing of responsibilities among the federal government and the states and localities. The relationship is encouraged and typified by federal grants-in-aid to states and localities. *(Ch. 3)*

criminal (law) cases Court cases that involve violations of the law punishable by fines or imprisonment. *(Ch. 13)*

crossover voting Voting in the primary election of the party with which one does not identify or belong. This occurs in states that use the open primary procedure (see *open primary*). *(Ch. 6)*

Declaration of Independence The document adopted by the Second Continental Congress on July 4, 1776, declaring the independence of the American colonies from Great Britain and justifying the Revolution. It draws heavily on the natural rights philosophy of John Locke (see *natural rights*). *(Ch. 2)*

de facto segregation Racial segregation that "in fact" exists but is not required by law. *(Ch. 4)*

defendant The person being sued or accused in a court of law. *(Ch. 13)*

de jure segregation Racial segregation that is required by law. *(Ch. 4)*

delegated powers Powers granted to the national government under the Constitution, as enumerated in Articles I, II, and III. *(Ch. 3)*

democracy A system of government in which citizens have a relatively high degree of control over their leaders. *(Ch. 1)*

direct democracy A system of government in which citizens participate directly in making decisions. *(Ch. 1)*

direct primary A popular election in which voters select the nominees that will run for public office in the general election. *(Ch. 1)*

dissenting opinion An opinion of a Supreme Court justice stating the reasons for disagreeing with the decision of a majority of the justices in a case. *(Ch. 13)*

due process clause A Fourteenth Amendment provision protecting people's basic liberties and rights from infringement (denials of life, liberty, or property without due process of law) by the states. *(Ch. 4)*

electoral college The assembly that formally elects the president and vice president of the United States in which each state's number of electoral votes equals its representation in Congress and the District of Columbia has three electoral votes. An absolute majority of the total electoral votes is required to elect a president and vice president. *(Ch. 2)*

entitlements Benefits provided by government programs to individuals or organizations based on eligibility criteria defined by law (for example, Social Security and civil service retirement benefits). *(Ch. 1)*

equal protection clause A Fourteenth Amendment provision prohibiting the states from denying people the equal protection of the laws—that is, discriminating against individuals in an arbitrary manner such as on the basis of race. *(Ch. 1)*

equal time rule A federal rule requiring a radio or television station that gives or sells time to one candidate for a specific office to make the same opportunity available to other candidates for the same office. *(Ch. 9)*

establishment of religion clause The First Amendment clause stating that "Congress shall make no law respecting an establishment of religion." *(Ch. 4)*

exclusionary rule The judicial doctrine based on the Fourth Amendment's protection against illegal searches and seizures, which provides that evidence obtained illegally may not be used in a trial. *(Ch. 4)*

executive agreement An agreement between the president, on behalf of the United States, and another country that does not require the advice and consent of the Senate. *(Ch. 11)*

ex post facto law A retroactive criminal law making actions that were not criminal at the time they were committed criminal offenses after the fact. Ex post facto laws are banned by Article I of the Constitution. *(Ch. 2)*

expressive (purposive) incentives Incentives to participate in or join an organization in the form of such intangible rewards as working for a just cause. *(Ch. 8)*

extradition The responsibility of the states to apprehend fugitives who flee across state lines and return them to the state having jurisdiction over the crime. *(Ch. 3)*

fairness doctrine A Federal Communications Commission policy, abandoned in 1987, requiring radio and television stations to give reasonable time for opposing views on controversial issues discussed on the air. *(Ch. 9)*

federalism (federal system) A constitutional division of the powers of government between the national government and the regional (state) governments in which both exercise significant powers. *(Ch. 2, 3)*

Federalists Advocates of a strong national government and supporters of adoption of the U.S. Constitution. *(Ch. 2)*

federal matching funds Federal money given to candidates seeking presidential nominations. To qualify for these funds, candidates must meet the requirements of the Federal Election Campaign Act. *(Ch. 6)*

federal supremacy clause Article VI of the Constitution providing that the Constitution and all federal laws and treaties shall be the "supreme Law of the Land." Therefore, all federal laws take precedence over state and local laws. *(Ch. 2)*

filibuster A congressional delaying tactic used by a minority to prevent a vote on a bill that probably would pass if voted on directly. The most common method of delay is to take advantage of the Senate's rule permitting unlimited debate. *(Ch. 10)*

fiscal year The twelve-month period, October 1– September 30, during which the financial operations of the government are carried out. The fiscal year carries the date of the calendar year in which it ends. *(Ch. 10)*

franchise The right to vote (also see *suffrage*). *(Ch. 6)*

free exercise of religion clause The First Amendment clause prohibiting Congress from interfering with the free exercise of religion. *(Ch. 4)*

free-rider problem A problem arising when the benefits of interest group activity (for example, cleaner air, Social Security benefits) are available to both group members and nonmembers—that is, nonmembers can receive the benefits of group efforts without paying the costs of membership. *(Ch. 8)*

full faith and credit clause A constitutional provision requiring the states to honor the civil acts, judgments, and public documents of every other state. *(Ch. 3)*

gerrymandering The drawing of legislative district lines in a manner that gives advantage to one political party over another. *(Ch. 4)*

government The institution and processes through which values are allocated and a society is ruled. *(Ch. 1)*

grants-in-aid Grants of funds from the federal government to states and local units of government to carry out federal policies. States also make grants-in-aid to localities. *(Ch. 3)*

Great Compromise (also known as the Connecticut Compromise) A proposal submitted by the Connecticut representatives to the Constitutional Convention of 1787 that broke the deadlock between the large and small states over representation in Congress. It provided for a popularly elected House of Representatives with representation based on a state's population and a Senate composed of two senators from each state elected by their respective state legislatures. *(Ch. 2)*

home style The manner in which a member of Congress presents himself or herself to constituents. *(Ch. 10)*

impeachment The power of Congress to remove the president, vice president, federal judges, and other federal officers from office. *(Ch. 11)*

implied powers Powers that Congress may exercise in carrying out its delegated or enumerated powers listed in Article I of the Constitution (derived from the necessary and proper—elastic—clause). The doctrine of implied powers was established in the 1819 case of *McCulloch v. Maryland. (Ch. 3)*

incumbency   Holding public office. Incumbency normally carries with it an electoral advantage. *(Ch. 6)*

independent   An individual who does not identify with a political party. *(Ch. 7)*

inherent powers   Powers that the federal government may exercise in foreign affairs, which do not derive from a specific grant of authority in the Constitution. These are the powers that the United States has by virtue of its status as a national government. *(Ch. 3)*

interest group   An organized body of individuals who share some goals and try to influence public policy to meet those goals. *(Ch. 8)*

iron triangle   (also known as a subgovernment)   A close-knit alliance of interest groups, congressional committee members, and executive agency personnel capable of exerting a powerful influence over an aspect of public policy. *(Ch. 8)*

issue network   A loose, flexible collection of groups, individuals, and public officials concerned about an aspect of public policy. *(Ch. 8)*

issue publics   Those members of the public affected by and aware of a particular issue. *(Ch. 5)*

joint committee   A congressional committee composed of a specified number of members from both the House and Senate that normally has investigative, research, or housekeeping functions. *(Ch. 10)*

judicial activism   A term used to describe judicial actions that expand the policy-making role of the courts by striking down or modifying the policies of the executive and legislative branches. *(Ch. 13)*

judicial restraint   The belief and practice that judges should restrict the policy-making role of the courts and show reluctance to set aside the judgments of the executive and legislative branches. *(Ch. 13)*

judicial review   A doctrine that permits the federal courts to declare unconstitutional, and thus null and void, acts of the Congress, the executive, and the states. The precedent for judicial review was established in the 1803 case of *Marbury v. Madison. (Ch. 2)*

jurisdiction   The authority of a court to try a case. *(Ch. 13)*

legislative courts   Courts created by Congress under the legislative authority granted to it by Article I of the Constitution. *(Ch. 13)*

libel   The creation and dissemination of written material that falsely and maliciously damages another person's reputation. *(Ch. 4)*

liberalism   Since the 1930s, a political philosophy favoring active government involvement in regulating the economy, providing social services, and assisting minorities and the disadvantaged. *(Ch. 5)*

limited government   The constitutional principle that governmental power is limited through restrictions imposed by the Constitution. *(Ch. 2)*

lobbying   Activities designed to influence the policy decisions of public officials. *(Ch. 8)*

lobbyist   An individual who seeks to influence legislative or administrative decision making. *(Ch. 8)*

majority leader   The chief strategist and floor spokesperson for the majority party in the House and in the Senate, elected by his or her party colleagues in the chamber. *(Ch. 10)*

majority opinion   The decision of a majority of Supreme Court justices, which states the reasons they reached the decision they did in a particular case. *(Ch. 13)*

material incentives   Incentives to participate in or join an organization in the form of tangible economic benefits. *(Ch. 8)*

minority leader   The chief strategist and floor spokesperson for the minority party in the House and in the Senate, elected by his or her party colleagues in the chamber. *(Ch. 11)*

muckraking   Investigative journalism that, early in the twentieth century, revealed wrongdoing in government and industry. *(Ch. 9)*

national (presidential) nominating convention   A political party convention composed of delegates from the states, the District of Columbia, and the territories that nominates candidates for president and vice president, drafts a party platform, and makes rules to govern the party. *(Ch. 6)*

natural rights   A belief that individuals are naturally endowed with basic human rights. The Declaration of Independence states that these natural rights include the rights to "Life, Liberty and the pursuit of Happiness." *(Ch. 2)*

necessary and proper (elastic) clause   Article I, section 8, of the Constitution which provides that Congress shall have the power to make all laws "necessary and proper" for carrying out its delegated or enumerated powers. *(Ch. 3)*

New Deal   The programs and policies of the Franklin Roosevelt administration designed to combat the depression of the 1930s. New Deal programs vastly expanded the regulatory and social service role of the federal government. *(Ch. 3)*

New Deal Democratic coalition   The electoral coalition forged by Franklin Roosevelt in the 1930s that provided the basis for the Democratic party's electoral successes. It was composed of white southerners, Catholics, Jews, blue-collar workers, union members, and blacks. *(Ch. 6)*

New Jersey Plan A proposal submitted to the Constitutional Convention of 1787 by William Paterson of New Jersey. It provided for a unicameral national legislature in which each state would have equal representation, a plural executive appointed by Congress, and a judiciary appointed by the executive. *(Ch. 2)*

news media The diverse array of outlets from which the public derives news, including national and local newspapers, weekly and monthly news magazines, television networks and stations, and radio stations. *(Ch. 9)*

nomination The official designation of an individual as a candidate for public office—for example, the selection of a Democratic or Republican candidate for president or senator. *(Ch. 6)*

open primary A type of primary election in which voters decide in the secrecy of the polling booth in which party's primary they will vote. Voters are permitted to vote in only one party's primary. *(Ch. 6)*

original jurisdiction The authority of a court to try a case in the first instance, in contrast to hearing a case on appeal. *(Ch. 13)*

oversight (congressional) Congressional surveillance and supervision of how executive agencies implement laws passed by Congress. *(Ch. 10)*

PAC See *political action committee.*

parliamentary system A system of government in which governmental authority is vested in the legislature, which chooses from among its members a cabinet headed by a prime minister or premier. The cabinet stays in office as long as it commands a majority in the legislature. *(Ch. 6)*

party identification A feeling of attachment or loyalty to a political party. *(Ch. 5)*

plaintiff The person bringing suit in a court of law. *(Ch. 13)*

pocket veto An act in which the president withholds approval of a bill after Congress has adjourned. It is a method of killing a bill without formally vetoing it. *(Ch. 11)*

political action committee An organization authorized by law to collect money and make campaign contributions to candidates. *(Ch. 8)*

political culture The fundamental beliefs and assumptions of a people about how government and politics should operate. *(Ch. 1)*

political efficacy A belief that one can be effective

and have an impact on public affairs. *(Ch. 5)*

political ideology An organized, coherent set of attitudes about government and public policy. *(Ch. 5)*

political party Any group, however loosely organized, that seeks to elect government officials under a given label. *(Ch. 6)*

political socialization The process through which people acquire political attitudes. *(Ch. 5)*

politics The process through which a society manages and resolves conflicts. Alternative perspectives include the acquisition, retention, and exercise of power, and the process of deciding "who gets what, when, how." *(Ch. 1)*

popular sovereignty The principle that government derives its power from the people. The Preamble to the Constitution, for example, states: "We the People of the United States . . . do ordain and establish this Constitution for the United States of America." *(Ch. 2)*

pork-barrel legislation Bills authorizing expenditures in the constituencies of members of Congress for projects that may not be needed but that enhance the reelection prospects of the members. *(Ch. 12)*

preferred position doctrine A doctrine used by the Supreme Court to determine the constitutionality of restrictions on speech. It holds that because free expression is essential for democracy, any restriction is unconstitutional unless the government can show that the speech constitutes an immediate and serious threat to society. *(Ch. 4)*

presidential coattails The ability of a presidential candidate to attract votes to other candidates of his or her party. *(Ch. 10)*

presidential primary An election held within a state to select delegates to the presidential nominating conventions. *(Ch. 6)*

president pro tempore The chief officer of the Senate in the absence of the vice president, elected by the Senate. Recent practice has been to choose the senator of the majority party who has the longest period of continual service. *(Ch. 10)*

prior restraint Censoring written material or broadcasts before their publication or presentation. *(Ch. 4)*

privileges and immunities clause A provision in Article IV, section 2, of the Constitution designed to prevent states from discriminating against out-of-state residents. It provides that "[t]he Citizens of each State shall be entitled to all Privileges and Immunities of Citizens in the several States." *(Ch. 3)*

probability sampling A procedure for selecting a sample of respondents for public opinion surveys in which every individual in the population being surveyed has the same chance of being chosen as everyone else. *(Ch. 5)*

procedural due process Protection from arbitrary deprivation of life, liberty, or property. The Fifth and Fourteenth amendments prohibit the states from denying people life, liberty, or property without due process of law. *(Ch. 4)*

proportional representation A system for electing legislators in which each party proposes a slate of candidates and legislative seats are awarded to the parties on the basis of their shares of the popular vote. *(Ch. 6)*

public agenda Issues that command the attention of public officials. *(Ch. 9)*

public interest groups A name given to interest groups that claim to advocate a broad public good rather than economic self-interest. *(Ch. 8)*

public opinion People's attitudes about an issue or question. *(Ch. 5)*

realignment A major change in the partisan identification of the voters. *(Ch. 6)*

reapportionment The allocation of seats in the House of Representatives among the states on the basis of population after each decennial census. *(Ch. 10)*

redistricting The redrawing of congressional district boundaries within the states to reflect shifts in population. *(Ch. 10)*

representative democracy A system of government in which elected representatives of the people make decisions. *(Ch. 1)*

reserved powers Powers not delegated to the national government by the Constitution and thus reserved or left to the states (the constitutional basis for the states' reserved powers is the Tenth Amendment). Although not specifically defined in the Constitution, reserved powers normally include states' police powers to protect the health, welfare, and morals of their citizens. *(Ch. 3)*

retrospective voting Voting based on an evaluation of the performance of a political party, officeholder, or administration. *(Ch. 7)*

revenue sharing The sharing of federal government tax revenues with the states and localities under which only minimal restrictions are imposed on the states and localities for the expenditure of such funds. Such a program was initiated in 1972 and discontinued in 1984 *(Ch. 8)*

rule making The development of rules and regulations by the bureaucracy for the implementation of government policies. *(Ch. 12)*

runoff (second) primary A nominating procedure used in some southern and border states when no candidate receives a majority of the votes in a primary election. A runoff or second primary is then held between the two highest vote-getters in the first primary to determine the nominee. *(Ch. 6)*

sampling error The error caused in public opinion surveys by using a sample of a population to generalize about the attitudes or behavior of the entire population. *(Ch. 5)*

select committee A congressional committee set up for a special purpose, and generally for a limited time, by a resolution of either the House or Senate. Most special committees are investigative, rather than legislative, in nature. *(Ch. 10)*

selective incorporation The process through which the judiciary has incorporated almost all of the protections of the Bill of Rights into the due process clause of the Fourteenth Amendment. As a result, most rights guaranteed against infringement by the federal government are also protected from state infringement. *(Ch. 4)*

senatorial courtesy A general practice of the Senate in which it only confirms judicial and executive branch nominations from a state approved by the senators of the president's party from that state. *(Ch. 13)*

seniority system The practice of designating as chairman of a congressional committee the member of the majority party with the longest continual service on the committee. *(Ch. 10)*

separate but equal doctrine A Supreme Court-adopted doctrine in the 1896 case of *Plessy v. Ferguson* holding that government-enforced segregation of the races was constitutional as long as the facilities for blacks and whites were equal. *(Ch. 4)*

separation of powers The constitutional division of government powers among three branches of government: the legislature, the executive, and the judiciary. *(Ch. 2)*

sequestration A procedure initially specified in the Gramm-Rudman-Hollings law of 1985 requiring automatic budget cuts (funds would be sequestered) if Congress failed to meet specified reductions in the federal budget deficit. *(Ch. 10)*

single-member district A legislative district in which only one person is elected—for example, all members of the House of Representatives are elected from single-member districts. *(Ch. 6)*

social compact A theory regarding the origins of government in which people, through a contract or compact, create a government. The compact specifies the rights and obligations of the government and its citizens. *(Ch. 2)*

solicitor general The third-ranking official of the Department of Justice responsible for deciding which cases the government will seek to have reviewed by the Supreme Court, reviewing legal briefs filed by the government, and presenting oral arguments for the government before the Court. *(Ch. 13)*

solidary incentives Incentives to participate in or join an organization in the form of such social rewards as companionship, status, and pleasure. *(Ch. 8)*

Speaker of the House The presiding officer of the House of Representatives, selected by the caucus of the party to which he or she belongs and formally elected by the entire House. *(Ch. 10)*

splinter parties Political parties that break away from one of the major political parties. *(Ch. 6)*

spoils system A pejorative term derived from the expression "to the victor belong the spoils" and used to describe the patronage system of making appointments to government jobs. *(Ch. 12)*

standing committee A congressional committee permanently authorized by the House and Senate. *(Ch. 10)*

stare decisis The judicial practice of following precedents of previous court decisions. *(Ch. 13)*

subcommittee government A term used to characterize the major role played by congressional subcommittees in the House of Representatives since a series of committee reforms was initiated in the 1970s. *(Ch. 10)*

suffrage The right to vote (also see *franchise*). *(Ch. 7)*

third party A political party composed of dissidents from the two major parties and independents. *(Ch. 6)*

Three-fifths Compromise A compromise reached between northern and southern factions at the Constitutional Convention of 1787 under which each slave would be counted as three-fifths of a person in apportioning congressional seats among the states. *(Ch. 2)*

ticket splitting When a voter casts his or her ballot for candidates of more than one party—for example, voting Republican for president and Democratic for senator. *(Ch. 6)*

trial courts Courts that hear or try cases in the first instance—that is, courts of original jurisdiction (see *original jurisdiction*). *(Ch. 13)*

turnout The percentage of the eligible electorate that actually goes to the polls and votes. *(Ch. 7)*

two-party competition Electoral competition between two major political parties, as between the Republicans and Democrats. *(Ch. 6)*

unanimous consent agreement A device used in the Senate to expedite business. An agreement may list the order in which bills will be considered and specify the length of time for debate on bills and contested amendments and when they will be voted on. *(Ch. 10)*

unitary government A government system in which all governmental authority is vested in a central government from which regional and local governments derive their powers. Examples are Great Britain and France, as well as the American states within their spheres of authority. *(Ch. 3)*

veto Disapproval by the president of a bill passed by Congress. When Congress is in session, the president must veto a bill within ten days, excluding Sundays, after its receipt; otherwise, it becomes law with or without the president's signature. *(Ch. 11)*

Virginia Plan A major proposal submitted by Virginia representatives to the Constitutional Convention of 1787 calling for a bicameral national legislature, with the lower house chosen by the voters and the upper house chosen by the lower house from among nominees submitted by the states. Representation in both houses was to be based on each state's population and wealth. *(Ch. 2)*

War Powers Resolution of 1973 A law that seeks to limit the president's ability to commit military forces abroad for unspecified time periods without the consent of Congress. Under this act, the president must report to Congress within forty-eight hours of the commitment of forces, and Congress must decide within sixty days whether to approve or disapprove of the president's action. *(Ch. 11)*

whip The assistant majority and minority leaders in both the House and the Senate, who are responsible for marshalling their party's members to support party strategy and legislation. *(Ch. 10)*

whistle-blower A person who calls public or official attention to bureaucratic mismanagement, waste, or wrongdoing. *(Ch. 8)*

winner-take-all (electoral) system Method of electing candidates to public office in which there can be only one winner—for example, as in the presidential, House, and Senate elections. *(Ch. 6)*

writ of certiorari An order issued by the Supreme Court, upon the approval of four justices, to bring up a case for review. *(Ch. 13)*

yellow journalism A type of journalism practiced in the late nineteenth century and characterized by sensationalism, partisanship, and often distortion. *(Ch. 9)*

ꝛ Index

Acknowledgments

Photo credits: ii—© 1988 James D. Scherlis; 11, 122, 137, 173 (left and right), 208, 232, 353, 360, 501—AP/Wide World Photos; 15, 87, 295—National Archives; 23 (upper left)—Courtesy of American Petroleum Institute; 23 (upper right and center left), 113, 167 (left), 255, 339 (center bottom), 345 (lower left), 351, 401, 455, 577—R. Michael Jenkins; 23, Jim Hubbard; 31, 37, 43, 69, 72, 79, 182 (top and bottom), 221 (left and right), 276, 303, 341, 343 (top and bottom), 346 (left and right), 388, 339 (upper left), 414, 420, 426, 472, 545—Library of Congress; 65—Courtesy of the John F. Kennedy Center for the Performing Arts; 104—Tribune Media Services; 118—Flip Schulke, Life Magazine © 1964 Time Warner Inc.; 129—Courtesy of the President's Committee on Employment of People with Disabilities; 142, 248—© the Washington Post Writers Group; 167 (right), 356—UPI/Bettmann Newsphotos; 184—Theodore Roosevelt Collection, Harvard College Library; 217—Courtesy of General Dynamics; 230 (left)—Courtesy of 1988 Bush/Quayle campaign; 230 (right)—Smithsonian Institution; 260, 339 (upper and lower right), 342, 345 (upper left), 348 (left and right), 354, 359—Jerry Orvedahl; 268, 285, 355—Washington Post; 305—C-SPAN; 328—David Valdez, the White House; 331—Courtesy of Republican National Campaign Committee; 345 (upper and lower right)—Courtesy of Washington, D.C., Convention and Visitors Association; 350—Jimmy Carter Library; 352 (top)—Courtesy of Austrian embassy; 352 (bottom)—Courtesy of Canadian embassy; 363—Air Photographics Inc.; 378—Dave Kaplan; 390—George Tames/New York Times; 411, 553—National Park Service; 463—U.S. Postal Service; 469—Federal Trade Commission; 484—Office of the Surgeon General; 497—Susan Biddle, the White House; 513—Courtesy of NAACP; 527—Reuters/Bettmann Newsphotos; 562—U.S. Coast Guard; 566—© Greenpeace; 573—Courtesy of Northrop Corporation.